AGENDA FOR THE NATION

KERMIT GORDON Editor

AGENDA FOR THE NATION

Papers on domestic and foreign policy issues by *Stephen K. Bailey*
Francis M. Bator
John C. Campbell
Kenneth B. Clark
Richard N. Cooper
Anthony Downs
Carl Kaysen
Clark Kerr
Henry A. Kissinger
Max F. Millikan
Edwin O. Reischauer
Charles L. Schultze
Marshall D. Shulman
Herbert Stein
James L. Sundquist
James Tobin
Ralph W. Tyler
James Q. Wilson

DOUBLEDAY & COMPANY, INC.
Garden City, New York

© 1968 by
THE BROOKINGS INSTITUTION
1775 Massachusetts Avenue, N.W., Washington, D.C. 20036

Agenda for the Nation was originally published in 1968 by the Brookings Institution. The Doubleday Paperback edition is published by arrangement with the Institution

Doubleday paperback edition: 1969
All rights reserved
Printed in the United States of America

Board of Trustees
Douglas Dillon
Chairman
Sydney Stein, Jr.
Vice Chairman
William R. Biggs
Chairman, Executive Committee
Dillon Anderson
Vincent M. Barnett, Jr.
Louis W. Cabot
Robert D. Calkins
Leonard Carmichael
Edward W. Carter
John Fischer
Kermit Gordon
Gordon Gray
Huntington Harris
Luther G. Holbrook
David M. Kennedy
John E. Lockwood
Robert S. McNamara
Arjay Miller
Herbert P. Patterson
Peter G. Peterson
J. Woodward Redmond
H. Chapman Rose
Robert Brookings Smith
J. Harvie Wilkinson, Jr.
Donald B. Woodward

Honorary Trustees
Arthur Stanton Adams
Daniel W. Bell
Eugene R. Black
Colgate W. Darden, Jr.
Marion B. Folsom
Raymond B. Fosdick
Huntington Gilchrist
John Lee Pratt

THE BROOKINGS INSTITUTION is an independent organization devoted to nonpartisan research, education, and publication in economics, government, foreign policy, and the social sciences generally. Its principal purposes are to aid in the development of sound public policies and to promote public understanding of issues of national importance.

The Institution was founded on December 8, 1927, to merge the activities of the Institute for Government Research, founded in 1916, the Institute of Economics, founded in 1922, and the Robert Brookings Graduate School of Economics and Government, founded in 1924.

The general administration of the Institution is the responsibility of a self-perpetuating Board of Trustees. The trustees are likewise charged with maintaining the independence of the staff and fostering the most favorable conditions for creative research and education. The immediate direction of the policies, program, and staff of the Institution is vested in the President, assisted by an advisory council chosen from the staff of the Institution.

In publishing a study, the Institution presents it as a competent treatment of a subject worthy of public consideration. The interpretations and conclusions in such publications are those of the author or authors and do not purport to represent the views of the other staff members, officers, or trustees of the Brookings Institution.

FOREWORD

This book presents eighteen essays on some of the urgent issues which will confront the new national adminstration and the new Congress when they take office early in 1969. It is addressed to all of those who play a role in the formulation of public policy—to elected and appointed officials, to opinion leaders, and to the informed and concerned public.

A word about the origins of the book may be of interest. Looking ahead to the presidential transition of 1960–61, the Brookings Institution prepared a series of detailed memoranda on the organizational and administrative problems which would be raised by the transfer of power to a new President and his administration. These memoranda were transmitted promptly after the election to President-elect Kennedy, and were used by him and his staff in organizing the work of the transition.

In anticipation of the 1968–69 transition, it was decided not to repeat the effort undertaken eight years previously, but to apply the energies of the Institution to an analysis of the substantive problems with which the new President and the new Congress would have to grapple.

With the aid of a special grant from the Ford Foundation, the project was launched in the spring of 1968. The initial menu of major policy issues to be considered ran to nearly forty subjects. This was clearly an excessive number, and the list was finally whittled down to eighteen. In the course of making the scope of the project more manageable, it was reluctantly decided to eliminate a number of subjects of very great importance. Thus, the reader will note that there are no essays dealing—in the domestic arena—with problems as important as the reform of state and local government, environmental pollution, mass transportation, health and medical care, or tax policy. In the international sector, only brief attention is given to the critical problem of world population policy, and there is no explicit consideration of our relations with regions as important as

Latin America or Africa, or with the important neighbor we tend to take for granted, Canada.

The authors of the essays exchanged outlines in order to minimize duplication of treatment. Those who wrote on domestic questions met together on one occasion, as did the authors of the foreign policy essays, to discuss the interconnections among their subjects. Though they were encouraged to declare their own policy views, the authors were told that their primary obligation in each essay was to clarify and deepen the reader's understanding of the issues. Two critics were selected to comment on the first draft of each essay; the authors, however, were free to accept or reject the comments and suggestions of the critics. The names of the critics of each essay are given, together with biographical information on the authors, on pages 615–20. The critics, of course, bear no responsibility for the final form of each essay, and in some cases would demur from the author's conclusions.

James L. Sundquist, author of the essay "Jobs, Training, and Welfare for the Underclass," wishes to acknowledge his debt to William L. Batt, Jr., Sar A. Levitan, Garth L. Mangum, Harold L. Sheppard, Jr., Gilbert Y. Steiner, Ellen Winston, and D. Richard Wenner, all of whom offered useful comments on earlier drafts of his essay. James Tobin, author of the essay "Raising the Incomes of the Poor," wishes to acknowledge the help of William Capron, Victor Fuchs, Robert Lampman, and Peter Mieszkowski, and of Harold Watts and his colleagues at the University of Wisconsin Institute for Poverty Research.

The essays were edited under great time pressure by members of the staff of the Brookings Publications Program—Mendelle T. Berenson, A. Evelyn Breck, Rosalie K. Epstein, Nancy C. Romoser, and Frances M. Shattuck. A special debt is due Herbert C. Morton, former director of the Brookings Publications Program, who managed the book through the publication process in its preliminary stages.

As always in Brookings studies, the views expressed in these essays are those of the authors. They should not be attributed to the Brookings Institution, the Ford Foundation, or to the Brookings trustees, officers, or staff members, except as some of the latter participated as authors.

KERMIT GORDON
President

October 1968

CONTENTS

KERMIT GORDON
Introduction 3

DOMESTIC POLICY

CHARLES L. SCHULTZE
Budget Alternatives after Vietnam 13

The Fiscal Dividend, 1969–74 *16* Savings from a Cessation of Vietnam Hostilities *28* Use of the Fiscal Dividend *35* Increasing the Fiscal Dividend *40* Conclusion *47*

JAMES L. SUNDQUIST
Jobs, Training, and Welfare for the Underclass 49

Questions of Strategy *53* Questions of Administration *66* Politics and Resources *74*

JAMES TOBIN
Raising the Incomes of the Poor 77

The Revolt against Poverty and the Negro Revolution *78* The Revival of Inequality as a Social and Political Issue *79* The Agricultural Revolution, Migration, and Contemporary Poverty *80* The Measurement of Poverty and the Objectives of Policy *83* Full Employment, Inflation, and Poverty *86* Structural and Distributive Strategies in Anti-Poverty Policy *90* Investment in Human Capital *91* Income Maintenance and Public Assistance: The Legacy of the New Deal *93* The Philosophical Conflict *97* Reform of Public Assistance *100* "Costs" of Redistributions to the Poor *103* The Credit Income Tax *105* Children's Allowances and Adults' Allowances *108* Negative Income Tax Proposals *110* Concluding Remarks *114*

KENNETH B. CLARK
The Negro and the Urban Crisis 117

The Intensification of Racial Hostility *124* Civil Rights and Foreign Policy *127* Questions for the Future *128* The Failure of Separatism *130* Alternative Programs *134* A Comprehensive Plan for Stabilization of Our Cities *136*

ANTHONY DOWNS
Moving toward Realistic Housing Goals 141

What Is "The Housing Problem"? *141* Meeting National Housing Targets *150* Summary of Policy Recommendations *171* Conclusion: Rhetoric Versus Reality *176*

JAMES Q. WILSON
Crime and Law Enforcement 179

Crime in the Streets *181* The Criminal Justice System *184* A Federal Role in Law Enforcement *196* Some Modest Proposals *205*

RALPH W. TYLER
Investing in Better Schools 207

Primary Education for All Children *208* Improving the High Schools *213* Building New Instructional Content *219* Teacher Recruitment and Training *222* Organizational Structures and Procedures *227* Educational Research and Development *230* Financial Support *233* The Costs *235*

CLARK KERR
New Challenges to the College and University 237

The Evolution of the Federal Role *238* Problems of the Next Decade *243* Higher Education and Federal Support Today *256* The Future of Federal Assistance *263* Recommendations *271* Summary and Conclusion *274*

HERBERT STEIN
Unemployment, Inflation, and Economic Stability 277

Unemployment and Inflation *278* Moderating Economic Fluctuations *288*

STEPHEN K. BAILEY
Managing the Federal Government 301

Reorganization: A Brief History 304 The Limitations of Existing Devices 309 Making the System Work: The Political Preconditions 326

FOREIGN POLICY

FRANCIS M. BATOR
The Politics of Alliance: The United States and Western Europe 335

A Time of Trouble? 336 Issues and Choices 352 Grounds for Optimism 370

MARSHALL D. SHULMAN
Relations with the Soviet Union 373

The Dual Nature of the Relationship 373 The Spiral of Interaction 375 Factors of Change in the International Environment 378 Soviet Policy in the Present Period 380 Policy Alternatives for the United States 392 Guiding Principles for the United States 402

EDWIN O. REISCHAUER
Transpacific Relations 407

General Perspectives 407 A Vietnam Settlement 411 The Prospects for China 415 China Policy 421 The Situation in the Less-developed Countries 425 Policy toward the Less-developed Countries 428 Japan's Role in Asia 433 Policy toward Japan 438 Conclusions 442

JOHN C. CAMPBELL
The Middle East 445

Lessons of Two Decades 445 Soviet Aims and Policies 449 Search for a Settlement 451 The Tide of Violence 454 Some Policy Choices 456 Keeping the Peace 459 America's Relationship with Israel 461 A Durable Basis for Policy 464 The Promise of Limited Measures 467 The Soviet-American Relationship 471

RICHARD N. COOPER
The Dollar and the World Economy — 475

The Present International Monetary System 476 Further Developments and Emerging Strains 479 The U.S. Payments Deficit 489 U.S. Policy Alternatives within the Existing System 497 Changes in the Payments System 501 Gold, the Dollar, and International Economic Cooperation 506

MAX F. MILLIKAN
The United States and Low-Income Countries — 509

The Foreign Policy Framework 510 Requirements for Effective Policy 526 Balance among the Instruments of AID Policy 532 Relations with Other Donors: Bilateral and Multilateral Approaches 543 Can We Afford It? 547

CARL KAYSEN
Military Strategy, Military Forces, and Arms Control — 549

The International Political Scene 552 Strategic Forces 559 NATO Forces 569 Other General Purpose Forces 575 Other Means of Keeping the Peace 579 A Summary of Force Sizes and Budgets 580

HENRY A. KISSINGER
Central Issues of American Foreign Policy — 585

The Structural Problem 585 The Limits of Bipolarity: The Nature of Power in the Modern Period 589 Political Multipolarity: The Changed Nature of Alliances 593 Bipolarity and Multipolarity: The Conceptual Problem 602 An Inquiry into the American National Interest 610

Biographical Notes — 615

AGENDA FOR THE NATION

KERMIT GORDON

INTRODUCTION

In the rhythm of America's national life, the early days of a new administration in Washington are marked by a renewal of governmental energies and a resurgence of hope. The nation has a sense that a page in history has been turned, and the new President has a blank sheet upon which to write. His defeated opponents rally round with expressions of goodwill and declarations of solidarity in pursuit of common goals. The new Congress, conscious of the structural disabilities which limit its own capacity to devise coherent national policies from a standing start, welcomes the impetus to the legislative process which is generated by presidential initiatives.

At the opening of a new administration—even in times more benign than the present—the public seems to turn away from the memories of the struggles, perplexities, and frustrations which clouded the record of the outgoing regime, and to nourish the hope that the new leaders, making a fresh and confident start, will find the therapies for the nation's ills which eluded their predecessors. The voters expect new diagnoses, new strategies, and new initiatives, and most are inclined to suspend their doubts while the new administration has a fair chance to show its skills. It is a time when a measure of faith is rekindled.

It is also a time when the political skies show broad patches of goodwill, when the barriers inherent in a system of checks and balances, which usually serve well their intended purpose of impeding vigorous and decisive governmental action, are temporarily lowered. This is not to say that a new President, during his honeymoon period, can write his own ticket. No President has been able to do that since Franklin D. Roosevelt in 1933, and the grim circumstances which made possible that awesome display of presidential power are not likely to recur. But during the early days of relatively smooth sailing, the new President will find the Congress and the country more responsive to his leadership than is likely to be the case later on. He

3

is able to define the national agenda; he can set the outlines of the debate on the issues; he can advance hard proposals for action which will possess the prima facie legitimacy which attends a new President's maiden venture in leadership.

Between the election and the inauguration, the new President and his lieutenants must make the jolting transition from the slogans and simplifications of the election campaign to the intricate task of constructing workable policies and programs. In designing the rhetoric of the campaign, the goal was to win the hearts of the voters; in hammering out the policies of the new administration, the goal is to solve problems. The problems are always vastly more complex, and the new administration is always considerably less confident of its ability to solve them, than the rhetoric of the campaign can admit. The full complexity and intractability of the problems will be seen more clearly in the cold light of the post-election scrutiny. Slowly and carefully, programs will be put together. Most of them will be recognized by their architects to be second-best solutions—constructs assembled out of delicate compromises designed to skirt the budgetary, administrative, congressional, political, and ideological pitfalls which lie in the path of those who seek to effect change in public policy. Most will represent incremental departures from the policies of prior administrations—perhaps modest deflections in direction, perhaps speedups or slowdowns in the pace of movement—though any new administration for understandable reasons will seek to emphasize the elements of novelty rather than the elements of continuity in its policies. And if the policies when finally unveiled are at no point inconsistent with the slogans of the victor's election campaign, the explanation must lie in an unusual combination of astuteness and good luck.

The shape and content of the election campaign foreshadowed the issues of greatest urgency which will confront the new administration in 1969. If there is killing in Vietnam when the new President takes office, his paramount task must be to stop the fighting. The brutality and horror of the war—made vivid as in no previous war by the immediacy of television; the corrosive and divisive effects of the war on American society; and the budgetary drain of the war which has shortchanged urgent domestic claims—all dictate that ending the war must lead all other tasks on the President's agenda.

Before it can formulate its domestic program, the new administration will have to think through, and find its own key to, the central paradox of American society in 1969: on the one hand, we are a nation which sees itself as wracked and divided over problems of poverty, riots, race, slums, unemployment, and crime; on the other hand, we are a nation which is clearly enjoying high prosperity, rapid economic growth, and a steady diffusion of affluence at a rate almost unimaginable a decade ago.

The paradox cannot be simply resolved. To some degree, certain of our social ills have been relieved by the effects of prosperity, aided by remedial public programs—to an extent greater than is widely perceived. To some degree, our problems have been aggravated by sustained prosperity; rapid growth implies rapid change, and change always has unsettling and destabilizing consequences. To some degree, our social problems have antecedents which seem to be unaffected, or only mildly affected, by economic forces. And finally, to some degree, we are prone to confuse a growing gap between aspiration and performance, caused by a more rapid rise in the former than in the latter, with a deterioration of performance.

At the start of the decade of the 1960s, the goals of steady prosperity and faster growth occupied the center of the public stage. They were sought not only for the direct benefits they would yield, but also in the expectation that many of our social and economic problems would be floated away on a rising tide of prosperity and expansion.

In broad terms, the economic goals of the 1960s have been achieved, though the record was seriously marred by the resurgence of inflation in 1966. Gross national product (GNP) corrected for price increases—the measure of our total output of useful goods and services—has grown by nearly one-half. (The output of the U.S. economy in 1968 was almost equal to the sum of the output of the United States in 1960 *and* the output of the Soviet Union in 1968.) Since 1960, the spendable income of the average American—after allowing for price increases and taxes—has increased by nearly one-third. By any reasonable standard, this has been a phenomenal performance, which few would have dared to predict a decade ago.

Yet, today, the mood of the nation is more troubled, and our internal problems seem more stubborn and incurable, than was the case a decade ago. The coexistence of growing affluence and growing social ills has led many to the conclusion that the vision of general prosperity as a solvent of social ills has been a chimera—that GNP has turned out to be a false god.

This challenge to the myth of the omnipotence of GNP has been a healthy step forward. But while not omnipotent, GNP is far from impotent, and there is danger that this important perception may be obscured

6   *Agenda for the Nation*

by the disillusion growing out of our current internal crisis. The record of the 1960s has in fact been a record of substantial advance in several important sectors of social concern, and there is little doubt that the advances have been substantially aided by general economic expansion.

A decade ago, for example, America was pockmarked with a large number of chronically depressed areas—communities apparently hopelessly mired in economic stagnation, heavy unemployment, and social decay. The depressed area problem was then regarded as one of our most debilitating social ills. It is so regarded no longer—not because all of the depressed areas have recovered, but because most of them have. Indeed, many of the communities thought to be far down the road to disintegration are today prosperous and expanding.

A decade ago, and even more recently, the nation was frightened by a specter called automation. New technology, it was feared, was displacing workers at so rapid a rate that we faced a future of massive and spiraling unemployment. The machines were taking over, and work was becoming obsolete; this alarming prospect required a fundamental reconstruction of the economic system to save it from collapse. Little has been heard of the specter of automation since unemployment fell to low levels.

In the 1960s, 10 million new jobs have been created; unemployment has declined by 40 percent; the number of persons living below the poverty level has fallen from 40 million to 26 million; and the number of households living in substandard housing has declined from 8.5 million to 5.7 million. Nor have these advances been limited to white persons; there have also been important gains in the economic status of Negroes. Though there remains a wide economic gap between Negroes and whites, nonwhite unemployment has fallen at the same rate as total unemployment—by 40 percent. The proportion of nonwhites living below the poverty level has declined from 55 percent to 35 percent. The share of nonwhite households living in substandard housing has declined from 44 percent to 29 percent. Nonwhites employed in white-collar jobs have increased by over 700,000, or nearly 65 percent. The proportion of nonwhite families with middle-income earnings—$8000 or more per year in dollars of 1967 purchasing power—has increased from 13 percent to 27 percent, and has reached 37 percent outside the South.

It is necessary—indeed, imperative—to recognize that Negroes in America are at the same time trailing very far behind and gaining rapidly. In the angry and polarized climate of racial politics, it is not easy for a participant in the debate both to condemn the persistence into our own time of the forces of discrimination, deprivation, and oppression which have held the Negro down for centuries, and at the same time to applaud the changes which have made possible the Negro's steady and substantial progress of recent years. Such a judgment may seem equivocal, but it is only what is required by a decent regard for the facts. In the words of a recent government report on the status of Negroes in the United States:

> Typically, Negroes are more likely than ever before to be earning decent incomes, holding good jobs, living in better neighborhoods, and completing their education. In many cases not only have Negro achievements reached all-time highs, but the relative gap between whites and Negroes has also diminished. . . .
>
> Despite these gains, in some instances striking gains, it should be noted—and stressed—that Negroes generally remain very far behind whites in most social and economic categories. Compared to whites, Negroes still are more than three times as likely to be in poverty, twice as likely to be unemployed, and three times as likely to die in infancy or childbirth. In large cities, more than half of all Negroes live in poor neighborhoods.[1]

The best remedy for despair about the future of the Negro in America is the first of these paragraphs; the best remedy for complacency is the second.

These gains in incomes, jobs, and housing—for Negroes and for the population at large—have been a joint product of sustained prosperity, remedial governmental programs, and a myriad of other forces. How much each of these influences has contributed to the result is an enigma; but it is a safe inference that the most powerful of these forces is prosperity. It operates directly and indirectly: directly on incomes, by expanding job opportunities and demand for better housing, and indirectly as well, by swelling the tax base and providing automatically the steady increase in tax revenues needed to finance remedial public programs.

But if prosperity and growth have had wholesome consequences in some sectors of social concern, they seem to have been unavailing or worse in others. Only the most disquieting examples need be mentioned: with crime increasing as poverty and privation diminish, it becomes steadily more implausible to ascribe criminal behavior mainly to material want; the deterioration of public education in many of our inner cities has so far defied the efforts of governments to halt and reverse the trend; the growing pollution of the environment not only runs counter to the steady improvement of private living standards, but is manifestly a baneful side effect of that trend. Sustained prosperity and growth are clearly necessary conditions to the further amelioration of many of our social problems, but

---

1. U.S. Department of Labor and U.S. Department of Commerce, *Recent Trends in Social and Economic Conditions of Negroes in the United States* (1968), p. V.

they are just as clearly not sufficient conditions. Where their effects are benign, they tend to operate more slowly than is tolerable either to the patience of the victims of injustice and deprivation or to the conscience of the more fortunate. That 14 million people have been rescued from poverty since 1960 is little solace to the 26 million who remain poor, and insufficient solace to the many who believe that any poverty is unconscionable in a rich society; and, as we have seen, prosperity and growth are helpless against some social ills. The responsibility of government to deal directly with specific social problems is not lessened by success in sustaining prosperity.

The essays in the first section of this book deal with some of the most urgent domestic issues with which the new administration must struggle. Charles L. Schultze analyzes the budgetary dimensions of the federal government's problems, and demonstrates that the end of the fighting in Vietnam will not quickly ease the government's budgetary bind. James L. Sundquist examines and evaluates alternative means of raising the employability and increasing the employment of the poor, while James Tobin analyzes proposals for direct support of the incomes of the poor by means which are both more efficient and less demeaning than the present welfare system. Kenneth B. Clark provides a diagnosis of the plight of the Negro in urban society which points to the breakup of the ghetto as an essential step in securing full citizenship for the Negro. Anthony Downs surveys the prospects and problems of attaining the national goal of "a decent home and a suitable living environment for every American family," and warns of the dangers of promising faster progress than can be achieved. In a somber review of the crime problem, James Q. Wilson finds no easy panaceas, though he identifies directions in which progress may be possible. Ralph W. Tyler examines the shortcomings of our schools and develops a detailed program for improving their effectiveness, and Clark Kerr reviews the problems of our expanding and rapidly changing system of higher education. Herbert Stein surveys the problem of maintaining prosperity and analyzes the difficult choices which must be made in pursuing both high employment and relative price stability. Finally, Stephen K. Bailey assesses the organizational and administrative capability of the federal government to perform its tasks effectively, and proposes reforms to correct manifest weaknesses.

Several of the authors concerned with domestic issues call for the expenditure of more government funds—in some cases, a great deal more. While it is most unlikely that the country will choose in the next few years to increase government spending on social programs on the scale urged in some of these proposals, it is a delusion to think that substantial progress can be bought with modest sums. However the programs are organized—whether in a centralized or decentralized structure; whatever instrumentalities are chosen—whether public bodies or entities in the private sector; the cost will be borne largely by the federal government. This recognition should redirect attention to Mr. Schultze's opening analysis. Post-Vietnam decisions on the defense budget—discussed by Mr. Schultze and in considerable detail by Carl Kaysen later in the volume—will have profound consequences for the availability of funds to finance domestic social programs. It is quite possible that the decisions of the new administration and the new Congress on the post-Vietnam defense budget will be the single most important factor in determining the scale on which the nation attacks its internal social problems. The vigor and courage with which the new administration seeks to curtail low-priority and obsolete federal programs, and the choice which is made between maintaining or reducing present federal tax rates, will also strongly influence the magnitude of the effort.

Though this volume arbitrarily divides the foreign policy essays from those which deal with domestic issues, the sharpness of the separation is misleading. It is now a commonplace that our domestic and foreign concerns are intertwined in a hundred ways. As was indicated above, Carl Kaysen's analysis of national defense policy has implications of major importance for the division of the federal budget between defense expenditures and outlays on domestic social programs. In his examination of monetary relations between the United States and other countries—an analysis of arcane forces which influence the economic welfare of the American people in ways which are important but little understood—Richard N. Cooper stresses the policy complications, internal and external, which are raised by the growing integration of the economies of the Western industrial nations; it is no longer fanciful to say that the rate of residential construction in Des Moines can be affected, through a lengthy but traceable chain of causation, by the actions of the Bundesbank in West Germany. Our foreign aid program—analyzed by Max F. Millikan in the course of his examination of the U.S. interest in the economic and social development of the low-income countries—is an important claimant for budget resources in competition with domestic and other foreign programs, and is closely intertwined with our internal agricultural policy.

A common thread can be discerned in the five remaining essays on foreign policy, which deal mainly with the political rather than the military or economic dimensions of our foreign relations. The theme is enunciated with greatest generality by Henry A. Kissinger in his concluding analysis of the central issues of American foreign policy. Kissinger finds that the age of the superpowers is nearing its end; that we are witnessing the emergence of a politically multipolar world, even though the world remains bipolar in a military sense; that this divergence is occurring because military power in the world of the 1960s no longer translates automatically into influence. Echoes of this theme, as it reveals itself in the relations of the Soviet Union to the other countries of the Soviet bloc, appear in Marshall D. Shulman's study of U.S. relations with the Soviet Union; and, as it colors transatlantic relations, in Francis M. Bator's analysis of the United States and Western Europe. In the view of John C. Campbell, writing on the Middle East, the opposing sides in the ominous Arab-Israeli conflict are considerably less amenable to influence by the superpowers than the logic of military power might suggest. And Edwin O. Reischauer, surveying our transpacific relations, concludes that the threat of hegemony by any power over Asia is empty, that "Asian countries cannot be controlled from abroad, even through communism or any other ideology."

The centrifugal forces loosed in the world by the waning ability of the superpowers to control events may, in the long run, work for good or ill. But for the present, in Henry Kissinger's words, the "international environment is in turmoil because its essential elements are all in flux simultaneously." Were the same statement made about the domestic environment, it would be just as apposite. The turbulence of our domestic life is a product of the rapid erosion of the institutional structures which channel and constrain social behavior. Both at home and abroad, we are being propelled in new directions by forces which we understand very imperfectly, toward destinations which we hardly perceive at all. As Marshall Shulman puts it, "The sense of some inchoate movement toward new crystallizing ideas whose outlines are still unclear is evident within societies as well as between them."

The essays which follow mirror the convulsions of a world in rapid flux. In a setting so turbulent, it is always a tempting option to postpone decision making, in the hope that the passage of time will bring greater certainty; but this is a luxury which governments are often denied. These essays are intended as a contribution to public discussion and debate on the problems which beset us, for governments make wiser decisions when the issues are widely aired and argued.

DOMESTIC POLICY

CHARLES L. SCHULTZE

BUDGET ALTERNATIVES AFTER VIETNAM

Seventy years ago, at the turn of the century, public expenditures in the United States—federal, state, and local—absorbed about 9 percent of the total national income. The federal government accounted for one-third of this total, and almost all of its expenditures were devoted to the centuries-old governmental functions—defense, post office, veterans' benefits, and interest on the public debt.

Today, 30 percent of the total national income is spent by the public sector—20 percent by the federal government (including its grants-in-aid to states and localities) and 10 percent by state and local governments. Defense expenditures take up 9 percent and the civilian programs of the federal government, many of which scarcely existed at the turn of the century, now account for another 11 percent.

The budgets of federal, state, and local governments have become major instruments of national policy, not only because they absorb almost one-third of our total income, but also because the programs they encompass touch upon the most critical national concerns. The quality of the air we breathe and the water we drink, our security and survival in an age of intercontinental missiles and "wars of liberation," the fate of our troubled inner cities, the provision of equal justice and opportunity to the poor, the safety and efficiency of our highways and air lanes, the promotion of economic prosperity and growth, the basic research which underlies our technological progress, public education—in short, almost every major national concern is critically affected by the budgetary decisions we make.

These budgetary decisions are of three kinds—all related, but each logically distinct.

First, the nation must decide how to divide its income between private and public purposes. With 30 percent of its income going to government,

70 percent remains for disposition by private consumers and business firms.[1] If public expenditures account for 30 percent of total income, they can also absorb 30 percent of the growth in the economy, while still remaining a constant fraction of income. Under normal full employment conditions, and assuming a 2 percent annual price inflation, the money value of the nation's income will grow by 6 to 7 percent annually, an increase of $55 to $65 billion a year during the early 1970s. Public expenditures, therefore, can rise by 6 to 7 percent, or $16 to $20 billion a year, without changing the fraction of national income devoted to public purposes. If public outlays increase by less than 6 to 7 percent per year, we are implicitly making a decision to change the division between the public and private sectors in favor of private spending. The converse holds true when public outlays rise by more than 6 or 7 percent annually.

When tax rates are left unchanged, the overall federal tax system, as a rough approximation, yields revenues which grow proportionally with national income. The federal payroll tax rate, used to finance social security programs, is scheduled under present law to increase significantly over the next fifteen years—from 8.8 percent to 11.4 percent. For this reason, total federal revenues will grow somewhat faster than income, unless the law is changed. But if history is any guide, the excess growth will be used to finance larger social security benefits. Federal revenues available to finance all other programs will, consequently, increase about in line with total national income. If state and local income, sales, and property tax *rates* are held unchanged, state and local revenues will also grow at roughly the same rate. Except for the social security program, therefore, total public revenues will rise in line with total national income, so long as tax rates remain unchanged. In the long run, assuming that revenues and expenditures are in "proper" balance to start with, a national decision to increase, decrease, or hold constant the proportion of income devoted to public purposes is equivalent, respectively, to a decision to raise, lower, or maintain tax rates.

The second kind of budgetary decision is the division of resources among public programs. What priorities should be placed on space exploration relative to aid to education? Within education, how should resources be divided between elementary and secondary education on the one hand

---

1. This is an oversimplification. While government expenditures account for 30 percent of total national income, some part of that amount, equaling approximately 6 percent of national income, is transferred back to individuals through such programs as social security and veterans' pensions to spend as they wish.

and higher education on the other? And, within elementary and secondary education, how much should be spent for the training of teachers, educational research, compensatory educational services in the inner city, and so forth?

Fiscal policy, the third aspect of budgetary decisions, primarily concerns the impact of the federal budget on economic activity. When private demands for consumption and investment goods are weak, threatening an increase in unemployment and idle plant capacity, then an excess of federal expenditures over revenues can help to restore overall demand to full employment levels. Conversely, when private demands are excessive, a surplus of federal revenues over expenditures can reduce inflationary pressures.

The problems of economic growth and stabilization, to which fiscal policy addresses itself, are discussed elsewhere in this book by Herbert Stein. For purposes of this paper, the central fact about fiscal policy is that it deals with the relationship between budget revenues and expenditures, not with the absolute level of those expenditures. Within reasonable limits, an increase in the share of national income going to the public sector need not be inflationary if it is accompanied by an appropriate increase in tax rates. A decrease in the public share need not lead to recession so long as tax rates are sufficiently reduced. Looked at another way, fiscal policy (and monetary policy) can help maintain a stable and prosperous economy with a share of public expenditures either higher or lower than the present one.

This is not to say there would be no transition problems during any major shift up or down in the public share. A radical increase in the federal share from 20 percent to 30 percent over a short period of time would indeed pose difficult fiscal problems, as would an equally large reduction. Moreover, should federal expenditures take either an exceedingly large or an exceedingly small share of total national income, long-term problems of fiscal policy would arise. A very large federal share would be most difficult to finance without discouraging private investment and economic growth. Conversely, when the federal share is very small, as in the 1920s and early 1930s, for example, reasonably attainable shifts in public expenditures or revenues may be so small compared to the size of the economy that they are incapable of offsetting fluctuations in private demand. But this qualification simply sets practical limits to the rate at which the public share can be changed and to the ultimate level it might reach. It does not invalidate the proposition that the public share of total spending can be raised or lowered without significantly affecting the efficacy of fiscal policy in pursuing the goal of stable prosperity.

In political debate, problems of fiscal policy are often intertwined with considerations of the size of the public sector. As the legislative history of the recent tax surcharge amply demonstrates, a presidential request for a temporary increase in taxes on grounds of economic stabilization is likely to touch off a major debate about the "proper" share of the federal sector. When fiscal stimulus is required, on the other hand, advocates of a larger federal share will seize upon the occasion to promote an increase in expenditures rather than a tax reduction. This facet of political reality has to be recognized—fiscal policy proposals usually generate debate about the size of the public sector. It is nevertheless still true that, from an economic standpoint, the nation can decide to enlarge or contract the share of the public sector without fearing that a higher or lower share necessarily leads to inflation or depression.

The Fiscal Dividend, 1969–74

An examination of the budgetary choices facing the nation can best start with an estimate of the fiscal dividend. The fiscal dividend is the difference between the automatic rise in federal revenues that accompanies economic growth and the unavoidable expansion in federal expenditures that stems from increasing wages and prices and from other factors. It measures the budgetary resources that will become available without explicit policy decisions. It can be used to expand federal programs or to reduce taxes. Cessation of hostilities in Vietnam would, of course, increase the dividend by removing one source of federal spending. The fiscal dividend is not an ironclad constraint, but to the extent we wish to expand outlays beyond what it makes available, we must be prepared either to raise taxes or to find existing expenditure programs which can be cut back to make way for new program expansion.

With an estimate of the fiscal dividend, we can proceed to consider two additional problems: What are some of the major potential claims against the fiscal dividend over the next five years, through the expansion of existing programs or the initiation of new ones? What policy actions might be taken to reduce the magnitude of built-in expenditure increases, thereby expanding the size of the fiscal dividend to meet the added claims upon it or to provide room for tax reduction?

Estimating the fiscal dividend over the period 1969–74 requires answers to the following questions:

1. Assuming high employment, by how much will the economy grow?
2. Under existing tax rates, what will be the increase in federal revenues accompanying economic growth?
3. What are the unavoidable—or "built-in"—increases in federal civilian outlays? To ask the question another way, what would happen to federal outlays in the absence of any major policy decisions? As pay in the private sector rises, so eventually must the pay of federal employees. Price advances raise the cost of carrying on the present level of government. As veterans return from Vietnam, education and training expenditures under the GI Bill will increase. These and similar built-in increases must be deducted from the growth in revenues in determining the fiscal dividend.
4. What increases can be expected in social security and Medicare benefit payments? Revenues from the payroll tax, which finances these benefits, will rise both because payrolls will be larger and because, under present law, several increases in the payroll tax rate are scheduled to occur in the next five years. On the basis of all past experience, we can expect those higher revenues to be used to raise benefit payments.
5. What is likely to be the saving in military expenditures given a cease-fire or a major reduction in the intensity of fighting in Vietnam? Although no one can now predict which of many possibilities will materialize—or when—some illustrative alternatives can be presented.
6. What is the likely course of non-Vietnam military expenditures? This estimate differs from the estimate of unavoidable increases in civilian programs. Most of the latter are open-ended, on-going programs, such as grants-in-aid for education, manpower training programs, administering the national parks, and so on. Barring a specific policy decision, they will continue. But a large part of military expenditures represents the procurement of major weapons systems. Once the system is delivered, procurement expenditures cease (except for spare parts). Consequently, an attempt to measure only the unavoidable changes in existing military programs would soon show an unrealistic decline in expenditures beginning several years from now, as existing procurement programs are completed and no new

ones take their place.[2] To avoid an unrealistically large estimate of the fiscal dividend, an attempt has been made to project the future course of military expenditures, taking into account not only unavoidable increases in pay and prices but also likely policy decisions on future weapons systems. I must emphasize immediately that the measure of the fiscal dividend can be significantly changed, up or down, depending upon future defense policy.

For purposes of estimating the fiscal dividend, I have assumed a balanced full-employment budget (national income accounts basis). This is not an attempt to predict the economic climate. It is only a convenient simplification. If the maintenance of full employment should call for a budget deficit in any year, then the fiscal dividend will be larger than I have estimated. The opposite would hold true should inflationary pressures dictate a budget surplus. (The estimates of the fiscal dividend presented here would be *systematically* biased only if the maintenance of stable prosperity consistently called for a budgetary surplus or deficit year in and year out. I do not think that is the case. But it is not my purpose to argue the point. Readers who believe a continuing deficit will be necessary can revise my estimate by adding to the fiscal dividend an estimate of the needed continuing deficit. Readers worried about continued inflationary pressure can perform the opposite arithmetic correction by subtracting their estimate of the required surplus from the figures presented here.)

Table 1 summarizes the major results for fiscal years 1971 and 1974. To illustrate the impact of a cease-fire in Vietnam on the budget, one "scenario" was chosen out of an almost infinite number of possibilities. A cease-fire was assumed to occur early in 1969, and a gradual return to the United States and deactivation of all American troops now in Vietnam was assumed to begin July 1, 1969. This set of assumptions was selected to show how a relatively optimistic outcome in Vietnam would affect the budget. The budgetary implications of some alternative possibilities are discussed at a later point.

As the table makes clear, federal revenues will grow substantially over the 1969–74 period, by $15.5 billion per year in the first two years and $18.5 billion in the succeeding three years. (Note that the 10 percent temporary

---

2. This is not to say that *any* decline in non-Vietnam military expenditures would be unrealistic. But such decreases should only be assumed to occur as the result of explicit policy actions, not as the inevitable consequence of a statistical projection technique. Compare the discussion of potential reductions in military expenditures later in this paper with those in Carl Kaysen's paper in this volume.

surtax of 1968 is excluded from all of the calculations.) Despite the large growth in revenues and the assumed cessation of hostilities in Vietnam, the fiscal dividend in 1971 will be relatively small, less than $10 billion. There are two principal reasons for this. First, without the 10 percent surtax there would be a substantial deficit in fiscal 1969. If the surcharge expires when Vietnam expenditures decline, part of the revenue growth will be needed to wipe out the deficit, under the assumption of a full-employment balanced budget. Should economic conditions call for a deficit in fiscal 1971, the fiscal dividend could, of course, be correspondingly larger. Second, I have assumed a large growth in built-in civilian expenditures and in non-Vietnam military outlays over the next two years. The reasons underlying these projections are spelled out at a later point. But their consequence is that a large part of the revenue growth will be absorbed by built-in expenditure increases.

In the succeeding three years, on the other hand, the fiscal dividend will grow rapidly. By 1974 it should lie in the range of $35 to $40 billion. The

TABLE 1. Projection of Fiscal Dividend, Post-Vietnam
(In billions of dollars; national income accounts basis[a])

Budget item	1969	Change 1969 to 1971	1971	Change 1971 to 1974	1974
Federal receipts[b]	172		203		259
Federal expenditures					
Civilian	106.5		126.5		146.5
Pay increases		1.3		1.5	
Price increases		2.0		3.0	
Social security benefits		9.0		12.0	
Other built-in changes		7.7		3.5	
Military	79.0		91		100
Pay increases		4.2		4.5	
Price increases		1.6		2.9	
Other changes		6.2		1.6	
Less: Vietnam expenditures	−1.0		−21		−24
Adjustment to NIA basis	0		− 1.3		− 1.7
Equal: Total expenditures[c]	185		195		221
Fiscal dividend	—		8		38

Source: Fiscal 1969 budget data are based on estimates in the "Summer Review of the 1969 Budget" (press release, Bureau of the Budget, Sept. 9, 1968).
  a. Federal expenditures and revenues as measured in the national income accounts differ slightly from those presented in the U.S. budget; but the national income accounts measures are more useful for analyzing the economic impact of federal activities.
  b. Revenues for all years including 1969 exclude the yield from the 10 percent temporary surcharge. Excise tax revenues assume the continuation of present rates.
  c. Total expenditures rounded to nearest billion.

annual growth in revenues after 1971 will be larger than in the prior two years simply because a relatively constant percentage growth is being applied to a growing base. On the other hand, the built-in growth of expenditures will be less. As time goes on, a larger and larger part of the federal budget is subject to discretionary control; less of it is determined by prior contracts and commitments.

The following sections briefly summarize each of the major sets of assumptions used in deriving the preliminary estimates of the fiscal dividend presented in Table 1. Later, I will discuss means of expanding the dividend substantially. (The reader who is primarily interested in the size and meaning of the fiscal dividend, rather than how it was estimated, may skip to page 35).

ECONOMIC GROWTH

Under conditions of full employment, the real output of the American economy will rise over the next five years by 4.5 to 5 percent per year. The civilian labor force will grow by almost 2 percent per year, most of which will result from the increase in population of working age, although a small part of the rise will reflect the release of some 850,000 men from the armed forces. A continued very modest decline in annual hours worked—as longer vacations are taken—will offset a small fraction of the labor force increase. Productivity of the private labor force should rise along a 3 percent trend. With the exception noted below, this projection assumes an unemployment rate of 3.75 percent. Taken altogether, these assumptions imply an average annual increase in real gross national product (GNP) and income of about 4.75 percent over the 1968–73 period.

Some slight modifications in these assumptions were made for the 1970–71 period during which the major part of the Vietnam demobilization is assumed to occur. An unemployment rate of 4 percent was assumed, rather than the 3.75 percent used in other years. The 3 percent annual growth in productivity was taken as a trend from 1966. Because of slack in the economy, 1967 productivity fell below that trend line—it increased by less than 3 percent over 1966. In the projections, productivity was assumed to recover the 1967 "loss." But most of that recovery was assumed to occur after 1971, on the ground that even with a highly successful transition after Vietnam the transition years would be slightly less prosperous than normal full employment conditions. Even mild economic sluggishness can dampen productivity growth. For similar reasons the ratio of corporate profits to GNP in 1970 and 1971 was held very slightly below its normal full employment level.

In short, full employment conditions were assumed for the period, with very modest downward adjustments in 1970 and 1971. The net result is that real GNP was assumed to grow by 4.5 percent annually between 1968 and 1971, and by 4.9 percent between 1971 and 1973.

Prices were assumed to continue rising over the period but at a decelerating rate. The overall price index for GNP is currently rising at an annual rate of 4 percent. The rate of price increase is assumed to drop to 2.25 percent by the middle of 1970 and then hold steady.

The results, in terms of projected GNP, prices, personal income, and profits, are shown in Table 2 for the calendar year 1970 and 1973 (which primarily determine federal revenue collections in the fiscal years 1971 and 1974).

TABLE 2. *Economic Projections*
(In billions of dollars)

Item	1967	1970	1973
Real GNP, 1958 dollars	673.1	765	880
Price index (1958 = 100)	117.3	128	137
GNP in current dollars	789.7	980	1,205
Major income components			
Personal income	628.8	778	950
Corporate profits before taxes	81.6	101	128

Source: Data for 1967 from *Survey of Current Business*, Vol. 48 (July 1968).

FEDERAL REVENUES

The revenue projections incorporate several assumptions. Corporate and individual income taxes were calculated without the temporary 10 percent surcharge, which is scheduled to expire on July 1, 1969. Should it be extended one additional year, through fiscal 1970, the extension would have only a modest effect on fiscal 1971 revenues. Should the surtax be retained through the period of the projection, an additional $11 billion in revenues would be available in fiscal 1971 and $15 billion in fiscal 1974. Federal excise tax rates on automobiles and telephones had been scheduled to decline in 1968 and 1969. The Revenue and Expenditure Control Act of 1968 (which also included the surcharge) extended these 1967 excise rates through fiscal 1969, after which they are again scheduled to decline. The projections, however, assume that the present rates are extended indefinitely. Should the rates be allowed to decline, as contemplated in present law, federal revenues in the projections would be reduced by $3 billion in fiscal 1971 and $3.5 billion in fiscal 1974. Table 3 summarizes the revenue projections.

TABLE 3. *Projection of Federal Revenues*
(In billions of dollars)

	Fiscal years		
Revenue items	1969	1971	1974
Federal revenues			
Individual income taxes	74.0	89.0	116.0
Corporate profits taxes	31.1	35.5	44.5
Employment taxes	34.4	40.5	51.7
Excise taxes	14.7	17.2	21.5
Other	13.9	16.1	19.5
Adjustment to NIA[a]	3.7	5.0	5.5
Total revenues[b]	172	203	259
Addendum			
10 percent surcharge[c] (NIA basis)	11.0	11.0	15.0
Scheduled excise tax reduction[c]	− 2.8	− 3.0	− 3.5

Source: Fiscal 1969 data based on "Summer Review of the 1969 Budget."
a. NIA: national income accounts.
b. Total revenues have been rounded to nearest billion.
c. Not included in the revenue estimates above.

BUILT-IN INCREASES IN CIVILIAN EXPENDITURES

The concept of "automatic" or "built-in" increases in the federal budget is not unambiguous. The effect of price increases on the cost of goods and services bought by the government, for example, has been included as a built-in increase. Yet, in any particular program, additional appropriations must be requested and enacted in order to meet the increased costs of operating the same program. Specific decisions have to be taken to request and enact those appropriations. And it is always possible to forgo the added appropriations, letting the real level of the program decline as prices rise. But this would imply a decision to change the real level of the program—that is, to lower it. Consequently, holding the real level of programs constant has been treated as the neutral case and the cost of meeting price increases defined as an automatic budgetary change. Similar considerations led to classifying federal pay increases (both military and civilian) as built-in.

The projection shows an $11 billion built-in rise in federal civilian outlays between fiscal years 1969 and 1971, excluding social security. Another

$8 billion of built-in increases are likely for the succeeding three years. While there are a large number of individual programs involved in these estimates, the major areas of increase can be briefly summarized as shown in Table 4.

Present law provides *pay increases* on July 1, 1969, to federal civilian employees sufficient to give them equality with employees in comparable occupations in private industry. On the average, federal employees were 3 to 4 percent behind private pay scales after their salaries were last increased, on July 1, 1968. Since the next survey of private wages and salaries will show an increase of at least 5 percent, federal salaries will have to be raised, conservatively between 8 and 9 percent—3 to 4 percent to catch up to the private sector and 5 percent to stay even as private wages rise. For future years, federal pay increases have been projected in parallel with private wage rates, estimated to rise by 4.5 percent annually. (Increases for civilian Defense Department employees are included under military spending.)

The effect on the budget of *wage and price increases*—assumed to level off at 2.25 percent a year by 1970—varies among programs. The cost of federal research and development contracts was assumed to rise at the same rate as private wages and salaries. Past experience indicates that construction costs will probably grow somewhat more rapidly than the general price level, and federal construction expenditures were increased accordingly. Prices of equipment and supplies purchased by the federal government, on the other hand, will probably rise less rapidly than the overall price index. The real level of federal grants-in-aid was held constant in the

TABLE 4. *Built-in Civilian Expenditure Increases*
(In billions of dollars)

	Fiscal years	
Expenditure items	1969 to 1971	1971 to 1974
Total[a]	10.8	8.4
Federal employees' pay	1.3	1.5
Price increases	2.0	3.0
Public assistance and Medicaid	1.2	0.9
Expenditures "catch-up" to program levels	3.2	—
Highway grants	1.0	0.4
Housing subsidies, net	0.1	1.1
Workload increases	0.4	0.6
Interest on the public debt	0.6	—
Other increases	1.0	0.9

a. In Table 1, the total increase was rounded to the nearest billion.

projection by assuming that the dollar value of grants rises sufficiently to offset increases in the general price level. Altogether, the assumed rates of price and wage increases will result in a $2 billion rise in federal civilian outlays between now and 1971 and a $3 billion increase in the subsequent three years.

Let me hasten to point out that there is no immutable law which says that all federal programs should be allowed to expand by precisely the amount needed to accommodate wage and price increases. The real level of each particular federal program should not be automatically protected against a decline. But I am attempting to measure the built-in growth in federal outlays on the assumption of no major policy changes, and have defined a policy change as a decision to vary real program levels.

Under *public assistance and Medicaid* the federal government shares with the states the cost of providing cash welfare payments and medical treatment for the poor. Within the limits provided in federal law, federal expenditures are determined by state policies on eligibility and size of welfare payments, and by the number of people becoming eligible for assistance under given eligibility standards. The projections assume that state cash payments will be increased in line with increases in the cost of living, and that recent increases in welfare caseloads will continue into the future, although at a lower rate than in the immediate past. Very sharp increases in hospital and medical costs have taken place in the last several years—doctors' fees at 8 percent a year and hospital costs at 16 percent annually. The projections assume a gradual reduction in the rates of increase over the next several years through 1973, leveling off at around 5 percent a year.

The social security amendments of 1967 provided for a freeze on part of the welfare caseload (that part dealing with Aid for Dependent Children). Early in 1968 the freeze was temporarily suspended for a year. The projections assume the freeze is permanently suspended.

Between 1969 and 1971 the combined built-in rise in federal expenditures for Medicaid and public assistance was estimated at $1.2 billion. Another increase of $900 million was projected for the succeeding three years. If the welfare freeze is reinstated, expenditures in 1974 would be about $600 million lower.

In many programs, expenditures lag behind program obligations or commitments, and so an allowance must be made for *expenditure "catch-ups."* Grants to state and local governments, for example, are first approved; then, as the states and localities gradually expend the funds, they draw upon the federal Treasury for the necessary cash, up to the limit of the grant approval. Similarly, contracts for the delivery of fighter aircraft are signed, but the actual expenditures are made as the contractor proceeds with production. In a number of important areas, federal program levels, as measured by contracts signed or grant commitments, will be significantly in excess of expenditures in fiscal 1969. As a consequence, even if 1969 program levels are held constant in future years, expenditures will necessarily rise as they catch up to program levels. Increases of $3.2 billion have been projected between now and 1971 on this account. Without further program expansion, expenditures would come close to matching authorized program levels by 1971, so no further increases have been projected for the succeeding three years. Programs of the Departments of Housing and Urban Development and Health, Education, and Welfare account for three-fourths of the 1969–71 increases in this category. In the Model Cities program, for example, large commitments are scheduled to be made in fiscal 1969, but significant expenditures under these grants will not occur until later years.

Federal grants to the states for construction of the interstate highways and primary and secondary roads are made from the *highway trust fund*. The revenues of this trust fund are derived from federal taxes on gasoline, diesel fuel, tires, and similar excises. Until fiscal 1967, federal highway expenditures tended to equal trust fund revenues. Since then, however, the growth in expenditures has been reduced, by administrative action, below the growth in revenues as an anti-inflationary measure, and the highway trust fund has accumulated $1.2 billion. Ultimately, barring a major change in the law, these funds must be used for highway grants-in-aid. In a post-Vietnam situation, therefore, highway expenditures should increase not only by the amount which economic growth adds to annual highway tax collections but also through the disbursement of these accumulated funds. An increase of $1 billion in highway expenditures between 1969 and 1971 has been assumed and, conservatively, an additional $400 million between 1971 and 1974.

The Housing Act of 1968 launches a large program of *housing subsidies* for low-income tenants and home owners. The long-run program, the first phases of which are authorized by the act, contemplates the building or rehabilitation of 6 million low-income housing units over ten years. As these units are completed, the annual subsidy costs will begin to rise. In the next several years, however, the rising subsidy cost will be partially offset as the subsidy technique (which results in federal budgetary costs being spread out over a number of years) replaces several direct housing loan programs (under which the entire construction cost is immediately reflected in the budget). On balance, housing subsidy expenditures are projected to rise by $100 million between 1969 and 1971 and an additional $1.1 billion over the subsequent three years.

In a large number of federal programs, *increases in workloads* are inevitable as population and national income grow. A rising number of tax returns places additional requirements on the Internal Revenue Service; growth in private ownership of pleasure boats raises the workload of the Coast Guard; rapid increases in civil air traffic require expanded air navigation and traffic control services from the Federal Aviation Agency. Overall economic growth raises the requirements for geographic maps and surveys, and increases the work of the Coast and Geodetic Service and the Geological Survey. The number of patent applications increases steadily. To gain some impression of the magnitude involved, major "workload-oriented" agencies of the federal government were identified (some twenty-seven bureaus or agencies with 1969 expenditures of $4.6 billion). As a rough approximation, their expenditures were extrapolated to 1971 and 1974 with the growth in real disposable income, population, or employment, whichever seemed most reasonable. In any given year, of course, there is no fixed relationship between the growth in expenditures of any agency and the growth of population or economic activity. But over the longer run, their expenditures will tend to rise as the economy grows, barring a decision to reduce the effective level of services provided. Growth of expenditures for these workload items was projected at $400 million for two years and a further $600 million in the following three years.

Even with no further increases in the public debt, *interest payments* will rise in the next year or so as the existing debt, originally issued at lower rates, matures and is refinanced at higher rates. In addition, even when the national income accounts budget is balanced, there is an increase in interest-bearing debt as the federal trust funds invest their growing surpluses in Treasury securities. Longer-term predictions of interest on the public debt depend heavily on the future course of interest rates. This projection, after allowing a $600 million increase in interest payments between 1969 and 1971, makes the convenient assumption that thereafter interest payments remain level.

Built-in expenditure increases were projected for several other areas:

veterans' compensation and pensions will at least keep up with cost-of-living increases, and veterans' medical services will reflect higher medical costs. Unemployment compensation will rise modestly even with a constant unemployment rate, owing to increases in the labor force and a higher wage base; federal retirement payments will rise, at a minimum, to reflect the growing number of retired federal employees. Increases of $1 billion between 1969 and 1971 and $900 million between 1971 and 1974 have been projected for these items.

SOCIAL SECURITY AND MEDICARE

The social security trust funds—Old Age and Survivors Insurance (OASI), Disability Insurance (DI) and Hospital Insurance under Medicare (HI)—present special problems. On the basis of the benefit schedules in present law, expenditures from the trust funds would rise by $2.6 billion from 1969 to 1971 and by $4.0 billion from 1971 to 1974. Revenues over the same period, however, would rise more than $6 billion by 1971 and another $11 billion by 1974. The growth in revenues stems both from rising payrolls and from the increases in payroll tax rates scheduled to occur in 1969, 1971, and 1973. In addition to payroll revenues, the trust funds receive interest on the Treasury securities they hold. With revenues and interest receipts running far ahead of benefit payments, these trust funds would build up very large surpluses—amounting to more than $63 billion at the end of 1972 and $110 billion by the end of 1975.

The past history of these trust funds has been that large surpluses are not allowed to accumulate. The Social Security Act is periodically amended to increase benefits and limit or eliminate the growth in the surplus. The surplus in the OASI trust fund, for example, remained constant, in the vicinity of $20 billion, for the eleven-year period 1955 to 1966. Benefit increases were legislated to match the growth in revenues. Between 1966 and the end of 1969, despite large benefit increases, the fund will grow by $8 billion. It is very doubtful if this growth will be permitted to continue.

These projections assume that benefit increases will be legislated sufficient to hold the surplus approximately at end-1969 levels. The trust funds will not be permitted to accumulate to the huge $60 and $110 billion levels which would be forthcoming in 1972 and 1975 in the absence of statutory benefit increases. Given the estimates of the payroll tax yield used in this paper, benefit increases of $9 billion between 1969 and 1971 and another $12 billion between 1971 and 1974 can be expected (see Table 5). These

28   Agenda for the Nation

are significantly more than would be required simply to take care of increased numbers of beneficiaries and rising medical costs—that is, the *real* levels of benefits will rise. The broader implications of the social security-payroll tax mechanism for the fiscal dividend will be discussed later.

TABLE 5. Increase in Social Security Trust Fund Expenditures, OASI, DI, HI

(In billions of dollars)

	Fiscal years	
Assumption used	1969–71	1971–74
Increase on basis of present law	2.6	4.0
Increase allowing for rising prices[a]	6.0	7.5
Increase necessary to hold surplus constant	9.0	12.0

Source: Estimates of benefit payments under present law from the *1968 Annual Report of the Board of Trustees of the Federal Old-Age and Survivors Insurance and Disability Insurance Trust Funds*, H. Doc. 288, 90 Cong. 2 sess. (1968), and *1968 Annual Report of the Board of Trustees of the Federal Hospital Insurance Trust Fund*, H. Doc. 290, 90 Cong. 2 sess. (1968); other estimates developed in accordance with assumptions explained in text. The estimates of trust fund revenues used in developing the figures in the last row of the table are slightly higher than those included in the two reports, since I am assuming a higher wage increase than is used in the reports.

a. OASI and DI benefits for fiscal 1971 were increased by 10 percent, reflecting an assumed 10 percent increase in consumer prices between calendar years 1967 and 1970. For fiscal 1974, OASI and DI benefits were increased by an additional 6½ percent, reflecting assumed consumer price increases between calendar 1970 and 1973. Hospital costs were assumed to increase faster than allowed for in the latest official projections—they were assumed to rise by 20 percent between fiscal year 1969 and 1971, and by another 25 percent between 1971 and 1974.

Savings from a Cessation of Vietnam Hostilities

The federal budget for fiscal 1969 estimates military expenditures, including military assistance, at $76.7 billion. An additional $1.3 billion must be added to this total to take account of the military and civilian pay increases which became effective on July 1, 1968. Total military spending therefore was projected at $78 billion. Of this amount, approximately $29 billion is identified as the cost of fighting the war in Vietnam.

The usual estimate of the fiscal dividend which would be made available from a cessation of hostilities in Vietnam assumes that the defense budget can be reduced by the $29 billion identified as the cost of Vietnam and, barring major changes in military policy, that non-Vietnam defense spending can be held at about $50 billion.

This set of assumptions is, I believe, seriously wrong on two counts. First, the true additional costs of Vietnam are less than $29 billion. Second, there are in process, already approved, large weapons systems procurement and other non-Vietnam military programs which will add very substantially to future defense expenditures. These expenditures are not inevitable, but halting them will require explicit policy decisions, reversing current programs.

Some of the $29 billion identified as the cost of the Vietnam war would have been spent in any event, even had there been no Vietnam. B-52s would have been flying training missions; fighter aircraft would have had to be replaced because of obsolescence and attrition from accidents; equipment would have worn out; naval task forces would have been engaged in training exercises, and so forth. In addition, many military expenditures which would have taken place have been deferred during the Vietnam war; construction of family housing at military bases and maintenance and normal construction work at military bases are cases in point.

On balance it seems likely that the net addition to total military expenditures attributable to Vietnam hostilities amounts to $20 to $22 billion. One indirect way to check this estimate is to ask the following question: If, in the absence of Vietnam, real military outlays remained at the level reached in the period prior to Vietnam, what would be the dollar value of military outlays in fiscal 1969? In 1964, the year immediately before our large-scale involvement in Vietnam, military spending was $50 billion. Taking into account pay and price increases since that time, military expenditures would now have to be about $58–$60 billion to maintain the 1964 real level of spending. The differences between this $58–$60 billion and the $78 billion total projected for fiscal 1969 produces an estimated $18–$20 billion as the incremental cost of Vietnam—a range very close to the $20–$22 billion estimated above.

Starting with a total of $22 billion as the current incremental cost of Vietnam, the budgetary savings from a cessation of hostilities were estimated by fiscal year on the basis of the assumption described earlier:

A cease-fire early in 1969, with a withdrawal of all American troops beginning on July 1, 1969, and continuing through July 1, 1970. The approximately 850,000 addition to the armed forces, between June 30, 1965, and June 30, 1969, will be deactivated. Ammunition and ordnance production lines will be kept running at presently high rates for a short period after the cease-fire in order to rebuild those inventories which have been depleted during the war.[3]

3. Large parts of the ammunition and ordnance inventory during peacetime are based on the need to bridge the gap between the start of hostilities and the reactivation of "hot" production lines. Once production lines are running at the level needed to take care of wartime consumption, these buffer stocks are not needed and may be eliminated. But after the war ends they have to be rebuilt before the production lines can be turned off.

Budgetary savings will grow from a small amount in the first quarter after the cease-fire to about $13 billion in fiscal 1970 and $21 billion in 1971.[4] (Thus, under this set of assumptions, almost all of the "savings" would be realized by fiscal 1971.)

To illustrate a more pessimistic scenario, the dates for cease-fire and withdrawal were moved back six months (cease-fire, July 1, 1969; withdrawal begins January 1, 1970) and the assumption was made that 100,000 of the troops, demobilized under the earlier assumption, are maintained in the armed forces and stationed in Southeast Asia. Under these assumptions, budgetary savings would be significantly less in fiscal 1970 and 1971 ($7 billion and $13 billion, respectively) and ultimate savings would be about $2 billion less than under the full-demobilization assumption used earlier.

Numerous other alternative outcomes are possible, including situations in which there is no formal cease-fire but the intensity of combat gradually diminishes. The first alternative, used in the basic projection, tends to present the optimistic limits of the possible set of outcomes. Other alternatives would generally imply a later or more gradual reduction in Vietnam costs.

The second, and equally difficult, aspect of projecting military expenditures relates to the future course of non-Vietnam outlays. As I pointed out earlier, it would be quite unrealistic to project military expenditures as built-in increases. Under this procedure weapons system procurement programs would gradually phase out, as the systems were produced. With no new procurement introduced, the projection would show an artificial decline in total military expenditures. The estimates presented here, therefore, represent an attempt to project non-Vietnam military spending on the basis of *currently approved military postures, force levels, and commitments.* The projections have been made on a conservative basis; they assume a significant stretch-out and deferral of a number of existing weapons system procurement programs.

First, there are now in process, at fairly early stages of development or procurement, a number of large weapons systems which, if continued, will significantly increase spending over the next three or more years. These

---

4. Table 1 shows a $24 billion rather than a $22 billion ultimate Vietnam saving in fiscal 1974. This stems from the way the calculations were done. Total defense expenditures were projected to 1974. These expenditures, both Vietnam and non-Vietnam components, are affected by increases in pay and prices. Consequently, a $22 billion Vietnam cost in 1971 prices would amount to $24 billion in 1974 simply because of rising pay and prices.

Budget Alternatives after Vietnam 31

systems fall primarily into three categories: strategic nuclear forces; Navy shipbuilding and associated weapons; and advanced tactical aircraft.

In the last several years decisions have been made to upgrade substantially the capabilities of the U.S. strategic offensive forces as a hedge against Soviet deployment of an antiballistic missile system (ABM), and other improvements in their strategic forces. A new missile, Minuteman III, is being developed and will be deployed. Under present plans it will carry multiple independently targeted reentry vehicles (MIRVs)[5] and penetration aids. The Minuteman II is being improved and the older Minuteman I phased out of the force. The estimated investment cost of the Minuteman II/III program is $4.6 billion, the largest part of which has yet to be expended.

The new Poseidon submarine-launched strategic missile has been developed to replace most of the existing Polaris missiles carried by our nuclear ballistic missile submarines. Thirty-one Polaris submarines will be converted to carry 496 Poseidon missiles at a conversion cost of $80 million per submarine. Funds for the first six conversions are included in the 1969 budget request. Expenditures will occur in subsequent years. Procurement of 253 new FB-111 bombers is getting under way, together with the development and procurement of a new stand-off air-to-ground missile system.

The decision to proceed with the deployment of the Sentinel "thin anti-Chinese" antiballistic missile system was made in late 1967. Procurement of long lead time items will occur in fiscal 1969 but the bulk of expenditures for this $5.5 billion program will occur in subsequent years.

A large Navy shipbuilding program is also getting under way. Four nuclear-powered aircraft carriers, at a presently estimated cost of $540 million each, are now planned. Construction of the first carrier is just beginning. Funds for advance procurement of the second carrier are included in the 1969 budget, with construction to begin in 1970. Construction of the remaining two carriers will begin at a later date. Practically all of the expenditures under this program are still to come.

A major destroyer construction program is also contemplated. The House appropriations bill defers construction of the first five destroyers in this program until 1970, but the committee report clearly indicated that

---

5. With MIRVs, one missile can carry a number of warheads, each of which can be separately targeted. MIRVs, in effect, multiply the capability of a given missile system. Penetration aids can be carried on missiles in the form of decoys, chaff, etc., designed to confuse potential enemy ABM defenses.

the program should go ahead, attributing the temporary deferral to the current budget stringency. Construction will begin soon on five nuclear-powered escort ships, at a total cost of $625 million and the House Appropriations Committee expressed concern that the planned number of nuclear escorts was too small. In addition, a decision has been made, and initial funds included in the 1969 budget, to develop and procure an advanced nuclear attack submarine. A new Navy fighter, the VFX-1, is under development to replace the Navy version of the F-111. Major expenditures under this program will begin to occur in the year 1970 and beyond.

One fairly predictable feature of most of these weapons systems is that their ultimate cost will be substantially higher than their currently estimated cost. The last conventionally powered aircraft carrier, the John F. Kennedy, cost $277 million. In 1967 the estimated cost of the first nuclear carrier, the Nimitz, was $427 million. By January 1968 that estimated cost had risen to $540 million. The cost of the Sentinel ABM system was estimated in 1967 at $4.4 billion. The latest published estimate is $5.5 billion. When President Johnson announced development of the Air Force's Manned Orbiting Laboratory, the cost was projected at $1.5 billion; the latest cost estimate is given as $2.9 billion. In January 1967 the unit cost of an Air Force F-111 was given as $6.2 million. A year later this had risen to $7.1 million.

In addition to approved programs, there are a number of new weapons systems in the development process about which procurement decisions will have to be made, one way or the other, during the next five years. An advanced strategic bomber, conceived as a replacement for the B-52, is under development. So also is a new strategic missile to be placed in hardened silos, a new main battle tank for the Army (being developed jointly with West Germany), a new Navy attack aircraft (VFX-2), a new antisubmarine plane (VSX), a new Air Force fighter, a new undersea long-range missile system, a sea-based ABM, and a long-range missile system for surface ships. In addition, there will be substantial pressure to expand the existing "thin anti-Chinese" ABM to cover other contingencies. The following quotations from the House hearings give the flavor:

Mr. Sikes: I have a greater apprehension about a possible attack from submarines than I have from Chinese ICBM's. . . . What steps would be necessary, at what contemplated cost, and in what time period to provide defense coverage against Soviet SLBM's [submarine launched ballistic missiles] comparable to Sentinel?

[Information requested follows: To provide defense coverage against Soviet

SLBM's comparable to Sentinel ICBM coverage would require additional Sentinel components with an estimated investment cost of (censored)] ....

Mr. Sikes: Now to stretch our imagination a little, if there should be a recurrence of the Cuban missile threat against the United States, will the Sentinel system provide defense against it?

General Starbird: Not as currently designed, sir.

. . . . . .

Mr. Sikes: Will the Sentinel system defend against FOBS [the fractional orbit ballistic system currently under development by the Soviets]?

General Starbird: It will provide only limited protection as currently designed against FOBS. However, it again could be augmented to take care of a FOBS threat.

. . . . . .

Mr. Sikes: ... I think the Russian threat is a much greater threat. ... I am not as alarmed about the Chinese threat as I am about the Russian threat. Am I wrong?

General Starbird: The Russian threat ... is a much more substantial threat and would require an augmented system.[6]

Knowledge that new weapons systems are being introduced into the armed forces and will be enlarged in future years is one thing. Translating this knowledge into estimates of defense spending is much more difficult. The estimates presented in this paper were developed on a conservative basis, along the following lines (see Table 6):

First, a combination of congressional cuts in defense appropriations and administration deferrals to meet the budget reduction which accompanied the surcharge is assumed to reduce the 1969 funds available to the Defense Department for non-Vietnam programs by about $6 billion from the January budget estimate. Should the Vietnam war extend beyond fiscal 1969, however, some of the funds withheld from non-Vietnam programs will have to be transferred to Vietnam programs in the early part of calendar 1969 to buy long lead time weapons. In projecting military expenditures including Vietnam, it was assumed that such funds would be indeed transferred to meet Vietnam requirements, and that actual 1969 military expenditures would be $79 billion, instead of the $78 billion carried in the official estimates.

6. *Department of Defense Appropriations for 1969*, Hearings before a Subcommittee of the House Committee on Appropriations, 90 Cong. 2 sess. (1968), Pt. 3, pp. 15-19 *passim*.

TABLE 6. Military Expenditure Projections[a]
(In billions of dollars)

	1969	Fiscal years Change 1969 to 1971	1971	Change 1971 to 1974	1974
Total, including Vietnam	79.0		91.0		100.0
Pay increases[b]		4.2		4.5	
Price increases		1.6		2.9	
Program increases		6.2		1.6	
Less: Vietnam savings	−1.0		−21.0		−24.0
Equals: Net total	78.0		70.0		76.0

Source: Fiscal 1969 estimate of military expenditures, including Vietnam, is equal to the $78 billion forecast in the "Summer Review of the 1969 Budget," plus a $1 billion upward adjustment for reasons given in the text.

a. Military expenditures include the military functions of the Department of Defense and the military assistance program.

b. Excludes potential cost increases from the planned conversion of military pay to a straight salary basis.

Second, most of the 1969 reductions were assumed to be deferrals and stretch-outs, rather than cancellations. (An examination of House Appropriations Committee cuts, for example, shows this to be the case.)

Third, fiscal 1970 was assumed to be a tight budget year, so that the Defense Department is allowed to make up only part of the 1969 cuts in 1970; I assume that only 60 percent of the cuts will be made up.

Fourth, the spending authority needed in 1970 to continue or to launch the approved programs described above adds about $6 billion to 1969 spending authority as originally budgeted. I assumed that practically none of this addition will be allowed in 1970, that one-half of the added funds will be removed in a rigorous budget review, and that the other half of the increase will be deferred until 1971.

Fifth, I assumed that after 1971 the phasing out of completed weapons programs will be matched by new ones, so that no net additions to spending authority for non-Vietnam purposes are allowed, except to cover increases in prices and in military and civilian pay.

From the resulting projections of spending authority, expenditures were estimated year by year. Since actual expenditures lag behind the provision of spending authority, they will continue to increase after 1971, even though spending authority levels off.

Just as in the case of civilian programs, allowance has to be made in the projections for increases in the pay of the armed forces and of the civilians employed by the Defense Department. The same basic assumptions were used. In recent years, the Congress has increased military pay by the same percentage as federal civilian pay, and the projections assume that this practice continues.[7]

The overall military expenditure total was first developed on the assumption of a continuation of the Vietnam war throughout the period, without further escalation. From this total, the estimated savings accompanying a cessation of hostilities in Vietnam can be subtracted to give a net projection of post-Vietnam military outlays.

Use of the Fiscal Dividend

The inclusion of built-in increases for civilian programs in calculating the fiscal dividend does not mean that the President and the Congress will have unfettered discretion in allocating that dividend. There are currently more than 400 federal grant-in-aid programs and a host of special credit programs providing loans for specific purposes. A wide variety of programs are directly operated by the federal government—flood control projects, national parks, watershed protection projects, and so on. Each of these has its own group of supporters, all of whom will be pressing for an increase in their program, particularly as Vietnam expenditures are declining. Some of these programs would take a high place on almost any reasonable list of priorities. But for purposes of estimating the uses to which the fiscal dividend can be put, one cannot assume that all of the dividend can easily be assigned just to high priority programs, or to some combination of high priority programs and tax reductions. Given the political facts of life, and the strong pressure exerted by individual program participants, the projected fiscal dividend should probably be discounted somewhat before calculating the amounts available solely for top-priority uses.

With that caveat, a brief survey of some of the more important claims upon the fiscal dividend may help to place the size of the fiscal dividend in perspective.

7. For the sake of presenting conservative estimates, one likely element of increased costs was omitted. The Defense Department has developed a new, simpler salary structure for officers and noncoms. A host of fringe benefits (allowances for quarters, special tax treatment, and so on) are converted to a straight salary basis. This new system is estimated to save budgetary costs over the long run. But it adds about $1 billion to military expenditures in each of the first several years after its introduction. Although it is highly likely that the new system will be introduced as part of the post-Vietnam transition, the projections developed here do not include it.

CLAIMS OF EXISTING PROGRAMS

In the first place, many of the newer programs inaugurated in the last five years have been significantly "underfunded." The most easily measurable kind of underfunding occurs when annual appropriations for a program fall below the amount authorized in the legislation creating the program. A sample count of fifteen programs, all dealing with relatively important social problems, indicated that actual program levels in fiscal 1969 were about $5 billion below the authorized amount.

When we expand our consideration beyond this relatively mechanical measure, the potential magnitude becomes very large. The Model Cities program, for example, aims at rehabilitating and providing a wide range of social services in specific urban slum neighborhoods. The 1969 budget requested $1 billion for this program. Some 130 to 140 cities would be involved, but only a fraction of the areas needing rehabilitation is included in each city's plan. If the program works, if it is chosen as the major vehicle for attacking the truly massive problems of our inner cities, substantial additional funds would be required. A full-scale program would cover four to five times the number of neighborhoods now involved (more cities and more neighborhoods per city), at an annual cost of $4 to $5 billion, compared to the $1 billion requested in the 1969 budget.

Improving the education of the poor, particularly children in schools where most of the population is poor, is one of the nation's most important and challenging problems. While knowledge of precisely how to accomplish this result is still rudimentary, most of the evidence seems to show that "compensatory education" cannot be effectively achieved without a large increase in per capita educational expenditures. At the present time Title I of the Elementary and Secondary Education Act makes grants to school districts for compensatory education in an amount which averages about $125 for each school child from poor families. Average per child expenditures on the part of state and local governments currently amount to about $600. To provide supplementary resources for compensatory education to raise average per capita educational expenditures on poor children by 50 percent—that is, from $600 to $900—for the roughly 10 million poor children of school age, would cost $3 billion, a $2 billion increase over present Title I outlays. Doubling per capita outlays, which may be necessary to make a real impact in compensatory education, would add $5 billion to current Title I expenditures. Making adequate provision for the education of the handicapped and extending the pre-school Head Start program to all poor children would require another $1.5 to $2 billion.

The Community Action Agency is the heart of the Office of Economic Opportunity's poverty program. In fiscal 1969 the budget requested slightly less than $1 billion for this program, compared with requirements ranging from $3 to $5 billion (estimated by using per capita requirements for a successful program in one of the better community action agencies, extrapolating those estimates to the rest of the nation on the basis of the number of poor people and then discounting the result by 50 percent on grounds that equally effective programs cannot be mounted throughout the country).

During recent years the emphasis in federal manpower training programs has shifted toward on-the-job training, with initial subsidies to employers to cover the costs of training expenses and lost productivity. A conservative estimate of training costs is $3,000 per trainee for one year. A three-year program to reach 1.5 million hard-core unemployed would require $1.5 billion a year.

In 1960 the United States devoted two-thirds of one percent of its gross national product to foreign economic assistance (including food aid). In fiscal 1969 the foreign aid budget request would have devoted a smaller fraction to this purpose, slightly more than one-half of one percent—and the Congress reduced that substantially. Simply to return to the point at which we devote the same fraction of our national income to foreign aid as we did in 1960, would require a $3 billion increase in budget expenditures by 1974. To reach the point in 1974 where one percent of our national income was used to assist the developing countries would require an added $7 billion in budget outlays. By the end of this century—now only three decades away—income per person in the United States, in dollars of today's purchasing power, will exceed $10,000. With current prospects, the income per person in a large part of the world will still be less than $400 per year, and, more to the point, it will still be rising very slowly. Whether any kind of meaningful international order can exist under those circumstances is, at best, an open question.

Other existing programs that would require substantial additional funds include: the control of air, water, and other environmental pollution; assistance in the development of urban mass transit systems; assistance to states and localities to improve law enforcement; the modernization of city hospitals and the development of additional health resources for poor neighborhoods, both urban and rural; and assistance to economically depressed areas. But in virtually every program, the budgetary resources now provided make possible only a relatively modest, and geographically quite limited, attack upon the problem.

NEW INITIATIVES

Public debate over the past several years has raised the possibility of two major new programs requiring sizable budgetary resources: federal income maintenance and federal revenue sharing with states and local governments.

James Tobin's paper in this volume discusses alternative possibilities for income maintenance programs. Present welfare programs suffer from a number of deficiencies. From a budgetary standpoint, three issues are particularly important: eligibility, size of payment, and work incentives. As of June 1965, of the 35 million people living in poverty only 16 million were eligible for welfare payments under federal standards. Of the 16 million, fewer than half were receiving public assistance, primarily because some state laws had more restrictive eligibility standards than the federal government. While the situation has improved since then, far more than half the poverty population is not assisted by any form of income payments. The problem is especially acute for those who have jobs but earn very low wages. Moreover, in many states, the average monthly welfare check is far below the subsistence level. In the program of aid to families with dependent children, for example, the average monthly check per recipient is currently $8.50 in Mississippi, $15 in Florida and Alabama, and $19 in South Carolina, compared to $46 in California, $45 in Illinois, $49 in Wisconsin, and $55 in Connecticut. Although recent changes in the federal law have begun to make improvements, incentives for welfare recipients to earn additional income are blunted because under present laws additional earnings generally reduce the size of the welfare check.

Correcting any or all of these problems is expensive. The negative income tax would require large additional outlays. Various detailed plans have been suggested, whose costs would range from $5 to $50 billion a year, depending on the level of income guaranteed and the rate at which income maintenance payments are reduced as the earned income of recipients increases.

The range of possible program costs from $5 to $50 billion is very wide indeed. The less expensive programs would provide a relatively low basic income and reduce income payments sharply as the recipients earned outside income. The cost of income maintenance programs begins to rise steeply when more than half of the poverty income is provided as a minimum and when substantial work incentives are provided. With work incentives incorporated into the program, recipients would be allowed to keep a significant proportion of their income allowance when they earn other income in order to make seeking and holding a job financially attractive, even though the combined income from federal payments and earnings significantly exceeds the poverty level.

An alternative route for improving the welfare system is to have the federal government assume the entire responsibility—substantially raising the level of benefits in some states, broadening eligibility standards, and increasing work incentives. Simply assuming the welfare financing now carried by the states, including medical assistance, would cost $4.7 billion. Raising the minimum benefit level, improving eligibility standards, and expanding work incentives by allowing welfare recipients to keep a significant fraction of additional earnings would cost many billions more. In fact, the cost of achieving any given nationwide level of income maintenance by this route would cost approximately the same as reaching similar objectives through a negative income tax.

In short, major improvements in income maintenance would absorb a significant part of the fiscal dividend. As income maintenance payments began to approach a reasonably high level, some offsetting savings could be made in the budget as certain special types of assistance—for example, distribution of surplus foods—became unnecessary. Nevertheless, the net costs would still be quite large.

Federal sharing of tax revenues with states and local governments is a second major new proposal. The claim on the fiscal dividend from such a program varies with the amount of revenue to be shared. But with 50 states and thousands of local governments, currently spending almost $100 billion per year, any revenue-sharing scheme which hoped to ease state and local fiscal problems significantly would have to exceed some minimum size—perhaps $5 billion per year.

The adoption of a negative income tax or federalization of the existing welfare system would be a form of revenue sharing. It would relieve state and local governments of part or all of the current burden of financing welfare payments. In states where welfare payments are currently very small, however, the fiscal relief from this approach would be less than that given by most of the revenue-sharing schemes which have been suggested.

Increasing the Fiscal Dividend

Ideally a projection of the fiscal dividend should be neutral with respect to future policy decisions. It should measure the difference between revenues under existing tax rates and the expenditures that would occur in the absence of substantial new policy decisions. This difference would indicate the budgetary resources automatically becoming available to expand public programs or reduce tax rates. For reasons explained earlier, however, the fiscal dividend estimated in this paper already assumes a series of future policy decisions in two areas—the defense budget and the social security program. A different set of decisions could produce a different fiscal dividend.

REDUCTIONS IN MILITARY EXPENDITURES

Decisions about the military budget depend fundamentally on three factors: the size and shape of strategic forces needed to provide deterrence against nuclear war or nuclear blackmail; the complex of U.S. interests and commitments whose safeguarding requires that we maintain conventional armed forces; and judgments about the force levels and weapons systems required to meet these first two objectives. The future shape of the defense budget, as it now appears to be developing, can be changed by decisions affecting any of these three elements. Carl Kaysen's paper in this volume discusses these precise questions. He puts forward a number of proposals based upon two central considerations: first, a series of initiatives designed by the United States to promote a meaningful limitation of U.S. and Soviet strategic forces; and second, a reevaluation of U.S. foreign commitments as they affect requirements for conventional forces. On the basis of his proposals, he develops a military budget that would be $15–16 billion lower than the post-Vietnam estimate presented here.[8] A reduction of this magnitude would require not only the adoption of recommendations along the lines which Kaysen suggests, but also a very rigorous screening of currently approved and proposed weapons system developments.

I have only one comment to add to Kaysen's exposition. If the military

8. Kaysen's reduced defense budget for the early 1970s amounts to $50 billion in 1969 prices. Adjustment of this budget to the pay and price levels of 1974 yields a figure of about $60 billion, compared to the $76 billion estimate presented in this paper.

budget in the early 1970s is not substantially lower than the level implied by current policy (my estimate), it will quite possibly grow well beyond that level in subsequent years. Because each side attempts to protect itself against uncertainty, strategic arms budgets can have a dynamic effect all their own. The present build-up of strategic forces and technological capabilities by the United States is designed to cover all bets in the preservation of our second-strike retaliatory capability. That is, it is designed not only to meet the highest likely Soviet threat, as estimated by intelligence sources, but to counter a "greater than expected" threat. As we build our own missile forces toward this objective, however, a Soviet missile force at the level toward which Soviet leaders now appear to be building would, from their point of view, begin to be marginal in terms of maintaining a second-strike capability. This is a particularly likely development when the actual deployment of MIRVs by the United States, or the capacity to deploy them rapidly, threatens Soviet defense planners with a manifold multiplication of the U.S. striking force. Moreover, it is much harder to determine the MIRV capability of enemy forces than it is to estimate other aspects of force capability.

Faced with this situation, the Soviet Union would have to strengthen its own forces. In other words, by building our own strategic forces on the assumption of a greater than expected threat, and in a way which sharply increases the uncertainties facing Soviet planners, we may well force them to construct that threat. In turn, we would then have to hedge our revised intelligence estimates with a new "greater than expected" threat estimate and a second round of improvements in U.S. strategic forces.

Similarly, as we go ahead with the deployment of the "thin anti-Chinese" ABM system, the pressures for expansion of that system will grow rapidly. The "thin" system contains most of the components needed for a system designed against a host of other threats. No major new breakthroughs are needed, just huge amounts of money. And to the extent that our development of a defense against Chinese ICBMs forces them to concentrate on submarine-launched missiles, then the original system will have to be augmented to meet the new threat which it itself created. A full-scale expansion, in an attempt to protect a major fraction of U.S. industry and population against a Soviet attack, would undoubtedly cost in the neighborhood of $40 billion and probably would provoke a counter response by the Soviet Union, negating the benefit of part or all of the investment.

In short, the future budgetary consequences of present strategic policy may prove to represent an unstable equilibrium. Either decisions will be made to reduce those expenditures, or they may themselves create a situation in which further expenditure increases will occur. To the extent that this evaluation is correct, the post-Vietnam fiscal dividend will either be significantly increased by policies that reduce military spending or it will be significantly eroded by further additions to that spending. There may be no intermediate position.

SOCIAL SECURITY BENEFITS

Calculation of the fiscal dividend assumed on the basis of experience that social security benefits will be increased in line with increased revenues. The financial mechanism of the social security system tends to generate large potential surpluses, which form the basis for benefit increases. Payroll tax rates are set to cover the actuarial cost of the social security system, taking into account projected growth both in the number of people paying payroll taxes and the number of beneficiaries. Since the aged population will grow relative to the working population, the tax rates which are established generate surpluses in the near future to cover the higher costs of later years. More importantly, the actuarial calculations assume level earnings; that is, wage rates are assumed to remain constant in the future. As wages rise, however, payroll tax revenues are increased much faster than benefits; a rise in wages for the typical worker will increase his payroll taxes immediately but his benefits only after retirement. As a consequence, the trust fund surplus grows much more rapidly than the actuarial calculations project. In turn, the sharply rising surpluses (actual and potential) give rise to legislation increasing benefits. But with higher benefits, future costs increase. To cover those future cost increases, the payroll tax rates are again raised. This, in turn, generates new surpluses in the succeeding years, leading to another round of benefit increases. The implications of this sequence are illustrated in Table 7.

Even with level earnings, tax rates are set to generate large increases in the surplus. A 3 percent annual wage increase greatly increases that surplus. Even if average benefit payments (and maximum taxable earnings) are advanced proportionately to wage increases, the system still generates huge surpluses.

In fiscal 1969 the social security trust funds are increasing their surplus

TABLE 7. Cumulative Surplus in the OASDI Trust Fund under Alternative Assumptions
(In billions of dollars)

End of year	Level earnings	Earnings increase at 3% per year	Earnings increase[a] at 3% per year, benefits increased proportionately
1968	28	28	28
1975	n.a.	108	92
1980	75	213	168
1985	99	349	250

Source: 1968 Annual Report of the Board of Trustees of the Federal Old-Age and Survivors Insurance and Disability Insurance Trust Funds.

a. Both benefits and maximum taxable earnings are increased in line with average wage increases.

at an annual rate in excess of $4 billion. By 1974 annual payroll tax revenues will be $17 to $18 billion higher than in 1969. Increases in social security and hospital insurance benefits to match the growth in the number of beneficiaries and in the cost of living would increase annual benefit payments by only $13 to $14 billion annually in 1974. Minimum benefits could be sharply raised, as a effective antipoverty measure, at an additional annual cost of $1 to $1.5 billion. (The current minimum for a single retired worker at age 65 is $55. This could be raised to, say, $90, and other minimums scaled accordingly.) Even after such increases, social security trust fund surpluses would be growing at an annual rate of $6 to $7 billion in 1974. There is no substantive reason why these surpluses could not be used as national priorities dictate. If an increase in social security benefits takes a very high priority, then benefits should be raised. But if other federal programs or tax reductions should be judged to have higher priority, then the trust funds could run a $6 to $7 billion annual surplus offsetting a similar deficit in the remainder of the government's accounts.

In short, if past practice continues, the potential large surplus accumulation in the social security trust funds will almost inevitably be used to increase benefit levels beyond the amount needed to cover cost-of-living increases and population growth. The fiscal dividend estimated in this paper assumes this outcome. But there is no a priori reason why historical practice has to be followed. National priorities should dictate the use of these funds. They can be used, as a surplus in the trust fund, to offset the economic effect of higher priority spending or of tax reductions on the rest of the budget.

REDUCING LOW-PRIORITY PROGRAMS

Another way of increasing the fiscal dividend is through a rigorous screening of existing federal programs, seeking to reduce or eliminate those which have low priority. The difficulty with this approach is that most programs that have low priority for the nation have very powerful support from a special constituency. Indeed, the continued existence of such programs in the face of the large budget deficits and mounting social needs of the past several years testifies to the potency of their support. It is impossible in a brief paper like this to provide a realistic treatment of the possibilities for program reform and reduction. But a few illustrations can be mentioned.

The farm price-support operations of the federal government are estimated at $3.5 billion in the fiscal 1969 budget, and recent official statements have indicated that this estimate will be exceeded. Because benefits are based on price support operations, they are distributed among farmers in rough proportion to the value of crops produced. Large producers benefit more from price supports than small producers. Sixty-eight percent of the cash receipts from farming in 1966 went to the 16 percent of farmers whose cash receipts exceeded $20,000. The average net income of those farmers, taking account of their nonfarm income, was $20,000. In effect, therefore, roughly two-thirds of the $3.5 billion federal price support costs accrue to the benefit of the top one-sixth of farmers, who have average incomes of $20,000. Very little of the benefits, on the other hand, go to farmers earning less than a poverty income. Most of the federal government's price support outlays are used to buy land out of production in order to keep farm prices up. If these payments were eliminated, farm income would fall by more than $3.5 billion as production increased and prices fell more than proportionately to the production increase. The dilemma is, therefore, to find a means of reducing federal subsidies to high-income farmers without producing a drastic fall in farm income. One possibility, often urged, is to put an upper limit on payments to any one farmer. A very low limit would induce many large farmers to withdraw from federal acreage limitations and sharply increase production, driving down farm incomes. Initially, therefore, the limit might be set relatively high, and gradually reduced as rising population and income called for increased farm production.

The space program accounts for $4 billion of the 1969 federal budget. Outlays on the manned lunar landing (the Apollo program) have been declining and will continue to do so. Decisions will have to be taken very shortly about the basic nature of the post-Apollo space effort. Maintaining and exercising U.S. manned space capability, particularly our Saturn V large-rocket capability, would probably require a minimum space budget of about $3.5 billion a year. A program which concentrated primarily on unmanned scientific experiments might be run for $2 to $2.5 billion. Our capabilities in the manned space flight area would then be left to the Air Force, with its Manned Orbiting Laboratory (MOL). The MOL program, however, employs a Titan III rocket with about one-third the lift capacity of the NASA's large and expensive Saturn V ($250 million per rocket booster).

The cheaper unmanned space program would probably yield almost as much valuable scientific information as the more expensive manned space alternative. Choosing the cheaper alternative, however, would mean closing down our large rocket, large payload capability, and allowing the personnel to scatter to other jobs. While it is hard to conceive of a major effective military use of very large space payloads, one can never be certain. Should the Soviet Union, for example, launch a large earth-orbiting satellite platform, any President of the United States would be under extreme pressure to reactivate our large rocket capability on a crash basis. The policy issues of whether or not to reduce the NASA program to an unmanned effort consequently pose most difficult questions. In summary, the fiscal dividend might be increased by $500 million per year by keeping the post-Apollo manned space program to a minimum effort and by another $1 to $1.5 billion by abandoning NASA's manned space program.

About $600 million of veterans' benefits represent disability compensation to veterans having low (10 to 30 percent) disability ratings. While evidence is quite hard to come by, it is highly probable that these veterans suffer no income impairment. The Veterans Administration is conducting a detailed study of income impairment among disabled veterans. If its results support the conclusions drawn above, these payments could be discontinued. An additional $100 million in veterans' benefits are paid for what appear to be unwarranted purposes; for example, the family of a veteran who is also a social security beneficiary can receive two burial payments, one from the Veterans Administration and one from the Social Security Administration. I leave to the reader's imagination, however, an evaluation of the political difficulties of carrying out these recommendations.

Other areas also warrant a searching reexamination. Should the federal government continue to make 2 percent loans to rural electric co-ops for building new generating plants? The 2 percent rate was set in the 1930s when interest on Treasury securities was also near 2 percent, and when less than half of American farms were electrified compared to over 95 percent today.

The federal maritime program subsidizes the U.S. merchant marine in a number of ways, to the tune of about $500 million per year and in a manner which is almost guaranteed to promote inefficiency. For every seafaring job supported by this program, the cost to the federal government is $7,000 per year. The construction of a merchant ship in U.S. yards is more than twice as expensive as it is in a foreign yard. The federal government pays the difference and carries on a sizable merchant marine construction subsidy program, at a time when the Navy shipbuilding program is crowding U.S. shipbuilding capacity to the point where prices are rising rapidly. Need this continue?

The President's Commission on Postal Organization estimated that reforms in the postal service could reduce costs by $1.5 billion. The principal reforms recommended would remove personnel appointments and the determination of wages and prices from the political arena. The Post Office would be reorganized, removed from the Cabinet, and established as a government corporation. Even if the commission overestimated the savings from these moves by 100 percent, there remains the possibility of a $750 million addition to the fiscal dividend (and better postal service) from the adoption of their recommendations.

Federal irrigation projects provide large subsidies in the form of cheap water primarily to middle-income and upper-income farmers. Many of these projects direct scarce water toward unproductive use in agriculture, and raise farm production when other federal programs are spending money to reduce it.

The impacted area school program channels $450 million a year into school districts on the basis of the number of children of federal employees attending public school in the district. But 70 percent of these employees do not live on federal lands; they are property-tax-paying residents of the school district. The argument is sometimes offered that the federal installations at which the employees work remove land from local tax rolls and depress school revenues. This argument is scarcely consistent with the zeal shown by congressmen to get federal installations located in their districts. The net effect is usually an increase in the local tax base. Some $300 million might be saved here.

Appropriate user charges on commercial and general aviation to cover the costs of federal air-traffic control and navigation services could bring in an additional $300 million, and at the same time, if properly assessed, would help relieve air-traffic congestion. Although commercial aviation, through a ticket tax, pays a large fraction of the federal costs associated with its activities, private planes used for business or pleasure pay less than 10 percent of the costs they cause the federal government to incur.

While these examples by no means exhaust the possibilities of budgetary saving, they suggest the kinds of issues involved and also the probable political difficulties in achieving substantial savings.

Table 8 summarizes potential additions to the fiscal dividend from adoption of the alternatives discussed in the last few pages.

TABLE 8. *Potential Fiscal Dividend*
(In billions of dollars)

Type of saving	Fiscal year 1971	Fiscal year 1974
Initial estimate of fiscal dividend	8	38
Potential additions to dividend		
Limitation on strategic forces and reevaluation of overseas commitments[a]	2-4	10-15
Increase in social security benefits *only* to match cost of living and to raise minimum benefits	2	6-7
Rigorous screening of existing programs to reduce or eliminate low-priority items	1-2	2-4
Potential maximum dividend	13-16	56-64

a. Figure for 1974 based on Kaysen proposals.

The estimates are necessarily rough, both in timing and magnitude. Decisions to achieve any of these savings would be exceedingly difficult to make. Most of the difficulties would be political, but some program cuts would raise very tough substantive questions. Nevertheless, the estimates indicate that the relatively small fiscal dividend in 1971 could be doubled if all of the necessary policy changes were undertaken. Even the much larger fiscal dividend of 1974 could be increased more than 50 percent by these decisions.

Conclusion

Several major facts stand out from an examination of the budget situation following cessation of hostilities in Vietnam.

1. The fiscal dividend during fiscal 1970 and 1971 will be relatively

small. Expiration of the temporary surtax, large built-in increases in federal civilian expenditures, the probability of increasing non-Vietnam military outlays, and sharp increases in social security benefits will largely offset the growth in federal revenues and the budgetary savings from a cessation of the war.

2. In the subsequent three years the annual fiscal dividend will increase rapidly, amounting to almost $40 billion by fiscal 1974.

3. Large claims will be made on the fiscal dividend for expanding high-priority social programs and launching new program initiatives.

4. Three major sets of policy decisions could expand the fiscal dividend substantially: First, a reexamination of U.S. strategic weapons policy and overseas commitments could reduce non-Vietnam military spending; second, some part of the rapid increase in payroll tax revenues could be captured for the fiscal dividend rather than being used in toto to raise social security benefits; and third, a rigorous screening of existing federal programs could produce significant budgetary savings.

Calculation of the fiscal dividend starts with one fundamental assumption, namely, unchanged federal tax rates. The United States, already the wealthiest nation in the world, adds the equivalent of a West Germany to its economic base every five years. With unchanged tax rates, about one-fifth of that growth will be used for federal programs, one-tenth for state and local spending, and the remaining seven-tenths for private purposes. If, as a nation, we decide that the social problems which confront us warrant the devotion of more than one-fifth of economic growth to public programs, there is no economic reason that prohibits our making this choice. But, in the long run, doing so means levying additional taxes upon ourselves by extending the surcharge, closing major tax "loopholes," or some other form of tax increase. Conversely, should we value a faster growth in private consumption or investment more highly than increased spending for public purposes, we can devote part of the fiscal dividend to tax reduction.

The budgetary resources available to meet public needs are not restricted by the size of the fiscal dividend. Within reasonable limits, we can devote either more or less of the fruits of economic growth to public purposes. The choice depends upon our evaluation of national priorities.

JAMES L. SUNDQUIST

JOBS, TRAINING, AND WELFARE FOR THE UNDERCLASS

The discovery of America's underclass—in the sense of a political and public discovery—can be dated from the middle 1950s.

In the preceding twenty years, economic thinkers and political activists had been preoccupied with other problems of the economy. In the 1930s, it was how to conquer the depression. During the Second World War, it was how to prevent a postwar depression. In the first postwar decade, it was how to stabilize prosperity and achieve a rapid and sustained rate of economic growth.

By the middle Eisenhower years, however, those problems of the macroeconomy seemed on their way to solution. Two recessions had occurred in the postwar years, but they had been relatively mild and recovery had been rapid. The economy was growing at a healthy rate—so healthy, indeed, that the primary concern of economic policy was to prevent inflation from getting out of hand. It was in those years of prosperity that a phenomenon that had previously been obscured began to catch the attention of analysts and politicians alike—that there were millions of people whom prosperity had passed by, a more or less permanent underclass that seemed fated not to share in the nation's growing wealth, even in the best of times.

First to come to public attention were the "depressed areas"—communities, areas, and whole regions lagging behind the rest of the country. Then, a little later, the figures on unemployment in the ghettos (particularly youth unemployment) became the subject of widespread discussion. From that time on, the spotlight of public attention focused with ever-rising intensity upon America's underclass until by 1964 it had become the foremost concern of the government's domestic policy. The President proclaimed an "unconditional war on poverty in the United States," and issues of class and poverty have since remained at the top of the national agenda—as the papers on domestic topics in this volume make clear.

The theme of the war on poverty was opportunity. The underclass was not to be rescued through "handouts"; Sargent Shriver, in presenting the President's program, was quite explicit about that. Rather, in the words of the preamble to the Economic Opportunity Act, the poor were to be lifted out of poverty through "the opportunity for education and training" and "the opportunity to work."

This paper considers those aspects of the government's policies and programs designed to provide opportunities for training and for work (programs for educational opportunity are discussed later in Ralph Tyler's essay) and some related problems of welfare policy and administration. To provide work and training opportunity, a series of specific programs has been enacted, many of them on an experimental basis and subject to change in design and nomenclature from year to year. The major programs for training or direct public employment are identified and their growth shown in Table 1. In addition to these were programs of public works and assistance to the development of depressed areas, which had employment of the underclass as one object.

What is the magnitude of the job and training problem?

The official unemployment figure, which has averaged about 3 million during the last three years, is not its measure. On the one hand, that figure includes well-trained workers who suffer unemployment only briefly, as well as secondary workers in families with good income. On the other hand, it excludes those who are employed but need training and better jobs in order to raise their earnings above the poverty level.

To get a better measure of the problem of unemployment and low earnings, the Labor Department has developed the concept of "subemployment," which is compounded of two groups: the long-term unemployed (those who suffer fifteen weeks or more of unemployment during the year) and those who earn less than $3,000 for year-round, full-time work. In 1966, a total of 9.1 million persons were classified as subemployed, 2.4 million because of long-term unemployment and 6.7 million because of low earnings. The total represented 10 percent of the working population, but the rate was 22 percent for nonwhite men as against 8 percent for white men. Using a slightly different definition, in October 1966 the department found the subemployment rate in ten urban slums was 34 percent. Low earners do not necessarily live in poverty, if a family has several such earners, but most of them do. Among the 29.7 million persons in families whose incomes were below the officially defined poverty level in 1966, Harold Sheppard points out, were 7.3 million workers.

TABLE 1. *Growth in Federal Expenditures for Training and Work-Training Programs, Fiscal Years 1963–69*
(Expenditures in millions of dollars)

Program	Expenditures							Number of people served in 1969[a]
	1963	1964	1965	1966	1967	1968[a]	1969[a]	
Training								
Manpower Development and Training Act[b]	50	104	222	275	275	434	407	275,000
Job Corps	—	—	54	258	339	306	295	98,000
Jobs in Business Sector (JOBS) program	—	—	—	—	—	35	175	140,000[c]
Work Incentive Program[d]	—	—	—	—	—	15	119	102,000
Other programs[e]	15	17	18	18	21	85	103	105,000
Work-Training								
Neighborhood Youth Corps:								
School and Summer	—	—	51	241	133	191	178	469,000
Out-of-School	—	—			131	168	181	93,000
Operation Mainstream[f]	—	—	—	—	13	41	46	22,000
Work Experience Program[g]	—	—	21	76	121	113	41	13,000
All programs	65	121	366	868	1,033	1,388	1,545	

Source: U.S. Bureau of the Budget, unpublished tabulations.
a. Estimated.
b. Excludes $10 million in 1968 and $16 million in 1969 included in totals for the JOBS program.
c. Number placed from beginning of program in February 1968 through August 1968.
d. Public employment of adults, and out-of-school teen-agers on public assistance.
e. Includes: Indian Manpower Activities, New Careers, Veterans On-the-Job Training, Opportunities Industrialization Centers, and Area Redevelopment Act Training (1963–66).
f. Public employment of elderly poor.
g. Public employment of unemployed parents of dependent children and other needy persons. To be replaced in 1968 and 1969 by the Work Incentive Program and Operation Mainstream.

An indication of the nature of the problem of the underclass, as well as its scale, is the rising number of fatherless families supported by public welfare. The rise in the case load of the aid to families with dependent children (AFDC) program is shown in Table 2. In most of these cases, the father has deserted. Desertion in turn can be traced to varied causes, but among those causes—and no one knows in what proportion of cases—is the inability of the father to earn enough to support his wife and children. A job paying a decent wage does not assure stability of family life, but it comes close to being a precondition of it.

How have we done, in providing opportunity for work and training?

The statistics, as James Tobin points out in his paper, show a steady movement of people out of poverty. The sub-employment rate of 10 percent in 1966 compares with 17 percent five years earlier. But, as Tobin also observes, aspirations have outrun performance. The war on poverty is under attack from many quarters, both from among the affluent and from among the poor themselves, and public opinion polls suggest that the way in which the war is being waged no longer has the support of a majority of Americans. What has misfired? Assuming that the goal of providing opportunity for the underclass is still valid, what can be done to make the national effort more effective?

The principal criticisms are of three kinds. First, there are questions of conception: some hold that the basic strategy of the war on poverty was

TABLE 2. *Growth in Monthly Payments under Program of Aid to Families with Dependent Children*[a]

	Families receiving aid (excluding those eligible because of unemployment of parents)[b]			Families receiving aid (eligible because of unemployment of parents)[b]		
Year	Families (thousands)	Recipients (thousands)	Total monthly payments[c] (millions)	Families (thousands)	Recipients (thousands)	Total monthly payments[c] (millions)
1936	162	546	$ 4.8	—	—	—
1940	372	1,222	12.0	—	—	—
1945	274	943	14.3	—	—	—
1950	651	2,233	46.5	—	—	—
1955	602	2,192	51.5	—	—	—
1960	803	3,073	87.1	—	—	—
1965	996	4,053	132.8	58	343	$11.5
1966	1,072	4,340	157.3	55	326	11.9
1967	1,232	4,938	195.2	65	371	14.5
1968	1,320	5,261	220.3	63	348	14.4

Sources: Figures for 1936 through 1960, *Social Security Bulletin: Annual Statistical Supplement, 1966*, p. 113; for 1965, 1966, and 1967, U.S. Department of Health, Education, and Welfare, Welfare Administration, *Welfare in Review*, Vol. 4 (March 1966), pp. 29, 31; Vol. 5 (April 1967), pp. 28, 29; Vol. 6 (May–June 1968), pp. 46, 47; for 1968, unpublished data from U.S. Department of Health, Education, and Welfare, National Center for Social Statistics.

a. Excluding vendor payments for medical care and cases receiving only such payments.
b. Before 1961, families with two able-bodied parents were ineligible for aid under this program. In that year they were made eligible (if the states so elected) in cases where the children were dependent because of the unemployment of the parents.
c. Figures are for the month of December except for 1968, when they are for June.

ill-conceived, and new objectives and approaches must be devised; others accept the initial strategy but would add the new objectives and approaches. Second, there are questions of administration: how the job and training and welfare programs can be coordinated with one another and with all of the other public programs designed to serve the underclass has yet to be worked out. Third, there are questions of finance: the nation has not yet found itself able, or at least willing, to raise and spend money on the scale that was implied when the programs were enacted and that is necessary to achieve the goals that were then established.

These questions will be considered in turn.

Questions of Strategy

The war on poverty has a radical objective—"to eliminate the paradox of poverty in the midst of plenty," the Economic Opportunity Act declaimed—but the means to that end were essentially conservative. The legislation built for the most part upon the methods and administrative structures of the past. The underclass would be given its new opportunities through more and better services of the kind traditionally provided—better education, better health services, better training and counseling, and so on, all improved through better community organization.

While one of the stated goals of the act was to provide "the opportunity to work," that goal was not to be achieved through any direct employment program. Rather, the opportunity would be the end product of the education, training, and other services provided. The underlying assumption was that the jobs existed in the private economy or could be brought into existence through economic expansion if only the unemployed and underemployed could be qualified to fill them. To help find the jobs for those who were qualified by the service programs, an intensified placement service known as "job development" would be assumed by the community action agencies.

It is true that some employment programs have been financed under the Economic Opportunity Act, but initially these had to be smuggled into the war on poverty under the guise of training. The principal benefits of the Neighborhood Youth Corps may be the employment and income it provides, but it is authorized as a "work training program" and priority must be given to projects with "high training potential." Even the adult work programs were authorized to provide "constructive work experience and other needed training." Some small-scale work programs were adopted in later years, on congressional initiative, but anything smacking of "make work" on an extensive scale has been abjured along with handouts by the "opportunity strategy" or "services strategy" of the war on poverty.

That is the strategy now under challenge. Many of those who have looked hardest at the facts of poverty, and who have been most deeply involved in administering the present programs, have despaired of the possibility of winning many skirmishes against poverty through the services approach. The obstacles standing between the worker and the private job—obstacles of geography, of education, of skill, of racial discrimination, of motivation, of poor health, and all the rest—can be overcome only slowly, with great difficulty, and with spotty results at best, and can the country afford to wait? Why not lift people out of poverty through the most direct and simplest means—by providing them with money through some new and universal form of income maintenance?

The prospects and problems of income maintenance and the forms that it might take are discussed by James Tobin in this volume, and I will not try to add to his analysis, with which in general I agree. It may be in order, however, to enter a caveat against those who see income maintenance as a panacea and who say (or imply, through their emphasis or statement of priority), "Now that we have found *the* answer, let's chuck all these other approaches that have failed." Even when income maintenance is accepted as sound public policy, it will still be equally sound public policy to reduce to a minimum the need for it. The development of human competence will always be a valid end, for both economic and noneconomic reasons, and services will be the means to that end. Income maintenance will be only a supplement to a services strategy, therefore, and not a substitute.

Public employment programs as a form of income maintenance are a strategic halfway house. Public opinion polls show them to be politically acceptable, even popular: a public job is not looked upon as a handout. For that reason, many who cannot bring themselves to endorse money payments to the able-bodied poor are willing to support large-scale employment programs. The Democratic platform of 1968, for example, promised only a study of income supplements for the working poor, but it gave an outright pledge to make the federal government "the employer of last resort" for those who could not obtain employment otherwise.

When the war on poverty was organized, Sargent Shriver proposed a large-scale public employment program, but it was rejected by the President as one that could not be financed at that time. In 1966, the National

Commission on Technology, Automation, and Economic Progress recommended creating 500,000 public service jobs as a beginning, and the Senate Committee on Labor and Public Welfare the following year approved a bill authorizing 200,000—a proposal rejected by the full Senate in the absence of administration support. Most recently, the National Advisory Commission on Civil Disorders (the Kerner Commission) proposed a program of public jobs to reach the level of 1 million in three years.

Part of the argument for public employment is that it is desirable as an end in itself—the work needs doing. The "Automation" Commission in its 1966 report estimated that, to meet the country's unfilled public service needs, 5.3 million additional employees "with relatively low skills" could be usefully employed. Nevertheless, in his 1968 message to the Congress on manpower programs, President Johnson went out of his way to deride public employment proposals as "make work." "The answer to today's problem," he insisted, lies instead in the training and employment of the hard-core unemployed by private industry, where six of every seven Americans now work.

Let us, then, review the prospects of solving the problem of subemployment through private industry and then return to the question of the desirability of expanded programs of public employment.

PRIVATE JOBS FOR THE HARD-CORE UNEMPLOYED

Private employers have developed, over the years, elaborate systems to avoid hiring the very people whom the government now wants them to employ. Responding to pressures for an efficient work force, they have designed their personnel systems with the express purpose of screening out the illiterate, the inarticulate, the inexperienced, the inept, the unconventional in appearance and dress, the applicants with police records. Among those who get by the personnel systems, supervisors are trained to detect and to fire the inefficient, the slow learners, the chronically tardy or absent, the uncooperative and the unreliable. But all those terms are the very definition of the "hard-core" unemployed; they are hard-core because they have been screened out of private employment (and public as well) for one or another of those reasons, for most or all of their working lives.

Yet when President Johnson appealed to the leaders of the business community, early in 1968, to organize a nationwide drive to hire the hard-core unemployed, they responded. Henry Ford formed the National Alliance of Businessmen, which organized the Jobs in Business Sector

(JOBS) program. Employers in fifty cities were canvassed; after six months 165,000 new permanent jobs had been pledged and an estimated 40,000 of them filled. In addition, 100,000 youths were placed in summer jobs.

What converted American industry? Among other things, certainly, the riots. The president of General Motors stood atop his building and saw Detroit in flames. "Absolutely terrifying," said another Detroit executive when he toured the devastated slums a few days later. Business leaders began saying to one another that they had a collective responsibility to help solve the problem of ghetto unemployment—if they didn't, who would? Only the government, obviously, through taxes levied on them. So they were receptive when the government proposed to cooperate by paying the extra costs that training and employing the disadvantaged would impose—costs that have averaged $2,800 per employee.

So far, experience is mixed. Some companies, like Lockheed Aircraft, insist that after the initial period of training the hard-core employees have performed as well, man for man, as employees hired according to the companies' regular criteria. Other employers, off the record, complain of absenteeism, high turnover, spoilage, inefficiency, and "backlash" from long-time employees. But, as in other experiments with mixed results, the success stories are sufficient to demonstrate that *under some circumstances* the objective can be achieved. The need is to identify and define the circumstances, through a comparative evaluation of the various experiments.

Some evaluation is under way, and already government and business experts are setting forth the do's and don'ts of how to salvage the hard-core unemployed. It is not easy for the companies to adjust to the do's in the how-to-do-it manuals. "Personnel departments," William Batt, Jr., has observed, "have to do exactly the opposite of everything they have done for 20 years." And the same goes for many others. Supervisors will have to tolerate the kind of performance for which employees have been fired in the past, while working patiently to improve that performance. Production engineers will have to fit the jobs to the workers instead of designing the jobs on efficiency considerations alone; in other words, they will have to preserve the very low-skill jobs they have been automating out of existence. Established workers will have to make allowances for their new co-workers, while not reducing their own productivity to the lower level that might appear now to be acceptable.

The manuals emphasize training in "human relations" and "sensitivity" for personnel staff and supervisors. They stress the need to eliminate the dead-end jobs so frequently reserved for the underclass and open genuine career ladders to the new recruits. They advocate and define "high support," which includes pretraining orientation, counseling, and assistance with the employee's personal problems whatever they might be—health, transportation, or possibly just an inability to get out of bed on time (one company discovered that only one in five of its new recruits from the ghetto even had an alarm clock). They advise the assignment of "coaches" or "buddies"—established employees, if possible from the same neighborhood, who keep in touch with the recruits on a 24-hour-a-day basis and take personal responsibility for helping them make good.

Transportation deserves special mention as a problem just beginning to be recognized. In almost every metropolitan area, new jobs are mainly in scattered suburban locations, while the hard-core unemployed are concentrated in the central city. Typically, the poor lack reliable private transportation (they have broken-down jalopies, or none at all, and many lack drivers' licenses) but the circuitous public transportation routes may require "two bucks and three hours," as one worker put it. Over the long run, and ideally, open housing legislation will enable nonwhite workers to relocate freely near their jobs, as white workers are now able to do, but at best the results will be slow in coming. In the meantime, new transportation arrangements must be devised. Many possibilities exist—all of them, of course, involving special subsidies—and varied experiments have been undertaken. The solutions are hard to engineer, but it is harder still to get them adopted, because urban transportation is a field where innovation is slow and monopolies are vigorously defended.

The complex transportation difficulties have led many to look for the solution to ghetto unemployment in the development of new jobs *in the ghetto*. But the realities of land and production economics suggest that the possibilities of ghetto industry, without substantial subsidies—and perhaps even with them—are severely limited. Vacant land is often scarce and costly. Existing commercial buildings are cramped and outmoded. The ghetto labor force lacks skill and experience. Insurance rates are high. So are the city tax rates. Transportation for materials and products is expensive. For all these reasons, ghetto industries are usually at a marked competitive disadvantage.

One large concern has won favorable national attention—and deservedly—by announcing plans for a factory in the Bedford-Stuyvesant section of Brooklyn. But the employment goal turns out to be only 300 workers by the end of 1969—hardly a far-reaching solution to the problems of a community of 300,000 that had a sub-employment rate, in 1966, of 28 percent of its labor force. A recent listing of other new ghetto enterprises showed planned employment totals of 50, 75, 275, 438, and so on. Yet companies like these are right now building plants elsewhere that will employ thousands. No wonder that blacks refer to the well-intentioned efforts of these companies in the ghettos as "tokenism."

If the prospects for ghetto industry in general are limited, the prospects for Negro-owned or Negro-operated industry—now so popular an idea—are even more so. The notion of self-help, as the constructive aspect of "black power," is inherently appealing, and Negro entrepreneurship obviously should be encouraged. Federal credit and technical assistance should be extended, and discrimination against Negro enterprises in such matters as surety bonds and other forms of insurance should be dealt with—if necessary, through federal legislation. Much can be said for a federal program to support and assist ghetto-based community development corporations that will have power to operate or finance commercial and industrial enterprises. But even with all these kinds of encouragement, to suggest that Negro entrepreneurship can produce much more than a token number of new jobs for the hard-core unemployed, at least for a long time to come, is pure romanticism. Ghetto autarchy is impossible. Even if the ghetto market could be walled off, in effect, through appeals to Negroes to "buy black," the market is not big enough to support significant manufacturing, and the number of white employees who could be replaced by black workers in retail and service establishments is limited. Any large-scale increase in Negro employment by Negro enterprises would have to come through those able to compete successfully with white-owned enterprises in the larger market *outside* the ghetto, and they are sure to develop only slowly.

With enough subsidy, of course, almost any enterprise can be made competitive. Urban renewal is already available as a technique for subsidizing land costs for ghetto industry. Through one or another form of federal subsidy, credit could be made available at rates below the market level. But the most effective form of subsidy would undoubtedly be tax concessions (accelerated depreciation or tax credits, or both) as has been proposed in various bills. Tight rules would have to be established to define the kinds of enterprises and the areas that would be eligible and to specify the hiring practices that would have to be followed, but presumably satisfactory criteria could be written, and the plan could be combined with one covering investment in rural and other areas of out-migration, which is discussed in a later section. Nevertheless, its effectiveness in solving ghetto sub-employment problems would still be restricted by the shortage of sites that could be made available without the mass displacement of residents.

If tax incentives are to be considered, the most promising form would appear to be the one proposed by the Kerner Commission's advisory panel on private enterprise and endorsed by the commission. The panel suggested that the hard-core unemployed, as identified and recruited by federal or local agencies, be given green cards (not to be confused with the green cards given foreign workers at the present time). An employer who hired a green-card holder, wherever the establishment was located, would then be eligible to take a tax credit equal to a share of the wages and fringe benefits paid the employee—75 percent for the first six months, 50 percent for the second six months, and 25 percent for the second year. Unless the employee remained on the job at least six months, no credit would be allowed. This approach goes directly to the objective, which concerns the employment of people and not the location of industry, and it offers incentives to a far wider range of employers than could be reached through subsidizing ghetto industry alone.

While this form of tax incentive appears preferable to one that subsidizes location, the question remains whether it is superior to the JOBS program organized through the National Alliance of Businessmen, under which the extra costs of employing and training the hard-core are paid through contracts between the Labor Department and the employer. The tax incentive scheme would be, in the advisory panel's language, "relatively simple, automatic and as self-enforcing as a government program can be." As compared with the contract program, it would undoubtedly induce much quicker and more extensive participation. Employers who have declined to accept JOBS contracts because of reluctance to submit to government supervision—and some big companies are among them—would find the tax concessions easy to accept. The employer would not have to negotiate with any government agency, satisfy its contract terms, open his employment practices to scrutiny. His only dealings would be with the tax auditors, and then only after he had claimed and received his subsidy.

The weakness of the tax incentive scheme is that it would inevitably cost the government more for any given level of results. In administering the JOBS program, the manpower agencies can satisfy themselves—through what is known as "red tape"—that every dollar contributes as much as possible to the purpose of the program. The contract can be negotiated so as to cover only the true added cost of employing and training the workers certified, and the employer's plans can be checked against program criteria. In contrast, the tax credit approach, for the very reason that it is "self-enforcing," could not be made to distinguish among jobs or employers or to offer differential incentives according to true costs. It would presumably have to cover all employment for which the hard-core are normally hired—including dead-end, menial jobs for which training is neither given nor required. In all probability, many employers would not change their personnel practices significantly, or employ more of the hardcore than they normally do; their tax accountants would simply keep records and compute the credit each year, and the subsidy would be paid for nothing. In short, a "tax loophole" would be created through which far more revenue would fall than the amount directly related to the purpose.

For that reason, it appears preferable to use the present contract approach if it can be made to produce enough results. It is still too early to judge how successful the JOBS effort will finally be. Voluntary organizations like the NAB have a way of losing vitality; after the novelty wears off, businesses may be less willing to donate the time of their executives. By early 1969, however, the ultimate potential of the JOBS program can be assessed with some degree of accuracy, and then the need for a supplemental public employment program, discussed in the next section, can be realistically faced.

THE GOVERNMENT AS EMPLOYER OF LAST RESORT

Since the "Automation" Commission in 1966 recommended a massive program of public service jobs to bring unemployment down to the minimum frictional levels, the notion that the federal government should be "the employer of last resort" has won widespread endorsement—most recently, as noted, by the Democratic platform.

Some advocates of guaranteed employment appear to interpret those words quite literally—as an *absolute* guarantee of a job to anyone able and willing to work. But an absolute guarantee presents so many administrative difficulties that it can be dismissed quickly as unworkable. To organize useful work takes time. Projects must be planned, supervision provided, and materials and equipment obtained, all in relation to a working force of reasonably stable and predictable size. Any person showing up on any day at a government hiring office could not be guaranteed the right to go to work immediately, if the jobs are to be genuinely productive work and not simply a disguised dole.

But, leaving the absolute guarantee aside, there are other difficulties that would attend any public employment program large enough to come even close to reducing unemployment to the frictional minimum. They would arise from the effect upon the wage structure of the private economy. The existence of an unemployment pool is a factor holding wages down. If public jobs were readily available at the statutory minimum wage of $1.60 an hour, then private employers would have to make their present $1.60 jobs more attractive, and raising wages would be one of the means. The effects would ripple upward through the wage structure, and the pay increases would in turn put pressure on price levels. Many families would be lifted out of poverty, but employers would find themselves with labor shortages and a profits squeeze, consumers would find themselves paying higher prices that would be blamed on "government spending," and public support for the program might be rapidly eroded.

The difficulties of government-private competition for labor would be reduced if the government could be truly the employer "of last resort"— that is, if it could close its doors to anyone who refused private employment on reasonable terms. But what terms are reasonable? Would a worker have to accept any job or would the private job have to be one "suitable" to his qualifications and, if so, how would suitability be determined? Who would be forced to become tomato pickers and who excused? If the manpower agency had available one restaurant dishwasher job and two eligible workers—one black and one white, say—who would be sent to the restaurant and who given the more attractive public job? Would migrant workers be compelled to migrate? What about the worker who quit? Who would decide whether the circumstances justified the resignation, and what would be the criteria? What about the worker who was fired? Would he be barred from the public employment program? All these questions suggest that the more practical course would be to make the public jobs an integral part of the labor market, available to any workers who prefer them, forcing employers to outbid the government for their labor and recognizing and accepting the inflationary impact that would follow. The effects would be similar to, and probably of a magnitude no greater than, those experienced each time the statutory minimum wage is raised. In any case, their severity would depend upon the scale of the public employment program. As long as some unemployment pool remained—and if the program built up gradually a substantial pool would remain for a time—the effects on the wage structure would be restrained.

In the five years that have passed since the nation set out to eradicate poverty, it has become clear that without an income maintenance strategy to supplement the opportunity strategy, that goal cannot be achieved. For those of the underclass who are employable, a large-scale public employment program is by far the best and most acceptable means of income maintenance. In the first place, a well-administered public employment program preserves morale and self-respect and imparts skills, habits, and experience that are transferable to the regular labor market. In the second place, it produces useful and necessary work; as Garth Mangum reminds us, the WPA of the 1930s constructed 651,000 miles of roads, 16,000 miles of water lines, 35,000 public buildings, 11,000 recreation facilities, and so on. With all the public work that now needs doing, there is no justification for belittling public employment as "make work."

To the extent that private employment of the hard-core unemployed can be stimulated through the JOBS program and related efforts, that objective is to be preferred. But the two approaches are not in conflict. They can be made complementary: the public employment program can serve as a training and screening organization from which workers are referred to private jobs as they are developed. If and as private employment expands, the public jobs can be easily retrenched. But it is wishful to believe that the JOBS program in itself can ever be a complete solution. The 40,000 jobs filled in the first six months of the effort—assuming that the placements turn out to be successful, and no statistics have been obtained on that—take the country less than one-tenth of the way toward the goal of 500,000 jobs the President set for the program, only one twenty-fifth of the way toward the Kerner Commission's goal of a million private jobs, and only one-fiftieth of the way toward the commission's goal of two million to be divided equally between private and public employment.

Because of the administrative and politico-economic complications cited earlier, the public employment program should begin on a modest scale and build up gradually, as experience and economic conditions dictate. An interim target might be the 500,000 jobs proposed by the "Automation" Commission as the initial number; that target slightly exceeds the 449,000 long-term unemployed (that is, unemployed continuously for more than fifteen weeks) who were counted in an average month in 1967. In addition to these, the program would draw upon the 1.1 million males between twenty-five and fifty-four years of age who were not in the labor force (that is, not actively seeking work) and the 1.9 million persons who desired full-time work but were working only part-time. The annual cost of 500,000 jobs would be $2.5 billion. This would be offset by some reduction in the cost of AFDC payments (depending upon how much desertion and public dependency would be prevented by regularized employment) and by the added revenues generated by the economic activity resulting from the employment program itself. All these figures, of course, assume government policies that maintain aggregate demand at levels preventing any significant increase in the magnitude of the country's unemployment and sub-employment problems.

A NATIONAL POPULATION DISTRIBUTION POLICY?

If the benefits of job and training programs are offered primarily in the cities, then the underclass will concentrate in the cities even faster than it has been doing and the progress made there will be canceled by the burden of the added population. Metropolitan and nonmetropolitan programs are thus interdependent.

A historian, President Johnson said recently, "may easily conclude that many of the social ills that plague America today had their roots in the desertion of the rural areas and the migration to the cities that gained force at the end of World War II.... Only in the 1960's have we faced the urban crisis. We would be a better nation today if, instead, we had faced the rural crisis in the 1950's. Now we must face both."

The concern is bipartisan. "Success with urban problems," observes the 1968 Republican platform, "requires acceleration of rural development in order to stem the flow of people from the countryside to the city."

This flow has been going on for a long time. In some rural sections, population has been declining for over fifty years. During the 1950s some 6.7 million persons moved to metropolitan areas; a million more moved during 1960–65. Conspicuous in the migration pattern was the northward and westward movement of the Negro, as shown in Table 3.

It is ironic but significant that the GOP reference to rural development comes under the heading "Crisis in the Cities" and the President's remarks occurred in the same context. Attention to the "rural crisis" might seem justified on its own merits: these, too, are communities in trouble. But urban-centered intellectual leadership has not seen the decay of rural and small-town America as an urgent national problem: the library shelves that are filled with penetrating studies of America's urban crisis are virtually bare of studies of the rural crisis. It was assumed, perhaps, that the inevitable—and the only feasible—solution to the problems of the rural poor was continued migration to the cities.

TABLE 3. *Net Negro Migration from the South*

Period	Number of migrants	Average annual rate
1910–1920	454,000	45,400
1920–1930	749,000	74,900
1930–1940	348,000	34,800
1940–1950	1,597,000	159,700
1950–1960	1,457,000	145,700
1960–1965	473,000	94,600
1965–1968	241,000	80,300
1910–1968	5,319,000	

Sources: Data for 1910–60, *Report of the National Advisory Commission on Civil Disorders* (Government Printing Office, 1968), p. 117; data for 1960–68, U.S. Bureau of the Census, unpublished.

But suddenly it became clear that this was just the trouble: too many of the rural poor were moving. Rural migration—especially black migration—had finally engulfed the cities. "Help!" cried the urbanists. "Do something about migration!"

But is this a proper concern for government? Should the United States have a national policy for the geographic distribution of its population—one that seeks to discourage further concentration? The answer would appear to be affirmative, if an effective policy could be devised: besides reducing the burdens on the cities, it would reduce the hardship on the migrants themselves—those among them who move involuntarily, only because they are driven to do so by lack of economic opportunity, and who suffer both financially and emotionally as the consequence.

The Congress made a start toward the definition of a policy in the Area Redevelopment Act of 1961 and the Appalachian Regional Development Act of 1965, which established the principle that areas lagging behind the rest of the country in economic growth should be assisted to catch up. These acts provided extra funds for "infrastructure"—the highways, public utilities, and supporting public services necessary for attracting industry—and funds for commercial and industrial loans on advantageous terms. Of the one hundred and one areas (excluding very small ones) classified as "depressed areas" when the Area Redevelopment Act was passed, ninety have now worked their way out of that category by reducing their unemployment rates to near the national average. But it can be doubted that the federal programs had much to do with those results. The loan funds have amounted to less than one dollar of every thousand invested nationally by American business and industry—hardly enough to make much difference in the aggregate. More important in reducing the unemployment rates were other factors: the retirement of the older unemployed and the continuing emigration of the younger, the voluntary movement of industry into depressed areas to take advantage of labor surpluses during a period when the national labor market has been tight, and strong state and local industrial development programs that offered publicly financed industrial buildings on concessionary terms as well as tax and credit incentives.

The improvement of unemployment rates in the depressed areas, taken by itself, can be misleading. Underemployment must also be taken into account—seasonal, casual, and part-time work and subsistence farming, all poorly remunerated. A method of computing the unemployment equivalent of underemployment has not been devised, but the Labor Department estimates that, if the rural labor force had been utilized as efficiently in 1965 as the rest of the country's labor force, it would have earned an additional $10 billion.

What are the means by which economic opportunity can be encouraged in areas of emigration? The first step is to equalize the accessibility and quality of public services, as is sought in present programs. Small towns need water systems and health services and better schools; regional growth centers need hospitals and vocational schools and airports; nonmetropolitan areas need federal housing assistance equivalent to that available in metropolitan areas; isolated areas need highways; and so on. Provision of a stronger infrastructure would help to induce private investment in areas of emigration, but nobody knows how much, and we may assume that private companies would still need some additional incentive if investment is to be sufficient to stem the population flow. Government loans and preference in federal procurement are the two means so far tried. Procurement preference has proved to be administratively and politically impossible; potential credit assistance has not really been tested, because the terms have not been attractive enough, but the political difficulties that would be encountered in liberalizing federal credit in order to subsidize rich and profitable businesses through appropriated funds, in an unequal competition with private lenders, need hardly be enumerated.

These considerations have led most advocates of a population distribution policy to conclude that the only really effective way to redirect investment in the long run is through tax incentives (tax credits, accelerated depreciation schedules, and other incentives) as have been proposed for ghetto industry. The administrative feasibility of tax incentives for investment—as well as their potency—has been proven in periods of national defense emergency. Some of the basic objections raised earlier in regard to the "green card" tax credit scheme would apply to an investment incentive: to the extent that the tax incentive was fixed and uniform, it would give some investors a subsidy beyond the minimum necessary to induce the investment. Yet there are two important differences. First, a tax incentive for investment would not need to be self-enforcing; eligibility could be controlled by an administrative agency charged with reviewing investment plans against the program criteria and issuing certificates of eligibility. Second, in the case of investment, there is probably no alternative that would be both effective and politically acceptable: a direct subsidy program for private plant construction would be beyond the range of practical consideration. If subsidies in the hundreds of millions, or billions, are needed in order to guide private investment toward the places where the people who need the jobs live, it seems clear that the tax incentive approach offers the most feasible means to that end—and probably the only one powerful enough to do the job.

Questions of Administration

Public programs for the training and employment of the underclass may be conceived in Washington and financed from Washington, but it is in the communities that they have to be administered, and there they comprise many links in a single chain. All of the links in that chain need to be designed in relation to all the others—in other words, they need to form a community manpower system.

THE DEVELOPMENT OF COMMUNITY MANPOWER SYSTEMS

The chain begins with "outreach." It is not enough just to open a neighborhood employment office or service center. Some of the sub-employed will walk voluntarily through its doors but others are too timid or too suspicious or alienated from the whole middle-class value system associated with education, training, and work. The recruiter must seek out the potential recruit wherever he is, and then it may take some time and considerable skill to win his confidence, overcome the psychological obstacles, and "reach" him.

Once the potential recruit is "reached," the appropriate service must be provided. He may need nothing more than counseling and referral to a job. He will probably need some kind of training, and that training must be designed in relation to the specific needs of employers in his community. He may need basic education. At some point he may require formal or informal instruction on how to apply for a job, how to dress when applying, how to fill out application forms and take tests. He may need health services, vocational rehabilitation, psychological services. When he is ready for employment, someone must arrange the placement, along with facilitating services such as transportation to and from the job, child care in the case of working mothers, and such counseling services as may be necessary to enable the new employee to hold his job.

Traditionally, the entire chain of manpower services has not been seen as a single system, and the various links have been the responsibility of different agencies, insofar as they have been of public concern at all. Individuals moved into and out of the jurisdiction of the separate agencies, with no one attending to transitions and hiatuses or accepting responsibility for the workings of the system as a whole. Except for the agencies serving small assigned groups (like vocational rehabilitation, parole and probation, and public welfare), each of the manpower agencies waited for applicants and from them selected its own clientele. Like the employers themselves, the service agencies inevitably "creamed" the manpower supply: they chose the applicants most likely to succeed. Those rejected did not automatically become the concern of any other agency. The range of education, training, and employment programs was not designed to fit the entire range of applicants—nor, for that matter, was it designed as a whole in relation to the whole range of needs of the employment market.

When the war on poverty was declared in 1964, however, a revolution in the administration of manpower services was touched off, and that revolution is still continuing. In the Office of Economic Opportunity and its local community action agencies (CAAs) there came into being for the first time a network of public bodies whose concern was exclusively with the underclass and whose interest extended to the totality of its problems. The CAAs were to bring an end to fragmentation; for that purpose, they were to develop comprehensive plans that would coordinate all of the agencies—federal, state, and local, public and private—that provided services to the poor. Neighborhood centers would provide a coordinated outreach for all agencies.

As was to be expected, the ideal proved unattainable. Few CAAs even made an attempt at comprehensive planning: they were too busy getting their centers established and initiating Head Start classes and other operating programs. But some coordination of manpower services was initiated, and the services were made available more extensively and more accessibly. The state employment service was induced, in many communities, to assign counselors to neighborhood centers, and the community action agencies developed manpower programs of their own, sometimes ancillary to the employment service but in many cases covering the whole range of manpower functions from recruitment to job finding, placement, and follow-up. For those who could not be placed in private jobs, the Office of Economic Opportunity financed the Neighborhood Youth Corps, the Job Corps, and small-scale public employment programs for adults.

The Labor Department, meanwhile, was striving to persuade or coerce the fifty state employment services to develop their own aggressive programs of outreach and service to the hard-core unemployed. Prodded from below by the CAA's and pressed from above by the Labor Department, the tradition-bound state employment services began to change—but slowly. Presently, the Labor Department began assigning its own "coordinators" to major cities, and out of this emerged the Concentrated Employment Program (CEP) in which, in seventy-six localities initially, an attempt is being made to administer the entire panoply of manpower services as a single system.

Under CEP, funds are set aside from various federal training and employment appropriations for the exclusive benefit of designated areas of concentrated hard-core unemployment. A local CEP organization is created to manage the manpower services, but it is placed (usually) under the CAA and in turn contracts with the state employment service for testing, counseling, and placement services and with other public and private agencies for training and for health, remedial education, and other related services. By concentrating on a limited "target area" within a city, so the theory goes, CEP is able to identify the individuals who need service, measure the breadth and depth of their problems, and develop some kind of program suitable for every case. Coordination is to be achieved through a central intake system, from which assignments are made, after an orientation period, to the various job and training programs. Continuity of attention to each individual is sought through assignment of a "coach"—a subprofessional from the neighborhood who assumes the role of personal counselor to the recruit as he enters the program and remains with him until he is settled into a permanent job. If he drops out along the way, the coach attempts to find the reason and arrange a second chance. As the JOBS program develops opportunities for the hard-core unemployed, CEP is conceived as one mechanism of supply.

The concept is sound, and the elements of the system should fit together more smoothly with each year's experience. Out of that experience in a limited target area a corresponding system for whole metropolitan communities should ultimately be developed. When large-scale public employment programs are adopted, they would be administered as part of those comprehensive systems.

The manpower system as a whole, however, is itself only part of a larger system that ideally should encompass all of the services and resources that can be brought to bear upon the problems of the underclass. The concept of an all-embracing system is now embodied in the model cities program, enacted in 1966, under which neighborhoods are designated for comprehensive redevelopment, covering every aspect of public activity affecting that neighborhood. The Labor Department has announced that a CEP will be established in each model neighborhood, and with the JOBS program (in the larger cities) it will presumably provide the manpower component of the model city plan.

The central administrative question, however, is whether the federal government will allow any local system to work. So far, it has followed an ambivalent course. On the one hand, it has set up a series of locally based decision-making mechanisms—including the CAAs, CEPs, and model cities. On the other hand, it has insisted upon launching programs that bypass these very structures and upon making the essential decisions itself. In the manpower field, it acts, most of the time, as though the manpower complex is one national system, to be designed, redesigned, and administered out of Washington. Great emphasis is placed upon cost-benefit analysis, and from the results of that analysis—or from more subjective criteria—funds are shifted from one kind of program to another, often precipitously. Federal administrators are impatient for results; rather than wait for thousands of communities to make decisions—many of which, by the law of averages, will be wrong—they find it preferable to make the one "right" decision themselves and organize their programs vertically, nationwide. When local authorities are given discretion to design programs, their proposals must be individually reviewed and approved, modified, or rejected by federal officials.

The federal government cannot have it both ways. It should decide whether the complex of manpower and related programs is to be conceived and operated as a national system or whether those programs are to be treated as federally aided community programs that have to be meshed by local leadership into community systems. Put this way, there is but one choice. It is in the communities that the manpower institutions operate; it is there that they must be designed in relation to the economy they serve; it is through those community institutions that the individual moves. It is in the communities, therefore, that the institutions must be effectively interrelated as manpower systems. Leadership and professional skill may now be insufficient to build and operate refined manpower systems in most communities, but the manipulation of programs and resources from Washington as though what is being administered is a single national system can only hinder the development of local capability.

Once the federal government acknowledges the development of community manpower systems as the primary objective, new administrative approaches must follow. Uniformity in the design of local programs must give way to flexibility. Federal agencies must shift their emphasis from a reviewing and approving role to a consultative role. They must find ways of feeding into the local planning process (often through the states as intermediaries) their general advice and technical information, their broader perspective, their evaluation data on local experiments. But, having done that, they must refrain from stultifying local initiative by substituting their judgment for that of local authorities on the substantive content of plans and projects. The focus of federal attention should be the planning *process* rather than the *product*. If the process is sound, the product is likely to be acceptable; if it is unsound, its supersession by a federal planning process is not a satisfactory remedy and the local process still must be improved.

The federal right of veto must be held in reserve, of course, because there will be times when the local planning system will break down and the national objective cannot be achieved without the assertion of federal authority. An obvious case in point arises in those communities where race relations are strained and effective minority group participation in the planning process—and in the benefits of programs—can be assured only by federal intervention. Other cases arise when local plans would result in the illegal use or gross waste of federal funds. The circumstances that warrant the assertion of federal authority do not lend themselves to precise definition. The extremes to be avoided can be identified: on the one hand, second-guessing of local judgments on substantive matters that do not involve any real federal interest (which also can lead to interminable delays while those local judgments are being reviewed); on the other hand, the passive relationships developed by those "old line" agencies that have accepted local judgments routinely without concerning themselves aggressively with the improvement of state and local planning processes. The middle course must be charted through experience.

The development and conscientious application of a new set of federal administrative principles will depend upon central control and leadership over all the participating agencies by the Executive Office of the President. Unfortunately, the Executive Office is not organized in Washington to exercise that kind of operating control and leadership over the government as a whole and is not represented at all in the regional centers where federal agency activities in relation to particular states and local communities must be harmonized. The strengthening of the Executive Office for these and other purposes is discussed in Stephen Bailey's essay.

Outside the metropolitan areas the organization of manpower programs is handicapped by the weakness of the institutional structure, both public and private. There the problem is not primarily one of organizing a multiplicity of services into a coordinated system, as it is in the cities, but one of filling a structural and program vacuum. The President's National Advisory Commission on Rural Poverty, reflecting what appears to be a growing consensus of officials and experts concerned with the development of nonmetropolitan areas, recommended the creation throughout nonmetropolitan America of multicounty development districts organized around growth centers. The federal government, which now is promoting and financing several kinds of multicounty development districts, needs to unify its own efforts. As the district organizations are created, the planning of manpower systems should be a major part of their responsibility.

A final word is in order about the Job Corps. If the range of services in a manpower system is to be complete, there is a place for residential training centers. Nevertheless, such centers are the most expensive form of training—$8,077 annually per enrollee in 1967, by Sar Levitan's calculation—and they can be justified only if the agencies that screen the applicants (usually the state employment services) have and apply sound criteria for determining which are the young people whose training needs cannot be met at lesser cost by community-operated programs, such as skill centers and Neighborhood Youth Corps work-training projects. Development and use of such criteria presumably would be expedited if the Job Corps were brought into the community manpower systems within which the other types of training programs are organized and operated. As Levitan suggests, however, to transfer the Job Corps as a whole to the states at this time would probably result simply in its liquidation in some states—those where the vocational education establishment lacked the capability to operate so innovative a program, and those where community mores would not permit the operation of racially integrated centers. As part of the devolution of responsibility for manpower programs to the communities, the Job Corps centers should logically be transferred (with continued federal support) at some point, but the transfer should take place gradually as the states demonstrate readiness to assume the responsibility, so that the continuance of the residential training program would be assured.

NATIONALIZATION OF PUBLIC ASSISTANCE

American welfare philosophy has expressed a dual objective. First, the doors of opportunity for every family to become self-supporting should be opened wide—an objective epitomized in the Economic Opportunity Act. Second, for those who cannot, for one reason or another, pass through those doors, assistance should be adequate—even generous.

The trouble is that the two objectives are in conflict, or at least appear to be. If welfare payments are generous enough, why should people bestir themselves to become self-supporting? This dilemma has resulted in the evolution of a double standard: welfare programs have been relatively generous to those classified as "unemployable," particularly the aged, and relatively restricted for those classed as "employable." Until 1961, indeed, no family could participate in a federally aided program if the head of the family was able to work. This policy, as noted earlier, provided an incentive to able-bodied but unemployed or low-earning males to desert their families. But only twenty-two states have taken advantage of the 1961 federal legislation that made families of unemployed parents eligible under the federal AFDC program; the others, presumably still fearful of the effects on motivation of providing assistance to the able-bodied, have chosen to reject the proffered federal assistance.

A corresponding situation arises in regard to the food distribution programs administered by the Department of Agriculture. Many counties, particularly rural counties in the South that need them most, chose not to participate in those programs—whether because of local administrative costs, simple lethargy, or a belief that provision of free food would reduce the motivation of the poor to seek work at home or migrate to the North. Hunger may be a national disgrace, and national policy frowns upon it, but the nation cannot move decisively to eliminate hunger if it continues to grant to states and localities a veto over the national policies and programs designed to wipe it out.

The traditional argument for local administration of public assistance has been that a family's need and its eligibility could best be judged by a committee of neighbors, and the requirement for a local financial contribution would be the best assurance against "welfare chiseling." But it is now clear that the committee of neighbors, whether or not the best informed, may also be the most prejudiced and the least sympathetic, and that local administration can vitiate the national purpose.

In those states that have assumed full state control over welfare financing and administration, the chance of maladministration is of course reduced. But the argument against permitting the states to veto national policy remains valid. Whether a child receives enough food for health and growth and whether a family receives assistance under conditions that enable it to remain united are matters of national concern. No one can say to what extent the disparity in welfare standards is among the reasons for the mass migration of the underclass from the South, but if a destitute southern family knows that AFDC payments are three, four, or even six times as high in northern cities, and food programs are available there as well, it can be assumed that this knowledge weighs on the scales in favor of migration. Perhaps the mobility of population is in itself a sufficient reason for national uniformity in welfare policy, but in the case of hunger it would appear reasonable to make a broader argument—that whether a child receives enough to eat should never be allowed to depend upon where his family happens to live.

The most direct way to assure that national welfare policies are carried into effect would be for the federal government simply to assume full financial and administrative responsibility, as HEW Secretary Wilbur Cohen and Maryland Governor Spiro Agnew, among others, have suggested. This would be a form of block federal grant to the states and localities, because they would be relieved of some $3 billion in annual expenditures for public assistance.

Short of nationalizing the public assistance system, uniformity of policy and standards could be attained in other ways. Federal legislation could establish and enforce minimum levels of payments—variable among localities according to differences in living costs—with full federal or federal-state financing, and possibly with further federal aid to particular states and localities that might wish to supplement the minimums. Extension of

AFDC to children of unemployed fathers could be mandated in all the states. In cases of noncooperation of maladministration, HEW could be authorized to undertake direct administration, as Agriculture has finally begun to do in the case of poor counties that have rejected the food donation programs. By administrative regulations, the federal government is now prescribing simplified eligibility procedures. Other changes—like the recent change to permit welfare recipients to keep a part of outside earnings without reduction of assistance payments—can be mandated by law. Nevertheless, the effectuation of national policies through a federal-state system is bound to be cumbersome at best. In the absence of some major advantage to be gained from divided administrative responsibility, a system of direct national administration is to be preferred. No such major advantage to be gained from divided responsibility for public assistance is apparent.

If public assistance is thus liberalized on a national scale, what is the answer to those who contend that motivation for self-support would be further undermined? The answer lies partly in the full development of the programs, to which this paper has been devoted, for a vast increase in opportunities for jobs and training and for the related services which help people to become employable and increase their earning power. It lies partly in the longer-run proposals outlined by Ralph Tyler to raise dramatically the educational opportunity for the children of the underclass. It lies partly in the encouragement of family planning to reduce parental responsibilities. It depends heavily on the eradication of racial discrimination. But even if all of these positive approaches to the problem of motivation were to prove insufficient—and that cannot be said until the country has pursued these approaches much further—it would still be unsound public policy to deprive multitudes of children of the sustenance they require to grow into healthy and self-sustaining adults in their own time in order to punish those of their parents' generation who may be considered to deserve such punishment in our time.

Politics and Resources

John Gardner made the point in his encounter with the governors at their 1968 conference. "We cannot solve the awesome problems that cloud our future as a nation without spending a great deal more money than we are now spending," said Gardner. "I am sure you understand.... We will have to raise new taxes." The governors understood no such thing. "Let 'em work for it, and not think they can threaten to burn and loot unless they get what they demand," said one, as quoted by the *Washington Post*. "Let's stop talking about spending all this money and start instilling in these people the spirit that made this country great," said another. "You have people who won't get on a bus and go five miles to work, and they are the ones who are hollering the loudest for welfare," said a third.

Gardner did not put a price tag on his new taxes and his "great deal more" spending. And the administration that launched the Great Society has scrupulously refrained from even hinting at the ultimate cost of all its programs. The nation's mayors have offered only loose estimates of the cities' needs for federal aid, such as a trillion dollars over a ten-year period. It is fruitless to try to be more precise, because the total need cannot be met within a decade, or even two, in any case. Limitations of manpower and of organizing capacity would set a ceiling on the effort, even if the nation's willingness to tax did not. What is important is to frame the issue in terms that can be considered intelligently at that critical moment when peace comes in Vietnam, for the alternatives then will be whether to make good on promises of jobs and income for the underclass or to reduce taxes for the comfortable.

The model cities program may be a means to frame the issue more clearly. In the fall of 1968, each of the seventy-five cities participating in the first round of planning—which includes most of the largest cities—will have submitted to the Department of Housing and Urban Development a five-year plan for the comprehensive redevelopment of its model neighborhood, complete with cost figures. For the first time, then, estimates will be available on not only what the cities need, but on what they want to do and believe they are capable of doing. Subject to the usual scrutiny for reasonableness and feasibility, these figures can be projected to cover all of the cities' slum neighborhoods, and then to cover other cities. To all this, a figure for rural and nonmetropolitan areas can be added, and at least a starting point will be at hand for a consideration of the national priorities. How much of the post-Vietnam bonanza—and Charles Schultze in this volume has shown that it will not be large in the first couple of years—will go to model cities and to counterpart programs for rural areas? How much for income maintenance? How much for public employment programs? How much will be given in block grants to the states? How much will be returned to the taxpayers—or will the sum total of all the needs compel the nation, as Gardner suggested to the governors, to consider even raising taxes?

These questions deserve the broadest kind of public discussion, based on the best available data. The moment of decision may come suddenly, and the country needs to be prepared. The President should move at once to end the secrecy about the country's long-range budget choices. Directly, or through a presidential commission or a joint presidential-congressional commission, he should lay before the country the estimates of needs and resources to meet the nation's goals, and state clearly the alternatives, so that the great debate can begin.

JAMES TOBIN

RAISING THE INCOMES OF THE POOR

The revolt against poverty and economic inequality in the United States began some time in the middle 1960s. Like many revolutionary movements, it arose and grew in intensity not when conditions were getting worse but when they were getting better, not when the ruling authorities were insensitive and oppressive but when they proclaimed commitment to the revolutionary cause. No doubt the natural progress of the American economy and the normal course of American politics would suffice, as they have in the past, gradually to raise the standards of life of the poorest fifth of the population. But neither the poor themselves nor their many sympathizers among the affluent majority are content with business and politics as usual. That is why the revolt against poverty is today the main item on the nation's domestic economic agenda.

It was not so eight years ago, when full employment and growth were the main economic issues. In terms of the aspirations of 1960–61, both private enterprise and public economic policy have performed very successfully. Unemployment, which was 7 percent of the labor force on the eve of the Kennedy administration, has been reduced well below the administration's interim full employment target of 4 percent. The growth rate of gross national product (GNP), adjusted for price changes, rose from 2.4 percent per year over the period 1953–60, to 6.5 percent per year over the period 1961–67.

As predicted, the restoration of full employment and the growth of national output significantly diminished the prevalence of poverty. By the income criteria of the federal government, 38.9 million persons, 22.1 percent of the population, were poor in 1959. By 1967 these numbers had been reduced to 25.9 million persons, 13.3 percent of the population.[1] What was

1. Bureau of the Census, *Current Population Reports*, Series P-60, No. 55, Aug. 5, 1968.

not predicted was that after this performance poverty and economic inequality would be more acute and divisive social problems than they had been for a generation, more compelling than at any time in this century save the depths of the Great Depression.

The Revolt against Poverty and the Negro Revolution

Aspirations have outrun performance. The major factor in widening the gap was the Negro civil rights revolution. Its essential message, to blacks and whites alike, was that Negroes count fully and equally as people and as U.S. citizens.

The determination that Negroes shall no longer be second-class citizens soon extended to the economic sphere. This is what gives the revolt against poverty its cutting edge—the disproportionately heavy burden of poverty and economic disadvantage on black people. And this is why the major battlefront of the war on poverty is the large northern city—that is where they live, the black people who aspire to a better life. It is statistically true that there are more whites than blacks among the poor, and that most poor people do not live in urban ghettos. Nevertheless it seems very doubtful that there would be either a revolt or a war against poverty in this decade if poverty were as rare and as unconcentrated among blacks as it is among white people.

TABLE 1. *Selected Statistics on the Prevalence and Distribution of Poverty*

	\multicolumn{4}{c}{Persons in poor households}	Percentage of poor persons living in central cities (1964)
	As percentage of all persons		Number (millions)		
Race	1966	1967	1966	1967	
White	11.5	10.2	19.5	17.6	23.8
Nonwhite	40.0	35.3	9.3	8.3	41.7

Sources: Persons in poor households—Bureau of the Census, *Current Population Reports*, Series P-60, No. 55, Aug. 5, 1968; percentage of poor in central cities—*Report of the National Advisory Commission on Civil Disorders*, Mar. 1, 1968, p. 127.

Prior to the civil rights revolution, almost all people of both races took for granted the second-class economic status of the Negro. Negroes were just not expected to enjoy the same standards of life, health, and education as whites; it was normal for them to put up with conditions that would be regarded as pathological for whites. Even optimists and well-wishers were content to reflect that time and education would slowly ameliorate the economic condition of the Negro. This racial double standard made the nation conveniently unconscious of the extent of poverty in its midst, and gave the national conscience a ready excuse for doing very little about it. (The nationwide attitude toward Negro poverty was similar to that of the ingenuously puzzled and indignant white residents of a northern Wisconsin county on learning that the federal government considered it to be one of severe poverty; it did not occur to them that the dismally low incomes of the many Chippewa Indian residents would count in this assessment.) When the Negro became a first-class citizen, the psychological and political dimensions of the poverty problem were suddenly magnified.

Poverty per se is by no means the only focus of discontent. The poor want more of the good things of American life, to be sure. They also want, especially for their children, the opportunities other Americans have for social, occupational, and economic advancement. Here again, the Negro revolution has revealed the vast failure of the society to live up to its professed ideals of equality of opportunity, a discrepancy that enrages middle-class Negroes no less than the poor. Essential as it is to raise the living standards of the poor, simply lifting the bottom of the income distribution will not set the situation right so long as Negroes feel that the institutions of the society conspire to confine them to the bottom.

The Revival of Inequality as a Social and Political Issue

The revolt against poverty has made the distribution of income, wealth, and economic power a live social and political issue in the United States once again. Periodically throughout American history the poorer classes have expressed severe discontent with their shares of the pie, regarding them as both inadequate and unfair. But for most of the postwar era—certainly after the war in Korea distracted President Truman from domestic reform—the issue of inequality was quiescent. Even John F. Kennedy and Lyndon B. Johnson tried not to revive it explicitly, although they presided over large increases in the scope and size of federal domestic civilian spending. They hoped to build a wide consensus in support of their war on poverty and related welfare measures. An essential part of this strategy was to rely on growth in the pie rather than on new ways of slicing it up. Corporate and personal income taxpayers would not be antagonized by demands to dip deeper in their pockets to pay the bills. As their profits and incomes rose under benign fiscal and monetary policies that sustained prosperity and encouraged steady growth, the yield of existing tax rates would grow too. In addition there would be savings in defense outlays as the cold war gradually thawed. These fiscal resources would permit a steady expansion of federal programs to aid the poor, even with occasional tax cuts for everyone else.

This strategy foundered for two reasons. One was the war in Vietnam and the associated jump in defense spending. The other was the impatience of the poor and their allies; they now want measures that will require actual sacrifices by the affluent majority; perhaps they want the sacrifices for their own sake. As Charles Schultze's calculations in this volume show, there is little prospect, even with optimistic assumptions about peace and the domestic economy, that federal fiscal resources for a major initiative in the war on poverty will develop painlessly.

The consensus which seemed so broad and so firm after the election of 1964 has broken down, and with it the faith that economic growth is the solvent for all potentially divisive domestic issues. In the coming years the issue of distribution may be squarely joined: Will the affluent majority explicitly tax itself to improve the lot of the poorest fifth of the population? Is the majority wise enough or frightened enough to do so? How can the poor, with so little national electoral force, bring effective political pressure for redistributive measures? If their disaffection cannot find political outlet, will it pour forth into the streets?

The Agricultural Revolution, Migration, and Contemporary Poverty

Poverty in the United States in the second half of the twentieth century is in substantial degree a final and painful phase of the liquidation of the nineteenth century agricultural system of the South. Ever since the Industrial Revolution, transfer of manpower from farm to factory, from country to city, has been a major feature of economic progress throughout the Western world.

So spectacular has been man's progress in extracting the basic necessities of life from the land that most of the U.S. labor force has been released for the satisfaction, and indeed the creation, of other wants. The percentage of the labor force in agriculture declined from 53 in 1870 to 27 in 1920 and to 5 in 1967. In urban occupations, which also benefit from the endless advance of science, the wages of labor steadily rise. But the gains in the standard of life of the industrial worker have not been available in the countryside. To enjoy them, the vast majority of farmers, farmworkers, and their children must leave the farm. In order to earn from agricultural work a standard of life comparable to that of the urban worker, a man must till an ever-increasing number of acres, using up-to-date knowledge and equipment.

Attracted by job opportunities and high wages in industry and in cities, discouraged by the prospects in agriculture, rural Americans have been migrating to towns and cities on a tremendous scale for many decades. Between 1959 and 1966 the number of farms fell by 20 percent and the number of poor farm households by two-thirds.[2]

But the process has by no means run its course. Net emigration from the farm is declining, but it is still nearly a million persons a year. There are still 1.7 million farms with annual sales under $5,000. And though a subsistence farm can probably produce at least as much as twenty or fifty years ago, the living it provides a family is poverty by modern standards. Moreover, the subsistence tenant farmer or sharecropper is often simply displaced from the land, as the landowner diverts it to more profitable uses under the competitive spur of modern technology or the incentives of federal subsidies. The same developments, of course, greatly curtail the demand for hired farm labor, a work force which is 27 percent nonwhite. The President's National Advisory Commission on Rural Poverty estimates that in 1965, 25 percent of rural residents, 13.8 million persons, were poor. They accounted for 41 percent of the poor population of the nation. Rural poverty extends beyond the farms to the villages and towns they once supported. Only a quarter of the rural poor live on farms.

Although the continuing obsolescence of rural labor is nationwide, it has been especially acute in the Southeast. The southern agricultural economy was built on highly labor-intensive techniques of cultivation, and the work force was organized in a feudal manner. It is of course Negroes, the descendants of men and women who were enslaved to the land, who are now too numerous for it to support. Therefore, the required migration is disproportionately a Negro migration, and in large part a migration from the South to the Northeast and the West.

Emigration from the South, and migration into metropolitan areas, by both whites and nonwhites, have declined in this decade. But 100,000 Negroes are still leaving the South every year, and the growing Negro popu-

2. *Economic Report of the President, January* 1968, pp. 132–38.

lation in the South will support continuing emigration. Negroes are becoming more urban and industrial in the South as well as the North and West. The nonwhite population of metropolitan areas is still increasing at 3.1 percent per year; two-thirds of the growth can be attributed to natural increase. Within metropolitan areas, nonwhites are increasingly concentrated in the central cities, while the white population declines in the central cities and grows rapidly in the suburbs.

It is not farfetched to describe the contemporary urban crisis and revolt against poverty as side effects and aftereffects of the industrial transformation of the American economy, perhaps the more frustrating, painful, and dangerous because the transformation is so nearly completed. The danger and pain are the legacy of peculiarly American institutions and developments: southern slavery, the Civil War, and the long survival in the South of a feudal organization of agriculture and of race relations. It is Negroes who must migrate to new jobs and urban locations. But their experience and education in the rural South have not prepared them for urban employment and residence. In a real sense, the population displaced from southern agriculture has become the social problem of the northern cities, and the centuries of southern neglect of Negro education and rights explode in violence on the streets of the North.

Several lessons can be drawn. First, the problems of the northern cities are national in origin, scope, and responsibility. No city can be expected to handle them with its own limited legal powers and fiscal resources.

Second, improvement of the social and economic environment for immigrants to northern cities and their families is going to be a prolonged and difficult and expensive task. These cities face, for some years to come, what amounts to a Malthusian problem, a large potential supply of new residents from immigration and natural increase. Efforts to improve the housing, employment, and welfare of ghetto residents can easily be swamped by waves of immigration, partly inevitable, partly induced by the improvements themselves. This does not mean that such efforts should not be made; it does mean that lots of running is required just to stay in the same place.

The objective is, after all, to improve the conditions of people, not of places. A welfare family in New York City or Milwaukee is certainly not living at standards other residents of those areas consider tolerable for themselves; yet the family is better off than in a tar-paper shack in rural West Virginia or Mississippi. A residential neighborhood may deteriorate as it passes from established workers moving to the suburbs to recent immigrants from the South. Yet both the new and the old residents are better off than before.

Third, urban poverty must be attacked not only in the cities but in rural areas, especially in the South. It is just as important to improve education in the rural South as in the ghettos of northern cities. Many of the pupils in southern schools will end up as school children and adults in the North. It is just as important to bring industrial jobs to the South—for example, through subsidies for the employment and training of men and women displaced from agriculture—as to urban ghettos in the North.

Finally, it is important to remove the artificial incentive to migration to the urban North provided by the immense differences among states in public assistance benefits and eligibility rules. This can be done only by nationalization of public assistance. The southern states do not have the fiscal resources, even on a matching basis, to pay adequate benefits, even if they had the political will to do so.

The Measurement of Poverty and the Objectives of Policy

The federal war on poverty, whatever else it has accomplished, has established an official measure of the prevalence of poverty in the United States. Adoption of a specific quantitative measure, however arbitrary and debatable, will have durable and far-reaching political consequences. Administrations will be judged by their success or failure in reducing the officially measured prevalence of poverty. So long as any family is found below the official poverty line, no politician will be able to claim victory in the war on poverty or to ignore the repeated solemn acknowledgements of society's obligation to its poorer members. A similarly binding commitment to a specific measure of full employment, the adoption of 4 percent unemployment as the "interim target" of the Kennedy administration in 1961, strengthened the political forces on the side of expansionary fiscal and monetary policy in the early 1960s.

The official count of the poor is based on annual income. A four-person nonfarm family, two adults and two children, is considered poor if its income is less than $3,335 at 1966 prices of consumer goods. Adjustments are made for family size, so that the 1966 poverty line varies from $1,635 for a single individual to $5,430 for a family of seven or more. Because farm families have less need for cash incomes, they are not considered poor if their incomes exceed 70 percent of the nonfarm standards. The standards themselves are based on estimates of the realistically minimal costs of nutritionally adequate food for adults and children. Generally speaking, a household[3] is taken to be poor if its income does not exceed three times the cost of this food budget.[4]

Since this measure of poverty has become so important in government policy, a number of comments on it are appropriate:

1. It is an absolute rather than a relative measure. The dollar amount of the cutoff line is, of course, recomputed for changes in the cost of living. But as time goes on, the official poverty line will fall further and further behind the average and median incomes of the population.[5] Thus it would be conceivable gradually to eliminate poverty, thus defined, without any equalization in the relative distribution of income.

On the other hand, there will certainly be strong political and social forces working to scale up the income definition of poverty as the majority of the population becomes more and more affluent. In terms of absolute real income rather than relative position in the national distribution of income, the Great Society counts as poor many people whom the New Deal did not, and some crusade on behalf of the "forgotten man" or the "other America" of tomorrow will further revise upward society's notion of a tolerable minimum standard of life.

2. Annual income is not a wholly satisfactory criterion of poverty, although a more sophisticated measure would probably not change appreciably the estimated prevalence of poverty. According to estimates made in 1964 by the Council of Economic Advisers, based on the Current Population Surveys of the Census Bureau, 69 percent of households with poverty incomes in 1963 also had poverty incomes in the previous year. This figure indicates considerable turnover, but the CEA also calculated that the estimated prevalence of poverty would not be changed by basing it on average income for the two years.[6]

The normal life cycle of income presents a somewhat different problem in the definition of poverty. The low incomes of some young people are not indicative of poverty: Consider impecunious students of law or medi-

3. The term "household" includes both families and unrelated individuals.
4. Mollie Orshansky, "Counting the Poor: Another Look at the Poverty Profile," *Social Security Bulletin*, January 1965, and Mollie Orshansky, "The Shape of Poverty in 1966," *Social Security Bulletin*, March 1968.
5. For four-person families, the national median income was twice the poverty-line income in 1959, two and a half times in 1966. Orshansky, "Counting the Poor," p. 6.
6. *Economic Report of the President, January 1964*, pp. 164–65.

cine with years of lucrative practice ahead of them. Neither are the low incomes of many old people who are living comfortably by gradually consuming assets they accumulated before retiring. Distributions of annual income exaggerate economic inequality by including differences due to age and position in the life cycle. Unfortunately we do not have good estimates of inequality of lifetime incomes.

When wealth is considered, along with one-year income, in the definition of poverty, the estimated prevalence of poverty among the aged is reduced by about a third. But the aggregate estimate of its prevalence is lowered only by two or three percentage points. Few people who have low annual incomes have much wealth.[7]

3. The strategists of the official war on poverty have focused attention on the poverty count: the number and proportion of households below the official poverty line and the number and proportion of persons in those households. But the importance of moving households from the wrong side of the arbitrary line to the right side should not be emphasized to the exclusion of other dimensions of progress in the campaign. Any increase in the income of poor families is desirable, even if it is insufficient to move them out of the "poor" classification. Indeed, it is probably more important to give $100 to a family with no income than to a family within $50 of the poverty line.

The aggregate poverty income "gap" is a useful and simple supplement to the poverty count in assessing the aggregate amount of poverty. The gap is the total of all the shortfalls of incomes of poor families below poverty-line standards. This was estimated at $13.7 billion, and 2.8 percent of GNP, in 1959, and at $11 billion, and 1.6 percent of GNP, in 1965.

Neither of these aggregate measures, the count or the gap, awards any points for increasing the incomes of the near-poor, those households falling, say, between one and one and a half times the poverty line. The line is, after all, arbitrary and minimal, and it would be a hollow victory over poverty just to move all the poor a few inches beyond it. Some income supplementation proposals spill benefits on the near-poor. Quite apart from the fact that this spillover may be necessary for reasons of incentive, equity, and continuity, the near-poor should not be considered undeserving beneficiaries.

7. B. A. Weisbrod and W. Lee Hansen, "An Income-Net Worth Approach to Measuring Economic Welfare," unpublished, Department of Economics, University of Wisconsin, 1967.

Full Employment, Inflation, and Poverty

Most poor households contain workers or potential workers. Fifty-four percent of the poor families in 1966 were headed by persons in the labor force; this includes 39 percent of families headed by females. Only 4 percent of poor family heads reported themselves as unemployed. Of male heads of households under 65 years of age, 82 percent had work experience in 1966. Unrelated individuals in poverty are mostly aged 65 or more, and mostly female; even so, 28 percent are in the labor force, including 2 percent unemployed.[8] Many more heads of poor households would have been in the labor force if job opportunities had been available, or if they had not been discouraged by disincentives connected with their public assistance or social insurance benefits. In the population at large, one of every ten persons not seeking work really wants a regular job.[9] About one-fifth of poor families had more than one earner. But unemployment rates were high for teenagers and other potential secondary workers.

Jobs, more and better jobs, are certainly the most appealing solutions for these poor families—let them earn their way out of poverty. This is undoubtedly the path that they would prefer. It is also, the public opinion polls tell us, the path that the general American public prefers. It accords with the work ethic of the society, strongly ingrained in both the poor minority and the affluent majority. Moreover, so long as there are socially useful tasks to be done, it is a national economic waste to leave willing and able hands unemployed or underemployed.

But this solution is easier said than done; otherwise the normal processes of the labor market would long since have absorbed most of the potential workers among the poor. Since the winter of 1965–66 labor markets have been tight in the United States, with the unemployment rate confined to the narrow range between 3.5 and 4.3 percent. Most of this unemployment may be regarded as transitional or "frictional." In an average month in 1967, only 15 percent of the unemployed had been out of work for as long as fifteen weeks, and only 6 percent for as long as twenty-seven weeks. In 1961, of the 3.7 million unemployed in an average month, two-thirds were

---

8. Orshansky, "Counting the Poor," pp. 10–12.
9. Robert L. Stein, "Reasons for Nonparticipation in the Labor Force," *Monthly Labor Review*, Vol. 90 (July 1967), pp. 22–27.

males 20 years of age or older. In 1967, of the 3 million unemployed, only 36 percent fell in this group, and 43 percent were teenagers. Job vacancy statistics are not yet available in the United States, but it is likely that over the last two or three years vacancies have exceeded the number unemployed. The index of help-wanted advertising shot up 20 percent in 1966.

The problem is that the vacancies and the unemployed do not match. They diverge in location, in specifications of skill and experience, in wages and other terms of employment, and in other dimensions—including race, sex, age—of the preferences of employers and the characteristics of potential employees.

Labor markets could be tightened still further, the number of vacancies increased, the rate of unemployment diminished. Tipping the balance of labor markets further in favor of workers, as against employers, is within the well understood capacity of federal fiscal and monetary policy. Since 1961 expansion of aggregate demand for goods and services has lowered the unemployment rate from 7 percent to 3.5 percent, the equivalent today of 2.7 million workers, while at the same time providing jobs for an increase of more than 10 million in the civilian labor force. The same techniques of fiscal and monetary policy that engineered or allowed this expansion could bring the unemployment rate down to 3 percent or lower.

Such a tightening of the labor market, like previous turns of the same screw, would be of particular benefit to the disadvantaged workers in poor families. As employers compete for increased work forces to meet the new demands for their products, they find workers tailored to their job specifications increasingly scarce and expensive. They reach further back in the queue of unemployed workers. They relax their requirements and broaden their preferences; they overlook deficiencies in education and skills and undertake themselves the expense and trouble of training. From 1961 to 1967, for example, while white unemployment fell from 6.0 to 3.4 percent, nonwhite unemployment fell from 12.4 to 7.4 percent. Workers at the rear of the queue gain not only in reduction of unemployment, but also in greater availability of full-time work and chances for advancement. In other words, private employers and free markets do much of the work of the war on poverty—without public expenditure and government bureaucracy.

Experience also shows, however, that tightening the labor market—increasing the excess of unfilled vacancies over unemployed workers—accelerates inflation. Skilled and qualified workers, whether organized or not, acquire greater bargaining power. Employers' adjustments to accommodate or train less desirable substitutes add to their costs. Reduction of unemployment below 4 percent has been accompanied by acceleration of the increase in the consumer price index from less than 1½ percent per year, 1960–65, to more than 3 percent per year, 1965–68. Reducing the unemployment rate from 3.5 percent to 3 percent would further increase the speed of inflation, perhaps to 4 or 5 percent per year. On the other hand, it would at the same time raise real GNP about $4 billion or $5 billion. More important in this context, it could be expected to lower the prevalence of poverty in the population by four-tenths of a percentage point, or about 2 percent. This is the same order of magnitude as the normal year-to-year reduction in poverty due to economic growth at a constant unemployment rate; a once-for-all half-point reduction in the unemployment rate would speed the attrition of poverty by about one year.[10]

How the society balances the cost in inflation of a monetary-fiscal policy aimed at tighter labor markets against the advantages in real income and poverty reduction is one of its most important and difficult political decisions. Some believe that we have already erred too far on the inflationary side; others, like me, favor pushing the unemployment rate still lower. But everyone would draw the line somewhere, if not at 4 percent unemployment, then at 3.5; if not at 3 percent, then at 2.5. At some point, certainly far short of zero unemployment, the distortions and inequities of inflation, and the risks that inflation will be constantly accelerating, will be deemed too great. Recent experience suggests that the political balance of forces in this country places this point somewhere between 3.5 and 4 percent unemployment. The inflationary pressures generated at such rates lead to restrictive monetary policies, as in the summer of 1966 and the winter of 1968, and eventually to deflationary changes of fiscal policy, as in mid-1968. Of course, the political balance is not immutable, and a greater understanding of the advantages of a tight labor market in the war on poverty may lead to a more inflationary resolution of the dilemma.

But even if the balance of forces determining fiscal and monetary policy changed in an expansionary and inflationary direction, total demand could not generate enough jobs to solve the problem of underemployment of the disadvantaged. Left to itself, the normal operation of labor markets cannot place these people in jobs unless the balance of demand and supply in

10. Estimates from Lester Thurow, *Poverty and Discrimination*, Chap. 4, to be published by the Brookings Institution. Experience with tight labor markets in recent years suggests that these may be underestimates.

many of them is tilted heavily in favor of excess demand and unfilled vacancies. This is why specific labor market policies, designed to match vacancies with unemployed workers, are necessary. This is, indeed, why they were inaugurated in 1961 and have been pursued with increasing vigor, if not with spectacular success, ever since. Elsewhere in this book, James Sundquist describes and evaluates these measures, and discusses government policy to create or to subsidize jobs tailored to the qualifications of the unemployed.

If the poor are employed, must someone else become unemployed? At first glance, this seems to be the implication if the economy and the body politic cannot tolerate the inflationary by-products of holding unemployment below a certain level. A good case could be made for the equity of some redistribution of the burden of unemployment, between black and white, poor and rich, unskilled and skilled. To equalize black and white unemployment rates in 1967 without changing the national average, for example, the black rate would have had to come down by 3.6 percentage points while the white rate rose by only 0.4 percentage point.

But in fact an increase in employment engineered by tailoring some existing vacancies to the type of workers who are in excess supply would not upset the balance of the labor markets. It is not these workers whose employment removes an important competitive check on the speed of wage increases. Indeed, filling vacancies with them reduces competitive upward pull on wages. Hence, successful labor market policy should dampen inflationary pressure even while lowering the unemployment rate.

If new jobs were especially created to absorb the disadvantaged unemployed, there would be no reduction in the excess of vacancies over unemployed. But there would be no increase either; the presumption is that unemployment would decline without increasing inflationary pressure. Of course the spillovers of demand from the newly employed workers into markets where products or skills are in short supply must be offset. Otherwise aggregate demand and inflationary pressure will increase. The necessary offset comes from sale of the products of the newly employed workers or from taxes levied to finance or subsidize the specially created jobs. These sales or taxes will cut down on spending elsewhere in the economy by roughly as much as the new employees spend. The conclusion is that policies to place disadvantaged unemployed workers in jobs, whether existing vacancies or new jobs, can reduce total unemployment at no inflationary cost. Therefore, these policies do not take jobs from other workers.

Structural and Distributive Strategies in Anti-Poverty Policy

The basic problem of poverty is that the earning capacities of many individuals and households fall short of socially defined standards of living. Continued prosperity and economic growth would, without any special governmental efforts, gradually narrow and eliminate these gaps. In ten years general economic progress would, it is estimated, diminish the prevalence of poverty by at least five percentage points. The response of poverty to economic growth might then diminish significantly, because most of the remaining poor would have personal disabilities isolating them from the mainstream of the economy. In any case, the prospective pace of attrition is not fast enough to satisfy the aspirations of the poor or the conscience of the nation.

Public policy can take two basic approaches to the war on poverty. One is structural: to raise earning capacities, equipping the poor of this generation and the potential poor of the next with the means to earn above-poverty incomes through normal employment. The other is distributive: to make up income deficiencies by direct government grants in cash or in kind or by subsidized employment.

The structural approach has two facets, the market and the individual. Labor markets, as currently organized, prevent many individuals from exploiting fully the earning capacities they have. Racial discrimination in employment and housing, restrictions on entry into organized trades, minimum wage regulations, failures of communication between employers with vacancies and potential applicants—these and other labor market imperfections bar some workers from competing for jobs they could perform and shunt them into unemployment, underemployment, or low-paid work. Public policy could try to promote more effective competition in labor markets, though not without encountering strong opposition from workers and employers who are sheltered by the existing barriers.

With respect to the individual, structural policy seeks to build up what economists call his human capital—the health, education, skill, experience, and behavior on which the future market value of his labor depends. This general principle is so clearly in accord with American ideals of fair play and equality of opportunity that it receives wide assent. An improved distribution of human capital poses a competitive threat to those who benefit from scarcity, but it is a diffuse and remote one. The trouble is that we are not very expert in making social investments in human capital. Adult education, training, and retraining are difficult, slow, and costly processes, as the review of past experience by James Sundquist makes clear. Our main hope must be in the education of children, where, as Ralph Tyler demonstrates, we are finding our belated commitment to equality of educational opportunity vastly more difficult and expensive to implement than anyone anticipated.

The two approaches, structural and distributive, compete for the taxpayer's dollar. But they are in an important sense complementary, for the following reasons:

1. There are some deficiencies of earning power that structural policy and economic progress can never wholly remedy: large families, families without breadwinners, blindness and other physical disabilities, obsolete skills, old age, and so on. Programs to maintain and supplement incomes are necessary to handle these cases.

2. The structural approach, even under the most favorable circumstances and with the most generous financing, is bound to take a long time. Labor markets and educational systems cannot be changed quickly. Furthermore, many of the necessary changes in these institutions will not bear fruit for a generation. Meanwhile people are poor.

3. It is tempting to dismiss the distributive approach as a palliative that deals only with symptoms, and to favor the structural approach as an attack on basic causes. But the metaphor is false. Poverty today leads to poverty tomorrow. Inequality of condition means inequality of opportunity. Poverty and inequality perpetuate themselves in children whose capacities and motivations to learn are impaired—perhaps by physical handicaps due to malnutrition or inadequate medical care before or after birth, perhaps by intellectually and culturally deprived homes and neighborhoods. Improvement in the conditions under which children are born and raised will increase, not diminish, their earning capacities as adults.

Investment in Human Capital

The principal objective of the structural strategy must be to increase the society's investment in human capital and to make the distribution of human capital much less unequal. The three major processes available are public primary and secondary education, higher education and vocational training for youth and adults, and experience in regular employment.

These processes, and policies to improve them, are discussed elsewhere in this book. I will confine myself to one suggestion before turning to distributive policy.

After high school, every youth in the nation—whatever the economic means of his parents or his earlier education—should have the opportunity to develop his capacity to earn income and to contribute to the society. To this end the federal government could make available to every young man and woman, on graduation from high school and in any case at the age of 19, an "endowment" of, for example, $5,000. He could draw on this "National Youth Endowment" for authorized purposes until his twenty-eighth birthday; the period of eligibility would be extended to allow for military service. Authorized purposes would include higher education, vocational training, apprenticeship, and other forms of on-the-job training. To be eligible, educational and training programs would have to be approved by the federal agency administering the endowment. The endowment would pay tuition and other fees to the educational institutions or employers operating the programs; the individual could also draw on the fund for subsistence while enrolled in an approved program.

For every dollar used, the individual would incur liability for payment of extra federal income tax after he reaches the age of 28. The terms of this contingent repayment would be set so that the average individual would over his lifetime repay the fund in full, plus interest at the government's borrowing rate. However, the government might decide to set less stringent terms and to subsidize the endowment, recognizing that some of the advantages of the program accrue to the nation as a whole and are not reflected in higher taxable incomes of the specific individuals assisted.

This proposal is a mixture of the GI bill of rights and the "Educational Opportunity Bank" proposed in recent years. It has a number of important advantages. Individuals are assisted directly and equally, rather than indirectly and haphazardly, through government financing of particular programs. The advantages of background and talent that fit certain young people for university education are not compounded by financial favoritism. Within the broad limits of approved programs, individuals are free to choose how to use the money the government is willing to invest in their development. No individual misses out because there happen to be no training courses where he lives, or because his parents' income barely exceeds some permissible maximum.

Every year 3½ million people become 18 years old and, under the proposal, they would acquire drawing rights in aggregate of $17½ billion.

Eventually repayments will cover most of the outlays. But meanwhile the government will build up a substantial claim. Since this is a social investment project it would not be necessary to meet the initial cash deficits by taxation. It would be entirely appropriate for the responsible government agency to borrow the funds in the capital markets, even though the monetary authorities would have to neutralize the inflationary impact by tightening credit and raising interest rates, temporarily displacing other investments, public and private, of lower social priority.

Income Maintenance and Public Assistance: The Legacy of the New Deal

The United States already has a large, complex system of income maintenance and public assistance. In 1967, cash transfers to persons by all levels of government totaled $48.6 billion, 8 percent of total personal income. In addition, other government expenditures provided benefits in kind to individuals or subsidized their consumption of certain goods or services. Among these expenditures the most important were $8 billion for health and hospitals and $3 billion for public housing and other welfare services. These transfers make an important contribution to the relief of poverty. It is estimated that slightly more than half of them went to people who would have been poor in their absence.[11]

A special Census survey for 1965 indicates that 55 percent of households receiving public cash income payments had other incomes below the poverty lines and that the total count of poor households would have been 42 percent higher in the absence of these programs. However, 31 percent of the households receiving transfers were still poor, and 32 percent of the pre-transfer poor, or 54 percent of the post-transfer poor, received no governmental payments.[12]

Why is the system so incomplete an antidote to poverty? The answer lies in the philosophy of the social security legislation of the 1930s, which

---

11. Figures from "U.S. National Income and Product Accounts," *Survey of Current Business*, Vol. 48 (July 1968), pp. 31, 32, 35, and 36, and from unpublished calculations kindly made available by Robert Lampman. He estimates also that $36 billion was transferred through the public educational system, of which $18 billion went to the pre-transfer poor. But in view of the long-established commitment of the nation to universal public education, without test of need, this "transfer" is quite different in nature from the others.

12. Mollie Orshansky, "The Shape of Poverty in 1966," pp. 26–30.

still provides the basic framework for social insurance and public assistance in this country. Its purpose was to provide protection against the unavoidable hazards of life. Some of the hazards are natural, biological; others, like involuntary unemployment, are incidents of our complex, interdependent industrial society. Some are highly probable, like outliving one's capacity to earn a living; others, like congenital or accidental physical disability, are very unusual. But they are hazards to which every individual and family is subject.

The major programs are the federal system of Old Age, Survivors, Disability, and Health Insurance (OASDHI) and the state-federal system of unemployment insurance. Over the years OASDHI has grown in coverage of the population, in scale of benefits and contributions, and in scope of contingencies insured. In 1967 the system disbursed benefits of $25.7 billion to a monthly average of 23 million recipients. Three-quarters of all jobs in the United States are covered by unemployment insurance or other public programs of unemployment compensation; and $2.2 billion in benefits were paid in 1967 to 5 million people.

These social insurance systems continue to be directed more against insecurity than against poverty. On the one hand, they protect people against economic reverses whether they are poor or not. The unemployed worker collects his compensation as a right earned during his employment and in a loose sense paid for by contributions levied on him and his employer. His benefits are not conditional on a showing of need; indeed benefits go up rather than down with his previous earnings. Similarly, OASDHI benefits must be earned in "covered" employment; their amount is positively related to pre-retirement earnings; no test of need or means is imposed; no reduction of benefits is made for property income or other pensions.

The other side of the coin is that these social insurance programs do not protect or assist chronically poor people. There is no unemployment compensation for the man who has never had a job, no OASDHI payment for the man with an insufficient history of covered employment.

Social insurance in the United States does, it is true, accomplish some redistribution of income in favor of the poor. In particular, transfers through OASDHI are the most important government mechanism for moving people, especially old people, out of poverty. The OASDHI system is a pragmatic mixture of contributory insurance and redistribution. There is no case-by-case actuarial correspondence between the contributions an individual and his employer make by payroll taxes during his working years and the benefits to which he is entitled. For some participants, the expected value, on a probability basis, of the benefits exceeds the contributions paid on their behalf. Others, correspondingly, pay more in taxes than the expected value of their benefits. Much of this redistribution is unsystematic and arbitrary. Much of it, however, is welfare-oriented, in the sense that the minimum benefits provided exceed the minimum tax contributions required.

Unfortunately OASDHI is not a suitable mechanism for redistribution. On the one hand, the absence of an effective test of needs and resources means that the beneficiaries may be better off than the contributors. Although the system contains a benefit-reducing "tax" on earnings by beneficiaries under 72, it contains no similar penalty for property income and wealth. On the other hand, the excess contributions redistributed are levied not in accordance with ability to pay, but by proportional taxes on total wages, salaries, and earnings from self-employment, up to an annual ceiling. The exemption of high earnings and of property income means that the transfers effected by the system are not financed on an equitable ability-to-pay basis.

The system as now financed and administered should, therefore, not be used for further income redistribution. It is true that minimum old age benefits are below the official poverty line and that increasing them would bring almost all old people out of poverty. But benefits would rise for all participants regardless of need. The same effect can be more equitably and efficiently achieved by a general system of income supplementation. A second-best alternative would be to use general federal tax revenues rather than payroll taxes to finance a welfare-oriented increase in the low end of the OASDHI benefit scale.

The social security legislation of the 1930s attempted to fill some of the gaps left by social insurance by providing for public assistance unrelated to previous earnings or employment. State and local governments spent $9.3 billion for public assistance and relief in 1967, of which $4.9 billion was for cash transfers and $4.2 billion for medical care. They financed more than half of the total with federal grants-in-aid. But these programs too are dominated and limited by the spirit of protecting people against the inexorable hazards of life. Thus public assistance is not available to everyone who is poor, but only to those whose poverty society recognizes as in large degree beyond their own control. The chief categories of needs recognized as legitimate are old age, blindness, physical disability, and absence or disability of one or both of a child's parents.

Several features of these categories are noteworthy. First, they were expected to dwindle in importance as, thanks to general economic prosperity and progress and to the widening of coverage of social insurance programs, more and more people earned protection against insured hazards and fewer and fewer people required assistance conditioned by need.

Second, the categories were carefully selected to minimize what insurance experts call "moral hazard"—risk to the insurer that some people will be induced deliberately to make themselves eligible for benefits.

Unfortunately these expectations have not proven to be true of the category of broken or incomplete families. Aid for Dependent Children (AFDC) was designed to help women who have to raise children without the help of a male breadwinner—principally widows, divorcées, wives of disabled workers, and mothers deserted by the fathers of their children. This category too was expected to decline relative to the population as more of these cases were covered by survivors' and disability insurance. It was never expected that the definition of the category would encourage desertion and paternal irresponsibility. The tacit assumption was that the institution of the nuclear family, the taboo on illegitimacy, and the ethic of paternal responsibility were too strong to be affected by financial incentives.

The enormous mushrooming of AFDC in recent years suggests that this has turned out to be a serious miscalculation. The number of cases rose by 25 percent between January 1961 and December 1965, a period of economic boom; only half of the increase can be attributed to liberalization of eligibility requirements.[13] Although the majority of AFDC cases are white, the increase is predominantly nonwhite, especially in the central cities.[14] No doubt the growth in the number of Negro households with female heads is a complex phenomenon, related to the matriarchal tradition inherited from slavery and to the submergence of the nuclear family in the extended family in rural agricultural settings. These traditions have left many urban immigrants unprepared for life in cities, where the culture and

13. *Welfare in Review*, Vol. 5 (May 1967), p. 10.
14. See Daniel J. Moynihan, "The Crises in Welfare," *The Public Interest*, Winter 1968.

economy are adapted to the nuclear family. Yet it is in the city that the Negro male encounters formidable disadvantages and difficulties. The incentives the man faces are certainly perverse when the government will help his children and their mother if and only if he disappears. Reform of this insane piece of social engineering has become a first order of business on the national agenda.

Social insurance and categorical assistance programs exclude able-bodied adults of working age, whether single or members of intact families, and their dependents. In 1966, there were 6 million poor households of this type, 54 percent of the total; they contained 17½ million people, 59 percent of the total. They are poor but few of them are eligible for assistance. Some local governments assist them from their own funds, and some states help intact families under the federally aided AFDC program when the breadwinner has become unemployed. But generally speaking, these people are not considered deserving poor with legitimate need for help. Able-bodied men are supposed to be able to take care of themselves and their dependents, no matter how large their family responsibilities. To give them assistance is regarded as an invitation to idleness at government expense, with ultimately incalculable damage to the national character and fisc.

The biggest issue the nation faces in the war on poverty and in the reform of its system of income supplementation and maintenance is how to handle this category. Can they be assisted in a way that preserves their incentives to work and to save to improve their own lot? Can they be assisted in a way that encourages them to form and maintain stable families? Can employment and training opportunities be found or provided for them? Do they need, and should they receive, assistance other than pay for employment or training?

The Philosophical Conflict

These questions are the battleground of a conflict among several American principles. One may be called the Puritan ethic: He who does not work should not eat.

Americans seem very firmly to believe themselves an indolent people, preferring idleness and meager subsistence to work and high income. In a society in which achievement and career success are so clearly honored and valued for their own sake as well as for their material rewards, in which wives work and workers "moonlight" not to eke out subsistence but to buy boats, vacation homes, and college educations, this appears a dubious collective introspection. Nevertheless, it has led to strong opposition in public opinion polls to unconditional cash assistance to potential workers, and to very substantial support for providing income via employment.

The second contesting principle is the social responsibility, accepted as an obligation of government since New Deal days, to see that no one falls below a decent minimum standard of living. How can this responsibility be discharged without making it a de facto or de jure guarantee? And how can such a guarantee be given without impairing the work incentive by which the Puritan ethic sets such store?

The third contesting principle is the American ideal of equality of opportunity. We like to think of the competition for career achievement, recognition, and material reward as a fair race, in which the success of every runner depends on his own talent and effort. This image underlies the strong conviction that the distribution of income and wealth resulting from competition in the marketplace is fair. Departures from it may be called for in the name of charity, but not in the name of justice.

This comforting view of the world assumes that everyone starts the race on a par, and America has had better cause than most societies to take pride in its record of individual opportunity and social mobility. Millions of immigrants came to these shores to escape limits on their social and economic status prescribed at birth. In a country free of the residue of feudalism, they could aspire to a better life. Most important, they could see their children surpass them in education, occupational status, and prosperity.

But this proud history does not mean that America has equality of opportunity and a fair race today. First of all, the concept has never fitted the Negro, the victim of America's own brand of feudalism and prescribed inferiority. Second, the inequalities of achievement and reward in one generation are inequalities of opportunity for the next. The United States allows vast differences in inherited material wealth and, what is probably even more important, vast differences in the health, informal education, and formal schooling which children bring to adulthood. The black son of a welfare mother in an urban ghetto and the son of a backwoods Appalachian subsistence farmer simply do not get the same start in life as the son of a suburban doctor or university professor. It is fatuous to pretend otherwise.

Some inherited inequality of opportunity is doubtless unavoidable where providing advantages for children is as important a motivation and incentive for parents as it is in our society. But this implies that children differ widely in their endowments. Distributing wealth and income in accordance with IQs or other genetic endowments is not inherently just. But actual inequalities far exceed innate differentials.[15] Public intervention is necessary to keep the race from becoming cumulatively more and more unfair and opportunity more and more unequal.

One obvious and recognized inequity is related to differences in family size. Wages and salaries are paid for work performed, without adjustment for family responsibilities or other dimensions of need. To do otherwise would certainly distort the allocation of manpower; family size should not be a factor in the assignment of jobs to men. Therefore, as between two workers of equivalent skill and wage, the one with the larger family is at a disadvantage, and so are his children. It is true that family size itself can be regarded as a voluntary decision, the more so as birth control technique is improved and widely disseminated. But if a poor family is too large, can we justify the children's sufferings on the grounds that they provide a salutary example for others? Discrepancies between earning capacity and family responsibility are inevitable in a society that entrusts economic decisions to the free market and child-rearing to the nuclear family. These discrepancies are particularly acute in the United States today; the prevalence of poverty rises dramatically with family size, in 1967 from 8.4 percent for families with one child to 35.0 percent for families with six or more children.

An increase in the legal minimum wage seems to many observers the obvious remedy for the inadequate incomes of the working poor. It is not. Employers can be required to pay higher wage rates but not to hire workers on whom they take a loss. The likely result of an increase in the minimum wage is to increase unemployment and involuntary part-time work among the very groups the measure aims to help. The way to increase the wages of the poor is to increase competition for their services and to increase their earning capacities.

15. Thurow, *Poverty and Discrimination*. Chaps. 5 and 6 show how inequality in education, experience on the job, and property ownership, together with racial discrimination, make the distribution of income much more unequal than the distribution of ability.

Reform of Public Assistance

The serious failings of the present system of public assistance can be summarized as follows:

1. *Inadequate coverage.* The restrictive categories of eligibility exclude millions of poor people, especially among the working or employable poor. Even within the eligible categories, many people in need receive no assistance because of state residence requirements, over-strict local administration, or simple ignorance.

2. *Anti-family incentives.* Eligibility rules for AFDC penalize financially the formation and maintenance of intact families.

3. *Inadequacy of benefits.* In most states benefits are inadequate. Under AFDC the states determine their own standards of need and decide how fully to meet them. The needs of a mother and three children, as estimated by the states, varied in January 1965 from $124 per month in Arkansas to $376 per month in Alaska. In most states actual benefit payments fall short of their own calculations of need. As a result, actual maximum payments to a mother with three children varied from $50 per month in Mississippi to $246 in New York. No state was paying benefits to families at the official poverty level.[16]

4. *Incentives for uneconomic migration.* The wide differences in benefits, eligibility rules, and administrative practices encourage migration to the wealthier and more liberal states, compounding the problems of northern cities. AFDC cases have more than doubled in New York and California since 1961, and these two states alone account for more than half of the one million increase in the case load since 1964.

5. *Disincentives to work and thrift.* Reduction of benefits on account of the recipient family's own earnings and savings amounts to a heavy tax on work and thrift.

6. *Excessive surveillance.* Complex administrative determinations concerning the eligibility, need, and resources of every applicant and recipient must be continuously made. The overburdened caseworker is a combination detective, social worker, advocate, and judge. This surveillance is costly; administration takes about 10 percent of the costs of public assis-

---

16. In August 1968, however, the maximum in New York was $344 per month.

tance. At the same time, the system often increases and perpetuates the recipients' incapacity to manage their own affairs.

7. *Inequities.* The present system gives rise to serious inequities. Unlike income taxation, which is designed to narrow but not to reverse initial differences in income, the present system changes economic ranks in an arbitrary and haphazard manner. Eligible households are made better off than ineligible households with the same or higher initial income. Households in generous states are better off than similar households in low-benefit states. Some taxpaying families are worse off than some households receiving aid.

This list of problems suggests the agenda of issues in reform of public assistance: How should benefits be related to household size and composition, and to the earnings and other resources of the recipient? How should assistance be financed? How should it be administered? Should there be a nationally uniform system?

I shall discuss these issues on the assumption that the objectives of the public assistance system are to reduce, indeed overcome, poverty; to reinforce measures to remedy the deficiencies of earning capacity that create the need for assistance; to treat recipients, nonrecipients, and taxpayers equitably—specifically to narrow income differences but not to reverse or to create them; to avoid financial penalties for work, thrift, and family stability.

In recent years a number of steps have been taken to remedy defects in the present welfare system.

Since 1962 federal legislation has permitted states to extend AFDC to families in need because of the unemployment of a parent. By 1968, twenty-one states had adopted this program, and 75,000 families were being assisted. Congress has not yet been willing to make the program compulsory for the states. The 1967 amendments to the Social Security Act imposed strict tests of "recent and substantial attachment to the labor force."

Three recent judicial decisions also work in the direction of extending eligibility. One, if sustained on appeal, will overturn residence requirements. One limits administrative discretion by establishing the principle that a citizen has a legal right to welfare benefits for which he meets the criteria. A third strikes down the practice of some states of denying AFDC when there is a "substitute father" in the house.

Thanks both to private initiatives and to public announcements, particularly in connection with Medicaid, more eligible applicants are becoming aware of their welfare rights.

Recent legislation has recognized the disincentive to work and self-reliance involved in 100 percent taxation—in reducing benefits one dollar for every dollar of earnings. States have had the option to disregard earnings of AFDC children, up to $50 a month per child or $150 per month per family. Now the states will be compelled to disregard all earnings of school children and the first $30 per month of other family earnings plus a third of the remainder. A two-thirds marginal tax rate is still very high—the President had proposed 50 percent—but it is an improvement over 100 percent. The 1967 amendments also required certain aid recipients to report to Department of Labor offices for employment or training.

Some states and localities are experimenting with streamlined methods of administration: greater reliance on declarations of applicants and less on investigation; greater use of flat cash payments and less of special appropriations for particular needs.

These are forward steps, but they leave untouched two major defects: the exclusion of the working poor, the inadequacy and diversity of benefits. The 1966 Report of the Advisory Council on Public Welfare recommended "a nationwide comprehensive program based upon a single criterion: need";[17] but neither the administration nor the Congress has yet seriously considered scrapping the existing categorical restrictions.

President Johnson proposed in 1967 to require states to pay benefits that meet the full need of eligible individuals by their own standards, under all federally aided assistance programs. The administration proposal also contained provisions to prevent erosion of the states' definitions of need. Unfortunately Congress ignored this recommendation, probably because many states would find it difficult to meet their share of the additional costs.

It is doubtful that the inadequacy of benefits in many states can be remedied without revamping the fiscal basis of public assistance. The Advisory Council on Public Welfare recommended in 1966 that all states be required to meet, or exceed, a minimum national standard for public assistance payments. A state's contribution to the cost of the required stan-

---

17. "*Having the Power, We Have the Duty,*" Report of the Advisory Council on Public Welfare to the Secretary of Health, Education, and Welfare, June 1966.

dard would depend on its fiscal capacity, as measured by state personal income and other economic indicators. The federal government would pay the rest of the bill.

Although nationwide standards of benefits, eligibility, and administration could in principle be imposed on the states, there are good reasons to move instead to a system wholly financed and administered by the federal government. The problem is national, and the population is mobile. It is no accident that the most successful social security program, OASDHI, is a federal program. Interstate differences in policy and administration have plagued the federal-state programs of unemployment insurance and public assistance. In the case of public assistance, state and local administrations differ widely in efficiency, sympathy, and impartiality. These differences can hardly be erased by federal edict alone. In particular, federal administration could make rural southern Negroes financially independent of the local white power structures.[18]

Another reason for nationalizing public assistance is to facilitate its integration with income taxation. As benefits and eligibility rules are liberalized, the need to mesh the two systems will become acute. Definitions of income and of household units need to be consistent. Otherwise there will be many anomalies and inequities, especially as individuals' circumstances change and they shift in and out of taxpaying status and in and out of eligibility for assistance. Later sections, therefore, consider how public assistance and income taxation could be integrated.

"Costs" of Redistributions to the Poor

From the point of view of the nation as a whole, a pure internal income transfer is, as a first approximation, costless. That is, no productive resources are used; no labor or capital or land needs to be diverted from other purposes, public or private. In this sense, transfers are fundamentally different from other government expenditures, which divert productive resources into, say, fighting wars or building schools. Transfer programs may, of course, have secondary consequences for the size and composition of national output. Administrative costs are real enough, though fractional;

---

18. See the eloquent testimony of John F. Kain before the U.S. Commission on Civil Rights, Montgomery, Alabama, May 2, 1968.

taxes and benefits may affect the behavior of the individuals involved, by altering their incentives to work, for example; and the beneficiaries of transfers may use the funds differently from the taxpayers. But exhaustive government expenditures have these consequences too, in addition to their primary claim on productive resources.

The costs that concern taxpayers are not the social costs but the additional taxes they will have to pay—or tax cuts they will have to forgo—in order to increase the incomes of the poor. There are many different ways in which this burden might be distributed among the non-poor. In the discussion that follows it is assumed that the additional taxes are federal taxes on personal income. A measure of the cost of a public assistance program is then the additional income tax which must be collected from the non-poor, taken as a group. This may be measured either in dollars of total additional revenue as of any given year, or in the equivalent increase in the effective average rate of tax on the personal income of the non-poor.

But under many proposals, benefits would not be confined to the poor. Indeed, it would not be fair or sensible to aid households with initial incomes of $2,999 at the expense of households with initial incomes of $3,001. Therefore, the burden on the non-poor as a group is a net figure, concealing some redistribution within the group from higher to lower income taxpayers. "Horizontal" redistributions may be involved as well, for example, between taxpayers with different numbers of dependents or different kinds of income. Some proposals draw a simple sharp line between beneficiaries and payers of additional tax, and in those cases it is possible to calculate the transfer between these two groups as well as the net transfer between poor and non-poor. The redistribution from non-poor to poor may be called the *primary redistribution* of a program of public assistance, and the transfers within the non-poor group the *secondary redistribution*.

The poor received $16 billion in 1966 and needed $27 billion. The poverty "gap"—the aggregate deficit of the incomes of the poor below their poverty thresholds—was $11 billion in 1966, less than 2 percent of total personal income, 69 percent of the actual personal income of the poor. This was the gap remaining after the incomes of the poor had benefited from existing governmental transfers, including $4½ billion of cash public assistance. It is an illusion, of course, to think that poverty could be eliminated by $11 billion additional expenditures. For if the government guaranteed everyone a poverty-line income, in the sense of making up any shortfalls, the poor would have no reason—and many non-poor very little reason—to earn as much as they do now. The poor would not lose by working less, or gain by working more. This would be the 100 percent tax rate implicit in old-fashioned public assistance.

Suppose the government pays every household its poverty-line income and takes back not 100 percent but some fraction of the poor household's initial income. How much transfer to the poor would then have to be made? How much would this exceed current public assistance? Initial incomes of the poor, before public assistance, aggregated $11.7 billion in 1966. Assuming that this figure is unaffected by the tax rate, the calculation is the simple one given in Table 2. Making up the $11 billion gap requires $15 billion with a rate of two-thirds, $22.8 billion with no tax. The table makes clear a general point: the redistributive cost of guaranteeing any level of income is greater the lower the tax rate—at least before allowance is made for the unknown incentive effects of the rates themselves.

TABLE 2. *Transfer to Poor Required in 1966 To Eliminate $11 Billion Poverty Gap, at Selected Tax Rates*
(In billions of dollars)

Item in calculation	Tax rate			
	2/3	1/2	1/3	0
1. Total poverty-line income	27.1	27.1	27.1	27.1
2. Offsetting tax on initial income of poor (tax rate × $11.7 billion)	7.8	5.9	3.9	0
3. Required benefit payments (1−2)	19.3	21.2	23.2	27.1
4. Current public assistance	4.3	4.3	4.3	4.3
5. Additional transfer required to eliminate gap (3−4)	15.0	16.9	18.9	22.8

The Credit Income Tax

The credit income tax, proposed by Earl Rolph and others, is a scheme for integrating public assistance with a vastly simplified and reformed system of income taxation. Radical as it is, the proposal deserves a serious hearing. It serves, moreover, as a convenient point of reference for considering less far-reaching reforms.

Suppose that every man, woman, and child in the country was entitled to receive $750 a year from the federal government, and obligated to pay the government one-third of his income (not including the $750). The $750 is a credit against the tax. It is also a guaranteed income, the final income an individual would receive if he had none of his own. Anyone else would end up with more final income, even though he would receive a smaller net amount from the government, or actually pay tax to the government. The system is summarized in Table 3.

Individuals with incomes of $2,250 would receive no net benefit and pay no net tax; $2,250 (more generally, the credit divided by the tax rate) can be termed the *break-even income*. If an individual has an initial income above $2,250, the government takes one-third of the excess. Symmetrically, if an individual's initial income is below $2,250, the government makes up one-third of the shortfall. The net benefits can be regarded as "negative income taxes."

TABLE 3. *Effect of the Credit Income Tax at Selected Initial Income Levels*

Initial income before payment to or from government	Gross offsetting tax (1/3 of 1)	Net benefit (+) or tax paid (−) ($750 − 2)	Final income after payment to or from government (1 + 3)
$ 0	$ 0	$+ 750	$ 750
300	100	+ 650	950
600	200	+ 550	1,150
900	300	+ 450	1,350
2,100	700	+ 50	2,150
2,250[a]	750	0	2,250
3,000	1,000	− 250	2,750
9,000	3,000	−2,250	6,750
12,000	4,000	−3,250	8,750

a. Break-even income.

Under the proposal, a family could pool its guarantee credits provided it also pooled its members' incomes. In the example of Table 4, the addition of another dependent would be worth $750 in reduced net taxes or added net benefits. Credits play a role in this scheme similar to that of personal exemptions in the present federal income tax. But there is one important difference. The guarantee or credit is of the same value, $750 in the example, whatever the income of the taxpayer. A personal exemption for a dependent is worth more to a high-bracket than a low-bracket taxpayer. The prevailing $600 exemption is worth $420 to a taxpayer rich enough to be taxed at a marginal rate of 70 percent; $84 to a lowest-bracket taxpayer; and nothing to a family too poor to pay income tax. To help large rich families but not large poor families is anomalous social policy.

TABLE 4. *Effect of Credit Income Tax on Initial Income of $6,000, by Selected Size of Family*

Size of family	Net benefit (+) or tax (−)	Final income
1	$−1,250	$4,750
2	− 500	5,500
3	+ 250	6,250
4	+1,000	7,000

Part of the logic of a negative income tax is that poor families should in equity be able to cash in their unused exemptions.

A simple proposal like the one illustrated in Table 4 is neutral with respect to the grouping of individuals. A person is worth the same—$750 in the example—whether he is a dependent member of a large taxpaying unit or a separate one-person unit. His income is subject to the same tax—one-third in the example—in either case. No set of individuals can gain at the expense of the government either by splitting into several units or by combining into one.

The average per capita net benefit or tax depends in a simple manner on average per capita income:

net revenue per capita = (tax rate × initial income per capita) − tax credit,

or:

$$\frac{\text{net revenue per capita}}{\text{initial income per capita}} = \text{tax rate} - \frac{\text{tax credit}}{\text{initial income per capita}}.$$

At the 1966 level of $3,000 personal income per capita, the average gross tax under the illustrative proposal would be $1,000, the average net tax $250. Thus the tax would yield the government 8⅓ percent of personal income (33⅓ percent − 25 percent) after all benefits or negative taxes were paid. (The federal income tax now yields about 10 percent of personal income, but little more than 9 percent after current public assistance transfers are paid.) Raising the guarantee from 25 to 30 percent of average income, that is, to the poverty line of $900 per capita, would require an increase of five points in the tax rate.

Real income per capita increases 2½ percent per year. Assuming the guarantee is held constant in purchasing power, net revenue from a credit income tax will rise as a share of personal income 2½ percent per year. Alternatively, this is the amount by which the flat tax rate can be reduced if no increase in revenue, relative to personal income, is needed.

A hypothetical redistribution to the poor is calculated in Table 5.

The proposal also involves, of course, a large secondary redistribution

TABLE 5. *Hypothetical Redistribution from Non-Poor to Poor in 1966, Comparing Existing Public Assistance with Credit of $750 per Capita and Tax Rate of One-Third*

Characteristic	Poor	Non-poor	Total
1. Number of persons (millions)	29.7	163.7	193.4
2. Percent of total population	15.3	84.7	100.0
3. Average income per capita			
a. Before taxes and public assistance	$ 395	3,471	$3,000
b. After taxes and public assistance[a]	$ 539	3,150	$2,750
4. Credit income tax			
a. Gross (1/3 3a)	$ 132	$1,157	$1,000
b. Net ($750 − 4a)	+$ 618	−$ 407	−$ 250
c. Final income (3a + 4b)	$1,013	$3,064	$2,750
5. Additional redistribution			
a. Per capita (4c − 3b)	+$ 474	−$ 86	0
b. Aggregate (billions)	+$ 14.1	−$ 14.1	0

a. These entries assume actual public assistance totalling $4.3 billion and an income tax that raises from the non-poor this amount and additional revenue of 8⅓ percent of personal income.

among the non-poor. A family of four would pay no tax unless its income exceeded $9,000. Benefits to non-poor families below the break-even incomes might total $29 billion. The burden would fall mainly on higher-income taxpayers, and among them mainly on taxpayers with income not now taxable. At present taxable income is only 46 percent of personal income. With this degree of slippage it would take a nominal tax rate of 70 percent to produce an effective tax rate of one-third. That is why the advocates of the credit income tax propose wholesale elimination of exclusions, deductions, and exemptions.

The uniform tax rate has great technical advantages; it eliminates all incentive to shift income, either in fact or in appearance, from one year to another or from one taxpaying unit to another. The structure is still progressive because of the tax credit or guarantee, which diminishes relative to income as income rises. As for progression in the rate structure itself, it is argued, the high rates applicable to high incomes are more apparent than real; the law is riddled with ways to escape these rates, particularly when the high incomes are derived from property. But marginal rates could be increased at high incomes.

Children's Allowances and Adults' Allowances

The credit income tax proposal can be modified in a number of different ways. The most important are the schedule of credits for households of varying size and composition and the structure of tax rates in relation to income.

A uniform per capita guarantee makes no allowance for economies of scale in family living or for differences in consumption requirements between adults and children. It favors large families, especially those with young children, as against single adults and small families. A high cash value for an additional child may be an undesirable incentive. For these reasons, it might be better to provide higher credits for adults, single or married, than for children, and also to reduce and eventually eliminate credit for an additional child as the size of family rises. An example is given in column 2 of Table 6. A schedule of this kind, however, introduces legal

TABLE 6. *Illustrative Schedules Relating Credits to Family Size*

	Household's credit or guaranteed income					
Size of family	(1) Constant per capita	(2) Guarantees near poverty lines	(3) Half of personal exemptions and minimum standard deductions	(4) Children's allowances Modest	(5) Children's allowances Anti-poverty
1	$ 750	$1,000	$ 450	$ 0	$ 0
2	1,500	2,000	800	0	0
3	2,250	2,600	1,150	200	1,800
4	3,000	3,200	1,500	400	2,400
5	3,750	3,600	1,850	600	3,000
6	4,500	4,000	2,200	800	3,600
7	5,250	4,200	2,550	1,000	4,200
8	6,000	4,400	2,900	1,200	4,800
9	6,750	4,400	3,250	1,400	5,400

Note: The table assumes that the first two members of a household are adults. If there is only one adult, entries in column 2 for households of two or more persons would be $400 less, and entries in columns 4 and 5 would be moved up one line.

and economic problems that the flat per capita allowance avoids. A youth's claim on the government may depend on whether he is an "adult" or a "child," and the value of a child may depend on what household claims him as a member. Nevertheless, it seems perfectly feasible to set up and enforce some reasonable legal definitions.[19]

An entirely different approach is to allow credits only for families with children. The United States is the only advanced country that does not

---

19. See James Tobin, Joseph Pechman, and Peter Mieszkowski, "Is a Negative Income Tax Practical?" *Yale Law Journal*, Vol. 77 (November 1967), pp. 1–27.

pay children's allowances. In other countries allowances are paid for all children, without regard to parents' income, although in some cases the allowances are taxable. But they are in almost all cases too small to be the major form of assistance to families in serious poverty. The purposes of the allowances are, rather, to improve "horizontal" equity between small and large families of the same incomes, whether poor or rich, and in some countries to raise the birth rate.

A children's allowance plan in this spirit is illustrated in column 4 of Table 6. Paid to the parents of all children under 19, of whom there were 75 million in 1966, these allowances would cost $15 billion gross, or about $12 billion net if they were subject to regular income tax. Of the net benefits, nearly 80 percent would go to families above the poverty line. If the program were financed by a uniform increase in income tax rates, the end result would be a modest but dubious redistribution from childless taxpayers to large families, and very little redistribution from rich to poor.

If children's allowances are intended to be of significant help to destitute families, they must be much more generous, as in column 5 of Table 6. Moreover, since no help is to be given to childless couples, the value of the first child would have to be very high indeed. To offer so large a financial incentive for women to start having children is risky social policy. With allowances on the scale of column 5, it is necessary to abandon the appealing idea of a universal payment subject to no test of need except the regular income tax. The net cost, of the order of $65 billion as of 1966, would exceed the yield of the federal income tax. Yet nothing would have been done for 18 million poor childless adults.[20]

Negative Income Tax Proposals

The credit income tax involves a large politically difficult secondary redistribution, which can be diminished in magnitude by abandoning the flat tax rate and by partially offsetting the credits or guarantees with a special high tax on low initial incomes. This is the technique of most negative income tax (NIT) proposals.

20. Recognizing these problems, Harvey Brazer has proposed a special tax that recoups part or all of the allowances, the fraction depending on the other income of the family. See his contribution to Eveline M. Burns (ed.), *Children's Allowances and the Economic Welfare of Children* (Citizens' Committee for Children of New York, Inc., 1968).

Consider, for example, the proposal made by Milton Friedman and others to pay each nontaxpayer half the difference between (1) the sum of his personal exemptions and standard deductions and (2) his initial income. The amounts that a household with no other income would receive are shown in Table 6, column 3. Benefits would decline by 50 percent of other income—that is, the income would be taxed at 50 percent. The break-even levels would be twice the entries in column 3. At those incomes households would begin to pay regular income tax, just as they do now. The tax rate would fall from 50 percent to the first-bracket rate under the tax code (14 percent in the absence of the temporary surcharge enacted in 1968).

If the Friedman plan were superimposed on existing public assistance, about half the poverty gap, $5.5 billion as of 1966, would be made up—a bit less because the break-even levels fall short of the poverty lines. To finance the plan, regular income tax rates would have to be raised two points. If the plan replaced current public assistance, as Friedman suggests, its net cost would be only $2½ billion or $3 billion as of 1966, but it would reduce the aggregate poverty gap only by the same amount.[21]

Column 2 of Table 6 shows a more generous schedule of guarantees. This too could be combined with a 50 percent offsetting tax on other income. Break-even incomes would range from $2,000 for a single adult to $8,800 for a family of eight. But the 50 percent tax rate would continue to apply at higher incomes until it produced the same tax liability as the regular income tax code. Above the "tax break-even" income the regular rates would apply. For illustration, the calculation of tax, negative or positive, for a couple with two children is given in Table 7. The tax break-even income is $7,920. For incomes above that point the normal tax calculation supersedes the special NIT calculation. The marginal tax rate falls abruptly from 50 percent to 17.1 percent, and then rises again with income.

The primary redistribution involved in this proposal is roughly the $17 billion required to close the poverty gap with a 50 percent tax, as calculated in Table 2. The secondary redistribution is difficult to estimate, but it is of the order of $5 billion. About half of four-person families, for example, had incomes below $7,920 in 1966 and would have benefited from the plan. Beneficiaries other than current recipients of public assistance would have been subject to higher marginal tax rates, 50 percent compared with 0 to

---

21. It is assumed that double exemptions for age and blindness would not be allowed for NIT purposes.

TABLE 7. Comparison of Effects of Existing Income Tax and Proposed Negative Income Tax, for Married Couple with Two Children at Selected Income Levels

Initial income	Net benefit (+) or tax (−)		Final income		Marginal tax rate	
	NIT[a]	1966 tax law	NIT	1966 tax law[b]	NIT	1966 tax law
$ 0	$+3,200	$ 0	$3,200	$ 0	50 %	0 %
1,000	+2,700	0	3,700	1,000	50	0
2,000	+2,200	0	4,200	2,000	50	0
3,000	+1,700	0	4,700	3,000	50	0
4,000	+1,200	− 140	5,200	3,860	50	14
5,000	+ 700	− 290	5,700	4,710	50	15
6,000	+ 200	− 450	6,200	5,550	50	16
6,400[c]	0	− 511	6,400	5,889	50	15.3
7,000	− 300	− 603	6,700	6,397	50	15.3
7,920[d]	− 760	− 760	7,160	7,160	50	17.1
8,000	− 772	− 772	7,228	7,228	17.1	17.1
10,000	−1,114	−1,114	8,886	8,886	17.1	17.1

a. $3,200 less 50 percent of initial income, or the tax under the 1966 tax law, whichever is algebraically larger.
b. Figures shown assume standard deduction of $600 or 10 percent of initial income, whichever is larger. The 10 percent deduction when applicable makes the effective marginal tax rate 10 percent lower than the nominal rate for the bracket; that is why the marginal rate is 15.3 percent in the 17 percent bracket and 17.1 percent in the 19 percent bracket.
c. NIT break-even income.
d. Tax break-even income.

17 percent now. This change could have serious disincentive effects, just as the reduction in marginal rate of tax from 100 or 66⅔ percent would improve incentives for public assistance clients.

A proposal of this type is, in effect, a credit income tax grafted onto the present income tax structure. The dip in the marginal tax rate creates some problems. Whenever marginal tax rates vary there is an inducement to shift income, both in appearance and in reality, to tax returns with lower marginal rates. This may mean the return for this year, last year, or some other person. In the present instance, there would be some incentive for concentrating income in time, in order to have it taxed at low marginal rates rather than at 50 percent. A more serious difficulty is the incentive for family-splitting: A father or potential stepfather with a good income may do better for himself and for a mother and her children by filing separately and paying regular income tax; if he joins the group, his income will be taxed at the 50 percent rate, depriving the mother and children of benefits they could otherwise claim. Although cases of this kind would be by no means as frequent or as serious as under AFDC, they point up the advantages of a uniform tax rate.

The two NIT examples both assumed a 50 percent tax rate. There is nothing sacred about 50 percent, or even about a constant rate. Lowering the tax rate in the more generous plan, while keeping the same schedule of credits, would increase the costs of both the primary and secondary redistributions. The Friedman proposal could be modified to change the tax rate to 25 percent while holding the break-even incomes constant. Then the guarantee levels shown in column 3 of Table 6 would be cut in half. So would the aggregate transfer: The government would be making up only a quarter of the deficit of each poor family. As an interim measure, Robert Lampman has suggested guarantee levels at a quarter of the poverty line, zero tax on incomes up to half the poverty line, and 50 percent tax thereafter. His purpose is to concentrate aid on the working poor.

Taxable income as defined for the federal income tax is so poor a definition of need that to use it as the base for negative income tax payments would be a travesty of common sense and social justice. Society does not want to pay benefits to people with low taxable income but with ample resources—wealth, tax-exempt interest, capital gains, pensions, social security stipends, college fellowships, large itemized deductions, gift receipts, and so on. Consequently, negative income taxation requires a much more inclusive definition of income as the base for the offsetting tax.[22]

Such a definition is feasible but admittedly involves a philosophical inconsistency. If taxable income as now defined is so obviously deficient as a test of need, why is it a good test of ability to pay? The illogic here is what leads Rolph and other advocates of the credit income tax to insist on a thorough reform, resulting in a single inclusive definition of income.

Americans, as noted above, are mortally afraid that some potential workers will choose idleness even at the expense of income. The total disqualification of households containing potential workers, as attempted in the present system of public assistance in most states, has proved disastrous. But does sufficient incentive to work remain after a tax of one-third or one-half is levied on earnings? Does the carrot need to be supplemented by a stick?

One possibility would be not to count potential workers in reckoning the guarantees to which the household unit is entitled, to presume that they have incomes at least sufficient to wipe out their credits. Thus if the credit

---

22. Detailed suggestions for this definition are made in Tobin and others, "Is a Negative Income Tax Practical?"

for a potential worker were $1,000 and the offsetting tax rate were 50 percent, he would be presumed to be earning income at a rate of $2,000 a year even if his actual income were lower. This presumption would deprive his family of the $1,000 but not, as under AFDC, of the amounts to which it is entitled on account of its other members.

The presumption should be removed, and the potential worker's entitlement restored, in any month for which a federal manpower officer in his locality certified that, whether due to temporary personal disabilities or lack of suitable job or training opportunities, he could not earn income at the presumed rate. In this manner, a federal program of creating, financing, and coordinating job and training opportunities could be meshed with a program of income supplementation.

Concluding Remarks

Poverty in the United States, as officially measured, has declined dramatically in this decade, thanks to the sustained expansion of the economy and the restoration of full employment. But the poverty that remains has become a greater threat to the social order. This is the decade of the Negro's claim to full equality in all aspects of American life. Although the economic conditions of Negroes have markedly improved during the boom of the 1960s, they suffer much more than their share of poverty, unemployment, and urban squalor. The transformation of the American economy and population from rural to urban is still going on. Ultimately it will be the engine of great improvement in the lives of Negro immigrants to cities and their children, as it has been for previous immigrants. But the transition is long, difficult, and dangerous.

The acute problem is the inability of many employable males to earn enough to support their children. The result is usually a family in poverty unrelieved by public assistance. With increasing frequency, however, the mother and children are left on their own, and "go on welfare." The basic solution in the long run is to build up earning capacities by education and work experience. Meanwhile, people are poor, and their children are raised under handicaps that may destine them to be poor too.

The present system of public assistance has failed. Inadequate in coverage and in benefits, perverse in its incentives, it fosters the very conditions it is supposed to relieve.

We urgently need a reformed and nationalized system of income assistance that does not exclude employable men and their families. In my opinion, this should be meshed with the federal income tax. The credit income tax seems the fairest and simplest solution. But it will take a long time to develop political consensus for so drastic a reform, and meanwhile something must be done. The merit of the negative income tax approach is that a workable and equitable system of aiding the poor can be introduced within the framework of present federal income taxation.

Which NIT proposal should it be? On some of the questions involved in a choice—for example, how high a tax rate can be used without costly damage to incentives—we will gain light from the experiments in negative taxation now being conducted in New Jersey by MATHEMATICA and the Institute for Research on Poverty of the University of Wisconsin. Meanwhile, I would venture the opinion that the tax rate should not exceed 50 percent. I also find it hard to justify guarantee levels significantly below poverty lines except as a temporary and transitional feature of a new system.

Together these specifications imply a system like the one illustrated in Table 6, column 2, and in Table 7. This is a costly proposal, and if the budgetary resources could not be found at once, it could be gradually introduced as follows: Keep the suggested break-even incomes, which for most family sizes are roughly twice the poverty thresholds. Start by making up, say, only one-quarter of the amount by which a household's income falls short of this break-even level,[23] and step up the rate gradually until it reaches 50 percent. During the transition the existing public assistance system would be gradually phased out. But states and localities that wished to augment the benefits available to the poor under the federal NIT system would be able to do so, perhaps even with some federal financial help.

The main obstacles to reform are ideological and fiscal. The widespread, if largely groundless, fear of freeloading can be met by making part, not all, of the assistance to families conditional on the willingness of employable members to present themselves for work or training, and by providing assistance in a way that rewards self-reliance. The budgetary cost is formidable, especially if we impose on ourselves the rule that taxes can never be

---

23. The guarantees would be half those in column 2 of Table 6; the tax rate would be 25 percent up to break-even incomes and then 50 percent up to tax break-even incomes. The total cost would be $14 billion, with no allowance for reduction of public assistance.

increased. But the war on poverty is too crucial to be relegated to the status of a residual claimant for funds that peace in Asia and the normal growth of tax revenues may painlessly and gradually make available. When asked to make sacrifices for the defense of their nation, the American people have always responded. Perhaps some day a national administration will muster the courage to ask the American people to tax themselves for social justice and domestic tranquillity. The time is short.

KENNETH B. CLARK

THE NEGRO AND THE URBAN CRISIS

The center of gravity of the civil rights movement has shifted almost imperceptibly from the South to northern cities. In the fifteen years following the Second World War, the more dramatic and flagrant forms of racial exclusion characteristic of the South had been modified by a series of federal court decisions, by civil rights legislation, and by executive orders. By the 1960s, it appeared that the task of achieving racial justice in America, and particularly the task of enlisting government in the struggle to relieve American Negroes of the burdens of racial segregation and discrimination, was about to be resolved. The 1963 march on Washington was widely interpreted as the opening of the final stage in major civil rights victories.

But, instead of orderly changes in the pattern of race relations, a series of northern ghetto rebellions erupted almost abruptly after the 1963 peak. In 1964, Harlem rioted. In 1965, Watts exploded. Every major northern city whose population included a substantial portion of Negroes has experienced ghetto turmoil in varying degrees each spring and summer since that time.

The nation faced an apparent paradox. Major disturbances in northern urban ghettos and significant progress in the civil rights movement seemed to coexist. It has become clear, however, that the progress which was real to some was an illusion to others. The court decisions, legislation, and other governmental actions which were allegedly dealing with longstanding racial problems did, in fact, address themselves to the conditions and the predicament of the southern Negro, particularly the middle-class Negro, but not the northern Negro ghetto residents. The evidence of discrimination in the South had been real—de jure segregated schools, segregation and exclusion in public accommodations, segregation in public recreation and transportation, and the symbols of social discrimination—the anachronistic "white" and "colored" signs in bus and railroad stations.

The end of such patterns of southern segregation, long enforced by law and custom, was not relevant to the depressed predicament of the masses of Negroes who had migrated to northern urban ghettos. The northern white was psychologically identified with the southern Negro's struggle against the more severe forms of southern racial segregation. His sense of identification had stimulated him to join the southern Negro in seeking to remedy these racial indignities. Once this was achieved, however, it became clearer to the northern Negro that his freedom from racial exclusion and cruelty imposed by laws and governmental action had obscured his predicament in the northern ghettos. His life was, in fact, as intolerable as that of the southern Negro.

Indeed, the civil rights victories won for the southern Negro, limited though they were, were mocked by the fact that the northern Negro was required to send his children to de facto segregated and inferior schools and to live in racially segregated and often substandard housing. He was still confronted with the fact of pervasive underemployment, and with inadequate health and welfare services. His children had a higher rate of infant mortality. They were more likely to be adjudged delinquent and to be subjected to the hazards of narcotic addiction. The statistics are clear that the poor Negro in the South and the Negro confined to northern ghettos is, compared with white citizens, subjected to substantially higher risk in his day-to-day life. He is more likely to be afflicted by the patterns of social and personal pathology. From the perspective of the northern Negro, particularly the Negro poor in the urban slums who is relatively more deprived than northern whites, the civil rights victories and racial progress of the 1950s and the 1960s must be seen as another source of personal and racial frustrations.

In addition, ghetto problems have been intensified because the distribution of Negro population in the United States has shifted significantly since the Second World War. Between 1940 and 1966, 3.7 million nonwhites left the South.[1] Most went to metropolitan areas. By 1966, 69 percent of all Negroes were not only living in metropolitan areas rather than in rural areas, but 37 percent (compared to 22 percent in 1940, 34 percent in 1960) were living in the North, most of them in cities. Almost all of the Negro population increase since 1950 has been in central cities—5.6 million

---

1. The statistics in the next few pages are from U.S. Department of Labor and U.S. Department of Commerce, *Social and Economic Conditions of Negroes in the United States* (October 1967).

of a total 6.5 million. Most of the increase in the white population has been in the suburbs.

Negroes in 1966 were 26 percent of the population in cities in areas of one million or more, compared to 13 percent in 1950. Only 4 percent of the suburban population is Negro. Negroes are increasing as a percentage of the total population in almost all of the largest cities. In New York, for example, Negroes were 10 percent of the population in 1950, 18 percent estimated in 1965; in Washington, D.C., 35 percent in 1950, 66 percent estimated in 1965; in Los Angeles, 9 percent in 1950, 17 percent in 1965; in Chicago, 14 percent in 1950, 28 percent in 1965.

Based on 1965 estimates, the fifteen cities with the largest percentages of Negroes were in this order: (1) Washington, D.C. 66; (2) Newark 47; (3) Atlanta 44; (4) New Orleans 41; (5) Memphis 40; (6) Baltimore 38; (7) St. Louis 36; (8) Detroit 34; (9) Cleveland 34; (10) Philadelphia 31; (11) Chicago 28; (12) Cincinnati 24; (13) Indianapolis 23; (14) Houston 23; (15) Kansas City 22.

The Report of the National Advisory Commission on Civil Disorders (Kerner Commission) showed that whereas the Negro population in 1966 in all central cities totaled more than 12 million, the Negro population in these cities will rise by 1985 to more than 20 million. Sixty-six percent of all Negroes will be central city residents.

It is clear, on the basis of these figures, that patterns of litigation, legislation, and other forms of governmental action that seemed appropriate to amelioration of the racially determined condition of the southern Negro are inappropriate to the predicament of the northern Negro who is afflicted by a pattern of racially determined forms of exclusion, discrimination, and oppression. In fact, these patterns have exacerbated the frustrations and, paradoxically, have increased the chances of a series of intense social disturbances in all cities in which a substantial proportion of Negro residents is confined to segregated residential areas.

The problem of the northern Negro, therefore, must be understood not in terms of laws which reinforce segregated education and housing, or discriminatory employment practices, but in terms of a pervasive pattern of racism. The fact of the ghetto—the involuntary restriction of the masses of Negroes to a particular geographic area of the city—underlies every other aspect of the problem. The ghetto results in de facto school segregation, which affects middle- and low-income Negroes alike, and the inferiority in education that is invariably related to it. Inferior education, in turn, reinforces the overriding economic fact of disproportionate Negro unemployment and underemployment.

In seeking to deal with this pathology, it has become very clear that as the techniques of litigation and legislation employed by civil rights groups proved ineffective in the North and for the southern poor, so the techniques of protest employed for civil rights by the southern Negro are weak in dealing with problems of the northern slum resident and the southern Negro poor. The direct-action civil disobedience approach, which worked in removing long-standing patterns of discrimination in public transportation and public accommodations in the South, did not work in dealing with the problems of poor housing, inadequate sanitation, and health services in the North.

This became clear when the late Martin Luther King, Jr., tried to transfer the strategy of Birmingham and Selma to Chicago. Chicago merely absorbed the thrust of the Southern Christian Leadership Conference (SCLC). Mayor Richard Daley initially welcomed King and the SCLC. He paraded with them in Chicago proper and provided police escort for King's demonstrations in all-white sections of the Chicago metropolitan area, but the mass protest approach of Negroes in Chicago as in other northern cities has not brought about any fundamental structural or functional change in education, housing, and employment.

The problems of the northern Negro, particularly the poor, are an integral part of the social, economic, and political patterns of the cities and did not need to be superimposed on the society or reinforced by law. Southern patterns of racial regulation, segregation, or discrimination were visible, public, and, in a curious way, superficial manifestations of a racism that had emerged out of the heritage of slavery. The disappearance of a number of the surface signs of racism in the South gave the appearance of social change that reflected to some extent fundamental change in patterns of employment and education. The northern patterns of racism, however, are an integral part of a continuing system that emerged in this century.

The Negro migration from the South to the North began in significant numbers during the First World War, when European immigration waned and war orders hit northern factories, and accelerated with the Second World War. In this process, the northern cities became "naturally" ghettoized. This "natural" trend was supported by the tendency of large numbers of Negroes to live among themselves to gain mutual support, as ethnic groups coming to America have historically done.

Other ethnic groups had been able to move out of the ghetto as their economic status rose. They were free to exercise choice, whether to stay within the ghetto or to disperse. The Negro had no such choice. His economic mobility was restricted through educational and job discrimination, and his residential mobility was restricted by the conspiratorial actions and policies of real-estate and banking interests, by government discrimination at federal, state, and local levels via loans, public housing, urban renewal— seen as "Negro removal"—local zoning ordinances, and the like.

Urban Negroes were required to experiment with a variety of methods in seeking relief. The National Urban League, founded more than fifty years ago, reflected an attempt to approach the problem through an amalgam of social service, negotiation, alliance, and appeals to governmental and industrial leaders seeking their cooperation in the alleviation of the predicament of the Negro. The techniques and methods of the Urban League institutionalized the earlier less coherent programs for Negroes in the city; their common denominator was an appeal to the conscience of white America. Essentially, this approach assumed goodwill. It sought to extend social service approaches of benevolence into the arena of race relations in the basic structure of American cities.

Parallel to this methodology was the more direct militancy of the National Association for the Advancement of Colored People (NAACP), which applied the strategy of litigation, legislation, and governmental action to the more primitive racial problems of the southern Negro. One of the recent developments on the civil rights front is the shift of the Urban League from the persuasive, benevolent-alliance approach to the more militant, direct-action approach of the NAACP and the SCLC. The NAACP, in turn, seemed less militant as it became more successful.

In fact, though their styles may differ, the Urban League, the NAACP, and the SCLC have become almost indistinguishable in their basic assumptions, their goals, and their belief that relief of the Negro can be obtained within the framework of American democratic institutions.

The effects of these methods, in ameliorating the conditions of the masses of Negroes, seem equally negative. Problems related to ghetto confinement and restriction have increased. The educational problems of segregated and inferior education become intensified as the Negro ghetto population grows. More Negroes are in school, but the gap in achievement between Negroes and whites widens the longer Negroes are in school. In 1965, Negro sixth graders were 2.4 grade levels below whites; Negro twelfth graders were 3.5 grade levels below whites despite a high (though decreasing) Negro dropout rate.

The following figures show the percentage enrolled in school, by age:

	1960		1966	
	Nonwhite	White	Nonwhite	White
16 and 17 years	77	85	83	89
18 and 19 years	35	40	39	48
20 to 24 years	8	10	14	21

Though the racial gap since 1960 has narrowed slightly for the younger group, it has widened markedly for the two older groups—from 5 to 9 percentage points for the 18–19-year-olds and from 2 to 7 points for the 20–24-year-old group.

The proportion of nonwhite families living in substandard housing has decreased since 1960, especially in large cities, but 3 out of 10 nonwhite households compared to less than 1 in 10 white households still live in such dwellings. In the South nearly half of all nonwhite families live in such housing.

Life expectancy of nonwhites in 1965 was lower than for whites in all age groups in the prime working years—with little change since 1960. In 1965 at age 35, nonwhites could expect to live 34.6 additional years, whites 39.2 years; at 55, Negroes 19.6, whites 21.8 years.

Although maternal and infant mortality rates for whites and Negroes have dropped sharply since 1940, the nonwhite maternal mortality rate in 1965 was four times that of whites; among nonwhite infants less than 1 month old, 25.4 per 1,000 live births would die, whereas 16.1 white infants would die. Further, the racial gap which had declined from 12.5 more deaths for nonwhite infants in 1940 to 8.1 in 1950, had risen to 10.3 in 1964, and in 1965 was still 9.3.

Absolute discrepancies in the economic status of the average Negro and white have broadened. The Negro middle class has gained, but the gap—and alienation—between the Negro middle class and low-income groups have widened, and the income gap between the Negro and white middle class has increased. The urban Negro ghetto is in a state of economic and psychological depression at a time of national affluence. Unemployment in a selected group of city slums studied by the U.S. Department of Labor in 1966 was almost three times the national average. The underemployed, and those who have withdrawn from the job market and are therefore unrecorded, push these figures far higher.

Nonwhite teenagers have the highest unemployment rates in the labor force—in 1967, more than 26 percent (more than double the white teenage rate) were recorded as unemployed. One-third of nonwhite families and one-tenth of white families are still poor and the nonwhite families are larger. White poverty since 1959 has declined more than Negro poverty.

The proportion of Negro families moving up economically is rising and the ratio of nonwhite to white family income is rising—from 54 percent in 1950 and 55 percent in 1960 to 60 percent in 1966. Nevertheless, the absolute dollar gap between white and nonwhite family income is growing: 1947, $2,174 more median income earned by whites than by nonwhites; 1960, $2,803; 1966, $3,036. Further, more Negro families had multiple earners so it took more persons in a Negro family to earn less.

The racial gap is evident also at the middle-class level. The disparity in median income between nonwhite and white men is greatest among college graduates, among whom an average Negro college graduate earns two-thirds of what his white counterpart earns. Negro elementary school graduates earn four-fifths as much as whites of equivalent education.

The conscience appeals, negotiations, persuasions, demonstrations, legislation, litigation, have brought no fundamental gain for the masses of urban Negroes. A relatively small proportion of middle-class Negroes has appeared to benefit from token promotion to higher levels of responsibility. Specific compensatory educational programs in open enrollment situations made it possible for a minority of Negro children to escape their inferior and segregated public schools. A depressingly small number of middle-class Negroes were permitted to purchase homes in previously all-white neighborhoods and suburbs.

These limited gains probably increased rather than decreased the frustration of the masses of Negroes who were still confined within the ghettos of American cities. As it became increasingly clear to the Negro masses that the promise of positive changes and the claims of civil rights victories in no way affected the realities of their own lives, and that even the more dramatic nonviolent demonstrations failed to lead to observable positive changes, the chances of riots increased. The last few years, therefore, have been characterized by the twin phenomena of intensified social disruption by Negroes and increasing resistance and overtly negative racial responses from whites. This polarization—the random and, at times, nonrational explosions among Negroes; and the cold hardening of "backlash" resistance, intensifying and revealing feelings and anxieties long suppressed among whites—characterizes the present pattern of racial instability in American cities.

The Intensification of Racial Hostility

To understand the nature of the contemporary form of the American racial problem and its relationship to the problem of the stability of American cities, it is essential that one seek to understand the dynamics of northern white racism and the Negro's response to this more complex form of racial hostility. When the major concern was with southern racial practices and problems, the majority of northern whites could either be indifferent or unconcerned or could pay lip service to the goals of racial justice in America. Many northern whites were able to deal with the basic problems of morality and conscience posed by racial injustice by contributing to civil rights organizations or by joining demonstrations in Selma or participating in the march on Washington.

When the center of gravity of the civil rights movement shifted to the North, and when Negroes began confronting whites with the more insidious forms of racism characteristic of the urban North, the reality of the basic ambivalence of northern whites toward the Negro erupted in the phenomenon labeled white backlash. The polarization phenomenon must be understood as a consequence of direct northern confrontation. Despite the absence of surface racist symbolism, there was no greater acceptance of the Negro as a human being and a citizen in the North than there appeared to be in the South. Public opinion polls show a gradual acceptance nationwide, particularly among the young, of the principle of integration, but there is also revealed a far less liberal view the more concrete and specific Negro demands become.

When white northerners are asked to vote on the acceptability of open occupancy laws, they tend to vote overwhelmingly against, as was clear in the vote in California in 1964, which defeated a ban against discrimination in housing by more than 2 million votes; 65.4 percent of those voting registered disapproval. Similar percentages were recorded in Akron, Detroit, and Seattle housing referenda.

When northerners are asked to vote on civilian police review boards, and when campaign discussion is permitted to be polarized along racial lines, the distinctions among northern white liberals, moderates, and conservatives break down. Forces in all these groups tend to combine to provide a majority against what they consider the encroachment and violence of the Negro population. In New York City in 1966, 51.4 percent voted against a civilian review board; 30.5 percent voted for. When white northerners vote and react against the demands of Negroes for racially nonsegregated schools, they tend to vote overwhelmingly for the continuation of segregated schools.

Northern school boards and school officials, with some notable exceptions, tend to resist, subtly or flagrantly, all programs and plans for school desegregation or any significant improvement in the quality of education for Negro children in their segregated schools. Northern housing authorities, in selecting public housing sites, continue to respect the wishes of all-white communities which desire to exclude Negroes and reinforce the walls of the ghettos. The patterns of racial discrimination in employment remain pervasive; they are reinforced by intensification of inferior segregated education and, in spite of overpublicized token employment or upgrading of some middle-class Negroes, by the continuation of gentlemen's agreements between management and labor to exclude Negroes from the mainstream of employment opportunities except in low-level and menial jobs. Indeed, one of the more disturbing facts that has emerged from the paradox of the coexistence of racial progress and continued racial stagnation in America is that, with the apparent lessening of the more flagrant forms of racial discrimination on the part of business and industrial management, organized labor has emerged as one of the most significant barriers to inclusion of the Negro in the economic life of the nation.

The more blatant forms of such exclusion exist in the craft unions and the railroad brotherhoods. Pervasive patterns of racial discrimination exist even in unions like the International Ladies Garment Workers Union, where there are substantial numbers of Negro members. The more progressive unions deserve the description only because they do not exclude Negroes. They cannot be characterized as progressive in the degree of influence available to Negroes. Few Negroes occupy policy-making positions in these unions or hold any power of office that suggests an aggressive concern with the economic condition or the mobility of the Negro worker. Organized labor in America is an integral part of American racism. Labor has contributed significantly to the subjugated condition of Negroes in America and to an unpragmatic limitation of its own strength and power.

As the Negro in American cities has been forced to face these realities, he has reacted with an increased volatility and an unwillingness to accept what he considers the clichés of law and order. He has also developed an intolerance of older methods of negotiations, of governmental intervention and other approaches now seen as primarily conducive to the convenience of the more privileged white society. More significant is that within the last three years, the Negro's disillusionment with the possibilities of progress through the more traditional and conservative methods has led, especially among the young, to an increasing rejection by a significant and articulate minority of Negroes of the goals of racial integration. This relatively small group of articulate Negro nationalists and racial separatists has increasingly dominated the pattern and form of racial dialogue. Although, as the Kerner Commission appendix revealed and a CBS poll corroborated, extremists have minimal support from Negroes themselves,[2] the mass media have responded to more dramatic racial separatist demands and violent rhetoric with disproportionate time and attention.

This nationalistic approach, feeding on the bitterness, disappointment, and frustrations of large numbers of Negroes and exploiting the drama of the violent eruptions in the cities reinforces these with the rhetoric of continued violence and increases the chances of further violence. It provides justification to whites for resistance and hostility to legitimate Negro aspirations. The circle of Negro frustrations, the exploitation of Negro grievances by Negro separatists, and the reinforcement of the rationalizations for white racism becomes complete.

A further disturbing ingredient is the possibility of a covert alliance between white racists and black racists, through which the former finance and in other ways exploit the most extreme black nationalist racketeers— thereby seeking to perpetuate a racial ferment that would be conducive to the entrenchment of racial segregation. Certainly, there would be no ideological barriers to such an arrangement. There is, at least, evidence that some of the more extreme black racists have hidden bases of financial backing which cannot be explained by the financial support of their limited followers. The perplexing expressions of support for George Wallace

2. One percent of Negroes interviewed would give active support to Ron Karenga; 2 percent to H. Rap Brown; 4 percent to Stokely Carmichael; 49 percent to Ralph Abernathy. "White and Negro Attitudes Towards Race Related Issues and Activities," A *Nationwide Study for CBS News* (Opinion Research Corporation, July 1, 1968).

from some black nationalists, who argue that a racial confrontation is overdue in America and that a vote for Wallace would be a means of bringing it about, are in many cases merely reflections of distorted cynicism or suicidal despair, but they make clear the curious interdependence of extremists.

Civil Rights and Foreign Policy

Another significant aspect of the racial problem is that, for the first time, the civil rights issue has become enmeshed directly in foreign policy problems. Indirectly, the negative influence of American racism—as, earlier, the positive influence of the American democratic dream—on the reputation of America abroad and on America's role of world leadership has long been clear. But now the problem has been intensified as some of the more extreme black nationalist leaders, such as Stokely Carmichael and Rap Brown and Ron Karenga, chose to appeal beyond the nation's borders and to relate the struggle for racial justice in America directly to the context of foreign policy. Stokely Carmichael's visit to Cuba and Hanoi and his declaration that American Negroes should be allied with enemies of America are the most obvious examples of this negative linkage of foreign policy and domestic racial issues.

To see this manifestation as merely a reflection of the traditional left's tendency to exploit the problems of the Negro in America for its own purposes probably would be an oversimplification. Rather, it reflects the initiative of Negro nationalist leaders themselves to exploit the unpopularity of the Vietnam war. The role of Negro soldiers in that war has intensified the issue. It is a fact that a disproportionate number of Negroes have been casualties in that war. And, probably for reasons related to conditions of racial oppression at home, a disproportionate number of Negroes have reenlisted. To complete the circle, more Negroes then become available again as potential casualties. In the light of such facts, it is understandable that black nationalist leaders would seek to tie racial oppression to serious and probing questions concerning the role of America as an alleged instrument of democracy in Asia and elsewhere in the world.

Asking such questions has not been confined to extreme Negro nationalists and separatists. Before his death, Martin Luther King, Jr., who was generally regarded as a moderate and as a leader of the nonviolent movement in the quest for racial justice, had devoted as much if not more time to speaking against America's role in Vietnam, on moral as well as pragmatic grounds, as to arguing for racial justice at home. Martin Luther King asserted persistently that racial democracy could not be obtained in America as long as the United States was embarked in what he believed to be a crassly imperialistic venture, a venture which deflected the billions of dollars needed to restructure American cities and to abolish ghettos and poverty in the United States. Further, the war has tended to solidify the right-wing whites and to divide the liberals, thereby contributing to confusion and weakness in the ranks of reform, and to racial polarization in the country at large.

Questions for the Future

The above perspective of the inextricability of racial, urban, and foreign affairs demands that any proposals for realistic changes or improvement in the conditions of the Negro in American cities take into account the fundamental problems of the political, economic, and military power dynamic operating within the American democratic system. The issues can no longer be seen primarily in terms of white attitudes toward Negroes or the traditional rhetoric employed by civil rights agencies and leaders. The problems of the ghettos are now clearly enmeshed in the larger problems of the future of the cities and the nation. They require prompt decisions. Assessments of need, establishment of priorities, and allocation of energies and economic resources and, of course, implementation on the basis of these are matters of urgency.

For example, will the nation commit itself to fighting a realistic war on poverty, to fulfilling the legitimate aspirations of Negroes for economic mobility, to abolishing ghettos, to reorganizing and improving urban schools, and to remaking our cities—whether or not billions of dollars are spent for war and space exploration? What type of reorganization in the American labor movement will be necessary to involve Negroes not in token numbers but in proportion to their numbers and needs? Is the apparent affluence of America solidly based? Can it absorb those white and Negro poor who so far have not shared its benefits?

These and other similar questions must be answered realistically if the problems of the Negro and our cities are to be resolved. One approach to this dilemma is to retrench on promises and to seek to reduce the frustration by demanding that the poor and the Negro adjust to their inferior status for an indefinite period. The arguments against this approach seem obvious.

First, it is no longer possible to withdraw these promises. The reality of American affluence is transmitted by the mass media and other forms of communication. This inadvertent publicizing of possibilities arouses the aspirations and demands of the white poor and the Negro poor. Any attempt to withdraw these promises on the grounds that they were rashly made or were not meant to be believed, especially by the Negro, would increase Negro frustration and the related eruptions of the cities and would intensify the racial polarization of Negroes, thereby strengthening the nihilistic black separatists.

Second, one cannot argue persuasively for retrenchment of promises or settling for almost unobservable increments without demonstrating that the economy has reached its ceiling of growth and cannot absorb those who do not now share its affluence. Such an argument could not be supported in the light of the repeated assertions by economists that our growth potential is high and rising. It would be difficult to support also in the light of the backlog of housing, school, hospital, and other needs which have been tabled or ignored in favor of allocation of resources to the military. In the absence of evidence of the economy's incapacity to adapt to need, Negroes will assume that the capacity is there, but that the nation does not intend to develop it in his behalf.

The social and urban problems and the problems of poverty in America are not in themselves insoluble. It is a reasonable hypothesis that, given the human and intellectual resources available to the American people, solutions are possible within the framework of American democratic capitalism. Not only are solutions possible but they would strengthen the foundation and structure of the system itself, eliminating poverty and abolishing slums and ghettos within a single generation. Yet, when these problems are seen primarily in terms of changing the status of the Negro in relationship to whites, they are frequently discussed as if they are insoluble.

If problems of poverty and slums are perceived primarily in terms of race, a reaction sets in awakening the long tradition of negative social attitudes and anxieties concerning the relative power of Negroes to that of whites, and the pattern of emotionalism which has historically dominated the question of race in America. Given the negative perspectives inherent in traditional American racism, it is not likely, therefore, that any realistic solutions to these problems will be found as long as they are defined in terms of race.

Problems of poverty and social change were not identified as racial in the early 1960s as the antipoverty program got underway. Indeed, the Appalachian region of West Virginia, rather than northern urban ghettos, served to symbolize poverty in the 1960 presidential primary race and election campaign. It was only after the antipoverty program focused on the problems of the urban Negro that the words Negro and poor came to seem synonymous, to the detriment of the white and Negro poor alike. As a result, the white poor often refused to participate in such programs, particularly in northern cities, and antipoverty and community action projects in many urban areas became almost exclusively Negro.

When the economic problems of other ethnic groups were seen as problems of economic mobility rather than of ethnicity, American society could facilitate mobility of these groups and their assimilation in the total scheme of American politics and economics. These groups, however, were not burdened with the tradition of slavery, with legal and governmental exclusion, and, above all, with the visibility of different skin color. The fact remains, however, that fundamental solutions to the economic and political problems of Irish, Catholics, Poles, Italians, and Jews did not come about as long as the definition of concern was ethnic identification. The struggle for assimilation in the larger American society was essentially a struggle to be free of a burdening and initially negative ethnic identification. The same problem with obviously greater difficulty confronts the Negro and whites concerned with the stability of our cities and society.

These are questions society faces: Is it possible to redefine the problems of our cities in terms that minimize race and emphasize the economic, political, and social imperatives for change? Is it possible to devise plans for eliminating or opening up the ghetto that will appear not only advantageous to ghetto residents but also advantageous—and non-threatening—to middle-class whites? Only if affirmative answers to these questions are found will it be possible to get the commitment to change essential to solving the problems of our cities.

The Failure of Separatism

The need for the strategy of redefinition is highlighted by the failure of the racial approach. All approaches that stemmed from racial inequities have reached their limits. The limitation of the racial emphasis is demonstrated in the rapid polarization reflected in the white "backlash" and the black separatist movement. Curiously enough, it is the racist reactions, white and black, that have demonstrated most clearly the fact that race is irrelevant, that the enemy transcends race. Extremism that relies on skin color as a definition of reality is the enemy of all those who are concerned with human dignity.

The frontal racial attack has bent back on itself, an observation validated and confirmed by the Kerner Commission's unwillingness to accept two opposing societies in American life, one black and one white. Biracialism as a viable way of life in the American economic and political system has been proved impossible as a historical reality in America. The major policy implications of this analysis indicate that any formulation of social problems that highlights race is doomed to defeat or, at best, to limited success.

Pathology is rampant in northern urban ghettos despite the efforts of the antipoverty program, in large part because racial definitions and anxieties have limited its implementation. The homicide rate and the delinquency rate in Negro ghettos, which are higher than in most other areas of the northern cities, have not decreased. The ugliness of the ghetto has not been abolished. The overcrowding has increased. Most Negroes are still restricted to ghettos by income and white resistance. Ghetto business continues to be unstable, inefficient, and for the most part controlled by absentee owners. Unemployment and underemployment remain high, particularly among males. The welfare system continues to reinforce family instability and to impose the stigma of charity. The educational system of the ghetto has decayed even further, encouraging extreme restlessness and violence as ghetto parents resort to overt manifestations of their anxieties and their loss of faith in the public school system.

If one judges the war against poverty as one judges other wars, as President Johnson did on March 16, 1964 when he called for "total victory" in "a national war on poverty," one must conclude that there have been some superficial skirmishes of advance, accompanied by wider stalemate and defeat. In a number of cities, as the poor prepared to organize and to confront the larger community, the leadership of these cities began to circumvent and defeat the outward thrust of the poor. The awakening of the poor seemed to be an unexpected consequence. Local governments viewed the organized poor as a competitor to be manipulated, controlled, or suppressed. The federal government responded with dismay to this troublesome phenomenon which threatened its political relationship with city hall. Despite the promises, the nation either seemed not to have intended basic social change in the conditions of the poor, or it was politically naive in its failure to anticipate the sense of threat which would affect established institutions. The federal government has been unable to persuade, and often has failed to attempt to persuade, local centers of power that their long-range interests in the growth of cities and their immediate interests in the stability of the ghettos would be served by positive social change as directly as would be interests of the poor.

Instead, when the poor moved beyond their assigned role as exotic indigenous to an attempt to influence major policy—in antipoverty programs, programs for community control of schools, and in welfare reform—the authorities have tended to view the movement with alarm and to seek to thwart it, causing a growing number of leaders of the poor to conclude with some justification that official plans for their involvement must represent a sham. There is, indeed, a sense in which involvement seems an attempt to draw the poor in as accessories to policy, but to reject them when they challenge the central controls of established economic, political, welfare, or educational leadership.

The key sign of effectiveness in antipoverty programs would be clear evidence of desirable social change, not mere participation of the poor in programs. The success of these programs will be judged by the immediate reduction and the eventual abolition of poverty itself. The poor who are able to work want jobs consistent with pride and self-respect, not permanent dependency on relief checks or a guaranteed annual wage without work. Those who are unable to work want security without the sense of social stigma. The poor want schools as effective in producing student achievement as the schools of the privileged suburbs. They want accountability for educational performance and full municipal services and adequate housing.

Federally financed community action programs, sporadic attempts at modification of welfare systems, and halfhearted attempts at school decentralization and community control have so far not resulted in many observable changes in the predicament of the poor. Indeed, most of these programs have tended to reinforce the dependency and the powerlessness of the poor. In no case has program effectiveness or change in the conditions of the poor served as a criterion for federal or local support. When the local community has resisted the organized program of the poor, the federal government has generally proved unable to protect the program effectively against such resistance. A study of twelve major city antipoverty programs conducted by this author under the auspices of the Stern Foundation indicated that all of the programs defeated or dissipated after open battle with the power structure—in Syracuse and in Mobilization for Youth and HARYOU in New York for example—were more promising of genuine change in the conditions of the poor than were those programs that were successfully implemented. The very inability of these programs to effect profound change—in Boston and Cleveland, among others—seemed to protect them.

Government has tended to set as its goal in community-action programs not the abolition of poverty but the avoidance of social chaos. In the halfway measures that attempt to achieve school decentralization, it has often not even set its goals that high. Rather it has sought temporary appeasement of dissident forces, only to shift to open combat when vested interests such as teachers and supervisors oppose even limited change. As the federal executive and Congress retreated in community action programs when local political interests insisted, so city boards of education have often panicked when entrenched professional interests resisted the coming of ghetto community control. If apparent peace and stability were to be achieved, the reality may be dry rot and stagnation, not vitality and growth. But even the limited goals of peace and stability have failed of achievement.

Policy makers have generally not recognized that neither peace nor stability will any longer be possible without the kind of fundamental social change in the balance of community power that reflects observable improvement in the conditions of those who are deprived and oppressed.

The fact is that the antipoverty programs have failed and part of the reason is the growing identification of the programs with the Negro. Attempts to deal with the causes rather than the manifestations of poverty have been resisted by both black and white racists and even by some of the civil rights organizations that found the continued existence of the ghetto useful for their own purposes. As a result, the antipoverty program was sucked into the existing pathology, while the pathology, in turn, was presented to the community at large as an excuse for inaction.

If the problems of the city are to be seen as the necessity of restructuring the city, the abolition of the ghetto as a racial prison must be related to the stability and viability of the city as a whole; it must not be regarded as a program whose goal is to do good for Negroes. Anything short of total commitment will lead us down a racial blind alley and hasten the further deterioration of our cities.

Alternative Programs

The alternative programs can be summarized as follows:

1. Attempts to maintain the stability of the ghetto, to resort to palliatives, to contain deterioration, to impose law and order constraints, to reduce the chances of social instability by increasing police and military power. The reliance on this strategy encourages the ghetto to find ways to outmaneuver the authorities by using gamesmanship to pursue an adversary relationship with the larger society. As the city seeks to contain and control the ghetto discontent, the ghetto will develop techniques for aborting and subverting these programs, and will adopt sporadic hostile tactics such as planned arson and disruption of transportation. Instead of collective violence, difficult-to-handle isolated random violence, which has already begun, will spread.

2. Attempts to deal with the ghetto by rehabilitation, seeking to make ghettos more habitable, reducing the proportion of deteriorated housing, reducing the number of rats, and similar campaigns. This method has the advantage of remedying some of the more obvious dehumanizing aspects of the ghetto, but it has the disadvantage of embalming the ghetto and of failing to address itself to the fundamental fact of the ghetto and its status as an area of involuntary confinement. The cleanup approach is necessary because no one can justify houses unfit for human habitation in the affluent American society. But it is a mistake to believe that ghetto rehabilitation addresses itself to the question of ghetto volatility or to the fundamental problem that underlies it—racial injustice. The fact that Watts is a ghetto without looking like a ghetto did not save it from eruption.

Ghetto confinement must be understood as the absence of choice, the imposition of a status inferior to that available to other American citizens, including the most recent European immigrants and refugees. As long as confinement exists, oppression exists, however clean the streets and habitable the homes.

3. The only realistic alternative to these options is the development of strategies to open up ghettos, to provide ghetto residents with the education and employment essential for the achievement of genuine rather than rhetorical freedom of choice. Once this freedom is established, it might be

necessary to develop a plan for systematic voluntary redistribution of ghetto populations designed to prevent proliferation of suburban ghettos and to free the suburban white from his unrealistic isolation. There is no reason to believe that the pathologies and psychological problems which now characterize urban ghettos will fail to manifest themselves even in suburban middle-class Negro ghettos. If we really mean to stabilize our cities, our suburbs, and our society as a whole, plans have to be developed with the clear goal of reducing present ghettos and preventing the establishment of future ones.

Among the arguments brought against the redistribution of the ghetto population from within the ghetto itself, the most strident come from the black separatists who maintain that redistribution is a device for reducing the political and economic power of Negroes. They assert that only with ghetto self-determination can the Negro develop the kind of power necessary for the achievement of justice. They and their white supporters, both liberal and segregationist, argue that this approach is parallel to the approach which led to the assimilation of other ethnic groups.

This is contradictory on its face, nor is it made more valid by the supporting arguments that American society is essentially pluralistic. Pluralism and assimilation are logically contradictory. The pluralism cited now by white ethnic groups is not separatist—it is to be seen rather as a freedom of choice within a context of essential assimilation. The fact is that white ethnic groups are not burdened by ethnicity and can use or reject it in their political and economic interaction. It is a romantic illusion and a misreading of the lessons of American racial history to believe, as some Negroes do, that power within the inevitable pathology of racial isolation and exclusion can facilitate the attainment of racial justice—even if the Negro rationalizes that belief on the ground that he desires to be isolated.

The attempts on the part of some industrial firms to make the ghetto more palatable by bringing subsidiary plants into it are also unrealistic. Such plans are based on the assumption that the ghetto is inevitable, will always exist, is unchangeable, and can be self-contained. Further, such palliative plans are contrary to the general movement toward greater efficiency of industrial production reflected in the location of plants in industrial parks which can take advantage of improved transportation to draw labor from a larger area. It would seem far more desirable for industry to move to industrial parks or suburbs only under conditions which ensure a larger competitive not racially restricted labor pool, at the same time insisting on basic conditions of open housing.

Black nationalist anxiety that seeks to maintain and reinforce the ghetto shows little confidence in the reality of black power. The power Roman Catholics have exerted by voting in blocs on issues of importance to them, the power of Poles or Jews or any other ethnic group wielded politically has never been dependent on geographic or residential isolation. It has been dependent on shared interests and a sure sense of identification of concerns. To the extent that Negroes do represent shared interests, their power to vote and to influence legislation and social change would be related to this fact, not to the artificial identity of ghetto confinement.

A Comprehensive Plan for Stabilization of Our Cities

The above analysis makes clear that piecemeal approaches to the problem of our cities and to the problems of the relationship of whites and Negroes will no longer work. What is now required is the development of a comprehensive plan that takes into account the inextricability of all components of this problem. Such a plan requires large decisions; the mobilization of adequate economic resources; the organization of city planning oriented to the needs of the people; a working relationship between cities and suburban areas; the solution of the problems of public school financing and of the organization and reorganization of public education in cities and surrounding metropolitan areas; and the solution of the problems of population redistribution and freedom of choice in mobility for all.

The logical first phase of such a comprehensive plan should seek to control the volatility and turmoil of the ghetto through a campaign of rehabilitation of housing to increase housing opportunities within and outside of the ghetto, and to clean up ghetto streets.

An increase in the efficiency of sanitation services seems capable of almost immediate solution. Crash techniques similar to those used to clean up after downtown parades, and techniques employed after natural disasters, could be models for an immediate program in all ghetto areas and for a long-range program to sustain the cleanliness of the streets. Such a mass cleanup would improve the health of the ghetto, but it would have an even more immediate psychological effect. It would demonstrate to the residents of the ghetto that someone cares.

If the streets are cleaned and if the areas of ghetto ugliness are transformed, there would be a strengthening of the self-image of the ghetto resident and a building of renewed confidence in the possibility of other solutions. It would be a mistake to believe, however, that this alone would be an acceptable substitute for dealing with the unsolved problems of housing, schools, and jobs. It must be seen as a first step, followed immediately by more rigorous code enforcement, and rehabilitation of ghetto housing for all economic levels.

The next stage in the opening up of the ghettos would involve massive reorganization of education, social welfare, and health services, and significant expansion of job and economic opportunities.

A dramatic improvement in the quality of schools which children are now required to attend is an essential immediate step. Attempts to decentralize these schools and to ensure the accountability of the schools to the parents are prerequisite. Strengthened ghetto schools should, in the long run, lead not to reinforced segregation but to growing desegregation as the gap between educational facilities and academic achievement in ghetto and other schools closes.

Parallel to a strategy of decentralization and community control is the provision of alternative forms of education for the ghetto resident. These alternative schools may be quasi-public, quasi-private educational models organized by business and industrial firms or by social agencies, schools run by state or federal governments. Such programs, like the parochial school system, enlarge educational opportunities for the ghetto child.

Further, the Defense Department, rather than reject adolescent males who now are below the minimum requirements for Army service, could continue and strengthen its compensatory educational programs to raise the level of academic competence. The success of the Defense Department's project to train each year 100,000 men rejected by the Selective Service system is a clear rebuke to the inefficiency of the public-school systems. These first steps to upgrade the quality of education must be followed by massive reorganization to remove the last vestiges of segregation. True quality education for both Negroes and whites requires desegregation.

The nonrational demands of black nationalists for racist curricular controls in the schools, and the persistent resistance to racial desegregation on the part of white segregationists, may be viewed as disturbing evidence of the negative consequences of past and present racially segregated schools. This pattern of black and white racism, a serious threat to the stability of the nation, can be resolved only by serious desegregation of American schools. Although clear upgrading of the quality of education available to Negro youngsters is a necessary part of the overall planning for desegregation, these problems cannot be resolved by better education alone. Even with the best intentions and the highest degree of emotional involvement of the Negro population in community-controlled schools, segregated schools can never be adequate to meet the needs of American society, which include increased educational quality and racial inclusiveness.

The psychological problems inherent in the history and dynamics of segregated education will not be ameliorated for either white or Negro children by even the best of segregated schools. The fact that race is irrelevant to the process of education must be reflected in the schools. The burden of the racial myth is that it is socially divisive and deflects energy from human effectiveness. Separatism, which is a form of ignorance and debilitating superstition, is inimical to the broadening perspectives that should be the goals of education.

Programs of social welfare and health services must be detached from the tradition of the charitable poor laws. The plans designed to achieve a guaranteed annual income and family subsidies represent a shift away from a public welfare approach toward the establishment of an economic base below which no American family will be required to attempt to exist. But the economic problem of welfare would seem to be less difficult of solution than the psychological problem. The chief psychological problems posed by all attempts to redefine welfare emphasize the need to provide support in ways consistent with human dignity and self-esteem; this need is not satisfied by hypocritical semantic changes which perpetuate the self-doubt, stigma, and feelings of inferiority now associated with the condition of being a welfare recipient.

It is possible to develop programs for economic support of families geared to training, child care, and other services essential to the improvement of the living conditions of the poor, and at the same time safeguard the self-image and self-esteem of the individual involved in such programs.

For example, the Head Start preschool program could involve parents of these children far more extensively than at present in paraprofessional roles that provide services for these children and at the same time provide for parental training in child care, nutrition, health, and the education of children; service, training, and supplemental income could be combined in a single program. Such a program would go a long way toward removing the stigma of welfare and at the same time enable the individual to make some contribution in return.

It would be important, in addition, for paraprofessional and service roles not only to guarantee a minimum family income but also to ensure that the jobs are not dead-end or patently make-work jobs, but provide an opportunity for upward mobility and differential achievement. Such achievement should be stimulated by incentives and reinforced by evaluation of the individual's contribution.

Paraprofessional roles will, of course, not cover the large number of welfare recipients who are old or handicapped or infirm. For these persons, who form a high percentage of those on welfare rolls, it is necessary as a minimum to abolish the term "welfare," and to substitute a designation associated with human dignity, like "insurance" or "family security." No American citizen should be deprived of a minimum economic base for living or of necessary health services because he cannot endure the taint embodied in the acceptance of needed aid. He must be assured of the psychological security enjoyed by others who seek and receive government support without stigma—farmers, veterans, small business firms, aviation interests, and others. Business and government must cooperate to provide jobs and job training for all who need and want them.

The psychological problems inherent in the relationship between the poor and the rest of society pervade not only the area of health and welfare but of essential municipal services. One crucial area of risk is the relationship between the community and the police and others responsible for the administration of justice. Improvement of the quality of human relations and acceptance between police and the residents of low-income areas is essential to any serious program for the restructuring of American cities. The problems of the police in low-income areas are complex. Police are, themselves, for the most part, products of lower middle-class families. Their status, like that of minority group members, is marginal. They are generally poorly educated and subject to the frustrations of the upwardly mobile; they tend to seek scapegoats and to interpret complex social problem in oversimplified terms. In addition, their task is more hazardous than that of most government employees. They tend to see the inhabitants of the ghetto as adversaries and inferiors. They do not behave toward these persons as they behave toward those they consider their equals or superiors. They act not with the courtesy they show to those they regard as worthy, but often with suspicion, arrogance, bellicosity, or indifference.

The residents of the ghetto, in turn, react to the police as adversaries; they tend to see them as occupation troops and either do not cooperate with them or often reveal overt hostility. As a result of this mutual suspicion and hostility, ghetto residents report a high degree of police brutality, verbal and physical. More pervasive than the claims of physical brutality—which at times can be directly substantiated—and the verbal abuses is the ghetto resentment that results from the fact that police services and protection provided to the ghetto are markedly inferior to those provided to more privileged areas. The chief victims of urban crimes—personal assaults, robberies, and homicide—are the residents of the ghetto. The noncriminal majority of the ghetto frequently claim that they are powerless to obtain from the police adequate protection from criminal elements. The crime statistics, particularly the unsolved homicides and burglaries, tend to substantiate these claims.

Furthermore, it has been stated with some justification that crime in the ghetto such as prostitution and narcotics traffic could not be so prevalent without collusion and involvement of the police. The problem of the ghetto community-police relationship, therefore, cannot be understood or dealt with in the simplistic terms of police brutality. It must be understood in the more complex terms of inadequate police protection and the more insidious and disturbing problems of corruption which seem to characterize police operations in ghetto communities.

Closely associated with these issues is the fundamental problem of the administration of justice. The evidence supports the contention that minority group members are subjected to bail when others would not be, and to higher bail than others, and are more likely to be convicted for similar offenses and to be given longer prison terms for minor and serious offenses, particularly if these offenses involve whites as adversaries.

Such racially biased administration of justice—prevalent in northern cities as well as the South—offends the sense of justice of the community, increases the incidence of racial disturbance, and thereby threatens the stability of the society as a whole. It would follow, therefore, that a comprehensive plan for stabilizing and increasing the viability of our cities would have to include a realistic program to eliminate all racial considerations in the operations of our courts and penal institutions.

The challenges inherent in the effort to make our cities more viable are awesome. But one must assume that they are not beyond the capacity of human intelligence, commitment, and resources. In the process of freeing America from its slums and ghettos and the associated pathology of human cruelties, the problems of environmental control, population control, sanitation, water and air pollution may also be solved. But these are far less difficult than the problems of educating human beings to accept and master the challenges of human conflict. Predictions of success in solving these are more difficult to sustain.

ANTHONY DOWNS

MOVING TOWARD
REALISTIC HOUSING GOALS

The Housing Act of 1949 set forth a national housing goal: "Realization as soon as feasible . . . of a decent home and a suitable living environment for every American family." Yet almost two decades later, the National Advisory Commission on Civil Disorders discovered that inadequate housing was one of the major complaints among residents of every area where civil disorders had occurred.

Consequently, the Housing and Urban Development Act of 1968 starts by declaring that "Congress finds that this (1949) goal has not been fully realized for many of the Nation's lower-income families; that this is a matter of grave national concern; and that there exist in the public and private sectors of the economy the resources and capabilities necessary to the full realization of this goal." The 1968 act further states that "Congress reaffirms this national housing goal and determines that it can be substantially achieved within the next decade by the construction or rehabilitation of twenty-six million housing units, six million of these for low and moderate income families."

This paper seeks to determine (1) whether these quantitative housing targets adopted by Congress represent a reasonable estimate of the nation's needs; (2) what actions would have to be undertaken by the public and private sectors to achieve those targets in the period 1970 through 1980; (3) whether these actions are likely to be carried out; and (4) what public policy recommendations can be derived from the above considerations.

What Is "The Housing Problem"?

According to the official national goal, every American household which does not enjoy "a decent home and a suitable environment" is part of the housing problem. Unfortunately, this statement utterly fails to convey the appalling living conditions which give the housing problem such overriding urgency to millions of poor Americans. In fact, most Americans have no conception of the filth, degradation, squalor, overcrowding, and personal danger and insecurity which millions of inadequate housing units are causing in both our cities and rural areas. Thousands of infants are attacked by rats each year; hundreds die or become mentally retarded from eating lead paint that falls off cracked walls; thousands more are ill because of unsanitary conditions resulting from jamming large families into a single room, continuing failure of landlords to repair plumbing or provide proper heat, and pitifully inadequate storage space. Until you have actually stumbled through the ill-lit and decaying rooms of a slum dwelling, smelled the stench of sewage and garbage and dead rats behind the walls, seen the roaches and crumbling plaster and incredibly filthy bathrooms, and recoiled from exposed wiring and rotting floorboards and staircases, you have no real idea of what bad housing is like. These miserable conditions are not true of all inadequate housing units, but enough Americans are trapped in the hopeless desolation of such surroundings to constitute both a scandal and a serious economic and social drag in our affluent society.

I am deliberately emphasizing this point at the outset of my analysis, because the remainder is necessarily dispassionate in tone and focuses primarily upon statistics rather than graphic descriptions of what life in substandard housing is really like. Yet behind the dry data lurk the faces of thousands of suffering human beings, whose basic need for decent shelter is not being met. Sadly, this failure is often *caused* by public policies that benefit wealthier Americans. I have tried not to let the moral urgency of meeting this need, and of righting the injustices underlying some of it, blur my vision concerning what remedies are actually possible in our society. But neither should the objective tone of the analysis obscure the raw human realities encompassed in "the housing problem."

HOW MANY UNITS ARE NEEDED?

Most experts measure inadequate housing by using the data for "substandard housing units" published by the U.S. Bureau of the Census. These include all units that are physically dilapidated and all that do not have hot water and full plumbing within the unit, regardless of physical condition. The number of such units has been declining in recent years, but is still very large, as shown by the following table:[1]

Year	All housing units (millions)	Substandard units (millions)	Percent substandard
1950	46.1	17.0	36.9
1960	58.5	11.4	19.5
1970 (estimated)	69.5	6.9	9.9

In the two decades from 1950 to 1970, the nation will have built 30 million new units, eliminated 10.1 million substandard units, and expanded the net supply of standard units by 80.7 percent (as compared with a 35 percent rise in population), but there will still be almost 7 million substandard units. Moreover, counting only substandard units as inadequate seriously understates the true severity of the problem. If we also consider all overcrowded housing inadequate (that is, all units with more than 1.0 occupant per room), then an additional 3.9 million units would be part of the housing problem by 1970.

Even more important, measuring inadequate housing only by the number of substandard housing units focuses solely upon the housing unit itself. *But housing broadly defined includes three basic ingredients: a physical dwelling unit, its inhabitants and their behavior toward the unit, and the surrounding environment.* Thus, improvements in physical dwelling units cannot be considered in isolation: they must be linked to changes in occupant behavior and to overall environmental upgrading if the housing problem is to be truly solved.

Another complicating factor is that many low-income households live in good quality units with decent surroundings, but must pay a large proportion of their income for rent or ownership costs. For example, in 1959, 77 percent of all households with incomes under $2,000 paid 35 percent or more of the income for housing. It may be desirable to provide some assistance to the many households which can afford to live in adequate housing only by spending more than some reasonable proportion of their incomes on housing. Careful budgetary studies have shown that this proportion should be about 25 percent, varying somewhat with income level and household size. Using this definition, at least 12 million households—and

---

1. These and other data concerning total and substandard housing units are from an unpublished report by Frank S. Kristof, "Urban Needs and Economic Factors in Housing Policy," prepared for the National Commission on Urban Problems, completed in May 1968.

perhaps many more—were part of the housing problem in 1966 (including those in substandard units).[2]

Finally, American standards of what constitutes "a decent home" and "a suitable environment" are constantly rising, so measuring housing needs by these definitions involves elements of both subjectivity and relativity that make precise accuracy impossible. Nevertheless, my rough estimate is that from 10 to 12 million households will be considered inadequately housed in 1970—or about one out of every six or seven U.S. households. To be conservative, I will use the estimate of 10 million.

To solve the housing problem, the nation must not only replace all this inadequate housing, but must also provide enough new or rehabilitated units to accommodate future population growth and to replace units that will be demolished. From 1970 through 1979, about 12.3 million net new households will be formed in the United States. In addition, about 5.4 million new housing units will be needed to replace the net losses from existing inventory caused by demolition, mergers, conversions, and other shifts. Therefore, the nation would have to produce about 17.7 million new or rehabilitated units in the 1970s just to keep even, and at least 27.7 million units to include elimination of all inadequate units.[3] And it would also have to create all the facilities and services necessary to generate "a suitable environment" for those units.

These calculations indicate that the official production target of 26 million units for the next decade—including 6 million for low-income and moderate-income families—represents a reasonably accurate estimate of the output needed to solve the housing problem in that period.

WHERE WILL NEW HOUSING BE BUILT?

Where would these housing units, facilities, and services be located? A recent study indicates that about 90 percent of all population growth from 1960 to 1985 will occur in metropolitan areas—10 percent in central cities and 80 percent in suburban rings.[4] I assume that future housing needs

---

2. Based upon a study conducted by SYSTEMETRICS for the U.S. Department of Housing and Urban Development, completed in July 1968.
3. Estimates of future household formation and needs to counteract net losses in the inventory are taken from the Kristof Report.
4. Projections from Patricia Leavy Hodge and Philip M. Hauser, *The Challenge of America's Metropolitan Population Outlook—1960 to 1985*, Research Report No. 3, National Commission on Urban Problems (Washington, D.C., 1968).

arising from population growth will be spatially distributed in the same way. Housing units likely to be destroyed or demolished in the next decade will probably be heavily concentrated within central cities. But replacement housing for these units will not be similarly concentrated, because the cleared sites will be occupied by new highways and nonresidential structures. Hence I have made an arbitrary spatial distribution of such replacement housing.

Information concerning substandard units, though inadequate, provides the best way to discover where housing deficiencies are located. In 1960, 64 percent of all substandard units in the United States were outside metropolitan areas, 21 percent were in central cities, and 15 percent were in suburban rings. However, the new housing units replacing these deficiencies will not be distributed in the same way. For one thing, continued population migration to metropolitan areas means that replacements outside those areas should be much lower than the proportion of substandard units there. Second, relocation problems will make it almost impossible to replace all the inadequate housing in central cities with new units located inside those cities. These problems are discussed in detail in a later section. Third, the replacement of all inadequate central-city housing units by new units within those cities cannot be achieved by 1980 because of the prolonged time required for clearance operations. Urban renewal projects now take an average of six to nine years from initial concept to final occupancy.[5] In 1967, the annual rate of construction of public housing, urban renewal housing, and interest-subsidy housing combined was less than 100,000 new units. At this rate, it would take over thirty years to replace all the housing units in central cities that were inadequate as of 1960, even if *all* public efforts were focused solely upon those cities. Certainly this snail's pace could be speeded up if housing were awarded a higher priority on the nation's agenda. But it is unrealistic to believe that even a major policy shift would accelerate clearance enough to permit complete replacement of inadequate central-city housing by 1980 without use of vacant land, most of which is in the suburbs.

A fourth factor in redistributing housing, which also emphasizes this need to build on vacant land, is the desire among city planners to reduce residential densities in central cities. Most plans for upgrading cities call for massive expansion of nonresidential land uses, such as parks, schools, and universities. Moreover, much central-city slum housing is inadequate

5. Based upon an unpublished study by members of the staff of the National Commission on Urban Problems.

precisely because of its sardine-can density, such as the 67,000 persons per square mile in Harlem.

These considerations all point to the inescapability of replacing many inadequate central-city housing units with new units built on vacant land in surrounding suburbs. But most suburban residents are not very eager to accept thousands of low-income households—many Negro—moving out of central cities. Their reluctance will have a critical influence upon the speed with which society tackles the job of replacing inadequate housing, and where future construction is likely to occur. Therefore, I have made a rather arbitrary distribution concerning the future location of replacement housing. The results are summed up in Table 1.

TABLE 1. *Housing Units Needed, 1970–80*
(In millions)

Type of need	Total needed	Central cities	Suburban rings	Outside metropolitan areas
For population growth	12.3	1.2	9.8	1.3
For replacement of units eliminated (net of other additions)	5.4	2.1	2.3	1.0
For replacement of inadequate units	10.0	1.0	5.8	3.2
Total	27.7	4.3	17.9	5.5

Sources: Patricia Leavy Hodge and Philip M. Hauser, *The Challenge of America's Metropolitan Population Outlook—1960 to 1985*, Research Report No. 3, National Commission on Urban Problems (Washington, D.C., 1968); distribution estimated by author.

HOW WILL THE TYPE OF HOUSING BE DETERMINED?

Up to now, the analysis has been solely in terms of undifferentiated housing units. This fails to provide guidance concerning the number of units of each building type, each kind of ownership or tenure, each size, and each type of financing. Many of these choices are best left up to private market forces. But others—especially those concerning type of financing—require public policy decisions. Hence the *quality* of future housing needs should be analyzed, as well as the *quantity*.

The best way to analyze quality is to focus upon those households which will require public assistance to achieve an adequate standard of housing. These consist of three main groups: those now living in inadequate housing because they cannot afford adequate quarters; those now living in adequate quarters but spending an inordinate fraction of their income to pay for those quarters; and households that will form in the future and enter one of the two preceding categories. The second group needs, not new or improved housing, but income supplementation. Consequently, my analysis will focus upon the first and third groups.

In 1960, considering housing in metropolitan areas only:

Most substandard units were occupied by low-income households—55 percent by those with annual incomes under $3,000, and 24 percent by those with annual incomes from $3,000 to $4,999.

A clear majority of even the lowest-income households lived in adequate housing, even so. For example, only 26 percent of all households with annual incomes under $2,000 lived in substandard dwellings (though many more lived in overcrowded or otherwise inadequate "standard" units).

Negroes occupied disproportionate fractions of all substandard housing in relation to either their total numbers or their incomes. Nonwhites comprised 10 percent of all metropolitan area households, but occupied 31 percent of all substandard housing units in those areas. And for "poverty-level" groups (annual incomes under $3,000), the proportion in substandard units was much higher among Negroes than among whites, even though their incomes were similar (44 percent compared with 25 percent for renter households, and 34 percent compared with 12 percent for owner households).

A very high proportion of large families (six or more persons) lived in inadequate housing.

Outside metropolitan areas, the same general conditions prevail, but substandard housing tends to be even more concentrated among the poorest groups and among Negroes.

Future population growth will undoubtedly create more households which cannot achieve adequate housing standards without public assistance. This will occur because housing of adequate quality, whether new or used, costs more than many low-income households can afford to pay. Moreover, the income which any household must attain to rent or buy adequate quality housing without spending too high a proportion of its total income on housing is significantly higher than the official "poverty level" as defined by the Social Security Administration, which is based on costs of an adequate diet rather than on costs of adequate housing. There are millions more "housing poor" households in the United States than "food poor" households.

Will future population growth increase the number of households that are "housing poor" and therefore need public assistance to procure adequate housing? Incomes will probably rise even faster than population in the next decade. Hence the number of new entrants into any given lower-income bracket will be more than offset by the number whose rising incomes take them out of that bracket. But these future income gains may be at least partially offset by an escalation in the "housing poverty level" resulting from rising costs and prices. The likely outcome of the race between consumer incomes on the one hand, and population growth plus housing costs on the other, is not clear. Nevertheless, I do not believe there will be any really significant increase in the number of households below the housing poverty level, even though the income figure representing that level will rise.

WHAT OTHER URBAN SERVICES WILL BE NEEDED?

Production of 27.7 million new or rehabilitated dwellings during the 1970s would not in itself achieve the nation's housing goal. For creating "a suitable living environment" for every American family also requires providing the many ancillary facilities and services related to housing. The facilities include sewer and water systems, streets, highways, schools, parks, shopping centers, public transit lines and equipment, public buildings, and other private buildings like churches, motels, small stores, and so on. The services include police and fire protection, garbage collection, street cleaning, operation of schools and recreational facilities, and operation of all the private facilities mentioned above.

Clearly, in a paper of this length, it is impossible to analyze all the problems and policies associated with creating this immense spectrum of facilities and activities. Even so, it is appropriate to make a few observations concerning this task. It consists of two essentially different parts: upgrading all the facilities and public services in existing neighborhoods, especially poorer parts of central cities; and creating the new facilities and services necessary to accommodate future population growth, largely in suburbs.

The Model Cities Program has already begun the extraordinarily complex, expensive, and frustrating job of trying to improve the overall environment in a sample of existing low-income neighborhoods. This program provides federal monetary incentives for each of a selected group of local governments to plan and carry out an intensive and highly coordinated upgrading drive in a relatively small part of its area. Each such drive involves activities by all city departments, the local school board, private social agencies, relevant state agencies (such as welfare departments), and key federal agencies. By trying to get all these "actors" to focus their efforts jointly in a well-coordinated attack on the problems in a single slum neighborhood in each city, the Model Cities Program seeks to overcome the excessive fragmentation and diffusion that have weakened the impact of past upgrading efforts. Therefore, a key national task is to carry out this program effectively and expand it. Greater emphasis should be placed on trying out really radical technical and institutional experiments, because we know so little about how to solve many key upgrading problems. For example, we have yet to discover an effective way to improve the educational achievements of children from the most deprived homes. Finally, there must be closer cooperation among the many federal agencies responsible for programs that affect Model City neighborhoods.

Providing adequate nonresidential facilities and services to accommodate future population growth seems strikingly different from upgrading existing deprived areas. Ironically, the same concern that causes reformers to advocate splitting large cities into small neighborhood-oriented jurisdictions simultaneously causes them to press for the merger of small suburbs into larger jurisdictions. This paradox occurs because, in both areas, the existing government is not responsive to the needs of the most deprived people in society. In big cities, this lack of responsiveness masquerades as the impersonal bureaucracy found in many large organizations. So the cure seems to be shifting the locus of decision making to small areas, in the hope that the obvious predominance of the deprived in those areas will compel the government to respond to their needs. However, it is not possible to deal with all the complexities of participation and representation issues here.

In contrast, in growing suburban areas political jurisdictions are already small enough to provide high responsiveness to their residents. But those relatively affluent residents deliberately seek to exclude most of the poor. In this case, the cure seems to be *reducing* local responsiveness by shifting certain policy responsibilities to a larger jurisdiction. Since that jurisdiction will incorporate the people now deliberately excluded, it will supposedly be far more responsive to their needs. Unfortunately, it is not really clear why this larger entity will be any more responsive to the deprived than large central-city governments are now. But there does not appear to be any other even potentially effective way to sensitize suburbs to a broader viewpoint. Therefore, "escalating" key powers to larger jurisdictional areas should certainly be tried in many metropolitan areas, and perhaps adopted generally.

In both central cities and suburbs, two other ingredients will be vital in creating proper facilities and services ancillary to housing. The first is more effective administration of existing institutions. This requires a greatly increased quantity and quality of state and local government personnel. The second consists of large infusions of financial aid from outside the local governments, for creation of adequate environments for new housing will be extremely expensive. A crude estimate of the cost of constructing the necessary ancillary capital facilities (such as streets, schools, water systems, and so forth) is that it will be at least two-thirds as much as the cost of the housing itself. This would amount to about $436 billion from 1970 through 1980. Studies indicate that about $196 billion would consist of private investment and $240 billion of public investment. This is an average public investment of $21.8 billion per year in new construction of facilities related to housing. This compares with $13 billion, my rough estimate of the amount spent on similar construction by all state and local governments in 1966. And these figures include no allowance for the immense expense of operating the new facilities. Thus, the public sector will have to expand its spending greatly to meet the nonhousing parts of the federal government's housing goals by 1980. Much of that expansion will require federal financing.

This conclusion should not be obscured by statements about the potentially increased role of the private sector in solving the urban crisis. No matter how much of the job of creating better urban environments is *performed* by the private sector, a major part of the *costs* of that performance must be borne by the public. And this is perfectly proper. The actions involved benefit society as a whole, and therefore should be paid for by society as a whole.

Meeting National Housing Targets

Creating 27.7 million new or rehabilitated housing units and the ancillary facilities and services they require by 1980 is a heroic target. If the United States actually reached this target, it would have virtually solved its remaining housing problem in slightly more than a single decade. According to the Housing and Urban Development Act of 1968, this is precisely what Congress wants the nation to do. And according to the official statements, exhortations, and policies of the Department of Housing and Urban Development, its leaders believe we can do it.

Yet the obstacles blocking attainment of this target by 1980 are formidable. From 1950 through 1959, an average of 1.5 million new housing units were built each year. From 1960 through 1967, the annual average was 1.4 million, and from 1966 through 1968 it will be about 1.3 million. In only three postwar years have over 1.6 million units been built; 1950 (the all-time high of almost 2 million), 1955, and 1963 (both under 1.7 million). Moreover, annual production of subsidized units for middle-income and low-income households has averaged less than 60,000 in the past decade. Therefore, meeting the targets in the 1968 act will require an annual rate of total production double that attained in the recent past, and 42 percent higher than the greatest ever achieved. It will also require producing ten times as many housing units for moderate-income and low-income households per year as in the past.

Theoretically, these enormous accelerations in housing production could be achieved only if, throughout *all* of the 1970s, the nation would simultaneously:

Attract vastly more private capital into residential investment. This would be virtually impossible unless we ended the war in Vietnam immediately, avoided any costly new foreign involvements, placed top national emergency priority on housing, and adopted monetary and fiscal policies that encouraged low interest rates and relatively little inflation.

Greatly expand the available supply of construction workers. This would involve major changes in existing union practices in the building trades.

Pace housing programs to avoid great dislocations between supply and demand.

Subsidize millions of households so that they could pay for adequate housing. This would demand annual congressional housing appropriations much larger than any ever passed before.

Overcome existing bitter resistance to relocation among low-income households so that millions of persons could be peaceably displaced through massive clearance programs.

Achieve a major change of attitude among middle-class Americans—both white and black—concerning their willingness to accept large numbers of low-income households into their communities, and similarly alter the unwillingness of present all-white areas to welcome Negro newcomers. Open up many "exclusive" suburban areas to provide vacant sites for housing lower-income households through fundamental changes in existing zoning laws and practices.

Remove the obstacles to the development of mass production techniques for building housing (such as myriad building codes), attract large-scale operators into the housing industry, and create better institutions in that industry to carry out federal programs.[6]

Slash administrative red tape and delays at all levels of government. This could be done only through basic changes in the incentive systems now built into all public institutions.

Expand local government revenues sufficiently to pay for all the ancillary facilities needed to support the new housing, and for their subsequent operation. This would require major shifts in the fiscal relations among federal, state, and local government institutions.

Merely stating these requirements indicates how unrealistic it is to believe they will all come to pass soon enough for the nation to reach its official housing targets by 1980. This conclusion is certain to be labeled as gloomy and pessimistic by many sincere and well-informed proponents of housing. They contend that the nation could reach these targets by 1980 "if only we would make the effort." Perhaps they are right. But I believe most Americans will conclude that the costs of making that effort are not worth the reward of eliminating nearly all inadequate housing by 1980.

After all, the vast majority of Americans at all income levels live in reasonably adequate housing now. Therefore, they would not benefit directly or immediately from wiping out inadequate housing, though they would receive many indirect benefits. Yet many of the profound institutional and other changes required to eliminate inadequate housing by 1980 would impose large costs upon this well-housed majority and drastically alter institutions they now cherish. Moreover, awarding the housing problem the top national priority—indeed, emergency status—necessary to reach the official targets by 1980 would necessarily downgrade efforts to attack other problems that many citizens believe are even more serious—such as poverty, the need for better quality education, and minority-group unemployment. In fact, focusing national efforts on housing might even raise unemployment generally, as pointed out later.

For these reasons, I do not believe the nation will reach the official hous-

---

6. Another major activity which could be added to this list is expanding the capacity of the building materials industry. However, limitations of both space and my knowledge prevent discussion of this possibility here.

ing targets by 1980. This conclusion seems to me an inescapable result of any thorough and realistic assessment of the true probabilities that all the key actors will behave in the ways necessary to carry out the actions set forth above. In the subsequent sections, I will try to support this conclusion by examining in detail each of the nine activities described above. In each case, I will first set forth the actions necessary to reach the housing targets in the 1968 act. Then I will indicate why, in my opinion, some of those actions will not occur in the near future. The purpose of these detailed examinations is not to dispute the desirability of attaining the official housing targets, or to attack those who espouse them. Rather, it is to develop effective policy recommendations which the nation might adopt concerning housing. For discovering what actions would be required to reach these targets by 1980 will also provide crucial insights concerning the actions necessary to solve the housing problem within a longer time-frame. In most cases, the basic policies and institutional changes required will be roughly the same regardless of what the ultimate target date may be—only the pacing and the annual magnitudes will be different.

Admittedly, I cannot determine the proper future pacing. I believe the nation's worst housing conditions are terribly bad, and improving them deserves very high national priority. Nevertheless, solving the housing problem is only one of the many pressing tasks facing the nation. Each of these tasks seems compellingly urgent to those who specialize in it; consequently, they often claim that it should be given top national priority. But, in my opinion, such specialists should not set national priorities—that is the task of our political leaders. Therefore, I will simply indicate what must eventually be done to solve the housing problem and what specific first steps could effectively be adopted within the next few years.

The principal challenges to the federal government regarding housing will not necessarily involve major new legislation. True, Congress must pass much bigger appropriations for many of the programs it has already authorized, and this implies a very different attitude of members of congressional appropriations committees toward the housing problem from the one prevailing in the past. But the really tough challenges will be effectively administering existing and new programs, and persuading key nonfederal actors to carry out their roles in attaining federal housing goals. These nonfederal actors are the local governments in major metropolitan areas, state governments, the three basic segments of the private building industry (lenders, labor, and builders), and the public at large. Thus, administration and leadership—rather than housing legislation—will be the crucial tasks which the President and his administration must undertake with unprecedented effectiveness.

FINANCING EXPANDED OUTPUT

Procuring the capital to invest in 27.7 million housing units involves four basic issues. First, is the required investment in residential construction compatible with the basic structure of the economy? Detailed analysis of the likely cost of creating that number of new housing units from 1970 through 1980 indicates that the total investment in housing required (in current dollars) will be about $654 billion. Assuming gradually increasing output, the annual investment rate will rise from about $37 billion in 1970 to about $85 billion in 1980. These requirements will amount to roughly 3.9 percent of gross national product (GNP) in 1970, and 5.1 percent in 1980. In recent years, the share of GNP devoted to residential construction has been from 3.0 to 3.3 percent, but it reached 5.5 percent in 1950. Similar analyses concerning gross private domestic investment and personal income indicate that high, but not impossible, fractions would have to go into housing. These could be attained only if current flows of capital into defense spending were significantly curtailed. Thus, if peace returns and defense spending drops off, it will be structurally possible to hit the 1980 target in terms of capital funds.

Second, will the financial institutions which have traditionally provided mortgage capital be able and willing to pour the required funds into housing in the 1970s? Prospects are not good for attracting such large flows of funds into housing through these channels. They include savings and loan associations, commercial banks, mutual savings banks, and insurance companies. A preliminary analysis of the levels of funds which each of these institutions (and others) would have to put into housing to finance 27.7 million units in the 1970s indicates: savings and loan associations would have to attract as high a share of savers' funds as they did before bank rates became competitive with association rates; American consumers would have to save about 7 percent of their personal disposable incomes throughout the decade—though they have saved a fraction of this size only twice since 1959; pension funds would have to overcome their past aversion to real estate and plunge heavily into mortgage investments; insurance companies, banks, and mutual savings banks would have to alter drastically their antipathy toward residential mortgages (especially for single family homes) during periods of high interest rates when other investments with lower processing costs and comparable returns become available.

Under current institutional conditions, these events are likely to occur simultaneously—if at all—only if there is a sharp slackening of business in all sectors of the economy relative to housing. But it is extremely unlikely that such a slackening would persist throughout the decade.

This raises the third basic question: what kinds of monetary and fiscal policies are needed to encourage large-scale investment in housing? During the postwar period, housing starts have risen whenever interest rates declined, and vice versa. Thus, the economic climate most conducive to massive investment in housing would be one with relatively low or declining interest rates. But interest rates normally fall during periods of receding general prosperity and rise when the economy is booming. This suggests that it is difficult to maintain both high-level prosperity and large-scale investment in housing at the same time—at least over a long period. How could it be done throughout the 1970s?

Some observers believe that huge amounts of money could be channeled into housing even during prosperity if interest rates on mortgage loans rose very high—to, say, 10 percent or more. Traditional lenders would then be willing to make mortgage loans even in prosperous periods, and consumer households would be encouraged to save more. But it is extremely unlikely that high enough mortgage rates can be either achieved or sustained. They are now illegal in most states, though existing usury laws are being changed. More significantly, these rates would probably tremendously reduce the demand for housing, thereby defeating this strategy. Finally, such rates would place severe strains on the huge savings and loan industry. Its large portfolio of past loans made at lower rates means it cannot sharply raise the rates it pays to savers without incurring financial losses. If mortgages could be made at 10 percent, there would be an immense pressure on banks and other savings institutions to raise their savings rates. But savings and loan associations hold over $100 billion in home mortgages; society cannot afford to let them collapse. For all these reasons, this strategy for sustaining a continuous high-level flow of funds into housing will not work.

An alternative might be to use fiscal policy to restrain general demand in the economy and to divert funds into housing. The government could utilize increased income taxes instead of high interest rates to "cool off" the economy. It could also invest all the proceeds of those taxes directly in housing. But when the economy in general cools off, housing demand drops, thereby weakening the desire of builders to create 21.7 million new unsubsidized units.

These considerations raise a fourth major financing issue: Can and will the public sector provide the necessary incentives or supplementary funds to make up for private capital deficiencies? In my opinion, the amounts of capital necessary to hit the target of 27.7 million units by 1980 are so vast (averaging almost $60 billion per year) that it is unlikely that Congress will appropriate any very large fraction of the total. Only a national commitment to this housing goal similar in determination to production commitments during the Second World War would move the federal government to shape the nation's fiscal policy as described above. Because of the current political climate of the nation and strong competitive spending demands for education and other social needs, such an all-out emphasis upon housing seems extremely improbable.

This analysis suggests that the investment capital needed to build 27.7 million new units in the 1970s probably cannot be channeled into housing unless the new administration and its successors elect to slow down economic prosperity significantly. That would injure the very households which many government housing policies are designed to aid. Moreover, it is unlikely that such a slowdown would last throughout the decade. Nevertheless, there are several milder public policies which the administration could adopt to encourage a larger flow of private capital into housing. They are set forth in a later section.

INCREASING MANPOWER

In 1967 there were 3.2 million U.S. workers engaged in all contract construction, but no separate data exist for workers in residential construction. Even this statistic is misleading. Thousands of manufactured components and raw materials go into construction, but the workers producing them are not included in this statistical category. Second, seasonal fluctuations mean that the number of construction workers each August is 20 to 45 percent higher than the number in February. Hence many more workers extract some earnings from construction than are considered fully employed therein.

This lack of accurate data makes it difficult to determine whether productivity in homebuilding is rising. Considering aggregate data only, it appears that the real value of each worker's hourly output has not increased significantly in nearly two decades. But recent detailed studies assert that this conclusion ignores significant improvements in product quality and that hourly productivity in construction has actually gone up more than 2 percent per year in the postwar period. If so, doubling the annual average output of housing in the next few years will require somewhat less than doubling the number of workers employed in residential construction.

Even this requirement means increasing residential construction manpower by at least 1 million man-years by 1975, and by even more in the late 1970s, if 27.7 million new housing units are to be built by 1980. But many of the skills required to build a house under present methods take a long time to learn, and there is a chronic shortage of apprentices in building trades unions (though most homebuilding is done by nonunion labor). This situation is likely to create a serious production bottleneck if government programs plus population growth suddenly expand the demand for residential building. Contractors and subcontractors will bid desperately for skilled workers, and wages will rise rapidly. Shortages of workers in key trades have already appeared in those few metropolitan areas where homebuilding has recently boomed. From 1960 through 1966 hourly rates in contract construction rose 25.7 percent, compared with 19.9 percent in all manufacturing. Total weekly pay also went up faster in construction, but by a smaller margin: 28.7 percent compared with 24.7 percent in manufacturing. However, the wages of on-site labor play a relatively small role in determining the ultimate cost of housing to its occupants. They comprise only one-fifth the cost of constructing a single family house, and one-tenth the total cost of occupying it (which includes property taxes, utilities, maintenance, and interest). True, many other costs of housing, such as property taxes, are proportional to construction costs; so on-site labor expenses have a "multiplier effect" on total cost. Nevertheless, if construction wages rose an average of 8 percent per year over the next decade instead of 4.3 percent as from 1960 to 1966, this would raise the cost of building a house by no more than 3 percent per year and the cost of living in it by about 2 percent per year.

These calculations imply that future shortages of construction workers are likely to have more important effects in slowing down the rate of housing production than in raising costs. The bottlenecks arising from such shortages will be aggravated by the unusually high rate of retirement which will prevail in this work force, because its members are relatively old. Consequently, the manpower required to build 27.7 million housing units by 1980 would not be forthcoming in time unless extensive public efforts were directed to increasing the flow of new workers into this field. Even if the ultimate target date for eliminating all inadequate housing is moved well past 1980, such efforts would have beneficial effects in increasing the output capacity of the housing industry.

PREVENTING DEMAND-SUPPLY DISLOCATIONS

To reach its stated housing targets by 1980, the federal government must increase the housing purchasing power of 6 million low-income and moderate-income households who could not afford adequate housing without subsidies. Hence they would form a *net addition* to the demand for adequate housing likely to arise out of future growth and other factors. The result would be an unprecedented level of demand for adequate housing. On the supply side, the federal government would simultaneously be stimulating the production of housing and expanding the total capacity of the housing industry. In theory, this two-sided approach should result in a close matching of rising demand on the one hand and rising supply on the other. But in reality some periods of significant dislocation would arise, with undesirable effects.

Some experts have contended that such dislocations cannot occur because all the programs of the Department of Housing and Urban Development (HUD) embody direct links between supply and demand. For example, rent supplements are not paid to households, but to developers who build or rehabilitate units. Therefore, a rapid expansion of the rent supplement program would automatically create an added unit for every low-income household thus newly put into the market. All other HUD subsidies similarly are attached to housing units. This linkage was expressly designed to prevent the kind of dislocation between subsidized demand and added supply described.

Nevertheless, major dislocations can still occur because HUD's programs must compete with all other nonsubsidized users of housing for labor, land, capital, and materials. If the production of subsidized units suddenly rose from its current annual average of 60,000 units to the proposed average of 600,000, then 540,000 "one-unit batches" of housing resources would be diverted from building housing for other people. Unless the total capacity of the industry expanded equally fast, this would result in rising prices of all major housing inputs.

Moreover, to reach HUD's 1980 targets, its programs must successfully "capture" large amounts of housing production resources while those resources are still limited in supply. Insofar as this occurred, many nonsubsidized seekers of new housing units would be compelled to continue living in existing adequate units. This would intensify competition for the present inventory of adequate housing, and the prices and rents of existing good quality housing would rise. This dislocation would injure many of the very households which HUD's programs are designed to assist—especially low-income renters. They would be less able than ever to bid competitively for existing or new adequate housing if rents and prices rose sharply. HUD cannot possibly subsidize all 6 million households at once. Thus in the first few years the number it benefited would be much smaller than the number which would suffer from the impact of its activities upon the existing inventory. Even at the end of the decade, all the poor households paying inordinate fractions of their incomes to rent adequate units would be permanently injured by the higher rents commanded by such units.

But what if HUD's programs have no initial surge? Their proponents argue that HUD will build up its activities gradually to keep pace with expansion of the housing industry's overall production capacity. Such gradualism would necessarily lead to one of two outcomes. The first is failure to build 6 million subsidized units by 1980. The second is a requirement for gigantic annual outputs of subsidized units toward the end of the 1970s in order to reach the target in that decade. For example, if HUD actually stimulated construction (or rehabilitation) of 200,000 units in the first year of its accelerated program and gradually built up to 600,000 units by the fifth year, it would have to generate 900,000 units in the tenth year to reach a ten-year total of 6 million. What would happen in the eleventh year? Would HUD suddenly cut further subsidies down to the ten-year average of 600,000 units, or to the current average of 60,000 units? If so, there would be a huge dislocation in the housing industry. Assuming HUD actually built up its subsidized programs to a very high level in the tenth year, some subsequent wrench of this kind could be avoided only if the nation made a permanent commitment to huge annual outputs of subsidized housing.

Thus, however HUD schedules its planned 6 million subsidized units, any attempt to build all of them within a single decade while still serving all other housing demands is likely to result in major imbalances between demand and supply in the housing market.

Other types of more localized imbalances between supply and demand are likely to arise wherever HUD's programs create a large number of adequate units in a very short period. However, these dislocations are inherent results of any attempt to attack the housing problem on a large scale. For example, if a large number of new adequate units are built on previously vacant land in some city, the demand for nearby inadequate units will fall sharply. This will lower the rents and prices of these surrounding units, thereby benefiting many poor renters not covered by HUD's subsidies (and injuring poor owners). In contrast, if the new subsidized units are built on land previously occupied by substandard housing, exactly opposite effects are likely. The number of households displaced by such clearance usually exceeds the number of new units built on the cleared site. The "excess" households displaced will increase competition for existing units nearby, thereby raising their rents and prices. Displacement connected with HUD's urban renewal programs has been causing precisely such injurious effects upon nearby renters for many years.

Policy implications drawn from these considerations are given later.

PROVIDING HOUSING SUBSIDIES

Whatever the number of households now living in inadequate housing, a large proportion have very low incomes. Consequently, any program aimed at providing adequate housing for all households must contain a large amount of "deep" subsidies that cover a large share of a household's total housing costs. But why should the government pay housing subsidies at all? Why not just raise people's incomes above the poverty level through various income maintenance and employment programs? Couldn't they then enter the market and obtain adequate housing without any special housing assistance?

They could not, for two reasons. First, the level of income maintenance adequate to remove people from poverty as defined by the Social Security Administration is too low. It does not allow a household to pay for adequate housing without spending an inordinate share of income on shelter, as pointed out earlier. Yet the cost of raising all Americans even to the "food poverty" threshold is huge, so large that society is certainly unlikely to adopt in the near future income maintenance schemes supporting even higher levels. Second, the supply of housing available to many low-income households in deteriorating central-city neighborhoods—especially Negro households—is highly restricted. There are many "frictional" factors inhibiting the market from increasing that supply in response to higher purchasing power, and these factors will not yield easily to public policy remedies. Therefore, suddenly raising the incomes of these people would simply cause their rents to go up sharply, as has already occurred whenever welfare rent allowances have increased. That is why housing programs per se must remain crucial ingredients in providing poor people with "a decent home and a suitable environment."

However, almost all the programs in the Housing and Urban Development Act of 1968 and in HUD's existing arsenal use "shallow" subsidies that do not cover most of a poor household's housing costs. Hence these programs will not reach really poor households directly. But HUD does have two "deep" subsidy programs available: public housing and leased public housing. In order to serve the majority of persons now living in inadequate units, HUD would have to expand these programs tremendously and alter them drastically to make this expansion acceptable in most communities. Specific recommendations to accomplish this are set forth in the final section of this chapter.

The average subsidy for all households receiving HUD assistance would be based upon both "deep" and "shallow" components. My crude guess is that about $800 per household per year would be required for all the households assisted by HUD's programs over the next decade. If 600,000 more households received such subsidies each year (HUD's target), the annual *added* subsidy cost would average $480 million. By the end of the decade, the *annual* cost would be $4.8 billion. This assumes that the federal government would pay only the marginal difference between the return demanded by lenders and the amounts which households in inadequate units could afford to pay. Moreover, this annual cost would continue into the future until all loans needed to build the new units were repaid, or until almost all families had sufficient incomes to take over full debt payments themselves. If consumer incomes rose rapidly, some of the initial subsidy receivers might be paying their own full costs by the end of the decade, so that the annual cost would decline somewhat. Disregarding this possibility, the *total* subsidy cost of a gradual buildup to the target of 6 million subsidized units by 1980 would be about $26 billion for the entire decade. This is 4.5 times all federal costs of urban renewal in the eighteen years from 1949 through 1966.

In reality, these subsidies to relatively low-income households would not be much larger than the housing subsidies which will be received by middle-income and upper-income households during the same period. All homeowners who pay federal income taxes already benefit from three hidden housing subsidies: they can deduct interest and property taxes from their federally taxable income, and the real benefits they get from occupying their homes are not counted as income. It has been estimated that in 1962 these subsidies amounted to about $2 billion per year for just the 20 percent of U.S. households with the highest income. Since the subsidy to wealthier families *rises* as their incomes increase and tax deductions become more valuable, their total annual subsidy may well equal $4.8 billion by 1980. Thus, extending these subsidies to lower-income households would rectify to some degree the present favoritism toward wealthier people.

OVERCOMING RELOCATION PROBLEMS

Earlier calculations indicated that constructing 27.7 million new housing units by 1980 would involve building about 4.3 million units in central cities. In most older central cities nearly all new housing construction requires prior clearance of existing units, because little usable vacant land is left. The present occupants of those existing units must be relocated first. Even large-scale rehabilitation requires relocation. But most of these occupants have very low incomes, and there is an acute shortage of low rent and low priced housing in these cities. One of the key causes of this shortage is the massive earlier demolition of low-income housing to make way for public improvements like highways and urban renewal projects. These improvements have in effect benefited their middle-income and upper-income users by imposing overcrowding and higher rents upon the lowest-income households—a stunning injustice typical of past public policies regarding housing.

Moreover, a high proportion of the households that would be displaced are Negro. They could find relocation housing only in predominantly white neighborhoods. Thus, massive relocation would speed up the already rapid white exodus from these cities by expanding the areas of Negro occupancy even faster than at present. Such displacement is vehemently resisted both by the Negroes to be displaced and by white residents and politicians. Even middle-class Negroes protest when poor Negroes are moved into nearby public housing projects. Consequently, the massive relocation necessary to build 4.3 million units in central cities before 1980 is now politically impossible in almost all metropolitan areas.

Two kinds of policies are needed to remove this crucial obstacle. The first aims at persuading the occupants of substandard housing to move willingly. They refuse to do so now because (1) present compensation practices fall far short of covering all the true costs of dislocation, (2) there is not enough available housing nearby for them to move into without paying much more or experiencing worse overcrowding, and (3) they resent being herded around without being consulted. One key remedial policy would be awarding both owners and renters "displacement grants" large enough to cover all of their dislocation costs. The Highway Act of 1968 authorizes such payments for road displacement, but they should be expanded and extended to all public programs. A second necessary remedy is engaging in politically sensitive negotiations with both neighborhood groups and individual residents, which will be much easier if generous cash compensation is available.

The third required ingredient is prior creation of adequate housing nearby for displaced families. Some observers have suggested a "roll-over" strategy, using mobile housing units near the housing to be replaced. Residents of the latter could move into the mobile units temporarily. Then they could return to new units on the same site after their original homes were rehabilitated or replaced. The mobile homes would then be moved near the next clearance site. But even this strategy requires more vacant land usable for temporary structures than is available in most large cities. Moreover, demolition and rebuilding now take too long for such a "roll-over" process to work on a large enough scale to allow construction of 4.3 million central-city units by 1980. Another strategy has been suggested: the creation of large "temporary way-station" housing projects on vacant suburban land. These would be occupied by displaced central-city households until new units were created on the sites from which they initially moved. After they moved back to those sites, a new group would move into the "way-station" projects until new units were built for them, and so on. But this policy implies that low-income households can be displaced en masse from one spot to another and back again. Years of relocation experience prove this is impossible. A majority of displaced households would refuse to accept such direction, particularly because it would mean leaving "the action" of the city slum and moving into a foreign suburban environment.

Therefore, the best feasible way to offset the impact of massive displacement upon the existing housing inventory is first to build new units for low-income households on vacant suburban land without trying to shift displaced households into those units directly. If these suburban units are made attractive enough, they will be filled with low-income households who will in turn vacate existing units somewhere. This will ease the market pressure caused by displacement of the households from clearance sites, particularly if the whole process is linked to an intensive housing information campaign in low-income neighborhoods.

If we optimistically assume that half of the 4.3 million new or rehabilitated units to be built in central cities by 1980 can be located on vacant sites therein, about 196,000 units per year must be created on land now occupied by existing housing. I estimate that all publicly supported housing programs have recently caused displacement of about 65,000 units per year in central cities. Therefore, reaching the planned housing targets will require at least tripling the amount of displacement recently generated each year by all housing programs. In large cities, this inescapably involves first building large numbers of new units for low-income households on vacant suburban land.

These considerations bring up the second set of policies needed to overcome relocation problems: those aimed at persuading middle-class Americans, both white and black, willingly to accept significant numbers of low-income households in their communities. These policies will be discussed in the next section.

OPENING UP THE SUBURBS

The hidden assumption in all programs aimed at rapidly improving central-city housing is that large numbers of new housing units for low-income people can be built on vacant suburban land. But up to now almost all suburbs (and many central-city neighborhoods) have vehemently resisted all publicly assisted housing—especially public housing, which is the major "deep" subsidy program now available. Three motives underlie this resistance. First, any influx of low-income households with children tends to add a net burden to local property taxes. Second, Americans who have "made it" into the middle class have traditionally sought to demonstrate their success by segregating themselves from those less affluent. This desire for relative economic and social homogeneity has important functions. It is much easier to pass on cherished values to one's children if they are reared in schools and neighborhoods where only children from families with similar values are found. And personal security is much greater when one lives in an area where nearly all others accept the same standards of public deportment. So each socioeconomic stratum tries to gain control of some local suburban government. It then sets zoning, taxation, education, and other standards which it regards as appropriate to "its own kind." The third exclusionary motive is anti-Negro sentiment, which is still strong among many whites. It is reinforced by their falsely imputing lower-class traits to all Negroes and by their fears that Negro newcomers will depress property values.

No attempts to open up suburban vacant land to low-income central-city households on a large scale are likely to succeed unless they effectively cope with all three motives for exclusion. The first—fiscal self-defense against higher property taxes—can be counteracted only by institutional changes that remove the economic penalties of accepting low-income residents. The following strategies are possible:

Creating grant-in-aid programs which attach bonuses to the incoming low-income households. These bonuses would go to the suburban governments and school boards concerned, thereby making it "profitable" for them to accept poor newcomers.

"Escalating" key taxation and land-use control powers away from individual suburban governments to larger entities, such as counties and metropolitan areas. If all households were within a single jurisdiction, no one would suffer a fiscal loss when low-income households moved from one portion to another. And each small part could not exclude any of the problem-creating uses which must go *somewhere*, but which most suburbanites do not want near them.

Shifting much of the burden for paying for certain expensive services—particularly education and welfare—from local governments to the federal government. This is also desirable because these services should partly reflect national rather than local policies, since they have nationwide effects. Then the fiscal penalties of accepting low-income households in any given suburb would be much smaller and overall property taxes lower.

The last strategy seems far more politically acceptable than the other two. Even so, it requires profound changes in present federal-state-local fiscal and institutional relationships. I do not believe society will adopt such changes fast enough to allow achievement of the "official" housing targets for the 1970s.

Even these profound fiscal changes would not in themselves open up the suburbs sufficiently. At least some escalation of land-use controls to higher levels of government would have to occur too. Yet this is sure to be bitterly resisted unless it is tied in with some kind of financing benefits like those mentioned above—and perhaps will be resisted even then. Again, prospects are bleak for accomplishing this change soon enough to help achieve federal housing targets in the 1970s. Nevertheless, the nation should place high priority on thus formulating and carrying out proposals for modernization of our obsolete local and state government institutions.

Counteracting the other two exclusionary motives in the suburbs will be almost as difficult. Desires to protect local socioeconomic status will probably remain dominant until land-use controls are escalated to bodies with bigger jurisdictions or the federal government is given the power to override them under certain conditions. Moreover, some degree of residential homogeneity along economic (not racial) lines at the neighborhood level is surely desirable. Racial discrimination in housing is already under assault by federal and many state and local ordinances. Fears about property values associated with Negro move-ins might even be mitigated by some form of federal or even private loss-limiting guarantees for nearby property owners over a specified time period.

Many observers believe that the best way to accommodate future growth is to create "new cities" outside existing metropolitan areas. Up to now, most developments labeled "new cities" are really large-scale, multi-land-use subdivisions within or dependent upon present metropolitan areas. Successful development of true new cities is beyond the capability of private enterprise acting alone. It requires special government powers to assemble land, bear some of the "front money" cost of the long development period, provide special incentives to attract industry, subsidize new housing for low-income residents, and establish viable relations with existing county and state governments. Moreover, new cities are a far more expensive form of growth than peripheral sprawl. The latter allows new subdivisions to use existing employment concentrations, utility plants, older housing for poorer households, and transport networks; all these things must first be built from scratch in new cities. It might be worthwhile to subsidize one or two experimental new cities to test the possibilities of large-scale, comprehensively planned construction using innovative technology, and to discover how much they might reduce environmental pollution. But it is doubtful whether any significant fraction of future growth will be accommodated in this way, though large-scale subdivisions near existing settled areas will probably multiply. Politicians deciding whether to spend billions on new cities or on existing metropolitan areas cannot help noticing that the latter already contain millions of voters, whereas there are none in as yet nonexistent new cities.

CHANGING OPERATIONS IN THE BUILDING INDUSTRY

At present, homebuilding in the United States is largely a localized industry dominated by thousands of small operators. This is true partly because there are over 8,300 separate jurisdictions with different building codes. Many of these also have differing subdivision regulations, zoning ordinances, and officials with whom builders must carry out specific negotiations. In addition, housing markets across the nation exhibit wide variations in climate, consumer tastes, topography, and soil conditions. A third reason is that land ownership is so fragmented that private assembly of relatively large parcels is time-consuming, expensive, and often impossible in the absence of any way to compel owners to sell or merge their holdings. The resulting fragmentation of the building industry has serious effects which keep costs higher than they might otherwise be and discourage comprehensive land-use planning. Nearly all builders have businesses so small that they cannot afford to experiment or do research that might cut costs. Also, they cannot sustain national advertising campaigns likely to persuade consumers to accept a standardized product. Even big builders have difficulty undertaking large-scale housing production.

Comprehensive community planning requires development of very large parcels under a single plan. Then the various types of land uses necessary for a balanced community can be laid out with full consideration of their interrelationships. This should result in a spatial pattern that provides nearly optimal efficiency for the area as a whole and maximum economies of scale in construction. A minimum size of at least 1,500 acres is probably necessary for such a development. But now almost every landowner controls a parcel that is tiny compared to this minimum. The result is a helter-skelter development pattern marked by ugliness, inefficient placement of related land uses, skipping over parcels in otherwise developed areas, and failure to take maximum advantage of land-use interrelations or possible economies of large-scale production. In theory, existing zoning arrangements take all such "external" relationships into account. But in practice, zoning laws are altered almost at will by powerful developers. Moreover, there is no effective way to coordinate the zoning in all the many small communities in each metropolitan area.

Several types of remedies are necessary to counteract these deficiencies. First, much greater uniformity of local building codes and other regulations should be required by each state. Second, a national agency—perhaps quasi-private—should be created to set standards for building materials and techniques so that each locality does not have to test every new idea. Third, the federal government should sponsor extensive research in new technology, as it has done so successfully in agriculture. Finally, development on a larger scale in at least some areas should be encouraged or even compelled. Clearly, it would be both impossible and highly undesirable to create a single detailed "master plan" controlling every development in an entire metropolitan area. But it might be practical to require developers in at least some parts of each metropolitan area to operate at a minimum scale—say, 1,500 acres—and to help assemble such parcels. The regulations governing such development could then call for the kind of comprehensive planning described above, as "planned-unit-development" zoning now does. The problems springing from such a requirement are no more severe than the objections originally raised against land-use zoning.

Another constraint blocking technological improvement in housing is insistence by building trades unions on retaining obsolete jurisdictional lines and work practices that render many promising technical ideas economically impractical. Entry into the industry of large manufacturing firms—which have industrial, rather than craft, unions—could conceivably introduce a new element of competition to offset these practices, if local union dominance of building codes and other regulations were ended by adoption of statewide standards. Such large firms would also be more likely to engage in research and development of new products and employ systems analysis and mass production techniques. It is true that the reductions in housing costs which large firms might make are often exaggerated. Many components that go into homes are already manufactured and marketed on a nationwide basis. Moreover, even large firms cannot overcome some of the basic cost-raising aspects of building houses. Yet surely some significant economies of scale and technical innovations would result from the entry of large firms into this industry.

The Department of Housing and Urban Development is promoting the entry of large firms into homebuilding also because they may be better adapted to its subsidized programs. Most small builders are oriented toward relatively rapid turnover of land and capital (whereas HUD's programs take years), close tailoring of their product to local markets (whereas HUD imposes many nationally standardized requirements), and small-scale, nonbureaucratic operations (whereas dealing with HUD requires expert paper-shufflers). Therefore, it is unlikely that most existing builders will ever be strongly motivated to participate in HUD's programs, particularly since the direct profits of doing so are limited. Nevertheless, small builders still have a huge role to play in meeting the nation's housing targets. Over three-fourths of the 27.7 million units needed in the 1970s will not be directly subsidized, so small builders are well suited to construct most of them. Furthermore, large manufacturing firms may prove to be not much more attracted to HUD's programs than small builders. Most big firms demand higher profit rates than HUD is willing to allow on subsidized projects. The 1968 act allows investors to gain sizable tax-sheltered cash flows, but these may not be tempting to large corporations seeking earnings to raise their stock values. However, individual investors in high brackets can indeed benefit from tax-sheltered cash flows. HUD should encourage such individuals and syndicates to participate in its programs by providing maximum technical assistance to limited profit as well as nonprofit housing sponsors (as in the 1968 act).

INCREASING ADMINISTRATIVE EFFECTIVENESS

If all HUD's new programs become burdened with the same administrative red tape snarling existing programs, the nation will not come close to producing 6 million subsidized housing units by 1980. In spite of recent attempts to cut processing time, "administrative overkill" is still the basic condition. Ironically, any potential savings to the federal government are more than canceled by the resulting delays. Moreover, these tactics cause most builders—even big ones—to shun government projects.

Whenever confronted by these facts, HUD blames Congress, with much justification. Congress must face the fact that higher risks of failure, mishandling of funds, and other errors are the inescapable price of moving fast to meet ambitious production goals—in housing or any other program. Reduction of administrative complexity is especially crucial in programs dealing with unsophisticated low-income households, and in attempting to encourage participation by private developers while restricting their profits.

This shift in viewpoint would not be just a trivial concession. It requires an entirely new method of rewarding program administrators at every level. Now, no matter how many new housing units an official expedites, he receives the same reward. But one visible error costs him serious penalties. In contrast, administrators should be given strong positive incentives —including spot promotions, financial bonuses, and special recognition— for their net productivity (total output minus mistakes) rather than for avoidance of gross errors. This may require a revolution in Civil Service regulations, but it is long overdue at all levels of government. In fact, the most crucial innovations which any federal agency can make in the immediate future concern better ways to administer existing programs rather than new program designs.

USING FISCAL REFORM TO SPUR INSTITUTIONAL CHANGE

Solving the housing problem will require both state and local governments to alter existing institutions radically and to receive large funds from the federal government. Therefore, it makes sense for the federal government to use the promise of large-scale assistance as a means of encouraging institutional change. Moreover, it would be irresponsible for the federal government to provide massive funds for state and local governments without demanding major institutional changes. Some programs have already attempted to do this. Generally, the more radical the changes they call for, the less successful they have been. However, the financial carrots offered have been quite small. Two kinds of fiscal incentives would be more effective. The first would be federal assumption of a major share of *all* costs of education and welfare. The institutional changes to be sought in return are described in the policies section. The second fiscal carrot would be federal revenue-sharing of a certain fraction of the income taxes collected from a state (modified by appropriate redistribution formulas among states) in return for basic state constitutional changes, such as those described in the discussion of opening up the suburbs.

The same political power which has prevented Congress from supporting programs to aid large cities or the poor on a massive scale might be arrayed against these institutional changes. After all, the people who live in deprived urban neighborhoods or occupy inadequate housing units form a minority of the total population—no more than 20 percent. Aiding them imposes an immediate cost upon the more affluent majority without providing any instantly perceptible benefits in return. Given these facts, how can sufficient political support be mustered for any of the programs or institutional changes suggested herein?

The only answer is through effective political leadership. It first must find those of the affluent majority who would directly gain from each specific change needed and persuade them to lend intensive support to that action. For example, many suburban industrialists would probably support middle-income and lower-income housing on suburban vacant land because they need more workers. Second, leadership must present to the public as a whole the most persuasive case possible for the entire set of institutional changes and programs needed to achieve its goals. Third, it must develop means of "packaging" key changes so that they become linked to other actions that provide clearly evident benefits to the majority described above.

Summary of Policy Recommendations

These are some of the policies that could move the nation toward its housing goals, even if those goals cannot realistically be achieved by 1980.

ANCILLARY FACILITIES

1. Forcefully carry out and expand the Model Cities Program, emphasizing more radical experiments and technical innovations and enlarging incentives for participation.
2. Prepare national public opinion for the large costs of both upgrading existing deprived neighborhoods and building adequate new environments for future housing.
3. Greatly improve coordination among federal agencies controlling components of the Model Cities Program.
4. Provide substantial federal aid for expanded administrative staffs of state and local governments and for improved training of such staffs.
5. Seek larger federal appropriations for facilities that will aid in both upgrading deprived neighborhoods and serving new population growth.
6. Sponsor comprehensive surveys and studies to measure accurately our real needs for housing and environmental improvements.
7. Have the Internal Revenue Service disallow all depreciation allowances, property tax deductions, and interest deductions on properties in designated "high deterioration" zones within large cities unless the owners' tax returns are accompanied by certificates of full code compliance issued by local authorities. Also, federal examiners of banks and savings and loan associations should not count mortgages on properties in such areas as valid assets unless they are similarly documented.
8. Obtain new legislation to support subsidized home and neighborhood maintenance services in designated "high deterioration" neighborhoods. These services would be operated through contracts with newly formed firms run by local residents.

FINANCIAL POLICIES

1. Attract large manufacturing corporations into the housing construction and ownership business by developing attractive tax credits and other incentives and removing obstacles to large-scale housing production (as recommended elsewhere in this paper). Such corporations could tap sources of funds not now used for housing, conduct national advertising campaigns to win acceptance for standardized housing, carry out large-scale production, engage in greater research and development activities, utilize industrial unions with less restrictive work rules, and bargain more effectively with building trades unions because of their size. The 1968 act aims at this objective by offering depreciation advantages to corporations and other investors, but more incentives will probably be needed.
2. Continue liberalization of state usury laws which now prevent rates on mortgage loans from rising to levels competitive with other investments in times of "tight money."
3. Use income taxation and other fiscal devices to "cool off" the economy as inflationary pressures mount rather than rely upon higher interest rates.
4. Develop a form of mortgage with variable interest rates tied to movements in the prime bank rate or some other index. To keep monthly payments constant, varying interest rates could take the form of changeable loan length.

MANPOWER PROGRAMS

1. Expand the supply of construction workers tremendously by overhauling existing apprenticeship practices in the building trades unions. Union agreements to allow low-skilled nonunion labor to work on local projects at wages which are less than union scale need to be made on a much broader basis.
2. Pay monetary fees to unions which participate in on-the-job training.
3. Set up special training programs to teach currently unemployed residents of central-city low-income neighborhoods the skills necessary for constructing housing.
4. Contract and subcontract as many portions of central-city housing tasks as possible to firms run by residents of low-income areas, especially Negroes.

SUPPLY AND DEMAND POLICIES

1. Apply major federal efforts to expand the production capacity of the housing industry, starting immediately.
2. Keep the buildup of subsidized demand generated by federally supported housing programs gradual enough to avoid major dislocations that might cause rising prices for all basic housing inputs.
3. Reconsider the stated national policy of trying to "lump" so much housing production in a single decade, and instead strive for targets which are both more realistic and less likely, if attained, to generate major dislocations in the housing industry.

HOUSING SUBSIDIES

1. Alter and greatly expand public housing and public leasing programs as follows: (a) Emphasize small-scale projects on scattered sites utilizing low-rise apartments, townhouses, and detached duplex or single family units. These characteristics should be promoted regarding both newly constructed and leased units. The key objective is not to overwhelm the local neighborhood or dominate the local public school with residents of public housing, but rather to have those residents form a relatively small part of both overall and school populations. This would help make public housing acceptable in many areas that now reject it. (b) Sell units within existing projects to tenants whose incomes have risen above existing eligibility, as allowed in the 1968 act. (c) Drastically reduce supervisory and administrative review requirements for "turn-key" construction of public housing. (d) Develop new public housing units in "mixed" projects with other publicly assisted units serving higher-income families. The public housing units should be physically integrated with other units as closely as possible and kept to a minority of each mixed project. Their tenants should be screened to minimize overloading with families in the most difficult circumstances. (e) Eliminate existing unit-cost restrictions on public housing and build many more amenities and better design into new units, thereby making them easier to convert to ownership and more acceptable in better areas. (f) Intensify social services in large projects inhabited mainly by "multi-problem" families; pay residents to run the services. (g) Improve project administrative procedures; encourage greater tenant participation, with monetary incentives for better maintenance.

2. Set up and carry out the many subsidy programs newly created in the 1968 act.
3. Seek much larger appropriations for existing and newly passed programs.
4. Set up locally run educational services to teach participants in new housing programs proper methods of housekeeping, financial responsibility, and management.

RELOCATION AND COMPENSATION PRACTICES

1. Speed up the entire site selection, acquisition, relocation, and demolition process.
2. Pay much higher compensation to most displaced households and businesses, whether owners or renters.
3. Link demolition of housing units in specific projects to "compensating" construction or rehabilitation of similar units nearby, or on vacant land in nearby suburbs if that is the only feasible location. An extreme version of this policy would be that no public agency—federal, state, or local—could tear down any housing unit without first putting up another one somewhere in the same metropolitan area available to the same income and ethnic group, and offered to the displaced household. Some such policy (though not necessarily on a one-for-one basis) would halt the current practice of constantly making the poorest big-city households worse off by reducing the total supply of low-priced housing.
4. Provide many more options for displaced low-income families to relocate in subsidized housing (assuming that more such housing is built).
5. Explicitly face the impact of relocation upon the ethnic change of big cities, and take account of it in planning, rather than ignoring it as at present.

POLICIES TO OPEN UP THE SUBURBS

1. Abolish the present "Workable Program" requirement that compels all cities to meet certain prerequisites to receive any federally subsidized housing programs within their boundaries (including explicit local legislative approval of such programs). If this cannot be done, make all forms of federal urban construction, planning, or other assistance (including sewer and water grants and highways funds) contingent upon adoption by local legislatures of Workable Programs. At present, many suburbs

deliberately refuse to adopt them so as to exclude all federally subsidized housing.

2. Seek legislative changes to enable public housing authorities in large cities to lease units outside the boundaries of those cities.

3. Persuade county or state public housing authorities to build new relatively small projects on unincorporated land outside central cities.

4. Provide planning grants to metropolitan housing agencies privately formed to build housing in suburban areas, and help those agencies get project funding under the new programs in the 1968 act.

5. Require that the new ownership assistance program in the 1968 act (which aids low-income households in home purchases via interest subsidies) insure that at least 30 percent of the units it subsidizes in any metropolitan area are located outside the central city in that area.

6. Offer grants to state planning agencies for studies of the socioeconomic impact of existing zoning ordinances and for developing "model" zoning codes or reformed zoning legislation.

7. Expand existing programs which set up housing information services in low-income central-city areas. These local offices should provide data on suburban housing available to minorities from both private parties and public agencies.

8. Put pressure on all firms receiving federal manufacturing contracts to help insure that workers of all races and creeds can freely obtain housing in the immediate vicinity of their plants.

9. Experimentally develop one or two "new cities" outside of major metropolitan areas, using the entire spectrum of HUD and other federal programs.

POLICIES TO IMPROVE THE BUILDING INDUSTRY

1. Provide funds for states to develop standardized building codes to apply to all communities in each state, with some elements uniform in all states.

2. Set up a single code-certification and testing agency (run by a combination of private and public members) to develop building and housing code standards, certify and test new products and processes (or approve such tests conducted by other bona fide agencies), review and certify existing codes insofar as they meet national standards, and act as a clearinghouse for other aspects of code improvement and standardization.

3. Expand HUD's existing research program (which is now under $20

million per year, as compared with over $7 billion in defense research, $600 million in agricultural research, and over $4 billion in space research).

4. Try to persuade building trades unions to break down some of their jurisdictional rigidities as part of overall market expansion and of new training programs.

5. Encourage states to formulate and adopt new land development regulations that would generate more large-scale, comprehensively planned projects.

6. Provide technical assistance and counseling to limited-profit corporations willing to participate in HUD's programs.

ADMINISTRATIVE REFORMS

1. Radically alter existing HUD procedures for application approval and project review. Initial cost calculations should be delegated to the long-term lender and merely reviewed by HUD. Much of this review process should be computerized. Later reviews of progress should be done on a randomized, sample basis like that used by the Internal Revenue Service.

2. Eliminate present congressional requirements to reduce HUD's staff.

3. Completely reverse the incentive structure of program administrators, as explained earlier.

FISCAL REFORMS TO ENCOURAGE INSTITUTIONAL CHANGE

1. Shift almost all welfare costs and a large fraction of basic educational costs from local governments to the federal government (perhaps via states) in return for adoption of reduced property taxes, more uniform property tax rates, broadening of educational district boundaries to link central cities and suburbs, shifts in educational fund allocation to favor the most deprived groups, reform of welfare regulations, standardization of welfare benefits, and shifts in powers to control land use to jurisdictions covering larger geographic areas.

2. Offer major revenue sharing of federal tax receipts to states for a five-year period in return for certain basic constitutional reforms, including escalation of land-use controls.

Conclusion: Rhetoric Versus Reality

The preceding analysis indicates that there are overwhelming obstacles to the construction of 27.7 million new or rehabilitated housing units—or even 26 million—by 1980. The same obstacles make it extremely unlikely that the United States will create 6 million such units for lower and moderate income groups by that date. In fact, adoption of the national priorities and policies necessary to reach these official targets might cause adverse effects that would injure more low-income households than the housing would benefit. What, then, should we think of the housing targets set forth in the Housing and Urban Development Act of 1968, and endorsed by HUD?

In my opinion, a fair appraisal must take into account the dilemma faced by responsible politicians in our democracy. In order to overcome widespread congressional and public resistance to new expenditures, the administration is tempted to exaggerate the potential effectiveness of anything it proposes. It therefore makes rhetorical promises that each new program will provide a "total solution" to the problems concerned. The antipoverty program will "end" poverty; the Model Cities Program will "completely renovate" slum areas; and HUD's housing programs will "wipe out" substandard housing—all in the very near future.

These rhetorical claims appear patently false to anyone who knows much about the problems concerned. Moreover, they have a devastating long-run impact upon the citizenry's confidence in government programs —and even authority in general. For such claims at first tend to generate great expectations among the relatively poorly informed persons suffering from the ills concerned. But repeated disillusionment eventually induces a deep cynicism toward all government programs. Even though most federal programs actually produce many benefits, they inevitably fall far short of carrying out the promises made in order to get them passed.

In setting a goal of 26 million new or rehabilitated units in the 1970s, including 6 million publicly assisted units, Congress and HUD have once more engaged in this dubious strategy. They have substituted rhetoric for reality, thereby almost guaranteeing the "failure" of their own programs to reach the overoptimistic goals they have set. I sympathize with their desire to spur the nation to higher housing production by setting idealized targets beyond our present capacity. Moreover, a great many of the policies that society would have to adopt to reach those targets are probably worth doing sooner or later. The sooner we adopt many of them, the more quickly we can achieve the national housing goal of "a decent home and a suitable living environment for every American family."

Nevertheless, I believe our housing targets should be both more realistic and more flexible. The nation cannot simply measure the housing needs that have accumulated throughout its history and decide to satisfy all those needs within a single decade, regardless of what happens in any other aspect of national life. Housing is both too important and not important enough for this approach to work. Its major importance in our economy means that how much housing we produce is inescapably bound up with other key aspects of national performance, such as the levels of employment, defense production, and spending on other social needs. But housing is not so crucial that we must shape our entire economic and institutional behavior solely to solve the housing problem in one decade.

Therefore, even though the targets in the 1968 act are an accurate measure of our current housing needs, I do not believe we should commit ourselves to reach them by any precise date. We should use them to identify the major directions of change needed to solve the problem, and start moving in those directions as fast as possible—as the rest of the 1968 act does. We should set precisely quantified targets only for the short run.

This approach is perfectly suited to the requirement in the 1968 act that the President report to Congress each year what his annual housing goal is and what progress the nation has made toward the previous year's goal. Even more important, this approach recognizes that government programs should reinforce the credibility of public authorities by producing results consistent with their official promises. Only in this way can housing officials build national confidence in their capabilities rather than contribute to growing public doubt that any government program can accomplish its objectives.

Furthermore, fostering such confidence is vital in moving the nation toward its basic housing goal of "a decent home and a suitable environment for every American family." The preceding analysis has shown the enormous complexity and depth of the changes in public policies and institutions at all levels necessary to reach that goal. Only outstanding leadership supported by strong public confidence will enable us to make those many changes as swiftly as the urgency of our housing needs warrants. Armed with such leadership, with the tools in the 1968 act and earlier legislation, and with a comprehensive understanding of what must be done on many action fronts involved, the nation can and should press toward solving the housing problem as fast as possible. We may not arrive at a solution within one decade, but we certainly can move much faster than in the past. The crucial role of housing in the lives of millions of Americans—especially those now suffering from miserably inadequate shelter—demands such a high priority effort.

JAMES Q. WILSON

CRIME AND LAW ENFORCEMENT

In this period of intense concern about crime, our ignorance about how to solve the problem may create special difficulties. Lacking a proven methodology for testing law enforcement proposals, we are in danger of turning a practical problem into an ideological one, passionately choosing sides over whether the right strategy is to arm or disarm the police, impeach or enshrine the Supreme Court, hire or fire prison guards. Moreover, in responding to the emotions that crime arouses, we may dangerously oversell our ability to lower the crime rate. Put another way, to induce Congress to supply funds that may make possible a 5 percent reduction in auto thefts we may have to promise (implicitly, to be sure) a 20 percent reduction in murders.

Now that the Crime Control and Safe Streets Act of 1968 has been passed and signed in response to mounting public concern, it is necessary to ask just how safe our streets are likely to become as a result. Leaving aside the gun-control provisions the act contains and the revisions in court procedures it attempts, this legislation supplies federal funds and a measure of federal leadership to deal with some of the deficiencies in manpower, training, recruitment, and planning that afflict state and local police departments. If wisely spent, the money will help at least the more energetic departments to improve their image, staffing, equipment, or procedures. As appropriations under this bill grow over the next few years, more departments will benefit. On a sufficiently large scale, these efforts may make possible significant gains in the size, facilities, and community relations of those agencies that know how to get federal dollars. These agencies, however, are probably only a small fraction of even the 320 or so police departments serving cities of over 50,000 population. More important, we cannot be optimistic that any of these changes will lower the crime rate or increase the apprehending of criminals.

The greatest opportunity afforded by the new federal involvement is that it may lead to experiments that will shed some light on the public safety problem that troubles most citizens. The greatest risk is that federal money will be pumped into the system without regard to whether it is in fact purchasing more of that desired safety.

Crime deterrence is not, of course, the only objective of law enforcement agencies. They have, in addition, important responsibilities for safeguarding individual liberties, providing community services, reducing or managing urban tensions, and handling large-scale disorders. Fulfilling these responsibilities better is eminently worthwhile, but doing so is not the same as reducing crime; indeed, in some instances it may be inconsistent with the latter.

Moreover, while the focus of public action as well as public concern is on the *police* role in crime deterrence, it is by no means clear that the police are the most important agency for that responsibility. The police have the most visible and dramatic functions, but most police work is not concerned with catching criminals or even dealing with crime. The fraction of police activity that does deal with serious crime typically begins after the crime has been committed, and those criminals who are caught are turned over to other agencies (courts, prosecutors, correctional systems) for disposition.

In sum, an adequate response to the public concern over crime must begin with a recognition that we know relatively little about how to prevent crime; that, to the extent that it can be prevented, it can be only as a result of the operation of a complex criminal justice system and not just by more intensive police activity; and that much experimentation will be necessary before we can make changes on the basis of much more than hunch. In this article, I shall examine the volume of those crimes most frightening to the public (primarily violent crimes among strangers occurring in public places), how such crimes and criminals are handled by the criminal justice system, and a few of the changes in that system that seem likely to produce the greatest increase in public safety. The underlying causes of crime, insofar as they are known, will be given only slight attention, because only broad social changes extending over long periods of time are likely to reach these causes. Poverty, broken families, inadequate education, and discrimination no doubt contribute to criminality, but these matters are best treated in the other chapters devoted to programs for social change. The focus of this paper will be on what, if anything, law enforcement institutions can do about crime.

Crime in the Streets

Attempting to deal with "the crime problem" as though it were a single entity is a mistake, for the label "crime" includes many acts that have little in common other than the violation of a legal code. Embezzlement, prostitution, murder, and auto theft are neither committed by the same kinds of persons nor best deterred by the same law enforcement strategies. Some types of crime may be decreasing at the same time that other kinds are increasing. Accordingly, measuring "the crime problem" by the total crime rate is misleading.

Common experience suggests that the kind of crime that produces the greatest anxiety is "street crime"—that is, crime involving violence or the threat of violence that occurs in public places (on the street, in business establishments, in subways or parks) and that is unpredictable or unexpected. A housewife whose purse is violently snatched by a stranger may be in some sense more seriously victimized than a man knifed by his mistress at the height of a bedroom quarrel—the former, unlike the latter, did not provoke or anticipate the attack and accordingly feels herself at the mercy of circumstance.

The most common street crimes are assaults and robberies. We can make only the crudest estimate of how many such crimes are committed every year. The number reported to the police (and by them to the Federal Bureau of Investigation) is an unreliable figure, primarily because not all victims are willing to call the police. Fortunately, the President's Commission on Law Enforcement and Administration of Justice carried out, through the National Opinion Research Center, a survey of 10,000 American households to find out how many had been victimized by any of several important crimes in 1965. Combining the number of crimes officially reported with the survey estimate of those unreported, we can guess at the true level of assault and robbery. In 1966, about 150,000 robberies were reported to the police throughout the country; the survey suggests that about half again as many robberies were in fact committed as police reports indicate. The total number of robberies may have been 225,000 in one year, though admittedly some of these may be minor thefts involving a schoolboy taking another's lunch money. There were also about 230,000 aggravated (felonious) assaults reported to the police in 1966; the household survey suggests there may be another 230,000 assaults which occur but go unreported, primarily because they involve relatives or "friends" who think of the assault as a private rather than a police matter or who fear the disfavor or vengeance of their assailant if they "squeal."

Assault occurs primarily among acquaintances; robbery occurs (we conjecture) primarily among strangers. One study in St. Louis showed that only 20 percent of all serious assaults known to the police occurred among strangers. A study in Washington, D.C., suggested that two-thirds of all known rape victims were attacked by persons with whom they were acquainted. There are almost no comparable studies of robbery, but in the household survey, robbery victims reported themselves as much more willing to notify the police than assault victims and much less likely to regard robbery as a "private matter." This implies, though it does not prove, that suspect and victim are less frequently known to each other in robbery than in assault cases. This conjecture is strengthened by the fact that while the apparent motive for assault is typically passion or rage, that for robbery is money.

Furthermore, robbery is more likely to be a street crime than is assault. A Chicago study showed that 62 percent of the female victims of assault were attacked indoors, and most of these (46 percent of the total) were attacked in their own homes. Over half of all robberies, by contrast, take place on the street and most of the rest occur in business establishments.

The causes of these crimes are not known with any certainty and, to the extent that we can make plausible guesses, it is not likely that society can do much in the short run (say, a generation or two) to reduce those causes significantly. We know that persons living in certain circumstances—young males with low income, little education, unstable employment, and living as part of a broken family in dilapidated housing in the central parts of a large city—are more likely to commit a crime, especially a crime of violence. But not everybody in these circumstances is criminal, nor do equivalent circumstances produce equivalent criminality in all cultures and societies (the slums of Dublin or London are less violently criminal than those of New York or Chicago). Nor does a lower-class milieu produce the same criminal tendencies at all stages of the life cycle. Of the young lower-class males who are criminal, a large fraction stop being so, for reasons we do not fully understand, by the time they are thirty years old. Even if we could be quite confident of the "causes" of violent crime, some are beyond our power to change. The largest reductions in crime would be made if we could change men into women and convert all persons who are sixteen to twenty-five years of age into persons who are thirty to thirty-nine. There are some things we could perhaps change, but no one would want to. For example, there is evidence that crimes of violence, like women's skirts, go up in periods of prosperity, but few people favor creating a depression (to say nothing of lowering hemlines).

Things we both can do and are willing to do will take many years to be effective and, in the short run, may even produce adverse consequences. For example, reducing the number of people in a lower-class status in our central cities will probably reduce the real, though perhaps not the reported, crime rate. But, as the other papers in this volume suggest, this reduction will not be easily attained, especially if the goal is changing the life-style of people and not simply increasing their incomes. Furthermore, progress made in this direction in the cities will induce more and more people to leave the rural countryside and migrate to the cities, thereby replenishing the ranks of those most likely to become a police statistic. Complicating the statistical problem is that in some of the rural areas from which migrants come (such as Mississippi), crimes against Negroes are greatly undercounted because such crimes are not taken seriously by sheriffs and police officers. By migrating to the cities, poor people leave areas where crime is not counted and enter areas where it is; the "national crime rate" accordingly goes up.

If the causes of crime are so complex and hard to understand, the changes over time in the rates of crime are equally obscure. Most studies agree that during the period immediately after the Civil War the rate of violent crime in the big cities was higher than at any other time in our history. Murder is the crime which is counted most accurately (but not with perfect accuracy, since some murders will be mistakenly counted as accidents or suicides). The murder rate during the last several decades, until recently, has shown a generally downward trend in the nation as a whole but a sharp upward trend in many, but not all, big cities. Since murder is overwhelmingly a lower-class crime, and since cities have steadily lost their middle class and acquired, we suspect, a larger lower class, it is not surprising to learn that though murder may be less common in the nation, such murders as remain may be increasingly concentrated in the cities. (Why some big cities have *not* had an increase in the murder rate is puzzling.) If murder, which we count fairly accurately, is a reliable index to assault, which we do not count accurately, then assaults may be following the same pattern as murder—down slightly nationally but up drastically in at least several cities. Unfortunately, we do not know that the murder rate is a good index to the assault rate. Thus, the only way we can get a reliable estimate of changes in the true rate of assault is to repeat (at, say, five-year intervals) the household victimization survey. Such resurveys are essential if we are to measure accurately the success of crime-prevention efforts.

The Criminal Justice System

The President's Commission on Law Enforcement drew attention to the way in which law enforcement agencies function together (or more commonly, fail to function together) as parts of a system. Each element of the system has at least three functions: a *crime-deterrence* capability, because people fear being arrested, or indicted, or tried, or convicted, or going to jail, or being on probation; a *crime-reduction* capability, because people while under arrest, or in jail, or on probation have their opportunities for committing additional crimes reduced in varying degrees; and a *crime-prevention* capability, at least to the extent that people who have been through the system have been "rehabilitated"—that is, induced to prefer noncriminal to criminal activities.

Many people ignore or discount the value of these various functions, emphasizing instead only one function. For example, some persons take crime prevention (that is, rehabilitation or reform) to be the major purpose of the system; if it fails to rehabilitate, then it has failed generally. But a system that rehabilitates no one may still be useful if it reduces crime by keeping unrehabilitated criminals under surveillance or in confinement. Conversely, a system which keeps almost no one in confinement may have a high deterrent value if the costs of coming into contact with the system at all are so high as not to be worth any gain from crime, however great (if, for example, all robbers were shot immediately by the police without trial).

Over the last hundred years or so, we have become, at least in principle, more concerned about the rehabilitation function of the system. This has led, in turn, to a reduction in the severity of sentences and the degree of confinement, and to increasing the length of time before sentence is imposed (in order that presentence investigations and psychiatric examinations can be carried out). But these steps may reduce the crime-deterrence or the crime-reduction capacities of the system. Such a loss would be tolerable if it were exceeded by a gain in rehabilitation. Unfortunately, so far we have no reliable way to measure the net result.

Ideally, one would like to be able to evaluate the criminal justice system by determining, at each decision point in it, the gains, in terms of various social values, and the costs, in terms of both these values and scarce resources, of alternative dispositions of the offender. But we cannot come even close to such an analysis. We do not know very much about even the effect of various dispositions on recidivism, that is, on the rate at which people become repeat offenders.

Rather than attempt to answer all the difficult questions that confront anyone trying to devise an ideal criminal justice system or even a comprehensible model of the present system, we will try to evaluate in crude terms the effectiveness of each element of the system in dealing with actual or potential street crimes of the sort that most concern us. At each step we ask what is done now, what are the results, and what changes, within the general legal framework that now exists, might be made to increase public safety.

THE COMMUNITY

Violent crimes in public places may be reduced if these places are more easily kept under public and police surveillance and if victims can easily call for assistance. It would seem reasonable that well-lighted, heavily trafficked streets and parks are less likely to be the scenes of surreptitious assaults than dark, lonely places. Many communities have embarked on ambitious street and park lighting programs partly to reduce crime. While there is as yet surprisingly little solid evidence that such methods have a substantial or lasting effect on crime, this may be more the result of a failure to study the efforts scientifically than a failure of the efforts themselves. At the very least, such methods, by making people *feel* safer, may bring more people out into public places and this, in turn, may reduce crime in those areas.

Bringing public places under surveillance mechanically is on first thought appealing but, unfortunately, suffers from high cost and high probability of error. Various alarm, sensor, and signal devices have been proposed by which citizens could call the police or intruders could be detected, but so far most of them would have a high false alarm rate, or would be prohibitively expensive, or both. Further research might overcome these weaknesses. In the meantime, some cities are experimenting with installing call boxes on street corners from which a citizen could call either police or fire services by opening a door and speaking into a microphone. Because one must use his own voice rather than just push a button, false alarms are less likely; because many cities already have fire alarm boxes installed on street corners, the cost of converting to a combined police-fire system is lower than for a wholly new alarm system. It remains to be seen, however, what gains, if any, these methods will produce.

Of greater usefulness, but presenting much greater organizational difficulties, is the mobilization of citizen auxiliaries to the police whose function, among others, would be to put more sets of eyes and ears onto the street to detect crimes, summon the police, and, by their presence, deter criminals. Getting a neighborhood involved in helping to police itself may be the single most effective addition to local police practice, but it is also the single most controversial one. The police themselves are often fearful that such groups will have one of two opposite defects—either they will be self-recruited vigilantes who, out of excessive zeal, abuse their authority and take the law into their own hands, or they will be organizations designed, not to police the neighborhood, but to police the police by reporting on official misconduct. These problems should not lead the police and the community to abandon efforts in this direction. Citizens' patrols have been organized in Harlem, Indianapolis, and Los Angeles on a volunteer basis, and more such efforts ought to be possible. If a civil defense and air raid warden system was possible given the (remote) possibility of enemy air attacks during the Second World War, a public safety patrol system ought to be possible given the much greater threat (at least in central city locations) posed by street criminals today. Assigning citizen alarm and radio systems only to the members of such units would certainly reduce the cost and probably the false alarm rates of such equipment.

All these methods are likely to be most effective against street crimes, and thus, even though the total volume of crimes of violence may not decrease substantially by using the techniques described above, any decrease that does take place may be in that form of criminality most productive of fear and public concern. One of the problems with current citizens' patrol experiments is that, like almost all efforts in law enforcement, no careful evaluation is being made. A success, or a failure, is likely to go unrecorded or else be recorded in unsystematic and unconvincing terms.

THE POLICE

The police can be effective against street crime, in theory at least, either by *deterring* the crime through intensive patrol and surveillance or by *apprehending* the suspect through a quick response to citizen alarms. Several experiments have been carried out to test the effectiveness of both measures, but few, if any, have been evaluated rigorously. Nonetheless, most of the available evidence, shaky though it may be, points to the possibility of reducing street crimes by more intensive police action. Yet many of the experiments remain only that—not sustained in the innovating city and not copied in other cities. The reasons are primarily economic and political—a shortage of resources with which to maintain high patrol coverage of city streets, and political conflict over the value and problems of patrol action.

The best known experiment has been "Operation 25" of the New York City Police Department. Carried out for a four-month period in 1954, it involved more than doubling the police force assigned to a high crime precinct (the 25th) in Manhattan, an area then composed about equally of whites, Negroes, and Puerto Ricans. Most of the additional men were assigned to walking beats—the number of foot posts increased from 55 to 89, the length of the average post was shortened, and no post was left vacant; previously, as many as two-thirds of the nominal posts in fact had no man assigned. Additional detectives, juvenile officers, traffic officers, and others were also employed.

Serious crimes in Precinct 25 declined during the experimental period compared to the same period the year before, and the reduction was greatest for street crimes. Street robberies (muggings) fell from 69 in 1953 to 7 in 1954; auto thefts fell from 78 to 24. Murder, primarily a "private" crime, did not decrease at all; in fact, it increased from 6 to 8. Felonious assault, also a crime that occurs primarily indoors, decreased, but the decline was relatively much less than that recorded for robbery, the number of assaults dropping from 185 to 132. Reported burglaries decreased also, the greatest decline being in those in which entry was made from the front (presumably because the front of buildings was more continuously under police surveillance). For almost all crimes, the percentage culminating in an arrest rose dramatically, with many of the arrests being made at the scene of the crime by the patrolman.

The major criticism of Operation 25, and of similar experiments elsewhere, is that no report was made of what increase, if any, occurred in the crime rate in adjacent precincts. Apparently such increases do occur, according to many police officers. But this objection does not mean that saturation patrol work is useless; it only suggests that the coverage must be far wider than one precinct. Of course, if all of Manhattan were given such heavy patrol coverage, perhaps the crime would be displaced into Brooklyn and the Bronx, and if all of New York City were so covered it would be displaced into Nassau County. But such objections require one to believe, first, that there is a constant level of criminality in society which must appear somewhere and second, that criminals are infinitely mobile, prepared to travel great distances to evade police surveillance. The first assumption can be proved or disproved only by experiment, but it seems unlikely. The second assumption can be directly challenged by facts we already have. Most crimes of violence and most street crimes are committed very near the residence of the offender. Professional criminals (jewel thieves, bank robbers, and the like) may travel great distances, but most crime, so far as we know, is committed by locals.

If there are some grounds for believing that close patrol deters street crime, why is there not more close patrol work? One reason is the shortage of manpower—to do for all of Manhattan what was done for Precinct 25 would have required several hundred more patrolmen than the department had. The other reason is political. In many places, "saturation" police patrol has led to complaints by community leaders, especially in nonwhite areas, that the neighborhood is being subjected to "harassment"—the excessive or unjustified stopping and questioning of persons.

The problems created by aggressive patrol have been alluded to in the reports of the President's crime commission and the National Advisory Commission on Civil Disorders. Some observers have concluded that, because these patrol methods create community tensions, they ought to be discontinued; but it would be a mistake to take this general view. In the first place, saturation and aggressive patrol are not the same thing—the former involves an increase in manpower, the latter an increase in police-initiated intervention in citizen affairs. And in any event, the problem is to weigh, in the specific case, the gains in public safety against the costs in police-community relations of these patrol tactics. Furthermore, community tensions and antipolice attitudes can result from real or apparent failure of law enforcement just as they can result from overly zealous law enforcement. The crucial task is to devise carefully controlled experiments to discover whether the increases in public safety that apparently result from methods such as Operation 25 can be duplicated in other areas and made permanent, and, as part of the experiment, to measure before and during the experiment public reaction in the neighborhood to the police methods employed.

Increased patrol effort is not the only way by which the police may deter or apprehend more perpetrators of street crimes, but it may be the most important method. Another is to increase the speed with which the police can respond to citizen calls for help. Studies done by the crime commission suggest that the faster the police can respond to a citizen call, the greater the likelihood of an arrest. In Los Angeles, for example, the average total response time in emergency cases resulting in an arrest was 4.11 minutes; the response time in similar cases not resulting in an arrest was 6.30 minutes. Many police departments have made major efforts to improve their communications system; one of the most advanced methods is that now being developed by the New York City Police Department where a computer is used to assist dispatchers in locating, assigning, and monitoring patrol cars. But there are limits to how large such gains can be. First, no matter how fast the police dispatch a car, a citizen must still find the means to call the police, and that may take some time. Second, since arrests occur primarily in cases where the victim can identify the suspect, gains in response time will have little value for crimes committed by unknown suspects (many street robberies are in this category). And third, because the police find improvements in communications systems to be relatively noncontroversial and even glamorous, they are likely to emphasize this approach to law enforcement (and to get financial support for it) over the more controversial patrol methods. Thus, the gains from shortening response time are likely to be rather quickly seized by most large departments while the gains, if any, from other methods are likely to be slower in coming.

Devising an optimal crime-deterrence strategy for a police department is made difficult by the absence, in the vast majority of departments, of any meaningful research and planning effort. Such "planning" units as exist often do little more than compile crime reports and analyze vehicle maintenance. Even with respect to the need most keenly felt by the police —additional manpower—many departments fail to make as convincing a case as they might. Typically, they speak of being "under authorized strength," but this is almost meaningless, for the "authorized strength" is an arbitrary force level determined by city councils or the like. The real problem is to show the consequences, in terms of response time, patrol coverage, and probable crime-deterrence value of additional manpower deployed in various ways. Operation 25, response-time studies, and other fragmentary bits of evidence suggest that substantial increases in police manpower are advantageous, but only carefully documented analyses and demonstration projects are likely to establish that advantage persuasively or, more important, to indicate how best that additional manpower can be used.

THE COURTS

Though much remains to be done, more effort in combating street crime has been made by the police than by any others in the criminal justice system. Major additional gains may require more expert attention to the courts and correctional institutions, perhaps the most neglected elements of the system.

When all crimes other than traffic offenses are examined, the vast majority of the persons arrested by the police have been arrested before. According to one estimate, 87.5 percent of the 5 million arrests made each year in the United States are of persons with a prior arrest record. This same study, done for the crime commission, indicates that a male who is arrested once (for a nontraffic offense) will on the average be arrested more than seven times in his lifetime. Even allowing for substantial error in these estimates, it is clear that the police are dealing with a large number of repeaters. *Therefore, considerable gains in terms of public safety can be made if, after the first arrest, the probability of a second offense is substantially reduced by court and correctional programs.*

A study by the FBI of "careers in crime," based on a sample of persons involved in the federal criminal process (and thus perhaps somewhat different from those involved in state and local criminal proceedings) showed that, of nearly 18,000 persons arrested in 1963, 55 percent were rearrested by 1966. Of those arrested initially for robbery, the principal crime with which we are concerned, it seemed to make little difference whether they had been placed on probation or had served a sentence and then been paroled—52 percent of the former and 45 percent of the latter were rearrested within thirty months. Recidivism was highest for the younger offenders—over 60 percent of those under the age of thirty when first arrested for robbery were rearrested for some offense. (Robbery, and crimes of violence generally, do not produce the highest recidivism rates; such rates are much higher for property crimes, especially auto theft and burglary.) A 1964 study by Daniel Glaser—*The Effectiveness of a Prison and Parole System*—of the persons who are returned to prison after release generally supports these findings. (The percentage returned to prison is of course lower than the percentage rearrested, since some who are rearrested are given probation, are acquitted, or otherwise dismissed.) His figures (for both state and federal prisons) show that the younger the prisoner, and the younger the age at which a prisoner was first arrested, the greater the chances of being reimprisoned. Of those imprisoned in California for robbery, 38 percent are reimprisoned within two years. Race does not affect these rates; Negroes and whites are equally likely to be reimprisoned.

To reduce recidivism, the court and correctional system should aim to provide each offender with that disposition, subject to the constraints of fair procedure and maximum sentences, most likely to reduce his inclination or opportunity to commit further offenses. But the system is rarely managed in this way at all; instead, judges, probation officers, prison officials, parole authorities, and others struggle to cope with the immediate organizational pressures facing them—primarily, how to deal with a very large volume of cases under severe budget limitations. Judges seek to get through their crowded calendars, probation officers to keep track of their large case loads, and wardens to find space and funds for housing their prisoners.

But the answer is not simply to ease these organizational pressures by supplying either more money or fewer prisoners, though these may be prerequisites. The result of simply decongesting the system would only be to make it easier for the system to contribute its share to the maintenance of a high recidivism rate.

Some persons believe that the problem begins with the courts because they give offenders "too many breaks" or "soft sentences" or because they have "tied the hands" of the police. These arguments are hard to evaluate. We do not know what effect severity of sentence has on the prospects of recidivism and we are only beginning to gather evidence on the effect of new court-imposed rules of evidence on the arrest and conviction of suspects. We do, however, have considerable evidence of the length of time elapsing between arrest and disposition and the proportion of persons receiving a nonpunitive disposition (such as probation, suspended sentence, acquittal, or dismissal). On the basis of these findings, we can see that for all offenses taken together, the probability that any given criminal suspect will be fined or imprisoned is quite small, even for crimes of violence of the kind that most concern us. In California in 1964, there were 18,746 reported robberies; about half resulted in arrests. Of those arrested, over 40 percent were released by the police without charges; felony complaints were filed against only one-third. Of these, about a fifth had the complaints dismissed at a preliminary hearing; of these, about a tenth were dismissed at arraignment and another 8 percent were acquitted after a trial. Of the 1,600 persons pleading or found to be guilty, 82 percent went to jail or prison. Thus, of the 10,000 persons arrested, only 13 percent were incarcerated.

These figures show that the problem is obviously not that the courts fail to convict the accused—fewer suspects fall out of the system at that point than at any other. The largest fall-out occurs with the police and prosecutors (who fail to charge suspects, often because they are discovered to be innocent) and at the preliminary hearing stage (where charges may be dismissed); how many of these dismissals at the early stages of the adjudicatory process are because the suspect is charged with a lesser offense than robbery is hard to say, but it may be substantial.

The time it takes to obtain a final disposition of a person charged with a crime is often quite long. In Washington, D.C., the median time required to handle a felony case from indictment to disposition was 4.8 months in 1966. Even if the suspect pleaded guilty, it still required a median time of 4.5 months to settle the matter. Ominously, the President's Commission on Crime in the District of Columbia found that the delay in disposition was increasing and, perhaps as a result, the number of felony prosecutions was declining despite the sharp increases in the number being committed. Between 1950 and 1965 the number of major crimes nearly doubled, the number of felony charges made by the police increased by 9 percent, but the number of felony prosecutions filed declined by 39 percent. One reason may be that an overworked prosecution and court system screens out all but the most serious violators and either dismisses the charges on the rest or reduces them to misdemeanors. Very few studies of state courts are available, but the impression one gathers is that the problem of delay is likely to be even greater in the state than in the federal system. Considering the delay in disposition and the small proportion of persons arrested who ever risk a penalty at all, the impassioned but largely uninformed debate over "tough" versus "soft" sentences may overlook the need to get some sentence imposed with reasonable dispatch. Assume that for every felony the sentence were two years in prison. It is likely that we could achieve a greater increase in deterrence by raising substantially the probability that every suspected felon would quickly have his guilt determined and then be quickly sent to prison than we would if we exposed a much smaller fraction of suspected felons to a much-delayed prospect of a twenty-year sentence.

It is widely believed that one factor reducing the chances of a conviction is the adoption by the courts of more stringent rules governing arrest, interrogation, and the provision of legal counsel. There have been six or seven studies of the effect of various court rulings and the results are equivocal; at the least, none shows that the exclusion of evidence taken through court-disapproved procedures has a dramatic adverse effect on the prospect of a conviction.

However, let us assume that such rules do have an effect, perhaps a great one, on police practices. For what crimes will the effect be greatest? In all probability, it will be for crimes *other* than those producing the greatest citizen anxiety. Most of the court decisions seek to limit the police power to interrogate suspects—by requiring that the suspect be warned of his rights, that free legal advice be available during interrogation for those needing it, and so forth. One purpose, though not the only one, of such interrogations is to obtain an admission or even a signed confession. Such evidence may be quite important when there is no witness to the crime, as, typically, in burglary. But violent crime typically produces an eyewitness—the victim. (To be sure, in murder cases the "eyewitness" is often dead, but the police solve the vast majority of all murders anyway.) An assault or a robbery gives the victim a look at his assailant—indeed, in the former case, he may know or be related to him. Prosecutions and convictions in such cases often depend on this testimony of victim-witnesses, and no confession is needed. (The problem with these crimes is often persuading the victim to testify.)

Perhaps because of such factors, a study published in the *Yale Law Journal* in 1967 of the investigative practices of the New Haven police showed that, in the vast majority of all cases, no confession or admission was necessary for prosecution, in the judgment of both legal observers and the police detectives interviewed after the conclusion of the interrogation. And warnings given to those interrogated seemed to have relatively little effect on whether or not the suspect made a statement useful to the police.

On the other hand, there is no doubt that most police officers believe these court rulings have seriously hampered their work, and their opinions should not be lightly dismissed—perhaps the effect has been great but of a nature that cannot easily be measured. For example, interrogation may be unimportant in getting evidence against the suspect but very important in solving other cases, finding accomplices, and the like.

Getting a conviction on a robbery charge may in some cases be made harder by court rulings. These rulings, like all rights enforced by our courts, impose some cost on society by letting guilty people go free. But we should keep the magnitude of this cost in proper perspective. The crime rate, so far as we can tell, was going up sharply *before* the court began issuing these rulings; therefore, the court rulings cannot be responsible for all, or even most, of the increase. Furthermore, a very large proportion of all persons arrested for crimes are juveniles, and until recently (1967) these court rulings did not apply to juvenile proceedings. Finally, the rulings cover persons in custody, and thus do not affect the robberies that are never reported to the police (about a third of the total) or the robberies that are reported but never solved by the police (about two-thirds of those known).

The major impact of the courts on the criminal probably follows from the disposition given those who are found guilty. (The majority of those found guilty, it should be noted, have *pleaded* guilty; for them, there never was a trial. In California, for example, of the 1,927 robbery suspects arraigned in 1964, 62.3 percent pleaded guilty.) To the extent that judges have a choice in a sentence, one would imagine an effort would be made to select that sentence most likely to reduce the chances of recidivism. Some effort, of course, is made. Presentence investigations probably occur in a majority of the felony convictions in this country. But the value of these inquiries has rarely been tested; often they produce reports that are little more than fact-filled biographies of the convict that offer no basis for choosing a sentence. They are likely to have value only if they can be used in conjunction with statistical prediction tables that estimate, for classes of offenders, the disposition least likely to produce recidivism, subject to the constraints of maximum sentences. Such tables cannot replace the individual case report, but they can make it more meaningful—more predictive and less anecdotal. To develop such sentencing guides, however, requires far more research—and after research, far better management of the sentencing process—than we now support. Attempts to use such sentencing guides, and to evaluate the results, have been made in California, Wisconsin, and elsewhere, and the results should caution us again not to expect dramatic improvements.

Furthermore, reduction in recidivism is only one of the goals of a criminal justice system. In addition, that system needs to express and strengthen the moral imperatives of the community as well as provide to the subjects of the system a sense of fair treatment. As James Fitzjames Stephens remarked eighty-five years ago in *A History of Criminal Law in England*, even if it could be shown that murderers would be deterred by a fine of one shilling, the moral horror which murder arouses (or should arouse) in us would require us to provide penalties greater than one-shilling fines. And some correctional programs, by treating differently men who have committed the same offense, may arouse in those men a profound sense of injustice—and may in fact *be* unjust.

CORRECTIONS

Once a person charged with committing a street crime, especially a vicious one, has been arrested, tried, and sentenced, the debate over his treatment reaches an intense pitch. Correctional programs are frequently described as either "tough" or "soft," in which, depending on one's views, the prisoner is either "abused" or "mollycoddled." As a result, almost any proposal to improve the correctional element of the system is opposed by liberals if it seems to involve expanding conventional prison facilities and opposed by conservatives if it seems to provide nonprison alternatives.

The debate here misses the point, or at best emphasizes ideology rather than the practical consequences of the system. If the goal is to reduce recidivism among perpetrators of street crimes, then we should develop a range of correctional alternatives suitable for different perpetrators with different prospects for correction. All too often, the choice in many states is between locking a person up in an overcrowded prison or assigning him to an overworked probation officer. In prison he "does time" and little else; when he's on probation, nobody knows what he does.

Can any program make a difference in the recidivism rate? The answer may be that in many cases the character of the institution makes less difference than the character of the person. First offenders committing crimes of passion may emerge from the worst dungeons and never commit a second offense, and professional burglars with long records may be unaffected by the most therapeutic environment. But for some persons, the correctional experience may be critical. And for almost all persons, truly substantial changes in the relevant institution may have an effect. One study suggested that merely changing a correctional institution from one that emphasizes pure custody to one that emphasizes "treatment" may have little effect on recidivism. Lowering the case loads of probation workers from 200 to 100 or even 50 persons may likewise have little effect. But other studies show that radically different correctional programs in which inmates are closely supervised in community-based treatment centers (permitting inmates to work at jobs or go to school during the day and report for supervision in the evenings and on weekends) may have significant results. A California experiment described by the President's crime commission managed, by this method, to reduce recidivism rates from 52 to 28 percent in comparison with a control group undergoing conventional correction. Equally encouraging (but not conclusive) results have been reported from experiments in New Jersey and elsewhere.

To many people, "community treatment projects" sound like "mollycoddling" or "social work." In fact, it could hardly be more different. The theory behind these programs is that the courts are now placing back on the streets thousands of convicted criminals "on probation" with almost no chance of meaningful supervision. Programs such as those in California and New Jersey are based on the assumption that closer rather than looser control over the probationer is necessary but that the control should prepare him for a return to civilian life. Daniel Glaser has tried to clarify these differences by noting that there are two basic aspects of the correctional effort—*control* and *assistance*—and four different combinations of these factors. The present prison system provides high control but little assistance; the conventional probation programs often provide little control and little assistance. The newer programs aim at providing both high control and high assistance.

Next to better community and police programs, there is no area where society has a greater opportunity to end criminal careers than in the correctional system, and yet even the most promising experiments in reducing recidivism are rarely duplicated elsewhere—again, because resources are inadequate and because the debate over such measures often arouses intense ideological controversy.

A Federal Role in Law Enforcement

Law enforcement has been, and no doubt will continue to be, primarily a local responsibility. The desire for "home rule" over police departments is especially strong. However, it is easy to exaggerate the extent to which this sentiment precludes federal action and even the extent to which it is relevant to the current efforts to control crime.

In the first place, the courts and correctional systems, where the need for innovation, planning, and careful experimentation is great, are seldom under local control. Indeed, most correctional systems are already state responsibilities, with few communities anxious to have prisons or treatment centers "close to the people." Citizens may fear, and rightly so, the prospect of a "national police," but they probably have little fear of increased federal leadership in (and money support for) devising correctional programs that will reduce recidivism. Second, the problems of crime, especially if under "crime" we include organized crime, civil disorders, and rioting, are increasingly national rather than purely local matters. Finally, there can be little doubt that, however strong may be localistic sentiments, the voters increasingly expect the federal government to take the crime problem seriously and to play a leading role in dealing with it.

Until recently, and perhaps even now, the federal government has been unprepared to play that role. Though there are some federal aids to law enforcement of long standing (such as the FBI National Academy that gives specialized training to local police officers), there has never been in Washington the law enforcement equivalent of the Office of Education, the Department of Housing and Urban Development, or the Department of Agriculture. The Department of Justice has traditionally consisted primarily of lawyers who are busy prosecuting, defending, or reviewing, not administrators or analysts charged with planning, allocating, or evaluating. Other than the Post Office, only the Department of Justice among cabinet agencies is headed by a "General" rather than a "Secretary." This structure has now been altered.

CRIME CONTROL AND SAFE STREETS ACT

The federal role in crime prevention has been substantially increased by the passage in 1968 of the Omnibus Crime Control and Safe Streets Act. Title I of the act creates a Law Enforcement Assistance Administration and a National Institute of Law Enforcement and Criminal Justice and gives to these agencies, both part of the Department of Justice, responsibility for providing financial assistance to aid in public protection, recruiting, and training criminal justice personnel, combating organized crime, preventing and controlling riots and civil disorders, improving police-community relations, constructing new physical facilities, and carrying out research and evaluation programs. The grants from the Law

Enforcement Assistance Administration will be made primarily to the states on the basis of federally approved "comprehensive law enforcement plans" prepared by state agencies; the research, training, and education grants of the National Institute of Law Enforcement and Criminal Justice may be made directly to governments, universities, and private organizations. For the first year, over $100 million is authorized; for succeeding years, $300 million per year. But only $63 million has been appropriated for the first year.

The most important effect of this legislation may not be the funds that are made available but the new institutional structure that is created. The Department of Justice will acquire three new presidential appointees—an administrator and two associate administrators of the Law Enforcement Assistance Administration—no more than two of whom may be of the same political party. The persons who fill these new positions will have an opportunity to create a strong federal presence in law enforcement at all levels; the fact that the bill explicitly acknowledges "local control" and requires that the administration act primarily through state agencies is important, but not controlling. In fact, as experience with most grant-giving agencies shows, energetic administrators, though they rarely override local powers, often create at the state and local levels energetic counterpart groups who, working together with federal officials, exert new pressures on the whole system. Typically, the distribution of powers in the federal system is changed, not so much by federal usurpation, as by the energizing, through federal initiatives and with federal money, of new sources of local leadership who then press both local officials for "action" and federal officials for more money.

The central question is, to what ends will this pressure be exerted? There are several risks—going on a shopping spree, emphasizing peripheral problems because the newly activated leadership thinks they are central problems, and multiplying demonstration projects that demonstrate nothing.

The shopping spree problem arises because certain things can be purchased more easily than others—almost by mail order—and therefore one can show "immediate results" from the sudden infusion of new money. The police are especially likely to suffer from this bias—ordering more patrol cars (or, for advanced thinkers, more scooters), better radios, larger computers, and shinier jails. Many of these things may be necessary but that must first be shown and not assumed.

Furthermore, since there are many unmet needs in law enforcement, new leadership groups are likely to press for attention to needs that have been neglected at the expense of those which may be more important. There may, for example, be a rash of efforts to send police officers to college, organize human relations training programs, open neighborhood police and legal offices, and form advisory and planning councils. Just as hardware is attractive to some because it is shiny and available, attempting to change the attitudes of members of the criminal justice system is attractive to others because current attitudes seem to be wrong or shortsighted. But it is by no means clear that attitudes fully, or even primarily, determine behavior; it is just as likely that attitudes are in large measure a result, not a cause, of the properties of the criminal justice system and that they either cannot be changed or, if changed, will not change performance. The studies of Albert Reiss and Donald Black for the crime commission show that most police officers express anti-Negro sentiments but they also suggest that most officers do not routinely display anti-Negro behavior. The crucial question is, what constitutes an effective law enforcement and order maintenance system? Creating, by experiment, such a system is more important (in my view) than changing the attitudes or communications patterns of people in the present system. Ideally, a better system will produce better behavior with respect to matters other than law enforcement as well.

Finally, many demonstration projects are likely to be funded but not carefully evaluated. Evaluation is difficult—sometimes it may be impossible—but important if such projects are to be the basis for general changes in the system. Operation 25 in New York was inadequately evaluated—crime rates in adjoining areas were not measured (or if measured, not reported) while the saturation patrol was underway, nor were citizen attitudes assessed. Most correctional programs—the California experiments and others are notable exceptions—tell us nothing about the effect of the programs. And the courts rarely give any systematic thought to the overall effects of their operation.

LIMITATIONS OF THE ACT

The success of the new federal partnership in law enforcement signaled by the passage of the Safe Streets Act, though depending primarily on establishing clear objectives and criteria, also depends on changing some of the restrictive features of that legislation. One is the limitation that no more than one-third of any grant may be used to pay the salaries of state and local law enforcement personnel (except for those in training programs). Even implementing the programs that now show some promise of success, not to mention new programs, will require massive increases in the number and quality of personnel in the criminal justice system. Suppose it could be shown that the rate of street crime in the highest crime areas of our large cities could be significantly reduced by doubling or tripling the number of beat patrolmen, reducing the case loads of correctional personnel who supervise offenders from 100 to 15, and hiring extra prosecutors and judges to expedite decisions. There is hardly a large city in the country that could afford (that is, could persuade local taxpayers to part with) the sums that such an effort would require for salaries alone. The new Law Enforcement Assistance Administration may develop and disseminate excellent ideas that no one can afford to buy. There is a grave risk that we may have oversold our ability to respond to the public safety crisis. It seems clear that in time, and perhaps sooner than we think, we shall have to provide generalized federal support for the salary structure of the criminal justice system.

A second restriction in the present act is an initial limit (which will, it is hoped, disappear in ensuing years) on the funds that can be used for correction, probation, and parole work. Special emphasis, on the other hand, is given to programs to prevent or control riots by police and auxiliary forces. While understandable perhaps as an immediate reaction to recent events, this restriction is for the long term a misstatement of priorities. Street crime will outlive riots by many generations—perhaps forever. Reducing the former requires an emphasis on correctional programs if we are to avoid allowing the present system to return its human products to the community unchanged.

A third problem, which has become increasingly familiar to the heads of other government departments dealing with social issues, is one of managing change. It is, however, more acute in law enforcement, for though we speak of the "criminal justice system" there is in fact no such system at all—or rather there are scores of local "systems" many of which are systems only in the sense that the output of one agency is the input of another. Forty thousand police agencies operate essentially as independent units, with scarcely any supervisory structure intervening between them and anyone in Washington interested in being of assistance to them. Requiring that police and other agencies make applications for projects through state planning agencies may mitigate this problem by calling into being nationwide what already exists in a few states—state coordinating bodies for criminal justice. But this scarcely solves the problem, for no one yet knows what a "state plan" for law enforcement should look like or what it might accomplish, and there is a desperate shortage of people who have the ability to create such plans, even assuming such creation to be possible.

One should proceed on the assumption that the state plans are not likely to be comprehensive sets of realistic goals toward which unified action can be directed. With proper guidance, however, they could assign priorities to the areas where intervention and experiment might have the highest return in public safety based on current best guesses. But to accomplish even this, the federal government will have to abandon a passive role. It will have to develop clear, substantive guidelines, even model plans, disseminate present knowledge and the results of new experiments as aggressively as possible, and take an active part in helping produce program ideas. To this end, the creation of federal technical assistance teams and a federal demonstration and dissemination center, or their equivalents, as part of the new Law Enforcement Assistance Administration, is of paramount importance.

OTHER APPROACHES

To the extent that we can do much about crime, it is not likely that the federal government can play more than a relatively small role, though if properly done, that role can be crucial. Primarily this is because many programs that have shown some success in reducing crime or recidivism (Operation 25, the California and other experiments in community-based corrections) require able and imaginative people to lead them. The supply of such people is not likely to increase very rapidly no matter how fast the appropriations may increase. To the greatest extent possible, therefore, we ought to be particularly interested in crime prevention programs that do not require creating large new agencies manned with extraordinary people. We ought, in addition, to look for programs that provide inducements for individual citizens to act, out of self-interest, in ways that will help to reduce crime. An example of such a program would be one to increase the financial cost of carelessness. Insurance companies in many cases reimburse people and business firms for stolen cars, television sets, fur coats, and jewelry no matter how careless the owner may have been with his property. There is no incentive to lock cars, put proper bolts on windows, or install alarms. Surely there must be a way to penalize persons for failing to take such precautions when the cost to society of retrieving stolen goods and prosecuting thieves is so great. To allow the negligent person to escape paying his full share of the cost is to encourage crime. Steps have been taken to induce auto manufacturers to make cars harder to steal; the next step might be to induce owners to lock their cars when they park them. One could reduce the amount recoverable on insurance if the car was unlocked or had the key in the ignition when stolen.

But even with respect to those programs requiring government management, it is by no means clear that the federal government can do the managing. There are too many police departments, courts, and correctional agencies for even a well-staffed Department of Justice to sort out unaided the proposals and approve the fund requests. Law enforcement is a field suited to regionalization, and not only to reduce congestion in Washington. Finding and developing new personnel, devising and testing new strategies, and enlisting private groups (business, university, and citizen) in public safety programs can best be done by creating a series of regional criminal justice centers—some based at universities, others organized as part of confederations of local law enforcement agencies, and still others perhaps patterned on the model of nonprofit research groups such as RAND. Recruiting able people will always be essential; the supply will never equal the demand at any price society is likely to pay; but the chances of getting more of them, organized into various independent centers of initiative, may be enhanced by encouraging regionalization.

This raises the thorny question whether the federal government should increasingly set standards for local law enforcement agencies. Some measure of federal influence will result from spending federal money in this area, whatever the localistic sentiments of the persons involved. Some would argue that we ought to go further than this and insist that state and local criminal justice systems measure up to federal standards before they get much federal money. Only in this way, the argument goes, will we produce a massive impetus to change and improvement in the badly decentralized "system" now confronting us. I am skeptical of this view, though not on grounds of ideology or constitutionalism. I do not think enough is yet known to warrant imposing many standards on anybody. One obvious standard, widely thought to be a good thing, is to require higher educational levels for police officers—the federal government might, for example, pay salary support to local departments only if their new recruits had two years of college training. I doubt that we have the faintest idea of what might be the practical consequences—the effects on crime prevention, criminal apprehension, community relations, or anything else

—of such a requirement. Ten years ago, a standard that in all probability would have been imposed would have been mobility (get patrolmen into squad cars and off the pavement—it's more efficient and professional). Today, we are increasingly desirous of putting more patrolmen back on foot beats—it helps them know the community, build better neighborhood relations, and deter street crime. The conventional wisdom is changing on this vital matter, but not on the grounds of much evidence. I suspect the newer approach is correct, but that is only an opinion. In sum, I believe that developing and testing strategies with explicit crime-reduction objectives ought to precede any thought of comprehensive federal standards. Standards can come, piecemeal, as knowledge accumulates.

In addition to devising such strategies (with heavy emphasis on those that can be operated by ordinary men, not geniuses), the federal government is probably the only agency that can take a serious fresh look at the extent to which we are creating crime, especially crimes of violence, by the current state of the criminal law. The use of violence to enforce gambling debts, or to collect on illegal loans, is an example, though perhaps affecting relatively few people. But theft to support narcotics addiction is probably widespread. Though addicts are interested primarily in obtaining money, not gratifying violent emotions, there is evidence that when they cannot get money by stealth they will take it by force. The price of narcotics, and thus the incentive to steal, is greatly inflated because many addictive drugs can be obtained only from criminal monopolies. Probably no one can judge whether enforcement efforts could be intensified enough to make narcotics prohibitively expensive even to persons willing to steal for them. What is clear is that enforcement efforts to date have not ended the traffic, and it seems likely that such enforcement as we have has increased the incentives for theft. It is possible to imagine a truly formidable crackdown on the narcotics traffic, of a nature never before attempted. It would require enlisting the aid of the governments of France, Mexico, and Turkey in closing permanently the clandestine laboratories and illegitimate farms which now supply the vast bulk of heroin consumed in the United States. Whether, given our other foreign policy objectives with respect to these countries, we are likely to assign drug control this high priority is questionable. Second, it would be necessary to multiply manyfold the border control measures now in effect, with the result that almost every passenger and every ship, aircraft, or automobile entering the country from certain areas would be searched. That private tourists and commercial importers would tolerate the inconvenience and intrusion this implies is hard to imagine. Finally, the number of agents assigned within the country to track down and arrest narcotics dealers would have to be increased sharply.

If these measures are not undertaken, or if they are undertaken and found wanting, we shall have to face squarely the problem that the crime commission ducked so badly—whether the present half-hearted war on narcotics produces costs in induced criminality that exceed the gains in a reinforced moral code. If it does, perhaps we should take steps to reduce the extent to which our laws produce an increase in those crimes we are now so concerned about ending. And what is true about narcotics may also be true about other forms of "consensual crimes" that occur because our laws have created a black market in which certain things can only be done illegitimately—gambling, homosexual practices, and so forth. Perhaps it is time to take a fresh look at the kinds of black markets we allow to flourish and which, by flourishing, often corrupt the police.

The central theme of the policy recommendations of this paper—that the federal government should primarily devise, test, and disseminate crime-prevention *strategies* rather than merely fund projects or organize programs—does not carry with it any promise of great success. For one thing, there are limits to what can be done about even the crimes most worrisome to us—limits arising out of ignorance, a commitment to the maintenance of civil liberties, and the presence of social forces we are powerless to change in less than a generation (if then). This means that we must learn to live with crime—hopefully, not as much crime as at present, or at least not with a crime rate that is increasing as fast as it now appears to be, but with a good deal of crime nonetheless. This is not an easy view for citizens or politicians to accept; politicians especially are likely to campaign against crime and exploit rather than solve a problem.

The easy path for such exploitation is to promise to end crime by, in effect, ending (or drastically curtailing) civil liberties. This would be a tragedy, not simply because we cherish those liberties, but also because limiting them is not likely to have much effect on the crime rate. The most substantial gains in public safety can be made through increased citizen involvement, more effective and community-involved patrol, speedier and more certain court dispositions, and more relevant correctional programs. Effective action in these areas is not likely to require more oppressive action. Protecting the rights of the accused is not the principal constraint on making the streets safer; passive citizens, insufficient or poorly deployed policemen, and ineffective correctional programs are far more important.

Some Modest Proposals

The tone of caution and even skepticism of this paper may strike the reader as stronger than the references to concrete proposals for action. This is neither unintended nor unprecedented. The President's crime commission, insofar as it dealt with recommendations to reduce crime by deterring, apprehending, or rehabilitating criminals rather than by eliminating the social and psychological causes of crime, was also mindful of how little we know of the efficacy of various strategies. All of us, I suppose, find it easier to speak confidently of solving general problems, such as poverty, than of preventing particular problems, such as street crime.

But, however proper a cautious posture may be, those searching for a program with which to begin the next administration or the next fiscal year will no doubt be impatient with any recommendations that seem to call merely for "more research." And the congressmen who must pass on any such recommendation are likely to be not only impatient, but derisive. They were elected, after all, not to study crime, but to stop it.

Let me conclude, therefore, by drawing attention once again, and perhaps more forcefully, to those steps that I believe can be taken now to deal with rising rates of street crime. We do not know enough about these programs to be confident they will work in all circumstances and we suspect that, if carried out generally, they will not produce benefits as large as those realized in the pilot projects. But they are a beginning.

First, the number of patrolmen on the streets of high crime areas must be substantially increased. More patrolmen are necessary not only to deter street crime but also to make possible the achievement of a variety of other police objectives as well. If the police are to emphasize their service function in the community, if they are to develop specialized units to handle family crises and derelict alcoholics, and if they are to devote more energy to police-community relations programs, they will have to be supplied with more resources—men, money, and equipment. No substantial increase in police resources—especially manpower, the most expensive resource—is likely without financial aid from other levels of government.

Second, the California experiments with intensive community-based correctional programs should be repeated and expanded in other states. Properly done, these correctional procedures are not something that can be added to an existing set of institutions (though they may have to begin that way); what is really called for is the complete redesigning of the correctional system so as to provide for the systematic management of offenders from arrest to release, with a variety of correctional options available, to replace the process of passing bodies from one agency to another.

Third, the criminal courts must be managed with a view toward obtaining speedier disposition of cases if the deterrent effect of the criminal sanction is to be preserved. This requires a variety of steps, ranging from the adoption of simple business procedures (careful scheduling, the quick preparation and distribution of reports and records, and eliminating bottlenecks caused by a shortage of judges, or prosecutors, or grand jurors) to a number of bolder programs that will lighten the load now being placed on the courts. Noncourt, or at least nontrial, disposition of certain offenders—chronic alcoholics, for example—will provide more time for attention to the serious offenders.

Fourth, incentives ought to be offered to both cities and citizens to reduce the ease with which various crimes can be committed. It should be made financially attractive to potential victims to lock their cars and homes and to safeguard the merchandise they display; it should be made rewarding for cities to light their streets and parks, provide street alarms and call boxes, and insist that security be one of the objectives of housing and building codes.

Finally, and perhaps most important, the President of the United States should use his office and prestige to enlist citizen interest and citizen action in crime-prevention programs. Citizen auxiliaries to the police can be formed without stimulating vigilante instincts. Indeed, it is possible that unless such auxiliaries are formed under responsible public auspices, they will come into being spontaneously under irresponsible private auspices. Such auxiliaries ought to be drawn from the neighborhoods they are to serve and used both to help detect and deter crime and to improve police-community relations. Business firms and foundations can help the released offender return to society through halfway houses, job opportunities, and educational programs. Since released offenders are, especially in big cities, disproportionately poor and black, private efforts to deal with crime can coincide with efforts to deal with poverty and race.

We end, thus, on a positive note. But though positive, the note is also uncertain. We shall be fortunate if we can even slow the rate of increase in crime; we shall be impossibly blessed if we can actually reduce the level of crime. We cannot afford to become recklessly impatient about progress in dealing with this problem. Just as there is no issue about which we should be more concerned, there is none toward which we should display more forebearance and stoicism.

RALPH W. TYLER

INVESTING IN BETTER SCHOOLS

Public education in the United States today enrolls more students, employs more teachers, and receives more financial support than at any previous time, yet we face serious problems in attaining the nation's educational aspirations. In 1966–67, more than 36 million children were enrolled in American elementary schools and 13 million youth were attending the high schools. In the same year over a million teachers were employed in elementary schools and 857,000 in the high schools. The expenditures in this year, the most recent for which information is available, were $31.9 billion. The numbers of pupils and teachers and the total expenditures have all risen sharply during the past fifteen years but, if the present birth rate continues, enrollments have probably reached their peak at 50 million and will decline steadily to perhaps 40 million by the early 1980s. The respite from the pressure of increasing numbers will enable the nation to mobilize greater effort for other problems.

During the past ten years schools have become central to personal and national aspirations. The shock of Sputnik stimulated the passage of the National Defense Education Act. Schools are now faced with responsibility for eliminating racial prejudice and discrimination. Crime and delinquency are recognized as deeply rooted in ignorance and inadequate education. The schools are urged to take a major part in their elimination. As public and private attacks are focused on poverty and unemployment, lack of education is found to be a critical factor thwarting efforts at quick solutions. The Elementary and Secondary Education Act of 1965 placed primary emphasis in Title I on the task of the schools in educating the poor. Never have schools been expected to do so much to so many.

These expectations are understandable in the light of the great changes taking place. Education has become essential for everyone. The rapid utilization of science and technology by agriculture, industry, business, the armed services, and the health services has profoundly shifted the structure of the U.S. labor force. At the turn of the century farm labor comprised 38 percent of the labor force; now it is less than 7 percent. Unskilled labor now represents less than 6 percent of the labor force and, as with farm labor, the proportion continues to decrease. Meanwhile the demands for educated people in the professions, the service occupations, management, engineering, and science exceed the supply provided by our educational institutions. Thirty percent of the nation's children of high school age fail to finish high school. There are 23 million adults in this country with less than an eighth grade education, and for this great nation the number of illiterate adults is appalling. These facts are only a few of the many that could be cited which clearly indicate the seriousness of America's educational problems. Seven of them are briefly discussed in this paper.

Primary Education for All Children

More than ever before, citizenship in our society requires education for adequate understanding of government and public problems and also for parenthood, constructive family life, personal and community health, and individual development. The uneducated child and the poorly educated youth are not promising adult assets in a modern technological society. Every child needs education, and the schools face a new task, that of reaching the children who would have dropped out in an earlier period.

According to the best estimates that can be made from scattered sources—local school testing programs, Selective Service Qualifying Tests, and rejection rates for military service—approximately one-fifth of the children in the United States do not attain the level of literacy required for available employment; a similar number may not gain the understanding needed for citizenship and satisfying personal lives. In rural and urban slum areas, 40 to 60 percent of the children in the sixth grade perform at second grade level or below on achievement tests. The educationally deprived are heavily concentrated among the poor, Negroes, Mexican Americans, Puerto Ricans, and American Indians. The schools have failed to reach the disadvantaged. Children from homes of poverty as they come to school belie our boasts that we have universal education and equality for all. Two-thirds are malnourished, three-fourths have one or more significant health problems, they have no place to study at home, and nearly half have no real family life. Lack of education among these groups is not a new phenomenon, but it is much more serious now than a few decades ago and is not likely to be balanced by other kinds of opportunities for learning, for employment, and for enhanced personal satisfaction. For most of these children and youth, education is the only means available for advancement, and they don't get it.

Our failure to educate most of these children is not due primarily to their inherent inadequacies, but rather to the inappropriateness of the typical school program. Experimental efforts at a number of research centers have demonstrated that almost all children, including those from urban and rural slums, respond to meaningful stimulation and learn quite complicated things, like a language. Among the majority of American children the school and its activities are an integral part of the learning begun at home, reinforced and developed by teachers and schoolmates, and fostered by opportunities to apply what they learn in out-of-school situations. For example, for the majority of children learning to read is an extension of language development begun in the home, with much conversation in standard dialect accompanied by the parents' reading aloud to them. The school provides a natural continuation of these language activities and, as the child learns to read, there are books and magazines at home on which to practice. Usually, too, there are parents and friends with whom to discuss what is read.

In contrast, most of the children who do not attain an education find the school alien to earlier experiences and a source of failure and rejection. Many children from minority groups have not had extensive experience with American standard dialect, they have not had parents read to them, they have not seen family or friends devoting major attention to reading. They find the school work in reading foreign to their home experience and frequently fail to carry on the tasks expected. In this way they lose the zest of learning and have an increasing sense of failure while in school. As they lose interest and confidence in the early months, they fall behind the majority of children more and more, so that they finish school or drop out without reaching a level of education on which to base a constructive life.

Until recently this state of affairs was, oddly, accepted and tolerated, as statistics on adult illiteracy reveal. Now that we see that an adult illiterate can find no constructive role in a modern society, we can no longer tolerate failure to teach children to read. Massive efforts are needed.

The Congress recognized the imperative need for educating disadvantaged children by boldly and responsibly offering categorical aid to schools having a concentration of children from homes of poverty. Title I of the

Elementary and Secondary Education Act of 1965 authorizes approximately $1 billion of federal funds for this purpose. This legislation has opened the door to a strengthened attack upon the serious educational problem and has allayed fears of "federal control," conflicts with "states' rights" and with "separation of church and state." Within two years of its operation approximately one-fourth of the schools receiving these funds were able to show some progress in educating the disadvantaged. Unfortunately, a majority of the efforts have not been highly effective. The programs developed have been for the most part only minor and relatively ineffectual modifications of ordinary programs—reducing the pupil-teacher ratio by four or five, providing an additional counselor, purchasing new audiovisual equipment. It is difficult if not impossible for most school districts to conceive of schools and programs widely different from the familiar ones. Comparing these ineffective programs with some of the experimental work under way suggests some possible explanations of the inadequacy of current efforts to educate disadvantaged children.

First, it seems clear that the added resources are grossly inadequate. By the time severely disadvantaged children enter elementary school, their experiences with language and with systematic learning have been so limited that a major reorganization of attitudes and habits is essential to enable them to perceive the meaning and significance of school learning, and to gain the confidence required to engage actively in it. For example, a majority of mothers encourage their children as they enter school for the first time to show what they can do in learning to read and to deal with numbers, whereas the typical advice given by the mother of a disadvantaged child is: "Don't get into trouble! Don't do anything that would make the teacher mad!" Hence the child avoids active involvement in learning, trying to be as passive as a six-year-old youngster can be. For him to acquire positive attitudes toward the work of the school, new language habits, and successful experience in active intellectual learning demands major changes in school programs and practices. These cannot be effected by expenditures of only 10 to 15 percent more than the ordinary school expenditures. In the early years of a new program, the costs per pupil are likely to be from two to five times the amounts currently allocated. The Head Start programs in the larger cities are costing about $1,000 per year per pupil for half-day sessions. This expenditure provides people to read to children, to converse with them, to stimulate their curiosity, to assist with health and nutrition, and so on. The Youth Corps programs are much more expensive because, as the uneducated become older, their problems are more difficult to attack.

In the second place, most of the efforts to help the disadvantaged have focused on children from six to seventeen years of age. Typically, children who are seriously deprived in their intellectual and emotional experiences in the first three or four years of life keep falling farther and farther behind the majority of their age mates as they progress through school. They are likely to be a year behind at the time they enter school and at least three years behind when they are in high school. What seems to be required is the early provision for deprived children of the kind of environment a good home and a good community offer its children.

The Head Start program is a small step in the application of this principle, but it does not go far enough. It has opened a way to attack the problem, but its full potential cannot be realized until it is part of a total effort to furnish constructive educational experiences for all children partly or wholly deprived of these opportunities in their early years.

Related to the other two, the third factor is the failure to arrange for the necessary major modifications of the school setting, the school program, and the kinds of personnel employed. The pattern characteristic of most schools, in which one teacher plans and conducts all the activities of the classroom, is not effective with children for whom the school is the major if not the sole systematic educational agency. Most of the projects have made only minor modifications, although experimental studies indicate the tremendous reorganization required in the tasks, the school setting, and the personnel in order to furnish educational environments roughly paralleling those of the homes and neighborhoods of the majority of American children. The children must perceive the tasks as relevant to things that are important in their lives. For example, the oral language development must help the normal communication involved in living and playing and doing their part of the work at home. The formal school setting should be changed to include activities in the school, the playground, the home, and the neighborhood in which the children can practice oral language. The school personnel should include mothers and other neighborhood persons who help guarantee that the school is related to the rest of the child's life. Free meals, at least breakfast and lunch in school, are needed for the ill-fed who cannot learn while hungry. In many cases, other children, older and younger, can be used to supply each child with an individual helper. Rather than set expectations of uniform achievement for all children, the program should place emphasis on each child's mastery of the particular knowledge or skill involved in his work so that he gains the basis for further learning and confidence in himself. A feature that will be hard to implement but necessary is to eliminate practices that hinder or discourage learning, such as "ability grouping," uniform courses of study and textbooks, and guidance practices that categorize individual children as "educationally incapable."

Enough experience is now available to justify supporting some ways of attacking this problem as likely to be successful and withholding support from other approaches as unlikely to produce significant results. The local school or even the state cannot effectively develop an educational program and secure the financial resources to mount it. Most disadvantaged children are found in areas where the resources are most limited—city slums, Appalachia, the poorest rural counties, the poor sections of the urban fringe—and where there are limitations in the availability of professional leadership and resources for developing new ideas.

To develop a nationwide program that promises success within a dozen years or so will require large-scale support by the federal government for local developments that are either designed by a central group or submitted for approval centrally. The cost for a comprehensive program directed to the 20 percent of children and youth who are not now obtaining an education would be at least $6.5 billion annually. This includes $1.4 billion for children aged three, four, and five who have not usually gone to school, allowing $600 per year for each of the 2.4 million. It also includes $5.1 billion supplementary educational support for the 10.2 million disadvantaged children already in school, at an average of $500 per year added to the amount now spent. Since the success of the program for the very young would result in decreasing problems as they progressed through the schools, eventually the need for supplementary support of older children would be a small fraction of the support needed in the first few years.

The estimated $6.5 billion is less than 20 percent of the $34.2 billion which the U.S. Office of Education projects for support of elementary and secondary schools in 1968–69. The results expected from the additional funds would, in the long run, much more than offset the cost of the program. It is clearly a wise and financially profitable economic investment. For both the economic and human values, it is time to make a massive attack on this problem.

Improving the High Schools

The second problem is education at the high school level. Society needs a much higher percentage of its youth educated beyond the elementary school. As the demand for unskilled and semiskilled labor has sharply diminished, there are increasing employment opportunities that require at least a high school education—health services, education, recreation, social services, science, engineering, administration, accounting. Such an education also contributes to constructive citizenship and to competence in other areas of living.

In spite of the need, the high school at present is failing to serve effectively more than half the youth who are of high school age. Over a million of them drop out each year before completing high school, and an equal number of those who remain make no measurable progress on standard tests in high school subjects. The dropouts include 60,000 unwed mothers and 80,000 already identified as delinquent. The largest part of the nation's expenditures for welfare and unemployment go to persons who dropped out before completing high school, and a considerable part of the cost of crime is associated with them.

Of those who remain in the high school to graduate, one-third do not develop the skills and attitudes required for higher level employment and for civic leadership. Many of them are from minority groups, but the largest fraction includes young people from white middle-class and working-class families of city, country, and suburbs. During the depression years the number of students who were learning little in high school was attributed to limited employment opportunities. With the present demand for people with training and education, it is clear that this is not the case.

Our current failure to educate approximately one-third of the youth enrolled in high school is not due primarily to the inadequacies of the students but to the inappropriateness of the program to supply them with the kind of learning required. They are concerned with becoming independent adults, getting jobs, marrying, gaining status with their peers, and helping to solve the ills of the world. They perceive little or no connection between the educational content of the school and their own concerns. "What has algebra to do with me?" they ask. "Why should I try to remember the chief battles of the Revolutionary War?" Even the high school science laboratory appears to be a place for following the directions of the laboratory manual to see if they can obtain the results reported in the textbook.

Because they do not see the relevance of the high school to their present and future lives, they do not become actively involved in the learning tasks assigned. They turn their attention to other things such as athletics, social activities, artificial stimulants, or they may become quiescent, enduring the school routine until they can drop out.

This problem has been recognized by many secondary schools over the years, but the steps taken have not been adequate to solve it. For fifty years the Smith-Hughes legislation has provided federal aid for vocational education in the high school, but even after significant revisions in 1963 only 10 percent of high school age students profit from vocational technical offerings.

Some schools have tried to provide a meaningful and relevant program for the student by broadening the offerings of the high school but without transforming the curriculum as a whole. Courses have been added, but within the same framework, so that the new courses were also outside the real concerns of the student. The history of Africa can be as lifeless as the history of Colonial America if both are seen as little more than events to memorize. Spanish can seem as irrelevant as Latin if both are treated as routines for acquiring vocabulary and remembering grammatical rules.

Another effort to attack the problem has been based on the assumption that the root of the difficulty was in the boy or girl, not in the school and its program. Hence, the focus of effort has been on counseling and other treatments administered to the student without making any basic shift in school attitudes and practices. Some students by dint of teacher and counselor efforts have been able genuinely to perceive the school tasks as being vital to them; but most of them, under stimulation, put forth more effort yet still viewed the school work as having no connection with life outside of school.

One factor standing in the way is the tradition that the high school should be an adolescent island outside the major currents of adult life. Modern society has increasingly isolated adolescents from the adult world. Yet this is the time of life in which young people are looking forward to being independent adults; they need opportunities to work with adults, to learn adult skills and practices, and to feel that they are becoming mature and independent. Hence, the restrictions on youth employment, the limited opportunities to learn occupational skills at home, the segregation of civic and social activities by age groupings, all add to the difficulty of the adolescent and increase his anxiety about attaining adult status and competence. The secondary school should help to bridge this gap.

Experimentation and research suggest practices that seem likely to increase the effectiveness of the high school in giving a functional education to more young people. Primarily these practices involve developing a close active relation, not simply a formal one, between the school and the responsible adult community, so that the student will find questions and problems outside the school that can be attacked by what he learns in school. The emphasis is upon learning that is relevant to his life, not upon grades, credits, and other artificial symbols.

What is required is a major effort to furnish high school students with significant adult activities—job programs, community service corps experience, work in health centers, apprentice experience in research and development, and in staff studies conducted by public agencies. It will be necessary to redesign the high school in order to open it to the community and to utilize many kinds of persons in education. The school will need to serve a wider range of ages and allow students to vary the amount of time devoted to studies. To supply a substitute for grades and credits as qualification for employment opportunities, a certification system will need to be developed to validate the student's competence in various major areas. This will also tend to reduce the emphasis upon purely formal requirements such as class attendance and the completion of prescribed courses.

This proposal is not simple and it may be misunderstood. It proposes to use work and other areas of life as a laboratory in which youths find real problems and difficulties that require learning and in which they can use and sharpen what they are learning. It does not propose to substitute learning on the job for the deeper insights and the knowledge and skills that scholars have developed. The teacher, the books, other materials of the school, and the intellectual resources of the community are to be employed by the student as he works on the problems of his job and carries through projects on which he is engaged. When he is actually doing work that he finds significant, he can see for himself with the aid of those who know the field that many kinds of learning are helpful and even necessary. Coordinators are needed to connect education with the world of work, and teachers need to learn to select the content of school subjects and assist students to use it in connection with the activities in which they are engaged.

The student is concerned with civic and social service activities as well as with gainful employment. In these areas he will meet problems that involve values, ethics, aesthetics, public policy, in fact, the many facets of real life. The opportunity is thus provided for the student to comprehend the perennial areas of educational concern—social-civic understanding and commitment, health, personal integrity, and the arts, as well as the skills of occupational competence.

To provide for the varied interests, abilities, and career plans of students, corresponding variations can be made in the selection of school assignments related to the job, and in the division of the student's time. For example, John Brown, a well-read student, who has been very successful in most of his previous school work and plans to enter a university, might work twenty hours a week for one year in an industrial laboratory and another year in a community service corps providing supplementary educational services to the children of an inner city area. He might be taking advanced high school courses, or he might be doing independent study in one or two fields. On the other hand, Tom Smith, a student who is skeptical of book learning and the relevance of schooling to his life, might work twenty hours a week in a data processing center for one year and another year in a community health center. His school studies should furnish a basis for finding other interests to be pursued in more intensive study, perhaps helping him to select a technical institute for further occupational preparation.

The proposal assumes an extension of the hours per day and weeks per year devoted to high school education. The present five- or six-hour day, even in concentrated vocational laboratories, is little enough to satisfy the level of skill now required for job entry. With the proposed variety of activities in and out of school, the student should be able to work eleven months per year without undue weariness. Since he would receive pay appropriate to the service rendered, summer vacation jobs would not be important.

Some of the major features of this proposal are currently used in imaginative programs of vocational-technical education in some high schools. Unfortunately, even in these cases the benefits are limited to the few students enrolled in these programs. But they demonstrate the feasibility of work programs, wider adult involvement in the education of youth, and closer relation between learning in school and activities outside. They also demonstrate ways in which federal funds may be used to furnish added support for constructive educational improvements.

It should be stressed that the proposal does not imply a sharp separation in educational goals and methods between elementary and secondary schools. Beginning at the fifth or sixth grade, opportunities should be provided all students to explore content and activities related to vocational-technical offerings, increasing in depth through grades eight and nine toward major field specialization at grades eleven and twelve.

Parts of the program have been employed in various places and subjected to impartial evaluation. The kind of education described here has been shown to arouse greater interest and effort in many students than classroom study alone, to increase student understanding of the subjects studied, and to develop maturity of responsibility and judgment. Community service corps experience such as that developed by the Friends Service Committee has been found to arouse in many students greater motivation to learn and to develop social skills, social responsibility, and maturity of judgment. Communities have constructed the Neighborhood Youth Corps program to serve a similar purpose with young people from backgrounds of poverty and limited opportunity. The involvement of a broad range of people in the educational activities of youth has proved helpful, as has the provision of a variety of patterns to include, in addition to full-time enrollment, part-time school attendance while holding full-time or part-time jobs, and enrollment in high school, full time or part time, after a period of work, military service, or other activity. This varied pattern of experience and competence can be utilized constructively in an institution open to the community, whereas it is likely to be a handicap to a school operating in isolation, with study confined to textbooks and related materials.

However desirable this program may be, national efforts may be required to eliminate or reduce the obstacles.

One major impediment involves making new institutional arrangements and training the personnel. For the development of cooperative work-study education, surveys of job opportunities in each community are necessary. Coordinators need to be trained to work out with employers the outline of job experiences and their relation to the educational resources of the school. Their primary concern is the utilization of job experience to enhance the student's development. The high school curriculum itself will need rebuilding to make it relevant to the problems encountered by students in their work, not only in business and industry, but also in public agencies and nonprofit institutions. In many cases, a community service corps will need to be established to provide young people with opportunities for social service. It will take three to five years to open the school to the community and to train coordinators who will serve as middlemen between the school and the community.

A second impediment is the fear by both school people and parents that a new and unorthodox educational program will not be recognized by colleges or employers. The criteria for college admission have broadened greatly from those of the early 1930s, which commonly prescribed the courses to be taken and required an examination based on specified textbooks, to the present policies that prescribe broad fields of study and examine a candidate's verbal facility and ability to handle quantitative relations. Furthermore, employers rarely look for particular courses or kinds of high school programs in considering job applicants. Nevertheless, the program recommended here would be more easily adopted and developed if there were an acceptable means for certifying the educational achievement of the students. Tests and other devices are now available to measure educational accomplishments in terms of most of the knowledge and skills that contribute to success in college or competence in handling a job. Federal government support of the development and standardization of the tests of competence in various major areas would help in gaining approval of the necessary changes in the school and also provide a means to institute the certification system.

A third obstacle is the lack of curriculum content and instructional materials for teachers to use in a program departing so markedly from the traditional high school courses. This is discussed at length in the next section. In addition, states will need resources to aid local high schools to obtain the materials and continue their development. The national interest in this aspect of secondary education might take the form of federal grants to state departments of education to support a high school curriculum resource center in each state.

A fourth impediment is offered by child labor laws, which in many cases will need to be modified to permit a student to do work related to his schooling. Similarly, practices and attitudes among employers and labor organizations will need to be changed, but earlier work-study programs and some of those developed for disadvantaged youth demonstrate ways in which they can be effected without too much burden to employers and other employees.

The provision of funds to get started, the development of appropriate measures of the student's educational achievement in the new program, and the establishment of curriculum service centers should furnish significant incentives to the hundreds of high schools concerned with providing a functional education for young people not now getting much from school. Their experience can be expected to influence another group of high schools to undertake the transformation. Within ten years practices and doctrines for these programs will be established, even though the number of schools involved to that time will likely be less than half the total in the country. When this situation is reached, a review of progress can be made to plan the next stage in still wider adoption of this kind of program. The problem is a national one, but the actual implementation is so dependent upon the initiative and resources of the local schools that the attack must depend upon the voluntary efforts of the local groups.

Building New Instructional Content

For many years the instructional content used in American schools has been less and less satisfactory, both from the viewpoint of the scholar and of the students in the schools. Much of the current content is obsolete. It has continued in the curriculum largely because of the respect of adults for what they learned in childhood and because of the veneration for things that played a significant role in the life of an earlier time. It is estimated that from one-third to one-half of the content of current textbooks is either false and distorted or is no longer considered important by scholars. Our children are being misinformed as well as educated.

A second criticism is that many textbooks are produced by rewriting older material to improve its language or its appeal to children, but the rewriting has commonly been done by those who are not themselves familiar with current scholarship. The result is a dilution and distortion of the earlier material which may have represented sound scholarship at the time. This leads to miseducation.

The instructional content currently in use is also unsatisfactory because it does not speak to the concerns of students. The changes taking place in modern society create new opportunities and problems. The experience of the past, the organized knowledge of scholarship, the modes of inquiry developed to seek answers to vital questions, can contribute much to students today in helping them to seize the opportunities available to them and to attack their problems. But for the results of scholarship to be effectively employed by children and youth, the most relevant aspects need to be selected and their significance made manifest. In many cases this has not been done. Our children fail to perceive the vitality of much of what they are taught.

The great importance of the quality and relevance of instructional content is not well understood by the public. Man's development and survival in modern society depend in large part upon his being able to distinguish fact from fancy, myth from reality, superstition from scientific generalization, and upon his ability to employ intelligent and systematic procedures in solving new problems. Scholars devote their lives to these problems, and a major function of the school is to bring their contributions to bear on the activities and problems of the common man. A school without contact with sound, responsible scholarship is no more sound a basis for education than street corner conversation. For the school to accomplish its mission requires it to provide fruits of sound scholarship that can be made relevant and be so perceived by the students.

Some public concern with the quality of instructional content in the sciences was aroused by the launching of Sputnik. The National Science Foundation instituted a series of grants to scientific groups to improve course content in their fields and is now spending several million dollars annually on such work. The Office of Education began under the National Defense Education Act to support efforts in other fields, although its grants are smaller than those of NSF. Earlier, the Carnegie Corporation provided funds for new work in mathematics, and other private foundations financed projects for developing instructional content.

These efforts are highly constructive and point the way toward further work. However, they are inadequate both in the level of support and in the range of criteria. Some of the projects, like those supported by the National Science Foundation, are focused primarily on bringing up to date the scholarly content of the material; they need supplementation to make the content relevant to the student. Some of the projects supported by other organizations aim to make the content understandable to students, and these have needed assistance in judging the quality of the scholarship.

The new instructional content can be best employed by teachers who are themselves familiar with the new materials and the ways in which they can be effectively used by students. Without this familiarity, teachers are treating the new content as dead material for students to memorize rather than as something relevant to use in raising questions, in seeking answers to the questions, and in guiding the student's own inquiry into matters of concern to him. Thus there are three problems—selecting authentic content, making it relevant to the pupils, and educating teachers to use it—that must be dealt with simultaneously.

It is clear that this problem can be solved only as each generation brings together panels of scholars and those engaged in elementary and secondary education in order to make selections of content that meet both criteria—authenticity and relevance. These materials will then need to be tested in a variety of school situations. On the basis of these tryouts, further selection and revisions can be made. In order to assure that an increasing proportion of teachers will be familiar with the new content, understand its function, and be able to use it appropriately, the preservice and in-service training of teachers will need to include experience with it, including opportunities to utilize it in work with pupils.

If school personnel demand authentic and relevant content, why will not the textbook publishers and other suppliers of instructional materials produce the content desired? Several factors can be noted. In the first place, most competent scholars have not worked on the selection of instructional content because it does not have significant status; recognition and promotion commonly come from achievements in research and not from working on course content. Second, since teachers and curriculum workers have not had available the kind of content needed, they have not demanded it in their purchases. A third factor is probably also influential: a tight budget. The pressure on the local budget is to provide salaries for teachers and other employees. As a result expenditures for instructional materials are a small part of the operating expenses of a school, and the proportion is diminishing. In this kind of market, producers work on low overhead and devote small amounts to research and development of new instructional content. As new content is developed, the free market mechanism should be adequate to provide for efficient distribution.

The building of instructional content as envisioned here is a very important part of improving American education. It is a task that must be done nationally, since the intellectual resources needed are to be found in centers throughout the country and since the content knows no state boundaries. A major attack upon the problem can be mounted by providing federal support for content development centers that bring together panels of scholars and those engaged in elementary and secondary education and that test in the field the instructional potential of proposed content. Twelve centers, each working in a major field of study, could in eight or ten years carry the task to the point where schools and producers of materials could keep the effort moving for another period of years with little additional support. The average annual expenditure of each center, including selection of content, preparation of experimental materials, and experimental testing is estimated at $3 million, a total of $36 million for the twelve centers.

Encouragement and support of the training of school personnel in the effective utilization of the new content will also be necessary. This is discussed in the next section, including the development of understanding and competence in the use of the new content. In addition, the twelve proposed centers should make every effort to involve teachers in their activities. One obvious opportunity would be in the field testing of new content, since for this teachers would need to be trained in the appropriate use with pupils. The centers, then, would aid in encouraging and supporting school personnel to learn how to use new content effectively.

Teacher Recruitment and Training

Now that the critical importance of education to the strength, welfare, and actual survival of the nation has been recognized, we would expect to find teachers as carefully recruited and as adequately educated as the members of other essential professions. This is not the case. There is a small cadre, perhaps 10 percent of the 2 million teachers in our schools, who measure up in every respect to the quality of the best professions, but the group as a whole is among the lowest in scholastic aptitude and in overall college performance among students preparing for professions. We cannot expect to solve our educational crisis without improving the quality of educational personnel. The problem of recruiting and training personnel required for quality education in the elementary and secondary schools is so serious and so pervasive that its solution is essential to the solution of all of the other problems we face.

The image most of us have of education is one of a teacher talking with a class of children. This is far too simple a picture. To achieve the educational results demanded to maintain and improve our society requires a variety of school personnel for the necessary planning, stimulation, and support for learning, evaluation of progress in learning, and replanning. However, in few schools can the needed variety of personnel be found. Although there is a great range of education, experience, skill, and understanding among the 2 million teachers, very few schools are organized to use different abilities on different educational tasks. Some schools have worked out imaginative ways of building teams of teachers and teacher aides for educating correspondingly larger numbers of children than the number typically found in a single self-contained classroom. Where this has been well done, the special talents, skills, and training of each teacher are exploited rather than having every teacher responsible for the same tasks. This also permits varied ways of grouping children appropriate to the kind of activities in which they are engaged: individual study, sometimes with the aid of technological devices; tutorial conferences of two or three children with one of the teachers; groups of a dozen working on special projects; or an assemblage of 50 to 150 viewing TV or a film, or listening to lectures or panels. Usually the team includes one or more apprentice teachers or internes who are able both to contribute to the work and gain valuable practice and experience.

Unfortunately, only a very small percentage of the nation's schools have developed such teams or other arrangements to exploit the range of abilities on their staffs. In most schools each teacher is responsible for all the activities required to stimulate students to learn and to guide and support their learning. Most teachers talk or lecture to students, give them assignments in textbooks, workbooks, or laboratory manuals, and grade the papers or other products. Except for a small proportion of classes, such essential teaching activities as the following are rarely observed: demonstrating or using tape or film to show the student what to do or how to learn; observing each student's effort to learn or using technology to record it, and analyzing with him what was satisfactory and where he got into difficulty; encouraging students to raise questions and to talk about their interests and what they would like to learn; planning later teaching activities on the basis of the difficulties of each student; finding places outside the classroom where the student can use and practice what he learns. When the teaching procedures are so severely limited, the learning is limited to those students who have already developed interest in the subject or interest in succeeding in school and have already learned how to use the books, the lectures, help from parents, and other instructional resources without a great deal of assistance from the teacher.

Educating children in a school not only requires the performance of a variety of tasks, but it also demands changes in the way tasks are performed, in terms of changes in society and changes in things to be taught. For example, slow readers can gain an idea of what they are to learn by a direct demonstration or a film better than by reading complex directions. The development of TV and its wide use by children furnishes new sources of information and experiences that teachers can use to illustrate and explain, rather than depending on the children's knowledge of the earlier classics. The "new math," the modern science courses, the new history materials all involve new approaches to learning and teaching. This fact of great change means that school personnel need to be able to devise and adapt new procedures. It has been found, however, that, when new educational problems are recognized and even after new plans of attack are designed by school systems or professional groups, only a minority of teachers change their procedures to test out these plans. Hence, the new tasks expected of schools today are not being effectively put into practice by most school personnel.

The facts that the total range of educational functions is rarely performed systematically and that inflexibility of practice is common have long been recognized but the efforts at improvement of school personnel have not been generally effective. Several reasons can be identified.

One is the tendency to equate school personnel with "the teacher," not recognizing the variety of persons needed. Even "the good teacher" is frequently visualized as a type, whether employed in rural, suburban, or central city school, and whether the children come from different backgrounds. The profession of medicine has reached the stage in which the various kinds of people needed to conduct diagnoses, therapy, emotional support during convalescence, and education of the patient and family are recognized. Until schools recognize the differences in the various aspects of the educational process and organize the tasks in a way to capitalize on differing abilities, time and energy will be wasted in seeking to find or develop "the good teacher."

A second factor is the process of recruitment. Most teacher training institutions and most school systems seek to recruit candidates from too narrow a range of persons, geographically, socially, educationally, and personally, hence limiting the supply and missing kinds of persons who have particular contributions to make.

A third factor is the tendency to separate too sharply periods of preservice and in-service education. The notion that a young man or woman can gain the necessary understanding and skills required to plan and guide learning and in the same few years in college develop the personal-social techniques required to deal effectively with students who seek to explore the limits of the teacher's authority seems preposterous. Yet this is implied when the candidate who completes his college years of preservice education is assigned on the first day of school a classroom where he must operate alone as the teacher. Perhaps this is one reason why more than one-fourth of all those entering teaching leave the profession at the end of one year.

A fourth factor that has frequently misled efforts to improve the education of teachers is the conception of the task as divided into two distinct parts, first gaining adequate subject-matter competence and then acquiring necessary professional understanding and skill. If a teacher is to guide learning effectively, he needs to be able to move quickly between a pupil concern and the resources of a subject that can help the pupil in dealing with the concern. He will not be able to do this if he considers the body of subject matter as separate from the skill to present it.

Finally, a major factor has been the limited time and resources allocated to the task. A few years of college training, a few months of graduate work, periodic enrollment in in-service courses are not likely to produce the results needed. Continuing education, both on and off the job, supported by resources of several kinds, is needed for the development of school personnel as it has become common in other professions. In general, teachers are willing to undertake in-service work to improve their competence, provided they respect the individual or institution offering to help. Unfortunately, in the past many in-service courses furnished little or no help to teachers in their continuing development. Now, the burden is largely on universities and school systems to demonstrate effective programs of continuing education.

In improving the quality of school personnel, one essential step is the differentiation of tasks so that recruitment and training can be focused on a variety of jobs. The proposals for both disadvantaged children and high school students involved the redesign of schools to employ a variety of persons. As these proposals are implemented, new kinds of recruitment and training will be required. These schools and higher institutions in the region interested in the problem could be the places for initial attack. The first step would be to analyze the new jobs and develop specifications for them. Then training programs for them could be designed, tested, and revised as necessary. These schools in the process of transformation would become centers of experimentation. Since they would represent a wide variety of communities and conditions, the latitude for experimentation would be large and the number of schools seeking a wide range of new personnel would encourage experimental efforts.

However, the success of these efforts and in many cases the opportunity to conduct the experiments will require sweeping modifications in certification and salary regulations. Some of the present certification requirements would not be relevant to personnel whose functions are different from those of the present classroom teacher. For example, some types of jobs would require very little formal education. Differentiation in job functions would mean differentiation in salaries. Opportunities for persons to gain and demonstrate the competence required for higher paid jobs would mean that their salaries would be increased on the basis of increased competence. At present, salary increases for classroom teachers are generally based on seniority or additional amounts of training. Some constructive moves to differentiate responsibilities and salaries have been made in various parts of the country, particularly in schools employing team teaching. It is very important to encourage the initiative, inventiveness, and devotion of teachers by rewarding them both materially and with public recognition for discovering ways to increase their productivity. Teachers are finding various ways of achieving greater efficiency, through the use of aides, volunteers, technological devices, and by acquisition of additional skills on their own part. The experience of the Office of Economic Opportunity with the use of paraprofessional personnel and aides indigenous to the neighborhood is indicative of some of these possibilities.

Some will argue that the needed changes in certification and salary regulations would be vigorously opposed by those organizations that represent the "guild" tradition, since the changes would appear to threaten "guild" control over the educational process and the supply of persons employed. The changes might also be opposed by some teacher-training institutions because of the changes implied for their work and influence. It is likely that some of the new programs would utilize high school and college for basic general education and leave specialized training to the employing centers. This would represent a shift that would probably be opposed by the institutions and organizations deeply involved in the present allocation of functions. However, most educational organizations and institutions are sincerely concerned with improvement and would probably recognize the possibilities for solving some problems by the proposed changes. They would be willing to experiment with new programs, including those novel to teacher education but utilized in some industries and in the health services. This might include training an individual to perform only a few tasks using special talents, but having him work successively with different age groups of students. Other experiments would have the trainee move successively through several major components of an educational program, such as planning, developing instructional materials, evaluating the student's progress, and replanning.

Since improving the quality of school personnel is a very important factor in solving the nation's major educational problems, it is a matter of national interest. The federal government does not operate the schools and colleges that are largely responsible for recruiting, training, and developing personnel, but national agencies can stimulate and support experimental efforts. Furthermore, they can adopt guidelines and provide panels for external, objective review so that more promising experimental efforts may be identified and aided. This would furnish momentum to the program.

The guidelines for supporting training projects should be related to the grants for the transformation of schools discussed earlier, so that schools would be strongly encouraged to seek a cooperative arrangement with colleges and universities to help in the recruitment and training of the personnel required for the new tasks. The guidelines should also emphasize the importance of experimentation based on analyses of the tasks rather than relying on present patterns.

The total task of improving school personnel is tremendous in scope and cost, with over 2 million people employed in our schools. Because of the cost, but even more because of the need for competent help in initial experimentation, it is proposed that the first year of effort be focused on no more than fifteen centers, each of which would include one or more colleges and several school systems and involve recruitment and training of several kinds of persons.

Organizational Structures and Procedures

Another urgent task crying for immediate action is to develop organizational structures and procedures at the local, state, and federal level that provide for effective policy making and necessary services and also are responsible to their clientele. The overlapping, heterogeneous multitude of school districts and the diversity in responsibilities and practices at all levels make the American "system" of education a jungle in which few people are able to find their way. The reason for this diverse and confusing situation is clear historically, since public education was adopted at different times and under different conditions in regions which were not originally part of a single nation. There is still considerable support for the point of view that education is primarily, if not solely, an opportunity provided as a privilege to individuals who wish to "get ahead," and hence the organization and conduct of schools is of sole concern to the families benefiting from them and the communities that contribute to their support. However, the growing recognition that education is the chief resource on which economic development is based and social stability is assured is resulting in greater public concern over the effectiveness and efficiency of the organization of education at all levels. The recent substantial increases in federal support have influenced the balance of policy making, but no clear assignment of responsibilities has emerged. The fundamental functions of an educational system in a modern nation cannot be well implemented by our present divided and confused allocations of responsibilities and resources.

For some years throughout the nation constructive steps have been taken in an effort to improve the situation, but the progress has been slow, and thus far the results have been small compared with the total problem. In 1930 there were more than 130,000 local school districts in the United States. This number has been reduced to about 20,000, but there are still far too many small ones, and very few steps have been taken to divide very large districts into sizes that can be more responsive to their clientele.

Most state departments of education have been weak, lacking both leadership and resources. They are being strengthened, but most of them still fall far short of having the resources needed to meet reasonable state responsibilities. With the states providing increasing support for the operation of the schools, the state legislatures are increasingly confronted with educational issues on which the recommendations of state education departments can have great influence. Yet few departments are collecting the necessary information and working on alternative long-range plans that are needed to give an intelligent base for recommendations.

Not only are the organizational structures for education unsatisfactory, but the responsibilities and roles of various groups and agencies are confused. In this chaos, pressure groups exert undisciplined force, and potentially excellent board members are loathe to accept membership. Nowhere are the respective roles of local boards of education, state boards, legislatures, federal agencies, the Congress, and the courts spelled out. These roles have not been recognized by appropriate legislation. In fact, they have not been formulated in any systematic fashion in spite of efforts for over fifty years.

Substantial improvement of the present condition requires action at all levels, local, state, and national, but steps to be taken locally and by the states can only be influenced, not directed, by national bodies. It is clearly important to reduce the number of local school districts so that none contains fewer than 5,000 nor more than 100,000 students. School districts with less than 5,000 students cannot normally get sufficient funds to provide the necessary staff and facilities for a program appropriate for the needs of the various pupils enrolled. Districts enrolling more than 100,000 students usually develop bureaucratic rigidities that greatly impede the task of adapting school programs and practices to the needs of the various sectors of the population. However, the reduction of the number of local school districts is legally a task of the states, and can be influenced only indirectly by the federal government in its allocation of categorical support.

Similarly, another necessary step is to upgrade the quality of local and state school board members and provide them with competent staff assistance, but this action is also one that can be only indirectly influenced by the federal government, using such means as the allocation of funds to the state departments of education to help the planning and administration of programs within the state that are partly or wholly supported by federal grants.

Another important action that would improve the American "system" of education is furnishing governors and state legislatures with more adequate staff to help them carry out their educational and policy-making responsibilities; this too is a matter for direct action by the states. The federal government can exert a constructive influence by supporting planning and evaluative studies in those state agencies where the federal programs in education can be aided by such studies. Federal legislation authorizing grants to the states that would serve to strengthen their roles in policy making and operation of educational programs holds promise of aiding in the improvement of state structures and procedures. The annual cost is difficult to estimate, but on the basis of the magnitude of federal grants now made to educational programs in the states, a total of $100 to $200 million would be likely to pay off in improved planning and more effective and efficient operation of programs.

At the national level, there should be no further delay in establishing a federal department of education of cabinet rank; at the same time the planning and coordinating mechanisms in the Executive Office of the President should be strengthened. A proposal of this sort has been debated for at least half a century, but now the arguments against it have largely disappeared. The first objection, that education in the United States is a state and local function and not a matter of national interest, has been disposed of by the increasing recognition of the central function of education in the strength and defense of the nation and by the tremendous increase in federal support for education. The second objection, that the federal government should be only a source of funds but not an agency of planning, coordination, and evaluation, has been eliminated by the activities now authorized and supported by the federal government, growing out of the recognition of the necessity for promoting and safeguarding the national interest in education with school programs operated by states and localities.

The third objection is that a cabinet level department of education would centralize too far the educational concerns of the nation, which are also represented in other agencies such as the Departments of Defense, Agriculture, and Interior and the Public Health Service. Representative Edith Green of Oregon recently presented a list of forty-two separate federal agencies, each of which has some responsibility for educational policy. There is no possibility of consolidating all of these educational functions into a single department, but a great improvement could be made by placing many of the most important programs in a single department. Educational policy making at the national level by Congress and by the executive branch would be facilitated, made more consistent, and be better understood by states and localities if the planning, the program development, and the evaluation of these major programs were under a single department, thus reporting to a single congressional committee in each house and having the benefit of advisory councils in common.

Furthermore, the Executive Office of the President should be furnished with additional staff responsible for helping the President and Congress to effect a more coherent system for human resource planning and execution in the federal government as a whole. One of the continuing responsibilities of this additional staff would be to help relate federal policies to state, local, and private programs in order to insure a healthy diversification of efforts rather than federal domination.

Educational Research and Development

Still another necessity for a dynamic and responsive educational system is an effective research and development structure. The educational problems already discussed cannot be solved successfully merely by doing more of what has been done in the past or simply by concentrating greater effort on the same activities. New approaches must be found. The value of R&D in furnishing successful new approaches and means of implementing them in agriculture, manufacturing, and medicine affords reason to believe that they can provide significant help in the field of education.

Successful research and development in other fields include a number of interrelated activities: painstaking investigations into existing practice; identification of needs and inadequacies; formulation of new techniques and approaches; development and testing in controlled situations of resulting new procedures and materials; widespread dissemination of information about those which prove to be effective; and marketing of the results.

Until the mid-1950s little research in education was conducted anywhere in the world. Most of it was done by university professors in their unscheduled time with limited funds for facilities and assistance largely furnished by a few of the private foundations. For the United States, the federal government has now become the chief source of funds specifically allocated to educational research, largely provided by the Office of Education, the National Science Foundation, and the National Institute of Mental Health. Until 1963 almost all of these funds were granted on the basis of specific project requests. Because some of the congressional authorizations and appropriations specified categories of research support such as vocational education, the mentally retarded, and science education, a variety of conditions and a number of offices were involved in obtaining grants. Colleges and state and local agencies feel the need for a central federal office to provide "road maps" for the identification of federal sources of research support.

Although grants to support specific projects contribute to obtaining new knowledge useful in designing and conducting educational programs, these projects rarely include the full gamut of interrelated research and development activities listed above. It was clear by 1963 that the results of widely scattered research projects were largely piecemeal and were not used on any systematic basis to guide further research, development, and educational practice. The outlook and procedures of most schools were little affected by research efforts and findings. In 1963 the Office of Education was authorized to support R&D centers, each focused upon a problem area of concern to schools. Nine of these centers are now in operation, each of which is part of a university, thus bringing the intellectual resources of the university to bear on the study of the problems. The average level of annual support for a center is approximately $1 million.

The Elementary and Secondary Education Act of 1965 authorized the establishment of educational laboratories that would seek to facilitate the development and use of research findings in the schools. For the past three years twenty regional educational laboratories organized as independent corporations have been supported by the Office of Education, at an average annual level for each laboratory of approximately $1 million. The growing pains of these new institutions—the R&D centers and the regional laboratories—have been many, but most of them have developed appropriate and viable structures and are beginning to attack some of the nation's most critical and vital educational problems. Hence, these institutions and others that will be needed as the support for educational research and development grows show great promise as parts of the needed nationwide structure and activities.

But these, although constructive and promising, are only modest beginnings. They fall far short of furnishing an educational equivalent to the experiment stations and extension services in agriculture or the network of medical research, medical schools, hospitals, and pharmaceutical manufacturers in medicine. What is needed now is to push vigorously to round out and complete the establishment in each state or region of a research and development structure so related to the schools both in policy making and in practice and so staffed and conducted as to furnish successful new approaches and means of implementing them that will assist the schools to meet their serious problems and to improve the quality of education.

The congressional authorization for support of the needed structure was passed in 1965. What is now required is much larger financial support for the units in existence. Furthermore, plans should be worked out for gradually expanding the number of units and for including in the network the producers and marketers of educational facilities, equipment, materials, and services, as well as private schools and other educational institutions that may not now be included in the network but do provide important educational services to American children and youth.

The third immediate need is to strengthen the activities in the Office of Education that serve to stimulate, coordinate, and aid in the guidance of the total R&D structure. The present services provided in this area by the Office of Education are constructive but inadequate. The staff is too small to serve such a nationwide enterprise. Funds are not available to carry on intensive communication with the nation's intellectual leadership concerned with the improvement of education in order to help in the identification of problem areas that need research and development attention but are not being attacked. Another important task requiring support is the systematic analysis and dissemination of the products and performance of the centers and the laboratories. For these organizations to become a more interrelated R&D network in the field of education, the Office of Education should serve as a central source of information. It should be possible for any responsible person in education to get from the Office of Education an evaluation of the activities of any or all of the units, in order to avoid duplication and to build an organized body of knowledge relevant to a problem as facts are discovered in various units. The present funding does not provide support for these essential central services.

Financial Support

Adequate financial resources to meet the great demands placed on the schools are not now available and are urgently needed. Quality education today requires more years of schooling, better trained personnel, more technological aids, and a wider variety of supporting services than was necessary in an earlier period, and these requirements are increasing. With the recent decline in the birth rate it appears that we shall not, for the foreseeable future, have to struggle to provide both for great increases in numbers of pupils and for marked improvement in the effectiveness and quality of education. But the need for more support for education comes at a time when cities and states are confronted with greatly increased costs of services that are pushing most of their revenue sources toward the limit.

The property tax, which has been the traditional source of local support for education, can no longer be increased in most localities. Furthermore, when it is used as a local revenue base for supporting education, it guarantees inequality in educational opportunity, since the assessed valuation of property in a district is not positively related to the number of school children who live there. However, because schools receive such a large part of their revenues from the property tax, it would seem necessary to continue to depend on it for the immediate future. A more equitable way to distribute the burden would be for the state to supervise assessments of properties and make uniform levies throughout the state for the support of education. The state could then distribute the funds collected in ways to assure equality of opportunity. In the case of school populations with concentrations of disadvantaged children, true equality of educational opportunity will be provided only by furnishing services substantially greater than for a similar number of middle-class children. Usually the revenue base is lower where there are many children from homes of the poor and of minority groups. Hence, the need for more financial support in these areas is most critical.

Another impediment to adequate financial support of education in many states is created by laws that were adopted under conditions very different from those of today. Archaic statutes and constitutional provisions at the state level have imposed tax limitations, unrealistic ceilings for bonded indebtedness, and provisions for tax referenda that make it almost impossible for many districts to obtain the funds needed to provide quality education.

The current efforts to increase the proportion of school funds provided from state revenues have helped improve the financial situation in some states, but the competition for funds to support other state services has limited the extent to which states have been able to contribute. Furthermore, although larger support can help to reduce the inequalities in educational opportunity among local districts in the state, there are also great inequalities in the revenue resources per school child among the states. For example, in 1967–68 the state and school districts of Mississippi levied a greater proportion of the total state income to raise the $413 per child spent on education than did New York State to obtain the $1,125 which was its average cost per child. Any large-scale reduction of inequalities throughout the nation can be achieved only through federal contributions to the financial support of education within the states.

The Elementary and Secondary Education Act of 1965 authorized a modest contribution of federal funds to local schools, but the total federal contribution is less than 8 percent of the expenditures of public elementary and secondary schools, hardly noticeable against the monstrous needs, and far too small to bridge the gap between the amounts required in many districts and the amounts provided from other sources. The federal government needs to increase its share of the financial support for American education through more consolidated and more flexible categorical grants, through special administrative grants earmarked for improving the capacity of state and local authorities to upgrade their own educational policy-making machinery, and through markedly increased funds for the education and retraining of policy-making, policy-coordinating, and policy-evaluating personnel at the state and local levels. This proposal is essentially a summary of the financial recommendations made in connection with the discussion above of the several problem areas. At this time, general federal aid to education is not recommended because the additional federal funds that can be made available now are not sufficient to support a vigorous attack on the problems identified earlier and also to help states and localities support educational programs that are not in serious trouble. When federal funds are furnished without specifying their use, the tendency in the states and localities is to distribute the money over the present programs where political equilibrium has established the formula for distribution; problem areas that have not previously been given adequate attention are likely to be overlooked again. For example, if block grants or general financial aid were afforded, the added income would go to the bargaining table in many cities for increased salaries, perpetuating the status quo rather than supporting essential improvements. The problems discussed in this paper are so critical for the nation's strength and stability that federal funds made available now should be largely, if not wholly, concentrated on their attack.

The Costs

The expenditure contemplated for the seven programs proposed in this chapter can now be summed up.

The cost for a comprehensive program directed to the 20 percent of children and youth who are not now obtaining an education would be $6.5 billion annually in the initial years.

The cost of the proposed reconstruction of the high school program involves three phases. The first is support of the training of coordinators or middlemen. If sufficient trained persons were available and all began at the same time, the annual cost for the three to five years needed to get the program under way would be $940 million. However, the coordinators will have to be recruited and trained, and it is unlikely that more than half of the schools will undertake the program in the next ten years. Thus a more realistic estimate would be $100 million the first year, $200 million the second, $300 million the third, $400 million the fourth, and $370 million the fifth. The second phase, development of certification instruments, is estimated at $2 million annually for six years. The third phase, grants to the state departments of education for state high school curriculum research centers, is estimated at a total annual cost of $20 million.

The building of instructional content would require federal support for twelve centers estimated to cost $36 million annually.

The proposed federal contribution to the task of improving school personnel would begin with $22.5 million the first year; the number of centers would increase gradually from fifteen to one hundred and the federal support to $150 million annually.

In the development of organizational structures and procedures for educational policy making, the federal grants to the states are estimated to range from $100 million to $200 million annually.

Costs for educational research and development would be as follows: To support and expand the present centers and laboratories, $60 million for fiscal 1970, with annual increases of $15 million, reaching $120 million in 1974. Additional R&D units should be established beginning in 1972, at $1 million per unit for the first year, increasing by one-half million dollars a year. The addition of four units each year from 1972 through 1974 would require $4 million in 1972, increasing to $18 million in 1974. Strengthening the central services to the nationwide R&D structure would require an estimated $2 million in fiscal 1970, increasing annually to $5 million in 1974. The total proposed in addition to present R&D amounts is $62 million in 1970, $98 million in 1972, $119 million in 1973, and $143 million in 1974.

The total of these estimates is somewhat more than $6.8 billion for fiscal 1970, growing to something over $7.4 billion by fiscal 1974. Ninety-five percent of the additional federal funding for the first year would be used to support the massive attack on making education effective for all American children, and this would also make a very significant contribution to equality of educational opportunity. By 1974, the whole financial situation of the schools should be reviewed again to determine what problems then require support. It seems reasonable to expect federal contributions focused in various ways to increase from less than 8 percent of the total cost to more than 25 percent within the next ten years.

American education can be rightly viewed with both pride and concern. Nearly all our children are enrolled in school; most of them remain in school for nearly twelve years. The proportion of youth attending college has increased more than twentyfold in the past century. The intellectual achievements of the ablest Americans rival those of other national groups. But the nation's need of education has risen and expanded greatly, so that conditions that were tolerable and seemed normal a generation ago must be improved or our development and stability will cease and the nation's very existence will be seriously threatened.

The seven critical problem areas discussed in this paper can be constructively dealt with if action is taken now. Judging by the past record, we can expect our schools to meet the demands they face if given the means and if aided in a basic reconstruction of the educational system.

CLARK KERR

NEW CHALLENGES
TO THE COLLEGE AND UNIVERSITY

Higher education in the United States is at the pinnacle of its effectiveness. It is also more beset with more fundamental problems than ever before in its history. Federal policy has contributed both to the effectiveness and to the problems. It may do so even more in the future, since the federal government may now stand on the threshold of both permanent and general support of higher education.

It is the best of times and it is the worst of times for higher education, and each could not be without the other. It is a season of success and it is also a season of despair, and they are the same season.

Higher education is not a unity; it comprises many types of institutions performing many kinds of functions and covers a vast diversity of endeavors. All together, there are 2,300 institutions of higher education, 1,800 of which are accredited. Beyond them lie many thousands of profit-making enterprises that give training above the high school level.

Higher education now enrolls almost 6 million students (on a full-time equivalent basis). This number will rise to 8 million by 1976 in the natural course of events; it could rise to 9 million if the federal government should adopt a policy of massive commitment to equality of economic opportunity. The portion of the gross national product (GNP) expended by colleges and universities is now a little over 2 percent and seems on its way to 3 percent by 1976—and federal funds will be the main source of this increase. The federal share of total expenditures is almost one-fourth and may need to rise to one-third.

The recent growth of higher education has been spectacular. The number of students has doubled in the past decade from 3 to 6 million; the increase equals the total growth of the previous three centuries, from the founding of Harvard to 1958. The portion of GNP spent by institutions of higher education has more than doubled from 1 percent to over 2 percent. This decade has seen the most dramatic increase in higher education of any past decade or any decade now in prospect.

The next decade will see a further, but less dramatic, expansion of enrollments by one-half or two-thirds. The following decade, ending in the late 1980s, will be marked by a more gradual increase as recent lower birth rates have their impact. There may even be years in the 1990s when total enrollments will decrease. Thus the decade just ahead is the most important one of those remaining in this century, in terms of growth and the change that growth makes possible and even necessary. This decade may see the evolution of new relations between higher education and the federal government.

This paper discusses the following themes: four historic stages in the relation of the federal government to higher education; the major current problems of higher education; the several ways in which higher education has served the nation and has become a prime national resource; the impacts of federal aid on the functions of institutions and the distribution of power within them; the major alternative methods by which the federal government may finance higher education; and, finally, my own recommendations for federal aid in the future.

The Evolution of the Federal Role

The federal government, now facing policy decisions for the next decade, has entered upon its role in American higher education by gradual steps.

THE DARTMOUTH COLLEGE CASE

The first step was unintentional. Most early colleges, including Harvard, had been founded with a special relation to the government of their colony or state. The Jeffersonians argued that the public interest was dominant, that the state had a natural right to control. The Supreme Court decided to the contrary in 1819. The state of New Hampshire was prevented from infringing upon the charter of Dartmouth College and changing the nature of the private college into a state university. Dartmouth was assured its independence and the trustees were confirmed in their control.

As a result, the movement for private colleges was accelerated and scores of them were founded in the period before the Civil War. The distinctive American pattern of many private institutions evolved, each able to go its own way, each started by private initiative, each financed wholly or largely with private funds. Public institutions, as a consequence, had a harder struggle for public funds and prestige. This pattern of private and public higher education, in which the private segment at its best has always stood for independence and quality, is unusual among university systems of the world, most of which were started by public initiative and are publicly financed and controlled.

The diversified American system creates special problems for federal policy. There are questions of the propriety and even the legality of public support for private institutions, some of which are under religious control. The selection of institutions to be supported is difficult; they vary greatly in the quality of their academic programs and in their contributions to social purposes. Accreditation systems, except for that of New York State, are private. Public support of private institutions presents problems of the degree of control that is necessary and proper, or even possible, over the expenditure of public funds by institutions not subject to basic public control. The most difficult problem, as will be noted later, is whether the federal government can and should give general institutional support to private, including religious, institutions to be expended at their discretion.

THE LAND-GRANT UNIVERSITIES AND SERVICE TO SOCIETY

The second step by the federal government came at the time of the Civil War. The Morrill Act of 1862 authorized grants of land to the states to provide colleges giving instruction in agriculture and the mechanic arts. Thus the Congress took the initiative in establishing land-grant institutions, but it worked through the states and did not create federal universities. The land-grant college movement built chiefly on the few state institutions which existed at the time. It borrowed from German universities the combination of teaching with advanced research, added direct service to agriculture, industry, and government, and thus evolved a distinctively American pattern, not only for the state institutions but also for the greatest of the private universities, which adopted a similar course. Nearly two hundred universities, public and private, now follow this pattern, and at least twenty of them have international distinction.

The land-grant model created great possibilities for cooperation with the federal government. Distinguished universities accustomed to giving service to the surrounding society were available to work with the government—willingly and competently. Thus, during and after the Second World War, the federal government turned to them for scientific research at the highest level of capability, while other countries relied more on government agencies, academies, or scientific societies largely separate from the universities.

The land-grant model also gives rise to problems for federal policy. The great universities are under state or private governance, not federal, and are less subject to federal control or even to federal coordination than those in other countries. They are independent to a degree hardly matched elsewhere. A national plan for university development is unlikely in the United States, although an actuality elsewhere. Consequently there may be more duplication of effort or absence of adequate effort than there would be if an effective national plan were in operation; but a national plan could, of course, be ineffective.

The public land-grant university is a chosen instrument of its state. The federal government has also, in effect, chosen its own special university instruments, both state and private. This approach has increased the great inequalities among institutions. In most states, the land-grant university has almost always been preferred over the teachers' college, for example. The quality of the chosen instruments has varied greatly with the wealth of the states and the state commitments to research and training at an advanced level. Among private universities, the Massachusetts Institute of Technology and the California Institute of Technology have benefited much more from their relations with the federal government than less preferred institutions which once viewed themselves as competitors. Private corporations have also followed the chosen instrument approach. One consequence is enormous variation in the facilities, quality, and effectiveness of institutions. A second consequence is that those not chosen demand equal treatment, particularly as the differences have become greater and more noticed. A third consequence is that concentration of effort has led to the development of many of the world's leading universities, to the great gain of the nation. A major problem is posed for future federal support: Should it be on the basis of merit or of equality, with present merit being enormously far from equal?

The land-grant model committed the university to a multiplicity of purposes. The earlier colleges had been more nearly single-purpose institutions devoted to the general education of undergraduates and the preparation of students for the professions. To these functions were added research and training in an ever-widening span of fields, and service to many and increasingly to all segments of society. This multiplicity brought confusion and even conflict. The purposes were not fully consistent with each other: for example, the general education of undergraduates conflicted with the specialized demands of research endeavors. The university was intertwined with the surrounding society and particularly with its powerful special interest groups. This reduced its objectivity and impartiality and made it more vulnerable to interference, outside control, and controversy.

All these added functions and relations required the university to become large, almost mammoth, compared with the small college from which it grew. It also became less governable, less unified, less stable, and less happy with itself—and thus more difficult for the federal government to deal with. The land-grant model has led increasingly to turbulence, not tranquillity. And this has posed problems for the federal government which authored it.

WAR AND SCIENCE

The third step came with the Second World War and the subsequent cold war. Military might was based increasingly on scientific capability. The United States, under emergency conditions, turned to the universities for the atomic bomb, radar, and much else. The results were phenomenal; and they were obtained from a handful of universities. Six universities at one time shared one-half of all federal funds spent for scientific research through universities. Special federal agencies were established to work with the institutions. By 1960, 75 percent of all university research was funded by the federal government, most of it in scientific fields. Thus was established one of the most productive relations in history—the nation became stronger, the leading universities more distinguished.

This relation also caused trouble for the universities that participated. Research and graduate training overwhelmed undergraduate instruction. Science rose far above the humanities, and some scientists liked this better than did most humanists. As scientists became attached to their Washington agencies, their loyalty to their academic institutions was reduced. Nonfaculty research workers became the fastest-growing element in the university population and grew to substantial numbers, but they were not admitted into the collegial structure. The institutions became more complex, as well as much larger, and thus more difficult to administer. Parts of universities became integral units or affiliates of the military-industrial complex.

Justified little step by little step, the university was greatly changed, at first, almost without realizing it. Flexner had complained in 1930 that the universities had become "service stations for the general public." By 1960, they were far more in the service—the very willing, even eager service—of the federal agencies than they ever had been of the general public. The modern university with all its built-in tensions, with all its imbalances, had been created. The process begun by the land-grant movement reached a new height—service to science had a more profound effect than had the earlier service to agriculture and industry.

Federal policy is now faced with some of the new problems created by the old success: how to encourage improvement in undergraduate instruction, how to satisfy the humanists and to a lesser degree the social scientists, how to give the university more sense of control of its own destiny, how to restore its unity and institutional integrity, and how to diminish the more abject instances of submission to secret research and international intrigue.

SPUTNIK AND THE "TIDAL WAVE"

The fourth evolutionary stage began in 1958, following Sputnik and facing the decade of the "tidal wave" of students. Federal aid took multiple forms in response to multiple problems. The National Defense Education Act of 1958 supported science training, but added language instruction and teacher training. Support for construction beyond research facilities began on a large scale in 1963. Assistance to needy students was greatly expanded in 1965. Support was increased to institutions as such, to selected budding "centers of strength" in the sciences, and to "developing institutions" which meant, in fact, largely Negro colleges.

Federal support, still confined to a limited number of institutions, reached $750 million by 1958. By 1968, it was six times greater—$4,700 million—going to 2,100 institutions and thousands of students through forty federal agencies. This was the decade when the federal government went beyond science and beyond the chosen few institutions.

Both quantity and quality of higher education were greatly benefited by this new federal support, but once again new programs brought new problems. Among them were the administrative difficulties created by many agencies handling many programs with little and sometimes no coordination; little sense of an overall policy and system of priorities, and no sense of how to integrate federal with state and private support of higher education; and a legacy of heavy dependence by all higher education on federal support and of great expectations of even more support in the future.

The first stage of federal involvement with higher education assured the integrity of the private colleges; the second initiated service to society; the third expanded scientific research; the fourth provided broadened support in the decade of assistance to growth. Each stage has given rise to problems, as every policy of importance inevitably does. The lesson for the future is to examine not only the purposes but also the problems of each new policy: this should lead not to inaction but rather to wiser action.

Problems of the Next Decade

Federal involvement with higher education—though federal involvement is only one of many forces at work—has resulted in a system which might be described, in part, as follows:

A strong private segment—numbering half of all the institutions of higher education, and including one-third of the students, about half of the universities of greatest prestige, and nearly all of the leading colleges—which sets standards for autonomy and quality and provides much of the innovative effort.

A remarkable series of multipurpose universities, some of them in the front rank around the world; they are more involved in the total life of society than are universities in any other nation.

A system with supreme strength in the sciences; of the Nobel Prize awards in science 5 percent went to Americans before the First World War, 40 percent since the Second. The Boston area and California have become the two science capitals of the world.

A system that doubled quantity and improved quality simultaneously in a single decade—from 1958 to 1968—with mixed financial support, amounting in 1968 to about a one-quarter share each for the federal government and the states and a one-half share for the private sector.

These are accomplishments of considerable note, but they have left in their train a series of questions concerning the policy of the federal government for the decade ahead:

How can the government aid the private institutions, including those under religious control, with public money; select among them in all their diversity; and at the same time preserve their autonomy, enhance their quality where it exists, and encourage their capacity for innovation?

How can it preserve the excellence of the distinguished universities, which are such a great national asset, while increasing their numbers gradually, and still accommodate the equalitarian pressures rampant in American society; and how can it help these leading universities to absorb and accommodate the myriad pressures placed upon them?

How can it preserve the strength in scientific research while offsetting some of the deleterious side effects of less attention to general education at the undergraduate level, of comparative neglect of the humanities and social sciences, of loyalties divided between the institutions and the federal agencies, of loss of integrity while in the hot pursuit of dollars?

How can it administer, in a coordinated fashion, a series of federal programs without establishing undue control in a single national agency; make creative use of the new dependence of nearly all of higher education on federal funds; continue to increase quantity and quality with federal aid?

These questions are legacies of past federal involvement in the development of American higher education. New problems of equal or even greater import arise from the current national condition, and federal policy is related and sometimes central to their solutions. Three problems can be classified as common to higher education as a whole, while others are more specifically related to certain types of institutions.

EQUALITY OF OPPORTUNITY

The first general problem is to provide more nearly equal opportunity to obtain a higher education than now exists. The principle of equality of opportunity has been part of the American heritage since 1776. After nearly two centuries, we still fall far short of its achievement. In higher education, however, the object is not an unattainable full equality of opportunity but rather some reasonable level available to all.

But our medium-range goal must be more modest than that. By the time students are ready for higher education, a reasonable level of opportunity means *economic* opportunity. This requires, first, that funds be available to students from the less affluent families and, second, that places in institutions of higher education be available to them. Equality of *cultural* opportunity requires action at earlier stages of life, to provide the motivation and academic achievement demanded for higher education. Inadequacies of that time can be only partially corrected, if at all, at the level of higher education. By then the problem has become almost solely one of economic opportunity.

The degree of equality of opportunity in the United States today may generally be described as follows:

Students with the greatest academic aptitude have good access to higher education. Of the top 10 percent measured academically, 90 percent go to college; of the top 20 percent, 84 percent enter. No great loss of the ablest talent now occurs.

In terms of income levels, the record is much less impressive. Forty-eight percent of all college students come from families in the top income quartile, 28 percent in the second, 17 percent in the third, and 7 percent in the fourth. Thus the chance that a student from the top half of the income range will go to college is three times as great as for one from the bottom half. In international terms, this is an excellent record; it ranks ahead of that in Russia and Japan, which stand next in line among the larger nations. It falls short, however, of what would be possible if economic barriers were removed and only the cultural barriers remained. A ratio of two-to-one by 1976—two centuries after the Declaration of Independence—is a reasonable goal. This would mean 1 million additional students (using the "medium" projection of Joseph Froomkin in *Students and Buildings*) with the requisite motivation and achievement, drawn largely from the lower half of the income range, and would provide 9 million instead of the 8 million students now in prospect. This ratio would also largely eliminate such top talent loss as now occurs.

Racially, the record is dismal. Half as many Negroes attend college as is true of the population as a whole, and half of these go to predominantly Negro institutions which for the most part are not yet in the mainstream of academic life. The comparative chance of a Negro becoming a medical doctor is one to eight. Even smaller proportions of Puerto Ricans and Mexican-Americans go to college. Students of Chinese and Japanese extraction, however, are more than proportionately represented in college attendance.

Geographically there is an imbalance of facilities. Rural and suburban areas are better served with four-year colleges than are urban areas. The deficit of colleges in urban areas may be conservatively estimated at from forty to fifty; Philadelphia is the area of the greatest lack. Among states, Arizona, Utah, and California have more adequate facilities than any others; some, particularly in the Deep South, have major deficits. The easiest and most effective way to provide equal access geographically (and perhaps racially as well) is to make community colleges as available nationally as they are already in California and Florida. This would require about five hundred additional community colleges. This figure is in addition to the forty to fifty urban four-year colleges mentioned above.

These inequalities have major consequences. Investment in human capital has taken its place with investment in physical capital in determining national wealth and also private income and status. The private return on this investment now runs from 10 to 12 percent, and, if social returns are added, from 13 to 25 percent, according to the analysis of Gary Becker of Columbia. Inequality of opportunity deprives the nation of its full growth potential and deprives individuals of the chance to make full use of their lives. It affects the level of cultural and economic attainment of major geographical areas. In the long run, it also has an impact on the distribution of income—the greater the equality of educational opportunity, the more nearly equal the distribution of earned income.

FINANCIAL PRESSURES

All institutions of higher education face a problem of rising costs. These costs rise faster than the general level of inflation. Central to this problem is productivity, which is both qualitative and quantitative. It is difficult to identify qualitative aspects of productivity in higher education because of the varied and changing nature of its products. Productivity in a quantitative sense does not rise in colleges and universities as it does in factories or on farms. Traditionally, better technology increases output per manhour which allows productivity to keep up with inflationary tendencies. However, in higher education the output of students taught per faculty member remains relatively constant. Mark Blaug of the London School of Economics found that in England productivity has actually declined slightly but steadily. Since salaries and other costs rise and are not offset by greater output, it takes more money each year per student enrolled even in a period marked by no general inflation. Since the Second World War the cost per student has risen about 5 percent per year for all of higher education; for leading private universities, about 7.5 percent, according to a recent study by William G. Bowen of Princeton. Beyond the productivity explanation lie several others. Faculty salaries have been rising faster than wages and salaries in general—they have made a net gain as against incomes as a whole; and faculty salaries amount to about half of total instructional costs. Graduate work has increased in importance and it is more expensive. Also the quality of the inputs has gone up—more books per student, better laboratory equipment, more counseling services, new fields of study—among many other improvements.

Past increases do not determine future increases. If funds are not available to support higher costs, the costs will not be incurred to the same extent. In the past twenty years vast new amounts of money came from public and private sources—to raise salaries, add graduate work and research, improve quality. Costs (and benefits) per student rose substantially. Higher education may not be given the same high priority claim on additional resources in the near future as in the recent past. Public opinion may not be as favorable, and other competitive priorities—such as elimination of poverty, improvement of primary and secondary education, renovation of central cities, and greater efforts at conservation—are rising to the attention of the nation.

Three additional reasons may cause the rise in costs to be dampened to a degree. First, faculty salaries lost ground to incomes generally in the 1930s and 1940s, but they have now generally caught up. Also, the "tidal wave" of students came when the pool of faculty talent was at a low point. Student enrollment will increase in the next decade at only about half the rate of the past decade, and faculties have already grown substantially. Hence, before long faculty salaries should rise with, rather than ahead of, wages and salaries in general—at about 3 or 4 percent a year instead of 5 or 6. A second reason that may retard the rise in costs is that the fastest growing segment of higher education is the community colleges, with lower costs per student. A third reason is that there is now more interest in efficient use of resources at the campus level and more pressure from the state capitols in this same direction. Projected rates of increase in costs could be offset by as much as ½ percent to 1 percent a year through more effective utilization of resources.

Offsetting factors will be the constant pressure for continued improvement in the quality of inputs—which should go on for a long time—and the prospect of a more generally inflationary situation in the near future.

All in all, it would appear likely that costs per student will rise over the next few years at about 4 percent per year, or a little less than the recent rate.

This rise in costs is putting pressure on the college budget. Resources tend to lag. Private endowments do not generally rise as they once did before the heavy income and inheritance taxes, although some recent efforts by major universities have had spectacular results; and accumulated endowments must be spread over more and more students. Tuition has risen, but it meets resistance if it rises faster than personal income rises. Offsetting this to a degree, however, is a considerable income elasticity for expenditures on education—as personal income rises, the tendency is for a higher proportion of it to be spent on education just as a lower percentage is expended on food. The income of state and local governments rises about as fast as incomes generally; and state and local governments have had many additional service burdens placed upon them in recent times. Thus attention has been turned increasingly to the federal government whose general income rises somewhat faster than personal income.

The magnitude of the financial problem before higher education is substantial. If the number of full-time equivalent students rises to 9 million by 1976 and cost per student increases cumulatively at 4 percent per year, total expenditures will more than double their current level. If the heavy burden of providing greater equality of economic opportunity is absorbed by the federal government, then it may be reasonable to expect the federal share of the cost of financing institutions of higher education to rise from the present 24 percent to 33 percent, which would amount to $15 billion out of the prospective total of about $45 billion. This $15 billion would equal total expenditures by higher education from all sources in 1965–66.

All institutions of higher education are under financial pressure, but the private institutions are under more pressure than the public. The ratio of tuition costs at private institutions over public has risen from three to one to about five to one. At the same time, many public institutions have narrowed their quality gap with the private institutions. These two factors are putting a ceiling on tuition increases by private institutions, and tuition is an important source of income to meet their institutional costs. Private institutions generally, judging by studies in New York and Illinois, are currently failing to cover their total costs of operation by the narrow but important margin of about 2 percent a year. If they go much beyond this, their continued operation is placed in jeopardy.

Special financial pressure falls on several other categories of institutions: those that emphasize advanced graduate work, particularly those with medical schools; those that begin to accept some students from low-income families; those that are trying to raise their position in the hierarchy of quality; and those public institutions in states that have reduced their support per student in higher education. Some of this pressure is alleviated by institutions which can (and all can) and more importantly do (and few do) improve the effectiveness of their use of resources.

NEW TECHNOLOGY

The third problem of nearly universal impact is adaptation to the new technology—new equipment to set up language laboratories, to renovate laboratories, to make available computer-assisted instruction, to give more access to more books. Some of this must be organized on a scale that goes quite beyond the capability of the small institution, and most of it is expensive. The new federal proposal of "networks for knowledge" is intended to encourage joint use of the new technology.

Additional problems are more specifically related to certain types of institutions.

PH.D. AND M.D. SHORTAGES

Two current deficits in the number of trained personnel can be relieved only by a small number of the 2,300 institutions of higher education—about two hundred with Ph.D. programs and some one hundred with medical schools in operation or in early prospect. The total supply of college graduates appears at the moment to be more or less in balance with demand. The overall manpower requirements of the nation are being and will be met by the prospective supply of college graduates, but this is not the current situation for recipients of the Ph.D. and medical degrees.

The output of Ph.D.s should at least rise at the same rate as total enrollment in colleges and universities, and preferably at a somewhat faster rate to make up for current deficits in college faculties and the greater demands of government and industry. Thus, with college enrollment by 1976 expected to be one-third to one-half greater than in the 1960s, it would seem reasonable that doctoral output should rise by one-half to two-thirds. Such increased capacity could be well utilized currently and in the medium run, although it might give rise to some surplus in the 1980s and 1990s when enrollments stabilize or even fall slightly.

The development and acceptance of a teaching doctorate, without research aspects, would greatly aid the supply of college teachers, and particularly of college teachers interested in general education.

The expansion of Ph.D. programs is very costly. Given the funds, the two hundred institutions (general and technical) now operating such programs could absorb most or all of the increase, since about forty of them now carry 70 percent of the effort, but some modest increase in the total number of institutions is both likely and desirable if it leads to a better geographical distribution of opportunities. Since the Second World War, an average of six institutions a year have added work at the Ph.D. level; however, at present a very large number (one hundred or one hundred and fifty) are lined up to enter the ranks at the first good or not so good opportunity.

The greatest and most enduring shortage is in the supply of medical doctors. The number of people in the United States and their demands for health care will keep rising beyond the time when the rise in the number of students has fallen off, together with the demand for college teachers. Over the past sixty years, the number of medical doctors graduated in the United States has increased one and a half times, while the number of Ph.D.s in science has increased twenty-five-fold. Part of this is explained by the great cutback that came in the decade after the influential report on medical education by Abraham Flexner appeared in 1910; and there has been an enormous improvement in the quality of the training since that report. But the output of medical doctors has continued to lag in more recent times as well. An increase in places for doctors somewhat beyond that for Ph.D.s is well justified—an increase by two-thirds to three-fourths. This will require expansion of existing schools and about twenty additional schools beyond those now in existence or announced for early opening. There are sufficient communities of appropriate size in the United States, and with universities of adequate strength now without medical schools, to accommodate this increase. An increase would lead to a better geographical spread of medical schools, which is an important goal in its own right since the potential quality of hospitals, the availability of specialists to consult, and access to refresher courses for practicing physicians all relate to the proximity of a medical school.

The further development of paramedical personnel at high levels of competence would be a quick, effective, and relatively inexpensive way of providing health care, and would relieve the demand on medical doctors.

To correct both of these manpower deficits will take several years of effort and large sums of money. The federal government is the most likely source of the money. Both Ph.D.s and medical doctors find positions in the national market, and it is only to be expected that the financing of their training will become increasingly national as well. The main problem for Ph.D.s is not so much quantity as the ever rising cost of quality, and particularly how to finance that quality; for M.D.s, it is not so much quality (with a few exceptions) as quantity.

THE CAMPUS AND URBAN SOCIETY

Higher education is facing the city for the first time. In Europe—in fact in most of the world—the university is a city institution; the capital city has the most famous university and each provincial city has its own university, usually of lesser note in proportion to the city itself. This has not been the American pattern. The religious denominations that started most of the early colleges preferred rural sites as more fitting and particularly more moral locations; the land-grant movement had a rural bias; and the boosters of new towns, as the population moved west, boosted local colleges. Many of the colleges and universities now in urban locations were once on the outskirts of the city and saw it grow up around them, often with the greatest of regret. The clientele was upper class and middle class, not working class and not from the most populous of the minorities. Higher education at first served the upper quarter and later the upper half of American families by income distribution. Attention was directed toward service to the historic professions of medicine, law, and theology and, at a quite lower level of status, teaching; later to agriculture and industry; and still later to national and international affairs and national defense. Except for occasional studies, as at the University of Chicago in the 1930s, and occasional institutes, as at Berkeley and Syracuse, the city was largely ignored. This neglect of the city paralleled the interests of the population at large.

Now national attention is being turned from the fields to the streets, from affluence to poverty, from white Protestants to minorities, from growth to welfare, from suppressing nature to designing the urban ecology. Higher education will not be far behind. It has followed in turn religion, industrialization, and national power—always with a lag, but it has followed the nation and it will do so again—some campuses more than others and, as always, some not at all.

Involvement in urban affairs poses very special problems for the campus —problems more intense than in its earlier relationships. There is the problem of quality; the students from the new ghettos are less well prepared, less motivated, less disciplined than those from the middle class, the farms, and the old ghettos. Research on local problems can be grubby; and service to local agencies meets a different level of competence from that at the federal or even state level. There is the problem of visibility; work by faculty members at the community level is less likely to meet the attention of their professional colleagues elsewhere. There is the problem of controversy that occurred only in minor degree in earlier relations. But the city is not a single interest entity that can easily be served; rather it is full of tensions and conflicts, and campus involvement with the city carries implications for involvement in local politics. This can scare a campus administrator into immobility. The intractability of the problems can discourage even those who are not scared.

Beyond these problems lies the heavy burden of involvements already undertaken by so many campuses with so many other aspects of society that one more (and a demanding one at that) may seem like one too many. However, elements of a campus that cry for academic purity and objectivity as against involvements with the military-industrial complex may also cry for engagement in the affairs of the city. Having served everyone else who has come along with a problem on which the campus might be of help, it would seem both out of character and almost immoral if the campus were not to make itself available to the city; it is too late to claim purity from the evils of the world.

The campus may approach the city in several ways:

It may assume the point of view of serving an *urban clientele*. This means location in the city to draw forth its students, to serve its needs for adult education, to provide additional centers for cultural programs, to act as a base for community renewal. The community college and the four-year college may best serve these needs; it has been suggested above that perhaps five hundred of the former and fifty of the latter are required to spread opportunities more equitably across the nation.

It may regard itelf as an *urban-grant* equivalent of the land-grant institution, with emphasis on the training of experts, the conduct of research, the giving of advice; this approach is the role for the university, not the community college or the four-year college. It can be done as well in

Princeton as in Trenton, in Urbana as in Chicago, in Westwood as in downtown Los Angeles. The professional schools have a special responsibility, particularly those of medicine, education, architecture and design, social welfare, and business. The medical school can (three in the Boston area do) work with local hospitals, public health officers, and community health centers; the school of education with the primary and secondary schools; the school of architecture and design with the urban planners; the school of social welfare with welfare agencies; and the school of business with small business generally and minority-run business in particular, and with programs for training, hiring, and integrating workers from minority groups. Rural life was once greatly improved by the interests of the colleges of agriculture and of home economics. Now the same opportunity lies open in relation to urban life. The students can be an asset. Their enthusiasm for new urban-related programs can be a force for revision of the curriculum, and their talents can be used as they become the new extension agents.

It may see itself as a *corporate entity*. Here the campus can be the good neighbor with an interest in parks and streets and community welfare and urban renewal generally, as the University of Chicago has been in the Hyde Park-Kenwood area.

It may become an *arena for the protagonists* as it permits or prohibits some of its members to use it as a base for attack on urban problems. This role of battleground, which the campus may have forced upon it by some of its students and staff, is one it never plays with much grace.

Federal attention is being turned to the insistent problems of the cities, but it is not yet clear to what extent institutions of higher education may be involved in federal policy toward the cities. The new federal Urban Institute has chosen to work through the office of the mayor and not directly with the campus. The federal approach to rural problems a century ago was through the land-grant university.

OTHER AREAS OF SPECIAL CONCERN

Three sets of institutions have quite special problems that require special approaches. The one hundred Negro colleges comprise the first group. They were started after the Civil War, often by religious organizations. They trained Negroes to enter middle-class occupations, particularly teaching. Now opportunities for Negroes have been opened up in once segregated white colleges. Some of the ablest of the Negro students are admitted or even recruited into the formerly white colleges, and even more of the Negro athletes. Negro professors are also being drawn into formerly white colleges. The Negro colleges are drained of some of their academically most able students and faculty members just at a time when their aspirations for higher quality are rising rapidly. Also the tone of some campuses is changing as they move from being ports of entry for the black bourgeoisie into being fortresses of black power. The president becomes less the revered emissary to white philanthropy and more the castigated Uncle Tom. Among all American colleges, the Negro colleges have the most insistent, almost insoluble, problems.

The second group consists of the seven hundred private liberal arts colleges. Until recently they have been at the heart of American higher education. Now the universities have surged ahead and the community colleges and state colleges are making a challenge. The private liberal arts college is particularly subject to the financial pressures noted earlier. It does not have state support or much federal support. Its tuition has risen faster than at public institutions. The financial problem alone, however, does not create the crisis. Most of these colleges are small to moderate, but current action in politics and culture is on the large campus; they are rural and suburban, yet the city is the mecca; they offer a general education, but more of the best students want specialization, particularly at the upper division level, with more library facilities and better laboratories; they offer a sense of community, but the local campus seems confining to many students who desire greater personal independence and to many faculty members who wish to be part of a national profession concentrating on published research. Despite their problems they constitute a great national resource for higher education. They stand for institutional autonomy, attention to the individual student, innovative possibilities. Public institutions depend on them as examples and follow them by choice, as, for example, in constructing cluster colleges on a few of the new public campuses. But the future place of the private colleges in higher education is now, for the first time, in some doubt.

The three hundred state colleges form the third group. They have come a very long way in recent years. For the most part they started as teachers' colleges, largely ignored. They are now bigger, better financed, better known. They have extended their efforts across the board from their earlier confinement to teacher training. Most of them give the master's degree, and such work has expanded faster than enrollments for either the first degree or higher degrees. They have vitality and increasing political power. Their problem is one of unknown destiny, of how far and how fast they can and should go. Many aspire to be full-fledged universities; these aspirations particularly animate and agitate the faculties. These colleges are too big to be liberal arts communities and usually too small to be great university campuses. They are caught between the rapid growth in numbers of the community colleges and the rapid growth in prestige of the universities. They have an identity crisis.

These three problem areas constitute two-fifths of higher education, with just over 40 percent of the institutions and just under 40 percent of the enrollments (2 percent in Negro colleges, 15 percent in private liberal arts colleges, and 20 percent in state colleges). Their problems are quite different from one another, with the Negro colleges caught among segregation and integration and separatism, the private colleges between a bright past and a cloudy future, and the state colleges between a cloudy past and a hoped-for bright future. In common, they have a sense of uncertainty—the last group has unfulfilled hopes, the middle has unfulfilled fears, and the first has unfulfilled hopes and fulfilled fears.

Higher education once expected to be free of major problems after 1968. The tidal wave of students would be over; the impact of the new attention to science would be absorbed. But new and more difficult challenges have arisen, a number of which have been discussed in this section. They are not the only challenges before higher education—student power and faculty unionization are two other illustrative issues in the area of governance—but these are the ones where the federal government may play a particularly prominent part in aiding solutions.

The period at least until 1976 will continue to be one of more growth, more change, new challenges; and perhaps a new set of federal policies to constitute the fifth stage of federal involvement with higher education. The quality of this involvement could be very high. New federal money is inherently very flexible. It is not so rigidly committed to what has gone before, as is income from tuition or state appropriations. Consequently it has the potential to draw higher education into newer directions in response to the challenges now arising from the current national condition.

Higher Education and Federal Support Today

The federal government now faces 2,300 institutions of higher education—big and little, single purpose and multipurpose, church-related and independent, segregated and integrated, private and public. All (or nearly all) agree on one thing and that is that they need more money. How they should get it and how they will spend it, however, divides them.

The first issue to consider is what percentage of the gross national product should be spent on higher education. In recent times it has risen from 1 to a little over 2 percent; for higher education to meet rising costs and enrollments will require 3 percent by 1976.

The second issue is the allocation of the cost. The federal government now provides almost one-fourth (24 percent), and this will need to rise to one-third, assuming that state contributions rise at the same rate as total personal income. This rate for state contributions may be too modest an expectation, however, particularly because many states now fall far below the best in contributions and thus can be expected to do better in the future, but the states are under great pressure for expenditures in many other fields. The private share, largely from parents and students, could then rise with increased enrollments and roughly with the general increase in average annual earnings of the employed labor force as applied to these enrollments. This could mean that the considerable income elasticity of demand for higher education as incomes rise, on the one hand, and the drawing forth of students from lower income groups, on the other, could be considered as roughly offsetting each other. The private share on a percentage basis, due mostly to the rapid rise in enrollments, would remain roughly at the present level of 50 percent, with the federal share rising to 33 percent and the state share falling to 17 percent.

A third issue is to what institutions and individuals, and for what purposes, and through what mechanisms, the federal aid should go. There are, unfortunately, no definite answers of scientific validity to these questions. Answers depend instead on historical trends, political pressures, and judgment, and are supplied by an accretion of largely unrelated decisions. An effort should be made to correlate goals and means in a more rational fashion. This is an unfinished—almost unstarted—task of considerable importance.

Federal aid to higher education first took the form of grants of land to the states. Money was first provided in 1887 and 1890 for agricultural research and extension and related fields. At the time of the First World War, support for ROTC and vocational education was added. During the depression temporary programs were introduced to subsidize construction, particularly of residence halls, and student aid. By the start of the Second World War, the federal government was spending $60 million on higher education, one-half for agriculture and one-third for construction.

The Second World War brought support of war-related science and the GI bill of rights. The GI bill produced a major impact. It greatly increased postwar enrollments, with diligent students. It also introduced the actuality of a college education into families and neighborhoods where the prospect had earlier seemed remote. The extension of a college education from the middle class and the well-to-do farmers to most, and increasingly all, of the population came with the GI bill of rights. The GI bill initially had three basic principles: support for the student, free choice of institution, and payment to the institution in lieu of tuition and for supplies. In the early postwar period, institutions of higher education were receiving $600 million from the federal government—a tenfold increase from just before the war—and half of this was for support of the GIs; most of the remainder was for science research.

GI support declined in the subsequent years; but science support continued to rise. The National Science Foundation was started in 1950, and the Atomic Energy Commission already had major programs in effect. By 1958 institutions of higher education were receiving $750 million from the federal government, over two-thirds of it for research.

The next decade saw the great expansion.

By 1968 the total expenditures were $4.7 billion; they went to nearly all institutions; and they were for many new purposes. Forty agencies were involved. The major ones were Health, Education, and Welfare, Department of Defense, Atomic Energy Commission, National Science Foundation, National Aeronautics and Space Administration, and Department of Agriculture. Of the total sums expended, two-thirds now come through the Department of Health, Education, and Welfare.

In terms of purposes, four major categories account for 96 percent of the expenditures, as follows: research, 33 percent; student aid, including training grants and veterans' education benefits, 36 percent; construction, 21 percent; institutional grants, 6 percent; other, 4 percent.

RESEARCH

Support for research currently amounts to about $1.5 billion a year, with an additional $700 million going to federal research agencies administered by universities. The federal government has taken four different approaches, and each continues at the present time.

The first type was for agricultural research (with extension also provided for), employing a formula that gave each land-grant university its proportionate share for clearly defined purposes. This has been more effective for extension work, because of its geographical aspect, than for research. Extension must reach the farmers wherever they are, and they are widely distributed. Research is most effective when concentrated in a few large centers which are themselves parts of distinguished institutions. Most of the important research results in agriculture have, in fact, come from a relatively small number of universities. The formula has been politically effective in getting congressional support from all states; it has been effective in giving service everywhere through extension; it has been less effective in research except for the successes at a few great centers—less money more highly concentrated would have been even more productive in actual results.

The second approach was to set up the Argonne Laboratory at Chicago, the Radiation Laboratory at Berkeley, the Lincoln Laboratory at Massachusetts Institute of Technology, the Jet Propulsion Laboratory at California Institute of Technology, along with a number of others. This approach began with the Second World War; $1.4 billion was spent on university-related research and development in 1944, most of it in the big laboratories. The early laboratories were parts of specific universities; some of them have been integral parts of their universities, like the Radiation Laboratory; others have been appendages, like Livermore and Los Alamos. More recently the tendency has been to set up interuniversity institutions like Brookhaven and the Kitt Peak observatory because of the strength of interuniversity rivalries.

The advantages of the university-related laboratory to the federal government were substantial. The universities selected had prestige. They had library and other useful facilities. They were often in attractive communities for scientific personnel. They stood outside the rules and regulations of the federal civil service. They had leading scientists readily available. The universities gained also. They became more important scientific centers. There were more jobs for graduate students. There were spin-offs of better equipment and library resources. Because of their surrounding environment the laboratories were probably more productive for a longer time than if they had been set up separately as government agencies or under corporate contractors.

Both the government and the universities, however, became involved in very complex relationships—with the university administrator in the front room, the government agent in the back room, and the scientist seeking to be supreme over both and usually succeeding. The laboratory approach has been used comparatively less frequently in recent years, in part because the research being supported expanded into fields where massive equipment was less often required.

The third approach was to approve individual project applications that originated with the scientists themselves, although some applications have always been informally encouraged. This has been the standard approach of the National Institutes of Health, Department of Defense, and National Science Foundation. The usual process has been to have applications analyzed at the staff level, with final judgments rendered by a panel of experts from the field. The federal agencies have acted much like private foundations, and they have acted with great effectiveness. Gradually funds have been spread to more and more fields and into many additional universities, partly because more funds were available and partly as a matter of policy in response to congressional and other pressures toward more egalitarian treatment. Generally merit has been rewarded; but it has been more difficult to get money for the new project than the old, for the young man than the established scientist, for the small project than the large.

The project system has given rise to major arguments about overhead allowances. The projects have committed time of faculty members; in effect, have assigned space provided by the universities; in fact, have put an extra burden on accounting and many other services. The universities have claimed that, as a consequence, they have subsidized the federal government rather than the reverse. If in fact they have, it has not been voluntarily but because it was the only way to keep the faculty members who could take their projects to more accommodating locations. The detail of reporting has been another burden. Overall, however, the universities which obtained the most money emerged stronger and those with the least became weaker—the good became better and the poor, poorer.

The fourth approach has been to give money to selected institutions to be spent as they see fit; this will be treated in detail in a later section.

Federal support of research has fluctuated with emerging national concerns—agriculture, atomic energy, defense, health, outer space, the oceans, the city—and in amount. It must be expected that federal aid for research will, in this sense, be "soft" money; and it should be if it is to be well spent on the basis of selection of the best of the current opportunities. The social sciences have never had their full turn—they now get somewhat less than 10 percent of the total; and the humanities may never have a turn, although the National Foundation for the Arts and Humanities now draws about $12 million a year.

The clear cost of federal support to research has been to undergraduate teaching. Faculty members have reduced their teaching loads; potential teachers have taken postdoctoral fellowships which have temporarily held them out of teaching, and many have become full-time research personnel on a permanent basis; the best graduate students have become research assistants instead of teaching assistants. The worst of the federal practices, from this point of view, have been the creation of permanent research professorships with no teaching responsibilities and the holding back of postdoctoral fellows from engaging in teaching performance.

The research support of the federal government, however, has been a clear gain for knowledge. It has, overall, been fairly and even superbly administered.

STUDENT AID

Student aid now totals about $1.7 billion a year and goes to about 1.4 million students. It takes three principal forms: fellowships and training grants to graduate students, amounting to about $400 million a year—heavily concentrated in the health professions and the sciences; scholarships and work-study subsidies for undergraduates, about $700 million a year—largely going to veterans and students from low-income families; and loans, about $600 million a year—partly through the institutions of higher education and partly through banks as guaranteed loans.

These programs are administered by a number of agencies under quite different rules. The programs in their totality do not give assurance to students in high school that financial assistance will be available to them if they need it. They must arrive at the college level before they know what their opportunities will be. About a million students with motivation and achievement are not now being drawn into higher education because of financial barriers.

CONSTRUCTION

Support for construction (58 percent in grants and 42 percent in loans) now totals about $1 billion. The first major aid to construction came in the Great Depression, particularly for construction of residence halls. At the end of the Second World War there was a major program, for moving war-surplus buildings to campuses to serve as living accommodations, classrooms, and cafeterias to help with the GI rush. Beginning with the Second World War there has been major help for construction of buildings for science and the health professions; federal money has become the main source for the health professions. Starting in 1950, low interest loans were made available for revenue-producing projects such as residence halls, student unions, and cafeterias, and this led to an enormous expansion of such facilities. The current program of general support for academic facilities began in 1963. It usually calls for a one-third matching grant by the federal government, and it is administered through state commissions.

Construction assistance has favored some endeavors more than others. It is tied to growth and thus has a tendency to aid the public institutions over the private. It is easier to get money for a new building than for renovating an old one, even when renovation would be cheaper and the building is better located than the new one would be; this has handicapped the older, private colleges. The program gives special support to community colleges, with a 40 percent subsidy rate and with 25 percent of the funds earmarked for them; but this special support may be inadequate if five hundred new colleges are to be added in the next few years. Urban institutions, strangely enough, have received a relatively small share, at least for the one year that has been studied, 1965–66. Institutions in metropolitan areas of over 500,000 population received only half as much money as their proportion of total enrollment would seem to warrant; the reverse might have been expected. There have been no announced policies on subsidy by size of campus, although campuses with over 20,000 students have in fact received less support than their number of students would indicate, or by rate of growth, whether excessive or not. Utilization rates of existing space have been little studied, although major improvements there are possible. Nor has the federal government, with all its involvement in construction, shown much interest in the rapid rise in building costs or in the technological sluggishness of the construction industry.

INSTITUTIONAL SUPPORT

The original GI bill gave support to institutions which accepted the GIs, with the institutions free to spend the money as they saw fit. Graduate fellowships under the National Defense Education Act and several other training grant programs provide institutional supplements to the campuses chosen by the recipients. This type of support goes to the institution automatically and with no strings attached, in proportion to its selection by eligible students. This might be identified as "student-choice" institutional support.

Other programs may be identified as "agency-choice" institutional support. The National Science Foundation has a program for institutions that "show promise" of strengthening their programs in science. Another NSF program gives an institution a percentage in addition to the grants received on merit, choosing the individual projects and permitting the additional percentage to be spent at institutional discretion. The "developing institutions" program was introduced by way of the Higher Education Act of 1965; it provides for general grants to selected campuses in need of improvement and seeking to improve themselves. In 1968, something over two hundred grants were made totaling $30 million, mostly to colleges in the South and many of them Negro. The average grant was about $150,000.

A third type of institutional support can be identified as "across-the-board," going to all accredited (or even all) institutions, for general support, as a matter of right. This type of support, which has not been given by the federal government in the past, is now favored by most of the associations representing institutions of higher education. Such support may be given according to many possible formulas. For example, it may be given on the basis of the number of students in science (the Miller Bill), or of the increase in students and costs per student (the Howard Bowen proposal), or of the total number of students by level of instruction.

Each of these types of institutional support has in common that somebody chooses the institution in its entirety somehow, and it is given money to spend more or less as it sees fit.

In summary, the research program of the federal government has been excellent, but it has unnecessarily as well as necessarily interfered with the teaching function. The student aid program has been helpful but has left out 1 million students who should be brought in and has not adequately explored the possibility of loan programs to encourage students from all income groups to assume more responsibility for their own support. The construction program has greatly aided growth but without a clear sense of what should grow and where. The institutional aid program has thus far been faltering, with no overall sense of who should choose which institution and why. Generally, the federal government has done better by research and construction than by students and institutions.

Two questions haunt all programs of federal aid: how concentrated or how extended should it be; and how flexible and how fixed should it be? In terms of value to the nation, research and graduate instruction are better concentrated into centers of great distinction, student aid and construction and institutional support are better extended as widely as reasonably possible; research and construction support is better made flexible depending on the needs and the opportunities of the time; and aid to undergraduate and to graduate students and to institutions is better made as certain and as fixed as possible.

Overall, federal support in the past and present has greatly strengthened higher education and the nation; but in the future there is both more to do and a chance to do better what is done already. There is also, of course, the chance to do less and to do it less well.

The Future of Federal Assistance

The nation now faces a new round of policy discussions on aid to higher education. Five general approaches to this aid are in contention. Each has its own set of impacts, both economically and politically, on who gains and who loses. Much money and power are at stake.

THE INFLUENCE OF MONEY

As much as $10 billion per year additional should and may become available by 1976. How it is spent will have many consequences. It will affect income distribution. If it is given to parents as tax relief, it will give direct aid to middle-class parents of college students, and subsequently to the colleges attended as tuition is raised. The prospect of higher tuition has led such colleges to favor tax relief. If it is given to the states to spend, it will tend to relieve the burden on state tax structures. Since state tax structures, relying heavily as they often do on sales taxes, are less progressive than the federal tax system, aid to states could bring some relief to lower-income families. If much of the new aid goes to students from low-income families, again the consequences are progressive.

The purposes for which the money is spent will affect the functions of higher education—the comparative attention to research, to teaching, to different kinds of service; and, within research, the choices of fields to support will help determine which progress and which decay. The rules for construction funds will strongly influence what activities grow (extracurricular activities, research, or teaching) and what kinds of campuses grow most and how fast. Should there be an across-the-board formula for support, its structure will affect the emphasis on undergraduate versus graduate instruction, on quality versus quantity, on conformity versus diversity.

The past effects of money have been quite dramatic—on the dynamic growth of agricultural productivity, on the flowering of science, on the flood of GIs, on the mushrooming of residence halls and student unions; and the future effects may be no less dramatic.

THE DISTRIBUTION OF POWER

Power is allocated with money. It has already been redistributed substantially by federal aid. The great beneficiaries have been the faculties, first in agriculture, then in atomic physics, followed by those in the medical schools, and in space science.

Faculty members were once quite dependent on the favor of the president who hired and fired and promoted. But the organized faculty gained somewhat in influence, and the individual faculty member gained greatly. He was happily faced by a sellers' market. He had a second source of funds in the agency in Washington. He became more mobile. The monopoly power of the president faded and even disappeared. Teaching loads went down, salaries went up, facilities improved. Faculty members became more like independent contractors. What happened in science and at Harvard had its impact, however muted, in the humanities and at Slippery Rock. Faculty members became more colleagues to be courted and less subordinates to be ordered, in keeping with the oldest traditions of the academic world. The sum of $1.5 billion a year for research, mostly to individual faculty members, has changed the relation of faculty members to the institutions of higher education. The federal government bought research, and individual faculty members took the money and bought their independence. A tight market for academic talent provided a favorable environment for this development.

The next great beneficiaries in terms of power redistribution have been the agencies in Washington and the congressional committees. The agencies in Washington have assumed some of the authority over funds and functions once held by the president of the institution and the trustees; the panels that advise them, some of the influence once held by committees on educational policy and research and buildings and space assignments of the organized faculty; and the congressional committees that set the priorities and vote the funds, some of the impact once held by committees of the state legislature, by foundations, and by major donors. Washington has drawn great power and influence into its many hands. Not so long ago, it was almost completely ignored by higher education, but not now or ever again. The sum of $4.7 billion a year has made the difference.

Students have gained some influence. Grants and loans to them, usually with free choice of institution, have allowed them to range more widely, particularly geographically and particularly at the graduate level, than would otherwise have been the case. This has taken some good students from poor institutions and concentrated them more heavily at the good institutions. As the students have made their freer choice, some institutions have risen and some declined. The students, by and large, have been informed and responsive consumers; they have shown good judgment in selecting institutions and departments—and superior performances have been rewarded by their selective choices. Students have gained influence in at least three other ways: the residence hall movement has concentrated more of them on campus where they can be a political force; the building of student unions has given them more to do and a place to do it; and the flight of the faculty from the campus in general and from undergraduate instruction in particular has created a vacuum which some activist students are now seeking to fill as they try to take over the abandoned area of education policy.

The individual faculty members, Washington, and the students have all risen in the hierarchy of power.

There have been losers: the president (and his staff) and the trustees; the state administrators and legislators; the big donors and the foundations, now that the federal government is the really big donor and the agencies are the really wealthy foundations; the organized alumni; and the special interests that worked most effectively through the state legislatures, the donors, and the alumni—agriculture, law, and medicine, although medicine has been able to substitute the National Institutes of Health and that is quite a substitution.

The day is largely past of the supremacy of the autocratic president, the all-powerful chairman of the board, the feared chairman of the state appropriations committee, the financial patron saint, the all-wise foundation executive guiding higher education into new directions, the wealthy alumnus with his pet projects, the quiet but effective representatives of the special interests. This shift of power can be seen and felt on almost every campus. Twenty years of federal impact has been the decisive influence in bringing it about.

The allocation of power is still fluid, and federal policy can still affect it. A continuation of categorical aid with a heavy emphasis on research and construction will tend to continue the current balance. A shift to aid through students would add to their influence. Federal support through tax relief would give parents more voice. Aid channeled through the states would turn authority in the direction of the governor, the state legislature, and the department of finance. Institutional support, and particularly across-the-board support, would give power to the president and the trustees and their advisors.

New federal funds will be coming along at a time when the governance of higher education is in crisis. This is not the first crisis. Colleges were once boarding schools of a strict type. Students fought this *in loco parentis* kind of control in a long series of battles that started well before the Civil War. A second and sharper crisis came at the end of the First World War, when faculties made their first great move for organized influence against the president and trustees. This is a battle that was won long ago in the greatest of the institutions, but still goes on in some other places. A third conflict has continued from the founding of Harvard to the present day, with shifting locations, as religious control has gradually yielded to lay authority in institution after institution.

The new crisis is more complex than these. The students are now demanding control or at least involvement and responsibility, rather than liberty alone. Faculty members are organizing into unions to confront the administration instead of senates to cooperate with it. New layers of coordination are being inserted within and outside the campus. But the crisis goes deeper. As the campus has become less of a community apart, it has lost some of its own internal unity and loyalty; students and faculty members belong more and more to many other worlds. As new purposes have been added, there is a contest over purpose that goes quite beyond anything in the history of American higher education over the relevance of some functions and the relative importance of others. Decisions are being made in more places and more of these places are external to the campus. If there is one set of imperatives for the governance of the campus, it is that the campus be allowed to make the maximum number of decisions about its own future, that it be allowed a sense of its own administrative integrity, that the president have enough authority to hold its disparate elements together and move them forward more or less together despite the inherent conservatism of some of the elements. This is not an easy set of prescriptions, and the federal government is only one of the several forces at work.

As the federal government moves toward more aid and possibly new forms of aid, its impact on power distribution is an important consideration.

The federal government has an interest in the health, effectiveness, and viability of the system of higher education itself. Therefore federal aid should be designed to strengthen the system as well as to add to the output of the system in terms of national welfare with these objectives: to draw forth, rather than replace, state and private support; to assist both public and private institutions; to maintain a margin for excellence, a premium for quality; to preserve institutional autonomy and integrity; to encourage diversity; to provide an incentive for innovation; to refrain from adding administrative complexity and building new tensions within the institutions and with the surrounding society.

Five major alternatives for aiding higher education have been used or are now being proposed: categorical programs, student aid, institutional support, tax relief to parents, grants to the states. The first two and, to a slight extent, the third have been the choices until now; the last two are the major new methods offered for discussion.

CATEGORICAL PROGRAMS

The research and construction projects described earlier have been the chief programs of this kind. Congress has set the categories. The agencies have decided on the individual applications.

The arguments for the categorical approach are: it is responsive to national needs—and this is the main argument; it is flexible not only to meet changing national needs but also to adjust to massive changes either abroad or at home; and this approach supplements state and private support for higher education and does not merely replace it.

The arguments against are: the federal government, not higher education itself, sets the important new priorities for higher education, and the federal priorities may and do upset the internal balance; federal controls follow federal projects; and flexibility for the federal government means uncertainty for the campus.

STUDENT AID

Past programs have aided veterans, low-income undergraduate students, and the ablest graduate students, particularly in high priority fields like science and public health.

Two new proposals are of particular importance. One made by Democratic Senator Claiborne Pell of Rhode Island would guarantee financial support for two years of college to all high school graduates in the United States on the basis of need. The second, coming from many sources, most recently the Zacharias Report, would establish an Educational Opportunity Bank making loans available to all students, the repayment of which would be a function of future earnings.

Aid through students is seen as having these positive aspects: it brings greater equality of opportunity throughout the population; it gives students a freer choice of institution, which will encourage diversity at the undergraduate level and quality at the graduate level; and it requires no direct interference by the federal government in the affairs of each institution.

The negative aspects are seen by some as these: it gives students more influence and may encourage them to seek more power; it means that the federal government, in varying degrees, subsidizes students and, since the students as members of the labor force gain in income from their education, they, as the beneficiaries, should pay their own costs; and it requires the institutions to get financial relief through the students when they should get it directly as a matter of right.

INSTITUTIONAL SUPPORT

This is the most difficult and complex single policy issue involving federal support to higher education. The present programs are largely for campuses with "promise" in science or among those which need "developing."

The main new proposal now being debated is the Miller Bill, introduced by Democratic Congressman George Miller of California, which would give support to a campus on the basis of its contribution to federal research programs, its enrollment of undergraduates in science, it production of advanced degrees in science. Howard Bowen of the University of Iowa has suggested that the federal government share *increased* costs both for more students and for higher quality.

The main reasons for institutional support are: it fosters the integrity of the campus, allows it to set its own priorities and spend its own money as it best sees fit; it gives direct financial aid to the campus and every campus needs such aid, and desperately; higher education and the associations that severally represent it can agree on this approach and are nearly united behind it; and it has appeal to every college and thus in every congressional district and becomes, as a consequence, a realistic possibility politically.

The reasons advanced against it are: it is difficult for the federal government itself to select and thus also reject institutions, but at the same time reliance on the judgment of private accrediting associations is of doubtful validity when it comes to spending public money; some of the money would go to institutions of very low quality, to others that do not really need it, and to still others that serve little social purpose; the money might just be used competitively to bid up faculty salaries and other costs without accomplishing other objectives; higher education may be able to agree on institutional support but not on the formula for distributing it, and the particular formula is the essence of the approach—how much emphasis it places on undergraduate versus graduate instruction, on quality versus quantity, on science versus other fields, on new efforts at quantity or quality as against existing levels; and that support of an institution in its entirety opens up opportunities for control of the institution in its entirety, just as state support leads to state control.

TAX RELIEF TO PARENTS

Such aid now exists to a slight extent since some parents may claim students as dependents past the usual age limit for dependency.

The most important proposal under debate is that of Democratic Senator Abraham Ribicoff of Connecticut, calling for credit for certain college expenses against tax obligations for families with incomes up to the level of $57,000.

The tax relief proposal recognizes: those who pay most of the taxes, the middle class, ought to have most of the benefits; expenditures on education lead to higher tax capacity in the future and this is a good national investment; tax relief to parents involves no control by the federal government over the campus; this is a middle-class society, the middle class has the votes, and through their votes higher education can be aided.

This proposal fails to take into account: the lack of equal economic opportunity lies in the lowest ranges of the income distribution; the real beneficiaries would not be the middle-class families but the private institutions that would raise their tuition; this approach does nothing to aid medical schools, community colleges, and other high priority endeavors; it does in a backhanded way what ought to be done forthrightly, if at all, which is to subsidize higher education.

GRANTS TO THE STATES

While such grants now exist in a number of fields, there are none for higher education.

The program could take the form of a sharing of revenues, unconditional grants, or conditional grants. Senator Jacob Javits, Republican from New York, has made one of the major revenue-sharing proposals, which generally follows the Heller-Pechman plan in that it allocates between 1 and 2 percent of aggregate taxable income from the preceding calendar year to states on the basis of population and average per capita income.

The points in favor of this approach are: it will strengthen the states and thus bolster our system of government as intended by the Constitution; it will foster income redistribution since the federal government relies heavily on income taxes and the states on sales taxes; it will draw political support from the governors and legislators of all fifty states.

The points against the proposal are: fifty states will have fifty different policies on higher education and some will be unenlightened; governors and their directors of finance will acquire even more control over higher education, and they have too much already; federal money will come in fact to replace some state money and higher education will not benefit to the extent it should.

Recommendations

Higher education now faces its last period of great growth for the foreseeable future. This period of growth holds within itself the potentials for change, for better or for worse, which can be greatly affected by the nature of federal support. At stake are great issues: the degree of equality of opportunity at this level, the adequacy of personnel for American health care, the quality of human resources for national scientific and cultural advancement, the direction of growth of higher education, the viability of the governance of the campuses, the general vitality of higher education as a national resource.

I should like to suggest consideration of a set of policies for the period to 1976, and I present them strictly as a private individual unable and unwilling to imply commitment by any other person or group but also grateful for the opportunity to discuss this range of policies with so many well-informed individuals and concerned groups.

POLICIES FOR RESEARCH

Research funds should increase at about 10–15 percent a year, as they did for a substantial period in the recent past, and should continue to be administered basically on a project system of grants through multiple agencies. This will recognize the increased output of Ph.D.s and M.D.s, offset modest inflation, permit expansion into more institutions and more fields (particularly the social sciences and humanities), and allow each institution an additional 10 percent on the basis of its total grants, to be used for small projects, young faculty members, and out-of-the-way areas of research. There should be no more full-time research professorships. Faculty time should not be charged so readily to research grants but be left more within the influence of the institution. Postdoctoral scholars and full-time research personnel should be encouraged to engage in teaching rather than being discouraged from this possibility—all to the end that the teaching function be supported, not decimated. All classified research should be placed in governmental laboratories and with private contractors, not on the campuses.

POLICIES FOR CONSTRUCTION

The federal rate of subsidy should be raised from one-third to one-half. Loans should be made available for an additional one-quarter of the cost, which will particularly help the private colleges. Funds for renovation should be more liberally provided, which will help the older private colleges. Liberal starting grants should be made available for the five hundred needed community colleges and the fifty needed urban four-year colleges. The federal government should consider policies on its support of different types of institutions, once they have grown beyond some reasonable size and if they exceed some reasonable rate of growth. The federal government should be more concerned with rates of space utilization, and the costs and the technology of construction.

POLICIES FOR STUDENT AID

Grants should be provided on the basis of need at least through the B.A. level, with free choice of institution. The availability and terms of these grants should be set on a national basis and known to all high school counselors well in advance. The grants should be combined with work-study opportunities which tie the student into the functioning of the campus. State and private funds should be encouraged to supplement the amount of the basic grant on a reasonable matching basis. Each participating institution should be given some grants to be extended according to its own rules to take care of meritorious situations not covered by the national rules.

Fellowships should be made available on the basis of ability to Ph.D. candidates of special promise in all fields.

A federal loan program should be developed to supplement basic grants and fellowships.

It should be expected that tuition will be raised in public institutions, once equality of opportunity has been assured, to close some of the gap that now exists with private institutions, and to reduce some of the discrepancies inherent in the current two-price system of higher education.

POLICIES FOR INSTITUTIONAL SUPPORT

Each institution should be given a grant roughly equivalent to full instructional cost for each student at that institution on a federal grant—"developing colleges" will tend to have many grant recipients. Campuses should be encouraged to use some of these funds to provide special assistance to disadvantaged students.

The federal government should assume additional responsibility for basic support at the doctoral level in a wide spectrum of fields, with careful limitation to programs of high quality. State colleges and comparable institutions should be encouraged to inaugurate a reasonable number of nonresearch doctoral programs.

Special funds should be available for grants to assist each state and each major region of a state to have at least one "center of excellence" at the graduate level—most but not all states already have at least one such center. Special funds should also be available to assist ineffectively small institutions to combine with each other or to affiliate with a larger institution.

POLICIES FOR SPECIAL PROGRAMS

Programs should be developed to assist libraries, and thus the humanities; computer-assisted instruction; "urban-grant" activities; international area study programs. Support and encouragement should be given to cooperative programs for liberal arts colleges in joint use of libraries, computers, research libraries, and other special facilities and programs to help assure their continued vitality.

POLICIES FOR MEDICAL EDUCATION

The federal government should assume most of the basic support for the instructional costs of medical schools, as it has already done for research. It should pay the full cost of construction for additional places in existing schools and for about twenty new schools, beyond the sixteen now going into operation, carefully located to give the maximum geographical spread of medical schools around the nation.

Summary and Conclusion

The total cost of all these recommendations would rise to about $15 billion a year by 1976, or about one-third the prospective total cost of higher education. The distribution of this amount would be about as follows if the suggestions given above were followed:

Research	$4.0–5.0 billion
Construction	1.0–1.5 billion
Student aid	4.0–5.0 billion
Institutional support	2.0–3.0 billion
Special programs	1.0 billion
Medical education	0.5 billion

There are, of course, infinite ways of designating the components in a federal aid package. This package gives to the federal government primary responsibility for support of research, of construction, of achievement of equality of economic opportunity, of training Ph.D.s and M.D.s, and of innovations. It reserves to state and private sources what might be called the "basic" support of individual institutions. The rapidity with which the $15 billion figure is approached can also vary. It would seem reasonable to try to spread the increase of $10 billion over present levels of expenditure rather evenly over the period to 1976. This would mean an increase of just over $1 billion per year in federal support of higher education.

These recommendations build on past experience with programs of federal aid and recognize the accumulated judgment of the many persons in and out of Congress who have helped design these programs over the years.

Federal aid to higher education will need to be evaluated and reevaluated. This is particularly important if it continues to be—and for the sake of the independence of higher education it should be—given through many agencies. A Council on Higher Education, or a broader Council on Education, could perform this function.

Higher education has been a great source of strength for the nation for more than three centuries. As society requires more knowledge and more skill, it becomes even more central. The United States now spends about 20 percent of its GNP directly for growth (15 percent on capital investments, 3 percent on research and development, and 2 percent on higher education). The role of higher education becomes ever more crucial to growth, as it does also for the achievement of equality of opportunity, improved health care, and the general political and cultural welfare of the nation. Higher education, as Woodrow Wilson once said of Princeton, is in the "nation's service."

The corollary of being in the service of the nation is that the nation has wishes about how it should be served. From religion to science, from agriculture to health, from depression to interplanetary probes, the nation has made its wishes known and higher education has obliged. Always there has been a constancy of effort toward the preservation and dissemination of knowledge without reference to temporal or geographical considerations that has been both remarkable and commendable. But around this central core, the flow of themes and emphases has been provided, not from inside the academic community, but from the massive interests of the nation of which it is a part. To understand higher education it is necessary to comprehend both the solidity of the central core and the fluidity of the current themes; to see the interchange between the eternal and the universal in the life of the intellect and the current and the particular in the life of the people.

The current and the particular in the United States today point in contrasting directions. They point to new service for higher education in achieving equality of opportunity, better health care, solutions to the problems of an urban civilization, ever greater economic growth, and an improved quality of life for the individual citizen. They point also to a backlash against the dissident students and professors, against the meritocracy of the experts that flow from the campus into positions above the common man, against the scientific and social changes that the intellectuals dream up in their laboratories and studies. In an as yet unpublished study for the Carnegie Commission on the Future of Higher Education, these themes of reaction draw substantial public support.

Thus it is possible to visualize either a new era of good works and good feeling, or a "collision course"—to use the phrase of David Riesman—between the ambitions of the academics and the disillusionments of the student customers inside and the public customers outside the campus. The signs of the times are mixed: Will it be thought that more money will bring more service; or that more money to higher education only means more trouble? It is by no means clear which response will be given.

Once the signs were clear when, in the two decades just past, higher education boomed along from 1 to 2 percent of the GNP as it provided the alluring new science and accommodated the great tidal wave of students. A further rise to 3 percent is more problematical. Yet it is as clearly needed, and the suggestions made here are in the optimistic belief that "more service" will be the dominant theme over "more trouble." If this should come to pass, then, by 1976, at the end of two more presidential terms and on the 200th anniversary of the Declaration of Independence, higher education in the United States will have reached a new peak of service to society and of strength for itself. It will be a season of success.

HERBERT STEIN

UNEMPLOYMENT, INFLATION, AND ECONOMIC STABILITY

Compared with past performance, the stability of the American economy in the last twenty years has been remarkable. Fluctuations in the rate of unemployment and in the rate of price increase have been smaller than in any earlier period of equal length. Still, it would be premature to file economic stability away in the small drawer labeled "Solved Problems," for several reasons.

There is no assurance that from here on fluctuations will always be as mild as those of the past twenty years. Optimistic statements made in 1929 about the New Era of economic stability warn us against overconfidence. The chance of a depression similar to that of the 1930s is as remote as anything in the sphere of human events can be. But there remains the possibility of recessions or inflationary booms more serious than those of the postwar period unless continuous attention is paid to preventing them.

If we could be certain of doing no worse than in the past twenty years, we would still want to do better. Even the relatively mild recessions and inflationary spurts of this period caused waste, inefficiency, and hardships that should be prevented in the future. Improving on this record will be difficult—much more difficult than improving on the record of the 1930s—but it should not be impossible if the American people place high value on doing so.

The main reason for present concern with the problem of "economic stabilization," however, is different. While fluctuations of the unemployment rate and of the inflation rate around their averages have been remarkably small, the averages themselves have not been. Unemployment averaged 4.3 percent of the labor force from 1948 to 1957 and 5.3 percent from 1958 through 1967. During the entire twenty-year period the average annual rate of inflation, as measured by the consumer price index, was 1.7 percent. There have been fairly long periods in American history when we did better than this in both respects, and many industrialized countries have had lower rates of unemployment than we in the postwar period. In any case, without regard to such comparisons, we want to do better, especially since we have become more keenly aware of the injury unemployment and inflation inflict on those parts of the population on whom their burden falls most heavily. Moreover, the more rapid price increases of the past two years may signal a long period of inflation more serious than that of 1948–66, or at least a troubled course back to a more moderate rate of inflation. Achievement of a lower rate of unemployment and a slower rate of inflation on the average over an extended period is the main problem of economic stabilization today.

Unemployment and Inflation

In the middle of 1968 the rate of unemployment was running between 3.5 percent and 4 percent, while the rate of inflation was about 4 percent a year. The unemployment rate was considerably below the 4.8 percent average of 1948–67 and the inflation rate considerably above the 1.7 percent average for the same period.

We now have to make decisions which will affect the future rate of inflation in the United States, not only for the year or for the presidential administration in which they are made, but for a longer period as well. One way of putting the choice is to ask whether our objective should be to maintain the present 4 percent rate of inflation, to return to the postwar average of approximately 2 percent, or to reduce the rate to zero. There are, of course, other possibilities, both within this range and outside it, but these are the three for which the most reasonable cases can be made.

There is no doubt that the government can, if it is determined to do so, achieve any of these inflation rates, including zero, on the average over a period of years. The means are at hand in monetary and fiscal measures to regulate the rate of growth of total money spending, which in turn controls the prices at which output can be sold and the wages at which labor can be employed. They cannot be employed with such precision as to sustain the rate of inflation at its target level year by year. But they can achieve the desired average over a period of years, which implies compensating for temporary departures in one direction by temporary departures in the other.

The primary question is what the consequences of these choices would be for the rate of unemployment. While there is much doubt and controversy about this subject, a few important points seem well established. There will be an interval during which unemployment will be higher if we reduce the inflation rate to 2 percent rather than permitting it to continue at 4 percent, and the unemployment rate will be still higher if we reduce the inflation rate to zero. The difference between 4 percent and 2 percent inflation, in terms of unemployment during this interval, will be smaller than the difference between 2 percent inflation and zero. Also, the difference in the unemployment rates will be smaller the more gradually the lower rate of inflation is approached. With the passage of time the differences in unemployment rates associated with differences in inflation rates will diminish.

After several years of rapid inflation, such as we have just had, there is a strong built-in tendency for prices and wages to continue rising rapidly. Some wages and prices are still catching up with price and cost increases that occurred earlier and some are being raised in the expectation of more inflation to come. If the rate at which total spending grows is held down to stem inflation, pressures from businesses and workers will continue to push up prices and wages and this will curtail sales, reduce output, and increase unemployment. However, these developments will in time moderate business and labor pressures, so that prices and wages rise less rapidly, thus further discouraging compensatory price and wage demands. If total spending continues to grow steadily at its new lower rate, the rate of unemployment will diminish.

Our experience with 4 percent inflation is still fairly new, so that although price and wage decisions are being made in response to it and to the expectation that it will continue, these expectations cannot yet be solidly entrenched. For example, labor and management have probably not come to think of 6 percent annual wage increases as normal, and therefore it may not take much slack in the economy to readjust wage and price behavior to be compatible with the lower rate of inflation that was our postwar average. To get down from the postwar average of around 2 percent inflation to zero would, for the same reason, involve more increase of unemployment than the reduction from 4 percent to 2 percent. Two percent annual inflation is now so familiar that price and wage behavior reflects expectations of its continuation that will not be easily shaken.

As price and wage demands and expectations become better adjusted to the actual rate of inflation, that rate will come to make less difference for unemployment. A credible case can be made for the proposition that in time the difference in unemployment rates will disappear, and the average unemployment rate will be the same for various rates of inflation and deflation, including zero, if all the rates are equally steady. On both theoretical and empirical grounds, this proposition has been disputed; but the argument need not detain us, since even if the proposition is valid it does not deny that the period required may be lengthy. We simply do not know how much or how long the rate of inflation influences unemployment. The influence is probably smaller over a period of, say, ten years than would be suggested by observations of the relationship from one year to the next; but it is probably not completely absent even over so long a period.

If unemployment were everything, the problem would be simple. We should then try to hold inflation to its present 4 percent rate, and thus assure a gain of employment for some significant period, if not forever. But unemployment is not everything. Inflation has its costs, or at least most people think it does, and these need to enter into the decision. These costs are mainly inequities resulting from the uneven pace at which different incomes and prices rise during inflation, with the consequence that some people receive less real income than they had expected and bargained for while others reap windfalls. There are some who consider these costs negligible relative to the costs of unemployment, at least short of the runaway inflation of which the United States has no need to be apprehensive. Unemployment imposes real costs involving the loss of real output, whereas the cost of inflation is a redistribution of output that benefits some while it injures others. The redistribution may be unfair, although it is difficult to define that objectively, but—so the argument runs—life is full of unfairness, and the injection of more may not worsen the net result. Therefore, it is concluded, we should give more weight to the tangible fact of loss of output than to the subjective and intangible claim of inequity.

This conclusion, however, almost certainly does not reflect common opinion in the United States. Even unemployment is regarded as an evil primarily because of its distributional effects rather than because of its effects on total output. We would not worry nearly so much about 1 or 2 percent additional unemployment if the effects were evenly distributed over the whole population. But the fact that its burdens are concentrated on relatively few, especially if the additional unemployment is prolonged, is the main reason for concern about it. If a permanently higher unemployment rate makes total output continuously 1 percent lower than it would otherwise have been, but total output grows by 4 percent a year in any case, we would reach in December 1969 the level of output we would otherwise have reached in September 1969, and in December 1979 the level we would otherwise have reached in September 1979. For an economy as rich as ours, an economy growing richer so rapidly, this is not a great loss. Many long-standing policies in the United States—including agricultural policy, tariff policy, and taxation—would be hard to explain on the assumption that the American people give total output greater weight than distributional considerations. Undoubtedly the emphasis on distributional considerations has increased recently as we have become more conscious of the numerous social problems our great affluence has failed so far to solve.

The distributional inequity of inflation diminishes if the rate of inflation remains steady for a long time, just as its employment-creating effects do. The reasons are much the same in both cases. As inflation continues, people more confidently and generally expect it, so that they enter into wage bargains and invest their savings on terms which take account of it. If inflation actually proceeds at the expected rate, they will get the real incomes they bargained for. However, the inequities of inflation probably last longer than its employment-creating effects, because they depend in large measure on contractual arrangements, such as pension plans, which are adjusted more slowly than the wage-price relations which mainly affect employment.

In addition to inequities, there are other effects which need to be taken into account in considering future policy about the rate of inflation. Rapid inflation here is undoubtedly harmful to our balance of trade, and although this may be offset in part by incentives to invest in the United States, the net effect on the balance of payments is probably negative. Policies such as adjustment of the exchange rate of the dollar might avoid these balance-of-payments consequences at little cost. But we have not adopted them up to this time, in part because their value is much disputed; while the policies we do follow in the attempt to correct our deficits plainly impede efficiency and curtail freedom. In these conditions the effects of rapid inflation on our balance-of-payments deficit, already ten years old, deserve heavy weight. Moreover, we cannot ignore the fact that rapid and continuing inflation is a temptation to direct government control of prices and wages. Most people who have had any experience with extensive wage and price controls would probably agree that continuation of the present rate of inflation is preferable to resorting to them. Nevertheless, controls seem such a simple and direct solution that we cannot be sure of avoiding them if inflation continues at a rate considered to be a serious problem.

This listing of the kinds of effects that should be considered provides no unique goal for the behavior of the price level. It does, however, suggest as a minimum the desirability of reducing the rate of inflation from the current 4 percent to the 2 percent we have averaged earlier. The 4 percent rate has not been in force so long that the country has become adjusted to it. For that reason, its continuation would impose serious and prolonged injustice on many whose incomes have been determined by an earlier and lower rate of inflation, while reduction would cause a smaller and briefer rise of unemployment than otherwise would occur. Moreover, this rate is above the rate of price increase experienced by most of our chief competitors in foreign trade, and its continuation is an obstacle to the restoration of balance-of-payments equilibrium. Finally, we cannot afford to validate the idea that every spurt of inflation will be built into the target for future policy. Doing so would make the task of preserving any steady rate of inflation impossibly difficult. To avoid such a development is ample reason not to accept the recently intensified rate of inflation as the standard for the future.

Whether we should go further and try to reduce our long-term average rate of inflation from 2 percent to zero is a harder question. Even in face of the large numbers who are dependent on assets and incomes the value of which was determined long ago in the expectation that prices would be stable, the case on equity grounds for attempting to halt inflation altogether is weaker. By now many individuals and businesses have made commitments, such as borrowing money at high interest rates, on the basis of expectations of inflation which public policy, if not official statements, encouraged them to hold. They might reasonably consider themselves unfairly treated by a policy-induced cessation of inflation. Furthermore, the cost in unemployment of trying to bring the inflation rate down to zero after all these years would undoubtedly be larger than that we would face if we were now to settle for 2 percent.[1]

[1] The point is often made that an increase of about 1½ percent a year in the consumer price index is "really" zero, because of improvements in the quality of goods and services that are not reflected in the price index. Of course, we do not know what the rate of quality improvement is. But even if the point is accepted, it does not much change the policy question, unless the rate of unmeasured quality improvement has increased, which is not usually claimed. Otherwise 1½ percent

One may ask whether it is necessary, or even possible, to decide the difficult question of the rate of inflation at which policy should aim. In view of all the uncertainties about the consequences of different inflation rates, is it not more sensible to feel our way day by day, as we now do, in making monetary and fiscal decisions, continuously balancing unemployment, price level, and other objectives in the conditions of the time? The trouble with this apparently reasonable approach is that it inevitably gives much more weight to the short-run consequences of inflation than to its long-run implications. An inflationary bias is thus built into the decisions, because the effect of a little more inflation in reducing unemployment is greater in the short run than in the long run. But decisions made on the basis of short-run consequences affect the choices that will be available later. Inflation resulting from day-by-day decisions is incorporated into expectations and commitments and cannot be counteracted without more unemployment than would have been involved in resisting the inflation initially. The purpose of a long-run goal for the price level is to give the future adequate weight in decisions. We should not now commit ourselves forever to a particular price level goal. We should be prepared to change the goal if pursuing it turns out to entail consequences persistently and seriously different from our expectations. But we cannot hope to avoid an accelerating and, in the end, futile inflation if we try to float the economy over every difficulty on a wave of inflationary expansion.

Before considering further the difficult choice of a price level goal, we should look at possible ways to reduce the costs of retarding the rate of inflation.

WAGE-PRICE POLICY

The most obvious possible means to brake inflation without unemployment is wage-price policy, perhaps better identified in the United States as "guidepost" policy. It is obvious because it has been discussed so much

---

inflation was always "really" zero, and people who were behaving in the expectation of zero-measured inflation were expecting a real price decline of 1½ percent. The question is whether we now want to seal the disappointment of their expectations by legitimizing a higher rate of inflation than they were counting on. Similarly, whatever the real rate of inflation was, we had persistent balance-of-payments difficulty with it, and we have to consider whether we should try to improve that situation by slowing down the rate. Finally, we have to ask whether we can adopt as a target something above what is commonly regarded as price stability, whatever the reality may be, without impairing what confidence remains in the government's intention to restrain inflation.

and tried so often, here and abroad, not because it has been demonstrated to be a solution to the problem. In fact, the main issue is whether wage-price policy is a reality or merely an incantation.

What is meant by wage-price policy is the effort by government to restrain the increases of wages and prices that, in the absence of such an effort, would occur in given conditions of demand, costs, output, and employment. The policy may be implemented or "enforced" by a variety of means, but these are usually understood to stop short of price and wage controls of the type invoked in the Second World War. It has been suggested here that if, after a period in which total spending and the price level have been rising rapidly, we now restrain both, wages and prices will tend to continue to rise for a time as if rapid inflation were still going on. The stronger this tendency and the longer it continues, the more unemployment there will be in the transition to a lower rate of inflation. If wage-price policy can help to shorten the time required for business and labor to adapt to the new lower rate of inflation, it will help to reduce the transitional unemployment. It can thus be regarded as a substitute for the brute fact of unemployment in teaching people that times have changed. An admission that decisions are based on imperfect foresight makes room for such an educational process.

The most recent round of wage-price policy in the United States opened with appeals by President Eisenhower, later made more specific and forceful by President Kennedy, for voluntary restraint by business and labor in making wage and price decisions. The initial basis of the appeal was the moral and patriotic responsibility of citizens, especially of powerful citizens, to act in a way that promoted the best interest of the nation. Participants in the economic process were asked to act as if there were no inflation, in the expectation that if they did so there would actually be none. Beginning in 1962, the policy enjoyed a rapid ascent, only to suffer an even more rapid fall by the end of 1966. The guidepost standards suggested by the administration were simplified and made more precise in an effort to mobilize public opinion behind them; in the process they also became more arbitrary. Instances of threats and coercion increased, and although never widespread, were conspicuous and provoked resentment. Finally, as the rate of inflation accelerated, the position that labor and business should act as if there were no inflation became untenable; the policy was abandoned or "suspended," although some signs of its revival have appeared recently.

The guidepost policy may have contributed to restraint of inflation during the early 1960s, although the evidence is subject to other interpretations. Moreover, there remain the questions of whether the policy could have survived much longer even without the spurt of inflation after mid-1965 and whether we would have had so inflationary a fiscal-monetary policy if reliance had not been placed on guideposts. The experience of other countries suggests that the life span of wage-price policies is short.

This has not been the only effort in American history to manage the economy by appealing for responsible behavior on the part of labor and business. Herbert Hoover tried to stop the depression in this way, Leon Henderson for a time tried to check inflation at the beginning of the Second World War with it, and the government recently tried it to reduce investment abroad, among other examples. The general lesson is that such efforts either wither or give way to mandatory controls. This does not suggest a cynical view of the moral or patriotic behavior of business and labor. It means only that the 3.2 percent wage increase guidepost, for one example, is not the stuff of which moral law is readily made.

There have been suggestions that wage-price policy might be made to work by involving Congress in it. Whether this would provide a real alternative to the choice among ineffective moral suasion, random harassment, and mandatory price-wage controls is questionable.

Despite these negative observations, it must be noted that political leaders of all parties and ideologies, and in many countries, have a strong tendency to resort to wage-price policy, and that numerous wise people think it has a contribution to make. Perhaps a more pragmatic and relativistic view of the world than is reflected here would reveal something in it. But most of its supporters would probably argue that it is unlikely to do much harm, rather than that it is likely to solve any serious problem.

REDUCING UNEMPLOYMENT AND ITS COSTS

The problem which confronts us is how, using noninflationary means, we are to reduce the average rate of unemployment and its concentration, or at least mitigate its evil consequences. We would face this problem even if unemployment and inflation were not linked, that is, even if in the long run the "equilibrium" rate of unemployment, and only that, could be achieved regardless of the rate of inflation, and inflation could be prevented without concern for attendant unemployment. If there is such a link, however, we seek to minimize the amount of unemployment entailed at each possible rate of inflation. In either case, we wish to relieve the injury caused by such unemployment as may exist.

The chief noninflationary ways to reduce unemployment and its costs are:

1. Improving the productivity of those job seekers whose productivity is lowest, so that they become more readily employable at effective minimum wages. These minimums are set not only by law but also, and more importantly, by relief standards and by the prevailing expectations of workers and even to some extent of employers, all of which reflect the average earnings of American workers. Persons whose productivity does not match the minimum cannot be employed. In the short run the most promising means of making such people employable is training, including repair of educational deficiencies left by the schools; orientation and counseling; and provision of job skills. In the longer run, reducing initial disparities in educational opportunity is essential.

2. Breaking the links that bind the minimum income people receive, the minimum wage at which they can or will work, and the minimum productivity needed for employment at the minimum wage. At present, society's desire to assure at least a basic income, expressed in relief programs and minimum wage laws, inhibits employment of people whose productivity is below the minimum. But this inhibition is not the necessary consequence of providing a minimum income. If the welfare system allowed recipients to retain, net, a substantial fraction of wage earnings, and if the minimum wage were abolished, people would have both more incentive to work at wages commensurate with their productivity and the legal right to do so. Alternatively, a subsidy could be provided for private employment so that work would be available at the minimum income even for those whose productivity is below it. A third approach, much the same as the second, calls for government to provide employment at the minimum wage for those whose productivity is below it.

3. Improvement of information about job availability. Not only unskilled workers but also many skilled and experienced people find that the most economical way to discover what jobs are available and therefore to make a reasonable decision about them is to remain unemployed and canvass the market. This helps to account for the long periods of unemployment often endured by well-qualified people. It is not that they cannot find some job quickly, but rather that they quite sensibly want a good view of the alternatives before making a long-term commitment. In the present state of the labor markets this takes a long time to achieve. Mod-

ernization of the employment service through methods, already available, of storing and transmitting information, could contribute significantly to reducing the average duration and total amount of unemployment.

4. Improvement of income-supplement systems, so that persons who have low earned incomes, for whatever reason, would be assured of some minimum level of income reflecting the society's consensus on the value of preventing poverty. This would reduce the concentration of the costs of unemployment on the unemployed.

The problems and possibilities of improving training, labor market information, and income supplementation systems are discussed in detail in the papers by James Sundquist and James Tobin in this volume. The point made here is that they can go a long way to reduce unemployment and its costs. Even if inflation were an effective and acceptable way to accomplish this aim, these measures would be required, because inflation will do nothing to improve the condition of the many poor people who cannot be employed or who would be employed only at low wages because of their low productivity.

Full development of programs for manpower training, improvement of labor markets, and income supplementation would still leave unsettled the trade-off between unemployment and inflation, at least as a transitional matter. However, development of these programs would alter the terms of the choice between inflation and unemployment. It would reduce the social costs of unemployment by relieving the concentration of unemployment on a relatively few people, a disproportionate number of whom have low incomes even when they are employed; and it would cushion the impact of unemployment by more adequate income supplements for the poor, including those who are poor because of unemployment. The effect of inflation on the poor is complex. Inflation may encourage employment of the unskilled if, because the minimum wage lags the price rise, it reduces the real cost of the effective minimum wage. But in these circumstances, those who are employed at the minimum, or who receive relief and other benefits at prevailing standards, will suffer from the lag. The more the poor are employed, the more they are covered by programs to supplement income, the more they will have to lose, and the less to gain, from inflation.

THE PRICE STABILITY GOAL

By the methods just discussed we should be able to make the world safer for anti-inflation policy. As we do so, we should be able to push further to slow the average rate of inflation. In any case, as suggested above, we should retreat from the recent 4 percent rate of inflation to the 2 percent which is our postwar average. That having been done, a decision to proceed further to stop inflation entirely would depend on the answers to two questions. First, has the transition from the 4 percent rate of inflation been accomplished without any substantial and persistent increase of unemployment? It is argued here that it can be, but the proposition remains to be tested. Second, are we vigorously and effectively developing programs for manpower training, labor market improvement, and stronger income supplementation systems, in order to reduce unemployment and relieve its consequences for those upon whom its effects are most concentrated? If both of these questions can be answered affirmatively, we can then gradually push on to eliminate inflation.

The government cannot avoid aiming at some price level; zero inflation would be the most satisfactory goal. Even after thirty years of rising prices, it is doubtful whether any goal for inflation other than zero would be credible. Acceptance of a goal such as 2 percent inflation would arouse suspicion that it was only a step toward acceptance of still higher rates. It would signal an increase from the only price level goal the government has ever espoused. Moreover, it would represent an increase from a goal that is intuitively if irrationally accepted as the natural meaning of stability to a goal that seems arbitrary and not obviously superior to many others. Private expectations are more likely to cluster around a target of no inflation, and private efforts will be more easily marshaled to achieve it, than any other goal the government might set. Furthermore, even if the government announces and achieves some goal other than stable prices, a great many people will for a long time act as if they expected prices to remain unchanged, simply because to act in any other way is difficult and expensive and requires more information and sophistication than most people have.

Moderating Economic Fluctuations

In the preceding pages the long-run or average behavior of the economy has been under discussion. Here the problem of reducing the short-run fluctuations of the economy, between booms and recessions, is considered. The questions are closely connected. For example, a policy which results in price stability (or in a specified rate of inflation) on the average over, say, a decade, will produce less unemployment if fluctuations of total spending and of average prices within the period are small than if they are large. Narrowing fluctuations in the economy is one way of reducing average unemployment. Moreover, given the same average rate of unemployment, a fluctuating economy probably produces less output than one that is stable. Thus if unemployment averages 4 percent for a decade, the total output in the decade would be higher if unemployment was 4 percent every year than if unemployment changed each year from 2 percent to 6 percent. Inefficiencies occur both in the swings and in the extremes. And, aside from their effects on longer-period averages of employment and output, short-run fluctuations create uncertainty and individual hardships that we wish to forestall.

The key to stabilizing the economy, in the sense of avoiding short-term fluctuations, is to stabilize the rate of growth of total spending by individuals, businesses, and governments for goods and services. If total spending grows steadily, the money value of output will also grow steadily, simply because, if spending and output are consistently defined, all output is sold and all spending is for its purchase. Growth of the total money value of output results from (1) an expansion of real output and (2) a rise in prices. Therefore, it is conceivable that the total money value of output could grow steadily, while real output moved one way and prices the other. In fact this does not happen, and both the growth of real output and the rate of change of prices tend to be fairly steady when total money spending is growing steadily. In these conditions, the rate of unemployment tends to be equally stable, although it may hover at either a high or a low level.

The determinants of total money spending are numerous and need not be gone into here. The essence of the theory of stabilization policy is that government controls certain instruments which can be used to prevent or offset unwanted variations in the rate of growth of total money spending originating elsewhere in the economy. There are three main instruments—the government's own expenditures, its taxes, and the size of the money supply. The government's own expenditures are part of total spending, and if other things are equal, total spending will increase with the size of government expenditures. Taxes affect the income that individuals and businesses have available to spend, as well as the profitability of certain kinds of expenditures; in general, if other things are equal, the lower taxes are the larger spending will be. The money supply is part of the total assets of individuals and businesses, and its size influences their willingness to hold other assets, including securities, and directly, or indirectly through interest rates, affects expenditures for the purchase of goods and services. Hence the textbook prescription for stabilizing the economy: when money spending is expected to grow too slowly, government expenditures should be increased, taxes cut, the money supply increased, or some combination of the three; and when spending threatens to grow too rapidly, these tools should be wielded in reverse.

There are two difficulties with this prescription:

1. The effects of decisions to change government expenditures, taxes, or the money supply follow their implementation with lags of uncertain length, so that the appropriateness of the decisions depends upon conditions at some future date, which can be forecast only imperfectly. Moreover, the magnitude of the effect of any action in particular circumstances is known only approximately. The possibility that a given decision will be an error, from the standpoint of stability, is therefore always present.

2. These instruments all have effects, other than their effects on economic stability, which also impinge on national interests. Therefore, decisions about using them will not be, and often should not be, made on the basis of their consequences for stability alone.

These difficulties aggravate each other. Because the correct prescription from the standpoint of stability is uncertain, other objectives receive greater weight. And because other objectives have to be considered, decision making is delayed, increasing the possibility that, when finally made, the decision will be wrong from the standpoint of stability.

The problem is to devise a strategy which will minimize errors in stabilization prescriptions, lessen conflict between the use of fiscal and monetary instruments for stabilization and for other objectives, and permit responsible choice among the objectives when conflict is unavoidable. In the strategy we have been following, use of the fiscal and monetary instruments is the outcome of a decentralized process in which the main participants are the Federal Reserve Board, the administration, and the Congress, or rather the committees and leaders of the Congress. Each participant decides the policy requirements for economic stability on the basis of its own estimate of the actual and prospective economic situation. Each gives the requirements for economic stability such weight as it considers appropriate relative to other objectives, including the balance of payments, interest rates on newly issued Treasury securities, interest rates on residential mortgages, credit conditions in general, the distribution of assets and liabilities among types of financial institutions, the level and composition of federal taxes and expenditures, in the short run and in the long run, and a variety of other considerations which may be summarized as "political." None of the participants gives exclusive or dominant weight to economic stability except in circumstances which are extreme from the standpoint of that goal.

The main characteristics of this strategy are decentralization, discretion, and a set of relative values, including stability and other objectives, which cannot be expressed in numbers but in which stability is clearly not dominant. That stability is only one among several objectives is the most important characteristic of the strategy and largely explains why it is decentralized and discretionary.

RECENT EXPERIENCE WITH STABILIZATION POLICY

As noted at the beginning of this paper, the American economy has been relatively stable in the past twenty years; government policy must be given a considerable measure of the credit for that. But if we seek to do better in the future, we must ask why we did not do better in these years. Two recent experiences with stabilization policy are instructive.

The United States went through a long period of relatively high unemployment from 1958 through 1964. Recovery from the 1957–58 recession was incomplete; it was followed by another decline in 1960–61, from which recovery was steady but slow. In retrospect it appears that policy should have been more expansive in 1958; or, failing that, should not have become so restrictive in 1960; or, given that development, should have become more stimulative earlier in 1961. Why didn't these things happen?

Errors of economic appraisal were partly at fault. The probable strength of the recovery which began in the summer of 1958 was overestimated, and the extent to which policy had turned restrictive by early 1959 was underestimated. But these developments are probably a minor part of the explanation. Other aims stood in the way of stabilization policy at every point. The administration's ideas of desirable long-run tax reform deterred it from initiating tax reduction in 1958. Balance-of-payments considerations inhibited both fiscal and monetary policy throughout. In the years 1958–60 concern with arresting inflation damped interest in stimulating a slack economy. In 1961 and 1962 the administration's plans for a big expansion of spending programs kept it from asking for tax reduction, while Congress was reluctant to approve its plans. When tax reduction was finally requested, action was delayed by disagreement between the administration and Congress over tax reform and over the desire of Congress to check the rising trend of government spending.

The rapid inflation in the three years after mid-1965 also reflected a mixture of errors of forecasting and conflicts with nonstabilization objectives. The extent of the inflation was not appreciated for some time after it began, and this prevented the timely application of fiscal and monetary restraints. But concern with rising interest rates always acted to moderate monetary restraint; while fiscal action was delayed both by the natural political aversion to tax increases and by congressional manipulation of the administration's 1967 request as a level for achieving expenditure reduction.

Thus it is clear that pressure to attain objectives other than stability has been a major factor in the inadequate use of fiscal and monetary policy for stabilization purposes.

FLEXIBILITY IN TAXATION

One great obstacle to more effective use of fiscal policy as an instrument of economic stability lies in the many important implications and consequences every tax or expenditure action has in addition to its impact on the overall condition of the economy. Such effects are inevitable with respect to almost all of the budget, and it would be unwise to try to subordinate them to the stability objective. Still, it should be possible without major sacrifice of other important objectives to make part of the budget, and through that its net position, more responsive to the requirements of stability. Probably the major possibility is to introduce greater flexibility into part of the tax structure.

What is needed is the ability to consider some tax changes freed as far as possible from the presumption that the change will be permanent and from issues of the structure and distribution of taxes. A common proposal for creating this ability is to give the President authority to raise or lower tax rates, within a specified range and for a specified period, when required for reasons of economic stability. This suggestion has received little attention from Congress. It involves a shift of power to the President which is not only naturally unpopular in Congress but also unnecessary for the purpose. Moreover, tying the request for the authority to its use as an instrument of stabilization lends it the appearance of a device for "fine tuning" which is not essential to it. Even if we ignored stability considerations and decided to carry out a budget-balancing policy instead, we would need more flexibility in taxation when expenditures are as variable relative to the national income as they have been recently.

One possibility would be to try to establish the practice of annual consideration, through the ordinary legislative process, of the size of a one-year surcharge on the basic rates of individual and corporate income tax. The President would recommend the rate of the surcharge, which might be zero or even negative, on the basis of whatever combination of considerations he thinks important. Congress would debate the proposal, and pass it, with or without amendments, or reject it. Congress might have objectives different from the President's. It might use the legislation in an attempt to force the President to change the expenditure side of the budget, as it did in 1968. In any case, both Congress and the President would have a vehicle for making an overall fiscal decision in a fairly routine way, without declaring or acknowledging any emergency, and with assurance that the decision would not bind the future. This does not guarantee that decisions made in one year would not influence decisions made in subsequent years, but it would be a move in that direction. Moreover, there is reason to believe, after the experience of 1968, that an across-the-board equal percentage surcharge of moderate size would be accepted as a distributionally neutral tax change and would not stir protracted debate over the question of its equity.

STABLE INTEREST RATES
OR A STABLE ECONOMY

The common concern with stable interest rates—usually meaning stable and low—has been another persistent limitation on stabilization policy in the postwar period. The traditional arena of the conflict between stabilization policy and interest rate policy has been federal debt management. A different and probably more serious aspect of the conflict between general stability and interest rate stability came to the fore during the inflationary experience after mid-1965. It arises from the prohibition against the payment of interest on demand deposits and the legal ceilings on interest rates that may be paid on bank time deposits and savings and loan shares. As a result of the relative inflexibility of these rates, the attractiveness of holding deposits in banks and thrift institutions declines when market rates of interest rise, because depositors can earn more elsewhere. This development weakens the anti-inflationary effect of restraint on the growth of the money supply, because in these circumstances people want to hold less money anyway. Also, the shift of funds out of the savings departments of banks and out of thrift institutions endangers those institutions and the borrowers, mainly the housing industry, who particularly depend on them. This process accentuates what would in any case be a special sensitivity of the housing industry to rising interest rates and credit stringency.

One important thing that could be done to soften the adverse impact of the variability of interest rates associated with a policy of economic stability is to abolish the limitations on interest rates paid by banks and other financial institutions. This would permit the rates on deposits to vary when market rates varied and would thus prevent variations in the latter from causing big shifts in the spread between the two rate structures. One result would be to dampen fluctuations in the desire to hold demand deposits and thereby to increase the stabilization effect of a policy of steady monetary growth or of any other policy seeking economic stability through management of the money supply. A second result would be to moderate shifts of funds between savings institutions and other forms of investment, reducing the threat which interest rate variations pose to those institutions and to the housing industry. If this were done, monetary policy might be less inhibited in pursuit of economic stability when that requires, at least temporarily, higher interest rates.

THE BALANCE-OF-PAYMENTS CONSTRAINT

The third objective that has compromised pursuit of a stabilizing fiscal-monetary policy—and potentially the most difficult—has been balance-of-payments equilibrium. Vigorous fiscal-monetary expansion has at times been checked by the fear that an increase of our imports and decrease of our exports would result. In addition, we have practiced monetary restraint in the hope of raising interest rates in the United States and discouraging capital outflow.

To devise means of meeting balance-of-payments requirements without diverting fiscal-monetary policy from the goal of stability would be a major contribution. The United States has already tried a number of ways: limitations on government purchases abroad; "Buy American" strings on foreign aid; a special tax on U.S. investment abroad; and controls on such investment. These efforts have had indifferent success in reducing balance-of-payments deficits and have impeded the economical flow of trade and capital. Other, more powerful, comprehensive, and nondiscriminatory measures, including variation of the exchange rate, deserve consideration. Each involves costs of its own. This problem is discussed in detail in Richard Cooper's paper in this volume, and only two points need to be made here. First, if other means can be found to manage the balance of payments, the gain in the effectiveness of stabilization policy would be great; second, we cannot count on relieving fiscal and monetary policy entirely of concern with the balance of payments.

Much the same can be said of the other conflicts which have been discussed. We should be able to make stability cheaper in terms of the sacrifice of other goals required to obtain it. That done, we should expect to achieve greater stability. But we shall still have to consider whether we want to give stability greater weight, and what kind of strategy would do so.

ALTERNATIVE STRATEGIES

Two alternatives to the present decentralized and discretionary strategy with its ad hoc evaluation of objectives deserve consideration. One would prescribe objective rules to guide monetary policy or fiscal policy or both. The most common proposals under this heading are that the money supply (usually meaning currency and demand deposits) should be caused to grow at a steady rate or at a rate within a range, such as 2 to 6 percent per year, and that the surplus or deficit in the budget as it would be at full employment should be kept constant. This may be called the "stabilizing rules" strategy. The other strategy would adapt policy as flexibly and frequently as seemed appropriate to changing appraisal of the economic situation and to requirements for economic stabilization determined in the light of that appraisal. This may be called the "stabilizing discretion" strategy.

The differences between these two strategies have been the subject of much discussion. But they have an important characteristic in common. Both are strategies for giving much greater weight to the stability objective in making fiscal-monetary decisions. The rules to be followed under the first strategy are chosen because they are the most likely to yield economic stability; one intent is to preclude the possibility of compromising the stability objective in the pursuit of other goals. The other strategy seeks to divorce discretionary decisions about stabilization from concern with other goals; the discretion is with respect to means, not ends.

A RULE FOR MONETARY POLICY?

The basic rationale for a rule of monetary policy is that it reduces errors of prescription and prevents diversion of policy from the stabilization objective. A priori it may seem unlikely that a rule could be specified in advance which would give better policy prescriptions than would be made on the basis of information available at the time of decision. The choices open under a discretionary policy would include adherence to a conventional rule and departure from it when evidence of the need to do so was clear. While presumably none would deny that the evidence might sometimes be clear, the problem is that its appraisal by those authorized to make decisions may be biased. Decision makers have a tendency to interpret evidence in ways that support decisions they would like to make. For example, they may wish to avoid actions which clearly focus responsibility on them, preferring a passive rather than an active posture, at least until conditions become critical, and hence lean toward interpretation of the evidence that justifies that posture. In particular, the monetary authority, the Federal Reserve, may tend to overweight considerations that are more important in the special world it inhabits than in the community at large, such as stability of money markets and balance-of-payments developments. Moreover, those in authority are inclined to have exceptionally high confidence in their own ability to foresee the future and adapt policy to it. This creates another kind of bias.

Whether a specific rule will give better policy prescriptions than come out of ad hoc decisions is an empirical question and cannot be answered a priori. There is substantial reason to believe that the American economy would have been more stable than it actually has been if a rule of steady growth in the money supply had been applied. The main contribution of monetary policy to economic stability in the postwar period was to approach steadiness of monetary growth more closely than in previous periods of equal length. The linkage between steady growth in the money supply and economic stability may not, however, be well enough established to justify advance commitments which limit freedom to make adjustments in the event stability does not in fact ensue. Although they have not been encountered in the postwar period, there may yet develop inflationary or deflationary pressures so serious and unmistakable as to demand forceful countervailing monetary policy rather than automatic adherence to the rule of steady growth in the money supply. The insulation such a rule might provide against the vagaries of discretionary policy in ordinary times might be dearly bought with the shackling of policy in an emergency which calls for stronger measures. Thus it does not seem prudent in the present state of knowledge to prohibit departure from the rule, even if it were possible to do so. But how and by whom should departures be decided? And how is the regime of the rule to be established?

Those characteristics of the Federal Reserve which provoke others to suggest a monetary rule make it quite unlikely that the Federal Reserve would itself espouse the rule. Congress, whose creature the Federal Reserve is in a formal sense, might establish the rule; the Joint Economic Committee has, in fact, shown interest in doing so. Congress would thus become the monetary authority to an important degree. While the natural inertia of Congress might safeguard against frequent or erratic changes in the rule, a more serious danger is that Congress would exercise its new authority to set a rule less conducive to economic stability than that of steady growth in the money supply. The obvious candidate is stable and low interest rates.

Even if it were clear that adherence to the monetary rule would yield the highest achievable degree of stability, the other objectives of monetary-fiscal policy would still be of concern. The most troublesome of these is the balance of payments. Since both fiscal and monetary tools are available, one possibility would be to adapt fiscal policy to the requirements of the balance of payments while monetary policy continued to play its stabilizing role. Thus if higher interest rates were required in order to stem the outflow of funds, that might be achieved by running a large budget deficit and, at the same time, maintaining an unchanged monetary policy. But would steady growth of the money supply be stabilizing if fiscal policy were producing variations in interest rates for the sake of equilibrium in the balance of payments? The proposition that the economy would be fairly stable if the money supply grew steadily implies that variations of interest rates originating in the private sector would not be destabilizing, and there is no reason to think that variations produced by fiscal policy would be any more so. But part of the argument for the rule is that it is destabilizing to try to compensate for unpredictable economic changes. If there are planned and foreseeable changes arising from fiscal policy, there may be a case for adapting monetary policy to them, even though adaptation to changes in the private sector is unwise. In fact, of course, the changes arising from the federal budget have often not been predictable.

The monetary rule will be examined again after a look at the problems and potentials of fiscal policy.

A RULE FOR FISCAL POLICY?

Postwar discussion has emphasized a standard version of a "modern" rule for fiscal policy that would require tax rates and expenditure programs to be so adjusted to each other that the budget would be in balance (or have a specified constant surplus or deficit) when the economy is operating at high employment. There would automatically be a deficit when the economy operated below that level, mainly because of the shrinkage of tax revenues, and a surplus at levels above it. Such a policy is intended to minimize the unstabilizing effects of budget variations by holding the relation between revenues and expenditures approximately constant when the economy is stable. The automatic variations of the budget surplus or deficit with fluctuations in the economy would tend to moderate economic fluctuations. Furthermore, this budget rule has been expected to discipline decisions to spend by requiring that they be matched by decisions to tax.

There is little doubt that adherence to this rule would have produced a more stabilizing fiscal policy than we actually had in the past twenty years. It would have prevented the large increases in the deficit during the Korean and Vietnam wars, and in the potential surplus (the surplus we would have had at high employment) in 1959–60. Also, experience suggests that, for stabilization purposes, to do better than this rule will be very difficult.

The "expenditure discipline" case for the rule is essentially a pragmatic one. It is believed that the political process results in overestimating the benefits of government expenditures, and therefore in excessive expenditures, unless the tax requirement is imposed. But this belief reflects a judgment about how high expenditures should be; and there are many who believe that the benefits of government expenditures tend to be underestimated, at least by comparison with the taxpayers' appreciation of the tax burden, and that on the whole we do not spend enough for public services. On this view, there is no good reason to put arbitrary limits on expenditures.

Whatever its merits might be if it were imposed, the concept of the balanced high-employment budget does not exist as a rule and there is no visible way to bring it to life as one. Those who initially proposed it hoped it would inherit the potency of what they believed to be the rule of the annually balanced budget. But the old rule is dead and had, in any case, nothing to bequeath. Any new rule would have to be established ab ovo, a very difficult procedure. This is especially true in view of the fact that it would have to be proposed and ratified by the President and Congress, the very parties it would be designed to restrain. Although Congress can lay down a monetary rule for the Federal Reserve, no institution has the power to impose a fiscal rule on the President and Congress.

No immediate alternative exists to a discretionary fiscal policy which reflects the weights Congress and the President place on numerous objectives from time to time. Still, the President might promote the idea that overall economic considerations, including stability and balance-of-payments equilibrium, should have a more significant role in fiscal decisions. The President bears main responsibility for these objectives, is more limited by them than Congress is, and has every incentive to try to get them accepted by Congress. To do this, he will have to demonstrate his acceptance of the limitations these objectives place on his own freedom. If Congress suspects that the President's concern with overall economic objectives is turned on and off as he finds convenient to support policies he wants on other grounds, it is not likely to be guided by those objectives. Moreover, if Congress thinks that the President is asking it to take strong, and often distasteful, action on the basis of weak forecasts of the economy, it will also be reluctant to accede.

THE COMBINATION OF MONETARY AND FISCAL POLICY

The foregoing recital cannot be said to point unequivocally to one best course of action. This should not be surprising. We have not been doing badly with respect to stability. Moreover, what is known about the subject, as well as much that is believed to be true but disputed, is adequately represented in the deliberations of policy makers. We cannot say that well-established truths have been neglected through ignorance, or that our performance cries out for change. Nevertheless, we can do better.

If we want more and better assured stability, we should devote our most manageable instrument to that purpose. That is, surely, monetary policy, because the competing claims upon it are fewer than the claims upon fiscal policy. There is also a presumption that steadier growth of the money supply would contribute to greater stability. A reasonable and cautious step toward steadier monetary growth is embodied in the recent proposal of the Joint Economic Committee, which calls on Congress to advise the Federal Reserve to hold the rate of monetary growth within certain limits (the Committee suggested 2 to 6 percent per year) and to explain to Congress when it allowed those limits to be exceeded. This is a fairly elastic rule, but it would safeguard against extreme variations in the rate of monetary growth that come about in passive response to market conditions rather than as positive policy of the monetary authority. Beyond this, Congress might advise the Federal Reserve that in exercising discretion, within the specified limits or outside them, it should be guided primarily by considerations of overall economic stability.

To tie fiscal policy down with a rule would be unwise amid the present uncertainty and disagreement about the effectiveness of monetary policy in stabilizing the economy. Furthermore, it would probably be impossible, starting, as we do, with no rules at all for fiscal policy. If steady growth of the money supply proves to be as effective an instrument of stabilization as many expect, fiscal policy will not in fact have to be bent much to the achievement of stability. But preserving the freedom of fiscal policy will provide a safeguard if that expectation is mistaken.

STEPHEN K. BAILEY

MANAGING THE FEDERAL GOVERNMENT

The President of the United States faces a crisis of public confidence in the capacity of the federal government to manage itself and to carry out with efficiency, equity, and dispatch its own legislative mandates.

The seriousness of this issue can hardly be overstated. In question is the capacity of an eighteenth century constitutional arrangement of widely diffused and shared powers and a nineteenth century system of political pluralism to deal effectively with twentieth century problems of technological, social, and economic interdependencies—at home and abroad.

Unless the President devotes substantial attention to making the system work—an effort involving persistence and the employment of high political skills—the consequences for the future of the American polity could be serious in the extreme.

The programs and policies of the government of the United States are currently carried out by a diverse collection of political, administrative, and judicial systems. (The last of these is not treated in this paper.)

The descriptive and taxonomic problems alone are almost grotesque in their complexity. One may list and classify the obvious. The federal government of 1968 contains: three constitutional branches—legislative, executive, and judicial; an Executive Office of the President with a half dozen major constituent units and scores of minor councils and committees; four operating agencies exclusively responsible to the Congress, which itself is divided into two houses, forty standing committees, and more than two hundred subcommittees; twelve cabinet departments; fifty independent agencies, nine of which are independent regulatory commissions with both quasi-legislative and quasi-judicial authority; fifty statutory interagency committees; 2.8 million civilian employees, 90 percent of whom are employed in federal field offices outside of the Washington, D.C., area; and 3 million military employees.

This gross breakdown suggests the magnitude and diversity of the enterprise, but it is only the tip of the iceberg. For federal policies are today carried out through a bewildering number of entities and instrumentalities: subdepartmental and subagency offices, branches, divisions, units—headquarters and field; hundreds of nonstatutory, but more or less permanent, intra-agency and interagency committees and commissions; grants-in-aid to fifty-five state and territorial governments and their hundreds of subdivisions, including tens of thousands of local governments, with more than 20,000 local school districts; a growing number of quasi-public, nonprofit corporations; scores of international and regional organizations; and myriad contracts to private industries, universities, professional groups, and charitable institutions.

Many of these subsidiary agents have their own separate identities, legal bases, and agenda of priorities apart from their instrumental (and often incidental) role in federal policy implementation.

This almost limitless diffusion presents internal problems of communication and control and often makes terms like "accountability" and "responsibility" words of art to cover a kaleidoscope of administrative fragmentation.

Even if the scene were not so cluttered, even if the formal structure of executive departments, agencies, and personnel were exclusively responsible for the implementation of federal policy, our constitutional system of shared powers and the pluralistic and oligarchical nature of political parties and interest groups would interfere with any neat model of hierarchical loyalty and public accountability. Elmer E. Schattschneider once commented that the history of the federal government could be written in terms of a struggle between the President and the Congress for control of the bureaucracy. But even this is too simple. For the struggle is not just between the President and the Congress: within the Congress, committee and subcommittee chairmen, often allied with powerful private group interests, exercise extraordinary control over the policies and administrative arrangements of subdepartmental and subagency units of the bureaucracy.

If we lived in a simpler and less apocalyptic age, such a complex arrangement might be tolerated without fear of untoward disruptions to basic social values. But this is not the case. The American national government is confronted with unprecedented factors that place an absolute premium upon improved managerial competence in the public sector:

Government decisions involve increased stakes and risks, while mistakes are much harder to retrieve.

Science and technology have penetrated national security, environmental, and social strategies in a way that imposes acute moral and philosophical burdens upon public policy.

The dimensions of public spending require a modern President to monitor spending, taxing, and wage-price relationships with unprecedented precision, and to take stabilization actions without regard to the costs to his political credit balances; he is now obliged to be a conscientious student of economics.

"People" problems no longer lend themselves to straight-line solutions, and a President finds that he must work overtime to compensate for failures of administrative response and to teach a new administrative style to reluctant bureaucrats and congressmen.

Shortened decision intervals and reaction times drive a President to form his calculus of strategy on the run, as it were, placing a premium on accurate and adequate information systems and analytic support.

The modern President lives with a relentless social criticism that generates dissatisfactions with the quality of life and leadership and tends to force his timing and priorities.

In this kind of world, the President, by the logic of his position, must have two overriding managerial concerns:

How can the federal government identify, mobilize, train, and release the energy of the most impressive talent in the nation for developing and carrying out federal policy?

How can staff and line arrangements in the executive branch contribute to more rational and imaginative policy inputs to political decision making, and how can they contribute to more effective and coordinated policy implementation?

These two concerns must be specifically related to the modern President's inevitable preoccupations in the field of public policy: national security, economic stability and growth, environmental management and control, and human resource development.

Concretely, in national security affairs modern Presidents cannot afford a series of "Bay of Pigs" episodes, nor can they afford contradictions between diplomatic and military initiatives. In domestic affairs, they cannot afford to allow brave legislative responses in the fields of environmental management and control and human resource development to be blunted by ineptness and confusion in implementation, as has been the case with much of the Great Society legislation of 1964–65. In economic affairs, Presidents cannot afford to return to earlier days when the varying power centers of economic stabilization policy making (notably key congressional committees, the Budget Bureau, the Council of Economic Advisers, the Treasury, and the Federal Reserve Board) went their separate ways. To do so would be to invite economic disaster.

The difficulty is that the magnitude of the political as well as administrative tasks in assuring some modicum of competence and coherence in these preeminent areas of public policy is staggering. For there are no organizational gimmicks capable of overcoming the enormous centrifuge of governance in our pluralistic society.

An attack upon the managerial inadequacies of the federal government should encompass at least the Executive Office of the President, the departmental and agency structure, the federal field office structure, the devolution system for the transfer of federal funds and functions to nonfederal agencies, and the federal personnel system. As we shall note later, none of these five points of attack can be negotiated without major presidential attention to the configurations of power dominating the Congress.

Before examining policy alternatives and recommendations relating to each of these separately and in combination, a brief review of federal reorganization efforts of the past several decades is in order, for future possibilities are inevitably conditioned by the legacy of the past.

Reorganization: A Brief History

Concern with the organization and management of the national government goes back a long way. The first study was commissioned by the Continental Congress in 1780. For the first century of this nation's history, however, investigations into these issues were feeble and intermittent.

It was only when the federal budget approached the billion-dollar mark, during the administration of President William Howard Taft, that a major attempt was made to examine questions of overall structure and procedures. And even the Taft Commission on Economy and Efficiency (the Cleveland Commission, 1910–13) devoted most of its energies to minute problems of internal management. The major fruit of its labors was the Budget and Accounting Act of 1921, which established the Bureau of the Budget (BOB) in the executive branch and the General Accounting Office in the legislative branch. The Bureau of the Budget was the first nonwartime centripetal staff agency available to the President for the conduct of his managerial responsibilities.

The 1920s witnessed a variety of additional proposals, both legislative and executive, focused on administrative reorganization. Most of the major recommendations got nowhere. Occasional authorizations were given to the President for minor reassignments of functions across agency lines, but Congress systematically pigeonholed or voted down any major delegation of power to the President for reorganizing executive branch functions.

In 1932, President Herbert Hoover submitted a message to the Congress calling for a massive reorganization of the executive branch. In a classic statement of the "practical difficulties of such reorganization," he commented as follows:

> Not only do different fractions of the Government fear such reorganization, but many associations and agencies throughout the country will be alarmed that the particular function to which they are devoted may in some fashion be curtailed. Proposals to the Congress of detailed plans for the reorganization of the many different bureaus and independent agencies have always proved in the past to be a sign for the mobilization of efforts from all quarters which has destroyed the possibility of constructive action.[1]

How penetrating this observation was can be judged by the fact that after the law was passed every executive order submitted by President Hoover to implement the act was disapproved. Furthermore, the law itself provided for key exceptions to the President's sphere and requested him to set up consolidations of the following governmental activities:

> Public Health (*except that the provisions hereof shall not apply to hospitals now under the jurisdiction of the Veterans Administration*), Personnel Administration, Education (*except the Board of Vocational Education shall not be abolished*) ... and to merge such other activities, except those of a purely military nature, of the War and Navy Departments, as ... may be common to

---

1. W. Brooke Graves (comp.), *Reorganization of the Executive Branch of the Government of the United States: A Compilation of Basic Information and Significant Documents, 1912–1948*, Library of Congress, Legislative Reference Service, Public Affairs Bulletin No. 66 (1949), p. 96.

both ... except that this section shall not apply to the United States Employees Compensation Commission.[2]

This was not the first nor was it to be the last of such explicit legal exceptions to the reorganization authority of Presidents.

The coming of the New Deal brought a totally new dimension to the policies and organization of the executive branch. A bevy of new laws created a host of new agencies and a variety of new functions within old agencies. And President Franklin D. Roosevelt had no institutional machinery for rationalizing and resolving emerging administrative issues, or for supervising in any meaningful sense the hundred-odd separate departments and agencies that reported directly to him.

In 1936, President Roosevelt created the Committee on Administrative Management under the chairmanship of Louis Brownlow. The report of the Brownlow Committee was probably the most sensible and impressive ever made on federal government organization. Many of its recommendations, notably those concerned with the independent regulatory commissions, the Civil Service, the General Accounting Office, and new cabinet departments, were largely ignored by the Congress. Its lasting contribution was the successful recommendation to create an Executive Office of the President (EOP) containing an expanded White House staff, the Bureau of the Budget (until then housed in the Treasury Department), and a National Resources Planning Board. Although the last was killed by congressional action in withholding appropriations in the early 1940s, the essential rubric of the Executive Office has remained. It is inconceivable that the government could have successfully negotiated the turbulent currents of the past quarter century without it.

The Second World War saw the inevitable proliferation of war-related agencies, most of which disappeared at the end of the conflict. But the experience of the war, especially the difficulties of relating separate military services to the consolidated demands of amphibious warfare and the serious problems of interrelating diplomatic and military initiatives and intelligence, led in 1947 to the National Security Act which created a National Defense Establishment, a National Security Council, and a Central Intelligence Agency. It would take time for these components to emerge into any kind of structural coherence, but the 1947 act set the foundation stone for the future.

In the immediate postwar years, the other major organizational develop-

2. Graves (comp.), *Reorganization of the Executive Branch* (emphasis supplied).

ment was the creation of the Council of Economic Advisers in the Executive Office of the President. This added staff resource has been of invaluable help to the President and the Congress in analyzing the state of the economy, in planning fiscal policy, and in acting as the major catalyst of interagency (BOB, Federal Reserve, Treasury) cooperation on fiscal matters.

Also in 1947 President Harry Truman asked Congress to create a bipartisan, twelve-man Commission on Organization of the Executive Branch of the Government.

The Commission (the First Hoover Commission) reported, and at length, in 1949. A number of its recommendations were adopted, under President Truman and later under President Dwight D. Eisenhower: the creation of a Department of Defense (replacing the National Defense Establishment); the assignment of the National Security Council to the Executive Office of the President; the creation of a cabinet-level department of Health, Education, and Welfare (HEW); and the centralization of increased authority in department heads, cutting away at some of the statutory authority that Congress had assigned at the subdepartment level. But many sacred cows were left undisturbed, and the commission's pleas for a "sharp reduction" in the number of federal administrative agencies fell upon deaf congressional ears.

A Second Hoover Commission was created in the mid-1950s; but its mandate, to examine governmental functions which should be discontinued, was preposterous, for it invaded the constitutional prerogatives of President and Congress. The commission's effective residue was little more than a chemical trace.

Aside from Secretary Robert S. McNamara's progress in transforming Defense from a *de jure* to a *de facto* department, the creation of an Office of Science and Technology in the Executive Office of the President, and the assigning of a White House role to the chairman of the Civil Service Commission, no substantial success greeted the John F. Kennedy administration's various attempts to reorganize the government.

President Lyndon B. Johnson has succeeded in adding two new cabinet departments: Housing and Urban Development (HUD), and Transportation. He also added the Office of Economic Opportunity (OEO) to the Executive Office of the President. During his administration a number of task forces have addressed themselves to questions of government organization—especially in the increasingly tangled thicket of intergovernmental relations as they relate to problems of poverty, race, welfare, urbanism, and education.

However, most of the underlying problems of organization remain. These have been illuminated time and again by presidential task forces, by congressional committees, by journalists, pamphleteers, and scholars. Congressional literature is particularly rich. Notable in recent years have been the studies of the Jackson Subcommittee on National Security Staffing and Operations and the Muskie Subcommittee on Intergovernmental Relations of the Senate Committee on Government Operations. More recently committees in both the Senate and the House have examined the adequacy of federal organization for mounting a coherent attack upon problems of the physical environment.[3]

Although these various studies, investigations, and proposals have differed in viewpoint and attack, there has emerged in recent years a consensus on two major issues: (1) the federal government lacks machinery for the effective development, implementation, and coordination of public policy; and (2) the conduct of the government's business is overcentralized in Washington.

Proposed remedies have included recommendations for the enlargement and restructuring of the Executive Office of the President; the consolidation of federal programs and functions into a few major departments; the strengthening of staff offices at the level of the secretary; making a departmentwide (secretary's) presence felt in federal field establishments; upgrading the quality and enlarging the power and discretion of federal field offices at home and abroad; devolving the conduct of federal business increasingly upon state and local authorities and upon private or quasipublic instrumentalities; and reform of the career services and upgrading of public personnel charged at various levels of government with the conduct and control of federal policy.

Whatever merit these various recommendations have had (and this paper will later explicate and endorse a number of them), they have tended to suffer from two overriding limitations: first, as commonly set forth, they have ignored the realities of congressional power, the rigidities of the present congressional committee structure, and the mutual defer-

---

3. See esp. *Managing the Environment*, Report of the House Committee on Science and Astronautics, 90 Cong. 2 sess. (1968); and *Report of the Joint House-Senate Colloquium to Discuss National Policy for the Environment*, 90 Cong. 2 sess. (1968).

ence patterns within the legislative branch, all of which affect the organization and conduct of federal programs; second, many of them have failed to articulate some of the administrative and policy costs and consequences possibly attendant upon their adoption. It is possible, for example, that unless extreme care is taken program coordination can be the enemy of program energy. "Keeping track" may be the enemy of "making tracks."

It may be argued, of course, that this dilemma is false; that topside planning and coordination is the precondition, not the enemy, of effective subordinate energy; that if program coordination is not rationally produced at the top it will be irrationally and wastefully accomplished through survival-of-the-fittest skirmishes at lower levels. This, in fact, is the author's own considered judgment. But to state the ideal is a far cry from realizing it in practice, and history suggests that arrangements constructed to achieve this ideal are inherently unstable—tending to veer toward the Scylla of a debilitating overcentralization on the one hand, or the Charybdis of programmatic anarchy on the other. All one can say at this moment is that historically in the United States more bones have been scattered around Charybdis than around Scylla. To change the idiom, constitutional and political beliefs and forces tend to run against generalist "kings" in favor of functional "barons."

The Limitations of Existing Devices

The validity of the foregoing proposition hardly needs elaboration. It can be readily documented by examining the weakness of centripetal devices now in vogue or recently tested in almost every level and branch of government.

First, there is the device of statutory or ad hoc interdepartmental and intradepartmental committees. There are thousands of them in the federal government alone, including a number in the Executive Office of the President. Most of them suffer from three chronic ailments: (1) confederationitis, (2) progressive deputization, and (3) implemental anemia. The first leads to common-denominator "paper" solutions for problems frequently calling for uncommon-denominator practical solutions. The second, marked by preoccupied secretaries requesting under secretaries to sit in for them, who in turn deputize assistant secretaries, who in turn deputize deputy assistant secretaries, ad infinitum, leads inevitably to a loss in the plenipotentiary capacity of the committee members, and to the necessity of referring every important issue back to each agency for topside clearances. The third means that, even if and when consensus can be reached within an interdepartmental committee, such consensus is not self-enforcing and can, in fact, be rendered inoperable by the failure of constituent units to implement the decision reached. When such committees are established by congressional mandate, further complications arise, for they cannot easily be disbanded nor their agenda adapted to new issues. If they become well-staffed and effective, they may interpose themselves between the President and his department heads and develop a policy line out of phase with both.

Necessary as such committees are, their numbers should be drastically pruned, and in any case they are no solution to most problems of program planning, coordination, and operational effectiveness that afflict the public sector.

Second, the "lead agency" notion, however attractive in theory, seems to have similar limitations. Bringing all relevant agencies together for specific program purposes under the chairmanship of the head of the department that has major concern or competence in a particular policy area would seem on its face to be a reasonable approach. But, since everyone likes to coordinate and few like to be coordinated—especially by one's peers—this device tends to degenerate into a simple interdepartmental committee with all of the inadequacies suggested above. Low-level issues may be thrashed out and clarified; tough issues of jurisdiction and authority rarely are, for disgruntled committee members have the option of appeal to centers of power in the presidency or in the Congress that can effectively override the decisions of the lead agency. The history of OEO, HUD, and HEW in that role is not encouraging, although some promise can be found in some of the lead-agency functions performed in foreign affairs by the Department of State.

A third device is coordination by presidential advisers, White House assistants, or by other representatives of the Executive Office structure. This has been attempted in various forms over the past decades. Sometimes the job has been given to individual men of considerable stature and ability (for example, Colonel Edward M. House, Harry Hopkins, "Jimmy" Byrnes, Sherman Adams, a vice president). The de facto "prime" minister, or executive vice president, device suffers, however—at least, in our form of government—from two intractable flaws. If he is strong, he tends to shield the President from issues, information, and forces essential to presidential judgment and power; if he is weak, he tempts others to go around him, thereby creating rather than solving problems for the chief executive.

More often, the President has used his "anonymous" White House assistants and his major institutional staffs in the Executive Office of the President to assist him in program planning and coordination. However successful this fairly flexible arrangement has been (and, if it had not been partially successful, the federal government could not operate at all), it has serious weaknesses. If the President defends his intimate staff too often, he has created a supercabinet; if he does not defend them at all, they are powerless. If he institutionalizes them, their time is preoccupied with managing their own subordinates, limiting their time and tolerance for intimate contacts with the President; if he does not institutionalize them, they become swamped by paper from below and expectations from above. And in many areas of public policy where the President himself is weak (programs under the jurisdiction of independent regulatory commissions; agencies like the Atomic Energy Commission and the Army Corps of Engineers that are effectively controlled by congressional committees), presidential staff, no matter how brilliant, are limited by legal and political reality.

This rather melancholy sample of centripetal coordinating devices and their weaknesses is not meant to suggest that nothing has been done or can be done to improve the coordination of policy planning and implementation in the federal government. There have been many evidences of at least partially successful endeavors along these lines. The Bureau of the Budget at its best is a remarkable and indispensable coordinating device, especially when buttressed by informational and analytical skills of cognate agencies like the Council of Economic Advisers and the Office of Science and Technology. Presidential assistants play out a daily drama of conflict resolution and program rationalization. The transformation of the Department of Defense under Robert McNamara is an indication of what at the departmental level can be done, in Paul Appleby's felicitous phrase, "to make a mesh of things." The development of analytical instruments like PPBS (Program Planning and Budgeting System) shows promise of making resource allocation choices more coherent and rational.

But enormous inadequacies remain and they cannot be redressed effectively without a sober recognition of the fact that the battle for improved federal management must be fought on a number of fronts simultaneously. The five major salients already identified need particular attention: the Executive Office of the President; departmental arrangements; federal field establishments; the devolution system; and personnel systems at all levels.

EXECUTIVE OFFICE OF THE PRESIDENT

The presidency is the only institution in the American polity where overarching and long-range public imperatives can be coherently analyzed and melded. This is true both because of the ubiquity of the presidential constituency, and because the President is mandated to recommend to the Congress a coherent program for allocating resources to and within the executive branch.

The structure of the Executive Office of the President must reflect the prime concerns of the nation as viewed from the vantage point of the chief executive. In the present age, as already noted, these prime concerns are four: national security, economic stability and growth, the integrity and viability of the physical environment, and the promotion of human welfare and of human resource development. In these four areas, the President must have at his disposal institutional arrangements that can help him plan wisely, sort options judiciously, and effect coordinated responses.

Because priorities change and, more important, because each President has his own leadership style, he must be given very substantial latitude in organizing, reorganizing, and adjusting the constituent units of his executive office. He must also have at his disposal substantial discretionary funds ($25,000,000 per year as a minimum) to permit him to tap selective expertise across the nation on an ad hoc basis, and to initiate in-house experimental capabilities for improving the planning and management functions of the office. The present discretionary funds of the President for "special projects" ($1.5 million) are totally inadequate.

If the President can secure from Congress the right to structure and manage his own office without restriction—including the right to make in-office appointments without Senate confirmation and the right to create, shift, and abolish constituent units and personnel assignments as he deems necessary for the effective conduct of presidential business—he will have won a major victory for effective public management. These prerogatives are essential if he is to have authority anywhere near commensurate with his administrative and policy-making responsibilities.

Granted this kind of authority and discretion, what should he do with it? Although each President will and must use them according to his own temperament and administrative proclivities, three weaknesses exist in

Executive Office of the President capabilities so glaring as to merit special emphasis.

First is the office's weakness in policy development. The presidency is perched on top of what one astute observer has called "a bottom-heavy administrative system." Policy proposals tend to emerge from levels of operational enthusiasm, which are likely to be the lower and middle governmental levels, coupled with discrete, single-interest segments of the private sector. Aside from ad hoc task forces (many of which have been extremely productive and catalytic), there is no effective agent or agency in the Executive Office of the President charged with the study of emerging public problems and the development of effective programs to deal with them in terms of continuing and changing presidential perspectives of the public interest. This is less true, of course, in the occult fields of economic stabilization policy and national security policy where the Council of Economic Advisers and the staff of the National Security Council have increasingly strengthened their policy-review capabilities. But in the increasingly troublesome and important areas of environmental management and "people" programs (health, poverty, education, welfare, housing, urban renewal, and the like) the EOP is patently deficient. Existing budgetary and legislative clearance reviews are inadequate. There is no underlying statistical and informational system of social and environmental indicators comparable to the economic indicators available to and through the Council of Economic Advisers. Whatever its original intent, the Office of Economic Opportunity has become an operational advocate, not a reflective center of governmentwide policy analysis. Since the demise a quarter of a century ago of the National Resources Planning Board, no presidential staff has concerned itself full-time with ecological interdependencies. The only gestures in this direction in recent years have been the Committee on Environmental Quality of the Office of Science and Technology, and a Water Resources Council independent of the Executive Office structure. The former is too small and weak to be effective (ideally, it should be reconstituted as a separate, strongly staffed office in the Executive Office of the President); the latter is limited by statute to water resources alone.

Whether effective policy analysis staffs in the environmental and human resource areas should be combined or kept separate, should be created inside the Bureau of the Budget or as a new and separate agency within the EOP (on balance, the author's choice) is perhaps of secondary importance. What is essential is that such a capability exist in the Executive Office of the President. Coherence and rationality in federal programming in these areas is impossible without such a capability. This is true in Washington; it is increasingly true in the complex arena of intergovernmental relations. State and local governments are federal partners in the purveyance of public services; their capacity to develop programs that effectively complement and implement national policies is today a matter of crucial importance. Too often they are bound by rigidities and categorical overprescriptions imposed by federal legislation and by administrative regulations and guidelines. There is a pervasive need to loosen existing categorical boundaries without destroying the basic thrust of federal categorical grants designed to promote the *national* interest.

One possible device to meet this need might be for the President to assign staff from his executive office and/or relevant departments and agencies to ride budgetary circuits in the fall of each year. Such staffs, with advance congressional approval, might be empowered to permit state and local governments to shift up to, say, 25 percent of approved categorical federal grants from one category to another; this would make the grants more relevant to varying state and local needs and would promote a series of useful dialogues between the partners of the federal system.

The second weakness of the President's office is the inadequacy of machinery for command and control within the sphere of his own executive competence. As suggested earlier, there are many areas of policy in which for reasons *de jure* or *de facto* the President has authority only to persuade and cajole, or in which he must repair to informal powers deriving from his political rather than his constitutional status. But even when his legal authority is clear, he lacks efficient means of enforcing his political will. Little is gained in strengthening the policy analysis capabilities of his office unless he can effect more coherence in policy implementation. It is true that knowledge can be power, and the President's directive responsibilities can probably be exercised with greater effectiveness if his policy analysis staffs are able to create information systems that include hard and systematic evaluations of federal programs. But the President's present span of control is so unwieldy, his budgetary flexibility is so limited, and his managerial universe is so ponderous that intelligence alone will not give his directives appropriate clout. If two or more agencies chart collision courses or if they determine to ignore presidential guidance, there is little the chief executive can do short of ultimate sanctions (such as firing) that often have prohibitive political costs.

It is this reality, of course, that has led a number of administrative reformers to suggest that the President needs one or more executive vice presidents or presidential coordinators to whom he can delegate command functions over parts of the executive branch, including his cabinet departments, in Washington and in federal field establishments. The inconveniences and political hazards of such devices and developments have already been traced. But the problem remains, and the need is real.

There is no single and easy solution to the problem, but if the President is given the kind of flexible control over his own office called for above, he should certainly use this elaborated discretion to experiment with a number of command-control devices. At the very least, he should create a team of two or three or four presidential "administrators" or "expeditors," removed from the day-to-day preoccupations of existing White House aides, who could be assigned on an ad hoc and short-term basis as troubleshooters to straighten out jurisdictional conflicts among agencies, both in Washington and (on an itinerant basis) in the field. "Ad hoc" and "short-term" must be underlined, for permanent and long-term portfolios for such assistants could only produce impossible tensions with cabinet secretaries, agency heads, and key legislators. Furthermore, they might easily create centers of power in the executive branch competitive with, rather than derivitive of, presidential authority. Such administrators or expeditors must be men of considerable personal stature. As surrogates for the chief executive in a system inherently unfriendly to surrogates, they must be skilled in mediation, soft of voice, wise in the ways of politics, and utterly devoted to the President—institutionally and personally. The President must be prepared to support their judgments in the overwhelming majority of cases while being willing on occasion to overrule them on appeal. This complex prescription may prove to be impossible of implementation, but it is the only one that, in the judgment of this author, gives promise of success.

The third and final major weakness of the presidential office is in communicating with the public and with state and local officialdom. Here, too, there are constraints. Too "open" a presidency can build impossible expectations, induce claimants to bypass channels of access to departments and to Congress, clog the President's information system, and preclude that measure of confidentiality necessary for face-saving negotiations. Too frequent use by the President of the mass media dilutes the President's "Nielsen rating" with the consequent danger of limiting his impact when real crises appear.

But inadequate communications, both inward and outward, can be equally perilous. Fresh ideas from creative citizens, and from public officials at all levels of government, can be lost or ignored. A public bewildered by complex public problems can be denied the clarifying and unifying voice of the President. In such circumstances, the chief executive can easily become vulnerable to surprise and miscalculations.

Adequately mandated policy analysis staffs and presidential expediters with sensitive antennae can remedy some of the existing defects in communication flows, but far more needs to be done to help the President develop effective techniques and policies. A public information competence must be built into the White House, possibly in an enlarged office of the press secretary, and at least one unit in the White House should be devoted to intergovernmental liaison with governors and with top officials of local government.

There are still other weaknesses in the Executive Office of the President. First, there are far too many statutory and ad hoc interdepartmental councils and committees with fuzzy mandates, little or no power, and only intermittent and unsatisfactory access to the President himself; these should be abolished or consolidated with more permanent staff operations. For example, the National Aeronautics and Space Council and the Marine Resources Council should probably be placed under a comprehensive Office of Environmental Analysis. The whole structure of citizens' advisory committees to the President should be reviewed and rationalized.

Second, the White House needs an even greater capability to identify talent for appointive federal positions in both domestic and international departments and agencies. It is an unfair strain upon the chairman of the Civil Service Commission to serve both as director of the President's personnel operations and as the policy chairman of the major career service of the federal government.

Third, the operational aspects of the Office of Emergency Planning (for mobilizing the services of all levels of government to meet emergencies of war or natural disaster) and the Office of Economic Opportunity should devolve upon other agencies (the General Services Administration for Emergency Planning; HEW and/or Labor for OEO), although in the case of OEO extreme care must be taken to insure that the innovative and flexible characteristics of many of its programs are not destroyed by transfers to more traditional and conservative bureaucratic superiors. It should be possible for some civilian counterpart to the "Green Beret" or Marine Corps mission-oriented services, often competitive with more massive and sodden bureaucracies, to be established (and disestablished) within existing departments or as functions of independent agencies. The Executive Office of the President is not the appropriate rubric for these kinds of operating line activities.

Fourth, the staff competence within the Executive Office (presumably within the Bureau of the Budget) for studying and recommending structural changes and procedural improvements throughout the executive branch organization, on a continuing basis, needs to be strengthened in quality, size, and funding.

All of these are important addenda to the three essential areas of concern identified earlier. Progress along all of these lines can best be promoted by giving to the President effective control over the organization, staffing, and missions of the Executive Office of the President. If this is to happen, as we shall note below, the President must ask for and receive the understanding, support, and assistance of the United States Congress.

DEPARTMENTAL STRUCTURE

One of the basic tenets of public administration is "span of control." In its simplistic form, at least in the federal government, it is a silly notion. The number of units reporting to a single administrator is not the essential factor in determining topside control. Ten units are too many if each has its own base of power in the legislature or in clientele groups of significant political influence. A hundred units are manageable if most of them lack an independent base of power, and if their mission is precise and low-voltage. Little is gained or lost in terms of "good management" in the executive branch if the Corregidor-Bataan Memorial Commission, the American Battle Monument Commission, the Commission of Fine Arts, the Foreign Claims Settlement Commission, and the Panama Canal Company are allowed to continue as independent, free-wheeling agencies. Those who would tidy up the administrative structure of the executive branch by putting everything under four or five giant-sized superdepartments, or under fifteen or twenty economy-sized regular departments, on the ground that only then can the President enjoy a manageable "span of control," overestimate the importance of the precept and underestimate the difficulties of achieving intradepartmental, let alone interdepartmental, coherence in anything as complex and diffuse as the federal government.

This is not to say, however, that the present structure of departments and agencies is either logical or efficient. Some regrouping and much internal reorganization, especially at the bureau level, is patently necessary. But since both of these kinds of moves involve political headwinds of gale force, a President should pick and choose a few major objectives and should calculate his political rations with extreme care.

The difficulty is that across-the-board generalizations about federal departments and agencies are inherently dangerous or irrelevant. Some are probably too large and heterogeneous (for example, HEW); some are too small and/or clientele-oriented (Labor, Commerce, Veterans Administration, parts of Interior, Agriculture, and HUD); some are too independent (certain regulatory commissions); some are too dependent upon Congress (Atomic Energy Commission, the Corps of Engineers, the FBI); some are miscast as cabinet departments (Post Office); some are too plagued with ingrown career service elitism (State); some lack the internal capacity or external support to generate and sustain high morale (Agency for International Development). A general diagnosis and a general therapy are, in short, effectively impossible.

It is possible, however, to raise questions about departmental and agency structure relating to at least two of the four overarching concerns of the President: environmental management and control, and human resource development.

This is not to say that all is well in the field of administering national security policy and economic stabilization policy—though the administrative machinery in the latter field has functioned relatively smoothly in recent years. While space does not permit an extended discussion here of problems in the national security area, it must be noted that the overseas mishmash of federal agency representatives still escapes effective control by the ambassador in the field or by the Department of State in Washington. The inflow of information and intelligence by cable and pouch has long since passed the point of digestibility. Horizontal and lateral clearances absorb an unconscionable amount of time and effort and involve delays that are sometimes dangerous. Some of these difficulties defy organizational rationalization; others might be partially obviated by an appropriate delegation of authority to regional assistant secretaries of state and by a more elaborate and effective staffing of the office of the Secretary of State. In 1962 the Herter Committee on Foreign Affairs Personnel recommended an executive under secretary of state, a further administrative option that deserves careful consideration.

On major and critical issues of foreign affairs the threat of apocalyptic consequences has a way of crystallizing small cadres of influentials under the immediate direction of the President. Emerging policies may not always be wise, and the ponderousness of the structure and the system of communications may at times create crossed signals of serious consequence (as when, in 1966, peace negotiations with North Vietnam were reputedly shattered by the President's unrecollected prior approval of bombing selected targets near Hanoi). But after a decade of review of national security machinery, the Jackson Subcommittee, although it has recommended a number of incremental improvements, has found no magic formula for a major structural reorganization. All that can be said is that the importance of the issue suggests that urgent and continuing attention must be given to the adequacy of staff arrangements for serving the President in this area of preeminent executive concern.

On the domestic front some major structural changes may well be needed in organization. Those involving the Executive Office of the President have already been discussed. At the departmental and agency level, four questions especially warrant hard analysis and viable answers:

First, how can the management responsibilities of cabinet secretaries and the heads of important line agencies be strengthened without throwing a wet blanket on the morale, energy, and discretion of subordinate operating bureaus?

Second, how can a gigantic hydra like HEW be split up without losing the benefits that logically accrue from reviewing health, education, and welfare as interrelated programs and values?

Third, how can the rule-making power of independent regulatory commissions be more effectively related to the policy mandates assigned by Congress to the President and to departments and agencies without jeopardizing the integrity of the quasi-judicial role of regulatory commissions?

Fourth, how can agency functions be regrouped in the human and environmental resource areas in such a way as to promote more coherent program planning and implementation without taking on more battles with vested interests than any single administration can afford?

Again, there are no simple answers to any of these dilemmas, but certain directions seem more promising than others.

On the first question, the *essential* controls of an agency head over constituent units are three, and only three: (1) control of legislative proposals; (2) control of budgetary totals; and (3) control of major personnel appointments and assignments. Each department secretary and agency head should have a staff, a management information system, and adequate legal and political authority to develop and maintain competence in these areas. The staff need not be large, but it must be highly competent and must be supported with a flow of information that will enable it to present rational policy alternatives to the agency head. With these tools of general, overall management at his disposal, an agency head can delegate to line subordinates a substantial amount of operating discretion. He can also be equipped to serve the President and the Congress in their roles of making politically accountable decisions. Many departments lack the staff, the information system, and the legal and political authority essential for responsible management. The President should urge, and Congress should support, reforms leading to the improvement of this condition.

On the second question, there is probably more to be gained than lost in splitting up HEW. The issue is not the number of employees; Defense, Post Office, Agriculture, and the Veterans Administration all have a larger civilian work force. The issue is the heterogeneity of constituent functions, the size of the budget (HEW's budget is five times greater than the next largest civilian agency), the extensiveness of mandated intergovernmental relations, and the limitations that the present structure imposes on attracting top-grade personnel to man programs of extraordinary national consequence—education, for example. A separate Department of Education would not only symbolize the importance of the federal government's commitment to an essential and growing public function; it would serve as a rubric for gathering together at least some of the educational activities being carried out by departments and agencies outside of HEW (for example, National Science Foundation, OEO, Veterans Administration, National Humanities Foundation, Bureau of Indian Affairs). A Department of Health and Welfare should have no more difficulty in relating to a Department of Education than HEW presently has in relating its disparate activities to cognate functions in HUD, Labor, OEO, in the human resource development area; or to Interior, Agriculture, and the Corps of Engineers in the area of environmental management and control. Granted that these difficulties are substantial, a strengthened program planning and implementation capacity in the Executive Office of the President could more than compensate for any loss in integrating functions now lodged unsuccessfully in the top echelons of an overgrown HEW.

On the rule-making authority of certain independent regulatory commissions, the analyses and advice of the Cushman Report (part of the Brownlow Committee study, 1937) and of the First Hoover Commission

(1949) need rereading and studied implementation. America will never have a coherent transportation policy until the rule-making functions (making general legislative mandates specific) of the Interstate Commerce Commission and the Federal Maritime Commission are integrated with the policy responsibilities of the new Department of Transportation. America will never have a coherent power policy until the rule-making functions of the Federal Power Commission and the Atomic Energy Commission are consolidated with those carried out by the Department of the Interior. There have been until now sufficient political barriers to changing the structure and functions of independent regulatory commissions to raise serious questions about the viability of new or reiterated recommendations. But the problem is real, and there are no inherent difficulties in separating rule making from the quasi-judicial functions (making judgments about the legality of activities pursued under laws and rules) of regulatory agencies, preserving the integrity of the latter while making the former subject to responsible and coordinated political control.

The fourth question, on the regrouping of agency functions in the human and environmental resource areas in the face of vested interests, is the toughest. It can be answered in practice only by sophisticated management studies buttressed by executive-legislative concordats. In the absence of major structural changes, some experiments in establishing multiagency operational task forces under the command of presidential designees might well be undertaken—at least where target problems are fairly precise and short-term.

FIELD OFFICES

Reforms in the Executive Office of the President and in the departmental structure of the executive branch in Washington can make a difference in the behavior of regional and district offices of the federal government. That difference, however, is likely to be minimal unless three additional steps are taken in the field itself: (1) locating regional offices of federal agencies together, at least in key functional areas of environmental management and human resource development; (2) selective upgrading of top field positions in order to permit an effective decentralization of decision making; (3) providing what Robert Wood has called "glue" money (federal grants to offices of governors, county executives, mayors, city managers) to enable responsible state and local officials to coordinate interagency and intergovernmental programs, including federal agency programs, that affect a particular area.

At present, the executive branch of the federal government in Washington is represented across the nation by hundreds of regional and district offices with different boundaries. The national map is, in fact, crisscrossed by a bewildering series of overlapping jurisdictions. Furthermore, some departments have no departmentwide representatives in the regions, but only program specialists representing functional bureaus. Others have departmentwide representatives whose missions are ill-defined and whose effective power over constituent departmental units in the region is minimal or nonexistent.

It might be argued that in ideal terms the federal government should start all over again and should divide the nation into, say, ten regions. For example:

Region	Regional Headquarters
New England	Boston
Middle Atlantic	New York or Philadelphia
Southeast	Atlanta
East North Central	Chicago
West North Central	Minneapolis
South Central	Dallas or New Orleans
Central	Kansas City
West Central	Denver
Southwest	Los Angeles
Northwest	Seattle

All federal departments and agencies with field establishments might then follow this regional pattern. Interagency and intergovernmental coordination could be promoted by propinquity. A single federal office building in each regional capital could house all major federal offices. A receptionist-information center on the first floor would provide citizens and state and local officials with one-stop guidance.

This resolution of the existing chaos points in the proper direction, but, as stated, it is as politically impractical as it is attractive. Powerful senators and congressmen have no desire to see federal field installations situated in their states or districts moved to another location. Any further rationalization of regions (and such rationalization is desperately needed, especially in programs concerned with environmental management and human resource development) will involve political bargains and trade-offs between the President and key congressional leaders.

Some agencies, notably HUD and HEW, have attempted in recent years to upgrade the position classifications of top field officials, and to devolve upon such officials enlarged responsibilities and greater discretion in decision making. The results to date have not been impressive, but, again, the direction is sound, and points the way toward eliminating some of the traditional reliance of the executive branch upon congressionally sanctioned patronage appointments in federal field offices.

Coordinating federal agency activities in the field is not a simple problem, even if a map with a single regional pattern were designed. Itinerant checks by Washington-based officials of the Bureau of the Budget and/or others from the Executive Office of the President should be continued and expanded. Federal executive boards, composed of representatives of all federal agencies located in a particular region who meet periodically to discuss common administrative interests, should be encouraged to play out their inevitably minor role in interagency communications. "Lead agency" conveners and expeditors should be encouraged to experiment with a variety of task-force and project approaches to coordination, including central information banks about federal programs in each region. The recently established Neighborhood Service Program instituted by HUD, OEO, HEW, and Labor is a worthy experiment.

However, the most promising devices for effecting the coordination and effective implementation of federal programs in the field are two: (1) improving the capacity, partly through federal grants-in-aid, of governors, county executives, mayors, and city managers to correlate and catalyze all public and private programs relating to broad substantive needs in their particular jurisdictions; and (2) improving the system of access and communication for these officials to those points of "ombudsman" power in the EOP, in departments and agencies, and in Congress most likely to redress administrative grievances.

THE DEVOLUTION SYSTEM

A vast amount of federal policy is carried out through a devolution system for transferring authority to nonfederal agencies—public, quasi-public, and private. The most prevalent form is the grant-in-aid to state and local authorities. Such grants-in-aid have increased more than two and a half times since 1960—from $7 billion in fiscal 1960 to an estimated $18.3 billion in fiscal 1968. Almost two hundred and fifty new programs were enacted in the period 1963–67 alone. But state and local authorities are not the only nonfederal instruments for implementing federal policies; an elaborate system of contracting out has been developed in recent years. Universities, private industries, and a host of specially created nonprofit corporations are engaged in implementing federal programs to the tune of billions of dollars a year. Through these contracts the federal government can command and reward talent far richer than that normally available through its own "in-house" capabilities.

The system is bound to grow, for it is the major device available for assuring that the federal government can, and does ". . . identify, mobilize, train, and release the energy of the most impressive talent in the nation for developing and carrying out federal policy." It also permits experimentation and promotes innovation in the search for answers to difficult policy problems. The trick is to let it grow without exacerbating problems of program coordination and democratic accountability.

Although a number of suggestions have been made in recent years to improve the devolution system (for example, the recodification of categorical grants into more general groupings; the development of uniform accounting and reporting systems at the state and local level; the simplification of federal administrative guidelines and regulations), hardly a beginning has been made in developing an adequate political theory and an adequate theory of public finance for the system as a whole. Perhaps this is too much to ask. Perhaps the system can work only on the basis of trial and error, experimentation and adjustment. Perhaps there is no way, in the abstract, of determining which federal functions should be carried out by the formal apparatus of the federal government, which by state governments, which by local governments, which by private industries and agencies, which by universities, which by newly created nonprofit corporations. But, in this author's opinion, far more concern should be evinced about such questions within the government and within the halls of academe. In this connection the work of the Advisory Commission on Intergovernmental Relations and the studies of the Senate's Muskie Subcommittee on Intergovernmental Relations deserve special praise. This work should be continued and should be substantially supported.

In the absence of an adequate theoretical formulation for the system as a whole, a special burden falls upon certain instrumentalities of the federal government, notably the Executive Office of the President and the General Accounting Office, for tackling the drudge details of developing effective central controls over a system whose very success may depend upon the extent to which such controls can liberate rather than bind subordinate energies.

In a broader sense, the creative extension and perfection of the devolution system must be a matter of preeminent presidential concern and programmatic leadership.

THE PERSONNEL SYSTEM

It is not in the province of this paper to discuss the public personnel systems of state and local governments, but a logical corollary of the devolution system just discussed is that the federal government has a high stake in the quality and efficiency of employees at all levels of government. The Muskie bills and the Johnson administration's proposed Intergovernmental-Personnel and Education-for-the-Public-Service Acts of recent sessions of Congress are a testament to this concern. They need to be implemented and adequately funded.

Within the federal government itself, the improvement of the machinery for career service and political executive recruitment, assignment, training, promotion, and termination is a patent and continuing need. Adequate salaries are part of the problem, especially at the higher levels. Presidential support for the recommendations of the first Federal Commission on Executive, Legislative, and Judicial Salaries, pursuant to the Federal Salary Act of 1967 (due in December 1968), should produce a major breakthrough in top salary schedules.

Much progress has been made in recent years under the leadership of John W. Macy, chairman of the United States Civil Service Commission, both in cutting away some of the rigidities and overprescriptions that have plagued the classified civil service and in improving the presidential machinery for identifying and recruiting talent for the top political executive posts of the government.

In spite of these impressive evidences of progress, much remains to be done to: reduce turnover; facilitate reassignments, transfers, and terminations; attract able talent from private life for short-term federal assignments; promote intergovernmental mobility; provide mid-career sabbaticals for educational and reflective experiences; increase dignity-producing discretion at lower levels of management; combine the best in the traditionally conflicting patterns of the career systems—on the one hand, the military and foreign service, where rank inheres in the man; on the other hand, a civil service system, where rank is in the job; and develop a system of collective bargaining that simultaneously protects the rights of the employee and the interests of the taxpayer-citizen.

There are no gimmicks to insure progress along these lines. The greatest hope lies in the willingness of the President and the Congress to give the White House office and the Civil Service Commission respectively the troops, facilities, resources, and encouragement needed to address such issues with courage and imagination.

In moving forward, all concerned must be aware of the perverse consequences of attracting and holding top-grade talents in the federal service. For, as Frederic C. Mosher has eloquently and elegantly documented in his recent studies, public employment at the higher levels is becoming increasingly professionalized. Professionalization is friendly to the qualified performance of precise tasks, but unfriendly to those accommodations and bargains that give coherence and direction to general public objectives. How to educate broad-gauged professionals for the public service; how to keep professional specialists accountable to politically responsible generalists within the executive and legislative branches; these are at present and prospectively among the most important unresolved issues of public management.

A final note: the caliber of talent attracted to the public service will depend in substantial measure upon the excitement that can be conveyed by presidential leadership. The federal personnel systems—career, civil service, and political—do not respond with vitality to "Whigs" in the White House.

Making the System Work: The Political Preconditions

To this point there have been only allusions to the peculiar nature of congressional influence and control over large segments of the federal administration.

However, the fundamental preconditions of reform in federal government organization are political—that is, they relate to changes in the locus of power within the Congress and between Congress and the President. Stated in another way, the present and traditional mode of conducting the government's business has been highly satisfying to a number of strategically placed congressmen, to certain individual agencies, and to a number of specific group interests (and often these three in combination); but the broader perspectives of Congress-as-a-whole and of the presidency as to what constitutes effective conduct of the public business in the public interest have been generally lost in the shuffle.

Organization is not neutral in its effect upon policy, and those who hold power do not lightly relinquish it. It is for these reasons that this paper began with the warning that if the President wanted to reform the system, he would have to be persistent and employ high political skills.

Fortunately, or at least insistently, events are dealing the President useful cards. Large groups of congressmen who now share minimally in the control of federal administration are recipients of increasing complaints from state and local officials and from affected citizens about the inconveniences and vexations of existing organizational arrangements and procedures. There are many members of Congress whose political fortunes are increasingly tied to presidential and congressional success in making greater sense out of the system as a whole.

Political reforms in the structure of Congress are the prerequisites of effective structural reforms in the executive branch. And political reforms are not easily effected. To accomplish them, a President must be willing to dip deeply into his reservoir of power and persuasion, and he must be willing to negotiate a series of trade-offs that, at least in the short range, may force him to request new structures and procedures rather than new programs and policies—to seek tidiness and effectiveness in preference to legislative splashiness.

In this context, the President and his allies in Congress must address themselves to four key issues: (1) the strengthening of central party leadership in the Congress; (2) the reorganization of congressional committees and subcommittees; (3) the modification of congressional powers over administrative policies and reorganization proposals; and (4) the financing of congressional campaigns, especially in the House of Representatives. The goal is not to make Congress subservient to the President: it is to subject atomized power to the discipline of general politics in these two branches of government.

STRENGTHENING CENTRAL PARTY LEADERSHIP

The weaknesses that afflict the presidency in bringing coherence to the management of the executive branch are paralleled by the weaknesses of congressional party leaders in bringing coherence to the management of the legislative branch—and the two are inextricably related. Central party controls over congressional committees and subcommittees tend to be weak and intermittent. Fragmented power in the Congress, buttressed by the principle of seniority in the committee system, is more than a match for the centripetal influences of party caucuses, conferences, policy committees, and floor leadership. Centrifugal tendencies are reinforced when the key positions of Majority Leader in the Senate and the Speaker of the House are occupied, as they are periodically, by philosophical Whigs.

Whatever is done, with or without presidential influence, to strengthen the capacity and the spine of central party leadership in the Congress will tend to improve the chances of flexing up opportunities for a more rational and coherent organization of federal administration. For the business of party leadership in Congress, like the business of the President, is the government as a whole. Just as there is a built-in propensity of subcommittee chairmen and bureau chiefs to want to magnify their control of specific programs and agencies, so there is a built-in propensity of party leaders to relate and homogenize conflicting interests and jurisdictions in the interest of a larger whole. Party leaders in Congress tend to be friendly to presidential perspectives, not because of any compulsive deference to presidential leadership but because, like him, they stand above the timberline on their respective mountains. At the very least, their staffs should be increased in size and competence to assist in reviewing issues of policy and structure that cut across existing jurisdictions in both the legislative and executive branches.

REORGANIZING CONGRESSIONAL COMMITTEES
AND SUBCOMMITTEES

Congress has undergone two reorganization studies in the past quarter century: one in the middle 1940s; one in the middle 1960s. As a result of the first (the LaFollette-Monroney Committee) a number of standing committees were abolished and/or consolidated, and Congress was provided with additional staff services. The second Joint Committee on the Organization of Congress (Monroney-Madden Committee) made a number of suggestions for curbing the arbitrary rule of committee chairmen and for vesting greater authority in committee majorities: appointing "review specialists" for each standing committee who would be responsible for examining the administration of laws under the committee's jurisdiction; providing Congress with more complete budgetary and fiscal data; dividing the House Committee on Education and Labor into separate committees on Education and on Labor and Public Welfare. These suggested reforms have made no progress. They deserve presidential concern and encouragement, for some of them (notably the first two) are inevitably related to the achievement of organizational reforms in the executive branch.

But the very fact that power centers in the Congress have not reacted favorably to the recent recommendations of their own joint committee is suggestive of the intractabilities and vested interests that must be overcome if centripetal tendencies in the federal government are to be strengthened.

Pending a climate friendly to a wholesale restructuring of the present committee and subcommittee system in Congress, the President and the party leaders in Congress should place their emphasis upon two more modest reforms.

First, three additional joint committees similar to and parallel with the Joint Economic Committee should be created: a Joint Committee for National Security Affairs (composed of representatives from the military affairs and foreign affairs committees in both houses); a Joint Committee on Environmental Management; and a Joint Committee on Human Resource Development. These three joint committees would not have legislative responsibilities, nor direct oversight responsibilities vis-à-vis any particular agency; they would be concerned with studies and hearings that would illuminate the crosscutting issues suggested in their respective titles. Working closely with the Committees on Government Operations and, through overlapping membership, with key legislative committees in each house, these new joint committees could perform a staff function for the Congress as a whole similar to that provided for the President by the existing and recommended staff units in the Executive Office of the President.

Second, the subcommittee structure of the House and Senate Appropriations Committees should be rationalized to provide a similar crosscutting view of the programs and activities of federal departments and agencies. Such a revision could be accomplished with a minimum of dislocation to existing centers of power within the two committees, and yet the effect of such a change could be quite salutary.

What is needed is a general strengthening of the power of the full Appropriations Committees relative to the power of their subcommittees. This could be accomplished by increasing the staff capability available to the full committee chairmen, and by reordering the missions of such staff in terms of interconnecting policy issues.

Short of this, or in addition to it, provision might be made for regular conferences of those subcommittee chairmen whose jurisdictions fall respectively under national security, economic stability and growth, environmental management, and human resource development. These conferences could be presided over by the chairman of the full committee or his designee, and special staffs could be assigned to each conference group. The task of each conference would be to discuss federal programs and organizational arrangements contingent upon appropriation actions of the several separate subcommittees, but in general interrelated terms.

If appropriately staffed, periodic subcommittee conferences of this type could give greater coherence to appropriations decisions affecting a number of programs and agencies of the executive branch and could be effective levers for promoting needed organizational and procedural changes.

STRENGTHENING PRESIDENTIAL DISCRETION
AND THE POWERS OF CONGRESS

Above all, the President should attempt to win from the Congress a greater measure of discretion in effecting organizational shifts and consolidations in the executive branch, especially within his own Executive Office.

Intermittently since the First World War Congress has given the President authority to submit reorganization plans to the Congress, with the provision that the plans would take effect within a certain period of time (currently sixty days) unless either house disapproves in the meantime. Although this arrangement is far preferable to having reorganization proposals run the full gauntlet of legislative delays and amendments associated with the normal congressional process, it gives to one house powers that should be exercised only by Congress as a whole. Furthermore, the reorganization powers of the President are granted for stated periods of time only. If the President is to be held responsible for the effective execution of the laws, his present authority to submit reorganization proposals should be made permanent, and such proposals should become effective within a stated period of time unless *both* houses of Congress have disapproved his recommendation.

In regard to his own Executive Office, his authority to reorganize, reassign, and consolidate agencies and functions should be plenary. Certainly in no case should Congress create *statutory* interdepartmental committees within the Executive Office of the President (or outside of it, for that matter).

Congress, through the oversight functions of its standing committees, through the appropriations process, through constitutional powers of confirmation, and through studies and investigations conducted by its Committees on Government Operations, will continue to have a variety of means of influencing the organization and procedures of the executive branch. It will still share with the President the overall management function. But the modifications suggested would give to the President a management capability commensurate with his responsibilities and would tend to modify parochial powers that are now exercised by congressional subdivisions.

CAMPAIGN FINANCING

Presidential campaigning has now become so expensive that no single donor or combination of donors is likely to be able to purchase undue advantage by making substantial contributions to a campaign fund. In many populous states, the same generalization can be made about United States senators. Nevertheless, in some states and in a number of congressional districts the dependence of candidates upon substantial campaign contributions from a few powerful donors can reinforce parochial and centrifugal tendencies in the American polity.

The consequences for federal administration can be delineated in the following flow chart:

$15,000 contribution from mining industry "x" to ⟶ Congressman "y" who becomes ⟶ chairman of a subcommittee with substantial control over ⟶ a bureau of the Department of the Interior charged with regulations over mining industry "x" making impossible ⟶ regulation of mining industry "x" in broader "public interest" terms by ⟶ the Secretary of the Interior, the President of the United States, and the Congress as a whole.

The division of labor in Congress, an inevitable consequence of the complex agenda of modern public policy, makes it essential that an individual congressman in positions of strategic authority over key aspects of the public business not be beholden to special minorities who stand to gain from his decisions. Otherwise, government is turned into a series of privately controlled but publicly sanctioned fiefdoms. This danger may, of course, arise from the existence of "balance-of-power" voting blocs in a particular constituency, but the lumpiness of campaign contributions is probably a more consistent cause.

Anything that is done to spread the base of campaign financing (including—perhaps especially including—the financing of primaries) will tend to dilute the passion of individual legislators for personal control over subunits of the federal bureaucracy. Thus presidential leadership in pushing for the public assumption of campaign costs is one of the preconditions of effecting greater rationality and coherence in the administration of the public business.

These, then, are some of the directions that must be followed if the American government is to operate with greater effectiveness and coherence in a time of increasing national crisis.

The precise recommendations are less important than the underlying strategic postulate. That postulate is that, if the system is to be made to work, the President must be prepared to meet head-on the political forces that inhibit the effective and responsible conduct of the public business.

FOREIGN POLICY

FRANCIS M. BATOR

THE POLITICS OF ALLIANCE: THE UNITED STATES AND WESTERN EUROPE

Some of the severest tests of statecraft come with the waning of great fears which have called forth great cooperative enterprises. The present state of Atlantic affairs is a case in point. The very success of Western Europe since the dark days of 1945-47 has eroded the foundations of transatlantic cooperation and weakened the impulse for closer Western European integration. The new administration will inherit an almost implausible quarter-century record of achievement. It will also inherit an atmosphere of apprehension and unease within the community of men concerned about Atlantic relations. And the new administration will certainly make, if only by default, choices affecting the Atlantic future as subtle as they are important—choices made more difficult because they lack the clarity and drama which marked the great decisions of the late 1940s.

The cause of our trial is familiar enough, and far from unwelcome in itself. It is the widespread change in perceptions of the threat of Soviet domination in Western Europe, powerfully reinforced by the failure of Moscow to create a monolithic empire in communist Eastern Europe. The apprehensions of the mid-forties are fading memories—I do not believe that the Soviet invasion of Czechoslovakia will reverse the trend—yet nothing has replaced fear as a vital part of the bedrock under the whole structure of Atlantic cooperation and, more important, as the most powerful and consistent goad to building of community.

Gone too are the peculiar conditions which gave shape and manageability to the Atlantic community. A partnership between one very large, very strong nation and several smaller, damaged ones imposes a certain natural hierarchy. It is by no means necessarily a hierarchy of merit. But it assures that the strong nation—in this case the United States—will be, though hardly the last word, the preponderant force on questions of both ends and means, as well as a powerful arbiter of quarrels within its own camp. With the success of European performance and American policy in the rebuilding of Western Europe, the question of leadership has become much more complicated.

A Time of Trouble?

The waning of a shared fear and of the semblance of hierarchy have contributed to symptoms of change and unrest which tend often to concern Americans more than the basic dilemmas they reflect. Britain is shedding Asian burdens and, some believe, reverting to an insular perspective. France has adopted a policy calculus which assigns positive value to divergence from the United States, and she seems to project for herself a solo role in Europe and the world which, while not in keeping with the raw facts of power, has a divisive effect on Atlantic politics. West Germany, still unsure of herself, feels obliged periodically to prove her independence. Finally, the North Atlantic Treaty Organization (NATO)—the most elaborate of our joint enterprises—is showing all the signs of stale middle age.

One effect of all this has been to persuade many observers of Atlantic affairs on both sides of the ocean that the alliance is now at a crossroad where hard and fundamental choices must be made on pain of imminent or eventual, if not precisely specified, disaster. Recent writings in the field—"Troubled Partnership," "End of Alliance," "Gulliver's Troubles," "Last Chance in Europe"—reveal more than an occupational pessimism, understandable enough among writers on international affairs. They evidence a common conviction that we are in trouble.

The new administration cannot chart its course by reference merely to symptoms. It will need to reexamine basic questions which define the American stake in Western Europe: What are the really essential U.S. interests in Western Europe? How are those interests threatened by the current malaise? Are there ways to solve the basic problems or to make them tolerable? Most important, the new administration must formulate an American position which, while it recognizes the limits of American influence, reflects the central importance of Western Europe to our security and to an environment conducive to the health of the American body politic, as well as the role Europe must play if chances for peace and for a decent civilization are to be kept alive on a globe where we, the Europeans—and, indeed, the Russians—constitute a small, rich minority surrounded by an enormous, desperately poor majority.

WHAT DO WE REALLY NEED FROM WESTERN EUROPE?

Twenty years ago our objectives in Western Europe were plain: to prevent expansion of the communist empire through military conquest or internal takeover, and to promote political and economic stability. With Soviet armies in the center of Europe, Stalin in the Kremlin, Western Europe in a state of collapse, and powerful communist parties in France and Italy benefiting from the spurious legitimacy conferred by the brave role communists played in partisan resistance to the Nazis, the danger seemed real enough. The extraordinary American response—considering that less than thirty years passed between the defeat of the League and the passage of the Marshall Plan—was informed both by the geopolitical notion that the United States could not afford to see Europe dominated by a single hostile power and by aversion to communism. It also reflected an underlying sense of community with Western Europe, built up through our involvement in two great European wars.

Relative to the fears of the forties, we have been enormously successful. The chances of a Moscow-dominated communist Western Europe are nil. Indeed, tight Soviet control of even established communist governments has in several cases proven fleeting, and, in any event, impossible to sustain without periodic resort to naked force. (Even revisionist historians have not claimed that it was Soviet policy to promote the growth of strong and independent friends.)

To an extent rare in international politics, the measures of the late forties solved the most pressing problems of the late forties. But these solutions have revealed a new set of problems, and it is in this context that one must raise the question: What are American interests in Western Europe in the late 1960s?

Though many formulations are possible, our central interests appear to be as follows:

1. Benign and constructive relations among the nations of Western Europe. At a minimum, we do not want Germany attacking France, or France attacking Germany.

2. Reasonably constructive, cooperative, and community-minded behavior with respect to those many issues of Atlantic relations where interdependence is not just a speechwriter's crutch but an economic and cultural fact. An adversary component in our relations is unavoidable, particularly in economics. The need is for a politics that exploits possibilities

for gain to all parties concerned, and at the same time settles conflicts in ways that do not drive any party to conclude that the game is not worth the candle. At the very least, Atlantic relations must not degenerate into harsh, beggar-thy-neighbor economics and political relations to match.

3. A wary, but open-minded and probing stance toward Moscow and Eastern Europe, with special sensitivity for those who have most at stake. This implies neither a rigid cold-war posture nor a complete relaxation which ignores the possibility of a lapse of sanity in the East. (At this writing it is impossible to foretell with certainty the net outcome of the Czech crisis. My own view of the evidence so far is that it demonstrates defensive anxiety in Moscow and not offensive hubris, and that this will become clear in Western Europe and even Germany in a matter of months. If I am wrong, then the question of alliance priorities will recede. I myself would give long odds the other way. Even so, our military position must remain appropriately hedged, in part to reassure the Germans and in part because defensive anxiety could conceivably turn into aggressive paranoia.)

4. Last, and for the near term I think least, we would like Western Europe to fill the American need for company in the world. This means more than sharing the material burdens in helping India or Latin America to grow. It certainly does not mean unquestioned support for every specific American action. For balance in our own politics and good sense in our conduct, we need neither straight men nor yes-men but responsible partners and critics who view the world in the round and can therefore advise and help, and on occasion reprove and restrain us.

It is relevant to ask what such conduct in foreign affairs implies for the domestic politics of the nations of Western Europe. No certain generalizations follow deductively. But as an empirical matter, tolerably effective welfare democracies—defined in terms of responsiveness to popular will and safeguards for minorities rather than specific machinery—are more likely to generate external behavior congenial to our interests than closed, less responsive, inner-directed governments. This is certainly true in relation to the first three tests above. At the very least, governments subject to popular opinion in prosperous industrial countries are less likely to indulge in a foreign policy of madness.

WHY ARE WE TROUBLED?

Measured by benign cooperation among nation states, organization for collective security and internal prosperity, and cooperative problem solving, this decade of Atlantic politics looks not at all bad, certainly as compared with any preceding decade in this century. Perhaps for the first time in modern history, the probability of any Western European nation resorting to military force against its neighbors is literally nil; that this has become a commonplace is a gauge of the progress we have made.[1]

Why then are we troubled? Much of the anxiety stems from a sense that none of the overarching visions designed to settle the Second World War and prevent a third is moving toward fulfillment. Early notions of Atlantic political integration have lost their hold. Western European political integration, the abiding faith of some of the best of our public men on both sides of the Atlantic, is at a standstill. Nor is there any immediate prospect of a final settlement of the Second World War which would heal the division of Germany. Measured against hopes and expectations of rapid movement in the direction of a grand design—not to speak of peaceful liberation of Eastern Europe and of an East-West settlement on our terms—the present architecture of Europe and the Atlantic world is disappointing.

It is tempting but wrong to dismiss such disappointment as the mere consequence of naiveté about the pace of change that is possible in the architectural relations among nations old and proud and deeply scarred. It is wrong, too, to take refuge in the belief that American interests depend not on structural arrangements among nation states but rather on their external conduct—that there is no necessary correspondence between structure and behavior. No doubt, in our enthusiasm, we have at times become overcommitted to particular architectures with respect to both our vital needs and tactical efficacy. But to stop there is to dodge the hard

---

1. Measured by the test of company in the world, the conventional impression is that we have not fared well. But this impression stems in important part from European reluctance to support America in Vietnam—at best an oblique test of companionship. Many Europeans think that the U.S. failure to provide company to France in Indo-China or Algeria and to France and Britain in Suez is an apt parallel. But that too misses the point, which is not how either party stands on a particular issue but that it stands at all, as distinguished from a posture of insular noninvolvement. And there is a more powerful test: aid to the development-capable nations of the third world. Here American failure during recent years overshadows whatever blame the Europeans deserve. We tend to forget that, while Europe is rich, it is not nearly as rich as the United States. Measured by the standard of the U.S. personal income tax, ours has not been a disproportionate share of the burden of common defense and aid to the poor. In any event, it is not at all certain that a fast uniting Europe—as against a fully united Europe—would do better. It is safe to say that the process of unification would tend fully to engage Europe's political energies for a great many years.

problem: The existing relations among the countries of Western Europe, between Western Europe and Eastern Europe, and between Western Europe and the United States are not in a state of long-run equilibrium. The existing architecture is not stable. Even where it appears most rigid, it may be all too brittle.

What are the sources of disequilibrium? Fundamentally, they lie in the failure of present structures to meet important aspirations of important constituencies.

- The Germans are deeply dissatisfied. However one measures it, whether against their wish for formal German unity or against their desire for a humane polity in East Germany which would allow easy intercourse between Germans on the two sides of the line, there is a large gap between what is and what the majority of Germans believe ought to be. German politicians will continue to regard this as an issue to which they must address themselves as a matter of high priority. And politicians of other nations will be forced to respond. This is not to say that the average German spends long hours brooding about these problems, but rather that this is an abiding dissatisfaction which will remain a potent issue in German politics as long as there is no sense of progress toward solving it. And it will amplify the political effects of other dissatisfactions.
- Many other Western Europeans are deeply frustrated. Some in positions of power and influence, including some Germans, believe that the existing structural arrangements among themselves—and, Gaullists would assert, between the United States and themselves—condemn Europe to an excessive dependence on America. They believe that it is neither fully safe, nor dignified, nor good for Europe's vitality to remain indefinitely a security ward of the United States. Many are concerned about American economic penetration, and worry that Europe's unique and ancient cultures will be submerged in a sea of Coca-Cola. Many more are concerned about how best to adjust to the harsh facts of scale in modern technology and defense, which raise basic questions about the future of the nation-state.
- Britain is becalmed, seemingly adrift in painful transition from paramount world power to important and influential island kingdom. And there is a widespread sense that in order to find a new role, she must make new connections.
- Many Americans also are dissatisfied. They regard as disproportionate the

American share of the burden of joint defense in Europe and elsewhere. They see us stalemated in our attempts to encourage a European system which will eventually preserve European security without major cost to us and guarantee an economically open Western Europe. And they, too, find it easy to blame the atomized architecture of Europe as the basic cause.

Responsible Europeans, Americans, and, we can be certain, Russians understand the hazards of a status quo which requires a continuing military confrontation between the United States and the Soviet Union in the center of Germany, with Berlin a perpetual irritant and potential trigger point. This concern is balanced by a vivid sense of the risks we would incur if American and Soviet troops were largely replaced in policing that line by two German armies under the command of hostile governments, neither of which recognizes the right of the other to exist.

Last, and a matter of no small moment for Atlantic and East-West politics, the shape of Eastern Europe is in flux. The Russian action in Czechoslovakia and its aftermath proved both that the Soviets are prepared to take strong, unpopular actions to maintain the status quo, and that even those actions will not assure stability if the subject people is sufficiently skillful and united. The resulting insecurities felt by Soviet and Eastern European leaders will be major factors in the stability of the entire continent.

In short, whatever the quality of Atlantic politics in the past, those who are content with the status quo must beware of the political weight of those who are not. The more so, because there is a strain in the politics of modern bourgeois societies which encourages change for change's sake. I believe it was the historian R. A. Nisbet who once suggested that boredom is one of the most underrated social forces in history. In domestic affairs, bread-and-butter interests tend sharply to constrain choices. But foreign affairs are a fertile field for politicians in search of issues, foreign and defense ministers and their speech writers looking for "policies," journalists in need of stories, and even satisfied publics with a weakness for drama. Except perhaps in Scandinavia, there is a streak of schizophrenia even in prosperous and satisfied welfare democracies. Six days of the week we act and vote as though the best foreign policy is no foreign policy at all. But on the seventh, our very leisure and prosperity are likely to promote receptivity to, if not outright demand for, novelty, even at considerable risk. Where thirst for drama reinforces genuine grievances about existing structures and genuine pressures for change among important political constituencies in an open international society, it is foolhardy to predict that things tomorrow will be the way they are today. It may not be right to despair because specific visions have not materialized. But it is certainly right to be concerned about the dangers—as well as the opportunities—inherent in both incipient change and prolonged rigidity.[2]

The sense that we are not in a stable and satisfactory equilibrium explains much, but not all, of our malaise. After all, we have faced painful and knotty problems before. The root of the trouble lies rather in a growing sense on both sides of the Atlantic that Americans and Western Europeans no longer share a plausible vision of the future which would provide us with a guide to action. Lack of a shared vision, of a concept of how to guide the forces which are at work, is at bottom what troubles people. For those who like to think of Atlantic political relations in terms of NATO, it is a case of an alliance in search of a purpose—a purpose which goes beyond what many have come to regard as mere guard duty. In terms of the broader political relations among the Atlantic nations, it is a matter of a search for a shared view about what to do and what to avoid with respect to the unsolved internal and external problems of Europe and the Atlantic.

IN SEARCH OF A VISION

Three grand visions of the future have at various times captured the political imaginations of various of our leading public men: Jean Monnet's united Western Europe; the Atlantic community; and, least congenial to most, a settlement of the Second World War through some scheme of U.S.-Soviet disengagement in Europe which would allow the unification of Germany. Each vision touched on the structural relations among Western Europe, Eastern Europe, the Soviet Union, and the United States. But the Monnet vision singled out as its defining theme the internal architecture of Western Europe and emphasized the search for a new European political identity. The Atlantic view stressed the American-Western European relationship and collective security. And the third vision was mainly concerned with the relations between East and West in Europe and the unification of Germany.

2. Whether one should worry that the confrontation between rigid structures and desire for change will yield malignant political behavior or that structures will change too quickly and abruptly, or be replaced by something worse, is, at this level of abstraction, a semantic game.

It is now clear that none of these three visions is about to be fulfilled—not even Monnet Europe, at least not in its strong form as an agenda for early, cumulative movement toward political unity.[3]

To start with the last, the idea of settlement through an East-West bargain entailing a unified Germany on terms short of a Soviet surrender never really caught on, least of all in Germany. Settlement by "compellence"—liberation and all that—was never a real possibility, even if we sometimes acted as though we believed in it. And settlement by barter—neutralization of the Federal Republic in exchange for unity under a freely elected government—was thought by most people almost equally unsafe. Not enough people ever thought that any such arrangement could provide either security or sufficient anchorage for a united but constrained, less-than-equal Germany. At the least, it would involve, indeed require, the indefinite active presence of the two giants in the center of Europe and their tacit cooperation as the senior guarantors and enforcers of the arrangement, a condition which has struck many as neither likely nor desirable. The leaders of postwar Germany have shown even less interest in this plan than governments elsewhere.

The idea of a neutralization bargain has been revived from time to time. And it might be revived again; one can find hints of something like it in recent speeches by Germans. But until now, it has not caught on in the West. One suspects it never caught on in the East either, although at times during the past two decades there has been some elaborate dropping of handkerchiefs.

The conception of an Atlantic community was and still is real enough in the sense of a defensive alliance among nations whose economies and institutions and citizens' lives are increasingly entwined. And the Atlantic nations remain by and large agreed, although one of them would deny it, on the need for collective defense against an external danger which is much diminished but still greater than zero.[4] (It is likely that events in Czechoslovakia will increase the sense of threat in the near term but, in my view, only in the near term.)

---

3. It is not my purpose to score specious points against the distinguished men who held these visions. In most cases, their hopes were balanced by a skeptical sense of reality. And enthusiasm, which in hindsight renders a man vulnerable to the charge of naiveté, is essential to the quality which, in case of success, one is wont to call genius.

4. The French are not a real exception. They are simply aware that there is no way in which the United States can withdraw nuclear protection from France and still provide it to West Germany.

Yet, as a motivating ideal in Atlantic politics, the vision of an increasingly comprehensive and institutionalized political structure—an Atlantic commonwealth—was never quite plausible either. Neither we nor the Europeans have been ready for it. Though many Americans are convinced of the need for a delegation of power to supranational entities in the long term, few members of Congress would today vote for any grant of sovereignty to an Atlantic council. This is not just a matter of habit and history; it also grows out of the lurking concern about whether effective governance of even fifty states, all on one continent, is feasible. (The fact that the boundaries of the security community explicitly defined do not coincide with the economic or the cultural community—witness Sweden, Japan, Portugal—would also pose problems.)

The Atlantic idea has enjoyed no greater credence on the eastern shore of the ocean. While much of the talk about what is not possible between partners of different square mileage or population is moonshine—neither Delaware nor Maine appears to feel disadvantaged by its partnership with New York and California—there is no doubt that close political integration between the United States and the separate nations of Western Europe would violate the deep will to autonomy of too many Europeans, whether nationalist or "European." To borrow Barbara Ward's affectionate remark, the idea is too much like sharing a bath with a genial elephant.[5]

The original prospects of the third vision—a united Western Europe—are especially hard for a sympathetic American to gauge in retrospect. Cer-

---

5. It is a different matter that some Americans, indeed some Europeans, are attracted by the idea of an Atlantic community precisely because of the intrinsic imbalance. Defining the American objective as maximum U.S. influence, and taking off from the minor premise that U.S. influence is an increasing function of European dependence on the U.S. strategic umbrella, they would have us try to sustain that dependence as long as possible, and not just because of the technical case for centralized command and control. This issue cannot be settled by resort to logic. I believe, however, that both premises are wrong. For one thing, one must distinguish between power and usable power. For another, what matters is not our influence as such, but how Europe behaves. Caring about the position of the football on the field, one must be interested not merely in how far one's team has moved the opposition, but where the play started. For both reasons, the notion that it is dependence on American strategic defense which will yield cooperative Western European conduct strikes me as implausible. In any event, this version of Atlantic community could hardly be expected to serve as a unifying ideal. It would have little attraction even for most Americans. This is true not because of an inclination to be softheaded about power, but because of a hardheaded understanding that even in international politics, gross asymmetry of direct power among partners is likely to produce either apathy or hubris in the weaker. In either case, irresponsible behavior is the likely result.

tainly it commanded the energy and enthusiasm of many of the great men of postwar Atlantic politics. One wonders what might have happened if Britain had early taken a strong lead, or if General de Gaulle had retired after extricating France from Algeria. Some might wonder, although I am not among them, whether things might have gone differently if the United States had not been preoccupied with centralized control of nuclear weapons. But in the end, it is not unreasonable to doubt whether rapid movement toward Monnet's Europe was in the cards, short of a prior cataclysm or highly risky shock treatment by American abandonment. This is in important part a matter of definition and tempo. Quite clearly, remarkable progress has been made in terms of some very political economics. But in the light of the very slow progress toward the near-term political version of Europe united, it is fair to infer that Monnet and the three other great Western Europeans—Schuman, De Gasperi, and Adenauer—underestimated the force of the separate European nationalisms and the difficulty of maintaining momentum in an enterprise aimed at a Carolingian Europe with its eastern borders on the Elbe. In the last few years, at least, the salient facts about Western European politics seem to be French resistance to any weakening of national sovereignty and a general shifting of attention to the East. Even the Germans, who for a long time and with good reason were reluctant to do so, have begun to turn eastward.

In any event, it is not explanation of the past which must concern us, but the search for a vision to goad and guide Atlantic politics in the future. For that, none of the three visions will quite do—at least not today. None is sufficiently responsive to both of the two great problems of Western Europe which make current arrangements unstable: (1) European identity and autonomy; and (2) healing the division of Germany and Europe. None will solve both problems on terms which, at the same time, can satisfy the need of Western Europe for security and can conceivably command early Soviet agreement on points where Moscow has a veto.

Settlement by neutralization would re-create a very large Germany, discriminated against and hence twice unequal. To be acceptable to Russians and Europeans, especially Germans, such an arrangement would have to engage the United States and the Soviet Union in the heart of Europe, and hence would preclude the kind of autonomy Europeans of both East and West want.

An Atlantic Europe would provide security from the East and an anchor for West Germany, but at the price of a very unequal partnership and no plausible prospect for either an autonomous Europe or reunification.

The question of Monnet Europe is more complicated; and, for the long term, the answer is surely open. In partnership with the United States—the terms of which would be responsive to practical need and would reflect an increasingly symmetrical interdependence—it would meet the aspiration of "Europeans" for identity and autonomy, as well as their desire for some secondary advantages of larger scale. It would provide a safe haven for West Germany. Where it fails, other than in denying the nationalist ideas of the Gaullists, is in not dealing with German unification concretely and explicitly, save after the cold war is so truly past history that the Russians might simply give away East Germany free, letting it join an organized, militarily self-sufficient Western Europe.

Ten years ago the school solution to this dilemma lay in the judgment, shared by a great many Germans, that the adventure of building Western Europe would provide West Germans a psychic and political substitute for unification. It was also judged, rightly at the time, that foreclosure of the option of unification-by-neutralization would not in any case cause Germans great pain, since they thought it too dangerous.

During the next few years, the dilemma may dissolve in a different way. In the past year or so, influential West Germans have begun to redefine what they mean by a solution to the German problem. There is under way a shift of emphasis from the objective of one nation-one flag to the more modest aim of assuring a decent life for East Germans and open intercourse among all Germans. To the extent that this new definition sinks firm roots in West German politics—which is a matter for German determination, not outside prodding—the basic flaw in the Monnet vision will disappear.[6] But for the present, even a blunter variant of the dilemma is too sharp to allow Western European integration to serve as a unifying goal for alliance politics. Inertia and Gaullist nationalism combine with the spectacle of at least intermittent movement in Eastern Europe to eclipse a vision which calls for an enormous burst of energy focused on building a political Western Europe as the priority task. Or so it seems now. This is all the more so, since many Europeans believe, whatever the truth, that a speeding up of movement toward coalescence in Western

---

6. I do not believe that the Soviet leadership would be so frightened by the prospect of a united Western Europe as to try to head it off by offering a bona fide unification-by-neutralization deal. I suspect such a bargain would scare them even more. To be sure, they might dangle it before the Germans hoping that their bluff would never be called. But if challenged to put up, they are likely to turn hard of hearing.

Europe might impede that loosening in Eastern Europe which is important to most Europeans and essential to West Germans if redefinition of their purposes is to take hold.[7]

If for the time being none of the three classic visions will serve to give Western Europeans and Americans a clear sense of where we are headed and how to get there, is there some other vision which will do? I believe not. The truth is, there does not exist today a design drawn in comparably sharp, architectural terms, which seems feasible and which will resolve the underlying problems and hence command the allegiance of a large majority of Western Europeans. It is important to recognize that this is not a consequence of American requirements or preconditions. It follows, rather, from the deep aspirations and concerns of Western Europeans—Germans and non-Germans—and from the fact of a Soviet veto over the fate of East Germany.

Yet among men who care about Atlantic politics, the search for a vision goes on. Not many believe that large moves or significant choices requiring an agreed blueprint are possible in the near future. But many do believe that, precisely because no near-term solutions to big problems are likely, we must fix on some conception which will soothe frustrations and help us hold on to each other in our workaday tasks. The fear is that in the absence of a sense of shared goals, the adversary element in our relations will tend to dominate internal Atlantic politics and produce a dangerous splintering in external affairs.

In response to this strong demand, there has emerged during the past few years a rather different vision of the Atlantic future, expressed for the United States by President Johnson in his European policy speech of October 7, 1966. Its goals are defined not in terms of a concrete, architectural outcome, but rather in terms of maximizing piecemeal movement in broadly indicated directions, as opportunity presents itself. It is a vision exceedingly flexible in both structural outcome and tempo. It allows for political integration in Western Europe but does not require it, and emphasizes the practical arrangements and the increasing closeness needed for efficient problem solving. It allows, but only at the end of a very long process, for some sort of growing together of the two parts of Germany, but in the meanwhile calls only for a further opening of relations between

---

7. If events in Prague were to produce a serious and prolonged freeze throughout Eastern Europe, the mood in Western Europe could easily change. Then only the Gaullists would stand in the way.

Western and Eastern Europe, and an improvement in the quality of life in East Germany and in the possibilities of intercourse between the two sets of Germans. It calls for increasing East European independence of the Soviet Union, but only at a pace which keeps down the risk of backlash. It allows for increasing autonomy in Western Europe's relations with the United States, even in defense, but only in step with the European capacity to manage a credible deterrent of its own—credible in the context of a prudent view of the risks (a function in part of U.S.-Soviet progress in bilateral arms control). It allows for some institutionalization of Atlantic politics, but looks mainly to increasingly close ad hoc cooperation on specific problems.

The premise of this view is that by working on a variety of concrete tasks, and by moving forward in small steps in directions only broadly defined, we will gradually resolve the larger structural problems, both by change in people's goals, habits, and tolerances, and by an evolutionary transformation in the environment. The theory is that problems will become soluble either because they will have been redefined or because arrangements now unacceptable become acceptable, and that the experience of solving small problems will make it easier eventually to solve big ones.

The difference between this process vision and the structural visions lies in large part in the specificity of priorities and of institutional outcomes, and—though here the distinction is less clear—in tempo.[8] The advantage of focusing on process, rather than on structure, is that painful choices are postponed and dilemmas bypassed. But there is a price. Even if widely shared and approved, a picture of the future which evokes only a blurred, romantic-abstract image of the architectural shape of Europe and the Atlantic—a vision, moreover, which indefinitely postpones structural solutions and provides no basis for concerted action on a grand scale—will not generate that sense of shared purposes, of élan and camaraderie, which would make the divisive strains in Atlantic relations easy to bear.

This, in my judgment, defines the central problem and central task of contemporary Atlantic relations: how to hold together and manage a constructive internal and external politics at a time when there exists no great shared conception of dominating and powerful purposes and when no

---

8. In one respect, the process vision is more demanding than the others; it implies a greater synchronization—for instance, between progress toward Western European integration and Eastern European autonomy.

such conception seems possible within the practical constraints which currently prevail.

PROSPECTS AND TASKS, AND THE AMERICAN ROLE

If large choices and movement were necessary or possible, the lack of a map with a clearly marked destination would be serious indeed. But the fact that there now exists no shared vision of structural solutions implies that for the near term no major moves are in sight.[9] The world could change, and quickly; one cannot discount the possibility of radical and wholly unexpected movement in international affairs. We must be ready to respond. But it would appear that the time is not now ripe for significant change: for major movement toward settlement in Europe, or toward tighter political organization of Western Europe, or toward more elaborate institutional arrangements between Western Europe and the United States.

What then are the tasks facing Atlantic politics, leaving aside for the moment the two great global problems of strategic arms control and relations between the poor and the rich?

There is still defense. Guard duty it may be, in the absence of a new taste for Western European adventure in the Kremlin; but it is exceedingly serious and sophisticated and expensive guard duty. There is East-West "bridge-building," and all the questions it raises about the proper balance between national enterprise and coordinated approaches. There is the political management of internal economic affairs, both European and Atlantic.

Each set of tasks offers opportunities for constructive and cooperative action. And each presents dangers. The second part of this chapter attempts to explore these opportunities and dangers in concrete terms. But there is a prior, general question about the proper role of the United States. Avoiding imprudence and rigidity in defense, immobility and splintering in Atlantic external relations, while assuring sensible management of our internal economics, depends heavily on how the United States plays its part.

9. For the proposition to be strictly true one must rule out large, unilateral moves by one or another of the participants not on the basis of agreement. More on this later. Suffice it here to assert only that the French couldn't pull it off; the Germans wouldn't and couldn't; and the United States wouldn't. The notion of a U.S.-Soviet condominium bargain over Europe is grotesque. It would be deeply damaging in terms of the most selfish American interests. And it is inconceivable in terms of our politics.

Much recent writing on Atlantic politics has laid the blame for the prevailing mood of anxiety on a lack of American leadership. On the face of it, there is a puzzle here, for the list of recent practical achievements in Atlantic affairs is long. For instance, neither the Kennedy Round nor the intense and fruitful negotiations about international money should be dismissed as mere economics; they reflect political progress of a major sort, in which American initiative has played a central role.

The puzzle turns on the definition of leadership. We are faulted not for failing to pull our weight in solving a host of practical problems in Atlantic relations. If anything, some of our friends in Europe feel that the United States has pulled too hard in the directions it prefers. Rather, the charge is that we have failed to generate that sense of momentum, of movement in pursuit of joint purposes, which the alliance must have to avoid falling apart. On this view, the only way the United States can demonstrate leadership is to take the initiative in generating a new, unifying vision which is addressed to the central problems of Atlantic politics.[10]

In my judgment, both the charge and the prescription miss the point. As we have seen, there exists no unifying vision which would provide the basis even for agreement in principle on how the great architectural dilemmas might best be resolved. Nor, in my judgment, would the balance and cohesion of Atlantic politics be served if the United States took the lead in stimulating a great debate on what we are about, an attempt at group therapy designed to clarify and blueprint the choices. Debate which cannot lead to action, and yet is bound to dramatize painful dilemmas for Germans, postponements for "Europeans," and frustrations for Europe-minded Englishmen and nationalist Frenchmen, is not likely to produce a healthy catharsis.[11]

The truth is, there is no occasion for immediate definitive choice with respect to such questions as how fast to get on with Western European political integration and in what form; how, if it should come to that, the

---

10. Another charge is that the United States has vacillated on specific proposals of its own making—for example, the ill-fated multilateral nuclear force.

11. Debate is sometimes urged in the hope that it will lead to agreement in the alliance to put a proposal to the Russians involving early self-determination for East Germans and agreement now on unification in a decade or two or three. The purpose would be to demonstrate that the blame for stalemate lies with Moscow. The notion that an American initiative in support of so transparent a ploy could unify the alliance strikes me as implausible on its face. We couldn't possibly get an agreed position out of Bonn, London, and Rome, never mind Paris. Serious governments are not willing to expose themselves to the charge that they are playing games.

West Germans might weigh tying themselves irreversibly into a political and self-defending Western Europe, as against keeping open some options for unity which would be closed if unity meant a complete East German switch from East to West; or even how fast it is right for Germans to redefine their purposes in the East. There is, furthermore, no way to act on the conclusions if the choices are made. No crossroad is in sight. And when and if one appears, neither our relatively secondary stake in many of these questions nor our limited margin of influence would justify a paramount role for the United States.

It is not that we have no interest in how these issues may eventually be resolved. We have a stake, a large stake. And on those questions which touch us directly—for instance, the military arrangements surrounding any change in the status of the two Germanys—we also have ample power to protect that stake. But, in general, our interest is at once congruent with that of the large majority of the Western Europeans, and not of the same magnitude. Cheer leading and arm twisting—and proposing non-solutions to problems which are insoluble in the near term and, in any event, more Western Europe's business than ours—will not advance American interests.[12]

What then is the appropriate American role in Atlantic affairs for the near term? Should we retire from center stage? The truth is we cannot. But we should resign ourselves to a role short on heroics. To be sure, we must continue to associate ourselves with the aspirations of our friends in Western Europe on the large issues, if only to quiet as best we can the natural fears about a unilateral American bargain with Moscow which would damage the chances for German unity or European autonomy. But our performance should be measured by progress on the many narrow issues where, in accord with the process vision, movement is possible, and by success in striking compromise solutions which will strengthen the fabric of Atlantic politics.[13]

---

12. In any event, conceptual thought about foreign policy, of the analytic variety, must distinguish among preferred outcomes, less-than-preferred but still tolerable outcomes, and feasible outcomes in the light of the limits of one's power or influence. Going for broke is not generally the best way to minimize regret.

13. On the first point, Americans should remember that the anxieties we may suffer about independent French initiatives toward the East are minor compared with European worries about exclusive Washington-Moscow dealings. This is especially true since the United States must retain a relatively free hand to carry on separate business with the Russians on strategic arms control and third world questions—questions on which Europe is not yet in a position to play a leading role. As a corollary we must

Much of this is a matter of style. In an environment of stalemate and frustration on the big questions, we must expect considerable *internal* sensitivity to even secondary external issues. It follows that, apart from associating ourselves with Western Europe's larger purposes, we should maintain a light-footed target-of-opportunity posture on the many fronts of Atlantic relations. The object is to avoid overloading the internal politics of any member of the alliance to the point where serious politicians are tempted or forced by domestic political concerns to question the basic articles of the transatlantic connection.

This is not a prescription for standing still. It is a prescription for maintaining a healthy tension between tranquility and advance. On many problems, it is true, there will be no movement at all without strong American leadership. Internal political strain for our friends will often be a necessary cost. But we should carefully calculate how hard we push which government on which issue and avoid becoming prisoners of our own blueprints. The accent should be on the political procedures by which issues are faced and compromises reached. Atlantic politics should be seen not as a series of discrete encounters, but as a permanent multiparty engagement in which progress may be indirect, but the ball is kept in play and the game goes on.

Issues and Choices

DEFENSE

Atlantic defense will present the administration with frequent and important choices. The number of American troops in Germany is only the most visible issue. Decisions will also be needed on nuclear arrangements within the alliance (tactical nuclear weapons in Europe, nuclear relations with Britain, France, Germany, and other countries, the role of the Nuclear Planning Group, and so forth); and on the future role and shape of NATO. All such decisions will contain dangerous traps, particularly if the question is viewed in terms of narrow military criteria alone. To avoid them we will need to keep sharply in mind what the problem of Atlantic defense in the late 1960s is all about.

1. The threat of a premeditated Soviet invasion of Western Europe is

---

make every effort to inform our friends, and to expose ourselves to their influence, always recognizing that since both they and we know that we cannot give them a veto on those special issues, no amount of consultation will still their fears.

no longer real to most Europeans, and—unless there is persuasive new evidence that Moscow is about to go mad—it cannot be made to seem real. An American attempt to boost NATO by playing on old fears, citing the Soviet performance in Czechoslovakia, will only make us look foolish.

2. Nevertheless, defense is still necessary. Even a prudent, risk-avoiding Soviet policy toward Western Europe must have some risk to avoid. And it must be risk sufficient to outweigh any conceivable gain, as well as the pain of a Western rollback of any East German move to alter the status quo. Both the Russians and our friends will measure that risk in important part by the West's military capacity for a credible response.

3. The danger lies not in a Soviet invasion in cold blood but in a sequence of escalation triggered by events in and around Berlin, where there is a direct U.S.-Soviet confrontation and where each country is likely to risk nuclear war to prevent a shift in the status quo in favor of the other. Our defense decisions must reflect both the generally low probability of serious military trouble, and the generally disastrous consequences if serious trouble were to occur. We should also take into account the indirect effects on the arms race. Throughout, we should remember that in the real world there exist no options altogether free of risk.[14]

4. An American role is still necessary. The fact that Western Europe is rich and populous enough to take care of itself would have more force if there existed a politically coherent United States of Europe. But it would miss the point even then. The most hardheaded definition of American interests, as reflected and reinforced by our commitment to the safety of West Berlin and West Germany, establishes that Americans and Western Europeans share, in Thomas Schelling's formulation, a common frontier.

---

14. Much of the conversation in these matters is confounded by ambiguity in defining "risk." Doves have in mind the low probability of trouble; sensible hawks, the disastrous consequences. Both are relevant to any judgment about how much to spend on defense. Since most people who emphasize low probability have in mind an invasion and/or an open-ended arms race, while those who worry about consequences are thinking, if they are sensible, about complicated situations triggered by risings in East Germany and troubles around Berlin, it is no wonder that conversations fail to converge. Yet it is important that they do converge. There are enough real uncertainties and perplexities: for instance, what to do when extra "insurance" moves the probability and the disutility of trouble in opposite directions (many of the arguments about defense versus deterrence raise just that issue); how to account for the intrinsic uncertainty even about the *direction* in which a change in doctrine or force levels will move the probability and the disutility of trouble in a world of response and counterresponse, where most of the future is at best only dimly foreseeable and it is the better part of wisdom to count on being surprised.

With respect to the security of Western Europe, we and the Western Europeans are in the same boat. Arguments about burden sharing, or who should man which oars, are necessarily secondary. Since we cannot jump overboard without certain capsize, our safety demands that the oars be adequately manned. The more so, since the American nuclear force is at present the only strategic force on our side capable of a retaliatory strike sufficient in certainty and scale to assure Americans and Western Europeans that, as long as American intentions are credible, the Soviet Union will be deterred from an offensive venture in Western Europe.

5. A substantial American conventional force in Germany is still necessary. Without it, the NATO order of battle is likely to become inadequate for the kind of graduated response required if strategic deterrence is to remain both credible and tolerably safe. But even if it were not so—it is a matter of political judgment what the Western Europeans would do if the United States pulled out—a large American contingent is still needed (a) so that Russians and Western Europeans will know that any trouble on the frontier or in Berlin would inextricably engage the United States; (b) to assure in advance that such American entanglement would be on a scale large enough to make the U.S. strategic force a vividly credible counter in everyone's calculations despite the vulnerability of American cities; (c) to give the United States sufficient direct power in the management of any crisis; (d) to provide, together with the other allies, close enough company for German forces so that the Germans will not be burdened with the possibility of having to manage alone a crisis in the middle of their country, and to render harmless any charges from the East, and allay atavistic fears in the West, that the Federal Republic is in a position to play a solo military role.

6. The central proposition is this: at least as long as there is no stable settlement—and, it may be, as a necessary aspect of any such settlement—the military situation in the center of Europe must remain a matter of international politics and multinational management. And the American nuclear force must remain manifestly relevant.

7. As is evident, the North Atlantic Treaty is still necessary. It follows also, despite the French, that it must continue to be embodied in a living institution. A conventional pact of mutual defense would not provide an adequate political frame for the continued presence of American, British, and other allied forces in Germany; it would smack too much of an occu-

pation, or of a Washington-Bonn axis.[15] It would not meet the need for the institutionalized company, vital to the political health of Europe, which the rest of us must provide for the dozen German divisions. It would fail to provide the smaller allied countries with a locus and a procedure for consultation and a vehicle for their small but important military contributions. Last, it would foreclose a great many opportunities for coordination in planning and management.

Yet none of the above propositions answers the tough operational question: How much defense, tailored to what kind of strategic doctrine, requiring how many American troops? Nor do they suggest answers to questions about the future shape of NATO and, in particular, about the European role in nuclear matters. Carl Kaysen's chapter addresses some of these questions in detail. Only two general points need to be made here.

First, there is nothing sacrosanct about the current level of American forces in Europe, but decisions on changes should take into account political as well as military implications. Obviously, much depends on the Warsaw Pact order of battle. If, after things settle down in Czechoslovakia, it reverts to the pattern of 1965–67, then, on the basis of personal involvement with the problem at that time, I think our security position *narrowly defined* could stand an appreciable reduction even if, as is likely, it would be followed by some reductions by others. But a judgment in terms of deterrence and conventional war-fighting capacity alone cannot settle the matter. Changes in American deployments—and American proposals pertaining to strategy—cast long shadows on European perceptions of American intentions and dependability. Ideally, we should be able to adjust the NATO order of battle, and the American contribution to it, on the basis of a shared assessment of the effects on deterrence, defense, arms control, and burden sharing. But that is easier said than done. In any event, whatever the rights and wrongs of the present distribution of the burden, the dollar cost to the United States of reducing forces later rather than sooner—of temporarily forgoing money savings that may be militarily justified—is exceedingly small when measured against the American defense budget (not to speak of GNP), and negligible when measured against the importance to the United States of confidence in the Amer-

---

15. Happily, it works with the French alone, but the kind of fuzzy arrangement Paris has with Bonn simply could not support the full weight of close to 300,000 British and American troops for any length of time.

ican commitment to the defense of Europe. In the absence of such confidence, the chances for a benign and cooperative Atlantic politics are slim.

This is not to say that we must not cut ever, or—if Eastern Europe is really quiet and there is no increase in the Warsaw Pact order of battle (net of the appropriate discount it is now safe to apply to Czech divisions)—even that we must not cut soon. But before doing so, we should apply at least three tests which go beyond the military calculus: How can we maximize the chances for a mutual reduction on both sides of the line? How can we assure the Europeans that we are moving to a safe plateau which will then be held, subject to agreed changes in the military situation? Any appreciable doubt about the credibility of the U.S. deterrent, which is a sensitive function of the U.S. conventional presence, is bound to stimulate a deadly serious argument among Germans about their commitment to remain dependent for nuclear defense on NATO, and hence on the United States. Last, is the timing right, given all the issues between ourselves and the Federal Republic, or do we risk so overloading German politics that a question of military management turns into a domestic quarrel about the American connection? Whatever we do, much will depend on style and procedure.[16]

Secondly, there is nothing sacrosanct about the present organizational structure of NATO. On the contrary, the administration will have to deal with a host of suggestions for reform, as well as the larger questions of role and purposes: Should NATO enlarge its political role? Should Atlantic external relations be coordinated and managed through the NATO machinery? If, as I believe, the answer must be in the negative, even with respect to European affairs central to NATO's agreed purposes, what reforms will keep it vigorous for its vital defense tasks? I would judge poten-

---

16. I think, for example, that we made a mistake in the spring of 1966 in linking the question of troop levels to a rigid, restrictive balance-of-payments offset arrangement. It was a mistake not only because there were available flexible schemes more palatable to the Germans and sufficient for the protection of our balance of payments. It was a mistake mainly because 1966 was the year of the NATO crisis, and of predictable internal strain in German politics; the year in which we needed German support on international money and the Kennedy Round; and the year in which we were going to administer a severe jolt to German politics in any case by going ahead (rightly, in my judgment) with the nonproliferation treaty. The fact that we managed to extricate ourselves from a deep hole by a precarious but on the whole successful diplomatic exercise (the so-called Trilateral Negotiations during 1966–67) is no defense for the initial mistake. Nor is there much defense, although there is explanation, in the fact that Germans, among other continentals, have taken an active part in lecturing the United States about living in balance-of-payments sin.

tial answers in the light of five rules of thumb: (1) No reform will work which fails to take into account that, while it is still necessary and important, by the test of political appeal NATO is middle-aged. (2) No reform is likely to entice General de Gaulle to rejoin the fold. (3) Changes in defense arrangements should be judged in precise, operational terms, not by slogans like "integration" and "independence." (4) No reform will work unless it reflects genuine European wants and needs, as revealed by their national politics without prodding from Washington. (5) Any change likely to command a consensus in Western Europe is not likely to damage the United States. On the contrary, we should be sympathetic and responsive to European ideas for a greater European role in NATO, whether it be through a European caucus in the Council, or evolution toward a full-fledged European Defense Community. We must not let secondary American interests, such as defense procurement from the United States, stand in the way. Responsible European behavior in Atlantic affairs is likely to increase with Europe's sense of mastery of her fate.

Two specific questions touching on Europe's role are likely to come up. First, should the next NATO commander be a European, with an American deputy for nuclear forces? This would give Europe a greater voice; the price would be the loss of the implicit but direct link between the principal military agent of the alliance and the American President who disposes of the paramount nuclear force. My prejudice would be to respond to any consensus in Europe. Second, what should be the U.S. stance toward the British and French nuclear forces? There is no easy answer. My own view is that we should continue to provide Britain with the technical help she needs to maintain the existing force of Polaris As, but to support London's present decision against trying for the more sophisticated Poseidon with its MIRVs. As to France, it would be a mistake (as well as politically infeasible, given the present French position on NATO) to offer General de Gaulle comparable technical help at this stage; at best, it would look like a bribe ten years too late. On the other hand, if Britain and France should ever decide to get together and then to come to us for technical help, we would face some difficult choices. In terms of internal command and control, a small but hard, tightly managed joint force, benefiting from American technical help, is preferable to separate national forces, although there would remain a question about coordination with the U.S. nuclear force. But the problem would be complicated by American politics and the McMahon Act; and it would pointedly raise the question of discrimination against Germany.

The right response, in my judgment, is a commitment to London and Paris, *if they ask it*, to provide assistance for any technically sound joint force which engages the Germans, Italians, and perhaps others, on terms consistent with the nonproliferation treaty; which has built into it the right kind of command and control; and which is seen as a good thing by a responsible German government, without any pushing and pulling by the United States, and despite the cross-cutting effects on its eastern policy and the general nervousness on both sides about any German role in nuclear defense. We should not try to dream up new solutions to the problem of nuclear management in the alliance; there is no good solution. The right policy for the United States is neither to propose that the Europeans get together, nor to resist if they, including the Germans, decide to do so. In the meanwhile, we should bend every effort to push forward with the Moscow negotiations on bilateral strategic arms limitations. The more progress we make, consistent with safety, the less painful and urgent will become the nuclear problem in Europe.

ECONOMICS

Much more than ever before, the economics of each touches on the prosperity of all. And because jobs and pocketbooks are directly at risk, it is both important and difficult for governments to put first things first.

The paramount task is to press on with the postwar effort to develop and strengthen practices and procedures, habits and institutions, which are both efficient in serving compatible economic goals and effective in resolving conflict. The important empirical truth which should inform each nation's conduct is that coordinated policies will generally serve everyone's goals better than any rule of devil-take-the-hindmost. Every unilateral action with consequences abroad (a change in interest rates or in customs procedures) and every international bargain (a new transatlantic air route or a tariff) must be judged, especially by the most powerful nation, not merely in terms of its specific outcome, but also in terms of the likely effect on the strength and efficiency of rules and institutions. The General Agreement on Tariffs and Trade (GATT) is far more important to us than any particular set of tariffs as such, or than any marginal change in the GATT rules themselves. The creation of a new reserve asset, managed through the International Monetary Fund, is far more important than whether it is called a new "unit" or a "drawing right." Some brinksmanship is unavoidable in negotiating bread-and-butter issues. But we should stay within safe limits except where essential rules and structures are at stake. To argue that the United States, because it is so powerful, can tolerate the jungle better than most, is to miss the point. Jungle economics breeds jungle politics and that we cannot tolerate.

What is the near-term economic agenda?

First, the central problem of international money and the balance of payments, the subject of Richard Cooper's chapter. It is central not because it should matter as such. It shouldn't; it concerns mere machinery. It is central because the Bretton Woods system has developed serious flaws which—save for the liquidity provided other nations by the American payments deficit—would already have exerted severe deflationary pressures throughout the world, with protectionist warfare the likely international result.

Great progress has been made since 1965 in reforming the international money rules. The United States has played a distinguished role, particularly in getting agreement on the Special Drawing Rights (SDRs) and in helping to introduce the two-tier system for gold. But more needs to be done. The only long-term answer is more intensive and binding coordination in the management of international finance, based on rules and practices less biased against deficit countries and better suited to our shared stake in prosperity and trade. Central bankers, especially, need reminding that "money is a good servant but a bad master."

If we wish to promote benign politics, as well as sensible economics, we must also sustain the momentum toward worldwide free trade. Protectionist pressures are as powerful as ever, and as pernicious in their results. The danger over the medium term lies in the hardening of two large trading blocs, one centered on the United States and the other on the European Economic Community, each relatively free within itself but in a state of economic warfare with the other. Whatever the economic costs, the politics would be poisonous. Thus, as the EEC expands, with its common external tariff and internal free trade, we shall have to keep up the pace of mutual tariff cuts, or slip backwards toward the jungle we all should want to avoid. The need is to cut all tariffs (on an accelerated, nonreciprocal schedule toward the poor countries) and—increasingly important as tariffs go down—the thick underbrush of non-tariff barriers as well. The implication is another ambitious round of trade negotiations starting in 1970 at the latest.

As the new administration moves toward that encounter, it should keep in mind three special considerations:

First, the political dangers of an allegedly benign version of the two-bloc world. If the Europeans won't go along with the international financial reforms required for adequate internal growth and increasingly free trade on a worldwide basis, we should, so the argument goes, settle for a dollar bloc open to all, letting those who remain outside organize a gold bloc and float their currencies against the dollar. The economic consequences would not be too bad. But for Atlantic politics and the American political interest a two-bloc world would be terrible, except as a short-lived, transitional arrangement designed to bring the gold-minded to their senses.[17]

Second, the demands of the poor nations for help in their exports of manufactures. We have an enormous stake in the economic growth of the development-capable poor countries, and their export earnings will play a critical role. Yet we must avoid bloc economics and politics. For each industrial country to give trade preferences only to its own less developed clients would be a great mistake. The recently developed American policy of support for temporary tariff preferences on the manufactures and semi-manufactures of all less developed countries by all industrial countries is, I think, the right answer. But we should beware of the notion that such a system, designed to stimulate poor country exports, provides a substitute for any significant quantity of aid. "Trade not aid" is an appropriate objective for the long term: Once a poor country has reached per capita income levels of several hundred dollars per year, it can manage adequate growth without extraordinary outside help. But as a strategy to speed the growth of countries whose incomes run at $80 to $200 per head, "trade not aid" is a mirage.

Third, agriculture. This will be the most difficult problem in Atlantic trade relations and the United States will have to exercise great patience. Europe is at a stage in its agricultural revolution where supply is bound to outrun demand at prices tolerable in terms of domestic politics, even though people are leaving agricultural employment in droves. The United States will be constantly tempted to delay trade liberalization in industry in the forlorn hope of getting Europeans to build still more warehouses and pay still more tax money in order to add some of our agricultural surpluses to their own. We should certainly push them to grant food to the underdeveloped countries, but that won't ease the pressure much, particularly

---

17. For a view of this entire range of issues, see F. M. Bator, "The Political Economics of International Money," *Foreign Affairs*, Vol. 47 (October 1968), pp. 51–67.

as the poor get better at growing their own food. Happily, prospects will change in time. The United States does have a long-term comparative advantage in highly capitalized, land-intensive, high-protein agriculture. And that is the wave of the future, at least until the chemical industry takes over.

The final item on the economic agenda is the so-called technological gap and the political problem of American investment in Europe. Here the United States must tread lightly. On the one hand—in terms of risk to livelihoods—this is strictly second-order business. Measured by income, jobs, and productivity, the economic performance of Western Europe during the past two decades has been superb. Whatever technological inferiority she may suffer relative to the United States does not impinge on the conditions which distinguish the political prospects of the late 1960s and early 1970s from those of, say, the 1930s.

Nevertheless, the U.S. advantage in the new, science-based industries is a significant political issue. So is American ownership and control of industry in Europe. Americans, with economists in the lead, tend often to forget that Europeans no less than Americans want circuses as well as bread, especially circuses widely regarded as symbols of prestige and power.

It is a different matter to know what to do. On the technological gap—a question of management and social mobility, of general education and economic scale much more than of science as such—there is not much the United States can do. In general, we should be sympathetic and reasonable in responding to sensible nonprotectionist European attempts better to organize to exploit economies of scale.

On American investment in Europe, there is more need for action, if only because direct investment in Europe has been our Achilles' heel in the international politics of balance of payments. There is some truth to the European charge that, in a fit of absentmindedness, the United States has been using short-term money borrowed in Europe to buy up Europe. Again there is no easy answer. To emphasize the case for multinational corporations, or for giving market forces free rein, only begs the problem of national control and influence. The near-term solution again lies in procedure: We and our European friends should together sort out our partly conflicting and partly compatible interests—their desire for long-term money, advanced American technology, and management; our need for balance-of-payments protection and for fair treatment of past investments made in good faith; their legitimate concern about the ownership and control of their advanced industries.

POLITICS

There is more to politics than defense and economics. And as in economics, the politics of one touches the politics of all. The American objective is a benign and constructive politics, where no nation is forced by the circumstances of its foreign relations to divide on basic questions of national existence and, in particular, on the question of the American connection. This holds for all the countries of the Atlantic; but the new administration will have to pay special attention to a number of well-defined problems in our relations with Britain, France, and Germany.

Britain faces two critical questions: Can she at long last get her economy right? Should she remain committed to joining the EEC or seek some other connection? The United States has a major stake in the answers. A frustrated and footloose Britain will do no one any good. In contrast, a prosperous and vigorous Britain, playing an active role in Europe and a limited but satisfying role in the outside world, would be a great source of strength to the United States—and not because she would play Trojan horse to America's Greece.

On the economic side there are strong grounds for optimism. Theories of what ails the British economy abound. Most of them make the mistake Karl Marx made in his labor theory of value: They assign exclusive influence to a single cause, be it the old school tie, the unions, not enough taste for risk or too much for a civilized life, or merely poor fiscal management. The truth is that a great many factors are at work. The right question is whether skillful economic engineering—effective use of the fiscal and regulatory instruments available to a modern government in a mixed enterprise economy—is sufficient to shift the British economy from the roller coaster of stop-and-go to a track of reasonably steady 3.5 to 5 percent growth, with the balance of payments in good order.

My own view is that, despite the drag exerted by some of the underlying social characteristics, reasonably skillful economic policy will do the job. The requirements are plain: Demand must be kept in balance with capacity, with enough slack to give wages policy a chance to keep British prices from running ahead of prices in Europe and America, but not so much slack as to produce intolerable numbers of unemployed or to kill off incentives to invest. The investment component of demand must be both allowed and stimulated to rise from 10–15 percent of GNP to 20–25 percent, with priority for exports and import substitutes and for activities with a potential for fast growth in productivity. Redistribution of income through the budget and other means must meet the tests both of incentive and of tolerable fairness as judged by the electorate. And, above all, the exchange rate must be right.

Given the devaluation of last November, none of this is impossible, or even unlikely. With sterling at the old rate of $2.80, no amount of deflation could be expected to provide a cure, not without years of waiting for foreign prices to catch up with British prices. With the pound at $2.40—and sufficient restraint on domestic demand to release the resources needed to meet the new, price-induced demand for British goods abroad and for import substitutes at home—the prospects are bright. It will take a while until speculators get used to the idea that sterling is not a dirty word. In the meanwhile, the major central banks may have some work to do in supporting the pound, as well as in dealing with overseas sterling balances as a part of longer-term monetary reform, and in stretching out some short-term British debt. But barring any major continental devaluations—which would open the entire structure of exchange rates for negotiation, though not the dollar price of gold—the $2.40 rate is likely to work fine in helping to fix Britain's basic payments position. Britain may well be on the threshold of her own economic "miracle." Miracle it would not be, only skillful economic management and a slightly undervalued currency.[18]

What about Britain and Europe? Here the story is more complicated. For the time being, the de Gaulle veto is a fact of life, and it is not clear whether time will make it easier or harder for Britain to become a full-fledged member of the EEC. In any event, there is bound to be talk in the interim about an alternative, perhaps a North Atlantic Free Trade Area (NAFTA), with the old Commonwealth and the United States as the founding members.

18. I do not mean to suggest that it is all clear sailing. It is not certain that, with labor and product markets organized as at present, a semi-voluntary wage-price policy can contain the rise in unit labor costs without intolerable levels of unemployment. If there is reason for being optimistic about the British case, it is in good part because the rest of us are not likely to do well either; and here it is relative performance that counts. For a full-fledged miracle, progress will also be necessary in market organization, in the training and mobility of skilled labor and of management, and the like. But there is no need for "fundamental" changes in British society or in the British character simply in order to permit a comfortably adequate economic performance. It is hard to exaggerate the enormous burden imposed by an overvalued currency. Both the German and the French "miracles" were preceded by their getting their exchange rates right. For a first-rate analysis of the British economic situation, see Richard E. Caves and associates, *Britain's Economic Prospects* (Brookings Institution, 1968).

The search for an alternative, already under way, reflects a widespread sense that Britain must make some new connection in order to cure her economic ills, and that an overseas, Anglo-Saxon arrangement might well be more attractive than joining up with the continent.

Neither proposition seems to me defensible. The notion that a new connection is essential to make the economics work is sheer nonsense. It is not necessary and it would not be sufficient. Indeed, it is an open question whether it would lengthen or shorten the odds.[19]

What about the case for NAFTA on its own terms? If it could be divorced from the larger question of Britain's political future—if it were merely an open-ended commercial venture, designed to enlarge the area of free trade and to put pressure on the more protectionist remainder to join the rest of us in a move toward worldwide free trade—it would represent a dangerous but thinkable strategy: dangerous because we would risk getting stuck en route in a two-bloc world. But short of a major change in the political environment, or clear prior evidence that the European option is closed, the economics cannot be divorced from the larger questions of politics. A British initiative in favor of NAFTA would reflect a sharp turning away from Europe. The possible economic gain would fail to balance the certain political cost. For, over the long term, Britain does need to make a political connection. And as a new political entity, NAFTA would be badly askew. Few Englishmen want their country to become the largest American state. And we, for our part, need no new states, and cannot afford to lose Britain as an independent source of vitality and influence in Europe. The probability that a close American political connection would soon produce either frustration or lethargy, or both, in London, should be enough to rule it out. But there is more to it: Europe without Britain playing an active role is much less likely to produce the kind of external and internal politics which is a vital American interest.

Diagnosis is easy; prescription is harder. Playing a waiting game will take considerable restraint on the part of London. No outsider can really judge, but my guess would be that it is politically workable if it encompasses an active engagement in all kinds of dealings with the other Europeans, and even more important, if the internal economics is right. (There is no contradiction; investors are perfectly capable of living with uncertainty.)

19. The only reservation I would make concerns the future course of tariffs. If the world should go protectionist, then being a member of some relatively large free trade club would become important.

What about the American role? On the economics, in the short run we must join in helping to hold the $2.40 rate. And we must avoid—for Britain's sake, as well as our own and that of the rest of the world—letting the American economy go slack. That in turn implies pressing on fast with international monetary reform.

On the political side we should politely discourage the people in London who will be drawing up schemes for an alternative to Europe, and continue quietly to associate ourselves with Britain's view of herself as a European power, albeit one which looks at the world in the round. This will require restraint in Washington. We must expect that London will generate a fair amount of anti-American rhetoric, and that she will line up with the other Europeans on a variety of bread-and-butter issues. Here too it will be important for us to put first things first.[20]

France presents two major traps for American policy. The first, shallow and not very dangerous, is to underestimate General de Gaulle's resolve and delude ourselves that if we are nice to him he will be nice to us. The other, much more hazardous, is to overestimate how much damage he can do and react with hostility toward France and all her works.

The first error may be largely behind us. Most Americans have learned that de Gaulle's commitment to his own special vision of France's needs and proper due is as fixed as any of Euclid's theorems. But the second is both more important and harder to avoid. To do so we must keep several points in mind.

1. France's capacity for damage to fundamental Atlantic security is exceedingly limited. Whatever the General may do—even if he should denounce the North Atlantic Treaty in 1969—NATO can and will survive for as long as most Europeans feel the need for American help in maintaining their defense—unless, that is, we lose our heads and withdraw. (It is a reasonable conjecture that if the other Western Europeans were suddenly to take a Gaullist line on NATO and American troops, Frenchmen would be among the most dismayed.)

2. As long as Washington and London refuse to play, the French simply

---

20. That is not to say that we must not take advantage of any political openings in Britain for a change in, for instance, her decision to abandon Singapore in the early 1970s. But American requests for continued British involvement east of Suez and elsewhere outside of Europe should be carefully tailored to British economic and political possibilities, and balanced by our priority stake in British solvency and her management of her relations on the Continent. At the margin, a British soldier is more valuable to us in the Far East than an American soldier, even if we foot the bill. But in my judgment British soldiers in Germany are even more valuable.

do not have the chips to deliver on any bargain with Moscow touching on the status of Berlin or the future of Germany. It is no insult to France to say that it is not in her power to act for the West either in legitimizing the division of Germany or in trying to negotiate German unity. It is not merely that American and British troops are in Germany by law. It is simply a fact of life that, until the cold war is past history, neither the Western Europeans nor the Eastern Europeans nor the Russians would join in a settlement which would re-create a unified German state without very close ties with its neighbors, or the United States, or both. Unless such a state were politically and militarily integrated with Western Europe, the Europeans would bend every effort to keep us from opting out. A Paris-Moscow hegemony in Europe is not in the cards. (That is why we should be relaxed about the talk of a European security conference without the United States. The Europeans would almost certainly not let it take place; and if they did, nothing much would come of it.)

3. This is not to say that French policy has been harmless in its effects on Western European and Atlantic politics. One can hope that the Germans have developed sufficient antibodies to remain relatively immune to the nationalist contagion. But even so, de Gaulle has effectively put a stop to progress toward Western European political integration. Perhaps even more important, he has hindered the growth of close working relations among Paris, Bonn, London, and Rome on which, lacking a Monnet Europe, a healthy European and Atlantic polity ultimately depends.

4. Nothing will more greatly multiply the price exacted by present French policy than American overreaction to it. The more we cooperate with de Gaulle in forcing Bonn, London, Rome, and the others to make a sharp choice between Washington and Paris on broad issues of "principle," the greater the risk of a balkanized Western Europe, an isolated Germany neurotically dependent on the United States, and a Britain with no place to turn. Small comfort then that more often than not Gaullist manners and U.S. power will have caused our friends to side with us.

5. It does not follow that we should simply appease Paris and let her have her way. But we must choose our ground with the greatest of care. We should fight only on concrete, specific issues where France does not have a veto by right of law or possession, and (a) where we can win without help from (and without undue damage to) others; or (b) where the other Europeans are likely to see things our way for their own reasons; or

(c) in the rare case where the importance to us of winning is so great that it justifies the use of leverage even at the risk of turning the American connection into a serious internal issue in Britain, Germany, or elsewhere.

Applying these tests, I think we were right to force a choice on international money and gold last year, and right also in pressing for large industrial tariff cuts in the Kennedy Round. The bread-and-butter interests of the majority of Europeans made those winning issues. We were also dead right not to respond to the French defection from NATO by trying to line up support for reading France out of the treaty proper and threatening to deny her the protection that her geography confers as long as we defend Germany. And it was right not to press the Germans to set conditions unacceptable to de Gaulle on the continued stationing of French troops in Germany. Doing so would have caused a damaging fight in Bonn about whether to thwart the United States or to eject French soldiers from German soil and thereby risk serious harm to the reconciliation with France which is one of Germany's great psychic needs. Last, it has been right to restrict ourselves to soft and hopeful words about Britain's entry into the EEC. On that, the French veto is absolute. We would do no one any good, and we could do considerable harm, by trying to force the others to challenge it.[21]

6. Here again, style is almost as important as substance. We must remain polite. Where possible, we must let the Europeans take the lead in fact as well as in appearance. And we must keep in mind the capacity of the present French government to overplay its hand and isolate itself. On the positive side, we should continue to make clear that there will always be an empty chair waiting for France.

In the end, we must remind ourselves that, even if she steps on our toes, a stable, confident France is likely to be better for us than a weak, turbulent France. We should be self-confident enough to ignore the anti-American rhetoric, particularly where it serves a therapeutic purpose in reviving the French spirit after a painful century. We should be ready to acknowledge the elements of truth and validity in any French position. We should never forget the widespread support in France and in Europe for many Gaullist policies—support which will outlast the General. Last, we should show not condescension, but genuine understanding of the pain caused

---

21. In both instances involving NATO the credit for American good sense belongs personally to President Johnson.

proud and great nations by the brutal facts of scale in defense and technology. In sum, except where our vital and specific interests are at stake, we should show the grace and forbearance which behoove a great power.

Germany is the one major country in the West with an external grievance of the first magnitude, and she is on the frontier. The danger is not that history will repeat itself; neither 1933 nor 1939 will come again. The danger is rather that external frustration will combine with a rise in activity by the small but vocal right-wing minority. This may not be so serious as it looks. Very likely we will all have problems with the old right as well as with the new left in the next decade. But the German right is harder for both Germans and others to tolerate. The risk is a level of anxiety about Germany among Germans and others which would make useless one of the great nations of Western Europe in the sensible management of Atlantic politics, and would make much more difficult a sensible evolution in Eastern Europe.

Beyond the general arguments already advanced, the following seem to me the right guidelines for U.S. policy:

1. We must avoid actions which would dilute German faith in American defense capacity and intent. We cannot and should not give in to every German whim. But we should think twice before encouraging irresponsible politicians and journalists in Europe who would try to profit by preying on German fears. And we should scrupulously apply the rules set out in the preceding section concerning issues on which we force Bonn to choose between Paris and Washington. German dependence on Washington is a mixed blessing. In nuclear defense, there is no alternative. But for healthy German politics, and necessary freedom of American maneuver on questions of strategic arms which do not touch on German safety or unity, it is in our interest that Paris and London play an increasing role.

2. It is not our part to take the lead in formulating strategy and tactics toward East Germany on matters which do not involve defense. We should make clear in Bonn that we stand prepared to play a strong supportive role: to help, to counsel, and, if the Germans wish, even to take the diplomatic lead. We should ask that they keep us and the others sufficiently informed. But the prime burden of deciding how to deal with East Germany should rest on Bonn.

3. Conversely, we should keep the lead on questions of strategic arms. We should always make a point of consulting on the large questions, especially those which could be thought by Germans to affect the pros-

pects for a German settlement. But we must retain control of tactics toward Moscow, and that includes responsibility for deciding precisely when to consult, given the danger of leaks. Responsible Germans will understand this. They will be anxious; but both we and they must learn to live with that.

4. In cases where arms control and the German future intersect, the particulars must govern how we and Bonn and others play the hand. There are no general rules except a presumption than anything which significantly reduces the danger of nuclear war carries a very high value indeed. Happily, I do not believe that there are many "either/ors."[22]

Above all, we should beware of so burdening German internal politics as to turn the American connection into a first order of domestic contention. We have a great stake in balanced German conduct in internal Atlantic affairs, and in the Federal Republic's explorations toward the East. Steady and sensitive American policy on matters of concern to Germany cannot guarantee such conduct; but it will sharply improve the odds.

It is not lack of interest, or even lack of space alone, which explains the failure to discuss Italy. Ten or fifteen years ago, she would have required full treatment. But in the interim, Italy has been a model friend and partner, both to us and to her neighbors in Europe. By putting first things first, and by behaving the way a reasonable welfare democracy should behave, she has managed to pull off a remarkable economic and, indeed, political feat. Yet it is important that the United States accord Rome the attention she deserves.

Much the same could be said about a number of the other nations of Western Europe. The old rule about the squeaky wheel getting the grease is not an inappropriate guide for a paper of limited length. But it is not a good guide for American policy. The new administration should take care

22. Neither of the two instances often cited to the contrary bears scrutiny. (1) The notion that an open nuclear option for Germany, of the sort ruled out by the Non-Proliferation Treaty, would constitute material for negotiating German unity or change in East Europe is silly. Few things would so worsen the prospects for East Europe, or for a German solution, than even a hint that Bonn was considering that particular ploy. (2) The notion that Europeans would be affected differently from Americans by strategic weapons limitations which would reduce American nuclear "superiority," flies directly in the face of the elementary logic of deterrence. No feasible amount of American strategic superiority would make American cities safe from a Soviet second strike. A prime purpose of the large American conventional force in the center of Europe is to make the American strategic force credible in relation to Europe despite that fact.

that it does not come to regard European policy as exclusively a matter of London, Paris, and Bonn.[23]

Grounds for Optimism

Where does all this leave us? What are the prospects in the Atlantic world? Clearly, there is no shortage of problems and troubles. Yet I think, in broad terms, there are powerful reasons for optimism.

The central truth is that the United States and Western Europe will for the foreseeable future enjoy a harmony of interests on the issues of peace and war. All of us share a commitment to avoid nuclear war which far surpasses the simple instinct for self-preservation. Violence against any of us would be enormously damaging to the high culture which we share and prize. For this reason, as well as our need for safety, we have a common interest in helping each other, and the Soviets and East Europeans, grow out of the cold war. And we share a deep long-term interest in ground rules for an international community which will provide for safe progress towards international objectives, while leaving most of our energies for urgent tasks at home.

One cannot of course count on objective interest to govern the behavior of governments; the modern world has known only too well the possibility of madness. But there exist powerful safeguards in Western Europe today which did not exist twenty or thirty years ago. Each nation has evolved into a welfare democracy of one sort or another. All exhibit a political and economic system which is more or less open and which is responsive to popular will, if not always directed by it. These are not surroundings friendly to madmen, to grand schemes of domination, or even to the traditional man on horseback. Evidently, not all hates and fears are gone. But we have so organized our societies that it is much less likely now than ever before that a narrow and hostile view of interest or ambition can capture the machinery of a major state and undo the progress of the past two decades.

---

23. I have not touched at all on one important organization and two countries of special significance. The European Economic Commission has a vital part to play in European and Atlantic affairs. We should not forget, for instance, that if it had not been for the Commission the Kennedy Round probably would not have succeeded. American relations with Canada require a separate chapter; they demand careful attention by Washington. And we would be foresighted to take a hard look at Spain.

Underlying that judgment are some large qualitative changes in the economic facts of life in Western Europe and the United States. Here, too, it is wise to hedge one's bets. None of us has solved the problems of affluence and some, particularly the most affluent of all, have failed even to solve the problems of extreme poverty; the New Left, and the young, have a powerful point. But it is a fair conjecture that the life of most Western Europeans is by now simply too good for serious trouble to arise. Although per capita incomes are still well below our own, they are, I think, well above the threshold at which concern for their preservation and growth begins to exert very strong pressure against political actions which could threaten them. The distribution of income in most of Western Europe, moreover, is not so skewed that the calculation of fundamental interest turns around as one moves up and down the economic scale. (This is in some contrast with the situation in the United States.)

Finally, there now exists the technical capacity and the institutional machinery in most of the countries of the Atlantic to avert the catastrophic economic fluctuations that so often nourished extremist politics in the past. This is important not only because it removes one large source of ferment, but also because it has produced over the past twenty years habits of international cooperation and experience which themselves act as stabilizers.

In short, whatever impact economics has on political behavior will, despite the adversary components, weigh heavily against nightmare politics. Even if one is not an economic determinist one must recognize that this is important. When combined with the political and cultural facts of current Atlantic life, it reduces the probability of really serious trouble generated within the Atlantic world to a point as low as the inheritance of man permits.

It does not follow that we and the Western Europeans face a comfortable and safe future. There are two great problems which transcend the difficulties of internal Atlantic relations: growing out of the cold war and effectively controlling nuclear arms, and ensuring the economic and political advance of the poor countries. We must face them together. The real nightmare for all of us, not over the next few years but over the next twenty-five, consists in a world split between a rich minority and an enormous majority of semi-industrialized poor—colored, angry, and equipped with modern strategic arms.

The internal dangers are simply not of the same order. They consist in irritation and mistrust, in shortsighted moralizing, in recrimination and estrangement. In avoiding this, much will depend on American behavior and, indeed, on the image cast by our domestic politics. A stable, dependable, reasonable line of American policy can go very far to limit turbulence in Atlantic affairs and to assure safe passage of the present period of transition.

MARSHALL D. SHULMAN

RELATIONS WITH THE SOVIET UNION

It is not easy to know what is essential and what is not in our complex relations with the Soviet Union, or how to act wisely when our knowledge on many points is uncertain, or how to respond with a sense of proportion and a due regard for our long-term interests. To begin with, it is difficult to know how to approach the problem most usefully in order to see it steadily and whole.

The Dual Nature of the Relationship

Perhaps one productive starting point for some fresh thinking is to clarify the *dual* nature of the relationship between the United States and the Soviet Union. That this is not well enough understood is evident from the extreme shifts of mood to which we have been subject in recent months and, indeed, from the many cycles of optimism and angry pessimism which have possessed us in recent years as one side of the relationship or the other has been in the forefront of our attention.

The dual character of the relationship arises from the fact that both conflicting and interdependent interests are involved. Some of our difficulties stem from not knowing how to define each set of interests or in not being able to keep both of them in mind at the same time. Is the conflict essentially between two ideologies, two political systems, two military machines, two giant nation-states? Is it absolute, in the sense that the conflict can end only in the elimination of one or the other as a state or as a system? As for the interdependence, does it imply a collaboration between the two giant states to maintain their dominant positions against all others, an acceptance of respective spheres of influence, a movement toward convergence? I will venture a short answer to these questions now at the outset in order to make my own approach to the problem explicit.

Fundamentally, the conflict is best understood as a competition between the two preeminent great powers for military power and for political influence. This national rivalry is enormously complicated by differences in ideology and in the historical experiences of the two countries, but these two factors are not primary causes of the conflict. The principal importance of the communist ideology today is that it deeply affects the Soviet perception of the world and provides the dynamism for a party bureaucracy. This function of ideology is a transitional factor which has been changing slowly over time.

The interdependent side of the relationship mainly arises from a common interest in avoiding nuclear war between the two states. Although this does not, at the present stage, imply common political interests or make military power irrelevant, it does impose some constraints on the conflict side of the relationship, which can therefore best be described as a *limited adversary relationship*. Both adjectives are significant, and both must be part of any true perception of our security interests.

As we seek to understand the balance between the competitive and the collaborative aspects of the relationship at any one time, it is not sufficient to deal with the two states simply as unified entities. The beginning of wisdom in the study of international affairs lies in understanding foreign policies as resultants of many and varied pressures and interests operating within each country. We know little enough about how this works within our own society and less in the case of the Soviet Union, but at least we have become aware of the great importance of bureaucratic, party, and professional interest groups in the Soviet decision-making process. Those involved in heavy industry, military affairs, agriculture, technology, and higher education, for example, are all strongly represented in the upper levels of political power and have been articulate and forceful in representing their respective interests. The balance between these interest groups may change greatly from one issue to another, and indeed, the predisposition of any individual political leader may not be a constant factor as he weighs conflicting considerations and seeks to accommodate contradictory pressures; and so we should not assume a simple and fixed identification of factions within the Soviet leadership. It is useful, however, to keep in mind the interplay of forces within the Soviet system and to be conscious, for example, of the bureaucratic self-interest of some groups in imposing dogmatic orthodoxy and in pressing for higher levels of military rivalry, often for domestic reasons but with foreign policy consequences.

This awareness prepares the way for another productive way of looking at the relationship between the two countries. The interplay of forces and interests on each side is affected by that on the other, with the result that a reciprocal process of stimulation is sometimes set in motion. For example, the claim of professional military groups for a share of the national budget is clearly affected by the actions of similar groups on the other side, and the guardians of dogma on one side provide fuel for the watch fires of the dogmatists on the other. The point here is that an awareness of the interplay of forces bearing upon the Soviet leadership can make us more sensitive to the way our own actions influence the Soviet decision-making process and how the spiral of interaction between the two countries works, whether upward or downward.

The Spiral of Interaction

That spiral of interaction has worked again and again over the years and helps to explain how we arrived at our present situation. A definitive history of the cold war remains to be written, although a considerable body of literature has appeared representing widely varying judgments about its origins and subsequent course. To attempt to resolve these issues here would require a separate volume, but we may at least observe how often the history of this relationship illustrates what Charles Yost has called "the law of disproportionate response to miscalculated challenges." In particular, it is useful preparation for our later discussion of policy questions to observe how the policy of containment went through major transformations as a result of the process of interaction over the last twenty years.

While some level of conflict was probably inevitable as the wartime alliance dissolved and the postwar adjustment to new power relationships began, it is evident in retrospect that the conflict was made more intractable than it needed to have been by actions on both sides. This is not to lessen the responsibility of Stalinist Russia for a brutal and callous exercise of power but to acknowledge some measure of responsibility on the part of the United States for an exacerbation of the conflict, resulting perhaps largely from the inexperience of the American people in international politics. Our wartime assumption that a common alliance with the Soviet Union against Nazi Germany meant a common acceptance of political goals, our failure to anticipate the territorial questions which were inevitably to arise in the aftermath of the war, and our rapid demobilization and withdrawal from Europe all made us vulnerable to a shock reaction when the Soviet Union asserted its claims to Eastern and parts of Central Europe.

These claims by the Soviet Union came to be understood in the United States as a reflection of a policy of unlimited revolutionary expansionism. History does not yet make clear whether this was an accurate perception or whether Soviet intentions at that point were limited to the flow of power into territories to which Russian national ambitions had long aspired. The reaction of the United States, in any case, was expressed in the policy of containment. In its early form, the notion of containment rested upon the assumptions that the repair of the vacuum of power in Europe was a necessary precondition for a negotiated settlement and that a check to the perceived communist threat to Western Europe and the eastern Mediterranean would buy time, during which the Soviet system and policies were expected to be modified substantially. On the whole, this seems to have been a reasonable response to the confrontation, once it had reached that stage, and it included constructive and generous assistance in the reconstruction of Western Europe; but in the course of the following years the guiding conception of containment evolved in several fundamental respects.

First, from an essentially territorial conception, containment tended to become an ideological crusade. Responding to the rhetoric of Soviet ideologues, perceiving Soviet expansion as revolutionary and unlimited in intent, deeply concerned about the risks of subversion, the United States blurred the issue between the actions of the Soviet state and the threat of "international communism." A period of heightened inner tensions in American society strengthened this view, and anticommunism became a central dogma of American purpose abroad.

Second, the military side of containment became more and more predominant. Political considerations were submerged in the overwhelming preoccupation with military force as the main instrumentality of policy. The high force goals for the North Atlantic Treaty Organization (NATO), the rearmament of Germany, the steep ascent of U.S. military appropriations, all reflected the assumption that the primary problem was the danger of military attack, or at least that the threat of military attack was the major obstacle to political stability in the world and especially in

Western Europe. Although these measures were taken in response to a large and worrisome Soviet military capability and uncertainty regarding Soviet intentions, in retrospect questions have been raised whether the response, because of its disproportion, weakened the political side of the Western alliance and unnecessarily stimulated further military response by the Soviet Union.

And third, the policy of containment was extended from Europe to Asia, particularly after the Korean war, and resulted in a network of military alliances against China as well as the Soviet Union. From an original effort to balance the Soviet ground forces in Europe, the doctrine was broadened geographically and blurred politically; in the name of preserving international order against what was seen as a Moscow-directed, internationally coordinated expansionist drive, the United States became involved in many former colonial areas in ways that were insensitive to local needs and unreflective of American political values.

As a consequence of these trends, the effort by the United States to contain communism, while it succeeded in removing any temptation to Soviet military expansion, acquired a momentum of its own, which has served to obscure the American purpose. By and large, the United States continued from the end of the war to maintain a comfortable margin of superiority in strategic weapons, and by virtue of its tendency toward overreaction (the "bomber gap," the "missile gap"), it became the pace-setter in the strategic arms race. To many in the world, the United States increasingly appeared to be an imperialist power, not because it sought to establish an American hegemony, but because of its overreliance on military force to contain a threat of communism.

Not that the communist threat was imaginary, but it was different in scale and nature from those reliable stereotypes of the ideology that never failed to produce legislative appropriations. (What cause has been so successful in loosening the public purse strings as anticommunism?) Perhaps it is inevitable in a democratic society that gross simplifications become necessary to galvanize a costly effort, but these simplifications tend to take on an independent life of their own.

It therefore becomes a necessary part of our task now to adjust our prevailing conceptions of the Soviet Union and the communist movement to the present reality. But before going on to grapple with this central question of how to characterize Soviet policy as it is today, we must consider a number of important factors of change in the international environment which deeply affect the terms on which the two countries meet.

Factors of Change in the International Environment

We find ourselves in a period in which many familiar notions about international politics evoke a feeling of staleness and irrelevance. The sense of some inchoate movement toward new crystallizing ideas whose outlines are still unclear is evident within societies as well as between them. The political and social consequences of changes in technology—weapons, communications, industrialization, and so on—are profoundly altering the context of Soviet-American relations.

What does national power mean today? In one sense, the power of the United States and the Soviet Union is preeminent among nations in terms of an unprecedented capacity for destruction, including the power to destroy each other. But the new weapons, by their qualitative increase in destructiveness, have introduced a discontinuity between force and politics. Because they are so clearly disproportionate to situations remote from the threat of general war, they do not exert a commanding influence over a large range of political actions. Therefore, Soviet and American power meet on two planes: a plane of bipolar strategic power and a plane of multipolar political power.

On the plane of bipolarity, the principal consequence of the new strategic weapons for the two superpowers is that their continued existence now depends upon each other's rationality. The balance of mutual deterrence takes some getting used to, but we have been learning to live with it. Experience has taught both the United States and the Soviet Union a considerable measure of sobriety, and in practice there have developed significant tacit restraints which have introduced some degree of stability in their military competition, although the quest for superiority and new technological innovations constantly threaten to undermine that stability.

But the effect of even this tenuous stability at the level of strategic weapons has been to allow lower forms of violence to flourish with less constraint and to release political forces whose manifestations we are witnessing in the ascendancy of nationalism, the fragmentation and blurring of alliances, and the decline of grand structural designs. Among the ambiguities of the various forms and levels of power (from uranium to geranium), it is increasingly difficult to apply any traditional balance of power conception as a regulating principle in international relations. The power of the United States and the Soviet Union to control these surging political forces is limited. Therefore while their relations with each other on one plane mainly concern the central question of peace and war, their political rivalry operates in a world of many forms and centers of power. In this polygonal setting, success in the competition depends increasingly upon how effectively each of them can relate its interests and ideas to the political forces at work in the world.

The drift of European politics illustrates how profoundly domestic forces have become the principal source of political dynamism in the present period and how relatively impervious to the influence of the major powers these forces are. Once the active theater of the cold war, and still the home of the most decisive territorial and political issue of that contest —Germany—Europe teases the political prophets. The resurgence of various forms of nationalism in Europe and the rejection of traditional values by a young generation in search of new values and goals make industrial Europe, notwithstanding its surface of prosperous stability, an uncertain factor in the Soviet-American rivalry. Whether Europe will emerge as a new world power, and if so, with what inclination; whether new coalitions will emerge in the major Western European countries, and if so, with what complexion; whether time will weave many strands of association between Eastern and Western Europe, interlacing a de facto settlement of the war's unfinished business—these are among the questions that shape the present form of competition between the Soviet Union and the United States in this still crucial industrial area.

In the nonindustrialized countries, too, domestic sources of change have progressively narrowed the range formerly open to external influences. In addition, the domestic preoccupations of the major powers have limited the resources which they are willing to make available for the modernization of the developing areas, and therefore the pace of economic competition in these areas has decelerated, with certain exceptions. However, innumerable potential sources of conflict remain in the former colonial areas, and the possibility of sparks igniting wherever the world interests of the two superpowers intersect in this fluid and explosive environment remains a major condition in the background of international politics.

The future course of Chinese developments will obviously have a significant effect on the ability of the United States and the Soviet Union to control their degree of involvement in conflicts in the developing areas, as well as on many other aspects of their relationship. Since this is the subject of another paper, by Edwin O. Reischauer, we will do no more than remind ourselves at this point that, among the conditions in the international political environment which will affect the course of relations between the United States and the Soviet Union, none may be more fateful nor more difficult to forecast than the future development of Chinese politics and power.

Soviet Policy in the Present Period

We come now to the question of how best to describe the main characteristics of Soviet policy in the present period and to identify the essential problems in relations between the United States and the Soviet Union.

In general terms, the Soviet leadership since Khrushchev has been cautious, pragmatic, and heavily preoccupied with domestic and bloc problems. It has sought neither a major confrontation nor an all-out détente with the United States; it endeavors to take advantage of opportunities presented wherever there has been a decline of American influence and a widening of divisions within the Western alliance; it has been making a steady effort to improve the economic and military underpinning of Soviet national power; and its decisions appear to have been made by a collective leadership, responding in varying degrees to articulate pressures from military and ideological interests within the party.

Deliberately eschewing the flair of the Khrushchev style, with its swings from sharp challenge to spirit of détente, the Soviet leadership moves ponderously in the middle ground, experimenting cautiously, compromising conflicting pressures. Its style of decision making is a new and important factor to take into account.

One other general point: through all its ups and downs, Soviet policy has reflected a long-term trend toward a further postponement of revolutionary action in favor of more traditional efforts to influence existing governments in a direction advantageous to Soviet state interests. In so doing, it has shown a realistic responsiveness to the fact that neither the advanced industrial nations nor the developing countries have shown much readiness for communist-type revolutions. Therefore, although the ideological goal of progress toward the ultimate world-wide victory of communism remains a part of every hortatory speech or document, it has in practice continued to recede as an operational guide to policy. (This fact has of course been a major element in the Sino-Soviet dispute.) Moreover, Soviet theorists have not yet come to grips with the assumption underlying the ideological goal of revolution that victorious communisms will automatically coexist harmoniously.

To go now from the general to the specific, let us begin with the military side of recent Soviet policy, which has been uppermost in our public attention. This aspect of Soviet policy has been more subject to tugs and hauls than any other, with the domestic economic reforms running a close second. As in the United States, the debate goes on at several levels: at one level, between the civilians and the professional military group as a whole; at another, within the military group, between the different generations and services and units within services. And also as in the case of the United States, the result often appears to be something of a "politician's compromise," affected more by budget battles than strategic theory.

Under Khrushchev, the Soviet Union fundamentally accepted the conception of nuclear deterrence, but it sought inflated political advantage from its early tests of an intercontinental missile, puffing up a myth about a "shift in the balance of power." The consequences were the "missile gap" issue in the 1960 American election campaign and the high first military budget of the Kennedy administration in 1961, overreacting to the uncertainty of what the Russians were actually up to. The result was that the Soviet Union was left farther behind in the strategic race than ever. Then, sometime within the following few years, the Khrushchev leadership made the decision to increase its rate of production of intercontinental missiles and to proceed to develop and install some kind of an antiballistic missile system. These decisions were continued in force by Khrushchev's successors, who also supported a high level of military research and development expenditure, approximately equal to that of the United States. At the same time, the leadership reversed earlier decisions which had had the effect of reducing Soviet conventional theater forces and gave greater attention to the mobility and firepower of these forces, in response to the increase in American local combat capabilities demonstrated during the intensification of the war in Vietnam. The Soviet military budget has risen steadily since 1965, but the political leadership has fought back pressures for a more drastic increase in military allocations in an effort to arrest a declining growth rate for the economy as a whole—an effort which has since proved successful.

The decision to go ahead with an antiballistic missile system particularly bore the marks of a compromise of a hotly contested issue. It was a partial concession to pressure from one segment of the military community, and it corresponded to a folk-wisdom feeling about the defense of Moscow. Over time, however, the decision appears to have been weakened by a growing realization of the system's ineffectiveness and its stimulating effect upon the U.S. military budget.

As the additional numbers of intercontinental missiles planned earlier began to make their appearance, as well as such products of research and development as an orbital missile, the question was raised in the United States whether the intention of the Soviet leadership was simply to try to catch up or whether it intended to try to achieve a decisive superiority in strategic weapons and to use this superiority to make political gains.

This question is at the heart of the current debate as to what level of military strength is required for the United States. According to numbers in the public domain, the Soviet Union almost doubled its stockpile of intercontinental missiles between mid-1967 and mid-1968 and by mid-1969 will have approximately 1,000 land-based missiles in place. This compares with a U.S. stockpile of 1,054 land-based missiles and 656 submarine-launched missiles, which the Soviet Union is also beginning to build. But of course numbers alone do not tell the whole story. They do not take into account important qualitative characteristics of the various weapons systems which favor the United States more than the numbers alone would indicate. But the question remains about the intent behind the rapid Soviet rate of increase: Does it reflect an aggressive intent, or is it simply an effort to catch up? And if the Soviet rate of increase continues, at what point would it begin to make a difference, either military or political?

The military side of this equation is dealt with by Carl Kaysen in another paper in this volume; in sum, the important point is that a decisive military superiority—that is, one which would enable either country to destroy the effective retaliatory capability of the other—is a practical impossibility for either side, and especially for the Soviet Union with its smaller economic and technological base. But this still leaves the political question: Would the psychological effect of some measure of superiority be such that the Soviet leadership might be tempted to follow a more adventurous policy or to accept higher risks in a crisis confrontation?

Of course no one can answer this question with certainty, since it depends not upon hard numbers but on very subjective calculations in particular circumstances. But we do have to make the best educated guess we can, because there are some serious risks in either gross over- or underestimation, even though the margins of time or of numbers are not fine. Any such guess is necessarily dependent upon our impressions of the present balance of pressures within the Soviet leadership and the possibility of changes in that balance. On the whole, the present leadership has shown caution about the risk of war, and when it has accepted some degree of risk, it seems to have done so in an effort to overcome its position of strategic inferiority. In the absence of an agreed leveling-off of the arms race, the Soviet leadership can be expected to push vigorously against an unfavorable balance, but it has shown a deep concern about the effects upon the Soviet economy of the further diversion of resources to military expenditures, and there is reason to believe it would be responsive to limitations on strategic arms. Before the Czechoslovakian episode began, the Soviet leadership had fought out the issue of whether to enter into discussions with the United States on a possible leveling-off of the strategic arms race, and agreement was reached at least to enter into such discussions. Although the militant and the military influences are clearly strongly represented, they have not had their way except in the intrabloc question of Czechoslovakia, and it is not clear as of this writing whether the effect of this exception will be to reinforce or to weaken these influences. While there can be no guarantee against a less moderate leadership in the future, this prospect may depend at least in part upon whether the actions of the United States appear either so irresolute, on the one hand, or so bellicose, on the other, that the case for Soviet militancy is made more plausible than it now is.

It should be mentioned that a complete account of Soviet military policy would also have to take into consideration a number of other important facets of the subject, including the military potential of Soviet space activities, the expansion of Soviet submarine and other naval forces, and the competence, mobility, and firepower of the Soviet ground forces and their Warsaw Pact complements, as demonstrated in the occupation of Czechoslovakia. Space does not permit us here to go beyond the central question of the level of Soviet strategic capabilities, with one exception—the political-military matter of "wars of national liberation," which will be discussed in the context of Soviet policies toward the developing areas. Let us turn now from military matters to some broad political aspects of current Soviet policy.

It would be a mistake to characterize recent Soviet relations with the United States with the word "détente," as so many of our European friends tend to do. Rather, the Soviet Union has avoided extremes of both tension and détente with the United States and has energetically tried to gain advantages from the decline of American influence, especially in Europe and the Middle East. Direct bilateral relations with the United States have remained correct but not warm. Certain limited measures of cooperation with the United States (the Moscow–New York air link, the treaties on nonproliferation, consular representation, and so on) have served as regulators of the level of tension but have been handled with reserve for a number of reasons. Too intimate a relationship with the United States would limit the opportunities for exploiting the "anti-imperialist" theme in various parts of the world; it would also leave the Soviet Union more vulnerable to Chinese charges of collusion with the imperialists. Further, the Soviet perception of U.S. policy in Vietnam and elsewhere has raised serious doubts about American intentions: seen from Moscow, U.S. policy is increasingly dominated by a "military-industrial complex"; it is pushing the arms race to higher levels; and it is increasingly prone to intervening militarily to arrest adverse (and inevitable) political trends. Of course the charge of "imperialism" is exploited propagandistically, but it also has genuine roots, so far as observers can judge, in the estimate on which Soviet policy is based. "Peaceful coexistence" is still the accepted political strategy, but its current inflection allows for a fairly high level of political struggle against "American imperialism" and "American monopoly-capitalism."

In practice, this has meant an increasingly active diplomatic effort in Western Europe, with the following apparent objectives: to encourage the reduction of American influence in Europe, to isolate the Federal Republic of Germany from other European countries and particularly from the United States, to prevent the erosion of the Soviet position in Eastern Europe and especially in the German Democratic Republic, and to encourage political movements and coalitions within the European countries more favorably oriented toward the Soviet Union. Although Soviet military power is in the background of this effort, it is not a major lever, except in Eastern Europe, and the keynote is the absence of threat, a differentiated détente applied with varying degrees of warmth to all countries except West Germany. The movement of Soviet and Warsaw Pact forces into Czechoslovakia undermined Soviet efforts to create a climate of reduced tension in Europe, and it also sharpened minatory pressures on the Federal Republic of Germany at the expense of any incipient neutralism in that country.

The main instrumentalities of Soviet policy toward Europe have been trade, technological cooperation, and cultural relations. The political slogan of opposition to "capitalist monopolies" is primarily aimed at limiting the influence of American-based international corporations and the appeal of West German technology and credits in Eastern Europe. It may be worth reiterating at this point that the purpose of this effort is not the communization of Western Europe in any foreseeable future; it is mainly intended to devitalize NATO and to move industrial Europe farther from the United States and thereby enhance the relative power position of the Soviet Union. Within this general purpose, the central issue is Germany. The Soviet Union has from time to time kept alive the possibility of encouraging neutralist trends in West Germany, but its main reliance has been on an unrelenting effort to isolate the Federal Republic by hammering away at the themes of "revanchism," "militarism," and "the revival of fascism." This approach has been sharpened in the recent past, as we have seen in the period following the occupation of Czechoslovakia, in a defensive reflex against the more flexible policy of the governing coalition in Bonn toward Eastern Europe, which the Soviet Union feared might be accelerating trends toward autonomy in that area and might serve to isolate and undermine the Communist regime in East Germany.

Another device which the Soviet Union experimented with in recent years to express its conviction that Western Europe should not be regarded as an American sphere of influence was the proposal for a "European Security Conference." The primary purpose of the proposal was to emphasize the slogan "Europe for the Europeans," which was intended to weaken the influence of the United States in European affairs; but since it also implied an encouragement of closer relations between Eastern and Western Europe and would thereby have increased the freedom of maneuver of the Eastern European states, the Soviet Union has been advancing the idea with caution as concern developed over the erosion of its position in Eastern Europe.

For the United States, Soviet policy toward Europe raises two questions: How successful is it likely to be? And to the extent that it is, how much does it matter? Let us venture a tentative answer to the second question first: If we visualize the worst outcome as a Europe in which the major countries were governed by popular fronts, moving toward neutralism or degrees of pro-Soviet orientation, and in which the democratic and moderate elements in West German political life were demoralized and rendered ineffective, the prospect would be a serious one by almost any reasonable starting premise for American policy. This is not because it would frustrate an American hegemony over Western Europe, which is not the American purpose, but because some reasonable degree of cooperation between a stable and prosperous industrial Europe and the United States is necessary for any progress toward an international order within which democratic values can survive.

In response to the first question, however, it seems fair to say that, if European politics should continue to drift in that direction, it is more likely to be a consequence of American incapacity than of Soviet manipulation. The rigidities of Soviet doctrine and policy have repeatedly frustrated its effort to increase its influence in Western Europe and have severely limited the capacity of Western European communist parties to translate their large electoral support into political influence. The irrepressible Soviet urge to demonstrate its primacy among the ruling communist parties has prevented a less sectarian broad-front appeal to Europe's middle classes, and the youthful radicals of Europe's New Left find little relevance in the sterile doctrines reiterated by Soviet ideologues. Out of the flux of European political life a new dynamism may emerge, but if it does it is more likely to exert a gravitational influence upon the communist world than to find its inspiration in the Soviet experience.

Another area where recent Soviet policy has sought to challenge American influence has been in the Middle East and the Mediterranean, where the Arab-Israeli tension has provided opportunities for Soviet exploitation and where the risk of direct involvement has seemed low or at least controllable. The potentialities of a policy that would deny the Arab crescent to the West have attracted Soviet attention since 1955, but of late the possibility of achieving a positive sphere of influence in this area has made the Soviet Union willing to accept higher risks and higher costs. The lure of positive strategic advantages has been strong—the natural resources in the region and especially its geographical centrality. The increase in Soviet maritime activity over the past decade has also stimulated Soviet interest in the Mediterranean, and the reopening of the Suez Canal has been a subject of particular interest since it would make available a more direct sea route to the Indian Ocean, where the recession of British power has opened new opportunities to a Soviet naval presence.

These tempting prospects had to be balanced against risks of encouraging higher tension which might lead to war between the Arabs and Israelis, with the possibility of an unpredictable response from the United States, which was deeply distracted by Vietnam. Moreover, it may have appeared to the Soviet Union that political gains could be achieved without actual hostilities. But once fighting did erupt in 1967, what became significant was the Soviet readiness to involve itself, however cautiously and ambiguously, with some personnel and with an increased naval presence in the Mediterranean and, afterward, its willingness to expend very large quantities of military supplies to recoup its damaged influence.

Here, too, the Soviet policy decisions bore the marks of vigorous internal debate between military and ideological "hawks," on the one hand, and cautious elements of the leadership, on the other, during which the continuing conflict between these opposing forces broke into an open skirmish. A central issue in the debate was what the costs would be in terms of the U.S. response, whether in the form of local intervention in the Middle East or generalized tension, and it is reasonable to suppose that this issue also played a critical part in the discussions that preceded the decision to move troops into Czechoslovakia.

The Middle East appears to be a special case, however, because of the inability of the United States to resolve the Arab-Israeli dilemma, and is not representative of Soviet policy toward the developing areas generally, except as an illustration of the basic strategy of seeking to draw nationalist leaders into a loose coalition against the West. On the whole, Soviet policy has tended to favor collaboration with nationalist leaders rather than encouragement of active revolutionary movements in the underdeveloped countries. The disastrous end of another experiment with weapons diplomacy, in Indonesia, where arms supplied by the Soviet Union were used to kill hundreds of thousands of local communists, was among a string of disappointments which deflated the optimism that had been sustained over a decade of active interest in the former colonial areas. These disappointments contributed to a general mood in the Soviet Union which shows some of the same weary preoccupation with domestic problems and disinclination to devote resources to the developing areas that is to be found today in the United States.

Until the Chinese became absorbed in their internal factional conflicts, their militant challenge to Soviet policies in the developing areas evoked at least a greater verbal revolutionary militancy on the part of the Soviet Union. It was in this context that Khrushchev talked quite menacingly about support for wars of national liberation in 1960 and 1961. One effect of this talk was that the United States began a great buildup in its local war capabilities during the early years of the Kennedy administration, prompted by the feeling that the active fight against communist expansionism was going to have to be waged in distant parts of the developing world and that counterinsurgency was the necessary answer to wars of national liberation. What was not well understood in this country at that time was that Khrushchev's speeches mainly expressed a lurch to the left in the Sino-Soviet polemic exchanges. After the removal of Khrushchev in 1964 and the intensification of the war in Vietnam, the Soviet leadership followed the American example of building up its local war capabilities. It reactivated its naval infantry (somewhat similar to the United States Marine Corps), improved the mobility and firepower of its ground forces, and greatly enlarged its logistical capabilities with more long-range planes, transport ships, submarines, and helicopters. The declared Soviet purpose was to prevent or offset any future U.S. interventions like that in Vietnam, but uncertainty over Soviet intentions persisted because of its continued declarations of support for wars of national liberation. What the Soviet role would be in practice is hard to say, for the open-ended commitment leaves the Soviet Union free to decide just when military, political, or economic involvement in any local conflict situation is required. As a matter of definition, any forces opposed to Soviet interests become counterrevolutionary, and those whom the Soviet Union wishes to support become national liberation forces. Given the prospect discussed earlier that many local conflict situations are likely to explode in former colonial areas during the coming decade, it is probable that the United States and the Soviet Union will find their relationship continuously roiled by some degree of involvement in these conflicts. Although the United States may be in a cautious mood after Vietnam and the Soviet Union may continue to be careful about direct involvements in such conflicts, the fact that both countries now have greatly increased local capabilities may lower the threshold of involvement, for capabilities have a way of begetting intentions.

Soviet relations with Eastern Europe and China belong somewhere in the twilight zone between Soviet foreign and domestic policy, for bloc problems tend in practice to be the primary responsibility of the party rather than of the foreign ministry. (In a less direct way, this is true of all major Soviet foreign policy decisions.) As a consequence, ideological considerations tend to have greater weight in relations with the communist bloc than with other countries.

Although conditions vary greatly from one country to another in Eastern Europe, and would require individual analysis in a more detailed account, it may be ventured as a general proposition that the Soviet Union is involved in a fundamental dilemma in the area which stems from the political effects of nationalism and economic modernization. While some of the communist parties in Eastern Europe have been able to harness nationalism to their own purposes—this is most clearly the case in Rumania—the effect generally has been to increase pressures for a greater degree of autonomy from Soviet control. The process of economic modernization has led the states of Eastern Europe to experiment in varying degrees with economic reforms, which in turn have involved political consequences—some decentralization, wider latitude in the political control of public life, and a growing interest in economic and technological contact with the West. The Soviet response, reflecting the vicissitudes of internal debates, has been a groping effort to find a pattern of control which would be resilient enough to accommodate some degree of local autonomy without jeopardizing local party control or the integrity of the bloc.

Meanwhile, the Western policy of "bridge-building" and the West German *Ostpolitik* were both proceeding on the assumption that the Soviet Union would accept a weaning-away of the states of Eastern Europe if the process were gradual enough. The use of troops against Czechoslovakia and the sharp Soviet response to the West German policy showed, among other things, that the Soviet threshold of response was lower than had been assumed. This reaction may have been peculiar to the Czechoslovakian situation, where acute strategic interests and ideological anxieties for the contagious effects of heretical political ideas combined to activate both military and ideological interest groups within the Soviet leadership. In any case, the experience has highlighted the contradiction implicit in the Western policy of building bridges to Eastern Europe within a framework of détente with the Soviet Union. While the situation remains inflamed, it seems likely that any bridges to be built will have to be cantilevered from the Western shore. The Soviet dilemma, however, will remain inherent in the situation, and the use of force can at best postpone the need for a more flexible accommodation of these irresistible pressures.

Yugoslavia is of course in a category of its own, as a result of earlier Soviet miscalculations. The effect of the Yugoslav example of demi-nonalignment and of economic and political experimentation will depend upon how successfully Yugoslavia meets its problems of federalism, succession, and a sagging economy. If the general direction of Soviet policy were to turn toward greater flexibility, as the Yugoslavs, the Rumanians, and the Italian Communist party have been urging, the position of Yugoslavia could be turned to advantage by the Soviet Union as a rallying point for neutralist tendencies in Western and Northern Europe. But for the orthodox elements of the current Soviet leadership, this course appears to involve too many risks.

With regard to China, the Soviet leadership has been playing a waiting game, hoping that the outcome of the factional conflict in Peking would be the emergence of those elements in the Chinese Communist party and the Chinese army that would be disposed toward a modus vivendi with the Soviet Union. In the meantime, the leadership has not sought to force the issue, responding minimally to the propaganda broadsides from Peking, comforted by the effect of the Cultural Revolution in reducing Chinese influence abroad. Even so, the Chinese have captured the imagination of the left wing of many communist parties around the world and of romantic revolutionaries outside the parties, and this continues to be a serious problem for the Soviet Union and especially for its ideologists, to whom the unity of the communist movement under Soviet leadership is a first article of faith. A victory of moderate elements in the Chinese party would ease one source of complication in the fragmented communist movement. If, on the other hand, the conflict in Peking were to result in the breakdown of central authority in China, the Soviet leadership would have to decide whether to intervene, knowing that the effect of such an intervention upon the international communist movement would make the experience in Czechoslovakia seem minor.

Before concluding this brief review of some main features of Soviet foreign policy in the present period, we should take account of some internal aspects of the Soviet system that are relevant to our inquiry. Although the character of the Soviet system is not a proper object of U.S. foreign policy, we are necessarily interested in how domestic trends may affect relations between the two countries. The stability of the regime, the balance of forces within the leadership, the degree of dependence of the regime upon external tensions, the effect of economic pressures—these are among the questions in which Russia's neighbors have a natural interest.

A subject of considerable speculative attention abroad has been the effect of advancing industrialization upon the Soviet political system. As the problems of administration have grown more technical and complex, there has been a tendency in recent years for the Communist party to separate the functions of specialists and administrators from the functions of the party, which now center on political control and fundamental policy making. This separation has also had the tendency to strengthen the role of the party bureaucracy as the guardian of ideological doctrine. The self-interest of the party bureaucracy is reinforced by the fear of irrelevancy and loss of control if the central task of economic advancement becomes the province of other groups and if foreign policy is steadily less revolutionary in practice. As a consequence, the increasing reliance of the leadership upon a pragmatic problem-solving approach to such major policy issues as economic reform has been accompanied, paradoxically, by an increasing insistence upon ideological conformity in the arts, among the nationalities, and in public discussion. The inertia of the party bureaucracy is still a powerful factor in Soviet behavior, favoring rigidity and militant zeal on selected issues. Whether this inertia will become so demonstrably a brake on economic progress that other forces in the society will be led to challenge and transform the bureaucracy, and to redefine the functions of the party in an advanced industrial society along more creative lines, is a matter of the purest speculation.

For the present, however, the interplay between these contradictory tendencies makes it difficult to answer the question whether the system intrinsically requires external tension for its political cohesion and whether it is inherently driven to external expansion. A simple answer would be that the system depends upon the balance of forces between the guardians of dogma and the pragmatists. The ideologues see the world in terms of conflict and have a vested interest in the tension of revolutionary élan; they require the dynamism of forward motion to preserve the muscularity of their movement. The economic pragmatists, on the other hand, have more to gain from economic growth at home than from tension abroad; their brand of communism would win and hold its support by effective performance. In practice, of course, this dichotomy is too simple, but it does illustrate the theoretical point that a communist system may or may not be inherently expansionist. Given the present balance of forces in the Soviet Union, the practical answer is that the direction of policy may depend primarily on external circumstances—that is, whether they invite expansion and militancy or not. These external circumstances may have a considerable influence upon the internal balance of forces.

Some writers have raised the question whether the structures of the two societies are moving toward convergence in response to the imperatives of industrialization. Because of the extreme differences in historical experience between the United States and the Soviet Union, it seems unlikely that this is happening in any significant way, but even if it were, it would be less critical to their relationship than the balance of forces within the two societies. Structural similarity between two countries would be no assurance of amity if competitive military interests and jingoists exerted a preponderant influence within either one or both.

In drawing this characterization of Soviet foreign policy to a close, we return to the question that is central to our own thinking: Is Soviet policy expansionist? For the present the answer would be yes, but we must clarify the sense in which this is true or may change in the future. Our experience does not warrant the stereotype of the Soviet Union as actively promoting the revolutionary overthrow of noncommunist governments or of a power committed to military conquest. On the other hand, it is clearly not a status quo power, except in its determination to hold on to its position in Eastern Europe, and it does not accept the present international order as a basis for stability. It is expansionist in the sense that it actively seeks to increase the political power and influence of the Soviet state wherever opportunities exist for such gains without undue risks—particularly, short of the risk of general war, as it calculates that risk in each situation.

If this correctly characterizes Soviet policy, the two significant elements are a competitive striving to increase its power and influence relative to that of the United States and caution regarding the risk of nuclear war. These are the elements that create the basis for a limited adversary relationship between the Soviet Union and the United States.

Policy Alternatives for the United States

We come now to the question of policy choices. Anyone who has had anything to do with any government knows what a conventional fiction it is to speak of governments making policy decisions as though this were a detached and rational process; more often than not, decisions tend to build up like coral reefs from the accretion of small unobserved deposits. And if in addition we take due account of the complexity of forces in the world largely outside the control of even the superpowers, and the contradictory considerations and domestic compromises under which any government has to operate, we are even less likely to approach the subject of policy alternatives in the expectation that detached reason will govern the course of events.

Still, there are choices to be made, and they will have fateful consequences. The more we try to stretch our political imaginations to anticipate what the consequences may be of alternative courses of action, or of inaction, the more rational our choices can be. Our concern is mainly with policy alternatives for the United States, but it would be a useful discipline to review first, very briefly, some policy choices facing the Soviet leadership, since they are part of the uncertainties we must weigh.

As we have seen, the central choice for the Soviet leadership is not between extremes but between degrees of inflection of the policy of "peaceful coexistence," which means in practice that their decisions will be based on calculations of margins of risks, costs, and gains of somewhat more competitive rivalry with the United States as against somewhat greater efforts to damp down tension. In a broad sense, these decisions depend upon whether the Soviet leadership as a whole is governed by a broad or a narrow view of Soviet self-interest, a long-term confidence in history, or an impatience for quick gains. But in a more immediate sense, the decisions may depend upon the balance of forces within the leadership, and this in turn may be deeply affected by such external factors as Chinese developments and the course of American policy.

The traditional bent of the communist movement is against letting itself be outflanked on the left, and so the outcome of the political struggle within the Chinese Communist party may be an important determinant. If the Chinese continue to mount a militant challenge to the Soviet leadership, the effect, by induction, upon Soviet policy will be toward a more active exploitation of unrest in the developing areas and a continuing reserve in its relations with the United States. However, although this has been the automatic response in the past, it is subject to a continuous tactical judgment on the part of the Soviet leadership whether an energetic use of the peace issue might be more effective than "out-Chineseing the Chinese," either in rhetoric or in practice. The leadership has wavered on this point, but if it were to decide to wage its intrabloc fight on the issue of Soviet peacefulness against Chinese bellicosity, an inhibition would be removed from a more thorough development of the strategy of peaceful coexistence and a more explicit acceptance of the evolution toward "creative Marxism," without regard for charges of revisionism. A movement in this direction would also encourage the evident tendency to turn inward, which is as strong in the Soviet Union as it is in other major countries in this period, and would enable the Soviet leadership to concentrate its attention and energies upon domestic economic and political problems. If this were to be the dominant tendency, those elements of the Soviet leadership concerned with the improvement of the Soviet economy would emerge as the strongest spokesmen for a policy of moderation and restraint abroad. Their natural interests, as we have seen, would argue for a downturn in the strategic arms race, but we should remind ourselves again that the extent of their influence as against those elements committed to activism abroad and military advantage may be more a matter of internal politics, tradeoffs and logrolling, than of detached analysis of policy alternatives.

Flowing from these general determinants are a number of clear policy choices toward particular areas. In Europe, the Soviet Union can decide to continue its effort to isolate the Federal Republic of Germany or to exercise an alternative option of seeking to encourage neutralist trends in that country; it can decide to continue to try to push the United States out of Europe or to work with the United States in the interest of European stability (and if it chooses the former, it can rely either on a broad-front "anti-imperialist" campaign or on the narrower support of national communist parties and the proletariat); in Eastern Europe, it can decide whether to accept a more flexible relationship, which would derive advantages from a network of closer trade relations between East and West, or it can continue to try to enforce a rigid control over a self-contained eastern bloc.

Among the many other specific areas of decision, one of the most influential will arise from the turbulence of the developing areas. The Soviet leadership can decide whether to ride the crest of revolutionary violence in the third world or to make an effort toward collaboration in international procedures to contain and pacify these conflicts. Which will be the guiding example: the gamble of the Middle Eastern adventure or the statesmanship of Tashkent? In the latter case, the Soviet effort to compose rather than exploit a conflict situation was dictated primarily by tactical considerations vis-à-vis the Chinese, and the decision in subsequent cases will depend upon how the Soviet Union weighs its triangular interests, against the Chinese along one side and against the West along the other.

Of course these questions are at best rhetorical in their simplicity, but they serve to remind us, in thinking about our own alternatives, that Soviet policy is a range of possibilities rather than a fixed constant and that we must remain aware how much our own behavior in turn is part of Soviet calculations.

In weighing our own policy alternatives, it may be useful to begin by identifying the main issues involved in relations between the United States and the Soviet Union which call for choices to be made. These would include the following: (1) military competition; (2) other matters involved in direct bilateral relations—trade, cultural relations, and so on; (3) political competition in Europe, West and East; and (4) political competition in the third world.

Let us now examine the main alternative approaches to each category of issues. For purposes of limiting our discussion, we will deal only with the nonextreme range of positions commonly represented in public consideration, but we will not attempt to fill in all the gradations and shadings between the major alternatives.

First, the military competition. Clearly, one major tendency in American thinking emphasizes the importance of military superiority over the Soviet Union. Starting from a skeptical view of present or future Soviet leaders, this approach argues that our military lead should be substantial enough in all significant categories of weapons to remove any temptation to Soviet use or threat of force for aggression. Further, it says that our military capability should be more than enough to deter; it should be large enough to provide for uncertainties and large enough to "prevail" in the event that the Soviet Union is not deterred. For the same reason (which reflects a lack of confidence in the rationality of the Soviet leadership in crisis situations), this position tends not only to favor the earliest possible deployment of the "thin," Sentinel antiballistic missile system but also to argue for moving ahead to a "heavy" ABM system oriented against Soviet weapons, in the expectation that the Soviet Union will not respond by greatly increasing its offensive capability. More generally, this approach urges a very high level of military research and development to guard against Soviet efforts to achieve shortcuts by technological breakthroughs, and it pushes for the earliest possible deployment of MIRV (the multiple individually targeted reentry vehicles) in our Poseidon and Minuteman III missiles in order to establish a clear superiority over whatever level of strategic force or ABM the Soviet Union may be building.

This approach goes further: it argues that the considerable advantage enjoyed by the United States in its economic and technological base means that it can outpace the Soviet Union in the military race and that, when this is demonstrably clear to the Soviet leaders, they will then be more likely to negotiate seriously or make concessions or, in any case, experience strains which will limit their capacity for expansionist activity.

The contrasting approach to military competition starts from a central preoccupation with the hazards of the arms race. This position argues that the quest for superiority inevitably results in a continuing arms spiral and that the risks of war from this spiral are greater than the risks of tacit or explicit arms control agreements. It tends to recommend a moderate and stable deterrence level of strategic weapons—that is, a limitation to what is required to ensure that we could retaliate against an attack with an "unacceptable level of damage"—and it assumes the Soviet leadership would not contemplate any policy that would result in substantial devastation of its country. This approach places more value on maintaining a stable military balance than on trying for superiority, arguing that superiority does not in fact confer any usable political advantage and that the quest for superiority only drives the competition to levels which are more costly, less stable, and therefore less secure. Those who urge this approach tend to doubt the effectiveness of an antiballistic missile system, particularly one oriented toward the possibility of a large-scale Soviet attack, and believe a deployment of the Sentinel system now costs more in terms of accelerating the arms race than it is worth. While they do not oppose a moderate level of military research and development to insure against future technological advances, they do oppose the immediate deployment of MIRVs on the grounds that for the near future at least the American strategic arsenal is ample and that the installation of MIRVs will force the Soviet Union into a new round of weapons-building and will greatly reduce the possibility of an arms limitation agreement. The more complicated on-site inspection system needed to detect multiple-warhead missile installations would be the stumbling block.

Those who argue for an arms-control approach to the military competition regard an effort by the United States to outspend the Soviet Union in a military race as reckless and ineffective: reckless, because it would give plausible grounds to those in the Soviet Union who have genuine doubts about our intentions or to those militant and military elements who would seize the opportunity to strengthen their own position, thereby modifying the Soviet system counter to our long-term interests; and ineffective, because they feel the Soviet control system can accommodate if necessary the social and political strains of putting a very high proportion of Soviet resources into defense, whereas an effort on our part to "overstrain" the Soviet economy would require so high a level of tension and mobilization as to have destructive consequences at home.

The differences between these two approaches center on the question of the meaning and usefulness of military superiority. The first approach reflects the traditional frontier confidence in the six-shooter; the second position reflects the belief that the destructiveness of new weapons has qualitatively changed existing conceptions of security.

The second category of issues that arise between the United States and the Soviet Union concerns other aspects of direct bilateral relations, and the alternative positions here carry over many of the differences reflected in the discussion of the military competition.

Those who argue for military superiority also tend to be deeply skeptical about détente, tension-reduction measures, and summit meetings on the grounds that these "atmospheric" changes work unequally to our disadvantage. While the Soviet Union has used previous periods of détente to build up its military capabilities, it is argued, the United States and its allies have tended to disarm unilaterally in a climate of optimism. In such a climate military appropriations are harder to get, conscription becomes politically difficult, and military laboratories tend to wither away and military scientists to drift away. Moreover, it is said, the spirit of détente may actually increase the risk of war by misleading the adversary about the firmness of our commitments and by tempting him into miscalculated adventures. In the present circumstances, a reputation for firmness in the use of our power to defend our interests is urged as a better guarantee of peace than a conciliatory attitude. Arguing by analogy from the experience with Hitler, this approach maintains that concessions to an adversary with unlimited aspirations only tend to feed his appetite; it is particularly wary of "salami tactics," by which political objectives are achieved slice by slice.

Correspondingly, from the point of view of this general approach, cultural relations with the Soviet Union are not encouraged on the grounds that such exchanges permit the Soviet Union to strengthen its power by borrowing liberally from Western technology, administrative experience, and so on, while Western scholars and students are severely limited in return. Trade with the Soviet Union is also regarded as disadvantageous: it helps the Soviet Union overcome shortcomings in the Soviet economy and thus lessens political strains which would otherwise circumscribe its freedom of action; it also hastens Soviet economic and technological advancement, which augments power that may be used against us. This position does not prohibit all business with the Soviet Union but urges that such business be conducted on the basis of normal short-term commercial credit; anything longer is regarded as a form of concealed foreign aid without any quid pro quo. For this reason, such sales as the "wheat deal," which was dictated more for domestic reasons than for requirements of foreign policy, are looked upon as unwise by this position; they make it harder to hold our allies to agreements prohibiting the sale of strategic goods and limiting longer-term credit.

Some who share this general outlook would not only warn against the dangers of détente but would go further to urge a more active political offensive against the Soviet Union. They would publicize the record of broken treaty obligations, keep alive the claims of the "captive nations," and take the political initiative in calling attention to the shortcomings of the Soviet system and in exploiting its troubles and contradictions.

The major alternative approach to other aspects of bilateral relations with the Soviet Union, on the other hand, accepts tension-reduction measures and a climate of détente as desirable even if they are more symbolic than substantive in effect. The argument is that tension-reduction measures, even if only symbolic, create a climate which makes more substantive agreements possible or at least results in tacit and reciprocal measures of restraint. Although recognizing that tension-reduction measures create complications for the Western alliance, this position would argue that tensions do more harm than good: they make problems more difficult to handle, increase diplomatic rigidities, strengthen the military influence in policy making on both sides, and encourage neo-Stalinist tendencies within the Soviet Union.

Those who share this general approach also favor an emphatic effort to enlarge cultural contacts and trade with the Soviet Union. Part of the case for the former rests upon a faith in the intangible value of the increase of mutual knowledge in dispelling misconceptions and misunderstandings and a faith in the dissemination of Western democratic conceptions through widened contacts. As evidence, it is argued that American understanding of the workings of the Soviet system has been greatly increased as a result of the cultural exchanges. As for trade, this position's argument rests upon a belief in the calming effect of increasing economic interdependence; some would emphasize the evolutionary effect upon Soviet society of increasing economic well-being (the so-called fat-man thesis), while others support an expansion of trade for reasons of economic self-interest. In any case, the volume of potential trade under discussion is not considerable.

As might be expected, those who share this general approach tend to eschew an active policy of political warfare on the grounds that it congeals differences, degrades international discourse, and isolates the United States from its allies by blurring the Soviet responsibility for the continuation of the cold war. Similarly, this approach tends to be reserved about pressing abrasive issues in the United Nations and would on balance prefer to operate within that organization to the limits that great power harmony permitted rather than press for action which would further estrange the Soviet Union from some degree of commitment to the United Nations.

The difference between our alternatives in this area is that the first approach would minimize direct bilateral relations with the Soviet Union whereas the second would seek to maximize them. Both accept some belief in the possibility of long-term changes in the Soviet system, although they may differ in their judgment of the pace at which this process is occurring, or is likely to occur in the future, and they may perhaps also differ in their assumptions as to whether that evolution is necessarily working in a benign direction. The first approach would put its reliance mainly on Western strength and firmness as an instrument inducing such change; the second would prefer a little more carrot and a little less stick.

The third category of issues concerns the political competition in Europe, West and East. The cornerstone of one of our alternative positions would surely be the fundamental importance of the Western alliance, which would imply primacy for the efforts to revive and strengthen NATO and for the maintenance of mutual confidence and intimacy in relations with the Federal Republic of Germany. There are, as the paper by Francis M. Bator in this volume shows, many approaches to the question of how this can best be done, but the relevant point for our discussion is that, to the extent that a contradiction is perceived between our relations with Western Europe and our efforts to improve relations with the Soviet Union or to advance the interests of arms control, the adherents of this position would resolve the contradiction clearly in favor of the Western alliance. One illustration of this problem is provided by attitudes toward the nonproliferation treaty. Adherents of this position would tend to give more weight to the adverse political effects of this treaty upon our relations with Western Europe and particularly West Germany than would those who give primacy to arms control or to improving relations with the Soviet Union. (This leaves aside for the moment the question whether the treaty is to be regarded mainly in its Soviet-American context or as a function of our other arms-control concerns.)

Another general proposition that would be advanced by many who share this approach would be that Western European integration or the

Atlantic association should be given primacy over efforts to bring Eastern and Western Europe closer together if these purposes interfere with one another. This choice rests upon the argument that the development of relations between Eastern and Western Europe belongs to a longer time perspective than the integration of Western Europe and, indeed, that the unity of Eastern and Western Europe can be achieved only on Soviet terms if Western Europe is not unified beforehand. Recognizing the Western European interest in developing closer trade and cultural relations with Eastern Europe, this approach would seek as unified a Western policy as possible on this matter and would not be constrained by considerations of a détente with the Soviet Union from encouraging an enlargement of Western influence in Eastern Europe.

The alternative approach to relations with Europe is essentially the converse of the first, in the sense that it would resolve the apparent contradictions in the other direction. Some who share this general approach would entertain proposals for a reduction in the Western military presence in Western Europe, possibly including demilitarization or denuclearization zones, in the hope of working toward a European settlement with the Soviet Union. Some would encourage the Federal Republic of Germany to move more rapidly toward juridical acceptance of the German Democratic Republic as part of such a European settlement. While the general disposition of this approach is to favor an active search for a formula to neutralize or "normalize" the situation in Europe, there are important differences as to how this can be done; some would accept a Soviet sphere of influence in Eastern Europe, while others see the primary purpose of such a formula as the withdrawal of Soviet forces from Eastern Europe and greater autonomy in that area.

It is obvious that the differences between the alternative approaches rest upon fundamentally different assessments of Soviet intentions and of the depth of the Soviet commitment to retain its position in Eastern Europe and particularly in East Germany. They also rest upon different assessments of the importance to the United States of internal political developments within West Germany and of Soviet prospects for deriving advantages from these developments.

Finally, we come to the issues involved in the Soviet-American competition in the third world. This can be dealt with briefly because it is discussed at greater length in chapters by Max F. Millikan, John C. Campbell, and Edwin O. Reischauer in this volume. The major difference here is between those who emphasize the continuing validity and importance of containment not only of the Soviet Union but of China at various points in the developing world and those who challenge either the feasibility or the desirability of this policy. The Vietnam experience of course exercises a dominating influence on this discussion, intensifying the convictions of those who hold either view. Those who favor a continuing or more active commitment by the United States against further wars of national liberation argue not only the strategic importance of particular areas but the general issue whether increased Soviet naval and local war capabilities reflect an intention to intervene more actively in Africa, Asia, and later Latin America.

The alternative approach argues that the United States has become overcommitted around the world and that it should contract these commitments in recognition that other states should assume a larger responsibility for the maintenance of international order or, in any case, that prospective threats to order will be less dangerous to American interests than it has tended to assume.

It is clear that these alternative approaches to policy reflect quite different assumptions about the processes of change within the third world and also about the nature of the communist challenge. The first approach emphasizes the military character of the challenge and its central direction from Moscow or Peking; as a consequence it tends to see the interests of the United States as deeply involved (the "domino effect"). The second approach, on the other hand, emphasizes the local political forces at work, whether communist or not, and either dismisses U.S. interest in the outcome or places its reliance upon the force of nationalism to preserve local independence.

This brief survey of some major alternative policy approaches to the various categories of issues involved in the relationship between the United States and the Soviet Union illustrates how deeply policy preferences reflect fundamental differences of assumptions, which are often not made explicit in public discussion. It is also clear that these differences in assumptions are not a purely intellectual matter but often reflect a natural tendency, in dealing with the unknown, to project hopes and fears according to one's temperament or political predilection. Although our knowledge may not be sufficient to dispel such differences, we should at least be conscious of the assumptions on which much of our thinking is based.

Since action cannot be postponed to a time of greater certainty, we must now turn to the question which originally prompted our discussion, keeping in mind the characterization of Soviet policy sketched in the preceding pages and the uncertainties that remain: What course of action on our part is most likely to move our relations with the Soviet Union in the direction we would like to see them move? We speak of directions rather than of goals, not only because we are conscious how many elements of this complex relationship lie beyond our power to direct, but because of a fundamental conviction that it is more consonant with the democratic spirit to regard change as a continuing process than as a movement toward total realization.

Guiding Principles for the United States

Starting from a recognition of the mixture of conflict and interdependence involved in the relationship between the United States and the Soviet Union, and of the interplay of internal forces within each of the two countries as it affects this relationship, what can we derive as guiding principles to govern U.S. policy toward the Soviet Union?

First, with regard to the military competition between the two countries, it is clear that we must never allow ourselves to lose sight of the inherent dynamism of this competition to edge closer to war. We have no choice in the immediate present but to learn to live with the possibility of mutual destruction and to seek some kind of equilibrium in this confrontation, but we must broaden our conception of security from its past reliance upon superiority. This means that we must go beyond a mutual recognition of the unacceptability of nuclear war as an instrument of policy to assert the mutual advantage in achieving a stable balance at the lowest levels possible. Even during the present period when the mutuality of this conception is not yet well established, restraint and a sense of proportion in our own military preparations are more consonant with our long-term interest than a policy which, by striving for maximum superiority, has the effect of stimulating military competition.

It is not easy to define how this restraint should be exercised in practice, because either too little attention to our military capabilities or excessive zeal in striving for superiority could encourage militant tendencies within the Soviet leadership. As a guiding principle, however, we should give great weight to our interest in the stability of the deterrent balance in strategic nuclear weapons.

This does not mean that both sides must have the same number of the same kind of weapons. Stability can be based upon an asymmetrical balance, which would enable each side to maintain a deterrent force that takes account of differences in its geographical situation and in the characteristics of its weapons systems. To maintain this balance at moderate levels means that the political authorities on both sides must exercise restraint upon the natural tendency of professional military interests to press for ever higher levels in the military competition.

If we conceive of our security interests in these terms, it is apparent that arms control must be an integral part of our defense policy. Arms control does not depend upon millennial changes in the Soviet system or our own; it does not depend upon a surcease of the political rivalry between the two countries. It does depend upon a recognition that we both have an interest in reducing the risk of general war, whether or not we may be engaged in clashing political interests. It is therefore vitally necessary to educate our people and our allies to understand the separation between arms control and the political conflict. As a beginning, we should not treat the talks between the United States and the Soviet Union to damp down the strategic arms race as an occasion symbolic of political harmony between the two countries; nor should this effort be suspended to indicate our disapproval of Soviet behavior in Czechoslovakia or to signify Soviet disapproval of our actions in Vietnam. This would be shortsighted, and when it comes to nuclear weapons, myopia can be a fatal illness.

The second set of issues concerns other forms of bilateral contacts between the two countries. The tone and scope of these relations should reflect our awareness of the limited adversary character of the relationship in the present and our desire to move the balance between interdependence and conflict in the direction of greater cooperation in the future. In the first instance, this requires the continuation and extension of good diplomatic channels of communication, characterized by privacy, confidence, and knowledge of each other's internal political life. This can be done quietly and constructively, without illusions of false harmony or exaggerated swings in the public mood.

Our earlier discussion spelled out the advantages and disadvantages of an expansion of trade and cultural relations with the Soviet Union. Legitimate points can be made on both sides of this controversy, but on balance the risks of these forms of contact would seem to be less significant than their possible long-term usefulness. Although these are not likely to exceed a modest scale for the present, or to achieve any major transformations in the relationship, they do contribute to mutual knowledge and insight and have already begun to influence prevailing stereotypes in the thinking of each country regarding the other. The entrenched police bureaucracy in the Soviet Union remains a formidable barrier to the extension of cultural relations, but it would be self-defeating for us to emulate this example. The present political leadership in the Soviet Union survived harsh infighting to make its way to the top, and the qualities that make for survival under those conditions are not necessarily those that make for broad statesmanship. Forms of contact that diminish parochialism on the part of the present or future generation of leaders seem more likely to contribute, on balance, to constructive relations in the future than to diminish our relative advantages in knowledge or techniques.

The Soviet interest in Western technology and administration provides a positive motivation to which we can usefully respond; such technical borrowing should have some effect in reducing the isolation of important segments of the Soviet population from the Western world. Further, new developments in science and technology offer some important opportunities for Soviet-American collaboration: desalting projects, weather and pollution control, oceanographic research and exploitation of ocean resources, international satellite communications, and many others. These projects would not only be of intrinsic usefulness; they would be a means of encouraging a shift in emphasis in the relationship over the coming years from conflict toward collaboration.

Whereas the two foregoing sets of issues concern the direct relations between the United States and the Soviet Union, the following paragraphs deal with policy toward the political competition between the two countries in Europe and in the third world. The preferred policy here must start with the probability that some level of rivalry is likely to continue for some time to come but that we should seek a clearer codification of the terms of competition. If what the Soviet Union means by peaceful coexistence is the competition between the two systems (or the "struggle," as it is more often expressed) by all means short of war, there is no reason why the United States should not accept this as the Marquis of Queensberry rule of political competition. Our ability to do this obviously depends upon the effectiveness of other aspects of our policy in various parts of the world.

In Western Europe this means first of all giving our attention to the sensibilities of our European allies, leaving them in no doubt about our continuing commitment to their defense. It also means an effort to understand the transitional forces which are in the process of transforming European thought and political life and to demonstrate that there is room for a European sense of identity in our common effort to create a world environment in which our shared values can survive. In particular, we must not lose sight of our vital interest in maintaining a relationship of confidence and common purpose with the moderate and democratic leadership of the Federal Republic of Germany against all Soviet efforts to weaken this bond, for the continued strengthening of democracy in Germany is essential to the future peace of Europe.

In Eastern Europe, we are obliged to recognize the dilemma implicit in "bridge-building" and should resolve it by rejecting a "spheres of influence" agreement. It is necessary to reconcile legitimate Soviet security interests in Eastern Europe with the right of the people of this area to determine their own forms of government. Over a period of time, the Soviet Union may come to appreciate that its security in Eastern Europe can be more effectively assured by military limitations guaranteed by the superpowers than by an effort to maintain political control over the area by coercion. This clearly represents a long-term process through a period of flux, during which we can give moderate and differentiated encouragement to many forms of functional arrangements across the continent of Europe.

In the third world, our interests are served neither by trigger-happy interventionism nor by withdrawal into complacent isolationism, the two extremes most actively represented in current American discussion, since both would have the effect of encouraging a more active and militant Soviet policy in these areas. What is required is an active extension of assistance to processes of peaceful change and development, without pressing for political alignment or relying upon military intervention as an instrumentality and while giving as much encouragement as we can to international instruments of peacekeeping and ad hoc arrangements for reducing the flow of weapons to troubled areas, including the Middle East.

This policy starts from the conception that political and economic access to these countries does not require political control; it emphatically rejects hegemonical rule as a backward step. This means that not every expansion of Soviet trade and contact should be regarded as against our interests, providing it does not involve the imposition of political control. This also means more discriminating attention to the internal political forces within other countries, instead of the automatic assumption that any local variant of communism is necessarily an anathema; it may in fact be a complicating factor rather than a prime cause of local turbulence. The issue for us, therefore, is not whether we should be a presence in the third world but what kind of presence is consistent with our purposes.

Finally, we come back to the question of the direction in which we would like to see our relationship with the Soviet Union move in the future. The important point here is that the relationship has to be visualized as proceeding through a series of stages over a considerable period of time. For the present, we are obliged to recognize and respond to the elements of conflict in the relationship, and perhaps the most we can reasonably hope to do is to take steps to moderate the arms race. In an intermediate stage, we can hope to codify and restrain the political rivalry and encourage some extension of economic and technological cooperation. It should be an essential part of our conception of the relationship that our current efforts are intended to prepare the way for a later stage of increasing political cooperation in strengthening international institutions and the international order, whenever later generations of Soviet leaders recognize an enlightened self-interest in this kind of world.

This stage may at best be decades away, for we should be under no illusion about the depth of the change required from the present rigid system of control in the Soviet Union by a tough and parochial political leadership. No one can predict with confidence whether that change will come about by a gradual process of evolution or by a series of convulsive advances and regressions. Specific policy prescriptions may therefore have less enduring usefulness than a philosophy of the problem which can inspire a constant sense of direction, through periods of tension and discouragement, toward a longer-term outcome.

That philosophy must reflect a sense of proportion about the conduct of a harsh political rivalry under conditions in which safeguards against the debasement and literal destruction of humanity are all too precarious. That philosophy must guide our political leadership to exercise constraints on the competition of forces within our own society, so that we may use our power with wisdom and restraint, toward the realization of an order among nations in which the fundamental values of human life can be made more secure.

If this is what we stand for, and if our day-to-day conduct is consistent with this sense of proportion, we shall find natural allies among the people of all nations, including the Soviet Union.

EDWIN O. REISCHAUER

TRANSPACIFIC RELATIONS

When we look across the Atlantic, we may find elements of uncertainty and change in our foreign policies, but when we look across the Pacific, everything seems in doubt. The outcome of the Vietnam war is still unknown; the reaction of the American people to this outcome is even less clear; developments within China are an enigma, and China's role abroad is uncertain; our chief alliance—with Japan—seems more threatened than our European ties; and the future of the 850 million people in the Indian subcontinent and the other noncommunist lands of South and East Asia is quite incalculable. Worst of all, we are not agreed on the underlying concepts for our transpacific policies. While the conceptual basis for our transatlantic relations needs some refining, our whole approach to Asia must be rethought and reconstructed almost *de novo*.

General Perspectives

Americans have come to assume that, as a nation, we have immediate, vital interests in the transpacific area, and in the past three decades we have fought three major wars in defense of these interests as we saw them. It is accepted as a truism that we are a Pacific as well as an Atlantic power. For most of our history, however, we saw no interests sufficient to justify large-scale wars in Asia. For a century and a half we were interested in our share of the trade with the noncolonial parts of Asia; we sought opportunities and protection for our missionaries; we came to champion the "open door" and territorial integrity of China as a way of keeping open this vast sector of humanity to private American trade, missionary activity, and at times investment; we inadvertently acquired a colony in the Philippines and perceived a strategic vulnerability resulting from this piece of transpacific territory; but none of these interests or involvements were seen by most Americans as a matter of vital national concern.

It was not until the early 1940s, when a rapidly modernizing, industrialized Japan threatened to establish hegemony over the whole of East Asia and this possibility became coupled with a threat of Nazi German hegemony over Western Europe, that we saw our vital interests menaced and became engaged in our first major transpacific war. We came out of that war with the dream that continued cooperation with the Soviet Union and the emergence of a friendly China as the dominant transpacific power would give East Asia stability. We soon awoke to the unreality of this concept and saw ourselves facing instead the threat of a new hostile hegemony in Asia. First we saw this as hegemony by an expanding, Moscow-dominated, international communist movement, which, by gaining control over the vast "third world," might tip the balance of world power decisively against the "free world." The victory of the Chinese Communists over the Nationalists was seen as part of this threat, and the Korean war fitted the pattern. Seen in this light, the stopping of a clear, conventional aggression in Korea was necessary to the defense of vital American interests.

The Vietnam war, despite its origin as an anticolonial, nationalist revolution, was also seen as part of the threat of communist hegemony in Asia, though carried out by subtler techniques of subversion and proxy warfare. Our involvement was based on this view and on the assumption that, unless this wave of indirect aggression were stopped at the dike we were manning in Vietnam, it would spread widely over Asia. In the course of the war, our concept of the source of the threat has shifted from a supposedly unified communist movement to a resurgent, neo-imperialist China; but the fear of hegemony by a hostile power over the half of the world's population that lives in East and South Asia is unchanged.

Today this whole conceptual basis for our transpacific policies is in serious doubt. If the threat of hegemony is real, then we probably cannot stop it by the methods we have adopted. We have found ourselves less able to suppress internal subversion and fight a guerrilla war in an Asian country than we had assumed. Far from preventing the flood waters of communism or Chinese domination from spreading by manning the dikes in Vietnam, we have become so deeply mired there that we could not meet similar challenges elsewhere in Asia without first extricating ourselves from Vietnam. The war has also proved far more costly to our world-wide position than we had ever imagined, and the divisiveness it has caused within our body politic much more disruptive. The early ending of the war has become a national imperative. Even if we are able to achieve this on terms satisfactory to us, the popular reaction against the war at home and abroad would probably preclude similar involvements in other Asian countries in the foreseeable future.

The threat of hegemony by any power over Asia, however, is empty, as the Vietnam war has shown. Vietnam may be a less-developed country, but it is no power vacuum. An Asian people, inspired by nationalism and armed with the techniques of guerrilla warfare, is no longer weakly susceptible to domination by foreign military forces. The Japanese army discovered this truth in the late 1930s in China. We and the French and Dutch had to relearn the lesson after the war.

The old imperialism is dead, and there is no room for new forms of imperialism. Asian countries cannot be controlled from abroad, even through communism or any other ideology. The postwar history of Asia, particularly the determined stand of communist Asians—Chinese, Koreans, and Vietnamese—against any foreign domination, shows that nationalism runs much deeper than political ideologies. There is no reason to believe that neo-imperialists, whether they be international communists or Chinese, can dominate other Asian nations any more successfully than we, the Japanese, or the French.

Nor would control over the less-developed nations of Asia, even if possible, give the controller increased power. These countries are for the most part deficit areas economically, draining rather than enriching a nation that tries to dominate them. Even though they are capable of generating great military strength within their own borders, this strength cannot be marshaled by outsiders. Nor do they have the industrial capacity to permit them or their dominators to project what power they have far afield. External control over less-developed nations in Asia would tend to weaken rather than strengthen the controller.

Thus we find the major objective of our past policies toward Asia, as epitomized by our involvement in Vietnam, impossible to achieve and unnecessary in any case. It may be true that the development of a hostile hegemony over Asia would be against our interests, but in this age of rampant nationalism this threat is only a remote one and therefore should not dominate our policies. We are in need of a new conceptual basis for our transpacific relations.

A multilateral balance of forces in Asia seems far more probable than any sort of hegemony and is fully compatible with our own interests. The achievement of this positive objective should be the major thrust of our efforts rather than the negative policy of preventing hegemony. We can perhaps best contribute to this outcome by consciously avoiding the polarization of power in Asia between ourselves and China and by helping to strengthen the other elements of a multilateral balance of forces.

We need also to distinguish clearly between immediate and long-range interests. Our frantic efforts to stop the supposed threat of hegemony made all problems in Asia seem to be matters of immediate concern. With this threat properly downgraded, our interests in the less-developed countries of Asia, including China, will be seen to be for the most part long range. Their trade and products are not vital to us; nor could they individually or collectively constitute any grave threat to our national interests in the near future.

Over the long run, however, the situation is very different. These countries hold half the population of the world. As distances shrink, and relations between all countries become closer and more fully integrated, and technical skills, including nuclear capabilities, spread, as inevitably will happen, this vast mass of people will come to have increasing impact on our own well-being. If the present great gaps in living standards and opportunities between them and us persist, producing growing resentments on their part, a time may come when a world divided between privileged and underprivileged nations will be in as serious trouble as is a city or country today which permits great discrepancies of opportunity between its citizens. Our chief interest in the less-developed countries of Asia, thus, is in their long-range growth into more prosperous, stable, and satisfied members of a world community.

By contrast we have immediate, vital interests in Japan. It is the third largest industrial unit in the world. Its 100 million people produce two-thirds as great a gross national product as the billion and a half other people of East and South Asia combined. It is growing economically far more rapidly than the rest of Asia as a whole—indeed, roughly twice as fast. As a consequence, our relations of mutual benefit with Japan are far greater than with the rest of Asia and will continue to be so well into the future. For example, Japan follows Canada as our second largest trading partner, accounting for roughly a tenth of our foreign trade. Its industrial power makes it a potential major weight in a world balance of power. It also gives it a capacity no other Asian country has to influence, through economic power and technological skills, the future of the rest of Asia, in ways either favorable or adverse to our interests. And because of geography and Japan's great potentialities, our relationships, both military and political, with most of the rest of the transpacific area are heavily dependent on the nature of our relationship with Japan. Friendship and close cooperation with Japan, as with Western Europe, are therefore matters of immediate, as well as long-term, concern to the United States.

A Vietnam Settlement

Such general principles may be easy to outline, but their translation into specific policies depends on what actually happens in the next few years in a number of highly uncertain and fast-changing situations in Asia. A discussion of the relative merits of specific policies must be subordinated to a consideration of the wide spectrum of possibilities in Asia and an estimation of the probabilities among these various possibilities.

To start with the Vietnam war, an early end may be imperative for the United States, but as of the present writing, the precise nature and timing of a settlement are far from clear. It is perfectly possible that the war will continue for some time on its present or on an expanded scale, that it will be settled through negotiation, or that the United States will in time withdraw unilaterally.

It is hard to believe that a continued or expanded war could lead to either a complete military victory or a complete military defeat for the United States. Much more likely would be a continued stalemate, which because of domestic and world-wide pressures on the United States would probably not be maintainable over the long run, thus producing at a later time one of the two other solutions—a negotiated settlement or withdrawal. The only other possible outcomes of a continued war would be war with China (which neither side could win) or, perhaps less likely, a nuclear holocaust with the Soviet Union.

A negotiated settlement would almost certainly entail the withdrawal of American military power from South Vietnam. What it produces for the South Vietnamese might be a noncommunist but more or less neutral South Vietnamese regime, a communist-leaning country, a chaotic disintegration of all central government, or a thinly disguised communist takeover. All of these seem perfectly possible end results, and it would be hard to assign degrees of probability among them.

American withdrawal might come suddenly because of the collapse of the Saigon government—we would have no other choice, since a puppet or colonial regime would not be a viable alternative today—or because of the collapse of the American home front as a result of violent antiwar sentiment. More probable would be a gradual American withdrawal if a negotiated settlement proves unachievable and domestic and international pressures make it impossible to prosecute the war indefinitely. Such a withdrawal would probably be achieved through a phased transfer of military and other responsibilities from the American forces to the South Vietnamese and a corresponding, step-by-step withdrawal of American and allied forces. This "de-Americanization" of the war is a relatively likely outcome and could produce either a collapse of Saigon or a settlement by Saigon with the Vietnamese Communists somewhere along the spectrum of possible negotiated outcomes outlined above.

What the result of the war proves to be within Vietnam is not in itself of vital importance to the United States. In hindsight, it now seems probable that, if we had never become involved in Vietnam, it would have developed into a unified communist state which would have served as a more effective bar to the expansion of Chinese power than the present war-torn country and, because of fears of Chinese domination, might have been relatively friendly toward the United States, in the Yugoslav style. Because of the war, such a favorable outcome now seems less likely, but in any case, the intense nationalism of the Vietnamese will probably keep Vietnam free of Chinese control or exploitation, and even a unified communist Vietnam, being after all only a relatively small and less-developed country, is not itself likely to prove much of a threat to crucial American interests.

Even though the actual outcome of the war in Vietnam itself may not be of vital concern to us, its impact on us and the rest of the world is of major importance. A humiliating, precipitate withdrawal by the United States or a negotiated settlement that was perceived by the American public as a "sellout" would probably produce a popular revulsion that could lead to dangerous rigidities in our foreign policies in general and might carry this country into a mood of isolationist unconcern for the less-developed nations of Asia and an unwillingness to make significant contributions through economic aid to their future development. (The current downtrend in economic aid appropriations is a clear sign of this danger.) The longer the war lasts and the higher its costs, the greater is the likelihood of these reactions of frustration.

A humiliating, precipitate withdrawal or a sellout would also have adverse repercussions throughout most of Asia, and these would be strengthened by any signs of isolationism in the United States. The communist countries of Asia and subversive elements in the noncommunist states might well be inclined to accept the Maoist doctrine that the United States is, after all, nothing but a "paper tiger" and might, therefore, be encouraged in their efforts to carry out subversion and revolutions throughout Asia, thus making the communist or Chinese ambitions of hegemony a little more plausible and the healthy development of the area somewhat less probable. Neighboring countries, such as Thailand, which depend on American defense commitments, would seriously doubt the continued value of these commitments and would look desperately for other roads to security. India would probably be encouraged to develop its own nuclear weapons, and the Japanese, too, would feel that they must put more emphasis on their own defense, possibly including a nuclear capacity.

Curiously enough, the same result would probably be produced in Japan by a long continuation of the war or its escalation. The argument would gain strength that American military adventurism endangers an allied Japan more than the alliance with the United States provides security, and as a result the mutual security treaty might be broken. This in turn could force the United States to withdraw to mid-Pacific, regardless of how the Vietnam war came out, and might induce the Japanese to go in heavily for rearmament, including the development of nuclear weapons. The result could be the reemergence of the historical and still perhaps most plausible of all possible threats of hegemony in East Asia.

To summarize the conceivable outcomes in Vietnam, we have three broad possibilities. The war may continue indefinitely or even escalate; but this course is likely to lead to a bigger and more dangerous war, a breakdown of our relations with Japan (and possibly with some of our European allies, too), or eventually a massive repudiation of the war at home—or probably some combination of these disasters. A second possibility is a forced, precipitate withdrawal or an obvious sellout, which would be such a humiliation for the United States as to undermine the confidence of Asian countries in us and to produce in the American public a sullen isolationist mood toward Asia, leaving us with little leverage to influence future developments in the transpacific part of the world. Both of these two categories of possibilities would be so disadvantageous to the United States as to be unacceptable as policy objectives.

This leaves us with a third, middle category of possibilities as the only acceptable outcome and the one that our government must do its best to achieve. The rest of this chapter presupposes this outcome, since the other two would so change the situation as to make further speculation at this time about American transpacific policies quite pointless. This middle category would be an ending of the war within a year or so, but in such a way as to leave Americans, despite a complete military withdrawal from Vietnam, still broadly concerned in the future of Asia and Asians still looking to the United States for a continuing, even if less conspicuous, role in their part of the world.

This general result preferably would be the product of a negotiated settlement which, whatever the ultimate outcome in South Vietnam, was not considered by Americans or Asians to be simply a sellout. A negotiated settlement might encompass an agreement between the United States and North Vietnam for mutual military withdrawal from South Vietnam, an agreement made largely between the Saigon government and the Vietcong for a cease-fire and steps toward the achievement of a mutually acceptable political system for South Vietnam, and, it is to be hoped, some international guarantees regarding these agreements and the security of neighboring countries, specifically Laos, Cambodia, and Thailand.

Failing such a negotiated settlement, the acceptable middle outcome would probably have to be achieved through a phased de-Americanization of the war—that is, a gradual unilateral withdrawal. To the extent that de-Americanization could be combined with a successful buildup of the Saigon government, both politically and militarily, and a resultant strengthening of Saigon's bargaining power, it presents perhaps the most realistic road to a middle-range settlement. Possibly such an outcome will be reached through a combination of the de-Americanization process and negotiations. It might even result from a precipitate pullout if, for example, a collapse of the Saigon government was seen as wiping out American commitments.

In any case, however, the matter of timing is crucial. In view of the repercussions of the war both within the United States and abroad, a middle-range outcome will have to be achieved within a year or at the most two, or else one of the other less desirable endings is likely to be unavoidable.

The Prospects for China

Assuming an ending to the Vietnam war of this general type, we should next look at the spectrum of possibilities among the other major variables in Asia. Of these China is probably the biggest and most puzzling. Its huge population—close to a quarter of humanity—combined with a rapid rate of economic growth in the first decade after the Communists took over in 1949 made it seem an incipient third superpower, or to more traditional minds a revived "Golden Horde" or "yellow peril." But in more recent years, the follies of the Great Leap Forward and the disruptions caused by the Cultural Revolution and Red Guard excesses have greatly slowed economic growth—at times to a standstill—and have even threatened centralized control. The country seems to be riven by a deep ideological struggle between Maoist fundamentalists, who stress the importance of right ideas (one hears clear overtones of the ancient Confucian belief in the innate goodness or, at least, perfectibility through education of human nature as the key to all social order), and more pragmatic men, who lay emphasis on technical knowledge and skills. In the course of this conflict, the command structures of both the government and the Communist party have been seriously damaged, and a new command system, apparently based in large part on the army, is still only in the process of development.

This situation gives rise to a wide range of estimates as to China's future stability and growth. Some, influenced by the century of disruption, warlordism, and civil war that preceded the Communist victory, predict the dissolution of China into warlord satrapies. In the light of Chinese success for over two millenniums in holding together the world's largest political unit and the general cohesiveness and remarkable political skills shown by the Communist leadership in the past two decades, this outcome seems improbable despite the present disorders. It may be that, in such a huge country, it will prove necessary to develop patterns of greater decentralization and increased local autonomy, but it is unlikely that such a relaxation of central control would proceed to the point where it seriously limits Chinese foreign policy or endangers, rather than enhances, the chances for economic growth.

But even granted the probability of continued unity, rapid economic growth seems unlikely in China in the near future. The damage done to the command structure must be restored before this would be possible. The reconstruction of the political system will at best require a year or two, and unless the struggle in Peking over basic approaches is resolved soon, the economic slowdown might continue much longer. It would probably take a clear victory by the pragmatists (who would be inclined to put more stress on technical education and skills and on sources of external aid in the Soviet Union or noncommunist nations) before a rapid growth rate could be restored. In our present state of ignorance, however, it would be useless to speculate as to how likely this is.

Thus political uncertainties in China preclude firm estimates regarding its economic prospects. A reasonable guess, however, would be that Chinese growth rates will stay below the average for the less-developed countries of Asia during the next five years. Compared with Japan, China will undoubtedly lose ground as an economic power. Its gross national product is only about two-thirds that of Japan at present, and over the next five years its growth rate is likely to be only a half or a third as high. The discrepancy in economic power between China and the United States or the Soviet Union is even greater—perhaps one-eighth of ours and one-fourth of the Soviets'—and these great gaps are not likely to shrink in the next few years. Thus, relative to the outside world, China is likely to become weaker economically during the next five years rather than stronger.

China's domestic political and economic prospects are of interest to us largely for their possible influence on its foreign policies. There can be no doubt about China's hostility toward the United States or, for that matter, toward most of the outside world. In part, this is the product of a fundamentalist belief in the Marxist-Leninist premises that capitalism produces imperialism and imperialism leads to war and that the only cure for this menacing situation is world-wide communist revolution. The United States, as the largest "capitalist" nation, is seen as the chief enemy —the major threat to China's safety and world peace; any country that cooperates with us is regarded as an accomplice; and the Soviet Union and other communists who tolerate "peaceful coexistence" are scorned as traitors to the cause.

Communist dogma, however, is not the sole source of Chinese hostility toward us and the rest of the world. It springs more deeply from a sense of national humiliation at the hands of outsiders—particularly the West. For long, Chinese thought of themselves as constituting the only nation of true civilization, the Central Country, surrounded only by barbarians. For most, if not all, of China's twenty-two centuries of existence as a more or less unified political system, it has been the largest political unit in the world, and for a thousand years (roughly 600 to 1600) it was the most advanced in most measurable terms. Deep Chinese assumptions of superiority have been rudely challenged during the past century by crude domination, exploitation, and constant humiliation at the hands of outside powers, mostly Western. The Chinese have a great hungering, not just for communist revolution throughout the world, but for the restoration of their country to the position of a great world leader—perhaps the greatest world leader, as the nation that sets the pace toward the promised land of the true faith.

The combination of communist belief and Chinese pride—the exact mix is debatable—helps explain China's hostility toward almost all of the outside world. It also underlies China's extreme sensitivity to the supposed American menace and its determined efforts to undermine the United States and most other nations through world-wide revolution. Maoists see this—in terms of their own revolutionary experience—as the mobilization of the world peasantry (the masses of the less-developed nations) against the landlords and city bourgeoisie of the world (the former colonial powers and the advanced nations in general). The question, however, is to what extent China is willing to translate these attitudes and hopes into action abroad and how successful it will be in its efforts.

First comes the question of China's will and capacity for military aggressiveness. Its traditional tendency to look inward rather than outward and its constant emphasis on revolution rather than military conquest suggest that conventional military aggression does not figure prominently in Chinese strategy. The very violence of China's rhetoric tends to strengthen (and perhaps purposely so) China's isolation and actual inward-looking stance. Nor have past military involvements on the part of the Chinese Communists been, at least in their own eyes, aggressive. Their participation in the Korean war was to fend off an American military threat to their Manchurian industrial base. As they remembered all too well, the Japanese road to imperialist domination had led from South Korea through North Korea into Manchuria. The Tibetan campaign was to bring back under control an errant province China had ruled, albeit loosely, for some centuries. The war on the Indian frontier, as the Chinese saw it, was to clarify a border line which the Indians, like their British rulers before them, had refused to respect. The provision of weapons and construction battalions to North Vietnam has been to help a fraternal country keep the American threat away from another of China's menaced borders. Thus the Chinese, for all their bellicose verbiage, have not in fact proved military expansionists.

China's capacity for military aggression also seems to be as limited as its will. Its huge populations, xenophobic nationalism, and experience in mass organization and guerrilla warfare make it an unbeatable adversary on its own terrain. It is very formidable in directly contiguous areas, as we discovered in North Korea and would probably again in North Vietnam if we pushed close to the Chinese frontiers there. But China does not possess the sea and air power or the logistic capacities to extend its military power far from home. The Chinese, with their massive land armies, could probably overrun nearby countries like Burma, Vietnam, or Thailand, but they probably could not hold them, much less exploit them successfully, if strong pressure were put on their lines of communication and there were, as seems predictable, determined nationalistic opposition within these countries. In fact, the weak Chinese economy might collapse under the strain of even such modest conquests. Successful occupation of a huge and much more distant country like India would be out of the question and conquest of overseas countries like Indonesia, the Philippines, and Japan a mere pipe dream—unless all naval power disappeared from the western Pacific.

The development by China of nuclear weapons does not change the military equation greatly. Peking will probably have a modest deliverable capacity within the next five years, and this in theory will give it a chance to play the game of nuclear blackmail against its nonnuclear neighbors. It seems very doubtful, however, that a Chinese nuclear threat will be credible enough to have much blackmail value. Neither the United States nor the Soviet Union could afford to let such a threat go unchallenged, and it seems altogether likely that they would see their interests in the matter coinciding in opposition to China's. Under these circumstances and in view of China's tiny nuclear capacity as compared with that of either the United States or the Soviet Union, it seems inconceivable that China would wish to initiate the use of nuclear weapons, and it is improbable therefore that its neighbors would feel themselves greatly menaced by them.

The reason why the Chinese have expended so much of their meager technical skills and resources on developing a nuclear capacity probably lies in their hope of enhancing thereby their claim to be a superpower and of deterring, even a little, what they regard as the American threat to China. They could not have hoped that their feeble nuclear arsenal, in the face of vastly greater ones, would give them much leverage over their neighbors. The impact of a Chinese nuclear capacity is much more psychological than military—in strengthening their own self-esteem and in stimulating desires among their neighbors, particularly Indians but also Japanese to some extent, to develop nuclear weapons, too. This double psychological influence has in large part already had its effect. The further development of nuclear weapons by China is therefore not likely to have a great added impact of any sort.

In this connection, the proposed development by the United States of a "thin" ABM (antiballistic missile) defense against China seems particularly unwise. It is obviously not needed to deter a Chinese nuclear attack against us and might therefore be interpreted by the Chinese as making an American nuclear attack on them more likely and by other Asians as insulating the United States from the Chinese nuclear problem. Thus, while not doing anything useful for the United States in terms of defense, it could increase Chinese fear and hostility and might help undermine the confidence of other Asian countries in our concern for their security.

China's economic capacity to extend its control over other countries is even more limited than its military ability. The almost exclusively Chinese population of Hong Kong and the largely Chinese population of Singapore make trade with China important to these two "city-states" (Hong Kong in addition is entirely defenseless against Chinese military power), but otherwise no Asian country has any important trade with China. Japan is China's chief trading partner, but a flow that amounted to about 13 percent of China's foreign trade in 1967 accounted for about 2.5 percent of Japan's. That Japan's trade should be about five times that of China's shows how small China's economic leverage is on the outside world. By careful concentration and manipulation, it can use its economic resources for political influence in some parts of the world (its efforts so far have been more in terms of promises than performance), but its capacities for wide and sustained economic influence are very meager when compared with those of the United States, the Soviet Union, Japan, or the major European countries.

This leaves political influence and subversion as China's chief means of acquiring influence or possibly control over other Asian countries. There can be no doubt about China's enthusiastic determination to spread subversion and revolution throughout the world, and it has considerable capacity to do so. During the past two decades, it has demonstrated its ability to exercise political influence, instigate subversion, train revolutionaries, and feed subversive and guerrilla movements with arms and supplies, not only in Asian countries, but as far afield as Africa.

China's record in these efforts, however, has been spotty. In the first heady decade of Communist rule, China's prestige and influence were high throughout much of the less-developed world, but both have dropped sharply in recent years. In part this has been a reflection of the troubles within China, in part the natural resentment of people everywhere to outside meddling. Each national group wants to march to its own drums. Appreciation for Chinese aid in starting a revolution can easily turn to fear of Chinese domination or resentment of Chinese arrogance, which is as great as that of any of the former colonial masters.

The large populations of overseas Chinese in Southeast Asia are considered by some to be a help to China in its subversive activities or in its more legitimate efforts to extend political influence. The influence of the overseas Chinese, however, is counterproductive to Chinese interests in some cases. In countries where the Chinese population runs high, such as Singapore (74 percent) and Malaysia (37 percent), direct Chinese influence or Chinese-backed subversion could be a very real threat. In areas with smaller Chinese populations, such as Indonesia (about 3 percent), popular resentments against the Chinese minority tend to offset China's influence and discredit Chinese-backed movements.

The threat of the spread of Chinese domination in Asia through political influence or subversion, while more real than the military and economic threats, is not very great and has its built-in limitations. To date no Chinese-instigated or supported subversion has succeeded, and some, as in Indonesia, have failed catastrophically. (Vietnam is not a case in point, since the revolution there has been from the first basically a native movement, and Chinese support has been significant only after it turned into a war between North Vietnam and the United States.) Nor is there any reason to believe that if a Chinese-backed subversive movement were successful it would remain for long under Chinese domination. The whole postwar history of communism points in the opposite direction. Thus subversion may prove a more feasible means than military aggression or economic pressure for China to bring down regimes in Asia that it dislikes, but it is not likely to be a way by which it can extend hegemony over Asia.

China Policy

All this suggests that the containment of Chinese expansionism is not as serious a problem as has been assumed and that a China policy which centers on this concept is largely misdirected. This is particularly true since close-in military containment and the effort to keep China politically and economically isolated (which has usually accompanied this policy) tend to increase and perpetuate the psychological pressures that have helped produce Chinese hostility toward us. They heighten Chinese fears of America's supposed aggressiveness and exacerbate the old resentments of Western failure to perceive China's greatness and accord it true equality. At the same time, they have no appreciable curbing effect on the chief area of the Chinese threat, which is subversive activities.

The reasonable choices in China policy are relatively narrow, lying in the spectrum between continuing our present stance and an effort at reconciliation and the relaxation of tensions. The choice should not be difficult. Our present stance heightens Chinese hostility but otherwise is unproductive. An effort at reconciliation might produce no specific results, but it would at least lessen the psychological pressures which help generate Chinese intransigence and at the same time reduce the heavy costs we pay in much of the world for what is generally considered to be an unwise China policy.

To be specific, we should drop our sham that China exists only in the form of the small, rump Nationalist regime on Taiwan and admit clearly that continental China ruled from Peking is the true, historical China. We should drop our use of the word "containment" as applying specifically to China and subsume it under our world-wide stand against aggression. We should drop our pretense that our embargo on trade helps limit China's capacity to be an aggressor and should make clear our readiness to trade with China in nonstrategic goods. The truth of the matter is that China does all the trade of which it is capable, principally with our closest allies—Japan, the United Kingdom, West Germany, Canada, and Australia. We should drop our effort to keep China out of the United Nations. The moral judgment implied in the blackballing of the largest nonwhite nation by the most powerful white nation is deeply insulting to Chinese and irritating to many other people in the world. Communist China would probably be a disruptive force if it entered the United Nations, but this would be less costly to us than our present blackball. In the long run, moreover, the educational value of China's presence in the United Nations in what it learned about the outside world and in what other U.N. members learned about China would probably more than outweigh its disruptive activities in the organization.

Such changes in American policies toward China should be accompanied by a relaxation of our close-in military containment. For example, we might remove our nuclear weapons from Okinawa, which are targeted on China but have been made obsolescent by Polaris submarines and intercontinental ballistic missiles (ICBMs). We also might eliminate all American bases in continental Southeast Asia in connection with the termination of the Vietnam war. This might not entail any curtailment of our capacity to stop Chinese aggression, because advances in technology are increasing our military mobility, but even if it did, this reduction in capacity would probably be more than offset by a decline in the likelihood of Chinese military action abroad. We should also favor, rather than oppose, an attitude of discreet respect and circumspect neutrality toward China on the part of its smaller neighbors. This is only natural and wise for small neighbors of big countries (for example, the attitude of Finland toward the Soviet Union), since by reducing tensions it would give these countries greater security than would open hostility.

China's responses to a changed American stance would probably not be great, at least at first. It would probably not be prepared to let de facto recognition grow into diplomatic recognition. It probably would prefer not to trade with us—it has its economic hands full with our allies. It probably would not choose to enter the United Nations. But such a change of stance on our part would reduce the psychological pressures on China and open the way to a more positive reconciliation at some time in the future. It might even facilitate the emergence of a leadership in Peking that would be more inclined to adopt a policy of peaceful coexistence with us. Incidentally, we should bear in mind that the Vietnam negotiations may offer opportunities for progress toward reconciliation with China and its engagement in a wider world order, through participation in an international settlement of the war, through arrangements for U.N. membership as a part of the settlement, or in other ways.

Peking, of course, has said that the only real way for the United States to relax tensions with China is to stop our "imperialist occupation" of Taiwan and hand it back. This probably is a correct description of its attitude. But this is not a point on which we can show much flexibility. The thirteen million people of Taiwan seem almost unanimous in their desire to remain free of Chinese Communist control. They have every right to self-determination, and Taiwan in fact has had a political experience distinct from that of continental China for almost three-quarters of a century. Given these facts, our historic relations with the Nationalist regime on Taiwan, and our firm belief in the right of self-determination, we could scarcely try to force Taiwan to rejoin China or acquiesce in its conquest by Peking, even though Taiwan's separateness does delay our reconciliation with China.

We should, however, clearly divorce our support of self-determination in Taiwan from Nationalist claims to be the only China or even one of "two Chinas." Our stand should be that we recognize the existence of two separate political entities, whatever their names; that both merit representation in the United Nations (Taiwan is among the top third of the members of the United Nations in population); that we would not oppose reconciliation between Taiwan and the mainland if it should come; but that in the meantime the unit ruled from Peking is obviously the country assigned the permanent seat in the Security Council. We should be ready to accept any names and theories the two Chinese entities and the United Nations devise, so long as they fit these facts. An independent Taiwan should be acceptable to us or a Taiwan which theoretically is part of China but has full autonomy and, on analogy with the spuriously labeled autonomous Ukraine and Byelorussia, a separate U.N. seat. If representation for the two Chinese entities does not prove feasible, we should recognize that the loss of Taiwan's membership in the United Nations would probably be less costly to overall American interests than the continuation of our blackball of Peking.

Since Taiwan is an island, we can at no great risk continue to guarantee its security from Peking, so long as the people and government on Taiwan really want this. But the Nationalist occupation and garrisoning of Quemoy and Matsu, two small island clusters close to the mainland, are another matter. They do not contribute to the defense of Taiwan but rather weaken it by isolating a large part of the Nationalist forces from the real task of defense. The chief role of these islands is as a symbol of the Nationalists' determination to continue the civil war and of their empty dream of reconquering the mainland. The United States should make it clear that it will not participate in the defense of these islands. It should also use what leverage it has to try to persuade the Nationalists to evacuate them as military and political liabilities.

Some people feel that an American refusal to continue the pretense that Taiwan is China might so anger the Nationalist regime that it would submit to Peking in an act of political suicide. Another not uncommon view is that when Chiang Kai-shek dies (he is now 81), his successor, quite possibly his Russian-trained son Chiang Ching-kuo, may "make a deal" with Peking. Either of these possibilities would result in a grave injustice to the inhabitants of Taiwan, 85 percent of whom are native Taiwanese who have no desire to be merged with continental China. But neither of these possible developments is at all probable, and in any case they are matters over which we have little control.

The inhabitants of Taiwan are a relatively affluent and well-educated people who are thoroughly capable of developing a prosperous and eventually democratic society. This obviously would be to American interests, somewhat offsetting the brake on reconciliation with China that an independent Taiwan constitutes. The pretense of the Nationalist government that Taiwan is only one of many provinces over which it has authority and its basically dictatorial nature stand in the way of this favorable development. The United States should look with sympathy on the growth of full democracy in Taiwan and the resultant preponderance of the native Taiwanese majority in the political life of the island. But there is little specific we can do to insure such developments. We should be clear in our own minds that the future of Taiwan lies primarily in the hands of the government and people on Taiwan to decide and that we can accommodate ourselves to almost any outcome without great menace to our own vital national interests.

To summarize the range of possibilities with regard to China, they run from a Chinese political breakup or a sudden shift by China to a policy of peaceful coexistence, at one end of the spectrum, to war with the United States or a massive Chinese impact on surrounding Asian areas, at the other end. If either of these extremes materializes, it would so change the situation in Asia as to require careful rethinking of American policies, but neither is at all likely, short of major escalation of the Vietnam war or an American pullout from all Asia. Much more probable is a general continuation of present conditions, with China slowly setting its house in order but playing a declining role for the time being in the rest of Asia and the United States relaxing military and psychological pressures on China in preparation for eventual reconciliation.

The Situation in the Less-developed Countries

Shifting to the other less-developed countries of East and South Asia, we find a very broad spectrum of possibilities. If the war in Vietnam escalates greatly, or if the United States as a result of the outcome in Vietnam withdraws its interest in and aid to other Asian countries, or if China proves to have a much greater capacity to extend its influence over these countries than the discussion in this chapter has implied, serious disruptions throughout Asia would probably result, and future developments would be quite unpredictable at this stage. If we assume, however, a tolerable outcome in Vietnam and developments in China in the middle range described above, the spectrum of possibilities becomes narrower and American policies more definable.

It would be impossible in the confines of this chapter to outline the economic and political prospects for all of the nations of the region. Each is a unique case with its own specific conditions that will largely shape its future: size, geographic location, ethnic and religious makeup, regional differences, cultural heritage, political and social traditions, colonial experience, and the present political and social situation. It would not be practical to attempt to list and analyze all these factors country by country, but a few generalizations may be of help.

Most of the countries of Asia are slowly solidifying as national units and therefore are becoming less susceptible to disintegrative forces. Where food deficits have existed, they are beginning to be overcome, and most countries show a promising trend toward economic growth, commonly at rates double or triple the rate of population increase. The development of educational and political institutions on the whole shows promise of bringing even more widespread and rapid development in the future. But almost all of these countries remain relatively unstable and susceptible to political upheaval, to subversion, and if there were a powerful attacker, to military aggression. Thus the long-run prospects for economic and institutional development are fair to good, but the short-term prospects for political stability are dubious.

A common view has been that either international communism or a neo-imperialist China might achieve hegemony over Asia by toppling one country after another in geographic succession in a falling-domino effect. Prolonged political instability, whatever its cause, could also so disrupt Asia that its long-range, healthy development would become impossible. Widespread disorders or upheavals would obviously be upsetting to all the countries in the area. Local wars, such as those between Indonesia and Malaysia and between Pakistan and India, have scarcely been helpful to either party. Efforts to stir up subversion from abroad could be a menace to almost any of the countries of the area, though we should remember that the Indonesian Communist coup backfired and that Chinese and North Vietnamese efforts in northeast Thailand and recent Chinese interest in the long-standing communist movements in Burma and in the Naga disturbance in India have not produced major results.

Some particularly weak countries are relatively open to domination or disruption by their neighbors. Thus North Vietnamese support for the Pathet Lao has for years threatened Laos, which has only a light population of two and a half million people, divided almost evenly between ethnically alien Montagnard groups and the Laos themselves, who are not ethnically distinct from the northeastern Thai. All of the long, thin, and extremely backward country of Laos lies completely in the shadow of the much more populous, better organized, more advanced, and far more aggressive Vietnamese state. It seems probable, therefore, that regardless of the outcome of the Vietnam war the Vietnamese will have a major influence over the future of Laos.

Most other Asian countries, however, are not very susceptible to domination or even subversion by their neighbors. Practically all are far more populous and historically and geographically more consolidated entities than Laos. For some, such as India because of its size or the Philippines because of its geographic isolation as an island group, domination or disruption by a neighbor is all but impossible.

On the whole, the countries of Asia have relatively little contact with one another and no great capacity to stir up trouble for each other. Pressures from other Asian countries are in most cases very minor compared with the influence of purely domestic conditions, such as regional, ethnic, or religious tensions, economic conditions, the efficiency of the government, and the people's attitude toward it. Political upheavals and revolutions resulting from such internal factors are much more likely than disruptions from external causes.

While it is in our interests to do what we can to discourage conflict and subversion between Asian lands, particularly when such disturbances threaten to involve the great powers, there is very little chance that a falling-domino process of disruption or subversion will occur on a large scale and even less that it will lead to any effective, exploitable control by a hostile power over much of Asia. The major military question we face in the less-developed countries of Asia is our role in cases of internal instability within those countries.

As we have seen in Vietnam, our capacity to control internal instability at a reasonable cost to ourselves or the country we seek to help is very limited. Our technological and economic aid may be important, but our efforts to help directly through military action are not very effective in cases of guerrilla warfare and may even be counterproductive. Our racial and cultural background is reminiscent of the erstwhile colonial masters and thus makes our opponents seem like better nationalists than the side we support. Our large-scale mode of operation and its economic consequences are likely to disrupt the local society, distorting the natural economy and spreading corruption. Our very participation may relieve the regime in power of the necessity of trying to correct the economic, social, or political ills that may in large part be responsible for the insurgency.

One general rule of thumb might be that, if an Asian regime is not able to control internal instability even with our economic and technological aid, it probably could not be saved by us through military intervention and, beyond that, is not likely to be worth trying to save. A more general rule would be that less-developed countries in Asia and elsewhere will probably experience frequent revolutionary upheavals, and many of these will be necessary stages in the development process, because these countries are going through rapid changes in their efforts to modernize but, for the most part, lack highly developed democratic institutions through which to effect political change without revolution. Coups d'etat and revolutions are the only way some societies have to get rid of undesirable governments and ineffective leadership. Thus the United States not only cannot suppress most internal instabilities in less-developed countries but, in its own interests and those of the countries concerned, should not try to do so even if it could.

Actually, political instability in the less-developed countries of Asia need be of no great concern to us. We do not even need to be particularly worried lest some of them adopt communist or other dictatorial forms of government, so long as their nationalistic ardor prevents effective prolonged external control over them. Freer economic and political institutions would probably be preferable, as being more conducive over the long run to healthy growth, and we should give what encouragement we can to the development of such free institutions, but we must realize that most Asian countries do not have the prerequisites in wealth, skills, education, or experience for efficient democratic government and that we do not have the capacity or, for that matter, the right to determine their institutions for them. Political instability will probably continue for some time in most of Asia, and economic and political systems, no doubt, will continue to change in response largely to internal forces. Under these circumstances, we should be careful not to tie ourselves to any specific regime in a less-developed country.

Policy toward the Less-developed Countries

As already indicated, America's only vital immediate interest in the area is the prevention of hegemony by a hostile power over most of Asia, and its only vital long-range interest is the economic and institutional development of these nations as healthy units in a world community. In the lack of any real threat of hegemony, the major policy questions the United States faces concern the means by which it can best aid the economic growth and political and social development of the nations of the area.

The various considerations discussed above suggest three basic principles for the elaboration of American policy toward the less-developed countries of East and South Asia. We should do our best, through economic and technological aid, to assist them in their long-range development; we should use our military power and political influence to give them as stable an external environment as possible for their internal development, attempting to minimize the threat to them of domination or disruption by an outside force; but we should at the same time try to avoid commitments to or direct involvement in the maintenance of stability within each country.

Of these three principles, the constructive one of providing economic and technological aid should undoubtedly be the central focus of American policy toward the less-developed countries, not only of Asia, but of the whole world. The problem of aid is dealt with more fully by Max Millikan in his paper on "The United States and the Low-Income Countries." It will be sufficient here to say that, in addition to increasing our efforts and improving our own methods for giving aid, we should do our best to encourage an increased participation in this activity by other advanced countries, such as Japan, the countries of Western Europe, and even the Soviet Union.

There is a tendency today to disparage aid programs, but despite considerable ineptitude in the past and some misdirection of effort, our achievements in this field in Asia have been promising and our skills have greatly improved. Taiwan is a brilliant success story; South Korea is not far behind; and Thailand is well on its way to sustained economic growth. India, with a half billion people, and Pakistan, with more than a hundred million, have made considerable progress but present particular problems of size that call for continuing, large-scale aid. Indonesia, another giant with more than a hundred million people, is an especially critical case, because the deterioration of the economy brought on by Sukarno's irresponsible policies has still not been fully stemmed. The Philippines has achieved only a disappointingly uneven record in both economic and institutional growth, and Burma, because of its political rigidities and self-imposed economic isolation, has gone steadily downhill. Vietnam, as well as Laos and Cambodia, will be in great need of constructive external aid when the war ends. Thus the needs are great and the problems many, but there is good reason to believe that a concerted effort by the United States, Japan, and the other advanced nations to help the economic and institutional development of the lower income countries of Asia can contribute greatly to the achievement of our long-range objectives in that part of the world.

We should be extremely careful, however, to draw clear lines that will prevent our future aid from growing into military involvement. The general perspectives of our problems in Asia, as discussed above, suggest that we should put much less emphasis on military aid, in contrast to strictly economic aid, than we have in the past. There may be cases, however, when it would be wise to provide arms or even military training to an Asian government. The more efficient, forward-looking, or democratic a regime is, the more it might merit aid of this sort. Further, the greater the external threat it faces or the more widespread the external support for an insurgency underway, the more reason there would be to provide such help. But there should be clear cutoff points and a periodic check to be sure that these are not being exceeded. In most countries, our aid efforts probably should stay entirely out of the military field. In the others to which we do give arms, a sharp line should be drawn either against providing constabulary or military training or at least against providing combat advisers.

Our military and political role in helping to provide a stable external environment without becoming involved in maintaining internal stability also needs careful definition. One element of this policy would be a nuclear guarantee (possibly joined in by the Soviets) of all countries against nuclear blackmail by the Chinese or any other nuclear power. Such a guarantee could be explicit or tacit, but in either case China and other nuclear powers should be made to understand that a nuclear attack by them would elicit a nuclear response by us that would destroy their nuclear capacity and possibly inflict other damage as well.

Another element would be the maintenance of sufficient military power in the western Pacific to give us the option, though not the commitment, to stop aggression by China or between other Asian countries if the attempt seemed feasible and worthwhile in terms of the specific situation. The existence of such an option would have a strong inhibiting effect on all would-be aggressors and particularly on those whose aggression would be most likely to prompt an American response, such as a North Korean attack on South Korea or an open Chinese attack on one of its neighbors. Some uncertainty as to American responses actually might be more advantageous than too clear a distinction between situations in which the United States would or would not respond.

Because of increasing military mobility, a credible military option of this sort could be maintained in the western Pacific in large part through bases in Guam, Hawaii, and the continental United States, but the continuance of American bases in Japan or at least close defense cooperation with that country would also probably be necessary, as is discussed below. It would be best, however, not to have this military option depend on bases in less-developed countries. The inevitable instability of such countries makes bases in them less secure over the long run, and the presence of American bases is more likely to involve the United States in problems of internal instability. Cases in point, besides Vietnam, would be the airfields in Thailand and in time possibly Clark Field and Subic Bay in the Philippines and the bases in South Korea.

The extension of this military option into the Indian Ocean area on a truly credible scale would probably require broader international participation, particularly if the United States were to give up its Southeast Asian bases. Bases in Western Australia and Australian naval participation might help toward this end, but ultimately, a truly international force is the only real answer. Similarly, the inhibitory role of military power in the western Pacific, too, might best be entrusted some day to international forces and eventually the United Nations itself. But all this would depend on long-range developments in the United Nations and elsewhere that are quite beyond prediction today.

Minimizing American military commitments to Asian countries would require relatively few changes in actual commitments, but a considerable change in attitudes. Our commitment through the Anzus treaty to the defense of Australia and New Zealand presents no problem, because both, as advanced, stable, and remote island countries, are easily defended. Japan, South Korea, Taiwan, and the Philippines, with which we have bilateral treaties, are all special cases, best considered individually. The Southeast Asia Treaty Organization (SEATO), organized in 1954, presents the greatest problems, having given us commitments to the continental countries of Thailand, Pakistan, and through considerable extension, South Vietnam and Laos.

We have no military commitments to the other South and Southeast Asian countries, only implicit concern in their future. When India was attacked by China in 1962, we quickly responded with offers of arms and supplies. When Indonesia underwent its upheavals in 1965, we stood aside and offered no comment, though the presence of our Seventh Fleet in the western Pacific no doubt insured that the Chinese Communists or other outsiders would not attempt to intervene. These are the patterns of noncommitment but helpful influence we should attempt to follow.

It would be best if the countries of this whole area were not involved in the broader world rivalries, such as those between the United States and the Soviet Union or China. In other words, an attitude of neutrality on their part should not only be tolerated by us but welcomed. So also should the present trend toward regional organizations. It must be admitted that such groupings are not likely to contribute much to internal stability or regional security within the next few years. But they can develop useful organs of economic and technological cooperation and a valuable sense of regional political solidarity that could give strength to all the participants. Over the long run these regional groupings can prove immensely significant.

The military commitments we already have to Asian countries must be handled on a case-by-case basis. Our relationship with Japan is treated in a later section. Since the Philippines and Taiwan are island states which we can easily defend from external aggression and since we have had particularly close historic ties with both, we can safely and properly continue our defense commitments to them, but we should be careful that we do not get involved in trying to maintain internal stability. The situation is particularly critical in the Philippines. Unsatisfactory economic growth, mounting corruption, increasing lawlessness, and declining morale all spell trouble. Our bases in the Philippines, our long emotional involvement in the islands, and the tendency of the Filipinos to resent our influence in their country but to rely on us to solve their problems are all likely to involve us in any revolutionary breakdown. We should take resolute steps—including possibly the relinquishment of our Philippine bases—to disengage ourselves from the internal instabilities of the Philippines, so that the local leaders will be forced to face their problems themselves and, if they fail to do so, a more competent leadership will replace them.

In the case of South Korea, the dangers of aggression are greater, but the risks of internal instability are less and the stakes are higher, because past history gives a world-wide significance to the communist-"free" balance in Korea and its geography involves it in the security of Japan. South Korea's recent spectacular success in both economic and institutional development has made the North Koreans extremely anxious to stop this growth before the North is completely overshadowed by the more populous South, in the manner East Germany is overshadowed by West Germany. Under these circumstances, we should continue our clear commitment to the security of South Korea so as to minimize the danger of aggression by the North. We should also probably continue our military presence in South Korea until there is less tension in the area than there is today.

Turning to continental South Asia, we should note that our military commitment to Pakistan has long since eroded away because of Pakistan's disinterest in SEATO. As we have seen, the settlement of the Vietnam war will probably entail the withdrawal of our military forces from and commitments to Vietnam and possibly our commitments to Laos, too. It is also likely to lead to a withdrawal from our bases in Thailand, which have been used exclusively for the bombing of Vietnam, and an understanding that we will not become directly involved in combatting insurgency movements in Thailand. The Thais have already made it clear that, while they appreciate our support, they do not want our direct participation in the small insurgency movements in the northeast or elsewhere in Thailand. Thus our post-Vietnam relationship with Thailand is likely to approximate our relationship with the other South and Southeast Asian countries: we would give aid, including arms and military training when appropriate, to a government deserving such support; we would maintain the option of coming to its aid militarily in the case of blatant aggression, if this seemed feasible and worthwhile; but we would not ourselves become involved in the suppression of internal subversion or revolution.

In summary, no clear prognosis can be given for the South and East Asian area as a whole, except to say that continued internal instabilities are probable, but wide hegemony by any power is highly unlikely, and long-range development for most of the area seems predictable. The United States should attempt to stay uninvolved in internal instabilities while contributing as much as it safely can through its military presence in the western Pacific to an external environment of stability and as much as it can afford through economic and technological aid to long-range development of the various countries of the region. Other advanced nations should be encouraged to participate, not only in aiding the development of this area, but in providing it an external environment of stability. But, basically, developments in this area should be left to natural local forces, especially since the greatest of these forces is nationalism, which works strongly against the spread of any hegemony over the region and for the development of each nation as an independent unit.

Japan's Role in Asia

Our relations with Japan, as we have seen, are of a different kind and on a different time scale from those with the rest of Asia. In fact, they bear more resemblance to our relations with Western Europe than with Japan's neighbors. As our second largest trading partner, Japan is of great and immediate economic importance to us. As our chief ally in Asia, in whose territory are located the bases that serve as the keystone for our military posture in the western Pacific, Japan is crucial to our whole military position in East Asia. Most important, as the third largest industrial unit in the world and the fastest growing major country, Japan is potentially a significant element in a world balance of power and an even larger factor in the future development of all of East and South Asia.

Japan is already the largest trading partner of many of the countries of Southeast Asia, and it shows signs of becoming a major source of economic and technological aid to the whole region. In other words, it is developing into our chief partner in the task of providing aid to the countries of Asia in their long-term development. The activities of both countries in this field increasingly complement each other, and each of us by our presence could help offset the fears of the countries of the region of domination by one or the other, if it alone were influential in the area.

Japan can also contribute to the multilateral balance of forces in Asia that is a feasible and desirable alternative to hegemony by any one nation or the present polarization of forces. As the one large, modernized and industrialized nation in the area, it lends a great deal of strength to regional groupings by its membership in them. The same is true of Australia and New Zealand, though on a lesser scale because of their smaller populations and less convincing geographic, cultural, or racial ties with the rest of the area. The three together could play a useful pivotal role between the other advanced nations and the less-developed countries of Asia. From this point of view, there is merit in Japanese suggestions that the advanced Pacific nations—that is, the United States, Canada, Japan, Australia, and New Zealand—should form a "Pacific Community" of donors with special interest in the less-developed countries of Asia but that Japan, Australia, and New Zealand should also continue as members of regional Asian groupings.

Japan could play an even more important pivotal role with regard to China. There is danger that a détente between the Soviet Union and the United States, however beneficial in the rest of the world, might in effect produce a sort of alliance against China, further isolating that great country and increasing the psychological pressures which help produce its hostility toward the rest of the world. A Japan nestled quietly under the protection of a Soviet-American "alliance" would contribute further to this political polarization in Asia. But a Japan that is a more independent influence might in time help bridge the gap to China and thus aid in the development of a multilateral balance of forces between China, Japan, the United States, and the Soviet Union, under which India and the other nations of South and East Asia would be freer from external pressure for their own internal development. The fact that the Chinese are very much more responsive to Japanese attitudes than to American or Soviet ones and are apparently more eager for Japanese friendship suggests the possible role of Japan in reducing political polarization and tensions between China and the outside world.

On the other hand, a Japan that sees its interests in terms at variance with ours could have an immediately dangerous impact on American interests. In relative terms it is essentially a stronger country today than it was when it threatened to establish hegemony over East Asia in the 1940s.

Its close alignment with the Soviet Union or China against us could produce a dangerous shift in the world balance of power.

Such a development is highly improbable, but there is a possibility that the Japanese might refuse us further cooperation in mutual defense and force a withdrawal of our bases from Japan. If this were to happen, the United States might not be able to continue to guarantee the defense of South Korea or maintain enough of a military presence in the western Pacific to inhibit aggressors. There would, of course, be strong pressures in favor of continuing our military posture through our relationship with South Korea, Taiwan, and the Philippines, but it would be much more costly, difficult, and dangerous to do so if Japan were uncooperative. Japan's technology and industrial capacity, its fundamental stability, and in some ways its geographic position, all make American bases in Japan more valuable than bases elsewhere in Asia, and, if Japan were uncooperative or hostile, it would in a sense lie athwart our routes to other potential bases in the area. In any case, if Japan, which benefits more directly from American efforts to maintain an environment of external stability in East Asia than we do ourselves, were to refuse its cooperation, it would probably not seem worthwhile to Americans to continue such efforts at increased costs to themselves. The United States, regardless of how the war came out in Vietnam, might in that case withdraw its military power to mid-Pacific and, because of the resultant lessening of popular interest in Asia, might further reduce or entirely eliminate its role as a provider of economic aid to Asia.

If this were to happen, the Japanese, forced themselves to provide fully for the defense of their country and its maritime life lines, would probably throw off their present strong pacifistic inhibitions and devote their energies to large-scale rearmament, probably developing in the process their own nuclear umbrella and a substitute for our Seventh Fleet. (Japan's present "self-defense forces" of some 240,000 men would be adequate only against a limited attack and are thought by most Japanese to be barred by their constitution from the defense of Japanese interests abroad.) The result would probably be some slowing down of Japan's own economic growth, a serious check on its efforts in the field of economic aid, growing hostility toward Japan on the part of its neighbors, less economic growth and probably greater turmoil among the other countries of Asia as a consequence of lessened aid from both the United States and Japan, and possibly even military rivalry between the United States and this one Asian nation really capable of being a military threat to our interests.

The road Japan takes over the next few years could thus have a profound impact on our interests and on the future of Asia as a whole. Fortunately, there is one very strong reason for believing that its choice of roads will be compatible with our interests. This is the fact that most Japanese actually have the same basic interests we do. All Japanese hope ardently for world peace, and most of them see this as best achieved in a multilateral world of independent nation states living under some system of international law, as symbolized by the United Nations. Most of them believe strongly in maximizing world trade. Most of them also favor a society with the greatest feasible room for individual freedom, organized politically along democratic lines. Their own government is a variant of the English type of parliamentary democracy.

At the same time, there are reasons why the Japanese may choose less favorable roads from our point of view. Many of them strongly resent the United States and are deeply suspicious of our policies. They are still not entirely free of the attitudes developed during the nineteenth century in their mad scramble for security from a technologically superior West and for equality with it. More recently our defeat of Japan, our occupation of the country for seven years, our continuing predominance in its foreign trade, and our military dominance in the western Pacific, all have made the Japanese feel, if not directly threatened by us, at least overshadowed and uncomfortably dependent.

The strongly Marxist tenor of much of Japanese intellectual life further sours Japanese attitudes toward the United States. While only a few Japanese are Communists, a great number of Socialists and less ideological Japanese join the Communists in believing that American capitalism produces irresistible imperialistic urges in us, which in turn menace world peace. Association with the United States through the mutual security treaty seems to these people to threaten Japan's security more than it protects it. The overwhelmingly unpopular war in Vietnam strengthens this concept and raises the specter of a Sino-American war in which the Japanese become involved because of our bases in their country. The bases themselves, of course, are a source of endless friction, as foreign bases are everywhere, and a constant reminder of the supposed danger of too close an association with the United States. It is small wonder that the security treaty is the most hotly debated issue in Japanese politics and the Vietnam war and American bases the chief targets of a wave of demonstrations that has mounted greatly in size and violence during the past year.

The mutual security treaty, which was renegotiated in 1960 amid massive demonstrations in Japan and a near breakdown of parliamentary government, runs for ten years, until June 1970, after which either side can terminate it on one year's notice. The opposition parties in Japan, therefore, have all along aimed at 1970 as the year to end or drastically reduce the defense relationship with the United States; the Socialists, the largest opposition party, unrealistically advocate "unarmed neutrality" in its place. Few Japanese seem to have considered seriously what the breaking of the treaty would mean for Japan. Instead, they appear to assume that the United States, driven by its supposed imperialist urges, would continue to maintain its military power around Japan in the western Pacific, thus permitting the Japanese to eliminate the irritations and supposed risks of the security treaty, while still benefiting from the American defense shield. They do not seem to have contemplated the possibility that the United States might withdraw to mid-Pacific, forcing Japan into a massive rearmament that would be extremely costly both in economic and political terms. The Japanese government seems to have a better understanding of the problem, but it has shown little skill or even will in educating the public.

In the early 1960's, dissatisfaction with the security treaty seemed to be waning, but during the past two years the escalation of the Vietnam war has reversed this trend, and the attack on the treaty has mounted greatly in intensity. Unless the war is ended by 1970 or shows clear signs of ending, the treaty may be seriously endangered.

Another factor is the growing nationalistic urge in Japan to get out from under America's shadow. This shadow today may in large part be only the psychological creation of the Japanese themselves, but it is nonetheless real to them. Some conservative Japanese would like to see Japan rearm fully in order to be less dependent on the United States for its defense. A few are even beginning to think that Japan, as the emerging third largest power in the world, must have the dignity of its own nuclear force. Some Japanese of both the left and right would like to see Japan go it alone in the French style, not realizing that American withdrawal to mid-Pacific would leave Japan militarily naked, with nothing like the surrounding North Atlantic Treaty Organization (NATO) cloak. Most Japanese would like to see their country cut loose from what they feel has been American dominance over their foreign policy. An ending to the Vietnam war that suggested a complete American withdrawal from Asia would, of course, greatly strengthen some of these tendencies. Thus there is a great ground swell of feeling, both on the right and left of Japanese politics, for less dependence on American military defense and greater independence of American foreign policy.

Policy toward Japan

American policies toward Japan must be formulated in the light of Japan's potential role in Asia and the sensitivities in Japanese-American relations. There is no reason for the United States to oppose either of the ground swells in Japan toward lessened dependence on American military defense and greater independence of American foreign policy. Only a Japan that feels independent of American domination in foreign policy will be able to see clearly the basic identity of Japanese and American interests or will be able to be an effective element in a multiple balance of forces in Asia. If a lessening of dependence on American military defense helps the Japanese gain this sense of independence of American foreign policy, this would be a helpful step. The danger is that in moving toward less dependence on American military defense and independence of American foreign policy, various misunderstandings of American intentions and irritations over the present situation might lead the Japanese to break the whole of the mutual security relationship, with the dire consequences for both countries outlined above. For this reason, it is vitally important that the United States clarify its attitudes toward Asian problems and also minimize existing irritants in its relations with Japan.

The most important thing we can do is to improve our own policies, extricating ourselves from the Vietnam war with the least possible damage, revising our stance on China, and putting our relations with the rest of Asia on a sounder, less military basis. Beyond that we should show understanding of Japan's desire for independence of our policies and sympathy for its initiatives. We cannot force continued cooperation on Japan or a larger role in Asia. Perhaps the less we say to try to convince the Japanese, the better. But by proper actions—that is, by reducing the reasons for their doubts about our policies and minimizing the frictions in our relations—we can make it easier for Japanese to see the general identity of Japanese and American interests, the great value to Japan of the defense relationship with us, and the importance of a greater Japanese role in seeking a balance of forces in Asia and aiding in the long-range development of the area.

Among the dangerous irritants in Japanese-American relations, those over China policy need special explanation. Most Japanese are deeply dissatisfied with their present lack of full, normal relations with China and blame this situation largely on the United States. This is not entirely fair. Whatever our historic role in helping produce the present relationship between Japan and China, the continuation or alteration of Japan's policy of recognizing the Nationalist government and trading with both China and Taiwan, under the slogan of "the separation of politics and economics," is, in fact, entirely in Japanese hands. What inhibits Japan from recognizing Peking is not the attitude of the United States but rather the attitudes of the Nationalist government on Taiwan and of South Korea and some of Japan's other important trading partners. However, if we were to shift our own stance on China, as described above, we would bring it more in line with popular Japanese sentiments, thus relaxing somewhat this particular strain on Japanese-American relations. We should be careful, though, to consult fully with the Japanese government well in advance of any steps we take, because China policy is a matter of the utmost sensitivity in Japan, and the Japanese government could be seriously embarrassed if it appeared to be either uninformed of our moves or left out on a limb in its own position toward Peking.

An even more serious irritant for both leftist and conservative Japanese is the friction surrounding our bases in Japan. A series of incidents in 1968, determinedly exploited by the left, has greatly exacerbated these feelings. The time has come for a serious restudy of the whole American base structure in Japan and other aspects of the defense relationship to see how potential irritations can best be minimized without seriously limiting the value of the mutual defense relationship to both Japan and the United States. If the problem were properly understood as being more political than military, the bulk of the dangerous irritants could probably be eliminated without significant loss in defense capabilities.

The greatest of the irritations is Okinawa (or the Ryukyu Islands). Okinawa contains one of the major American defense complexes in the western Pacific. It is also inhabited by 960,000 Japanese who were once resentful of their treatment by other Japanese as second-class citizens but are now the most unambiguously patriotic of all Japanese because of twenty-three years under American military rule. One can hardly imagine a more unsound situation than for the United States to be ruling almost one million citizens of its major Asian ally in the only "semicolonial" territory created in Asia since the war. This situation is intensely irritating to Japanese of both the left and the right.

For long the Okinawan situation was justified on the grounds that an uncertain political climate in Japan endangered the future of our bases there and that, therefore, a firmer grip was necessary on our Okinawan bases, just in case we lost our bases in Japan. But this is to state the problem backwards. If we were to lose our bases in Japan, our "colonialist" grip on Okinawa would be one of the major reasons for this disaster, and if the mutual security treaty were broken, the 960,000 Japanese living in and around our bases in Okinawa would soon make them quite ineffective, if not untenable. We shall either continue to have a friendly defense relationship with Japan and bases in both Japan proper and Okinawa, if these are needed, or we shall have effective bases in neither and a hostile Japan to boot. It is high time that we solved the Okinawan problem. The islands must be returned to Japan by 1970, or at least a clear, early date for their return must be fixed by that time.

One problem complicating such a solution is the presence of nuclear weapons in our Okinawan bases. Nuclear weapons cannot be introduced into our bases in Japan proper without specific agreement by the Japanese government, and the Japanese public, which has been understandably sensitive to the nuclear problem since the atomic bombings of Hiroshima and Nagasaki and has become greatly aroused over the whole military relationship with the United States since the escalation of the Vietnam war, is not likely to tolerate an agreement which permits retention of nuclear weapons in the Okinawan bases after the islands have reverted to Japan. On the other hand, some conservative elements in Japan seem to hope that we will insist on our retention of nuclear rights in Okinawa even after reversion, as a step toward overcoming the nuclear "allergy" of the Japanese public, so that some day Japan itself can develop nuclear weapons. This, of course, is not in American interests. Nor do nuclear weapons on Okinawa seem necessary or even desirable, as we have seen in our discussion of China. This is a point we should concede to the Japanese in an effort to eliminate the Okinawan problem before it gets out of hand and contributes to a general breakdown in Japanese-American relations.

Economic matters also figure among the irritants in Japanese-American relations, though basically they are elements of strength. Close to 30 percent of Japan's trade is with the United States, which is a figure commensurate with our economic position in the world but is so large as to make Japanese particularly sensitive to and apprehensive about our trade policies. After several years of intensive efforts by the Japanese to expand their trade with the Soviet Union and China, Japan's trade with the whole of the communist world is hardly more than a quarter of its trade with us, and these proportions are not likely to change greatly in the foreseeable future.

The Japanese maintain "voluntary restrictions" on their exports to the United States in a number of fields for fear that a sudden flooding of the American market by them might result in stiffer restrictions on our part. These self-imposed restrictions, they realize, constitute orderly marketing procedures, but they chafe at the situation and worry about it. On the other hand, American businessmen resent the extremely stiff quantitative restrictions Japan places on imports in many fields and the even narrower limits it has placed on the introduction of investment capital. Japanese promises of liberalization in both fields have so far produced irritatingly few actual changes. There are numerous other frictions over economic matters. For example, Japanese fishing in Alaskan waters and for "American" salmon in the North Pacific lead to annual bickering and negotiations. In the long run, the salmon problem can probably only be solved by a rational division of the fish in the manner of the Convention for the Conservation of North Pacific Fur Seals.

Frictions over economic matters are only to be expected between such great trading partners, and in fact, the trade between the two countries has grown steadily and spectacularly to the benefit of both. In dealing with economic matters, however, the United States should realize the special Japanese sensitivities and should be particularly careful not to discriminate against Japan in ways not used against the industrialized nations of the West.

In summary, the chief problem in Japanese-American relations is that each side tends to take the other for granted. We have let our preoccupation with policies toward far less crucial areas in Asia endanger our much more vital relations with Japan. The Japanese have so taken us for granted that they have not even envisioned a situation in which we do not continue to be overwhelmingly their chief trading partner and do not tacitly provide a large portion of their military security. Neither side, in its own interests, can safely go on in this way. We, for our part, must realize that a major element in America's transpacific policies, perhaps the most important element, should be efforts to maintain and strengthen our mutually beneficial relationship with Japan. At the same time we should recognize and welcome Japanese desires for independence of our foreign policies and lessened dependence on our military defense.

Conclusions

We can draw from this survey of our transpacific relations five broad conclusions. The first is that an early but tolerable ending of the Vietnam war is absolutely essential. The second is that the maintenance of a friendly, cooperative relationship with Japan underlies the achievement of all our other transpacific objectives. The third is that, in place of the present political confrontation between ourselves and China, we should seek a relaxation of tensions, the development of live-and-let-live attitudes, and the emergence of a multilateral balance of power in the area. The fourth is that, once we have successfully extricated ourselves from Vietnam, we have no other vital, immediate interests in the less-developed nations of Asia, only a long-range interest in their development over time as healthy, independent states, and that therefore we should be more relaxed and much more patient in our attitudes toward Asia. The final conclusion is that we have less control than we once imagined over developments in the transpacific area. Our role there can be no more than marginal—to try to help desirable trends and inhibit undesirable ones. There can be no American Master Plan for Asia. Outside of the field of economic aid, a lessened American role actually may be more helpful than an increased one.

China's relationship with the outside world will be determined fundamentally by the attitudes of the Chinese themselves, their success in handling their domestic problems, and the attitudes other Asians develop toward them. Our efforts at building an encircling alliance against China and maintaining a close-in line of containment have probably done more to stimulate Chinese aggressiveness than to contain it. The chief contributions we can make toward inducing China to move in a desirable direction are to relax our psychological and military pressures, reduce the political polarization in Asia between China and the United States, open doors for reconciliation so that the Chinese can come through them when they are ready, and in the meantime, encourage the Japanese and others to establish such contacts with the Chinese as will help them adjust to the outside world and find their place in a multilateral Asian balance of power.

In the other less-developed countries of East and South Asia, it is primarily their own nationalism and skills in meeting their domestic problems that will determine their success in avoiding external domination and developing the strong economies and healthy societies they all yearn for. Our economic and technological aid and that of Japan and other advanced nations can, of course, be of help. In most cases, however, military alignment with us, by increasing strains in a country's relations with China, may threaten its security more than it aids it. In no country can we ourselves maintain internal stability, nor in most cases would it be in our interests to do so if we could. Our military role can be only marginal—to preserve the freedom of the seas, to maintain insofar as possible an external environment of stability, and to serve as a reserve force to discourage blatant aggression.

Our defense relationship with Japan, our huge trade with it, and the budding partnership between us in facing the problems of Asia are all matters of immediate, vital concern to us, but their future will be determined in large part by Japanese attitudes over which we have, at best, only an indirect influence. All we can do is minimize the specific strains in our relationship, particularly those in the touchy defense field, modify our own transpacific policies in ways which reduce Japanese doubts about them, and show understanding of Japanese sensitivities toward what they feel is our undue influence over their country. A fruitful partnership can only be between nations that feel themselves equal. Since the discrepancies in size between the United States and Japan have been greatly magnified in Japanese minds by recent history, we must make conscious efforts to redress the balance in our relationship.

Our overall transpacific objective should be to reduce the political polarization that has involved us in a disastrous war, keeps alive mutual fears of hegemony between us and the Chinese, and contributes to unhealthy tensions throughout the whole area. To help achieve a multilateral balance of power, we should strive to increase the relative influence of other powers in the area and in this sense reduce our own. A larger Japanese role would be one essential element. The further development of India and the other countries of the area as healthy independent entities, some of them perhaps banded together regionally for added influence, would be important. A greater Soviet and Western European presence would be desirable. If these other elements of a multilateral balance emerge, the alleged threat of Chinese hegemony would recede even further, and the political polarization of the area between China and the United States would gradually fade away.

All of these policies suggest the desirability of a lower profile in the American transpacific presence than has been characteristic of the past two decades. A better term might be the Japanese phrase "low posture." We cannot control the vast forces of Asia; we can only seek to understand them and then, when necessary, attempt to redirect their thrust. We must move with the dominant forces, such as nationalism, not against them. Again to adopt a Japanese metaphor, we should approach the problems of Asia in judo style, not trading blow for blow with the forces of Asia, but so adapting our stance as to let these forces work for us.

JOHN C. CAMPBELL

THE MIDDLE EAST

The problems of the Middle East have a persistence which would be little short of boring to the American public, as well as to the old hands in the State Department, were they not charged with those special types of explosives which produce international crisis and war. The crises pass, and the problems remain unsolved. The conflicts remain unreconciled. But the demands of the situation change, and the United States must periodically assess where it stands, what its interests are, and what is to be done.

The new administration will have to find answers to hard and pressing questions. We might list a few. Should the United States try to mediate between the Arab states and Israel if the effort by the United Nations has run its course without success? Should we provide more arms to Israel, in particular the advanced types of aircraft and missiles it desperately wants? Should we continue to support our Jordanian friends, who are under relentless pressure from, among others, our Israeli friends? Can the United States really do much to stabilize the situation in the Middle East without the cooperation of the Soviet Union, and is it worth trying to get that cooperation? How should we react, if at all, to the growing Soviet military presence?

For answers to such questions, past policy is no infallible guide, for the old problems have new dimensions. Yet, like the *hodja* who rode out of town seated backward on his donkey, we have to know where we have been before we can think clearly about where we are going.

Lessons of Two Decades

American policy in the Middle East since the Second World War has been bound up in two problems which brought us into the politics of the area from two quite different sets of circumstances. The first is the problem of coping with the expansion of Soviet power, or as official statements usually put it, helping to safeguard the independence of the Middle Eastern nations. In brief, considerations of global strategy and balance of power pushed the United States into the Middle East with its Truman Doctrine in 1947 and have kept it there ever since. As conditions in the area have changed over the years and as political leadership in Washington has shifted, differences have appeared in approach and in emphasis but not in the basic policy of keeping the region free of Soviet domination.

The second problem has grown out of American involvement in what is perennially listed on the UN agenda as the question of Palestine but is now better described as the conflict between the Arab world and Israel. The United States from the start recognized a special relationship with Israel because of the American role in its creation, the sympathy that it enjoyed among the American public as the refuge and the hope of a cruelly persecuted people, and the intimate ties between a sizable and influential body of American citizens and the people of the new state. At the same time, the United States wanted to develop friendly relations with the newly independent Arab countries and to pursue interests there important to its global strategic position, to its economy, and especially to the needs of European allies. And with the Arab world, too, the United States had bonds of culture and good will dating well back in history.

As the Arab-Israeli conflict persisted and as Western relations with the Arab states came under heavy strain during and after the transition from colonial rule to independence, it was inevitable that some of the elements making up U.S. policy should run into mutual contradictions and that a goodly amount of partisan heat should be generated in the public discussion of that policy. One school of thought regarded a pro-Israel policy as reckless gambling with vital interests in security and oil. Supporters of Israel stressed moral and humanitarian considerations but also pictured democratic Israel as America's truest and most reliable friend in the Middle East. Some of the contradictions and much of the partisanship remain today.

With many zigs and zags and with failures to match its successes, the United States developed an overall policy aimed, first, at maintaining tolerable relationships with all Middle Eastern states, generally supporting their independence against any attempt by the Soviet Union to move in, and, second, at keeping the Arab-Israeli conflict within bounds while avoiding a clear choice of one side that would alienate the other. This was a policy at first carried out in cooperation with other Western powers. The Soviet breakthrough to the Middle East and the fading of British and French influence after the disastrous Suez adventure in 1956 changed the ground rules, but the United States stuck to its general purpose of safeguarding the peace and its declared policy of impartiality between the Arab states and Israel.

The policy has been notably successful in Turkey and Iran, two societies with long and continuous experience as independent states and periods of strong leadership by rulers determined on fundamental reforms. Living in the shadow of Russia, they were not hesitant to cooperate with the United States. Neither has been immune to internal crisis in the past two decades and both may find more trouble ahead. Iran's remarkable progress based on booming oil revenues rests on the precarious political base of the one-man regime of the Shah, who has not created durable political institutions and whose fascination with modern arms bodes no particular good for his own country or its weaker neighbors. Nevertheless, Turkey and Iran represent success stories. Our aid has helped them, and they in turn have helped us. An increased desire for greater independence of policy has recently led them to more normal relations with the Soviet Union, but that should be no cause for undue concern as long as they see their Western ties as fundamental to their interests.

In the Arab world it has been a different story: a crumbling of the old order without sufficient cohesiveness to build a new one; a condition of simmering unrest periodically boiling over into civil strife or conflict with neighbors; a bewildering variety of forms of government from survivals of traditional absolutism and tribal factionalism to the latest models of "Arab socialism" and Caesarism; above all, a great uncertainty where political loyalties lie, in the vague idea of a single Arab nation or in the reality of an Egypt, Syria, or Saudi Arabia, each with its own institutions and national interests. From all the evidence, the Arab world seems unable to produce a Bismarck or a Prussia to bring it strength and unity; as a result, much of its energies have been consumed in internecine strife. But the dream of unity, nonexistent on the map, exists as an active element in Middle East politics.

The great difficulty in this sort of situation is the inability of any outside power, no matter how strong or how benevolent, to maintain an essentially status quo policy under the pressure of dynamic local forces which a rival outside power is only too happy to turn to its own advantage. Added to the deep hatred between Israel and the Arabs are the bitter feelings of Arab nationalists against what they see as Western imperialism and also the conflicts which divide Arab states and factions from each other. Alignments among the Arab states have shifted from time to time but there has always been a polarization of conservative forces, which had interests running parallel to those of the West and no taste for Egyptian leadership or domination, and of radical forces increasingly hostile to the West.

American attempts in the fifties to build defensive alignments against the Soviet Union amid these clashing elements seemed to make a mockery of our proclaimed impartiality, at least for the radical Arab nationalists led by Gamal Abdel Nasser, who regarded American policies as openly partial to all whom they opposed: the Zionists, the European imperialists, and the conservative Arab regimes. The Soviet Union, on the other hand, as the enemy of their enemies, perforce became their friend. The working alliance between revolutionary Arab nationalism and Soviet power and diplomacy has proved to be a formidable combination.

Looking back, one can see how American policy in the Arab world, whether deliberately or not, came to focus on Cairo. The United States went through many phases in its relationship with Egypt (later the United Arab Republic) without ever finding firm footing. When we tried to work with Egypt in promoting a "free-world" alignment covering the Middle East, King Farouk's government and then Nasser's rejected the proposals as not compatible with independence. When we tried to organize defense without Egypt by pushing the Baghdad Pact and later the Eisenhower Doctrine with other Arab states which were willing to cooperate, we were in fact choosing to back its enemies and rivals and helped provoke Nasser's turn to Russia. This plunge into Arab politics resulted, in 1958, in the disappearance of pro-American regimes in Lebanon and Iraq. Later, less concerned with alliances and alignments, we tried to establish normal relations with Cairo and provided considerable economic aid, but this experiment also came to grief. By the mid-1960s, Nasser apparently became convinced that America was intent on destroying him as leader of the Arab world, perhaps a reflection of his own failure to clean up the rag-tag royalist armies in the Yemen war and of his inability to challenge Israel.

This account of American experience in the Arab world may seem a story of arbitrariness and pique on the part of one man. It was in fact a series of actions and reactions, a clash of national interests as the two sides saw them. Whether the clash was inevitable and the conflict irreconcilable is another matter, and one which bears on our policy for the future.

Formal American-Egyptian relations, finally, were a casualty of the war of June 1967. The place of the Arab states, and particularly of the UAR, in an American policy for the Middle East now faces the United States again as it seeks to deal with the aftermath of the war. Before taking up that question and the related question of relations with Israel, it would be useful to consider the role of the Soviet Union, so that perspective on the broad range of American interest is not lost in obsessive concentration on the one point of most frequent explosion.

Soviet Aims and Policies

To those inclined to the belief that the cold war is a thing of the past it is worth pointing out that the Soviet Union, whatever it may be doing elsewhere, is not practicing détente with the United States in the Middle East. It has eased the pressures on our allies, Turkey and Iran, promoting economic cooperation and in Iran's case even providing military aid, but for the obvious purpose of weakening their ties with the United States. In the Arab world, using the twin themes of anti-imperialism and anti-Zionism, the Soviet Union seeks to consolidate the footholds it has gained and to spread its influence to other countries. From about 1966 on, it has bolstered this strategy with new military capabilities: a sizable naval force now permanently stationed in the Mediterranean, access to facilities in Egyptian and Syrian ports, and increased all-purpose forces for action well beyond the frontiers of the USSR. Russian warships have appeared for the first time in the Persian Gulf. "Cold war" may no longer be the right descriptive phrase, but there is still a grim competition for position and influence.

To state these facts is not to say that the American response should take the form of urgent military buildup and organization for defense. The aim of Soviet strategy is not military conquest of the Middle East any more than it is the spread of communism. In essence it is a political strategy intended, as it was in Khrushchev's day, to weaken America's influence and to establish the Soviet Union as the preeminent outside power in the region. It uses military dispositions along with ideological propaganda, manipulation of communist parties, diplomacy, and economic aid as its instruments.

The Soviet leadership has been increasingly aware of the advantages the United States has derived from the range and flexibility of its military power. Russia, for all its nuclear might, has been by comparison a muscle-bound Eurasian giant. It wishes to act like, and to be recognized as, a power with world-wide reach. What more logical place than the Mediterranean, where for nearly two centuries Russian rulers have wanted to sail their men-of-war? Where else in the third world can Soviet naval forces be so close to home and yet make their presence felt in a wide area where Soviet influence has already made substantial gains? The purpose of the Soviet buildup is not to shoot it out with the Sixth Fleet, for which it is no match, but to neutralize the effects of the American military presence, to hearten pro-Soviet regimes against the threat of U.S. intervention, and to overawe pro-Western and neutral states.

Some Western analysts of Soviet behavior believe that the creation of long-range conventional forces, against the background of the strategic nuclear balance, heralds an adventurous policy of intervention in local conflicts the world over at the risk of limited war. The possibilities of Soviet military intervention to protect or impose a particular regime, leaving to the United States the decision to initiate or shy away from a direct clash, deserve serious attention. But the record of the past is consistent and compelling: Soviet leadership, whether exercised by Stalin, Khrushchev, or their successors, has shown a great wariness of any situation which might pit Soviet and American forces against each other in combat. Neither they nor we wish to test in practice whether a limited Soviet-American war in some part of the third world would remain limited.

In the absence of an established international order and of any basic agreement between the two great powers, military strength and balance form the background against which the game of political action and diplomacy is played. We have no choice but to maintain our own position. Concentration on military factors and on the Soviet Union, however, will give us an inadequate and distorted picture of the tasks ahead. We have seen from experience that deployment of military power does not produce proportionate political gains. The key to the problem of the Soviet threat and how to meet it is to be found in constructive relationships with the peoples of the Middle East. Both the Soviet Union and the United States are trying to protect their interests or pursue their ambitions in an area where success or failure depends largely on the attitudes, actions, and decisions of local leaders and peoples. The test of policy throughout the Middle East (including the Persian Gulf area, now that Britain has announced its intention to withdraw) will lie less in the stroke and counterstroke of the cold war than in the ability to navigate amid the complexities of regional politics and to find common ground with these societies as they move haltingly into the modern world.

Today it is still competition. Whether that competition can be limited by Soviet-American agreement is a question for the future. A new test may not be far away, as increasing armed action across the cease-fire lines between Israel and its Arab neighbors threatens a renewal of the war and the danger of great-power involvement.

Search for a Settlement

Whatever opinion one may have of U.S. diplomacy in the weeks preceding June 5, 1967—and some of the criticism has been sharp—the war itself clarified many things in the Middle Eastern picture for the United States, as it did for others. The prospect of a major Arab and Soviet victory, military or political, had evaporated. The leader of the struggle against "American imperialism" in the Arab world had suffered a crushing defeat—not by America but by tiny Israel—which could not be hidden from the Arab peoples by any amount of propaganda. The Soviet leaders, faced with the danger of military involvement, had hastened to assure Washington that they were staying out. The United States did not have to decide on military action to stop the war or to save Israel, because the war was virtually over on each front by the time the United Nations Security Council passed its cease-fire resolutions. Israel had saved itself.

That the war could open the way to resolution of deeper and longer-term problems was the hope of Israel, of the United States, and of others whose representatives came together in the United Nations to debate what was to be done. Would the Arab states, having experienced the reality of an encounter with Israel's power, forsake their dream world in which Israel did not exist and accept the need to live in peace with a sovereign Israeli state? If they did, would Israel be magnanimous in victory? Would both sides, recognizing that the old jerry-built structure of armistice agreements, demilitarized zones, and ineffective UN supervision had not worked, be ready to reach agreement on a new and firmer foundation for peace?

The United States, as President Johnson's speech of June 19, 1967, indicated, decided that an effort to achieve agreement should be made. The five points of that speech called for a settlement which would include the right of each nation to live, respect for the independence and territorial integrity of all in the context of recognized and secure frontiers, free navigation of international waterways, justice for the Arab refugees, and international control of the arms race. It was a statesmanlike plan.

It was conceivable that shock at the magnitude of their defeat or an abandonment of their cause by the Soviet Union could have led to early acceptance by the Arabs. In fact, the shock was not all that great, and the immediate Soviet reaction to the outcome of the war was to rebuild Arab military strength and Soviet prestige in the Arab world as quickly as possible and to back the Arab demand for unconditional withdrawal of Israel's forces. As various resolutions were debated at the United Nations, the Arab League at Khartoum decided on the need for a political solution but on a basis of "no negotiations with Israel, no recognition of Israel, no peace with Israel." A positive note was discernible, but the accent was on the negative.

One point is worth special emphasis. At the end of the fighting Israel's forces were at the Suez Canal and the Jordan River and on the Golan heights in Syria. The declared intention of the Israeli government was that they should stay there until peace could be negotiated: the terms of any withdrawal would be a part of negotiations which would also cover other points in dispute. Thus the occupied territories were to be used as bargaining power to induce agreement on a peace settlement.

The United States, in putting forward its own recommendation for a package solution, implicitly adopted that same view. It was a different stand than the one President Eisenhower had taken in 1956, when he insisted on Israel's evacuation of Sinai and the Gaza Strip. This time there were reasons for a different policy: Israel's attack on Egypt in 1956 came out of the blue by prior and deliberate Israeli decision, whereas the responsibility for the war crisis of 1967 lay, if anywhere, more on the Arab side; more important, the return to the armistice lines in 1956–57 had not brought peace, and there seemed no sense a decade later in merely putting things together again for a new war in the future. The reasons were understandable, but without the assurance of a rapid and successful negotiated settlement, the American move threw some doubt on the principle that territory cannot legitimately be acquired by force of arms and also on the often repeated statements of the United States itself upholding the independence and territorial integrity of all states in the area. This was, as a matter of fact, one of the President's five points. But on what line did Israel's, or Jordan's, or Egypt's territorial integrity begin?

This point, of course, was made much of by the Arabs and their supporters, whose entire campaign stressed Israel's withdrawal as the first requirement in any settlement and indeed a matter of right and justice wholly apart from a settlement. The UN Security Council resolution of November 22, 1967, which was passed by unanimous vote and raised no protests either from Israel or from the Arab states (except Syria), left the point not wholly clarified—it mentioned withdrawal of forces but also "secure and recognized boundaries"—but without some obscurity, a resolution could hardly have been passed at all. In any event, all governments concerned were free to put their own interpretations on it and did so.

Under the UN resolution Gunnar Jarring of Sweden set forth upon his task, as Special Representative, to persuade Israel, the UAR, and Jordan to negotiate a comprehensive settlement. The difficulty of his assignment (about which he had no illusions) soon manifested itself in Arab rejection of Israel's demand for direct negotiations, a reflection of the basic dispute on recognition, and in endless controversy over "acceptance" of the UN resolution by the two sides; and the deadlock held month after month. But events in the Middle East did not stand still awaiting the results of quiet diplomacy. While officials of the three states talked with Jarring, President Nasser made fiery speeches to his people to the effect that what had been taken away by force must be regained by force. His missiles sank an Israeli destroyer, and heavy exchanges of fire took place across the Suez Canal. Israel's new "security borders" were no more immune to raids and counterraids than the armistice lines had been. Meanwhile Israel began to write some of its own terms of settlement where it had the power to do so: it joined the former Jordanian sector of Jerusalem to its own sector in a united city; it established a number of Israeli settlements in the occupied territories; and it refused to allow Arabs who had fled across the Jordan during the war to return to their homes on the West Bank.

The United States, with its real interest in a settlement and its close ties with both Israel and Jordan, could not avoid involvement. It urged restraint, cajoled, occasionally deplored, sometimes warned, and pressed all concerned to cooperate with the Jarring mission. As the situation deteriorated, however, it had to deal increasingly with urgent specific questions: how to keep Israel from acts which made a settlement all the harder to attain; how to get Jordan to check terrorist activity against Israel; whether and how to meet requests from both sides for more arms; above all, what to do if the Jarring mission should never get off dead center.

After a year of tireless and patient negotiating efforts, Ambassador Jarring has achieved no breakthrough toward a settlement. Israel's government, facing a general election in 1969 and divided in its views on what to do about the occupied territories, has been unprepared to abandon its demand for a process including direct negotiations leading to a signed agreement, reluctant even to declare its unqualified acceptance of the UN resolution for fear of pressure for withdrawal before its conditions are met. The governments of Jordan and the UAR speak of the need to "implement" the resolution, by which they mean that both sides, on the basis of separate talks with Jarring, should proceed with various actions and declarations. Moderates on both sides might be able to come close to agreement on actual terms of a settlement; the governments themselves appear to be a little less rigid than before with some prodding from outside. But nationalist pressures hold the governments on the politically safer line of yielding as little as possible, and the impasse on procedure enables them to avoid compromise on matters of substance.

The Tide of Violence

While the possibility that Jarring will yet work a miracle cannot be excluded, in the more likely contingency that the prospects for a settlement fade the United States will no longer be able to take refuge in continued support of the UN conciliation effort as the sole answer to a situation that has left conciliation behind. New decisions will have to be made, and the troubled atmosphere and dangerous situation will not make them easy.

Briefly, the situation is one of rising violence. The cease-fire lines along the Suez Canal and the Jordan River have witnessed unceasing fire, including artillery duels and air operations. The UAR and Syria are rebuilding their armies with Soviet weapons and Soviet training toward the declared goal of renewing the war at some later day. Meanwhile, much of the initiative for violence has now passed into the hands of the guerrilla organizations of Palestinian Arabs, which from training bases in Syria and the UAR and operational bases in Jordan are trying to carry on a "war of national liberation." Their aim, they make quite clear, is not just to liberate the Israeli-occupied areas but to redeem their homeland of Palestine, that is, to destroy Israel. The effect on the prospects for an Arab-Israeli settlement is obvious, for that aim of reversing the decisions of 1947–48 undermines the position of any Arab government which would be satisfied with a reversal of the military verdict of 1967.

These armed *fedayeen* are grouped in several rival organizations, some with ties to Arab governments but none really controlled or controllable by anybody. Their exploits, highly exaggerated in their own announcements and in the Arab press, have been hailed enthusiastically in the Arab world. These young heroes, so the comment runs, are the only ones doing anything for the Arab cause; they are puncturing the myth of Israel's invincibility and restoring pride in Arab valor. Money pours in to support them. Israel's security measures, however, make their forays a highly dangerous proposition. The Arabs of the occupied West Bank and of Gaza have remained largely passive though by no means reconciled to their situation, and in any case, the limited space and open vistas of Palestine are not ideal territory for the strategy of Ho Chi Minh or Che Guevara. But some fedayeen get through, they plant their bombs and mines, and they take Israeli lives.

Israel's retaliatory strikes, carried out by their regular military forces against fedayeen bases and populated areas in Jordan, are intended to cripple the fedayeen terrorists in their lairs and to deter future attacks by demonstrating that they and the governments that support them will be repaid tenfold or more in casualties and damage. Reprisal has been accepted theory and standard practice since David Ben-Gurion began it in the 1950s, despite the fact that the results give more substantiation to another theory: that a massive strike may give the Arabs pause sometimes, but in the end it only breeds more violence.

The rise in violence tends to close the minds of leaders and the public on both sides to any serious consideration of negotiation or peaceful settlement. Those who have tried to nurture the possibilities of agreement are silent, while each side by its acts gives substance to the image which the extremists on the other side have of it: aggressive Zionism bent on carving out an empire from the Nile to the Euphrates; fanatic Arabism determined to annihilate the state and the people of Israel. Both sides may pay a heavy price. Regardless of the intention of Israel, the militarization of its own society in the name of security will in time raise the question of the survival of the democratic order. For the Arabs the absence of any prospect other than permanent war foreshadows further disasters, even though they cling to the conviction that their numbers will tell in the end.

Where will the cycle lead in the next few years? Israel is not likely to lose its military superiority in that time, and if the Arab armies were to attack in desperation, they might get worse than another bloody nose. Israel, should it choose not to wait, might launch a preventive attack on the UAR or take more territory from Jordan for greater security. Or a war might just happen, the end product of a series of blows and counterblows.

A more likely outcome in the next year or two is that, impotent to challenge Israel in the field, the Arabs will turn inward upon themselves, not constructively, but in anger and frustration. Governments will be overthrown as factionalism runs riot, economic progress slows down, and the one appeal of every demagogue who seeks or seizes power is for whipping up the struggle against Israel. Neither the radical nor the hitherto moderate or conservative Arab states will be immune from this virus.

Some Policy Choices

What are the choices for the United States? One is to withdraw, ending our special ties with Israel and Jordan and forgetting about a settlement. Perhaps the Arab-Israeli dispute could be left to find its own level, with each side forced to make the necessary adjustments. The war in Vietnam has led to a deeply questioning attitude toward the totality of obligations and ill-defined "vital" interests which could involve this country in similar situations at other points on the map. As both national budgets and international payments show continuing deficits, Americans increasingly ask whether we have the resources to meet these commitments and the social crisis at home. The United States cannot be the policeman of the world, they say, and the politicians of both parties nod their heads in agreement.

The Vietnam war has its lessons on the making and interpretation of commitments and on the scale of military involvement in peripheral wars. But the lessons will be lost if we follow no guideline except retrenchment and retreat. The United States need fear no further Vietnams unless it deliberately chooses them. It will not be invited to serve as policeman in the Middle East, and it should know enough to stay out of local quarrels and to avoid identification with particular regimes insofar as possible. But it does have, and will continue to have, commitments and interests in the region.

The United States has a clear obligation to defend Greece and Turkey as members of the North Atlantic Treaty Organization. It has a more vague bilateral security agreement with Iran. These ties would be undermined by a retreat from responsibility in the Arab-Israeli area. Besides, there is little doubt that we would not permit the destruction of Israel, although no treaty to that effect exists. And if we cannot avoid responsibility for coping with a world crisis when it develops from events in the Middle East, what is gained by refusing to help guide events so that a crisis may be avoided? Our commitments are part of the pattern of policy, understood in Moscow and in the Middle East, by which we uphold what are our only vital interests in the area: that events there lead to no major shift in the world balance against us and to no catastrophic war.

Time and the changing dimensions of war and politics have perforce altered some of our notions about what is vital. This country has interests in trade, in transit rights, and in the production and transport of oil. It has close relations with a number of Arab countries based on a common interest in stability and in existing arrangements for security and mutual economic benefit. It has bases and other important military installations. None of these, however, is an interest we should try to protect against local vicissitudes by military force.

Because oil is often cited as the one reason for America's presence in the Middle East, a few words may help to put it in perspective. The Middle East, with Arab North Africa, accounts for over 40 percent of the noncommunist world's oil production (1967) and contain's about two-thirds of the entire world's proven reserves. Produced in large part by U.S. companies, it is important in terms of investment, revenue, and the balance of payments. But it is not essential as fuel to the United States. For some years to come it will be indispensable to the industrial life and progress of Western Europe and Japan, but the responsibility for assuring continuing access to it falls mainly on those consuming countries. They have bargaining power against cuts in production or shipment in that the producing countries need the markets as much as the consumers need the oil. Europeans also have a hedge against closure of pipelines to the Mediterranean or of the Suez Canal in the increasing North African production and in the use of supertankers which can make the long haul round the Cape of Good Hope.

In a political crisis one or more Arab countries may embargo oil, but it is most unlikely that all of them plus Iran would do so simultaneously. Soviet seizure of Middle East oilfields or collusion with producing countries to shut off the supply to Europe and Japan is a remote and unreal prospect. Nationalization of the producing companies is always possible, but that would be no disaster if the oil continued to flow on reasonable terms to its natural markets. In the end, the protection of U.S. and Western interests rests on the nature of the relationships the United States and other Western nations can establish with the governments and peoples of the Middle East. This is the province of diplomacy and other instruments of policy, demanding not a withdrawal from the Middle East but a heightened understanding of it.

An alternative to withdrawal is to continue on present lines: encouraging the parties to negotiate, urging reason and restraint, supporting Israel solidly, supporting Jordan in a limited way, and waiting for Nasser to see the light. This way has helped to hold things together. But a combination of pragmatism and hope offers little chance for a more stable situation and has not headed off the violence. Jordan could be the first breaking point.

Of all the Arab states, Jordan under King Hussein has been the one which most needs a peaceful relationship with Israel and might go some distance to get it. Yet while the search for a settlement has gone on, Israel has rained severe blows on Jordan in answer to raids by the *fedayeen*, tangling with the Jordanian army and further straining the already weak position of the king. The more his authority is put in doubt, the stronger become the *fedayeen* and those political forces in Jordan which decry his pro-Western orientation and see no course but to get arms from the Soviet Union and answer the attacks of Israel. The radical regime in Syria, no friend of King Hussein, sends *fedayeen* over into Jordan and fans the flames. For the United States these are worrisome developments. Hussein and a moderate Jordan, which we have supported diplomatically and with arms and economic aid, have been a hope for maintaining a balance in the Middle East and a chance for peace. If no settlement comes, we should not be surprised to see the king fall prey to intolerable pressures and the country turn sharply to the left.

Jordan could even lose its independence, becoming an object of struggle among its Arab neighbors and perhaps of a new military push by Israel. One could argue that we need not be unduly concerned with the fate of Jordan, that disorder is nothing new in the Arab world, and that if the Arabs choose to indulge in it they will thereby relieve some of the pressure on Israel and its friends. This is short-sighted. It cannot be in our interest to see Jordan or any other Arab country relapse into destructive chaos induced by and feeding on hatred of a neighboring nation.

A third choice for the United States is to take the initiative alone to bring the Arab states and Israel, by mediation, persuasion, and pressure, to an agreed comprehensive settlement. That might make sense near the final stage of negotiation when an extra push could bridge the remaining gap. As matters stand, with the gap as big as all outdoors, the promise of success would be slight and the loss of American influence and future bargaining power serious. It would be wiser to continue support of the UN conciliation effort until some change, either between the disputants or among outside powers, creates new opportunities to go forward—here the key would be a move in which the United States and the USSR both take part.

Fortunately, other courses are possible. Without writing off the effort to promote a settlement, we could concentrate on the need to keep the peace on the existing cease-fire lines. We could choose full and consistent support of Israel as the simplest and most effective way of achieving that end and also of bringing the Arabs to see the need for a real peace. Finally, we have the option of staking out a new position which does not abandon hope of settlements, general or partial, but is responsive to the realities of what may be a long period of stalemate. These are not necessarily exclusive alternatives.

Keeping the Peace

The history of the Arab-Israeli dispute well illustrates the rule that nothing is more enduring than the provisional. The armistice lines of 1949 were intended to be temporary pending a political settlement. They lasted for eighteen years, with the one temporary break in 1956, as de facto boundaries between Israel and its Arab neighbors. They were buttressed by international arrangements for observation and peacekeeping: first, the UN Truce Supervisory Organization (UNTSO) with headquarters in Jerusalem and observation posts on the borders; and after 1956, the UN Emergency Force (UNEF) stationed on the Egyptian side of the armistice line and at Sharm-el-Sheikh at the Strait of Tiran, the narrow passage connecting Israel's southern port of Eilat with the open seas and a crucial item of dispute in the two crises of 1956 and 1967.

Neither side was happy with the armistice lines. Both violated them. UNTSO had limited authority: it could observe, it could pass judgment, but it could not prevent violations of the armistice and the parties could refuse to cooperate. UNEF helped keep the Egypt-Israel border quiet, but it was there on the sufferance of Abdel Nasser (who in May 1967 decided to suffer it no longer). Still, the lines endured. The UN Security Council debated the more flagrant instances of recourse to force, although the conflicting views of the great powers prevented it from doing anything about them, and the diplomacy of successive secretaries-general surely helped to keep the peace as well as it was kept.

Since then Israel has won a war, the balance in the region has changed, and there is a new territorial status quo. It is labeled as temporary, due to be changed as peace is negotiated, but for all we know it may last another eighteen years. Israel is settling down in its new position. For security it vastly prefers the present cease-fire lines—shorter, more easily defensible, farther from the centers of population—to the old armistice borders. Some groups in Israel demand outright annexation of the occupied territory. Others would give some of it back if security could be achieved some other way. If representatives of the Arab states will not sit down at the negotiating table with Israel, Israel may decide to negotiate with representatives of those Arabs now under its control, those who are in the occupied areas of Palestine. According autonomy to the West Bank and perhaps the Gaza Strip as a Palestinian Arab entity linked to Israel could provide a way out of the Palestine problem consistent with Israel's security and its character as a Jewish state. Its proponents say it could open up channels to the rest of the Arab world and eventually lead to peace. All the lessons of nationalism, however, point to the emptiness of these hopes. A satellite Arab state in Palestine would get neither the acceptance of Arabs outside, Palestinians or others, nor the enduring support of its own citizens. It would be a further block to any possible settlement.

Meanwhile, if the world is stuck with the status quo, should not the United Nations try to keep the peace by putting greater authority behind the cease-fire lines it established in June 1967? It is hard to believe, against the magnitude of the danger of a war that is potentially global, that a desultory mediation effort, a few UN observers, and an occasional Security Council resolution condemning resort to force represent the total international endeavor to preserve the peace.

Some UN members have proposed that observers, like those now stationed along the Suez Canal, be placed on the line between Israel and Jordan where most of the action is. A more ambitious measure would be to station UN peacekeeping forces on both sides of the cease-fire line with substantial authority and a guarantee against summary removal by order of the host countries. The difficulty is that the consent and cooperation of the parties would be essential to any such plan. The Arab governments will oppose anything which seems to give permanence to the present cease-fire lines, and Israel has never favored the presence of UN troops on its teritory. Israel, indeed, is decidedly unimpressed with the previous record of the United Nations in the Middle East and has deplored its propensity to "meddle" in matters best left to the parties concerned. All this is very discouraging, though it should not deter us from seeking to make the role of the United Nations as effective as possible.

The exchanges of raids and reprisals pose a problem, an almost daily one, to which we have found no answer. The governments act in accordance with the pressures on them, pressures reflecting the imperatives of national will and the instinct for survival. In contrast, American appeals for restraint are politely received and filed away. With ingenuity and forcefulness we may be able to make them more effective. To Israel and Jordan we should stress defense as opposed to incursions across the cease-fire lines and show our willingness to provide equipment and training for handling infiltration and threats to internal security. We should leave Israel in no doubt that the United States would oppose any military move for further acquisition of territory. Greater selectivity and attention to timing in meeting various requests may strengthen our influence with both sides.

Inability to stop the violence by diplomatic remonstration or by any existing UN authority or action drives one back to the nature of the conflict itself: Can anything be done to remove the causes? The maximum answer, a real political settlement, has been unattainable. The minimum is an improvement of the atmosphere through convincing the disputants that their fundamental needs—security or return of territory or whatever—can be met in some other way.

America's Relationship with Israel

A major question relevant to a policy of enforcing the cease-fire lines has to do with the permanence of Israel's presence in the occupied areas: whether the United States and the international community should help to consolidate and appear to guarantee the acquisition of territory and of subject populations by force. The question is central to the possibility of reaching a modus vivendi in the Middle East, and it bears directly on the nature of America's relationship to Israel.

Some Americans advocate a policy of full and frank support of Israel as a matter of the highest priority. They believe that the government should acknowledge that the peace and security of the Middle East and American interests there can best be preserved by a strong Israel backed by the United States with arms, political and financial help, and a guarantee against attack. To the earlier arguments that Israel deserves support as a sturdy democracy friendly to the United States they would add the fact that Israel now counts for something in the military balance. The picture of a beleaguered fledgling state uncertain of survival in a hostile environment has given way to that of a strong, self-confident national community capable of defeating any potential enemy other than a great power. If the United States makes sure that Israel retains its military superiority over the Arab states in conventional arms and the territory it needs for security, it is argued, there will be no war in the Middle East and no need for the United States to fear military involvement; and Israel will feel no compulsion to make nuclear weapons.

The objection to such a policy is that it takes little account of the wider interests of the United States. This country would lose much of its independence of choice in the entire area. It would be committed to the needs of Israel's security as Israel interpreted them. It might be left with only remnants of useful or tolerable relationships with Arab countries, from Lebanon to Kuwait and perhaps across North Africa as well. Even without waving the red flag and pointing to the political gains the communists would make, we may note that the Soviet Union would have little incentive to reach agreements with the United States about the Middle East. And U.S. arms deliveries to maintain Israel's superiority would surely be matched by Soviet deliveries to the Arabs.

An American policy of full support for Israel might be defended on the ground that only the radical Arab states, which are anti-American and pro-Soviet anyway, would be hostile; the conservative and moderate Arab leaders, whose main fear is of Nasser and of communism, would not be alienated and would tend to align their states with the West, with Iran, and even in an indirect way with Israel to protect themselves against the main enemy. This is a debatable thesis, in view of the elemental force of Arab nationalism, but even if its logic were unassailable, the United States would still have to decide whether the relatively advanced areas of the Arab world, Egypt and the Fertile Crescent, should be simply dismissed as of no consequence to the American position in the Middle East for the indefinite future.

The argument comes back to the unresolved questions of twenty years of American-Egyptian relations. The figure of Abdel Nasser looms less large now than before 1967, but whether a successor regime would be more hostile and abusive, or less so, we cannot tell. Over the long run Egypt will have to come to terms with the rest of the Arab world by compromise rather than by conquest. It will need the assistance of international institutions such as the World Bank. It will even need a Western connection to provide some balance to the tie with the Soviet Union, whose ultimate aims are incompatible with Egypt's own. America therefore has an interest in keeping communications open and in not assuming a state of permanent hostility. Whatever the character of today's regimes, the long-run interests of the people of Egypt and of Syria and Iraq are not incompatible with ours, but the surest way of making them so would be total support of Israel.

Actually, the choice of policies is not such a clear-cut matter as the preceding paragraphs suggest. The United States has a good relationship with Israel. Common interests are many. The American people recognize that in serving its own interests Israel has often served ours as well. They admire Israel for its remarkable achievements. But there is a difference between a sympathetic and cooperative relationship and an exclusive one, between willingness to act on the conviction that Israel has the right to live and an American carte blanche to Israel to realize an undefined manifest destiny.

An administration in Washington doubtless feels more comfortable at home when it is following a policy favorable to Israel. The organized American Jewish community exerts a potent political influence, not primarily in votes at election time, but rather in its financial contributions to political causes and in the prominence of its members in the media of communications and other fields of public and private life. Its voice comes through loud and clear at the White House and in the Congress. This is a political reality. Yet it is by no means the sole reason for our great interest in Israel, and it would be wrong to say that American policy in the Middle East has been consistently determined by "Zionist pressure" on behalf of a foreign government. At times in the past American policy has run counter to that of Israel, as when President Eisenhower, at the close of the election campaign of 1956, opposed Israel's attack on Egypt and insisted on the withdrawal of Israeli forces behind the existing armistice lines. We may even be permitted to hope the day may come when candidates for high office will no longer feel compelled to go through the ritual of extravagant statements of support for Israel, which only complicate the sober working out of sound American policies.

We must, of course, understand the mood of the people of Israel, for like the feelings and the psychoses of the Arabs it is a significant political fact. The prewar crisis in 1967 was a time of supreme peril, the climax of twenty years of living under the threat of extermination. They felt alone, with no real assurance of help from the United States, the United Nations, or anyone else. They then summoned their strength and spirit to repulse the threat. But the swiftness of their victory and the relief and rejoicing it brought were mixed with a grim feeling of "never again." Hence much of the hardness in Israel's postwar attitude, the insistence that guarantees of security be in its own hands and not in the paper pledges of others. Hence the determination to hold the present lines of defense until the Arabs offer equivalent security by making peace.

A Durable Basis for Policy

The United States cannot be indifferent to another nation's will and determination to survive. Americans have an obligation to themselves, however, to find a position on which this country can stand during an indefinite period in which there is no settlement in the Middle East. That position should rest on two propositions which represent at the same time the surest foundations of peace between the Arab states and Israel and the means by which this country can establish durable relations with both sides. Each proposition depends on the other. The first is that Israel should be treated as a sovereign state free from belligerent acts on the part of its neighbors. The second is that the territory lost by the Arab states in the war of 1967 should be returned. The first, Arab acceptance of Israel, implies a reciprocal obligation on Israel: to cooperate in dealing adequately with the plight of the Arab refugees. The second, return of Arab territory, should include provision for demilitarization of those areas and for reasonable minor adjustments in the old armistice lines, mainly in the Israel-Jordan sector, to give them more stability as recognized international boundaries. Two specific areas should be exempted: the occupied sector of Jerusalem, the status of which must be regulated in accord with the interests of Israel, Jordan, and the world religious communities to which the city is sacred; and the Gaza Strip, which was never a part of Egypt and probably should be put under international administration at least for a time. Jerusalem may be the toughest problem of all, but the unity of the city should constitute one firm base for a solution; unfettered access to holy places, including direct access by Muslims to the Old City from Jordanian territory, should provide another.

The first proposition is held by virtually the entire international community, which does not accept the idea that the Arab states, whose representatives sit with those of Israel in the United Nations, can deny to Israel the right of existence. The second rests on the UN Charter and on a record of policy in the Arab-Israeli dispute which the United States has followed since 1950. The President's "five points" and American support for the Security Council resolution of November 1967 were not inconsistent with that policy, for the resolution envisaged within a reasonable time a comprehensive settlement of which Israeli withdrawal would be a part. But as the prospects for settlement recede, the perspective changes. Israel remains in the occupied territories.

Abba Eban told the United Nations on October 8, 1968, that when permanent boundaries are agreed upon the consequent "disposition of forces" will be carried out "under the final peace." Where those boundaries might be he did not specify (for obvious bargaining reasons, one could say, since negotiations had not begun). The United States, however, is not engaged in this negotiation. It need have no hesitation in stating its own view that the permanent boundaries should be in the vicinity of the old armistice lines rather than the present cease-fire lines.

The form of Arab acceptance of Israel and of the new frontiers is another crucial question. Israel's insistence on signed contractual documents specifying definite Arab obligations *to Israel*, not just pledges to the Security Council or statements to the world at large, is well known. The peace Israel wants is one which spells out a relationship "with far-reaching political, practical, and juridical consequences," as Eban put it. The terms appear to include diplomatic relations and borders open to trade and travel. It is reasonable in the abstract, but the real question is what can reasonably be required of the Arab states, given the whole history and setting of this problem. Surely they should be obliged to pledge in some way to accept Israel as a sovereign state within the agreed frontiers, to live at peace with that state, and to refrain from belligerent acts including infiltration and terrorism. They cannot, however, be expected to sign a treaty dictated by Israel or to accept a series of restrictions on what are the normal attributes of any state's sovereignty. It is a fiction that somehow a treaty will bring peace to the Middle East regardless of deeply rooted Arab attitudes. The fact is that distrust and hostility on both sides will remain whatever the form of settlement and that the best chance of tempering and gradually wearing down these feelings is to search for a form that contains the elements of compromise and can gain international support. The United States should hold no brief for Arab intransigence or Arab vows to fight again after a temporary period of peace. It cannot condone an Arab position based on the Khartoum formula of no recognition of Israel, no negotiations, and no peace. But neither should it be tied to an Israeli position which the Arabs see as a demand for capitulation.

The United States, in its general advocacy of a negotiated settlement through the Jarring mission, has not taken a public position in any serious way divergent from that of Israel. An American stand showing greater independence, stressing the temporary character of Israel's occupation of Arab territory and the still to be determined status of Jerusalem, would clear the air and give the lie to those who charge the United States with 100 percent backing of Israel no matter what the rights and wrongs. Whatever their governments might say, the record would then be there for the Arab peoples to see, now and in the future.

It is especially important that Israel take account of America's reluctance to commit itself to an Israeli security policy based only on the military considerations of the present situation, for such a policy offers no way out of the arms race and the cycle of war. "Secure and recognized frontiers" are the words of the UN resolution. The only real security comes from recognition by the world community (and by the Arab states) of frontiers deemed reasonable and durable and worthy of guarantees, not from a concept of maximum physical security imposed on others. The issue of willingness to give up, at the appropriate time and with the necessary assurances on the Arab side, the strategic lines of defense won in 1967 is a test of Israel's view of the future. A positive answer would provide the grounds for American and international action to curb Arab military operations and also to support and guarantee the consolidation of peace in the Middle East. We may deplore the acts of violence on both sides which ignore the current cease-fire lines. But neither the United States nor other powers can make the firm commitments to maintain these temporary lines that they could to guarantee frontiers agreed upon in connection with an Israeli withdrawal.

This approach to Israel's security also provides a key to the vexing question of whether to sell advanced American weapons to Israel. The current request for F-4 aircraft may well be granted, since 1968 is an election year in the United States and the sale would give Israel a needed boost in morale and in military strength at a time when there has been an obvious buildup in the UAR. The important question is the long-range one. Should the United States, having become Israel's main supplier, continue to meet all such requests in the future, abetting an uncontrolled arms race, without regard to the political situation?

If we assume no agreement on arms control, an Israel which had given up its forward positions or declared its willingness to do so on condition of Arab acceptance of its sovereign existence should have what it needs to maintain its deterrent power. But an Israel which gives no sign that it will ever give up the occupied territories should receive no special consideration from the United States.

The whole question of the arms race is crucial to peace, but we have done no more than grasp at the corners of it. Neither Israel nor the UAR will even think of limitations on arms, though the race is a heavy burden on them, so long as their conflict has its life-and-death character. Control is especially difficult since the Soviet Union for over a decade has used arms deliveries as its most potent political instrument. The United States has had no alternative but to use them in the same way, in order to help keep Israel from exposure to certain aggression and to buttress friendly regimes in Jordan, Saudi Arabia, and elsewhere.

Only if the dangers or the costs of the arms race bring changed views in Cairo or Moscow can the United States do much to control it. The UAR will not change unless domestic crisis cuts down its ambitions or the Soviet Union checks the flow of arms on easy terms. Nasser has not been comfortable in a situation in which his dependence on Russia increases but a decisive edge over Israel is as remote as ever. Moscow's caution is perhaps a stronger ground for hope, though a comprehensive system of control, which would have to cover other supplying and receiving nations—the Russians might insist on including Turkey and Iran—would be immensely difficult to obtain. Yet the Soviet Union is already in agreement with the United States to keep nuclear weapons out of the hands of local governments. It has shown circumspection in meeting Nasser's requests for weapons, as has the United States with respect to Israel. Here at least is an opening for further diplomacy.

The Promise of Limited Measures

If hope for a comprehensive package settlement recedes into nothingness, what next? It does little good to condemn the obduracy of leaders in Jerusalem or Cairo. Each side has weighed the consequences of yielding positions and getting on to serious negotiations against the consequences of living with the situation as it is and as it may become. Yet if the whole is unobtainable, perhaps one can chip away at the mass of problems in piecemeal fashion. Partial settlements or even unilateral actions could perhaps resolve some troublesome disputes and open the way to broader agreements later on. We cannot expect Israel and the Arab states to give way on principles in little deals if they will not do so in a big deal, but both may see something to be gained through practical de facto arrangements which finesse the questions of principle. There are also some matters in which states other than the disputants have specific interests of their own at stake and could press effectively for solutions.

Four possible areas of limited settlement are (a) separate bilateral general settlements between Israel and individual Arab states, (b) economic and other special arrangements, (c) the problem of refugees, and (d) the Suez Canal.

As time passes and the political picture changes, separate bilateral arrangements between Israel and one or more of its Arab neighbors may become possible. Jordan, with its survival at stake, could some day come to the decision to conclude a separate peace with Israel, moving without President Nasser's express consent. Or a government in Cairo might conclude that its urgent and primary tasks lay in Egypt rather than in an unending struggle over Palestine and that it was worth paying a price to do away with the humiliating Israeli presence on Egyptian territory. In either case (and in that of Syria, too, if the time ever comes when a Syrian government decides to talk reason instead of unceasing propaganda), the basis of a deal is there, especially if certain difficult issues with special international aspects are left for future settlement. All this is a large order, dependent on changes of heart or of government perhaps only slightly less improbable than a general settlement involving all parties.

It may be more practical to encourage modest bilateral arrangements or unilateral moves which do not face frontally the question of formal peace and recognition. Here the main opportunities lie in the economic relations between Israel and Jordan. The existing traffic in persons and goods across the Jordan River could be broadened by the independent decisions of the two governments. Tourism, in the past an important source of revenue to both Israel and Jordan, could be expanded with a minimum of practical cooperation. Another possibility is for Israel to make available transportation routes and port facilities so that Jordan's trade would have access to the Mediterranean. Israel might well make economic sacrifices in return for a political breakthrough.

Such economic arrangements, to be sure, would be much easier to put through if Israel would first make a significant gesture on the political side. It could improve its treatment of the people of the West Bank. With appropriate arrangements to avoid prejudicing its security, it could turn over a portion of the West Bank to provisional Jordanian administration. That would be a clear and convincing sign of an intention to come to an eventual settlement with a Jordanian state that again spanned the Jordan River. It would be a bold stroke, not easy for Israel to take, but surely a more hopeful direction for boldness than that of annexing territory or of creating its own Arab satellite state in Palestine.

Another matter which need not await a comprehensive political settlement is the fate of the Palestine Arab refugees. Years of debate and resolutions in the United Nations have made the world aware of the dimensions of the problem as the refugees, by now numbering over 1.3 million, continue to subsist on UN charity in the countries surrounding Israel. The June war, by creating over 300,000 more refugees, made the situation worse, but it so changed the political landscape that some movement now seems possible toward making it better.

For two decades the refugee problem has been locked into the conflict which produced it, the partition of Palestine and the creation of Israel. No room for compromise has been found. If both sides hold to their former positions, it is hard to see where the justice generally recognized as due the refugees is going to come from. But new facts are at hand, the most important being Israel's physical control, through occupation of the territories where they reside, over roughly one-half of the refugees of 1948 vintage.

Here again the problem is one that principally concerns Israel and Jordan, and both are in a position to take certain steps that do not require an overall settlement. First of all, Israel could permit the return to the West Bank of all those Arabs who fled to the East Bank at the time of the war of 1967 and wish to come back. Such an act would provide a modicum of justice to the refugees and at the same time a sign of Israel's recognition that the West Bank will remain Arab and will not be used to make room for Jewish settlement. Israel on the West Bank and Jordan on the East Bank could undertake programs of development which would create jobs for refugees and absorb them into the economy. Israel could provide them with additional financial help as part of the compensation so often mentioned in UN resolutions as due the refugee community for its abandoned property. The same bold approach could be made in the miserably overcrowded Gaza Strip toward helping refugees settle on the West Bank or elsewhere. Recent Israeli statements show at least a new openness of mind on these matters.

The world has a humanitarian concern and also a financial one. Those countries contributing to the UN Relief and Works Agency (UNRWA), the agency which bears the bulk of the responsibility for providing food, services, and education for the refugees, are going to be looking impatiently for ways in which these unfortunate human beings can be given a choice for a new life and a helping hand to get there, and for ways in which funds can be used to reduce and eventually liquidate the problem itself rather than merely to alleviate and perpetuate conditions of misery and hopelessness. The U.S. Congress, as the chief provider of funds for UNRWA, may not be prepared to wait indefinitely.

Finally, something might be done about a problem where local deadlock directly prejudices the interests of many nations and of world commerce: the closed Suez Canal. Israel accomplished in 1967 what Britain and France failed to do in 1956. It put its military forces in physical possession of the east bank of the canal. Thus it gained a strong defensive position against any Egyptian attempt to return to Sinai, denied to Egypt a major source of revenue, and acquired a valuable bargaining counter for reaching the kind of settlement with Egypt it wanted, including the right of Israeli ships to use the canal. Until some move toward satisfaction of its demands takes place, Israel is content to leave things as they are. The UAR, which is receiving payments from the oil-rich Arab states to replace canal revenues, has been content to do the same.

Meanwhile other nations, suffering serious inconvenience and financial loss, are not so content. British losses in shipping costs have been high, although Middle East oil is still available by supertankers making the long haul round the Cape. The Soviet Union is inconvenienced by inability to send naval vessels through to the Red Sea and the Persian Gulf and to move its shipments to Vietnam by the shortest sea route. The United States has no pressing interest in reopening the canal, other than to help serve the interests of friendly countries and of international trade. In fact, it might prefer to have it remain closed in order to keep the Soviet Union at a disadvantage.

Two strong considerations, however, argue that an effort be made at some point to reopen the canal. The first is that, regardless of momentary advantage or disadvantage, the Suez Canal is an international waterway of present and future as well as past importance and cannot be allowed to fill up with sand and be forgotten. The second factor is that this is an area in which the impasse between Israel and the UAR might be broken.

If the Cairo government wished to clear and reopen the canal, perhaps with the help of other countries, the obvious bargain would be for Israel to agree not to interfere in exchange for the right of passage for Israeli ships. Forces of both sides might be pulled back a few miles and a UN force established to patrol the evacuated zone. All parts of such an agreement would deserve the strong support of the United States.

All these are speculations, not meant as specific proposals but as illustrations of the point that a variety of opportunities for partial settlement are there to be pursued even though the general questions of peace and recognition have no chance at all.

Thus, several avenues are open to American initiative: to help check the current rise in violence, to establish a more tenable position for the long run in relations with both Israel and the Arab states, and to explore the possibility of limited or partial settlements. The United States can do much on its own. Its success, however, will surely be affected by the looming presence of the Russians.

The Soviet-American Relationship

From Israeli friends an American listener will hear that, unless the United States gives full support to Israel, the Arab radicals inevitably will win out in one country after another and that the real victor will be the Soviet Union, the real loser the United States. From Arab friends the same listener will hear that it is American support for Israel that drives all Arabs into the radical camp and into the arms of the Russians and that there is no surer way to sacrifice American interests in the Middle East. Perhaps two conclusions can be drawn from these conflicting pieces of advice. One is that, despite the self-interest of the speakers, what they say has enough validity to illustrate the "heads you win, tails I lose" character of some of the choices before us. The second is that the United States, looking beyond any simple formula, must reach its own conclusions on Soviet interests and policies in this region and on their interaction with its own.

Ironically, after twenty years of pursuing its aims in the Middle East by trying to thwart the Soviet Union and hold Russian influence to a minimum, the United States now seems more and more dependent for the attainment of those aims on some substantial measure of agreement with its adversary. One example: we have favored and worked for a general Arab-Israeli settlement through the Jarring mission, all the while knowing that probably the only way it can be brought about is by concerted Soviet and American pressure on the respective parties. Another example: we have found no answer to the spiraling arms race in the area, in which the two great powers and others are arming all and sundry, other than to appeal for a system of arms control which must rest on Soviet cooperation. A third: effective UN action to keep peace on the cease-fire lines today requires a foundation of American-Soviet agreement.

Above all, the world cannot permit a "fourth round" to imperil the peace of all, and "the world" in this case may mean the United States and the Soviet Union. Both have compelling reasons to resist being drawn into military operations by their ties with Israel or the Arab states. An established pattern of consultation would enable them to see and forestall approaching danger well ahead of time.

The argument that all depends on consultation and negotiation should not be overdrawn. Waiting for the men in the Kremlin to make agreements which would serve our purposes may mean waiting forever. They will move toward agreements only when they feel it will advance their own purposes. That point has not yet been reached in the Middle East, and an early summit meeting would not be likely to bring it nearer. Whether and when it will be reached depends both on the success the United States has with its own policies in the area and on the problems and difficulties that beset the Soviet Union. On both counts we may be permitted a feeling of tempered optimism for the future if not for the present.

Positions and policies which may serve the United States in what is likely to be a period of transition have already been described: maintenance of our military strength; full cooperation with Turkey and Iran; equitable dealing with both sides in the Arab-Israeli conflict in the hope of contributing to the settlement of differences as that becomes possible; friendly relations with the moderate Arab regimes without losing contact with the radicals; avoidance of polarization which locks local conflicts into those of the great powers; increasing ties with peoples regardless of changes in political regimes.

On the economic side, we should be ready to help those nations that need and can profitably use such help—bearing in mind that in the Arab world the main need is not for outside aid (other than technical) but, once the situation permits, for a more equitable distribution of income from the vast oil wealth, which nature has distributed so unevenly. Americans are wont to put faith in bold regional economic schemes as a way toward peace in troubled areas. But we should have no illusions about bridging political differences with huge nuclear desalination and power plants, though in the long run they could dramatically raise living standards. All in all, the policies called for in the near future will not require a vast outlay of material resources from the United States. The crucial requirements are imagination, steadiness, and highly competent diplomacy.

If the United States encounters difficulties and setbacks—as it will—so will the Soviet Union. Given the heavy demands on its resources, the Soviet Union will not be able to pour large sums into challenging the United States in its strong suit of wide-ranging naval and air power or into meeting the pleas of Middle Eastern clients. Syria and Iraq have deep economic troubles. If Jordan should turn to the left, would Moscow be ready to replace subsidies paid in the past by London, Washington, and the conservative Arab states? As for Egypt, to assume responsibility for the continuing growth of its economy would be to take on the task of Sisyphus; and not to do so would raise trouble with Cairo. If the Soviet presence grows, moreover, friction with the Egyptians will also grow, as is already apparent in the military field.

The Soviets may win propaganda victories in the Arab world, but unless they can deliver victories over Israel or guarantee the fulfillment of promises the Arab leaders have made to their own people, they may pay the price of Arab frustration. They must already have doubts about the stability and reliability of their client states. Arab nationalism, which Moscow has done so much to encourage, is hostile to domination by all outside powers, including the Soviet Union. The ideological ties, the common devotion to the ideas of socialism about which much is heard from both sides, would fade away once the "Arab socialists" saw behind the proclaimed solidarity a Soviet attempt to impose its own type of socialism on them. Moreover, the radical Arab states are engaged in competition among themselves, causing their patron to do a balancing act in order to maintain influence with all of them. In the conservative oil-producing states there is little chance for Soviet gains short of revolution, and the revolution itself would be nationalist rather than socialist.

All this is no prediction that Soviet policy will come to grief in the shifting sands of Arab politics. It is merely an indication that the Soviet Union is limited in what it can accomplish and may see its troubles mount and its victories turn sour. The day may come when its leaders will begin to count the costs of cold war competition in the Middle East and measure them against the results. Both powers may in the end come to the reasonable conclusion that neither is going to dominate the Middle East and that the aim of denying it to the other may be achieved with less danger and at much lower cost by tacit or explicit agreement than by frenzied competition.

The United States should by no means act as if that day were here before it arrives. Official Soviet thinking is encrusted with habits and slogans of the past. There is no steady progress toward greater liberalization at home or greater cooperation with the United States in matters of foreign policy. The struggle against imperialism and the inexorable forward march of socialism are concepts which have reality in the Soviet leaders' minds, so far as we can read them. Yet these same leaders can coolly assess the national interest in terms of risk and of cost, and they have made agreements with the "imperialists" when areas of common interest have appeared.

Whether and when the two great powers will find common ground in the Middle East, beyond the urgent interest in avoiding nuclear war, is an open question. We should work to enlarge the possibilities of agreement, being tough or conciliatory as the changing situation may demand and always recognizing that the Middle East is not the only or the determining factor in the Soviet-American relationship. Should the trend be toward agreement or away from it, the United States can best prepare for either contingency by establishing and maintaining a durable position of its own in relations with the peoples of the Middle East.

RICHARD N. COOPER

THE DOLLAR AND THE WORLD ECONOMY

International monetary relations were badly unsettled in the winter and spring of 1967-68 by devaluation of the pound sterling and thirteen other currencies, a massive rush to buy gold, and a flight from the French franc, all in rapid succession. These disturbances were aggravated by failure to keep the world's two largest free enterprise economies on an even keel. Inflationary demands rose sharply in the United States after 1965, and Germany, in contrast, experienced its first true recession since the end of the Second World War. As a result, the balance-of-payments deficit of the United States became alarmingly large.

Such developments do not directly touch the man in the street, except perhaps by making him vaguely uneasy. But he should not be indifferent to the nature and operation of the international monetary system—the formal rules and the informal conventions which govern international trade and payments—for they in fact strongly influence his opportunities for employment, the prices he pays, and the wages he receives—in short, his standard of living.

In these terms, the present international monetary system has served the world extremely well. The past two decades have seen unparalleled growth in world production and trade, and in standards of living. Even the laggards in economic growth, such as Britain, have grown rapidly by historical standards. And while the less developed countries have not shared fully in this rapid growth, taken as a group they too have performed well by the standards of the past. Furthermore, the world economy has been maintained on a relatively smooth course over the period, and inflation in major countries has been moderate.

While there is ample room for self-congratulation, there is also a danger of becoming smug. The year 1929 also followed a prolonged period of prosperity. Although the present international monetary system has done well, it contains tensions—internal contradictions, Marxists would call them—that threaten the continuation of this prosperity unless new and imaginative policies are adopted to cope with them. The pages that follow attempt to describe the formal features of the present international monetary system, to outline the unexpected developments and strains that emerge from it, to discuss the U.S. balance-of-payments deficit as both a cause and a consequence of those strains, and to consider measures that might be adopted, both within the present system and by changing it, to relieve the strains.

The Present International Monetary System

The basic outlines of the present monetary system, agreed upon at an international conference in Bretton Woods, New Hampshire, in 1944, were in direct response to the economic and political disasters of the 1930s. At that time, economic depression and financial collapse had been transmitted rapidly from one nation to another. Each country felt itself trapped in a web of relationships which it was too small to influence and from which it could not escape. Some, such as Germany, turned to radical political solutions and broke sharply with the international order; others, to varying degrees, stayed with it and suffered the economic consequences.

The postwar international monetary system was designed therefore to protect from international intrusion the commitment, recently adopted by virtually all major governments, to maintain full employment, and to do so while fostering efficient use of the world's resources. More fundamentally, its aim was to introduce monetary order into a world of interdependent nations: to define and police certain rules of international behavior. The rules of conduct called on each nation to specify a fixed and single rate at which its currency would exchange for others and to eliminate artificial restrictions on the freedom of its residents to make payments to other countries for the purchase of goods and services. These rules approximate those that prevail within a single country with a single, freely usable currency. There were several important differences, however. First, the injunction against restrictions did not extend to purchasing securities, making loans, or establishing businesses—movements of capital, in the economists's jargon. Second, exchange rates between currencies were not absolutely fixed. They were permitted to vary within 1 percent on either side of the declared parity, allowing some flexibility. More important, exchange parities could be changed occasionally, but only under conditions of fundamental balance-of-payments disequilibrium and only with international agreement. In principle, such changes could be either upward or downward; in practice, with only three exceptions, all changes have been downward, despite the fact that balance-of-payments surpluses have been quite as numerous as deficits.

The logic of fixed and only rarely changed exchange rates in combination with freedom from controls over foreign trade in goods and services required adequate international reserves to finance the inevitable imbalances in payments—differences between total payments to foreigners and total receipts from foreigners, before allowing for the residual financing. By long tradition, gold provided the most important form of international reserve. It was almost universally acceptable among banks and governments, and could therefore be used to settle residual debts between one country and another. But, for reasons to be given below, gold was likely to be insufficient in amount and inappropriately distributed among countries to fulfill this role adequately in the new system. The International Monetary Fund (IMF) was therefore established to police the new rules and to provide occasional financial support to member countries, through its own lending operations, to make adherence to the rules possible. Only when it became clear that a country's foreign trade position could not be indefinitely sustained—when it was in "fundamental disequilibrium," in the undefined terms of the IMF—would a change in exchange parity be in order.

The main features of this system for dealing with financial interactions among countries can be etched more sharply against the background of the principal alternative arrangements that prevailed at various times and to various degrees in earlier years. These systems involve, respectively, completely fixed exchange rates, flexible exchange rates, and extensive resort to direct controls over international transactions.

Under the pre-1913 gold standard, national currencies were tied to gold —immutably, it was thought—at fixed prices, and this in turn implied fixed exchange rates between currencies, except for a small margin arising from the cost of shipping gold from one country to another. Under this system, a country experiencing a deficit in its international payments would finance it by selling gold. The outflow of gold in turn would reduce the domestic supply of money, tending to push interest rates upward and to produce a decline in business activity. Unemployment was likely to result, at least temporarily. In addition, swings in the business cycle were transmitted rapidly from country to country, for a downturn in one country would reduce its imports, causing payments deficits and inducing contractions elsewhere. An attempt was made to restore this system after the First World War, but even then countries were becoming more desirous of gearing monetary policy, still in its formative stages, to stabilization of the domestic economy, an assignment that often conflicted with balance-of-payments requirements. Engulfment of the world in the Great Depression strongly reinforced this desire and doomed continued acceptability of an international gold standard.

In the years immediately following the First World War, and again for a brief period in the 1930s, flexible exchange rates seemed to offer relief from the rigors of the gold standard system. Exchange rates, far from being tied rigidly one to another, were allowed to vary freely from day to day according to the dictates of supply and demand, like prices in the commodity markets. This arrangement was not fully satisfactory either. In the unsettled postwar years, speculation for or against a particular currency, by keeping its value too high or depressing it excessively, often impeded needed processes of adjustment and contributed either to economic depression or to rampant inflation. Later, in the 1930s, some governments deliberately depressed the international value of their currencies to stimulate domestic employment—but at the expense of employment in other countries. In neither period did flexible rates prove workable.

Direct governmental controls over international transactions—regulations concerning which payments could be made, to whom, and for what —first came into prominence during the First World War. They were revived by several countries, notably Nazi Germany, in the 1930s and became widespread during and after the Second World War. Such controls badly disrupted the trading world. To mitigate the obvious inefficiencies they introduced, such as resulted when two countries in serious payments difficulty restricted trade with each other, pairs of countries entered into bilateral trading arrangements. These usually led to trade discrimination, often became instruments of diplomatic manipulation, and always were highly disruptive of political relations between participants and nonparticipants. By the late 1940s it was widely recognized that extensive and indiscriminate use of direct controls did not represent a viable system of international trade and payments.

The framework of the present payments system was designed to provide exchange stability, yet, by allowing for changes in parities, to avoid the straitjacket of the gold standard. It was designed to preclude the need for controls over trade by providing adequate financing for temporary balance-of-payments deficits, yet also to provide a suitable mechanism for correcting lasting imbalances. Above all, it was designed to provide a forum and a frame of reference in which international economic cooperation could supplant economically disruptive and politically damaging competition among national policies designed to protect each nation's balance of payments.

As noted at the outset, this system has been highly successful. Thanks largely to vast improvements in the use and direction of domestic economic policies, depressions have been avoided and economic growth has been both substantial and relatively steady. Although many less developed countries have countered the trend, direct controls by the major industrial nations were drastically reduced by the mid-1960s. Serious balance-of-payments disturbances have not disappeared, but the system has provided enough flexibility to prevent these, until recently, from becoming a substantial bar to progress. International trade has flourished.

Further Developments and Emerging Strains

The payments system laid down in 1944 was not entirely realized in practice, however, due to certain subsequent developments. Chief among these were the emergence of the U.S. dollar as an international currency and, indeed, as a widely accepted reserve asset, like gold; and the great increase in the degree of economic interdependence between nations, especially as reflected in the international mobility of capital. Both these developments, which will be discussed below, represented natural but nonetheless significant departures from the basic design. First, however, a word should be said about the role of gold in the present international payments system, as a prelude to discussion of the dollar.

GOLD

The payments system outlined in 1944 depended heavily for its efficient operation on the use of international reserves, of which far and away the most important component was gold. But at the close of the Second World War most of the officially held gold was in the hands of the United States; by 1947 the U.S. share exceeded 70 percent. The U.S. Treasury determined the world price of gold by offering to buy or sell gold at a fixed price of $35 an ounce, plus or minus a small commission, in dealings with other monetary authorities "for legitimate monetary purposes." It also supplied gold to U.S. users, such as dentists and jewelers, to fill the gap between U.S. production and U.S. consumption.

The international monetary system could not function properly with gold so heavily concentrated in the hands of one country, particularly a country that had a surplus in its international payments. Reserves elsewhere were simply not sufficient, even when supplemented by the meager lending powers of the IMF, to finance the large imbalances of the late forties which would have developed in the absence of stringent controls over international payments.

The maldistribution of gold, however, merely aggravated a difficulty which was bound to arise, though possibly not for a long time. For use of gold as a commodity and use of gold as an international money, at a fixed and unvarying price, are basically incompatible in today's world. The demand for gold as a commodity is affected by the growth in world income and by the prices of those commodities, such as silver, platinum, and palladium, that compete with gold in desirable properties. Recently the commodity demand for gold, even apart from speculative demands, has risen sharply.

The demand for gold as a monetary reserve could also be expected to grow rapidly. As noted above, the international payments system depends heavily on the financing of international imbalances. The more successful the system—the more rapid the growth in income and trade—the larger these financing requirements would be, even though they might not rise proportionately.

New supplies of gold amount to just under $1.5 billion a year. Seventy-five percent of newly mined gold comes from South Africa, and this is supplemented from time to time by gold sales by Russia. Given a fixed price for gold, new supplies—apart from sales by the USSR, which depend largely on harvest conditions there and are entirely arbitrary as far as western needs are concerned—depend on the costs of mining gold. With wages and other costs rising and with the best mines gradually being exhausted, an expanding or even steady production of gold depends crucially on technological improvements in mining. Despite technological advances, production has declined in most gold mining countries, with the important exception of South Africa. And even there production has leveled off in recent years.

A payments system based on gold reserves thus confronted the world with a grim prospect: inadequate supplies to satisfy competing private and official demands at a fixed price of $35 an ounce. That being so, speculators have gambled on a rise in the price of gold, and private speculative demands in the mid-sixties added heavily to the already large demand for gold for industrial and artistic uses.

Raising the official price of gold offers a way out. A higher price would at once increase the value of existing production and stocks, and would undoubtedly stimulate new production. There are four standard objections to this course of action. First, revaluing by the stroke of a pen $40 billion in official gold, plus large additional amounts in private hands, would be strongly inflationary, creating pressures that in practice could be compensated by restrictive monetary and fiscal policies only with difficulty, if at all. Second, the distribution of the capital gains would be heavily skewed in favor of the wealthy countries, which hold most of the monetary gold; and the principal continuing beneficiaries of the price increase would be South Africa and the Soviet Union, both of which have already benefited greatly from what amounts to a commodity price support scheme for their major export product. Third, a once-for-all price increase would offer only a temporary solution to the problem of inadequate supplies; eventually (though perhaps not for a long time) a further increase would be required. Finally, and most fundamentally, revaluing gold would ratify its continued use for international settlements and would impose the real costs of taking gold from the ground merely to store it in vaults under the ground. We learned long ago that it is not necessary to use a valuable commodity for settlement of domestic debts, and substituted instead banknotes and other forms of legal tender.

A similar substitution can be effected for settlement of international debts, and it is currently in the process of being worked out. It is a more rational method, for it avoids diverting a useful metal to monetary purposes; but it is also more complicated than a rise in the official price of gold. Two steps have been taken toward this solution, the first carefully planned and under discussion for some five years, the second adopted hurriedly under crisis conditions. The planned step involves creation of a man-made substitute for gold for use in international settlements; the unplanned step separated official gold from private gold, and allowed supply and demand to determine the price of the latter.

The proposed substitute for gold takes the form of a Special Drawing Right (SDR) on the International Monetary Fund. It is to be created and allocated among countries by international agreement in amounts that seem to be required to serve the purposes of the international monetary system. SDRs have been approved, and the required changes in the IMF and in national laws may be expected to take effect in 1969. SDRs should be created soon thereafter, although there is reluctance among some European countries to create them so long as the United States is running a large payments deficit.

SDRs will be transferable among all members of the IMF, like cash, and they will be convertible into the currency of any member. They will not circulate generally, however; like gold in the major countries, they will be used for settlement only among central banks. Nor will they supplant monetary gold, at least for a very long time. But they can substitute for gold where it counts, as increments to international reserves, and can thereby free the payments system from its dependence on gold.

Widespread belief in this dependence led in the winter of 1967–68 to heavy speculation on an increase in the price of gold. Central banks sold over $3 billion worth of gold to private markets in an effort to keep the free market price of gold from rising substantially above the official price of $35 an ounce. Then in a historic decision in mid-March, the major central banks split the market for gold into two distinct parts: an official sector in which gold transfers would take place at the official price, and a private market in which the price of gold would be governed by supply and demand, without official intervention. The decision furthermore seemed to break the link between these two markets, at least temporarily. In view of the new SDRs, central banks stated that they no longer saw any need either to sell to the private market or, more significantly, to buy from it. Following creation of this two-price system, the private price of gold rose above $35 an ounce. But it rose remarkably little, considering the fact that South Africa virtually cut off its gold sales. Users' needs were thus supplied by small producers and, evidently, by substantial dishoarding.

The two-price system leaves unsettled the question of what happens if the gap widens between the two prices, when and how official gold will be disposed of, and what becomes of any "capital gain" arising from disposition of the gold. These questions may become important at some time, but they are not urgent today. One proposal would have all monetary gold turned into a central account in exchange for transferable certificates, the gold to be disposed of later by joint decision. But central banks are not likely to agree to such a proposal until they have had several years of successful experience with SDRs.

THE DOLLAR AS AN INTERNATIONAL CURRENCY

The shortage of monetary gold would have been far more acute had it not been for another, much earlier development—the emergence of the U.S. dollar as an acceptable reserve asset. Rebuilding war-depleted reserves around the world required some redistribution of gold from the United States in the late 1940s, but even such a redistribution would have been inadequate to support the large growth in trade that subsequently took place. Fortunately, many countries were willing to build up their reserves with dollars—in practice, bank deposits and U.S. Treasury securities. The dollar was widely acceptable in settlement of debts. By using dollars, foreign monetary authorities could avoid gold transaction costs, and in the meantime earn interest on their unused dollar balances.

A more technical reason for emergence of the dollar as a reserve currency lies in the detailed functioning of the payments system. Under the pre-1913 gold standard, gold circulated freely, major banks converted gold into national currencies at a fixed price, and exchange rates were held within narrow bounds. After the Second World War, only the United States and Switzerland officially bought and sold gold for domestic currency at a fixed price, and there was no inclination in some countries, including the United Kingdom and the United States, to permit residents to deal freely in gold. But all adherents to the IMF rules were obliged to keep their exchange rates within prescribed margins around parity, and they needed a mechanism for doing so. Most countries adopted the method of holding the exchange rate with the *dollar* within the prescribed margins by buying and selling dollars against the local currency. By virtue of this arrangement, the dollar became an "intervention currency," and countries needed at least working balances in dollars for day-to-day intervention in the exchange markets. Thus the surpluses countries earned initially took the form of dollar accumulations. It was convenient and profitable to retain reserves in this form and the dollar also became a reserve currency. (The British pound played a similar role for countries within the sterling area.) Formal symmetry among national currencies thus gave way to marked asymmetry, dictated not merely by differences in national size but also by the mechanism itself, with the dollar playing a pivotal role.

Use of the dollar as a reserve currency relieved the potential shortage of international reserves, for reserves could grow despite limited gold supplies to the extent that other countries accumulated dollars and so long as the United States did not regard such dollar liabilities—for dollar reserves of other countries represent claims on the United States—as an equivalent loss to its own reserves. But emergence of the dollar in this role also posed two problems for the payments system.

First, relief from the gold shortage was purchased at the price of a gradual weakening of the credibility of continued convertibility of dollars into gold at a fixed price. The U.S. Treasury stands ready to convert foreign official dollar claims into gold at foreign initiative. But as the dollar claims grow, the Treasury's ability to do this lessens. Dollar claims of official holders exceeded the U.S. gold stock for the first time in 1965. There is, of course, no magic in equality between the U.S. liabilities represented by those claims and the value of the U.S. gold stock, not least because of large foreign *private* claims on the United States. Just as commercial banks thrive on having short-term liabilities to their depositors far in excess of assets which can be quickly mobilized, in confidence that not all depositors will wish to withdraw at the same time, the United States as banker to the rest of the world need not have liquid reserves as large as its liabilities. Indeed, *total* U.S. claims on foreigners, including private U.S. investment abroad, far exceed foreign claims on the United States.

Nevertheless, the U.S. payments deficit has persisted for more than a decade. With U.S. gold reserves declining and U.S. liabilities to the rest of the world increasing, a number of central banks have become restive about accumulating and holding additional dollars, and the possibility of large-scale conversion is there. If foreign dollar reserves continue to rise, the gap between them and U.S. reserves will continue to widen, possibly posing a threat to the stability of reserve holdings; if they do not continue to rise, the world will sooner or later face a reserve shortage. The new SDRs, once they come into being, can solve this dilemma.

The second problem posed by the emergence of the dollar as a reserve currency concerns the apparent absence of restraint on U.S. payments deficits that this role implies. Indeed, U.S. payments deficits have been large and they have become a source of controversy and strain. The complaints have taken on political overtones. The United States has been accused of "printing" international money to finance its ventures abroad. General de Gaulle regards the reserve currency role of the dollar as merely one aspect of American hegemony, and he has referred to the "exorbitant privilege" of the reserve currency countries to finance payments deficits through foreign accrual of their national currencies. Two particular abuses of the international printing press have been alleged: the sharp rise in American investment in Europe, and the large increase in overseas expenditures associated with the war in Vietnam. The first development gave rise to the charge that the United States was buying up Europe and that the purchase was being financed by European central banks; the second to the charge that Europeans were financing an American military adventure about which they were not consulted and of which a great many of them disapproved.

Willful abuse of the "privilege" is not required to create a problem for the international monetary system, for the net flow of dollars to central banks around the world results from myriad decisions of businessmen and individuals about how and when and where to spend their money, rather than from world demands for additional reserves. While U.S. monetary, fiscal, and other policies can influence these flows, U.S. authorities may find it inexpedient to make their ideas about world reserve needs the sole or even principal criterion for exerting such influence. As has been plainly illustrated during the past several years, monetary policy has been called on to serve a variety of objectives, and the monetary authorities have occasionally found themselves caught between equally persuasive considerations for easing the monetary reins on the one hand and for tightening them on the other.

By converting unwanted dollars into gold, foreign central banks may attempt to exert pressure for measures which reduce the U.S. payments deficit; France did this gradually after 1963, with the silent approval of many other European countries. But they undertake these actions only at the risk of compromising more rapidly the convertibility of dollars into gold, on which the payments system is thought to rest. Moreover, the use of gold conversions to influence U.S. policies that in turn influence the course of the world economy represents a clumsy and ineffectual method of coordinating economic policies. Cooperation in framing policies would be preferable.

The absence of satisfactory, smoothly operating methods for controlling imbalances in international payments is perhaps the major weakness of the present international payments system. But because of the pivotal role of the dollar in international finance, for the United States this weakness takes the particular form indicated here: the haphazard linkage between the supply of additional reserves, provided by U.S. payments deficits, and the demand for them, combined with the great disruption that would result from applying the IMF prescription for fundamental disequilibrium to the United States. In dealing with its payments deficit, the United States has had to thread its way delicately between a desire to reduce the deficit and a desire to avoid measures for reducing the deficit that would be destructive of domestic objectives or international order.

GREATER ECONOMIC INTERDEPENDENCE

More significant for the long run than the strains associated either with gold or with use of the dollar as an international currency, and certainly more perplexing for policy, is the growth of economic interdependence among countries, a growth that will result in more intense clashes between national and international considerations in framing economic policies. This interdependence is due in large measure to vast improvements in transportation and communication which make the world smaller in every sense but the physical. International transport has become faster and more reliable, and it has also become cheaper relative to the value of the goods shipped. Business familiarity with foreign markets has increased greatly and, combined with rapid communications, permits firms to take advantage of market opportunities that in previous times would have been ignored.

But the growth in interdependence derives also from the success of the payments system itself. Among industrial countries, tariffs have been sharply reduced and quantitative restrictions on trade in industrial products have been virtually eliminated. Currencies have become more readily acceptable, and the risks and uncertainties in dealing with other countries have diminished.

Improvements in communication and increased familiarity have been especially significant for the movement of funds between countries. The rapid growth of the Eurodollar market from the late fifties and the even more rapid growth of the international bond market since the early sixties are both consequences of these developments. By the end of 1967 total deposits in the Eurodollar market—a market made by European banks (including branches of American banks) in dollar deposits and short-term claims—amounted to $16 billion, more than the total money supply of many individual European countries. The international bond market brings together long-term borrowers and long-term lenders outside of any single national securities market. Borrowers are large firms of international reputation, many of them American, plus a number of governmental entities that find it too difficult or too costly to float issues in their home markets; lenders come from all over the world, with roughly half the funds coming immediately through Switzerland, on behalf of customers elsewhere. Most of the issues are denominated in U.S. dollars. Although smaller than the Eurodollar market, the international bond market has grown even more remarkably, from less than $200 million of new issues in 1963 to well over $3 billion in 1968.

Both markets have become large enough to influence developments in national financial markets. Short-term investors can elect to hold their funds in their national currency or to place them in Eurodollars. Which option they choose depends on relative yields and risks. Similarly, long-term investors can put their funds either directly into national markets or into the international bond market. The existence of these new options tends to tie national markets together, making it increasingly difficult for national interest rates to get far out of line with those prevailing in the international market, except in periods of heavy speculation on changes in exchange parities, or through the use of restrictions to isolate national markets from international influences.

Interdependence has also grown outside the areas of trade and financial flows. Business firms increasingly look beyond national boundaries for locations. People move across national boundaries more readily in response to economic incentives, a fact that leads, in the case of the skilled, to the "brain drain." In short, the strictly national orientation of economic behavior, at least within the industrialized countries, is declining; the revolution in communications and transportation is increasing the responsiveness of capital, labor, and commodities to differences in earning opportunities spanning national boundaries. The extent of this responsiveness should not be exaggerated; there is still much attachment to traditional locations and sources of supply. But these attachments are gradually weakening as firms and individuals develop an increasingly international outlook.

The implications of these developments are profound, in two respects. First, the great increase in the international mobility of capital makes the international payments system as laid down a quarter of a century ago all the more difficult to operate effectively, for the prospect of changes in exchange parities gives rise to huge speculative flows of capital. This condition in turn has strengthened official inclinations against changes in exchange rates, both to discourage speculative flows and to avoid rewarding the speculators.

More basically, however, high economic interdependence circumscribes governmental freedom to pursue widely divergent economic policies. When nations are effectively separated by barriers of ignorance and uncertainty, language and law, custom and customs, the responses of business and labor to divergences in national policies remain minor and tolerable. But as foreign commerce and international capital flows become more sensitive to such divergences, the impact on other countries of one country's policies becomes more important. Policy differences tolerable in the past begin to strain both the ability of nations to pursue divergent policies and the functioning of the payments system itself as countries take actions to protect themselves from unwanted side effects.

The constraints imposed on local government by the mobility of business and individuals are familiar to Americans. Taxes and business regulations in one community cannot differ widely from those in surrounding areas or even in distant competing areas, for firms and individuals are free to locate where taxes and regulations are less onerous, and they have shown increasing readiness to do so. Whatever their legal powers, the actual freedom of state and local governments to regulate and to tax is sharply curtailed when labor and capital can locate where their interests are best served and when the product of their effort can be sold anywhere, unimpeded by barriers to trade.

The constraints on national policies imposed by international mobility of men, goods, and money are not yet so binding. But the movement is clearly in that direction. The growing constraint on monetary policy as an instrument of domestic stabilization provides one example: tightening money to curb a domestic boom often pulls in capital from abroad, while easing monetary policy induces capital outflows; in both cases, the effect of monetary action on domestic expenditure is tempered. Businesses have shown increasing willingness to locate in response to tax incentives, and this in turn produces strong pressure for tax "harmonization," for example within the European Common Market. International mobility even exerts pressures on the redistributive and social policies of countries, as illustrated by the exodus of British physicians in response to low salaries and other restraints imposed on them under the National Health Service.

These developments pose a key question: How is the average degree of monetary tightness, or of business regulation, established for the community of nations as a whole? Without international cooperation, the resulting national policies may well work to the disadvantage of all. In particular, interest rates are likely to be higher than may be in the interests of most countries, each nation having responded defensively to developments in neighboring countries. Business regulation is likely to be less comprehensive than is desirable. Just as increasing constraint on freedom of governmental choice at the local level has led to a gradual extension of federal authority within the United States—authority which reaches beyond the mobility of goods, capital, and labor and hence is not so circumscribed by *national* mobility—so increasing constraint on national policy imposed by higher *international* mobility calls for increased international cooperation and, on some issues, even for joint decisions among nations.

Reactions to this increasing interdependence, and to the constraints on national policies that it implies, have pulled in two directions. On the one hand, it has stimulated much closer communication among governments on their economic policies. Central bank officials from eight major countries meet monthly in Switzerland to discuss topics of common interest, and government financial officials meet six or seven times a year in Paris to review the economic outlook and to recommend to each other monetary, fiscal, and balance-of-payments policies compatible with the collective interest. On the other hand, measures have also been taken to insulate national markets partially from international repercussions, to reduce the interdependence. Taxes and other measures have been introduced to counter the effects of monetary policies on international flows of capital. Moreover, extra-territorial application of national rules and regulations—such as when the Securities and Exchange Commission imposes its disclosure requirements on certain Canadian firms or the U.S. Treasury extends its regulations prohibiting trade with mainland China and Cuba to the foreign subsidiaries of American firms—is simply another manifestation of the same phenomenon. National regulatory authorities, frustrated by the actual or potential movement of firms outside their jurisdiction, reach across national boundaries to accomplish their mandates, in the process irritating the countries with foreign-owned firms within their borders.

The U.S. Payments Deficit

Although the U.S. payments deficit has been the focus of international financial discussion during much of the past decade, it cannot be considered apart from the matters dealt with in the preceding section. It has been an irritant in the payments system, a proximate cause of its strains; but it has also been a consequence of those strains, which are more fundamental features of the system and which would have become manifest, if with different timing, had the U.S. deficit been half its actual size.[1]

SOURCES OF THE DEFICIT

The sources of the U.S. payments deficit are complex and diverse. If undue emphasis is laid on single causes and the complex relation among components of the balance of payments is neglected, the deficit can be attributed in the late fifties to a deteriorating competitive position of American products in world markets; in the period 1960–65 to an enormous increase in capital outflows, which more than offset a marked improvement in the competitive position; and since 1965 to large increases in military expenditures at home and abroad, with some resulting deterioration in the competitive position. Even in the most recent period, however, the United States has not been "living beyond its means," by false analogy to a family consuming more than it is earning. A better analogy would be to a dynamic corporation that is borrowing heavily at short term to supplement its own large earnings in financing an ambitious investment program. Indeed, Americans increased their net claims on foreigners very sharply, from $45 billion in 1957 to $49 billion in 1962 to $68 billion at the end of 1967.[2] U.S. investment abroad reached such a magnitude, in fact, that it began to alarm some foreigners. In effect, Americans were lending long (and acquiring equity) by borrowing short to cover some of the new investment, the remainder being financed out of domestic savings. The character of American investment operations vis-à-vis the rest of the world has led some observers to emphasize the role of the American capital market (taken broadly, to include individuals, firms, and banks) in providing financial intermediation for the rest of the world, converting liquid (for-

---

1. I will bypass the important but technical question of how the U.S. payments deficit should be measured. Several concepts vie for leading place, and this fact alone illustrates the difficulty in characterizing simply and directly the international financial position of a country whose financial role in the world is as complex as that of the United States. Differences among the various concepts hinge principally on how various types of capital flow should be treated. The reader interested in these matters might consult my "The Balance of Payments in Review," *Journal of Political Economy*, Vol. 74 (August 1966), pp. 379–95.

2. Net claims on foreigners are calculated to include the U.S. gold stock, which declined by nearly $11 billion during this ten-year period.

eign) savings into long-term (foreign) assets. But a large amount of U.S. savings has also been invested directly abroad.

Although partisans of one view or another argue that since expenditure X is the cause of the payments deficit, expenditure X should be reduced to improve the deficit, in strict logic there is no relationship between the proximate cause of the deficit and the most desirable or least costly method for correcting it. To take an obvious and relevant example, most observers might agree that the buildup of U.S. military forces in Vietnam was largely responsible for the payments deficit during the past few years, but it does not follow that the appropriate means for reducing the balance-of-payments deficit is to withdraw the forces; that should be decided on grounds transcending balance-of-payments considerations. Similarly, an increase in domestic demand that cuts the unemployment rate from 4½ percent to 3½ percent may be expected to worsen the trade position, and indeed did so after 1965; but moderating unemployment may be judged a socially desirable development which should not be reversed on balance-of-payments grounds.

PAST AND PROPOSED BALANCE-OF-PAYMENTS POLICIES

The American government early expressed concern about the size of the payments deficit. The extraordinary tightening of monetary and fiscal policy in 1959, leading to the recession of 1960–61, can be attributed in part to balance-of-payments concerns. Subsequently, deliberate deflation was rejected as a balance-of-payments measure on the ground that it was far too costly both to the United States and to the rest of the world. But many other expedients were adopted instead. Some involved the manipulation of monetary or fiscal policy, as when the administration held short-term interest rates above normal recession lows in 1961–62, even while attempting to reduce long-term interest rates. These were supplemented by the wage-price guideposts, aimed at inhibiting cost and price increases in a period of economic expansion. Other measures were designed to restrict particular balance-of-payments outflows. The major measures in this category are:

1959 and subsequently: foreign aid expenditures increasingly restricted to procurement of U.S. goods and services.

1960: abortive attempt to recall military dependents from Germany.

1961: first military offset agreement with Germany, under which Germany agrees to purchase arms in the United States to offset U.S. troop costs in Germany.

1962: Defense Department applied price differential in favor of U.S. goods and services, shortly thereafter raising it to 50 percent and higher on big contracts.

1963: interest equalization tax applied to U.S. purchases of foreign securities; later extended to cover bank and other lending.

1965: voluntary program established to restrict lending to foreigners and business investment abroad.

1968: mandatory limits placed on outflows of enterprise capital and retained earnings of U.S.-owned firms operating abroad.

1968: tax on foreign travel requested, but rejected by Congress.

Broadly speaking, the administration attempted first to limit the balance-of-payments impact of government programs, without, however, reducing their scale; it then turned to restrictions on private capital outflows. Other measures sought to promote exports, travel to the United States, and foreign purchase of U.S. securities. Steps were also taken to improve the appearance of the balance of payments (on a particular measure of the deficit). Finally, the presence of the deficit influenced countless minor government decisions, and perhaps private ones too, in the direction of restraining expenditures abroad.

Because a large payments deficit has persisted, still other means have been proposed to reduce it. These include a tax or other restrictions on foreign travel by Americans, a tariff surcharge on imports, tighter restrictions on private capital outflows, greater emphasis in the federal tax system on indirect taxes (which can readily be refunded to exporters), and drastic reductions in foreign aid and overseas military expenditures, the last aimed especially at Europe. These diverse proposals, typically advanced by different groups, reflect agreement on the desirability of reducing the deficit but sharp disagreement on the most desirable way to do it.

These disagreements arise on two distinct grounds: differences in social priorities and differences in assessment of the effectiveness of various methods. In the debate over policy, the two grounds are often commingled. Thus businessmen typically oppose existing or new restrictions on capital outflows *because* (they say) foreign investment really helps the balance of payments rather than hurting it, returning more than enough in additional exports and earnings to cover the investment outflow in a short period of time. AID officials oppose cutting foreign aid on balance-of-payments grounds *because* (they say) that will help the balance of payments only negligibly, since virtually all foreign aid is currently tied to purchases of U.S. goods and services. A debate that is really about social priorities is focused on alleged effectiveness. In fact, the evidence for both these claims is doubtful. The most complete quantitative study to date on the relationship between direct investment and the balance of payments suggests that at best an additional representative dollar of direct investment in Europe would not be recouped in the balance of payments for six and one-half years, and that under ordinary circumstances the period would be over ten years. Direct investment outflows that continued to grow at 25 percent a year, as those to continental Europe did from 1960 to 1966, would in aggregate never help the balance of payments. Similarly, the difference in impact on the balance of payments between tied and untied aid is far less than that dichotomy would suggest, since on the one hand untied aid was often spent in the United States, owing to the convenience of purchasing here or the competitiveness of American products, while on the other, tied aid is frequently substituted for funds that would have been spent in the United States in any case.

Even if it were true that direct investment abroad is completely recouped within a period of six years, a decision to restrict new outflows is not obviously foolish. It was noted above that the United States was not living beyond its means. To carry the analogy with a family one step further, it has been investing its savings (and more) in foreign equity and debt. But that the typical family should never reduce its purchases of stocks to improve its cash position or even to take a vacation is a precept that surely most businessmen would neither recommend nor follow themselves.

The internationally minded business community has focused on reductions in overseas military expenditures as a substantial source of improvement in the balance of payments, thereby implying basic changes in foreign policy.[3] Some domestically oriented businessmen have urged the use of import quotas, but this position looks suspiciously like a self-serving protectionist measure clothed in a balance-of-payments rationale.

CRITICISMS OF RESTRICTIVE MEASURES

Many observers are skeptical of the effectiveness of past and proposed piecemeal corrective measures and are unhappy with the inefficiencies to which they give rise.

3. The military posture proposed by Carl Kaysen in this volume, entailing a substantial withdrawal of forces from continental Europe and a reduction in commitments elsewhere in the world, would permit such improvement. It is recommended on grounds other than the balance of payments.

The skepticism results, first, because there is thought to be a high degree of substitutability among international transactions, so that patchwork restrictions and artificial incentives simply induce rearrangement of existing transactions without altering appreciably the overall payments position of the country. As indicated above, tying foreign aid to U.S. goods and services leads aid-receiving countries to use foreign aid to buy goods and services that they would have imported from the United States in any case, thus freeing earned foreign exchange for purchases elsewhere in the world. Similarly, restraining or taxing some types of capital outflow may merely change the form of capital outflow without reducing the total. Imposition of the interest equalization tax on foreign bond issues in the United States was followed by a sharp increase in term bank lending; when the tax was extended to cover term bank lending direct investment outflows greatly increased; and so on. As long as money is substantially cheaper in the United States than elsewhere, foreigners—and American firms abroad—will be tempted to borrow here, one way or another. Most forms of capital outflow initiated by U.S. residents are now restricted in some way; but no similar restraint applies to the right of foreigners to bring their capital home from the United States, nor of course to foreign funds which might normally be expected to come to the United States. The extent to which these loopholes vitiate restraints depends on the overall substitutability of one type of funds for another. This substitutability is undoubtedly a good deal higher than officials reckon when they impose new and selective restraints, especially in the long run; but it is also less than complete, even in the long run.

A second ground for being skeptical about the effectiveness of the measures taken or proposed is quite different; it hinges on the alleged refusal of other countries to allow a decline in their payments surpluses or a rise in their payments deficits—changes that are obviously necessary if the United States is to reduce its payments deficit. This refusal is said to rest in part on a desire by other countries to add to their international reserves (or a reluctance to part with the reserves they have), in part on mercantilistic objections to a deterioration in their trade balances. For example, after years of arguing that the United States had maintained excessively easy monetary policy, Germany in early 1966 tightened its own monetary policy after an increase in U.S. interest rates—pleading a weakened balance of payments. The German economy lapsed into recession, generating the largest current account surplus in its long history of surpluses. U.S. exports to Europe declined as a result. Other countries, too, have been quick to prevent or to reverse a worsening of their payments positions. But surpluses in the rest of the world imply, apart from small increments to monetary gold stocks up until 1966, a corresponding deficit for the United States. Indeed, this is simply the obverse of the point discussed in the preceding section, that the dollar has come to make up for the deficiency in additions to monetary gold.

Unhappiness with piecemeal measures stems less from their ineffectiveness than from the inefficiencies they produce. Tying foreign aid, for example, can greatly reduce its real value to recipient countries. In some cases, the price of aid-financed imports has been increased by 50 percent or more as a result, so that the real value of a dollar's worth of aid is correspondingly reduced. Balance-of-payments considerations also distort the allocation of foreign aid; because donors emphasize the direct financing of imported goods, recipient countries have leaned unduly toward development projects with large import requirements, and thus away from the use of local goods and services. Similarly, the 50 percent advantage American suppliers enjoy over foreign suppliers in government procurement has not only swollen the government budget (and thereby lent some truth to congressional charges of government inefficiency), but has also shielded American suppliers against healthy competition from abroad. Restrictions on capital outflows may inhibit the use of capital where it is most productive.[4] Finally, promoting arms sales around the world, while perhaps not "inefficient" in the narrow sense of the economist, hardly seems conducive to efficiency in a larger social sense.

While many economists agree in condemning what has been done, they disagree among themselves on which "efficient" techniques of adjustment should have been undertaken. Three broad schools of thought can be distinguished. The first emphasizes the total supply of dollars available; so long as this is "too great," dollars will flow abroad through one channel or another and will end up being acquired by foreign central banks. The only sure way to stop the deficit is thus to reduce the total supply of dollars

---

4. This is the most complicated and debatable of the efficiency points. Efficient allocation of real savings among countries requires the corresponding transfer of goods and services. But if the surplus on goods and services were large enough, there would be no balance-of-payments problem. Moreover, funds move abroad for reasons other than the search for the socially most productive uses; taxes, tariffs, industrial incentives, and business regulations all distort international capital flows, and the efficiency argument for freedom of capital movements presupposes more harmonization in these policies than now exists.

relative to the supply of foreign currencies, which is to say, maintain tight money.

The second school of thought insists that adjustment in exchange rates is required. The numerous ad hoc measures taken or proposed to improve the payments position represent devaluation of the aid dollar, the government procurement dollar, the investment dollar, and the travel dollar relative to other currencies, but only for certain transactions and by varying amounts. These should be consolidated into a single, uniform depreciation of the dollar relative to the currencies of the surplus countries, thereby avoiding inefficiencies of the type described above.

While the first school of thought emphasizes adjustment in the quantity of dollars and the second adjustment in their price, the third argues that the U.S. payments deficit represents a vast misunderstanding, fostered by the way it is officially reckoned; that it does not represent "disequilibrium" in any important sense; and that it is simply a manifestation of the position of the United States as a financial intermediary in the world economy. The United States no more has a deficit than a commercial bank does when it accepts sight deposits and lends a portion of them at long term to businesses and home-owners. On this view, all the measures that have been taken are erroneously aimed at a non-problem, and they run the risk of greatly disrupting an international financial system that is functioning well in a misguided attempt to improve that system by reducing the deficit.

Whatever one's shade of opinion on these issues, there is certainly enough justification for caution on further piecemeal measures. The United States is not simply one country in a world of many, able to assume a given world economic environment when it takes measures to improve its own payments position. Such measures have wide-ranging repercussions abroad, and these feed back onto the U.S. balance of payments, often reducing the effectiveness of the measures. Furthermore, some steps may badly damage international relations, and at a minimum set an undesirable example for others. Put another way, the potential damage caused by measures taken by the United States to reduce its payments deficit exceeds the gains by much more than would be the case for any other country, and this fact should give American officials pause in adopting new measures.

To its credit, the U.S. government has avoided deflation, with its very high attendant costs per dollar of gain to the balance of payments; and it has avoided restrictions on private imports, a move which in isolation might set off a round of protectionism reminiscent of the interwar period. It has undoubtedly moved too far and too unevenly in restricting government procurement to U.S. sources, although the domestic politics of foreign aid perhaps dictated virtually complete tying to preserve the foreign aid program at a tolerable level during the early and middle sixties. And the restraints on private capital outflow have failed to follow canons of comprehensiveness and efficiency.

U.S. Policy Alternatives within the Existing System

Disagreement persists on the proper course of action for the United States because of the great difficulty in comprehending the complex role of the United States in the world economy. Disagreement has also persisted, however, because of an uneasy sense that actions likely to have a major impact on the balance of payments would necessarily transform the existing international order, but not in a clear or well understood direction. Uncertainty has urged caution, and caution has prescribed first aid rather than major surgery.

At the same time, the continuing deficit and the implied weakening in the liquidity position of the United States have led to considerable uneasiness both at home and abroad. This uneasiness has been reinforced from time to time by a feeling that international financial relations have gotten out of control; created by uncertainties, the uneasiness in turn creates uncertainties in a payments system whose purposes emphasize certainty and stability. The uneasiness is contagious, and could lead to hedging behavior or even to irrational actions on the part of governments as well as firms and individuals. For psychological reasons, therefore, the United States, as the pivotal country in the international payments system, must behave in such a way as to restore some sense of control. This behavior involves not only measures aimed directly at the balance of payments; it equally concerns domestic economic policy, an ability to keep the U.S. economy growing, with neither excessive unemployment nor excessive inflation. (The income tax increase of 1968 was helpful in this regard, but it came two years too late, after much damage had been done.) But it also involves some demonstration of ability to control the country's balance-of-payments position. This does *not* mean reducing the deficit, as officially measured, to zero; that is neither necessary nor desirable. It does mean establishing a sense of deliberateness, of being on top of things. Sometimes this might involve a conscious decision to run a deficit and to finance it out of reserves or official borrowing; at others, reducing the deficit would be appropriate.

Yet few means are available to the United States, within the framework of the existing system, to reassert this sense of control over the balance of payments. Two approaches are discussed here, both involving the use of monetary policy (defined more broadly than is customary) as a regulator. Both propose greater weight for external considerations in framing economic policy, but the first presses toward closer international coordination of policies whereas the second consciously retreats from it.

On the first approach, general monetary policy would be geared much more closely than it has been to the balance of payments. To reduce a deficit, monetary conditions would be deliberately tightened with a view to retarding capital outflows or attracting capital inflows. Assigning general monetary policy to this role, however, requires other instruments of economic policy to be sufficiently flexible to take over some of the roles it is now expected to play, such as stabilization of the domestic economy, stimulation of investment, and so on. The monetary authorities cannot be expected to pursue many divergent aims simultaneously, nor should they be blamed for not succeeding at such a hopeless task. If the domestic economy softens when the balance of payments is weak, the Federal Reserve will face a dilemma, as it did in 1960 and again in 1967, in directing monetary policy. Given present perspectives and objectives, such dilemmas have been resolved generally (but not wholly) in favor of domestic objectives, and given the practical constraints on other actions this was generally the right thing to do. But future dilemmas can be avoided or eased by providing other, equally flexible instruments suitable for the attainment of domestic objectives.

Fiscal policy could be made sufficiently flexible to perform most of the task of maintaining domestic economic stability. Far greater flexibility would be required than fiscal policy has had in the past; measured from the time each should have taken effect, it took over three years to get the tax cut of 1964 and two and a half years to get the tax increase of 1968. In 1962, President Kennedy requested presidential authority to make uniform reductions in the personal income tax, subject to congressional veto. This idea, or something like it, including tax increases, should be revived. Alternatively, the President might propose annually an appropriate tax surcharge (positive or negative) for examination and action by Congress in that year, with a view to implementing quickly any necessary tax changes. Monetary policy might still have to be used for short-run adjustments; but more flexible fiscal policy, desirable in any event, would partially relieve monetary policy from its role in domestic stabilization.

While the flexibility of monetary policy makes it valuable for economic stabilization, the level of interest rates maintained by monetary policy influences other aspects of the domestic economy. If monetary policy is more responsive to external considerations, other measures will have to be used to compensate for unwanted side effects at home. For example, some analysts have argued that the United States should maintain an easy monetary policy along with a tight fiscal policy, at full employment, so as to encourage private investment for economic growth. For this aim, changes in tax structure, such as the investment tax credit, provide a potential substitute for monetary policy. Another practical problem arising from the higher interest rates that might well result from giving greater weight to international considerations is the increased debt burden placed on state and local governments, school boards, and other bodies that rely on the bond market to finance public services. Again, larger federal grants or tax-sharing arrangements could be used to compensate for this higher debt burden in areas where local tax resources have already been stretched to their limits. These examples illustrate the close connection between balance-of-payments policies and more strictly domestic aims and policies.

For monetary policy to be an effective regulator of the balance of payments, it must not be neutralized by foreign actions. If other countries view monetary tightening in the United States as a signal for deliberate monetary tightening abroad, the United States may derive no help to its balance of payments. The possibility is not merely theoretical. Many other countries use fiscal policy even less flexibly than does the United States, and they rely even more heavily on monetary policy for domestic stabilization. Caught between already high tax rates and strong political pressures for rising government expenditures, several important countries have compensated for the resulting fiscal expansion through tighter monetary policy. Such countries may welcome tighter monetary conditions in the United States because they are thus enabled to curb excess expenditures at home, something they could not otherwise do through monetary action because of the large capital inflows which would be induced by relatively easy monetary conditions in the United States.

Under these circumstances, linking U.S. monetary policy to the balance of payments would help ease the stabilization problems of some other countries, but it would not help the U.S. balance of payments; on the contrary, it might hurt it in the long run, by slowing down the rate of inflation abroad. The United States would in effect be taking on the task of stabilizing both its own economy (through fiscal policy) and certain foreign economies (through monetary policy). These policies, moreover, would lead to a higher level of world interest rates. This development in turn might aggravate the difficulties of domestic economic policy in still other countries, whose monetary authorities would have to tighten credit defensively for balance-of-payments reasons; and it would hurt countries heavily dependent on foreign capital.

Thus the suggestion that the United States devote monetary policy increasingly to the balance of payments needs to be reformulated: U.S. monetary authorities should give greater weight to the world's monetary requirements in framing monetary policy. The U.S. balance of payments is too narrow a focus, for the United States sets the monetary tone for the world. Such a reorientation raises the question of the extent to which there should be foreign consultation in the framing of U.S. monetary policy, both to achieve closer coordination in the formulation of monetary policy for the world and because, as implied above, world monetary requirements depend in part on the success other countries have in managing fiscal policy. Major countries have a legitimate interest in the "domestic" policies of their large trading partners, and their mutual concern for a prospering world economy is best served by considering the formulation of policies jointly rather than separately.

If domestic tax policy at home and abroad lacks sufficient flexibility to relieve general monetary policy from its domestic roles, an alternative approach is possible. This approach reduces reliance on close international coordination of economic policies. The internal and external roles of monetary policy might be separated through institution of a flexible tax, such as the interest equalization tax (IET), over external capital transactions. With adequate coverage this tax could be varied according to the amount of capital outflow thought to be consistent at any point in time with the overall balance-of-payments position. Such a tax would insulate domestic from foreign monetary conditions, thereby giving monetary policy greater scope for domestic purposes.

Under the IET Extension Act of 1967 the President received discretionary authority to vary the IET from zero to 22½ percent on equities and long-term bonds, with correspondingly lower rates for loans with shorter maturities.[5] The present tax covers only securities of developed

---

5. This tax is levied on the total value of the transaction at the time it occurs, but the tax schedule is designed so that a maximum tax of 15 percent is equivalent to about one percentage point in yield over the life of a loan.

countries, and it does not cover direct investment outflows. When interest rates are lower in the United States, U.S. firms will be tempted to finance their foreign investment through their home offices. At present this loophole is blocked by the mandatory controls on direct investment outflows, but that program is inherently temporary and must soon be replaced or discarded. One possibility would be to extend coverage of the IET to direct investment outflows and retained foreign earnings.

Even then the substitution of such a flexible tax for monetary policy would be far from complete; short-term bank lending, suppliers' credits, and individuals' deposits abroad would be stimulated by large discrepancies between U.S. and foreign interest rates. To cover all these sources of outflow effectively would require full registration of all foreign exchange transactions, a prospect not pleasant to contemplate.

Finally, the IET would not, of course, cover *foreign* capital; that already inside the country could be withdrawn freely, and that outside need not enter. An IET covering only U.S. capital outflows would thus represent only one side of the supply-demand "scissors" when it comes to influencing international capital flows through changes in monetary conditions.

These weaknesses are not decisive. Money and capital markets are not yet so perfect that each form of capital movement represents a perfect substitute for any other, and some effective separation of national financial markets can undoubtedly be preserved in this way. A tax on a broad class of capital outflows, flexibly used, would affect international capital movements much like general monetary policy, and general monetary policy could continue largely to serve domestic ends. But like the income tax, this kind of tax would require extensive reporting and surveillance.

Either of these approaches would furnish an important instrument of control over international capital movements, and either could influence them for a long time. Neither, however, would be suitable for correcting "fundamental disequilibrium." That would require more basic remedies.

Changes in the Payments System

Whether either of the foregoing courses of action, or some combination of them, proves to be adequate for the United States, it remains incontrovertible that correction of payments imbalances under the existing system has been clumsy and inefficient. Recent U.S. measures are not isolated exceptions. Other countries too have relied on a host of restrictions over international transactions, including trade as well as capital movements, to correct or prevent imbalances; and some have resorted to a degree of domestic deflation that was undesirable on other grounds. Any sharp adjustment from one situation to another is bound to cause some dislocation. But the jar from discrete changes in exchange rates sanctioned under the present monetary system is apparently too great to be borne willingly. Considerations of internal politics and national prestige often strongly inhibit changes in exchange parities. They therefore tend to be delayed too long, postponed in fact by the use of restrictions on international transactions; and the prospect of discrete devaluation stimulates currency speculation by offering a one-way option under which speculators can gain but not lose. Finally, the pressures for adjustment bear heavily on the countries in deficit, but only lightly on countries in surplus, since the ability to finance deficits is inherently limited whereas the capacity to accumulate reserves is not.

It would be reassuring if we could expect the magnitude of payments imbalances to diminish in the course of time, so that we need not worry so much about methods for correcting them. Unfortunately, the recurrence of balance-of-payments disturbances is inevitable. They will arise because of the differential effects of national growth on trade, because of divergent national choices between inflation and unemployment, and because of differences among countries in the mix of economic policies. As a result of the first factor, some countries' imports will grow more rapidly than their exports, and as a result of the second some countries' price levels will rise more rapidly than those of their major competitors. Unless countries gear *both* their rates of economic growth and their employment levels to the requirements of the balance of payments, imbalances will develop sooner or later and adjustment will be required. This will be true even when national economic *policies* are far more closely coordinated among countries than they are today, so long as national *aims* with respect to growth, employment, inflation, and even the distribution of income are inconsistent with the maintenance of payments equilibrium.

Can correction of payments imbalances be made smoother and more efficient? The present system could be made to operate more efficiently if capital were not free to move in anticipation of the discrete changes which it dictates. Tax regulators, as described in the preceding section, would reduce anticipatory movements of capital. But even they could not eliminate currency speculation because of the inseparability of trade from short-term credit and the possibility of speculation through postponement or advancement of payment for imports and exports—a practice that has often plagued Britain. Moreover, changes in parities would remain inhibited by an often misguided conception of national prestige.

A second possibility would be to concentrate corrective measures on trade (including some services as well as goods), to the exclusion of capital transactions. During the 1960s both Britain and Canada used import surcharges in an effort to restrict imports and thus to improve their payments positions. Such surcharges contravene the General Agreement on Tariffs and Trade, and they were used only temporarily in these cases. But surcharges could be regulated, and rules of conformance imposed regarding broad coverage and uniformity, to avoid their use for protecting particular industries. It would be possible and desirable, if this route were taken, to go even further and permit the simultaneous subsidization of exports at the same rate of surcharge applied to imports. Such action would take advantage of the essential similarity in effect on trade between the imposition of uniform surcharges on imports and subsidies to exports on the one hand, and an equivalent change in exchange rate on the other. Speculation on anticipated changes would not be wholly absent under this kind of system, but it would be far less than at present because of the inherently greater cost of speculating in commodities.

This kind of system would mark a sharp break with past practice, which has attempted to maintain a fairly clear (though somewhat artificial) separation between trade policy and financial policy. Many economists would find such a system repugnant, even though Keynes recommended something similar forty years ago.

A third possible way to correct imbalances in payments involves abandonment of the system of fixed exchange parities in favor of completely flexible prices, determined in the market, at which one national currency exchanges for another. Three advantages are claimed for flexible rates. First and foremost, they would provide a system of adjustment to balance-of-payments disturbances devoid of the numerous inefficiencies and slippages accompanying alternative methods. The currency of a country experiencing an increase in payments or a fall in receipts would depreciate, and this depreciation would both stimulate exports (because they would be more competitive) and retard imports, thus restoring balance. Second, the adjustment would be gradual, rather than once-for-all, so that speculators would not enjoy a one-way option; they would have to decide how far depreciation of a currency would go, not merely whether it would occur. Finally, flexible rates would insulate national money and capital markets from one another by introducing greater exchange risk.

A system of flexible exchange rates is intellectually attractive, but it would mark a radical departure from the present international monetary system, based on fixed but changeable exchange parities, a system which it has already been noted has performed extraordinarily well by historical standards. Moreover, flexible rates are historically untested except during the hyper-inflations of the early 1920s and the deep depression of the early 1930s. On neither occasion did they perform outstandingly, and on both they were abandoned as soon as more stable internal conditions were re-established. The economists' claim that a system of flexible rates is smooth, neutral among objectives, and socially costless reflects the assumptions underlying their idealization of such a system, and we cannot be sure that these assumptions are valid in the real world.

A system of flexible rates between major currencies might eventuate, however, if the pressure becomes too great on other instruments of policy, and while that development would by definition represent a "failure" of the existing system, it should not be regarded as a disaster. It would indicate that the mechanism for payments adjustment and the degree of international cooperation under the present system are not up to the strains that are placed on it. A switch from fixed parities to flexible rates is most likely to come about as the result of a financial crisis, during which the United States, with a large payments deficit caused or aggravated by heavy outflows of capital, suspends convertibility of the dollar into gold, thereby confronting other countries with the choice between maintaining existing exchange rates and accumulating dollars on the one hand, and, on the other, pegging their currencies to gold and allowing their currencies to appreciate in terms of the dollar.

Indeed, to some this outcome looks sufficiently attractive that it has been urged as a basis for U.S. policy, implying the creation of a "dollar area" of countries whose currencies were linked to the dollar, with flexible rates between these and currencies outside the area. Such an arrangement would relieve U.S. authorities from preoccupation with the balance of payments, for dollar area countries would accumulate any dollar earnings they chose not to spend, whereas incipient imbalances with the rest of the world would be self-correcting through changes in the exchange rate.

Objection to encouraging this route to flexible rates is primarily political rather than economic: it would mark a sharp unilateral rejection of international economic cooperation by the United States. Moreover, it should not be assumed that the major trading nations would maintain rational policies during such a crisis. An alternative outcome, which should be even more offensive to the advocates of flexible exchange rates than the present system, would be a large-scale return to protectionism and controls over international transactions. Such a development would involve not only considerable economic inefficiencies, but by greatly increasing the scope for using commercial policy for political ends would be highly divisive among nations.

Two variants of flexible exchange rates—more modest in the degree of departure from the present system—have been suggested. The first would enlarge the range within which exchange rates are permitted to fluctuate around parities. Under the IMF rules, the range is 2 percent for each currency with respect to the dollar (hence 4 percent between any two other currencies), but in practice it is narrower. The range of permissible flexibility might be widened, without changing parities, from 2 to 6 or even 10 percent. Such a step would fall short of complete flexibility, but it would increase the scope for market-directed exchange rate adjustment between countries in payments imbalance while at the same time preventing wild movements in rates generated by speculative excesses. It would also inhibit large interest-sensitive short-term capital movements, which disrupt national monetary autonomy. It would not, however, cope with substantial and persistent sources of imbalance.

A second variant is designed to introduce greater long-term international price flexibility but still to retain major features of the present system. This proposal would involve changes in exchange rate parities in small steps, with slight but continuous depreciation for countries in deficit, appreciation for countries in surplus. The gradual change in parities would alter the competitive trade positions of countries in the direction of equilibrium. Small adjustments would avoid stimulating the very large movements of capital associated now with relatively large prospective changes in exchange rates. A sliding parity, as this variant is called, would not avoid speculative capital movements altogether, since the prospect of steady (if gradual) appreciation of a currency would add to the attractiveness of assets denominated in that currency. Monetary policy would not therefore be freed from concern about the balance of payments. This proposal might, however, be combined with wider exchange margins to yield some of the benefits of each.

To bring any of the adjustment processes described in this section into effective existence requires the cooperation of many countries. These methods are not at the disposal of the United States alone, and hence they do not offer immediate improvement in the U.S. payments position. But international discussion of further improvements in the payments system should involve an open-minded examination of all these devices for improving the mechanism for correcting imbalances, as well as of balance-of-payments objectives, which must be compatible among countries before any corrective mechanism can work. Such discussion might have the not incidental consequence of removing the moralizing tone that often surrounds consideration of balance-of-payments deficits and of increasing general tolerance for payments imbalances when the alternatives are viewed realistically.

Gold, the Dollar, and International Economic Cooperation

The international monetary system has performed extraordinarily well, but it is subject to certain strains. Some of these strains are well on their way to resolution; others are likely to become more acute. The United States can provide direction both by its own behavior and by its efforts to persuade others to adjust their behavior.

We should place increasing reliance on man-made money as a substitute for gold money for use among nations, as we did years ago for use within nations, to satisfy the growing demand for international reserves. Great strides have been made in this direction during the past few years, with agreement finally reached in 1968 to establish Special Drawing Rights at the International Monetary Fund. It now remains to get SDRs into circulation. Gold will continue to play a significant role as monetary reserves for some time, but it will be one of steadily diminishing importance. The only questions concern the pace at which gold is displaced and the future disposition of existing monetary gold stocks totaling $40 billion, over twenty-five times current annual production. These issues are likely to arise only after several years of satisfactory experience with SDRs, combined with a private market price of gold above $35 an ounce and rising. At that point central bankers might well reenter the market as sellers of gold— not to drive the price down, but to moderate the rise. A rise in the official price of gold is neither necessary nor desirable.

The question of the dollar is more complex. Even more than is the case with gold, its role depends on how useful the SDRs are in practice. Some central banks will want to continue to hold dollars for reasons of convenience and yield. Others will switch to SDRs, a prospect that should not be regarded with dismay by the United States, even if it involves some reduction in U.S. reserves.

Private dollar holdings are another matter. The dollar plays a central role in world commerce—a role too useful for the world to give up while there is no obviously superior substitute in the wings. A common medium of exchange, like a common language, smooths the path of economic and social intercourse among nations. Expansion in world trade implies expansion in holdings of liquid dollar assets by foreigners and a continuation of extensive use of the dollar in international trade and payments.

Large private dollar deposits—domestic as well as foreign—carry the threat of large withdrawals, analogous to a run on the bank, if at some future time large numbers of private holders should become skittish about the value of the dollar relative to other currencies. Under the present system of fixed exchange rates, any such run should be covered by central bank cooperation on the scale required—either directly through present swap arrangements between central banks, amounting now to nearly $10 billion, or perhaps indirectly in the future through powers granted to the IMF to lend on a scale and with a speed that it is not now able to do.

The fundamental weakness of the present payments system—its lack of an orderly and efficient procedure for correcting payments imbalances that will inevitably arise—remains unresolved. How this deficiency should be remedied cannot be decided on technical economic grounds; it depends on the broad political direction we want the community of industrial nations to take. Do we want the payments system to encourage, even to compel, close economic cooperation among major countries—or to preserve the widest possible degree of national economic autonomy?

A system of flexible exchange rates caters to national autonomy, both by introducing more uncertainty into international transactions and by permitting individual governments greater freedom of unilateral action. To work, however, it requires both abstention from interference with the movement of exchange rates, and public willingness to accept whatever short-term changes in cost of living and distribution of income such movements may bring about. In practice, such forbearance is unlikely, even if national insulation were desirable or, in the long run, possible.

A system of fixed exchange rates seems to cater to economic integration among nations, but it may not survive conflicts in national objectives, degenerating instead (given present resistance to discrete changes in exchange parities) into unorganized and disorderly attempts to correct deficits in international payments. A system of sliding parities—gradual movements in exchange rates among major countries—offers a welcome escape from this dilemma. It would exert pressure toward closer economic cooperation among countries, since parities would not be permitted to change rapidly. But it would also provide a mechanism for gradual correction of lasting payments imbalances. Serious consideration of this proposal should be high on the agenda of the new administration.

The United States should respond to the pressure for coordination of monetary policy by improving the flexibility with which fiscal policy can be used to stabilize the domestic economy, so as to relieve monetary policy from this task. Other major countries should be pressed to move in the same direction. Success here would permit closer effective coordination among countries in framing monetary policy, with respect not only to balance-of-payments requirements, but also to world monetary requirements.

Pressures for coordination of policies would go far beyond this, however, eventually encompassing business regulation, government aids to business and labor, and even domestic taxation. Growing economic interdependence outmodes the nation-state as an instrument of control and calls for international—perhaps supranational—formulation of policy. Perhaps we can respond suitably as the growth in interdependence requires joint action. But the pressures may outpace our capacity to respond suitably, evoking instead defensive and mutually damaging national reactions. Allowance should therefore be made for some deliberately *dis*integrative responses, so as to slow the move toward greater interdependence in an orderly, rather than a disorderly, way. Such responses may involve the coordinated national use of taxes or other impediments to capital movements—not so much for balance-of-payments reasons as to preserve some independence for domestic monetary and other policies. It may even require occasional use of import surcharges. Restrictions or taxes on international transactions insulate national economies somewhat from international influence, and thereby weaken the integrative pressures of trade, capital movements, and business investment abroad; but they also provide occasion to define and police rules concerning acceptable types and durations of such measures, and thereby strengthen the machinery for intergovernmental cooperation and even joint effort—illustrative of the "process vision" of international cooperation outlined by Francis Bator. Discussion of this range of delicate issues with other major countries should also be high on the agenda of the new administration.

MAX F. MILLIKAN

THE UNITED STATES AND
LOW-INCOME COUNTRIES

There has been mounting confusion, uncertainty, and debate in the United States during the last few years over what should be our relations with the ninety-odd countries of the underdeveloped areas of Asia, Africa, and Latin America. These countries, which include some two-thirds of the world's population, are all desperately poor in contrast to the more developed countries of North America, Western Europe, Russia, and Japan. Virtually all share the problems of an effort to make the transition from traditionally rigid societies to modern participatory ones.

Before the Second World War, our concern with these countries was marginal. In the fifties and early sixties, we focused attention on the underdeveloped world, partly because most of the postwar international crises had their proximate origins there—from Korea, Suez, Cuba, and the Congo to the Dominican Republic, Rhodesia, and Vietnam—and partly because we viewed the underdeveloped world as a principal arena of the cold war. We developed a new range of foreign policy instruments (including technical assistance, capital grants and loans, food for peace, cultural exchange programs, information programs, and the Peace Corps) and new forms and emphases for the more traditional instruments of diplomacy and military assistance to deal with this essentially new dimension of our foreign policy concerns.

The doubts and uncertainties voiced of late about our policies toward the third world have been reflected in sharp cuts in the foreign aid program, which encompasses the principal new instruments for dealing with these countries. Proposals are rife for further reduction and reorganization of this program, but the organizational debate conceals deeper foreign policy issues. The uncertainties have been accentuated by the domestic controversies generated by our involvement in Vietnam, by the strains on our economy posed by a mounting government budget and balance-of-payments difficulties, and by the growing recognition of the urgency of many domestic problems. Faced with an increasing confusion of purpose, we badly need a new articulation, in the light of changes in the international environment, of the range of U.S. concerns with the low-income countries. While virtually all the elements of such a fresh articulation are to be found in one place or another in doctrines developed over the past twenty years, a new emphasis and balance among those elements is required as a foundation for the more pragmatic discussion of instruments and organizational alternatives which follows.

The Foreign Policy Framework

From the enunciation of the Truman Doctrine in 1947 to the present, it has been conventional to distinguish sharply between a hard-nosed concern with the U.S. national interest and a moral and humanitarian concern with poverty. In my view, continued emphasis on this distinction has led to some distortion of the problem. Analysts of the U.S. interest have often focused quite narrowly on the short-run impact of the international distribution of power on our security position. Recent changes in our perception of the forces at work in the world have rendered the cold-war security arguments of a decade ago decreasingly persuasive.

On the other hand, doubt in some quarters as to the validity of U.S. intervention in the political and social affairs of other countries has led us to focus our humanitarian concerns on the war on hunger and disease and to depoliticize the rhetoric of aid activities by shying away from discussions of the quality of political and social life abroad. Meanwhile, the force of the foreign projection of our humanitarian motivation has been weakened by the recognition of our crucial moral and welfare problems at home.

Our sense of disquiet about our activities in the underdeveloped world has been greatly increased by the feeling that pursuit of our alleged security interests through military assistance, counterinsurgency activities, and even open warfare in Vietnam has been in sharp conflict in some countries with our professed moral concerns with people and their welfare, with open societies, and with government by consent of the governed. Both at home and abroad a gap has been perceived between our actions in defense of our security interests and the rhetoric with which we define our moral purpose. We have supported regimes that are repressive, engaged in military programs that restrict rather than expand popular participation, and strengthened the resistance of some traditional regimes to the kinds of changes that the social and political development which we profess to favor in fact requires.

One reaction to this gap is to urge that we cease the actions, which many no longer perceive as necessary, and that we abandon the rhetoric which in view of past actions is no longer credible; that is, that we withdraw or greatly reduce our activities in the underdeveloped world, concentrate on reconstructing our own society, and suspend all but token efforts in the third world until we understand better the revolution of modernization that is in progress there.

The alternative to this view, and the thesis this writer would strongly support, is that when reexamined in the light of an updated appraisal of the world situation and a corrected interpretation of both our national interests and our moral and humanitarian values, most of the dilemma disappears. Properly understood, U.S. long-term security interests, economic interests, cultural and social interests, and historical moral concerns with the welfare of common men everywhere come together and can be advanced by the right kinds of policies toward the low-income countries. There will, of course, continue to be conflicts in detail in particular places and at particular times among our objectives. We will have to live with these. We will have to tolerate for a long time to come a high level of instability and frequent outbreaks of local violence and political upset in the underdeveloped world which may impinge unfavorably on a number of our perceived short-term interests. But over the next few decades we have a compelling interest, both national and moral, in the emergence of a compatible and congenial environment in a more and more interdependent world of increasingly modernized states.

Thus viewed, the broad interest of the United States parallels that of many other governments and peoples, especially in the less-developed countries. There are some leadership elements who do not share our growth and social development goals enough to make cooperation possible. But with many others in the third world, though we will have frequent frictions and differences on means of implementation, our national interests properly defined are not competitive, and our moral values are not a unique American export. There need be no arrogance in cooperative efforts to pursue mutual goals of modernization and participation, particularly when both parties are aware that both have unsolved problems. To see what this means, we must explore further the content of U.S. security, economic, and social and civic interests in the less-developed world as they are affected by recent changes in the world environment.

U.S. SECURITY INTERESTS

U.S. security policy is treated in another paper, but it has been such an important component of past policies in the less-developed world that it must be reviewed here briefly. In the bipolar postwar world of the fifties, as Europe stabilized politically and exhibited vigorous growth economically, both the United States and the Soviet Union came to look upon the underdeveloped world as an important—perhaps as the most important—arena of conflict between what was viewed as a still monolithic international communist movement and a still reasonably cohesive "free world." While even the largest of the underdeveloped countries did not then and do not now possess the resources to pose a serious direct security threat to either of the super powers, even a marginal addition of manpower and economic resources to one bloc or the other was regarded as dangerous by its opponent. More important, it was believed that the transfer of even a relatively small country would have symbolic and psychological consequences which might set off a dangerous chain of reactions. Whether this was a correct appraisal even then is not at issue here. It was widely enough held to have a significant impact on U.S. policy and in particular on the allocation of U.S. military and economic aid resources.

Several developments of the past decade have changed this appraisal markedly. The first and most frequently noted is the fragmentation and dispersion of power among countries in both the communist world and the free world. Fragmentation in both camps has meant that the capacity of each to control those it believed were its clients in the underdeveloped world has been greatly reduced. Czechoslovakia, far from being an exception to this generalization, supports it strongly. Further, the psychological consequences of additions of states to either fragmenting group are now less clear and less serious.

Secondly, both Americans and communists have discovered painfully that those whom they believed to be clients in the underdeveloped world are much more resistant to their influence and much less subject to their control than they had expected. In some cases, as with Castro, Sekou Touré, Nasser, and Ayub Khan, the leadership, pursuing its nationalist objectives, has refused to follow dutifully the sponsor's line. In other cases, leaders regarded by one side or the other as potential clients have been unable to maintain their own positions of authority, as happened with Sukarno, Nkrumah, and Diem. It is interesting to note that several autocratic and repressive leaders, whether of the left like Sukarno or the right like Trujillo, have fallen before pressures for participation from elements of the population which a few decades ago would have been apathetic or powerless. Participation has sometimes been anarchic, has frequently produced conflict, and has seldom been channeled by effective institutions in constructive directions, but it has been growing, and has frequently thwarted communist and traditional authoritarian efforts to control and suppress it.

The conclusion that increasingly emerges is that the "two-camps" model does not apply as we once thought it did. The United States, the Soviets, and the Chinese have experienced great difficulty manipulating their presumed clients, hence the security interests of each are much less likely to be predictably affected by switches of the international posture of individual countries, particularly of the smaller ones, than was believed. This suggests that we can afford to take a much cooler view about particular threatened or actual shifts of leadership in individual underdeveloped countries, even when the threat is of a shift in a strongly leftist and anti-Western direction. There are likely to be many more such instabilities in the underdeveloped world over the next two or three decades, and we no longer have a cold-war case for rushing in on what appears to be the anti-communist side of each.

This change in our perception of the environment does not mean that we no longer have any security interests in the third world. In the first place, there are a few cases like South Korea and Taiwan—and some would add Vietnam—where we have commitments of such long standing that to retreat from them now would severely damage our reputation for reliability and constancy in our dealings with other countries. Fortunately, in the first two cases cited recent economic and social progress has been so dramatic that the conflict between our security interests and our moral principle is no longer severe.

Secondly, there are a number of larger underdeveloped countries each of which has the capability over the next decade or two to acquire significant nuclear capabilities. None of these has the potential capability in the foreseeable future to pose a direct major threat to the United States. Nevertheless, the consequences of the employment of nuclear weapons anywhere in the world are so difficult to foresee and the risks of even a slight chance of escalation are so perilous that it is urgent that we do everything in our power to avoid serious alienation of these countries from the international community. Economic development will not insure their cooperative behavior, but great-power assistance in their development efforts combined with increased effectiveness of international peacekeeping machinery will greatly reduce the risk that they will behave in internationally irresponsible ways.

Thirdly, we have a generalized interest in reducing the level of tension and violence in the world, particularly as between states. The fact that we may have limited interest in the specific outcome of particular disputes does not, of course, mean that we are indifferent to processes of adjudication of disputes which avoid violence. It does mean that in pursuing our security objectives in the third world we can and should place much greater stress on operating with and through the United Nations and other international organizations than we thought possible a decade ago. However, the effectiveness with which these international institutions can operate will continue to be dependent on the extent, quality, and cooperativeness of bilateral relations between each of the super powers and the majority of states in the underdeveloped world outside the security area. We can afford to be cool and avoid involvement on one side or the other in specific disputes, but we cannot afford to be indifferent and unconcerned.

Similar considerations apply to our concern with internal stability and civil violence within the borders of underdeveloped states. Experience should have taught both the United States and the communist states that effective insurgency can seldom be generated from outside unless there are genuinely serious tensions and frustrations within the society of the target country. We should also have learned that where such tensions exist, our active participation in counterinsurgency programs runs a serious risk of increasing rather than reducing these domestic tensions and frustrations. Again this does not mean that we are indifferent to the level of civic order and violence within countries of the underdeveloped world. The distinctions between internal disorder and external aggression, always obscure, are getting harder and harder to draw in an increasingly interdependent world. Whatever our degree of involvement in particular disputes, the dangers that internal violence will spill over into the international arena will continue to be severe. While there is profound truth in the current cliché that we cannot and should not be the world's policeman, there is equal validity in the observation that we have a deep interest in devoting some of our resources and energies to helping to channel the changes that modernization inevitably brings in orderly and constructive rather than violent and anarchic directions.

We may frequently be faced with a choice between long-term tension reduction and short-term stability. Modernization requires revolutionary change in the structure and distribution of power, and stabilization measures which inhibit or delay change may make an ultimately destructive explosion more likely. This analysis suggests that in these cases we should be much more relaxed about short-term instabilities and much more concerned about long-term tension reduction than we have been in the past.

This view of our long-term security interests implies that we can adopt somewhat different priorities than were implied by our earlier cold-war focus on short-run stability. With this reinterpretation, our security interests are less likely to be in conflict with other economic and social goals. As Carl Kaysen explains, our security requirement for military and communications bases in the low-income world is no longer dominant, and history has largely destroyed whatever case there once was for competing with rival great powers for loyal clients. Thus we can and should support governmental regimes in underdeveloped countries dedicated to the economic development of their countries and the diffusion of participation in decision making and the wider sharing of the benefits of social and economic development whatever their international political posture. More important, we need no longer in most cases support for security reasons regimes which are either not interested in these goals or incapable of promoting them. In a very few cases, we may be constrained by past commitments from following criteria based on our human values, but the number and importance of these unpleasant cases, if Vietnam should somehow be resolved, should shrink to insignificance.

U.S. INTEREST IN ECONOMIC DEVELOPMENT

U.S. support for the economic development efforts of the underdeveloped countries has since 1947 been based in part on the notion that this was a worthy end in itself which deserved American attention and resources. It started in the original Point Four program with the notion that the main requirement was for a transfer of American technical know-how. We moved in the Eisenhower and early Kennedy administrations to a recognition that in some countries substantial capital assistance was important. There was a phase of emphasis on human and institutional development and most recently the favored focus has been on agriculture, nutrition, population control, and education.

But the defenders of aid have always felt that they had to build their case on a presumed relation between economic development and other U.S. security and political goals. When the two-camps model was at the forefront of our foreign policy thinking, there was a presumption that if we could create a few showcases of how productive our system could be, this would discourage fence-sitting neutrals from opting for a communist development strategy and thus implicitly for a communist political system. As the two-camps model began to lose its persuasive force, this was modified to a vaguer argument that economic development would bring with it a reduction of tensions and of the disposition to violence. The case was even made in some official and private statements of the rationale that economic development by itself would result in an almost automatic growth of democratic institutions and a rapid spread of popular participation.

Unquestionably, some part of whatever disillusionment currently exists with respect to the effectiveness of our aid programs is attributable to the disappointment of exaggerated expectations as to both the speed and extent of these presumed favorable effects of economic growth. Continued crises in the underdeveloped world have forced a recognition of the fact that many of the roots of conflict both within societies and between nations are traceable to deep forces unrelated to economic conditions. Beyond this, economic growth itself, by shaking up the stable patterns and expectations of traditional society, may at least in the short run be destabilizing. There have been cases like Stalin's Russia or pre-Castro Cuba in which substantial economic growth as measured by the conventional indicators has been accompanied by increases in repression and autocratic measures. In other cases, as in the Middle East, growth has provided resources for the more vigorous conduct of international conflict. One conclusion some observers would draw is that since growth has so far not turned out to be the miracle cure for many ills of the third world that some of its advocates had suggested it would be, the case for devoting substantial U.S. resources and attention to it has been largely demolished.

In the view of this writer, this reaction has gone much too far. While we badly needed increased sophistication about the difficulties and limits of economic growth and its complex relations to our other long-run goals relating to the world environment, it still deserves a high priority as both a U.S. and an international objective of policy.

In the first place, the above argument, of course, leaves untouched the case for economic development as an end in itself. Most Americans will not be at ease living in a world about which they will be increasingly well informed—two-thirds of whose people do not have access to the most elementary material requirements of civilized life—if they feel the United States can do anything about it. The level of family income that the U.S. government defines as drawing the boundary between intolerable poverty for an American and minimal access to basic necessities—about $3,000 in most U.S. communities—is five to ten times the average family income for the entire population of most countries in the underdeveloped world. The only effective thing we can do about it is to devote a modest share of our resources and a more substantial amount of effort and energy to the promotion of economic growth in the underdeveloped world. Even the narrowest interpretation of our moral responsibility to the rest of the international human community, namely to help combat hunger and permanently crippling malnutrition—and on reflection most Americans would think our responsibilities are broader than this, as explained in the next section—would call for economic development assistance substantially larger than we are now supplying. For as will be explained later, significant nutritional improvements in most of the low-income world can be accomplished only in the context of vigorously expanding economic activity.

Our short-term foreign-policy lenses have led us frequently, in the past, to write off too casually our long-term national economic interest in the growth of the economies of the low-income countries. It is, of course, quite true that currently European markets, investment opportunities, and sources of supply are quantitatively much more crucial to the welfare of the U.S. economy than those of the underdeveloped world. We are decreasingly dependent on raw materials and tropical products from the underdeveloped world. In any case, access to these imports is related to the economic growth of the supplying countries only indirectly if at all. At present levels of income in underdeveloped countries, opportunities are limited for mutually beneficial trade and investment. This is especially true in the poorer of the low-income countries. But if in the next twenty or thirty years per-capita incomes in some of the larger countries were to double, a wholly achievable target, the world economic environment for the United States could be substantially improved. We have seen in parts of Latin America and most notably in Japan, now our second most important trading partner, how rapid domestic economic growth can, in a decade or two, radically alter trading opportunities. If economic growth stalls or is retarded in a large part of the third world, prospects for the expansion of trade, for access to markets and investment opportunities, and even for international monetary stability are bleak. Even if growth is accelerated, an improving international economic climate is far from assured. Political disruption, restrictive practices, and a breakdown of international cooperation would still be possible, and would unquestionably occur at some times and in some places. But without growth these unhappy prospects are much more than possible—they are virtually assured.

U.S. INTEREST IN SOCIAL AND CIVIC DEVELOPMENT

Our final interest in the modernization process in low-income countries is our concern with the fuller participation of the common people of these countries in political, social, and economic activities in an atmosphere of freedom and opportunity. Our national interest in a compatible and congenial world environment for the United States and our humanitarian interest in an improved quality of life for average men everywhere are thus brought together. The dichotomy between national interests interpreted narrowly in power and security terms and humanitarian interests interpreted equally narrowly in terms of feeding and housing the miserable has led to a neglect both at home and abroad of this rich dimension of national purpose. It has something to do with the spread of the idea of democracy. This word has been identified by some with too narrow a range of peculiarly American institutional forms, and has been used by others, as in the various peoples' democratic republics, to label societies which violate its spirit. It also relates to what is sometimes called political development, but this term likewise has acquired many inappropriate overtones. Elements of it have been identified by the Congress in provisions of the various foreign assistance acts, perhaps most notably in Title IX, Section 281, of the Foreign Assistance Act of 1966, which directs that "emphasis shall be placed on assuring maximum participation in the task of economic development on the part of the people of the developing countries through the encouragement of democratic private and local governmental institutions."

This notion of expanded popular participation as an aspect of modernization encompasses a number of elements. Three in particular may be noted. First, is the notion of broadened participation in decisions affecting the quality of life of the people, whether they be political, economic, or social decisions. Second, is that of increasing opportunities for people to acquire and use productively the full range of modern skills, to participate in the psychologically satisfying processes of modernization. Third, is the notion that there should be the widest possible participation in the distribution of the economic and social fruits of development by all elements in the world's populations. We and our colleagues abroad in both developed and underdeveloped societies are only beginning to have some understanding of what this participatory dimension of our common goal requires. At a minimum, we are beginning to see that it requires in all cultures a greatly enriched pattern of institutions for channeling creative and innovative energies in constructive rather than destructive directions. It requires greatly accelerated progress in education, a massive expansion of facilities for communication, transport, and sources of energy. It requires greatly increased capabilities of both governmental and nongovernmental institutions at national, regional, and local levels to respond effectively to the demands it generates. And it requires, if it is not to be disruptive, a rough balance among these economic and noneconomic elements of the modernization process.

Accepting this goal of expanded popular participation broadens our moral and humanitarian objectives beyond the elimination of hunger, disease, and material deprivation to a deeper concern with the widespread diffusion of fundamental human satisfactions. Most Americans share with many people abroad a faith that in the long run this multi-dimensional human development will greatly increase the prospects for a world environment of more open, more cooperative, and more liberated societies. Interaction with such societies can enrich our own culture intellectually, aesthetically, and socially as well as economically. Those who would have us promote these participatory goals more vigorously in the low-income countries, as Title IX of the Assistance Act enjoins us to do, must recognize that in many traditional societies as presently constituted these are profoundly revolutionary aims. Their effective pursuit may well be resisted by present power holders who regard themselves as our friends. Where they are so resisted, we have little option but to keep our distance and wait for internal historical forces to change the situation. But where, as in an increasing number of countries, our help in social and civic development is sought, there is much we can do in cooperation with the leadership to promote it. In any case, we can be reasonably sure that in the underdeveloped world, as in our own cities, if the increasing demands for participation in the development process and in its benefits are not or cannot be met for significant numbers of people in many countries, the prospects for continued improvement in aspects of the international environment that will matter to us most over the rest of this century are slim indeed. The potential resources of the low-income countries are likely, to be sure, to remain too small to permit even high levels of frustration and disaffection there to pose direct challenges to the physical security of the United States. But the prospect of the division of the low-income world into a series of mutually hostile closed societies with restricted human access and interchange is a disaster. We should be willing, in our own interest, to devote substantial resources to avoid that disaster, whether it touches our consciences as members of the world community or not. Fortunately, we have been moving in the last decade away from and not toward the world described by George Orwell in *1984*. The troubles the low-income countries have been experiencing are ascribable more to their political and economic difficulties in handling effectively greatly expanded demands for participation than to increased attempts to suppress it. But with a slowing of growth and development rather than an acceleration, this trend could easily be reversed.

RELATIONS AMONG U.S. LONG-RUN INTERESTS

The complex interactions among our long-run security interests, our interests in economic growth, and in social and civic development in the low-income world should have begun to emerge from this discussion of the three interests. First, we are increasingly recognizing that short-run stability in certain country situations or an antirevolutionary bias of some traditional leadership groups may be inconsistent with the growth of a more stable world environment in the long run, and that the latter, not the former, is our true interest. This recognition changes not only our military assistance but our economic assistance priorities as well.

Actually, if we look at the recent distribution among countries of our economic-aid resources, we are not likely to find that—apart from Vietnam, where our large economic-aid program is closely related to an American war effort—the altered appraisal of our security interests suggested here as rational would change the distribution of funds very much. Ten years ago our economic aid was rather heavily concentrated in countries around the periphery of the communist world, believed to be in danger through either aggression or subversion of falling into the enemy camp; and a number of our major aid recipients were countries which did not then look promising either economically or politically. The pattern has changed in the last decade in two respects. In the first place, both Latin

America and Africa, neither of which have been menaced seriously by widespread threats of incipient communist take-over, have received a significantly larger share of our attention and resources. In the second place, several countries, aid to which was justified primarily on short-term security grounds a decade ago and which did not look economically or politically promising—South Korea, Taiwan, Pakistan, and Turkey—have, in the last few years, exhibited an extraordinary acceleration in economic growth and a substantial extension of popular participation in the modernization process.

The fact, however, that the change in the rationale here proposed would perhaps result, Vietnam aside, in only limited changes in intercountry priorities of attention does not mean that the change is unimportant. An alteration in our explicit rationale for doing the things we are now doing would be most useful to resolve some of the doubts in the public and congressional minds about the wisdom of our present course of action and to alter the image held abroad of the objectives of U.S. foreign policy. There are a few countries, most of them rather small, where the cooler and more relaxed attitude here suggested toward our short-run security interests and greater emphasis on economic and perhaps especially on social and civic development would alter both intercountry priorities and intracountry program design. A few such changes would be enough to persuade skeptics that alterations in U.S. foreign policy rationale were real and not merely rhetorical.

Clearly our long-run security interests in the low-income world, redefined as suggested above, result in less sharp security priorities among the underdeveloped countries than some of our earlier preoccupations. If we are concerned to forestall the alienation of any large potential nuclear power and to reduce the prospects on all three continents of a generalized spread of interstate conflict and intrastate violence, our priorities will be guided much less than they once were by considerations of geographic proximity, strategic zones, specific ideological orientation between the left and the right, and even historical commitment and alliance. If, on the other hand, we have reason to believe that these longer-run and more generalized strategic interests will be advanced if a significant number of countries having an important share of the population of the low-income world exhibit rapid economic growth and a spread of effective popular participation, then our strategic priorities come into much greater harmony with criteria based on the prospects for economic and political development than in the past. To a confirmed skeptic, concurrence cannot be proved between our long-term strategic interests and widespread economic and political development. Indeed, many historical instances of the failure of this relationship can be cited. Cuba was relatively prosperous when Castro took over, and while the Italian and German fascist aggressions followed severe economic depression, they were preceded by substantial histories of democratic development. Similar instances are bound to occur in the future whatever our posture.

What is nevertheless being asserted here is that, on balance, the prospects for a stable, orderly, and cooperative international environment in the underdeveloped world are substantially better if most of it is prospering economically and exhibiting a widening range of civic participation than if it is economically stagnant and politically autocratic and repressive. This is partly because a leadership successfully coping with internal economic and political development problems is under less pressure to divert attention to foreign military adventure; partly because there will be fewer groups in the population whose frustration with working through existing institutions threatens to explode into violent revolt.

With respect to the relation between the two goals of accelerated economic growth and widened popular participation in the development process, there have been cases in the past in which substantial economic growth as measured by the usual aggregate indicators has not brought with it much improvement in the quality of the life of the bulk of the population. Economic growth can at least for a time be focused on a limited sector of the economy and benefit a narrow class of the population, as has happened in several of the oil-rich countries. Indeed, there are many circumstances in which pursuit of the goals of equitable distribution and widened participation in decision making will slow the growth of the economy as measured by the rate of expansion of aggregate GNP. These conflicts between equity and productivity when they arise are fundamental conflicts of values which must be resolved by the political process of the host country. Outside expertise can help formulate the alternatives, but the final choice is a domestic political responsibility.

Nevertheless, one conclusion is beyond serious question. In the very low-income countries, effective social and civic development is impossible in the absence of vigorous economic growth. While improvements in the quality of life of the average man involve much more than increases in his material standards of living—education, the acquisition of new skills, increased opportunities for social and economic mobility, an increased role in the making of social decisions—they require resources beyond the capacities of a subsistence economy. Nutrition, health, jobs, schools, roads, communications, governmental services cannot be supplied or equitably distributed at the levels of income and productivity characteristic of the bulk of the low-income countries. Continued and accelerated economic growth is a *sine qua non* for the expanded range of goals which it is here argued should characterize U.S. policy toward the low-income countries. But the economic growth objective must be pursued in the context of greatly expanded U.S. and international attention to a widened spectrum of mutual objectives relating to the requirements for broader effective popular participation in all of its forms.

THE EXTENT AND LIMITS OF U.S. INFLUENCE

Before the question whether it should continue to be a major thrust of U.S. foreign policy to help promote economic, social, and civic development in the low-income countries can be answered affirmatively, two more questions must be posed. One is the question of our capabilities to affect significantly the development of the low-income world, and the second is the question of the willingness of the peoples and the governments of that world to work with us toward these ends.

With respect to economic growth, the record of the past decade or so is conclusive. In the face of an unprecedented expansion of population at a rate of 2 to 3 percent a year, the less-developed countries on which acceptable information is available—and they constitute the bulk of those in the free world—have achieved an average rate of growth of per-capita income of about 2 percent a year. This is better than the United States and most of the other developed countries were able to sustain over comparable periods of their development history.

The respectable overall average was high partly because of a few remarkable success stories with sustained per-capita growth rates over 5 percent a year like Taiwan, South Korea, Thailand, Mexico, Israel, and Peru. In the face of this impressive record, the widespread impression that the rate of development has been disappointing is puzzling. Some of the large countries like India did not meet the ambitious targets they set for themselves, but even India has grown much more rapidly since independence than ever before.

A significant fraction—a fifth to a sixth—of the investment throughout the less-developed world which made this growth possible was financed by foreign aid supplied either bilaterally or via international institutions.

In the countries where U.S. aid has been concentrated, the fraction of investment financed by aid is significantly larger. In short, I know of no serious question being raised by anyone who has carefully studied the problem whether a contribution of resources from the developed countries as a group constituting a relatively light burden on their economies—less than 1 percent of their gross national products by the most liberal estimates—can make the difference between stagnation and growth in most of the low-income countries. The contribution of capital assistance to investment can be roughly quantified, but of equal importance in its effect on growth is the contribution of technical assistance to the productivity of investment.

On U.S. capabilities to help with social and civic development, we must be more modest. The institutional forms with which we are familiar are in many cases not well-suited to the circumstances of the low-income countries. Beyond this many of our social, political, and economic institutions are currently undergoing reexamination here at home.

Nonetheless our efforts in education, public administration, community development, local government, cooperatives, and the development of transportation and communication have already had important effects on the quality of life in a number of developing countries and could have much more significant effects if we cooperated more actively with recipient governments in pursuing these goals.

This leads directly to the second question whether the less-developed countries will welcome a more active concern on our part with other than the strictly economic problems of their development. They will not do so in most cases if they feel we are trying to export institutional solutions which are not performing well within our own society. On the other hand, the peoples and even the governments of many low-income countries share our interests in social and civic development so long as we do not presume to have all the answers to precisely how that development is to be accomplished. The charter of Punta del Este underlined the noneconomic goals of development in Latin America with relatively little controversy. There is reason to believe that the same extension of the development concept might be widely welcomed elsewhere if we could convince our colleagues abroad that our interest was in the substance of participatory activity and not in particular ideological labels or institutional forms. We must be prepared to recognize that sometimes these goals can be as effectively promoted in single-party as in multiparty systems, in formally socialist as well as capitalist states, and that even states which call themselves communist like Yugoslavia and Czechoslovakia have pushed some distance in the directions in which we are interested. The fact that Americans are now aware of problems of bringing about an adequate level of participation by elements of their own population should make discussion of these problems with foreigners easier rather than harder.

THE NEED FOR A DIVERSITY OF COUNTRY STRATEGIES

Emphasizing the differences among the low-income countries is important in concluding this discussion of the rationale for our concern with them. They can be discussed as a group because they all share in one form or another a concern, which in most of them is of recent origin, with the modernization process, economic, social, political, and cultural. But they differ so radically in so many fundamental ways that the effort to design and legislate a common strategy for all is doomed to failure at the outset. They range in size from mini-states like Guyana and Mauritius with less than a million people each to a subcontinental state like India with over a half billion. They include still predominantly subsistence economies like Somalia and Paraguay and countries with thriving modern industrial sectors like Brazil and Turkey. They include countries with ample foreign exchange resources like Venezuela and Libya and countries with chronic problems of foreign exchange earnings like Pakistan and Jordan.

The policies of these countries defy a simple classification along a spectrum of left to right or from dictatorship to democracy. Some countries have a strong sense of national integration, a common language, and a long democratic tradition like Chile, and others like the Congo are hardly yet countries at all. In some, power is held narrowly by a small elite, as in Liberia and Burma. In others, the regime is dedicated to expanded popular participation as in India and Tanzania. There are those in which U.S. influence and advice is eagerly sought as in contemporary Indonesia, and others in which it is suspect as in Cambodia. This is only an illustrative sampling of the range of country variation that must be taken into account in the design of U.S. and international policies to cooperate with local governments and institutions in furthering the development goals of particular countries. This diversity has profound implications for the organization and orchestration of the various instruments of U.S. and international policy to which we now turn.

Requirements for Effective Policy

Much attention has been devoted in this essay to our foreign policy posture toward the low-income countries because without agreement on this no organizational reshuffling, national or international, of our various policy instruments will be viable. If we can achieve widespread consensus on the underlying philosophy of our relations with the third world, many alternative organizational arrangements can be made to work. These include among others a continuation of something essentially like our present aid and foreign policy structure. If the President and the nation conclude that the interests outlined above do not justify a level of effort and attention which would reverse the downward trend of the recent past, much of what follows is inapplicable. In this event, we can maintain dwindling bilateral programs to support our few remaining specific security interests and discharge our commitments to places like South Korea, Vietnam, and parts of Latin America, and we can pay our conscience money in modest contributions to international organizations.

In what follows, however, it is assumed that the more positive set of interests outlined above is accepted as valid and that the public and the Congress will provide whatever support is needed to implement this posture. One of the troubles with foreign aid is that some of its proponents have tried to be too clever in shaping their arguments to meet the presumed prejudices of some members of the Congress and of the public. Unless there is widespread acceptance of the case on its genuine merits, no organizational tricks or catchy labels will have any lasting effect.

Whatever specific instruments and organizational patterns are adopted, four general requirements must be met.

First, the President and the Secretary of State must take the lead in explaining just what it is the United States is trying to do and in giving guidance to the whole foreign policy machinery of the government on how the United States proposes to do it.

Second, we must mobilize the full range of the public and private, domestic and foreign analytic and research resources to which the United States has access to improve our understanding for each of the more important low-income countries with which we are dealing. We must understand the economic, social, political, and psychological forces at work in the society, the critical obstacles to effective modernization, and the alternative ways that outside human and financial resources can be brought to bear in helping the country to deal with those obstacles.

Third, we must work out, in close cooperation with the host country and with other donors, both national and international, coordinated country programs in which the role to be played by each major instrument—capital grants and loans, technical assistance, food for peace, cultural exchanges, information programs, and military assistance where appropriate—is specified, priorities established, relations between the various external instruments and appropriate host country activities determined, and the consistency and effectiveness of the whole joint strategy evaluated.

Fourth, we must be prepared to adopt a realistic time perspective recognizing in the organization, funding, and staffing of the program that its effective horizon is not one or a few years but at least one or two decades.

Stated thus in summary form these sound perhaps like somewhat bland and toothless platitudes, though as I shall try to suggest, their full acceptance would have very far-reaching practical consequences.

PRESIDENTIAL REFORMULATION OF POLICY

First, the persuasive reformulation of foreign policy doctrine toward the low-income countries by the President, the Secretary of State, key congressional spokesmen, and public leaders could have at least two crucial operational implications. One is that in the absence of such a reformulation, the widespread demands for a new look at foreign aid may be met by an unproductive fiddling with organization charts and agency labels which will not touch the heart of the problem. A clear articulation of a strategy for the future could focus the push for novelty where it belongs and leave the government free to retain those organizational patterns of the aid effort developed over the past seven or eight years which are substantially better than any of the proposed alternatives. The principal virtue of many proposed alterations is an appearance of change and a recognition of the unsatisfactory state of present foreign aid doctrine.

Another implication follows from the fact that the various instruments of our policy toward the low-income countries other than aid, such as diplomacy, commercial policy, cultural exchange programs, information activities, and the Peace Corps, have not in the past been designed with a view to their potential contributions to modernization and especially to its social and civic dimensions. The Food for Peace Program has been reoriented in the last couple of years to focus it more on the promotion of agricultural development abroad and less on surplus commodities disposal. This is a substantial step forward, but a still broader consideration of its role in modernization is needed. These various non-aid instruments have, of course, other purposes which must continue to be served, but their potential contributions to economic growth, and especially to social and civic development, have not yet been fully exploited—in part because of a lack of articulation of doctrine and of policy direction from the top levels of government.

UNDERSTANDING THE ELEMENTS OF MODERNIZATION

With respect to the second requirement for more probing applied research and analysis, the Agency for International Development (AID) has taken an important and unrecognized lead in the last seven years. This leadership both within the federal establishment and with the academic world has broadened our understanding of the obstacles to economic growth, especially in the eight or ten countries where the bulk of our development assistance has been concentrated. Recognition of the major advances in the sophistication of our economic diagnoses in which AID has pioneered and the World Bank has played a role leads to the conclusion that this effort must be continued and reinforced.

There is now urgent need for a parallel analytic effort in foreign missions, in foreign affairs agencies in Washington, and in the research community at home and abroad, on the nature of and requirements for popular participation in social and civic development in the variety of cultures and political and social systems in the less-developed countries. We need to devise research techniques for measuring and evaluating progress in social and civic development which can gain the same degree of international acceptance that national product accounting already enjoys. The President's Scientific Advisory Committee issued a call in 1961 for a greatly expanded program of technical, economic, and social research on the development process. In spite of the notable progress which has been made in economic analysis, this recommendation has never been effectively implemented. Any reorganization must make provision for meeting this need.

INTEGRATED COUNTRY PROGRAMMING

Planners abroad and development analysts at home have become increasingly aware of the interdependencies and pervasive interconnections among economic, technological, institutional, and social elements of the modernization complex. It cannot be dealt with as a series of independent parts which will add up, but must be treated as an organic process whose elements must be kept in balance if the whole system is to function effectively. The main responsibility for seeing that the pieces fit together—that transport is available when and where needed, that skills match jobs, that institutions are ready when there are functions for them to perform, that technical advice is at hand when farmers are ready to use it—rests on the development agencies of the low-income countries. But country programming is also essential for those who contribute resources and help from outside.

Integrated country programming was not applied successfully to the less-developed countries by U.S. agencies until AID was formed in 1961. Since then, the country programming process has been greatly improved as applied to the economic problems of the countries in which development assistance has been concentrated, both within many of the field missions in concert with host governments and in Washington. A comparable integrated country programming effort in collaboration with interested governments is now called for in social and civic development. The progress already made in designing with local planners country strategies to take account of the relations between major economic sectors is now seriously threatened by proposals to break up AID into separate functional organizations dealing respectively with such areas as agriculture, education, and health, or into independent agencies concerned with technical assistance, capital grants, and the promotion of private investment.

These proposals usually recognize the need for coordination and propose a special office in the White House or the State Department to perform this function, but our experience with this way of dealing with the problem has not been happy. Even in AID with its strong organizational focus on the country program, there has to date been wholly inadequate progress in designing strategies which recognize the relations between different kinds of technical assistance, between technical assistance and capital development, between the promotion of participation and the strengthening of institutions, between local units and central government agencies, and indeed across the whole spectrum of the noneconomic elements of the modernization process. An organizational structure which permits and encourages this country programming process is critical in Washington but especially in missions in the field where the principal contact with host country planners takes place.

In field missions, the establishment of the country team has been a step in the right direction, and in a few instances where enlightened ambassadors have devoted their energies to making the team work effectively, it has had some good results. The experiment which has been launched in the Latin American area of partially integrating Washington AID personnel and the State Department regional bureau around country units deserves careful study to see whether it can be extended to other regions. In any case, a movement from the present position toward the dispersion and multiplication of separate agency interests in low-income countries is a movement in the wrong direction.

An interesting suggestion which deserves further study is that for the low-income countries the process of congressional authorization and appropriation for the whole range of foreign policy activities might be organized much more explicitly around regions or large countries rather than as at present around separate and somewhat unrelated functions.

This country programming requirement also has implications for the issue of the extent to which and the rate at which we should transfer our development assistance activities to international organizations, which is discussed later in this essay. The past structure of international organizations was sharply divided by functions—the International Bank for Reconstruction and Development (IBRD) and the regional banks for capital financing of projects, the U.N. development program for generalized technical assistance, U.N. Food and Agriculture Organization (FAO) for agriculture, U.N. Educational, Scientific, and Cultural Organization (UNESCO) for education and science, U.N. Industrial Development Organization (UNIDO) for industry, U.N. Conference on Trade and Development (UNCTAD) and General Agreement on Tariffs and Trade (GATT) for trade, the International Monetary Fund (IMF) for monetary policy. Such a structure was not well-suited to recognizing and dealing with the interrelations among these activities in particular countries. The pervasive presence of these interconnections is currently forcing more consideration of them on the international agencies. The IBRD in particular has recently taken important steps both to undertake more integrated country analysis itself and to coordinate its activities with those of the other international agencies. The United States should support the transformation of the IBRD from a project bank to an institution concerned with development strategy. But it will be some time before the Bank or any other international institution will be equipped to take over completely the country programming process. There is a powerful case for the United States as the largest donor to continue to take the lead in emphasizing the systemic character of the modernization process in all its dimensions.

A REALISTIC TIME PERSPECTIVE

On the requirement of continuity and a longer time perspective in U.S. policies toward the low-income world, the record of our performance over the past twenty years has exhibited more consistency and persistence than would be suggested either by the exhausting annual process of congressional presentation, review, authorization, and appropriation or by the drastic reorganizations and relabeling every few years. Top aid agency officials have estimated that as much as half of the time of the senior staff in Washington is devoted to the preparation, presentation, and defense of the AID program before congressional committees, including at its core the authorizing committees of the two houses and the two appropriations committees. In addition, a substantial number of ad hoc inquiries, probes, and reviews by other units of the Congress are usually involved. Much of this activity is useful and necessary to internal management as well as external support. But there is evidence that there is growing dissatisfaction with the annual review procedures among congressmen themselves. It is hard to believe that, if the Congress genuinely accepted the long-run role of an aid program in U.S. foreign policy, more rational and efficient and less disruptive ways of insuring accountability to Congress and responsiveness to legislative direction could not be found, as they have been for military programs.

Uncertainties as to organizational continuity are perhaps even more disruptive of individual morale and effectiveness and of institutional learning than the tribulations of the annual review process. In the course of twenty years, we have gone from ECA to TCA to FOA to MSA to ICA to DLF and finally to AID, to list only a few of the alphabetical labels attached to the entities that have been involved in aid. Any private business or domestic government agency which was subjected to this degree of uncertainty and disruption through time would be unable to perform its functions successfully. In view of these obstacles to the conduct of what must inevitably be a long-term and frequently slow-acting program, it is indeed remarkable that development assistance has achieved the results described earlier. The period of greatest effectiveness has unquestionably been the last few years when the cumulative advantages of seven years of a basically uninterrupted organizational structure could begin to exhibit themselves. But major improvements in the quality of aid administration could be accomplished if the federal government were to recognize service in development agencies, national and international, as an established career with a prospect for stability and advancement.

A number of conclusions follow from these considerations concerning time perspective. First, changes in the present organizational structure should not be proposed solely to symbolize a new administration's determination to set out in fresh directions. Second, any new organizational structure proposed should be presumed to persist in broad outline for at least a decade. Third, the administration should enter into consultation with the congressional leadership on ways of streamlining congressional review and supervision of the operation that will reduce the inefficiencies and impairment of organizational morale implicit in the present arrangements. Whether this consultation should involve a fresh attempt to secure multiyear authorizations for parts of the program or some other technique for improving the present practice will have to be determined in consultation with the congressional leadership. Clearly no changes of this sort can be brought about, or if brought about can be lasting, unless the fundamental philosophy adopted by the President for the program as a whole is accepted by the Congress. Fourth, the aid legislation should be redrafted to remove the innumerable restrictive provisions and limitations which have been added over the years, most of which are now irrelevant to the purposes of the legislation and reduce sharply the effectiveness of the fund appropriated.

Balance among the Instruments of AID Policy

In addition to diplomacy, the major foreign policy instruments used during the sixties in dealing with the low-income countries are: (1) military assistance, which apart from Vietnam has recently declined sharply from the level of around $1 billion a year in the early sixties; (2) development loans and grants both bilateral and through multilateral organizations running somewhat over $1 billion a year and comprising three forms of capital assistance: capital for large projects, assistance to broad sectors like agriculture and education, and program assistance for general imports to support development programs as a whole; (3) food aid averaging about $1.3 billion a year; (4) technical assistance, both bilateral and through international organizations, running between $300 and $400 million a year; (5) supporting assistance to aid a small number of countries believed to be directly menaced by communist aggression or subversion running over $500 million a year; (6) trade and other policies to promote and stabilize the export earnings of the less-developed countries; (7) governmental support and encouragement of private investment and of the activities of other nongovernmental organizations; (8) a variety of programs with other objectives but having important effects on development like the Peace Corps, cultural exchanges, and information programs.

MILITARY AID AND SUPPORTING ASSISTANCE

Military assistance, apart from our very extensive activities in Vietnam which are now part of the regular defense budget, has been falling consistently over the years. Foreign aid described as utilized for essentially military purposes declined from 79 percent in 1952 to 17 percent in 1968. This change is partly in language, since in the early fifties it was believed that Congress would support economic assistance only if it had a military rationale, while today the reverse is probably nearer the truth. More importantly the change is a reflection of changes in our perceptions of the national interest described earlier in this essay. If the diagnosis there given of the trend in our perceptions is accurate, the levels of military assistance may be expected to decline still further in the future.

A shift from an interest in supporting one side in a conflict to reducing the general level of violence in the low-income world suggests a greatly reduced logic for bilateral military assistance. Further, the argument advanced by Senator Fulbright that aid inevitably sucks us in as parties to disputes from which we should remain aloof, which probably has very little weight as applied to economic assistance, is a great deal more persuasive with reference to military assistance. Indeed, the present mood of the Congress as expressed in the Conte-Long and Symington Amendments to the Foreign Assistance Act of 1967 is to direct that such leverage as our economic aid programs give us with recipient countries should be used to inhibit rather than to support the expansion of their military budgets. Whether these particular amendments prescribe what will turn out to be workable techniques for achieving the ends they seek, their objectives are certainly consonant with the foreign policy posture suggested earlier.

Ninety-five percent of the $630 million requested in the President's budget for fiscal 1969 for supporting assistance was designed for four countries, Vietnam, Korea, Laos, and Thailand, with nearly $500 million planned for Vietnam alone. Apart from Vietnam, there may continue to be a case for the availability of relatively small amounts of money to be used in support of political objectives unrelated to development in low-income countries. If the appraisal of our altered strategic interests given earlier is correct, however, the amounts should be minor in aid budgets over the next decade.

DEVELOPMENT LOANS AND TECHNICAL ASSISTANCE

Among the instruments available to promote our long-run interests in the economic and social development process, three—development loans and grants, food aid, and technical assistance, including contributions for these purposes to international organizations—involve substantial financial resource transfers from the U.S. government to the low-income countries. The remainder—support of private activities, trade and commercial policy, and the collection of other non-aid instruments—may involve indirect costs in American human and other resources but pose negligible direct burdens on the U.S. taxpayer through the federal budget.

A key question is whether over the next decade our national interests in the low-income countries can be pursued with present or reduced levels of resources allocated to aid. The answer is clearly in the negative. United States and other developed country official economic aid rose rapidly during the late fifties. In calendar 1961, the total supplied by noncommunist industrial countries as reported by the Development Assistance Committee of the Organization for European Cooperation and Development was a little over $6 billion of which the U.S. share was $3.4 billion. Communist country aid added perhaps $300 million more. From 1961 through 1967, the figures rose slightly in money terms, mainly because of increases in European contributions. In terms of real resources, they probably declined, partly because of persistent price increases in the supplying countries, and partly because the spread of the practice of tying aid to purchases in the contributing country reduced the opportunities of the recipient countries to buy in the cheapest market. Further, in the decade of the sixties the burden of payments of interest and amortization on past indebtedness mounted for many of the less-developed countries, reducing sharply the net foreign resources available to them from new aid allocations. A tendency in the United States to stiffen terms on new aid loans threatened to cut in advance the value to them of future aid prospects. The drastic reductions in the U.S. aid appropriations in fiscal 1968 and fiscal 1969 and the rise in the share of this reduced total taken by Vietnam means that the aid resources at the disposal of countries other than Vietnam will be sharply reduced in 1969 and 1970.

The need for food aid in the period ahead is somewhat uncertain. An agricultural revolution is in progress in the cereal producing countries of Asia which is already yielding dramatic increases in productivity. The future needs for food aid depend on how the race comes out between burgeoning agricultural productivity in the underdeveloped world and the rapidly swelling demand for foodstuffs there. The course of demand depends partly on population growth and partly on the growth of non-agricultural output and incomes in the low-income countries. Measures to inhibit population growth, to which the United States is now devoting greatly increased attention in technical assistance activities and which are beginning to show real promise, will, if successful, permit an increasing share of the investment resources of the low-income countries, supplemented by aid to be devoted to raising standards of living rather than to preventing starvation for millions of additional people.

Whatever happens to the need for food aid, the need for capital assistance will grow over the next decade as an increasing number of countries can use it productively. Some countries like India are clearly operating their existing industrial plant at substantially less than capacity because of shortages of foreign exchange with which to purchase the essential imports required to utilize it fully. Others are now capable of boosting their growth rates markedly if additional capital resources were obtainable to finance the purchase of plant and equipment. Still others, while not yet in a position to absorb productively large increases in capital resources, will develop additional absorptive capacity over the next decade. The World Bank has estimated that an additional $3 or $4 billion of aid from all sources could now be productively employed by the less-developed countries. For the United States to supply its fair share of this increase would require more than double our present level of official capital aid, which would still leave the aid burden below 1 percent of our gross national product. And there is evidence that the total cost of the aid required to generate self-sustaining growth will be a good deal lower if it is applied in adequate amounts over a relatively short period than if it is stretched out in smaller dribbles over a longer time.

A few countries have been successful enough in their growth efforts to have already graduated from the list of recipients of capital assistance, and appear now to be able to sustain their economic growth without further concessional aid. This group includes Taiwan, Iran, Israel, and Greece. Several others like Turkey and South Korea may be able, if they are given a last push of substantial help, to obtain independence from concessional aid within the next five years. Others, including some very large ones like India, Pakistan, and Brazil, which together account for about 40 percent of the people of the less-developed noncommunist countries, have set the stage by launching over the past decade a pattern of growth which with adequate external help could be greatly accelerated during the seventies.

Without substantial capital assistance continuing for a number of years, however, they probably cannot even sustain the developmental momentum they have achieved. The reason is either that, though their savings have been growing rapidly, they will not be able for another decade or so to save enough to finance the necessary investment, or that the growth in their exports has not yet reached the point where they can pay for the level of imports that rapid growth requires. Others, like Indonesia whose initiation of a serious developmental effort has been delayed by inadequate leadership and political turmoil, appear now to be ready and eager to get started on serious development programs. To do this, they will need levels of help they have not enjoyed in the past. Finally, a number of other states, including several of the African countries, are so far behind that they will require further investments in human capital and in basic social and economic infrastructure before significant growth can even be started.

The main financial requirement for aid is likely to come in the near future from a relatively limited number of the larger countries in the middle group just described whose earlier development efforts have brought them to a point where they are ready for a spurt of a decade or so of rapid growth. At this stage, substantial foreign capital resources are most critical. The evidence of our experience since 1950 is conclusive that for countries in this group there is a minimum threshold of capital assistance below which they limp along without much per-capita development. On the other hand, a level of capital assistance substantially above this threshold may, by activating unsuspected reserves of initiative, energy, and innovative ability within a country, produce a dramatic economic boom which may greatly shorten the period during which aid is required. Such a boom, in turn, may lay the groundwork for an extension of popular participation in the development process which could not occur in a more stagnant economy. Something like this response appears to have happened in Taiwan, South Korea, and to a limited extent in Pakistan, and could happen over the next decade in a number of other countries if aid levels were above the critical minimum threshold.

Thus, if resources for capital assistance of the United States and other developed countries are limited, probably the most efficient use of the resources is to concentrate them in relatively few countries and to try to do an adequate job in each. The United States has been following that policy for the last few years. Before the recent cuts in the U.S. aid budget, it was already concentrating 80 percent of its development loans in eight countries—Pakistan, India, Korea, and Indonesia in Asia; Turkey in the Middle East, and Brazil, Chile, and Colombia in Latin America. Aid to some of these countries, notably India, the largest, was already well below an efficient level. In no way can our strategic, economic, and social interests in the development of the low-income countries be effectively advanced without a higher level of resource transfer than was achieved in the mid-sixties, which is a much higher level than is implied by recent aid appropriations.

The relation between development lending and some of the other less expensive instruments listed at the beginning of this section might be explored further. The principle of concentration is much less applicable to technical assistance than to development loans. Technical cooperation with host country efforts in agriculture, education, health, population control, public and private administration, institution building and participation can have important effects in countries which have not yet developed the absorptive capacity for large amounts of capital, such as many of those in Africa. Technical assistance also continues to be important in countries like Taiwan, Iran, Greece, and Mexico which have become economically self-sustaining but still have problems of making their economies and their institutions more responsive to the needs of their people. But if capital assistance is not available at the times, in the amounts, and in the places where it is critically needed in the development process, the beneficial effects of many admirable technical assistance activities can be frustrated or rapidly dissipated. For example, improvements in educational technique are of little use if the economy does not provide the resources to build schools and pay teachers or the jobs in which those with newly acquired skills can put them to work; agricultural improvement is of no avail if urban incomes are not rising enough to permit city dwellers to buy more food; more efficient and more honest government administration does not help much if a country does not have the resources to finance programs for the government to administer.

PRIVATE RESOURCES FOR DEVELOPMENT

The suggestion is sometimes made that if only we can find ways of stimulating a greatly increased flow of private capital investment into the underdeveloped countries, by U.S. measures to make private capital export more attractive and by inducements to host governments to improve what is described as the investment climate, a good part of the burden of public aid appropriations could be avoided. But this suggestion misconstrues the relation between public development lending and private investment opportunity which historically and analytically have more often been complements than substitutes. Private investment to supply local markets is not very attractive whatever the inducements or the political climate, in countries where purchasing power is very low or the supportive overhead facilities of transport, communication, energy sources, and engineering services are nonexistent or primitive.

The best stimulus to private foreign investment activity in an underdeveloped country is a period of sustained and vigorous growth in domestic per-capita incomes, which in many cases requires injections of public capital to get it going. In addition to the economic reasons why at the takeoff stage of development substantial public capital flows are a necessary condition—often a precondition—for private investment activity, there are political reasons. Countries faced with severe shortages of capital and foreign exchange are likely to react to these difficulties by multiplying the governmental restrictions, controls, licensing, and regulation which are so frightening to the foreign private investor. The climate for foreign private investment has been best where national sensibilities have been soothed by the sense of confidence that results from successful development efforts and an expansion of domestic industry supported in part by foreign public resources.

Active policies by AID, the Treasury, the Export-Import Bank, and other government departments are important to foster and promote private capital flows to the less-developed countries. But devices for more ingenious combinations of private entrepreneurial skills with public resources to make their employment more attractive deserve further study. As development proceeds, frequently an expansion of private capital flows ultimately makes possible the graduation of a country from the class of aid recipients. But in the lower-income range of countries these measures are unlikely to be effective in the absence of an adequate public development lending program.

TRADE POLICY

Finally, the hope of avoiding the level of aid appropriations, earlier suggested as unavoidable if we are to promote our development objectives, sometimes rests on the notion that where the central problem facing an underdeveloped country in its development efforts is the acquisition of sufficient foreign exchange for necessary imports, policies to promote the export potential of the country may be a substitute for aid appropriations. Again, unquestionably, such policies are urgently needed. The long-run economic viability of any developing country, even of some of the very large ones, is likely to be dependent on its exports growing much more rapidly than its gross national product. Fortunately, the focus of attention in the underdeveloped world, which was very heavily on domestic investment to produce substitutes for imports in the early postwar period, has been shifting to export promotion, regional trade agreements, and a search for foreign markets. This shift has been signaled by the formation of the U.N. Conference on Trade and Development, by the pressures from the low-income countries for preferential treatment of their manufactured exports in the developed countries, and by schemes to stabilize the prices of the more traditional raw-material exports.

Most of these pressures for trade expansion deserve our full support. Our tariffs and those of the other developed countries on processed raw materials and on light manufactures from the underdeveloped countries are nominally often quite low, but our policies including a variety of non-tariff restrictions have for a number of reasons been more protectionist than appears from the tariff schedules. A strong case can be made for acceding to a demand made by the less-developed countries that some preference be given in the timing of contemplated international tariff reductions to low-income country manufactures, though there are some technical problems in implementing this proposal. The United States should do what it can to encourage common-market arrangements like the Latin American free trade area among groups of underdeveloped countries. Commodity price stabilization schemes may boomerang unless accompanied by effective measures to prevent world supplies from persistently exceeding world demands for products like coffee, cocoa, and some of the metals, but we should support arrangements which combine removing some of the effects of commodity price fluctuation with promotion of the diversification of exports.

Important as these trade measures are to the long-run viability of the developing economies, no serious observer has suggested that they can be an effective substitute over the next decade for capital assistance. With the exception of oil and some of the minerals, the markets for the traditional raw material exports of many of the underdeveloped countries cannot be expanded enough to provide the foreign exchange they need for rapid growth. Thus their long-run prospects for international balance depend on their doing as Japan did, namely finding new products, many of them manufactures, in which they can develop a comparative advantage. But this is a long process in which substantial investments in capital goods, machinery, training and organization, market knowledge, and in some cases imported raw materials must be made many years in advance of the hoped-for payoff in foreign exchange earnings. Part of the investment required to cover this period of reorienting economies to new and different types of export performance must be made through foreign aid. So once again we come to the broad conclusion that trade expansion, far from making aid unnecessary, requires it as a handmaiden.

This review of balance among the instruments of aid policy is not intended to suggest that, if we appropriate adequate sums for the more expensive items of capital assistance and technical cooperation, the other dimensions of the problem will take care of themselves. We need much more attention to private enterprise promotion and trade expansion to further our interests in economic development and much more concern than we have had with the social and civic dimensions of all our policy instruments. And, of course, unless recipient governments take the necessary self-help measures to raise complementary domestic resources and to make foreign resources fully effective, aid will not be productive. What we are suggesting is that none of these things are substitutes, individually or taken all together, for public economic aid, and that if the levels of such aid are inadequate, the other tools are very unlikely to have the desired effects.

DEVELOPMENT INSTRUMENTS AND THE PROBLEM
OF POPULATION AND FOOD

The realization has been growing rapidly of late in the developing countries that unless they grapple more effectively with measures to contain the growth of population, their attempts to raise living standards will be largely frustrated. The dramatic decline in death rates which relatively inexpensive modern public health measures have already brought about in the low-income world has not yet been matched by a corresponding fall in birth rates such as has occurred in virtually all developed countries. The result has been a rate of growth in the world's population in the last few decades of close to 3 percent per year, unmatched in any other period of history. Indeed, population is now growing as fast each year as it did in each century until about 1600. At present rates the world's population will more than double by the year 2000, and most of the increase will be in the low-income countries.

While the performance of the underdeveloped countries in increasing production by 4.5 percent a year has more than kept up with the population explosion of less than 3 percent annually in the last decade, yielding a slow improvement in per capita standards of nearly 2 percent a year, more than half the resource cost of this growth has been required merely to meet the subsistence needs of the extra people appearing on the scene.

Several changes both in practice and in knowledge in the last few years give us hope that we may be able to bring this problem under control by the end of the century. First, while as recently as five years ago there were almost no effective government programs for family limitation in the low-income countries, some twenty-five countries, including some of the large ones, now have such programs, and many more are under consideration. Second, while it was widely believed until recently that tradition, cultural practices, and religious scruples were major barriers to the adoption of birth-control techniques, recent attitude surveys combined with the experience of the new programs have shown that where effective, safe, and inexpensive methods are available a majority of couples of child-bearing age in rural as well as urban communities are eager to use them to limit their families. We do not yet know how far birth rates can be reduced simply by providing people with the means to do what they are already motivated to do, but we can do much more with techniques and organization before we are blocked by motivational obstacles than we once thought.

Third, there have already been marked advances in contraceptive techniques, notably the intra-uterine devices and the contraceptive pill, which have had an important effect in countries like Taiwan and South Korea. These techniques are not suitable in all circumstances and have disadvantages, but an expansion of research effort, which is urgently needed, could accelerate the availability of a spectrum of methods which would speed adoption. Finally, in the United States and other aid-giving countries, after some years of uncertainty about policies toward technical assistance in the population field, we have settled on a vigorous promotional effort in all the countries that want it.

At best, this is a long-term program which will probably not show marked results in a sharp drop in world population growth for ten or fifteen years. Fortunately, so far as the basic problems of nutrition are concerned, the revolution in agricultural technology which gives us hope of increasing food production more rapidly than population for at least a few years gives us a little extra time. The two proximate objectives of a limitation of population and an expansion of food supply are interdependent. An improvement in child nutrition will probably, by sharply reducing infant mortality, make parents more willing in the long run to limit the number of births.

More broadly, however, neither the expansion of food production nor the improvement in nutrition is possible in the underdeveloped countries without greatly accelerated industrial production. The new agricultural technology on which increased food production depends requires very heavy industrial inputs. The new miracle seeds in wheat, rice, and coarse grains flourish only with heavy applications of fertilizer, with radical increases in irrigation calling for pumps, wells, piping, and other industrial products, and with extensive efforts in pest and weed control. All this takes mechanical equipment. The man who was formerly a subsistence farmer must now sell much of his output in order to buy the necessary industrial inputs. Unless incomes are rising rapidly in the nonagricultural parts of the economy, money demand for the new marketable surplus will not be adequate, and the technological revolution in agriculture will be brought to a halt. Put another way, people can eat better only if their incomes are substantially higher, and their incomes will be higher only if the entire economy and not just the agricultural sector is prospering.

Further, it is clear that population limitation also ultimately requires general economic development. While existing motivations will lead to some reduction in birth rates where the means are made available, over the longer run more fundamental changes in attitudes are required which are closely associated with education, urbanization, and rising standards of living.

These higher levels of exchange between urban and rural, industrial and agricultural sectors in turn mean much heavier burdens on facilities for transportation, communication, and other social overheads. In short, all parts of the economy must be growing in rough balance. But a rapid growth in imports is required, not just of fertilizer and agricultural inputs but of the whole range of things that a flourishing economy needs from abroad. In turn exports must grow, which requires capital investment in new export industries, training in new skills, improvements in the effectiveness of all kinds of institutions, and a massive broadening of participation in the development process. The fallacy of the notion that even if we were interested only in the war on hunger, we could concentrate our attention solely on agricultural productivity and population control is thus revealed. Development is a seamless web, and while it can take many forms, isolated attention to one or two of its dimensions is unlikely to be either efficient or productive.

Relations with Other Donors: Bilateral and Multilateral Approaches

Two broad questions have come up recurrently in the discussion of aid policy over the years and deserve a fresh look here. The first has to do with the appropriate sharing of the burden of development assistance among the more developed countries. The second relates to how far the United States and the other developed countries should conduct development programs bilaterally with the recipients and how far development lending and technical assistance activities should be channeled through a variety of international organizations. The two questions are quite distinct, though they are related and sometimes confused.

With regard to the first, it is sometimes suggested that the burden of aid on the U.S. budget could be reduced if other developed countries could be persuaded to carry an increased share of the aid load. In the light of the record of the last few years, this suggestion is both grossly inequitable and practically unfeasible. According to the records of the Development Assistance Committee (DAC) of the Office of Economic Cooperation and Development (OECD), which included Japan and the United States as well as virtually all the developed countries of Western Europe, the United States ranked tenth in 1967 in its share of gross national product devoted to public and private development assistance, ranking behind France, the Netherlands, Portugal, West Germany, Great Britain, Belgium, Switzerland, Japan, and Australia in that order. U.S. ranking in official governmental aid as a percent of gross product was somewhat higher, but it was still well below many European countries such as France, Belgium, and the Netherlands. Since real per-capita income in the United States is roughly twice that of the average for all other members of DAC, the principle of ability to pay, enshrined in our own progressive income tax, would suggest that in equity our relative contribution should be larger, not smaller than that of the others. With a good deal more than half the income of the noncommunist developed world, we had until 1967 been supplying publicly and privately only about half of the flow of resources to less-developed countries. The sharp cuts in fiscal 1968 and fiscal 1969 aid programs have undoubtedly reduced our share markedly below even the inequitable levels prevailing until 1967.

A strong case can be made for larger contributions from most of the developed countries. Targets set by the United Nations, by DAC, and by the recent meeting of UNCTAD, have suggested as desirable something in the neighborhood of 1 percent of gross national product in public and private resource contributions from the developed to the underdeveloped countries. For the middle sixties, the DAC countries averaged about eight-tenths of 1 percent of GNP, with official contributions representing 0.05 percent, and with the U.S. contributions significantly lower than these averages. In the face of this record, it is clearly unrealistic to expect other countries to increase their contributions while the United States is cutting its contribution from the low levels of the sixties. If, on the other hand, we reverse the recent trend and increase our aid levels substantially, it would be reasonable to expect additional contributions from other donors. Since gross national products are growing through the developed world at a rate of 4 or 5 percent a year, a constant percentage of gross national products would represent an expanding flow of aid over time rather than the constant or shrinking one which has characterized the sixties. Once the United States has reached its reasonable share, it might even be appropriate for it to make further increases explicitly contingent on matching contributions from others.

The question of the best international coordination and management of these aid flows is more complex. We have been channeling a gradually increasing fraction of our official aid through international agencies and now furnish nearly 10 percent of our nonfood aid this way. The OECD countries (Western Europe, Canada, Japan) provide a larger share in this form bringing the average for all OECD countries up to about 11 percent. With respect to another 25 percent or so of economic and technical aid, bilateral contributions are coordinated to a greater or lesser degree through multilateral consortia, consultations, and the like. Senator Fulbright and others have proposed that we should move much more rapidly in the direction of turning over a major part of the administration of our development assistance to such organizations as the International Bank, the U.N. Development Program, and regional banks like the Inter-American Development Bank, and the newly established Asian and African Banks. The United States would then administer bilaterally only those programs whose scale and character was dictated by immediate U.S. security and other special considerations.

A number of virtues are alleged for this proposal. If our interests have in fact shifted in the fashion described at the beginning of this essay toward those which are less parochial and more widely shared in the international community, the disadvantages to U.S. security interests of losing control are greatly reduced. It is argued that international administration would insulate us from involvement in domestic controversies in the low-income countries and thus avoid undesirable U.S. entanglement with particular factions and pressure groups abroad. It is further argued that the application of self-help and other conditions to the granting of aid, which are necessary to make the aid productive and effective, would be much more acceptable to the recipient countries if the conditions were imposed by international organizations than by national agencies suspected of having unrevealed political motives. A related suggestion is that the image of the United States in the underdeveloped countries would be greatly improved if its presence abroad were less visible and if it demonstrated a willingness to forego the special uses of its power and influence which bilateral-aid arrangements give. There are strong elements of validity in all these arguments which suggest that we should continue to give increasing resources and responsibility to international agencies and help them in any way to discharge their responsibilities more effectively.

Some counterarguments, however, suggest that it will be difficult and perhaps not wholly wise to move too rapidly or radically in this direction.

First, I have explained above the basis for my conviction that the allocation by all the developed countries of substantially greater resources to the development process than have been provided in the recent past is critical to the advancement of long-run U.S. moral and national interests. It seems unlikely that the U.S. public and the U.S. Congress will or should in the present state of effectiveness of many of the international institutions be willing to transfer to them the whole of the enlarged scale of resources required to do the job. If we were content with limited or token programs, as I suspect some of the advocates of largely international administration would be, this objection would lose its force. But if we feel that expanded levels of effort are required to promote both U.S. and international interests, I suspect we will continue to have to mount bilateral programs of some magnitude for some time to come.

A further consideration has to do with our relative contribution. Because of our level of income which in the aggregate is roughly half that of the free developed world but in per-capita terms is twice that of the average of the other developed countries, we should be supplying not half of the aid resources being furnished the low-income countries, but closer to 60 or 70 percent. If our contribution to international agencies rises above the 30 to 40 percent to which it has been limited in the past, their international character may be gravely compromised. If, because of their regional and commercial interests in particular parts of the world, the other developed countries are unwilling, as they probably are, to increase radically the share of their development aid administered through international institutions, which is already larger than ours, this problem will be greatly exacerbated.

There are other considerations. If the United States were overwhelmingly the dominant influence in international institutions, the alleged advantages of multilateralization in host country receptivity to influence and in improvements in the U.S. image would be open to serious question. In any case, the U.S. image can be most effectively altered abroad not by organizational and institutional rearrangements but by changes in the way we behave and the objectives we pursue in foreign countries. In fact, to limit bilateral programs to those in which there is an obviously dominant and narrow U.S. security or political interest would contribute strongly to the further deterioration of our image.

It is sometimes argued that internationalization is desirable because international organizations can handle aid more efficiently than U.S. agencies. The record to date does not seem to bear out this contention.

The International Bank has a good reputation in the appraisal and management of large capital projects, but the regional banks are too new to have demonstrated the quality of their talents and the long-standing U.N. technical assistance program has not been as effective as a number of bilateral ones including ours. In the circumstances, we can for the time being probably mobilize American talents for technical assistance, concentrate American capital where it will be most productive, influence social and civic change most constructively, and have the best chance of applying the volume of human and financial resources required effectively to promote our interests in the modernization process by continuing substantial bilateral programs. At the same time, we should redouble our efforts to put these programs in a multilateral framework, both by supporting and financing the expansion of international institutions and by fuller participation in consortia, consultative arrangements, and devices for international programming.

Can We Afford It?

If the long-run interests outlined earlier are accepted as valid, and if it is agreed that to promote those interests effectively we would need to allocate substantially larger human and financial resources to the task than we have been doing for the past few years, perhaps roughly doubling the level, the question remains whether in view of all of our other domestic and international responsibilities we can afford it.

Let us dispose first of a widely used argument that a larger aid program would pose intolerable strains on our already dangerous balance-of-payments position. We have so effectively tied aid to procurement in the United States that the estimate is that this year more than 94 percent of the expenditures of our economic aid program will be made in this country. While some aid shipments may replace export earnings we would otherwise enjoy, some untied aid disbursements find their way back indirectly to U.S. purchases. Whatever these incalculable offsets, the burden that aid places on our balance of payments is unlikely to be currently very important. However, the tying arrangements we and other countries have adopted reduce the efficiency of resource use, and it is to be hoped that more fundamental solutions to our balance-of-payments difficulties can be found.

The drain on our resources involved in aid levels up to as much as twice as large as recent appropriations would be relatively small either as a fraction of our national income or in comparison with other programs in which the federal government is now engaged—like defense and domestic welfare. Aid to European countries in 1949 at the peak of the Marshall Plan was more than 2 percent of our GNP for that year. The budget proposed by the President for 1968–69 calls for a level of assistance to the low-income countries of only about one-half of 1 percent of GNP or about one-fifth of what Charles Schultze estimates in his paper is the current net cost of the Vietnam war. The maximum increases which have been proposed in the U.S. contribution to bring our public and private aid up to the target level of 1 percent of GNP are $2 or $3 billion at the most. These figures compare with a projected annual increase of our GNP of $50 or $60 billion each year over the next few years or $35 to $40 billion at constant prices, and with the projected increase in federal tax revenues at existing rates which Mr. Schultze estimates as rising from some $15 to some $18 billion a year. A glance at the magnitude of various other public programs proposed in this volume makes it apparent that even a dramatically expanded aid program would be one of the smaller ones. Since the low-income world is so much poorer than we are, the small cost to us will in many cases be vital to their economic and social modernization. We can certainly afford it. Whether the modernization is worth the limited cost and inconvenience it involves depends on the value the United States places on the interests outlined at the beginning of this paper.

CARL KAYSEN

MILITARY STRATEGY, MILITARY FORCES, AND ARMS CONTROL

The fundamental aim of American military policy since the end of the Second World War has been defensive: to prevent the advance of communist power led by the Soviet Union. From our promise of military and economic assistance to Greece and Turkey in early 1947, this aim has led us to steadily widening commitments and to deployments of American forces over most of the globe. Over the same period, revolutionary changes in military technology have drastically altered the old geographic parameters of warfare and led us—and the Soviet Union—to create vast new forces of entirely novel kinds.

Both the international political scene and the technology of warfare have been changing rapidly in the recent past; both can be expected to go on changing in the near future. Changes already experienced and those in prospect require a reexamination of the goals of our military policy and the purposes and nature of the forces and deployments related to them. It is the argument of this paper that the proper conclusion of such a reexamination is that our security interests and needs require great changes both in the underlying rationale of our military policy and in the force structures and deployments which are the concrete expressions of that rationale. The new political and technical realities point to the futility of a quest for security primarily through increased military strength and to the increasing importance of political factors and arms-control arrangements and agreements. Indeed, by giving weight to these factors in the next five years, we will have a better prospect of achieving higher levels of real security—that is, lower risks of harm to the United States and its vital interests, with armed forces and military budgets as much as a third lower than they are now—than we will have by continuing to follow the line of our past policy in a radically altered situation. In plain words, the course of arms limitation, restrictions in deployments, and arms control is not only cheaper than that of continuing competition in arms and military confrontation; it is safer.

Our military strategy in the past has been shaped by three chief goals, all interrelated, but nonetheless of different importance. The first was to deter and defend against a direct attack on the United States. The second was to deter and defend against both a direct attack on Western Europe and the use of the threat of military force, including the threat of attack on the United States, as a weapon in the indirect conquest by political means of some or all of Western Europe. The third, and both later in time and lesser in importance, was to oppose expansion of communist power in any part of the world, especially when it took the form of a takeover by communists, with overt or covert assistance from the Soviet Union, of the government of a previously noncommunist state. This strategy had its origins in the events in Europe in the first years after the end of the war; by the end of the Korean war in 1952, it had settled into a hard mold from which it is only just now shaking loose. It has been given formal expression in a series of multilateral and bilateral treaties binding the United States in mutual defense pacts with nearly fifty nations, several of which are involved in more than one treaty, beginning with the Rio pact of 1947, covering nineteen Latin-American powers, and including the North Atlantic Treaty Organization (NATO), with fifteen members (1949), the Southeast Asia Treaty Organization (SEATO), with eight members and two protocol states (1954), the Central Treaty Organization (CENTO), with four members and U.S. "association" (1955), and bilateral defense treaties with Japan, Taiwan, and South Korea.

Each of the three major goals can be associated with a corresponding aspect of the level, structure, and deployment of U.S. forces, though this correspondence is somewhat artificial, since the various elements of our forces are interrelated and serve more than one goal. The first has led to the creation and maintenance of a long-range strategic striking force, equipped with thermonuclear weapons and capable of world-wide action. We have also created defensive forces against enemy strategic attack, but our main reliance has been on an offensive force. The size and composition of our offensive force has been shaped by the concept of U.S. strategic superiority. In its crudest form this has meant a larger and more effective force than that of the Soviet Union, which even now remains the only other nation with significant long-range striking power. The subtler meanings of the notion of strategic superiority will be explored below. The second goal is reflected mainly in the sizable long-run deployment of U.S.

forces in Europe under the North Atlantic Treaty Organization, though the strategic forces make a vital contribution to it as well. These forces constitute a major military establishment in all arms: the equivalent of nearly 5 divisions of combat ground forces, several battalions of medium- and short-range missiles with nuclear warheads plus support troops, an air force of some 900 tactical aircraft and 85,000 men, equipped with a very large number of tactical nuclear weapons, and the Sixth Fleet in the Mediterranean, a major fleet (built around two carrier task forces) of some 50 ships, 200 aircraft, and 25,000 men. In addition, the backup forces for NATO in the United States amount to nearly 4 army divisions trained and equipped for European service, a sizable portion of the 475 ships, 2,500 planes, and 240,000 men of the Atlantic Fleet, and some part of the tactical air strength in the United States. Indeed, the combined U.S. forces in Europe form a more powerful military establishment than that of any nation save the Soviet Union.

Reflections of the third goal in our military deployments are more diffuse, more variable in time, and thus are less easy to specify precisely. The very size of the forces we maintain, other than strategic offensive and defensive forces and those committed to NATO, is perhaps the most important expression of this third goal. So are such specific deployments as two divisions and some air force units in Korea and a marine division scattered throughout the Pacific; the size and far westward patrol range of the Seventh Fleet in the Pacific; the existence and mission of Southern Command in Panama; the restructuring of the U.S. strategic reserve under Strike Command, in order to create a capability for rapid response with conventional ground and tactical air forces on minimum notice any place in the world; and the world-wide network of military assistance agreements and military training missions both within and without the framework of mutual defense treaties. The great spread of U.S. air bases, communication facilities, and related installations around the world in part reflect this same purpose, although they also serve as support for forces deployed in Europe and the United States. Finally, of course, the most recent powerful and pointed expression of this third goal has been our commitment of more than half a million American troops to a war in South Vietnam to halt and reverse the partly political, partly military, process by which the joint forces of the guerrillas in South Vietnam and the communist government of North Vietnam had begun to take over the South, and to discourage further communist penetration in Southeast Asia.

The International Political Scene

The greatest changes in the international political scene have been those affecting the relations between the United States and the Soviet Union. The Soviet Union is no longer the unchallenged leader of a unified bloc of thirteen communist governments—all but Cuba forming a contiguous mass from Eastern Europe to East and Southeast Asia. Nor is it still the political headquarters of a single world-wide communist movement controlling a network of legal and illegal communist parties and exercising significant political influence in many important countries in both the third world and the U.S. alliance system. The political and ideological split between the Soviet Union and China has not simply bifurcated the communist world; it has shattered it into fragments. And even the largest and most powerful fragment in both economic and military terms—the Warsaw Pact grouping (minus Albania)—though still led by the Soviet Union, no longer shows the unity of purpose and unquestioning submission to Soviet leadership it once did. On the other side, of course, our own dominant role within the American alliance system has also diminished, though it never equaled that of the Soviet Union in terms of command. The result is that the edge of the Soviet-American confrontation is much less sharp, as allies on both sides take a political stance between those of the two superpowers.

On the military side of the confrontation, there has been an increasing mutual recognition by both superpowers of the sharp limitations on their use of military forces directed at each other to achieve or advance political goals. The succession of crises involving some greater or lesser degree of Soviet-American confrontation, Berlin in 1961, Cuba in 1962, the Middle East in 1967, has underlined the reality and strength of the political constraints on the direct use of military force. These constraints are essentially the product of the nuclear age; their working will be examined in some detail in the discussion of strategic forces below.

Profound as these changes are, they have by no means removed the sources of conflict between the United States and the Soviet Union. Mutual ideological hostility still exists on both sides, but it is especially important in the Soviet Union, where it has a much more significant role in the internal political process than in the United States. Direct conflict of political interests over the German settlement in all its ramifications remains, although it, too, has become less sharp. Neither side publicly accepts the legitimacy of the role and activities of the other in the underdeveloped world, but the tendency, respectively, to interpret every action in terms of communist aggression and conspiracy or capitalist encirclement and neo-imperialism has diminished somewhat in intensity, again perhaps more here than there. Many of these conflicts, moreover, are becoming those traditional among great powers and losing their intense flavor of religious war.

These changes are not only the result of mutual appreciation of the political implications of the facts of military technology; they also reflect deeper currents within both the United States and the Soviet Union, currents that are flowing with equal or perhaps greater strength within the other NATO and Warsaw Pact countries as well. In any modern industrialized nation in which the government is responsive to popular will—whether through the mechanisms of democracy or through other less sure and sensitive means—the primary pressures of popular opinion will ordinarily be focused on internal problems of economic and social welfare. Extraordinary events and circumstances are required to sustain wide public interest in foreign policy. Even the governments of the Soviet Union and its Warsaw Pact allies, far as they are from democracy, are gradually becoming subject to and responsive to popular pressures and demands, and thus the same political forces that give primacy to internal problems in the West are operating to some degree on them. Expensive and risky foreign and military policies demand political justification in popular terms, a demand that becomes increasingly difficult to meet, even on the Soviet side.

These trends are both deep and slow-acting; it cannot be asserted with any confidence that they will not be reversed in the shorter or longer term. Between the early and final drafts of this paper, Soviet and other Warsaw Pact forces invaded Czechoslovakia to reverse the Czechs' unacceptably rapid program of liberalization in internal politics and economics. It is difficult to assess the full results of this venture now; yet several preliminary conclusions can be set down. First, the operation was defensive in character and provides no basis for inferring an increase in Soviet readiness to act against NATO or the United States directly. Second, the slowness with which the Russians are pressing their demands on the Czechs and the restraint they are showing in the face of stubborn resistance from Czech leaders and people—in contrast to their behavior in Hungary in 1956—appear to indicate some Soviet reservations on the political effectiveness of military force. Third, disunity within the Warsaw alliance and between the Soviet-oriented communist parties and the Soviet Union has increased sharply. Thus, on the basis of present evidence (late 1968), it seems no more correct to view these events as a reversal in the trends sketched above than as a confirmation of them; yet they could presage such a reversal.

On the United States side, a hardening of our own policy toward the Soviet Union and the communist world, shown by, say, an attempt to achieve "military victory" in South Vietnam and to make concrete in terms of military deployments the notion of maintaining U.S. "military superiority," might also reverse these trends. The political future is unpredictable; but the choice of policy by the United States is a major independent variable in the system. If we ourselves choose to deemphasize military means in foreign policy, we can hold back further increases in our military forces and in some cases (which will be detailed below) reduce them unilaterally. We can actively seek arrangements and agreements, both bilaterally with the Soviet Union and multilaterally, that will permit still further reductions in military forces on both sides. Choice of such a course can make a major contribution to a general movement in the preferred direction of more security. Though this is obviously not a risk-free course, it will be argued below that it is in fact less risky than its alternatives.

In pursuing this path, we should not expect that the Soviet Union will quickly and simply forego all efforts to project its power in diplomatic, economic, and military terms into the noncommunist parts of the world. No more can we expect that it will abandon its determination to maintain the borders of the present communist world or discontinue its search for whatever degree of unity under its own leadership over whatever part of it that appears feasible. Quite the contrary, we should anticipate continuing evidences for some time of Soviet efforts at playing the role of world power: further deployments of Soviet ships outside the waters adjacent to its territory, such as have recently been observed in the Mediterranean; wider patrols of Soviet missile-launching submarines; continued arms shipments on credit terms and dispatches of military training missions to countries of the third world. Many of these actions can be seen as responses to earlier similar ones on our side. In none of these areas would an increase in Soviet activity reach the level of our own for some time, even if that had already begun to decline. What can be anticipated is that, first, those forces which have increasingly limited the political effectiveness of our own activities in these areas will operate in the same way on the Soviet efforts, and second, the Soviet leadership, which—for all its ideological commitments—appears to be a group of rational men capable of attending to the facts of experience, will learn from this experience, however slowly, even as we have ourselves.

The relations of East and West in Europe have displayed the same tendencies toward softening, perhaps to an even greater degree than bilateral Soviet-American relations. Two points have been central in this change. The first is the increasingly low probability assigned by European governments on both sides of the dividing line through Germany to the prospect of a massive westward military movement by the Soviet Union and its Warsaw Pact allies. Even the understandably nervous and dissatisfied government of the Federal Republic, with the strongest cause to be discontented with the European status quo, does not act—in terms of military budgets and force levels—as if it gave high priority to the Soviet military threat. The second is the decline in the belief in "negotiating from strength" in Europe. This change, which has come about fairly gradually over the last decade, is of fundamental importance. Some of the NATO partners, especially the United Kingdom, never believed that the pressure of Western military power could bring about a new settlement that would reunify Germany; some of them, including the Scandinavian countries and perhaps France, were content with the status quo. But Germany and the United States, which both desire a change in the status quo, have come slowly to recognize that change can come safely only through political means and that change is least likely when the two alliance systems confront each other as if at the brink of war. This change in point of view is the product of a number of factors. First is the great success of U.S. and NATO policies over the two postwar decades: the nations of Western Europe are prosperous and confident; despite a variety of internal troubles, they feel more successful and secure than they could possibly have expected in the first years after the end of the Second World War. On the other side, the communist regimes of Eastern Europe are more disunited and more torn by internal pressures than the most confident observer would have predicted a decade ago. The communist parties of Western Europe have become increasingly cautious as they attempt to survive and retain political relevance in an atmosphere of economic growth and even some increase in economic equality and social mobility. All these changes have robbed communism of the dynamism it appeared to possess in the first decade after the war and increased the confidence of the Western European nations in themselves and in their capacity to deal with the Soviet

Union and its allies in political terms. Another consequence of the success of our policies, of course, is the increasing assertiveness of European governments and their decreased willingness to accept American leadership unquestioningly.

None of this has changed the vital U.S. interest in Western Europe or the disproportion between the present military power of the Soviet Union and its allies and that of the Western European nations apart from the United States. But it has changed the immediacy and character of the military element in American-European relations in a way that is highly relevant for our military policies.

The Chinese-Soviet split and the expansion of the American commitment to South Vietnam to the level of a major ground war have highlighted the position of China in U.S. security policy. Old feelings and anxieties arising out of the "loss" of China in 1949 have been revived, and a variety of semiofficial pronouncements in recent years interpreting our role in the war in Vietnam as a necessary step in the containment of the aggressive, expansionist foreign policy of the People's Republic has reinforced these sentiments. This essay is written on the assumption that in the near future the war in Vietnam will be on the road to settlement. The details of such a settlement are impossible to predict with any confidence but will probably not include any close continuing military relations between South Vietnam and the United States. It is from this assumption that the international relations and security interests of the United States in South and East Asia will be discussed. A major feature of the Asian scene will continue to be the presence and voice of Communist China, by far the largest power in the area or the world in terms of population, located centrally and thus bordering on a great number of other states, the strongest militarily of all states in the region and the only one possessing even a few nuclear weapons. Yet, despite its central position and its military superiority over its neighbors, China, during the near future, will remain a basically weak nation, inferior in economic potential to Japan and in no way comparable with the two superpowers. China will undoubtedly continue to build up her nuclear forces and develop a modest missile capability at a pace determined to some extent by internal political events. But at the most anxious projection, these forces will not in the near future reach a level in terms of size and survivability that will permit a Chinese government however faintly rational to run even a small risk of inviting attack by the strategic forces of the United States or the Soviet Union. For this period, both will maintain a credible first-strike capacity against China.

The limitations of Chinese military strength go much farther than this: large as her army is, she does not have the capacity to project her power much beyond her own territory and the areas immediately adjacent to it. With a tiny navy, made up mostly of coastal defense vessels and an air arm whose major element is a defensive fighter force, China's military power is important chiefly in a defensive or internal context or very close to its borders. Chinese foreign policy since the effective end of the Soviet alliance reflects no different estimate of her own strength; she has been as cautious in deed as she has been violent in exhortation and denunciation.

Even after the settlement of the war in Vietnam, major points of conflict between China and the United States will remain and are unlikely to be settled soon. Chief among them is the issue of Taiwan, or what China views as the occupation of Chinese territory by a puppet government managed and supported by the United States. Even if we can stop pretending that Taiwan is China, move to a "two Chinas" policy, or even beyond that to a "China plus independent Taiwan" policy, and try simply to avoid for as long as possible facing the problem of China's right to a UN Security Council seat, it is unlikely that China will change its position. But it is equally or more unlikely that China will try to reoccupy Taiwan by force, as long as elements of U.S. forces are deployed in and near the Formosa Strait.

Further, China will certainly continue to exercise propaganda and political pressure against the noncommunist states of Asia and even occasional military pressure against those with vulnerable borders such as India and Burma. Her influence on the large overseas Chinese communities in Singapore, Malaysia, Thailand, and the Philippines will continue to provide a means of creating political unrest in all those countries; she will continue to hold Hong Kong under threat.

Nor are the prospects good for untroubled peace in Asia, aside from the activities of the Chinese People's Republic. North Korea will probably continue border harassment and infiltration against South Korea. North Vietnam will continue to seek to expand its influence in South Vietnam and Laos, probably successfully, and in Thailand and perhaps Cambodia, with much less certain prospects of success. Peace between India and Pakistan will continue to be uneasy; so may it be among the Philippines, Indonesia, and Malaysia.

Despite these alarums and excursions, there are only two fundamental questions for the United States. The first is whether such conflicts, at the scale we have depicted, involve the security interests of the United States to an extent that they must be settled favorably to us at whatever cost. The second is, short of such a broad commitment, what, if anything, can we do about controlling or preventing them by military means. Our answer to the first question is no; and accordingly, the second can be answered in the course of considering future military deployments in the western Pacific and Asia. There are, of course, some contingencies in Asia that we would and should view as threats to vital U.S. interests. The most important of these are a direct attack on Japan and a massive invasion of India. Both seem impossible for the Chinese to undertake alone and highly unlikely as joint Soviet-Chinese enterprises. The continued independence of South Korea and Taiwan, unless they should choose otherwise, is also vital in view of both our past commitments and our success, after long and expensive efforts, in building them up into viable, self-supporting states. But here again, neither the repetition by North Korea of the 1950 invasion, this time without Soviet or probably even Chinese help, nor the invasion by China of Taiwan in the face of the Seventh Fleet seems more than a remotely possible contingency.

In the rest of the world, only Latin America shows a reasonable prospect of relative peace and this only in terms of international wars. Coups and revolutions will probably be as frequent in the next eight years as they have been in the past eight, and there is no guarantee that they will not be more violent. Africa will probably continue to display coups, civil wars, and guerrilla struggles against the white powers of the southern tip. It is not unlikely that some of these will erupt into international wars. But here and also in Latin America, we must again pose the double question: Are our interests sufficiently involved so that we must insure by whatever means an outcome that we favor in such struggles? Short of that, what can we accomplish by what kind of military force?

Only in the Middle East are the prospects of war so high, and the degree of American commitment clearly so great, as to raise the prospect of U.S. military intervention, if all else failed and the Arab countries were really about to overrun Israel. Perhaps, by the end of the four- to eight-year period we have in prospect, military struggles between black majorities and white minorities in southern Africa may arouse the profound and widespread emotions among the American public that the defense of Israel now does. But, with these possible exceptions, the general answer to the first of our two key questions appears to be in the negative for the rest of the third world.

This discussion of contingencies in the rest of the world should not be read as arguing that only Europe matters. It does underline the point that, aside from the remote possibility of an attack on Japan, no single contingency in any other area is of the same order of importance. Further, it emphasizes the limitations in many cases on U.S. military force in preventing developments that we clearly view as undesirable. Thus, to take a sharp example, suppose Brazil were "going communist" as a result of internal strife and the appearance of a left-wing faction in the army as well as among the populace. American military intervention on a large scale might be able to prevent the particular group from succeeding at that time, but only at very large costs in terms of our longer-run relations in all of Latin America and with considerable likelihood that the government we had aided would prove unstable.

In sum, if we compare the likely prospects in the next presidential term of, say, eight years with the experience of the past eight years, we see a significant change. It is not, alas, that the prospects for disorder on the international scene in general will be fewer and for world-wide peace greater. Rather it is that the confrontation between the United States and the Soviet Union will be less salient in both international and internal politics for the great powers and, accordingly, that there will probably be less U.S. involvement in violence.

Strategic Forces

The changes in the world political picture that have been sketched in the preceding pages affect our whole military posture, since they alter its underlying political rationale. Also vitally important are those changes in military technology, current and prospective, that affect primarily the capabilities of the strategic forces of the United States and the Soviet Union, both offensive and defensive. These changes call sharply into question the concept of "strategic superiority," which has long had wide currency, if not official standing, as the basis of our military policy, and make more delicate and difficult for both sides the task of maintaining an effective deterrent balance.

Over the past decade the United States and the Soviet Union have each, more or less, become increasingly aware that the chief utility of its strategic forces was to prevent its adversary from using his forces. Each began to realize that any attack would be met by a counterblow so devastating as to convert a decision to attack into a suicide pact. And so the strategic equilibrium commonly termed "mutual deterrence" was recognized.

For our (or the Soviet Union's) strategic forces to provide effective deterrence, they must be in such numbers, of such nature, and so deployed as to be capable of delivering the required counterattack *after* the other side has struck; thus effective deterrence is measured by the usable strength of the survivable second-strike force. We were perhaps earlier than the Soviet Union in recognizing this, but we were far from perceiving it from the first. Once we recognized the need, we sought survivable forces in different ways as technological possibilities changed over the period. Increase in the size of the force, geographical dispersal to increase the number of targets presented by a given force, active defense, hardening to survive attack, warning and movement capability to take advantage of warning, all played a part in the quest for a secure second-strike force. Equally essential, if surviving forces are to be usable, are means for ensuring the survival of a complex network of reporting and communication facilities, command organization, and commanders, all of which occasion their own technical and organizational problems. At the present time, with missiles having displaced aircraft as the most important component of a second-strike force for both sides, hardening, combined with concealment and mobility for the sea-based portion of a force, provides the main means of ensuring survivability. The Soviet Union, with smaller and less effective sea-based forces, depends more heavily on hardening.

Only the United States and the Soviet Union have built up large strategic forces with second-strike capabilities; in comparison, the forces of the small nuclear powers are insignificant. The United States and the Soviet Union can be expected to retain their unique position for some years to come: no other nation seems both willing and able to commit resources on the required scale. This, and the more general disproportion between the conventional military power of the two superpowers and that of other nations or groups of nations, leads us to concentrate the discussion of strategic forces on the bilateral relations of the two. This neglects the small nuclear forces of the three other countries now possessing them, France, Britain, and China, and the possibility that they may be used in ways that will trigger great power conflict. If the number of nuclear powers should grow, this possibility will clearly become more important and directly relevant to the stability of the relations of the two great powers. For the present and the near future, however, we can pass them over without damage to our argument.

Strong and survivable long-range striking forces provide each superpower with something more in relation to the other than deterrence against direct nuclear attack, though the precise specification of the extra effect is difficult. First, they provide a substantial incentive for each nation to refrain from initiating any military action against the other, lest the conditions under which rational calculation can be expected to dominate decision and action disappear in one or both. This incentive is stronger the larger the forces and interests involved and thus becomes a kind of built-in brake on the occurrence of military incidents in situations where the military forces of the superpowers face each other directly or could readily do so in their world-wide movements. By extension, the same incentive operates with respect to political confrontations that might in turn lead to military action, but more weakly the more remote the military steps appear to be in the chain of potential actions and reactions. Together these effects add up to a kind of indirect or second-order deterrence, which could tend to stabilize the behavior of the two superpowers in relation to each other over a wide range of actions and prevent unilateral attempts by either to change the status quo forcibly or suddenly.

The history of the last two decades, however, makes the strength, steadiness, and symmetry with which these incentives might operate questionable and emphasizes their relation to broader military and political contexts. In the earlier part of the period, the Soviet Union seems to have acted at a higher margin of risk than the United States; more recently, the reverse appears to be true. These changes are not the simple consequence of shifts in the balance of strategic forces; on the contrary, if there has been a shift, it has probably been a steady movement against the United States over most of this period.

In analyzing the concept of effective deterrence and trying to understand the relation of forces on which it depends, it is conventional and useful to detail a spectrum of possible strategic purposes and the striking forces appropriate to them, stretching from what might be termed a credible first-strike at one end to a minimum deterrent at the other. A first-strike force would be one whose size, reliability, accuracy, control arrangements, and so on, were such, in relation to the adversary's forces, as to make possible an attack that would, with a high degree of assurance, destroy essentially all of the adversary's forces and still leave the attacker a substantial unspent reserve force. In this context, "essentially all" of the adversary's forces has the sense that whatever residual might escape destruction would not be able to inflict major damage on the attacker or prevent his reserve force from being used to a very substantial extent. For a first strike to be further characterized as "credible," the relation of forces described above would have to be clearly perceived by both adversaries, and the "high degree" of assurance involved might have to be set at 99 percent or more. In such circumstances, it is just conceivable that the superior adversary could use this power for what has been termed "compellance," as opposed to deterrence: the threat of a strike used as a means of compelling specified behavior by the adversary.

At the other end of the spectrum, a minimum deterrent force would be one which would provide high assurance of the survival of an effective, usable force (for a second strike) large enough to inflict unacceptable damage on the adversary, defined in terms of some level of expected casualties, urban and industrial destruction, and so on.

Since 1961, our strategic forces have been programmed in terms of deterrence-plus. We have never sought a first-strike capacity, and indeed, in his first budget message, Secretary of Defense Robert S. McNamara denied both the possibility and desirability of attaining one: the Soviet striking capacity was, and would be, maintained at a high enough level to make a U.S. first strike irrational. But in the first two full budgets of the Kennedy administration—which laid down guidelines governing the size of the strategic striking forces that are still in effect today—the programmed missile and long-range bomber forces were larger in relation to projected Soviet forces than would have been required for minimum deterrence alone, even allowing for a generous margin of uncertainty on the growth of Soviet forces, their effectiveness, and the post-attack performance of our own programmed forces. The margin over deterrence was justified in terms of the idea of "damage limitation" should deterrence fail —a contingency that could not be ignored. Were warning of preparations for a Soviet strike or the actual launching of one received in sufficient time, U.S. missiles could be launched against Soviet missile sites and airfields, thus limiting to some extent, depending on warning time, the damage that the Soviet strike would inflict. A large enough effort at "damage limitation," of course, shades off into a first-strike posture; a small enough one becomes indistinguishable from the safety margin for deterrence.

The decisions of 1961 and 1962 called for the buildup by 1965 of a U.S. strategic force of nearly 1,800 missiles capable of reaching Soviet targets; somewhat more than a third were to be submarine-launched. In addition, some 600 long-range bombers would be maintained. This was projected against an expected Soviet force of fewer than a third as many missiles and a quarter as many bombers capable of reaching the United States. Further, the Soviets were expected to possess an equal number of shorter-range missiles and a much larger number of medium bombers, which could be used against European targets and, possibly, against the United States as well. Unknown, and unknowable, at least for some time to come, is whether the Soviet Union's original force goals in 1961–62 were as modest as our estimates of them at the time—or even more so—and whether their rapid recent buildup, discussed immediately below, was a response to the tremendous acceleration in growth of our long-range striking forces brought about by the Kennedy administration. In any event, until 1967 it was possible for the administration to deny any wider aim for its strategic posture than deterrence, to argue the futility of seeking to achieve a first-strike force, and yet to avoid the sharp edge of the question whether we were maintaining "strategic superiority" over the Soviet Union, as that term is used in congressional and public discussions. Recent changes in Soviet deployments have given a new bite to this question; anticipatory changes of our own have raised an even broader question of how stable our deterrent posture will be in the years ahead.

The last two years have shown significant changes in the Soviet strategic forces. The number of their intercontinental and submarine-launched ballistic missiles has grown rapidly. As of late 1967—as estimated by Secretary McNamara in his 1968 budget presentation—the number of land-based missiles had grown to 750, or nearly half our total, and most of the growth had taken place in the previous year. This indicates that the number might well continue to grow rapidly and by mid-1969 might be as large as ours. The total number of Soviet missiles targetable against both the United States and NATO countries is already nearly equal to the total number of U.S. missiles that can reach Soviet targets. Further, the Russians are currently building up their missile submarine fleet both qualitatively and quantitatively, so as to achieve—on the pattern of the United States—a substantial force protected from a first strike by concealment and mobility. In addition to these changes in their offensive forces, the Russians have been slowly deploying an antiballistic missile defense system around Moscow.

So far, we have not responded to these developments by planning an increase in the number of our missile launchers. Rather, we have concentrated on programs for upgrading our present forces by replacing existing missiles with new ones designed to use present launching platforms. The new missiles will be superior to the old in three respects. First, they will be significantly more accurate, which means that a smaller warhead can be used to achieve a particular level of destruction against a specified target, a fact which is significant for attacks against hard targets. Second, they will contain a variety of decoys and other penetration aids that will make more difficult the defensive task of an ABM system. Finally, and most significant, they will ultimately contain several independently aimed warheads within a single missile (MIRVs, or multiple independently targeted reentry vehicles). These, in turn, will make the task of the defensive ABM even more difficult. In addition, they raise a new, and as we shall see, somewhat frightening possibility of multiplying greatly the number of warheads that one or the other side can launch without changing the number of visible missile launchers.

We have also made the decision to deploy a "thin" ABM system, primarily as an area defense against light attacks—such as might be within the capacity of China in the near future—rather than as an effective defense against a major Soviet attack. However, the Senate debate on the appropriation for this system (June 1968) cast serious doubt on the continuance of this rationale as the governing one for deployment.

While the recent and projected changes in Soviet and American strategic forces have not altered the fundamental strategic situation from one of mutual deterrence, they may have set forces in motion which can undermine the stability of the relation in coming years. Within the Congress, pressures are already beginning to mount for action to offset the large increase in numbers of Soviet missiles, so as to maintain a margin of "strategic superiority" rather than accept "parity." As the planned deployment of the ABM system goes forward, congressional and public pressures to upgrade it can be expected to rise; demands will be made to add local defenses of missiles and cities to the present area-defense system. We will then face the dilemma of either publicly and explicitly accepting strategic parity with the Soviet Union or giving in to these pressures and beginning a new set of developments in our strategic forces, with consequences that are unpleasant to contemplate.

The core of the case for accepting parity has already been put above, but it bears repetition and a little elaboration. In essence, we cannot expect with any confidence to do more than achieve a secure second-strike capacity, no matter how hard we try. This capacity is not usefully measured by counting warheads or megatons or, above a particular level, expected casualties. Whether the result comes about with twice as many American as Soviet delivery vehicles—as has been the case in the past—or with roughly equal numbers, or even with an adverse ratio, does not change its basic nature. Further, any significant change in deployments by either major adversary requires a long period of time and announces itself either explicitly or through intelligence means in its early stages. The other side, therefore, has notice and time within which to respond. The present level of research, development, and production capacity for weapons on both sides is such that each has the power to respond to a change in the deployments of the other in a way that leaves it "satisfied" with its new position in relation to the adversary. Each, accordingly, feels it must anticipate such a response. And so the arms race goes on. The expected result of the process can be no more than a new balance at higher force levels, larger expenditures, and most likely, unthinkably higher levels of destruction in the event that the forces were ever used.

The other and even more troubling consequence of following the competitive path is that the stability of mutual deterrence becomes far less certain. First, a rapidly changing situation itself creates problems. Deterrence is at bottom a political and psychological concept. It rests on the perception and interpretation of the military situation by political decision makers; and it is as much open to influence by changes in their operating environment or the attitudes they bring to their perceptions as by changes in the hard technical facts. This inevitably marks it with a certain elusiveness. How great a capacity to wreak death and destruction on an adversary is enough? Can it be measured in absolute terms in millions of dead and acres of destruction or only in the fractions of one side's population, industry, and urban area? If one side's destructive capacity grows while the other's remains constant at a high level, does this reduce the effectiveness of the latter's deterrence? Questions such as these clearly have no unique, well-defined answers for all decision makers in all circumstances. What is clear is that constant or slowly changing force structures, whose technical performance characteristics are reasonably well understood—subject, of course, to the important fundamental limitation that no one has experienced their use in war—provide a much more stable basis for mutual reliance on and acceptance of deterrence than a rapidly moving process of qualitative and quantitative competition.

Second, the current technical developments in weaponry could introduce significantly new elements of uncertainty into the situation that in themselves diminish the stability of deterrence. Antiballistic missile defenses and multiple independently targeted warheads carried by a single missile both have this effect. At present, each adversary has a reasonably clear idea of the other's deployments, with enough detail to permit a confident estimate of the balance of forces. Once MIRVs become widespread, it will be much more difficult for each side to know how many warheads, as opposed to launchers, the other has. How great the uncertainty will be depends, of course, on the specific technical possibilities: two warheads per missile would create one situation; ten, quite another. Further, MIRVs increase the asymmetry between first and second strikes, moving us toward the instability inherent in a situation in which neither side has a survivable second-strike force. The mutual deployment of large ABM systems, too, will reduce each side's belief in the adequacy of its second-strike force and generate strong impulses to compensate for uncertainty by building still larger offensive forces.

The combination of ABMs and MIRVs opens up an even more alarming prospect. If both were reasonably effective, then each side could believe it had a first-strike capability: its MIRVs could be used to attack the adversary's fixed missile launchers and its ABM defenses to intercept weapons launched from the adversary's mobile systems. The deterrent stability permitted by our present technology of relatively invulnerable offensive forces and no defense would vanish.

These frightening possibilities still lie in the future. For the next several years, nothing that is currently happening or in prospect justifies anxiety for the continued effectiveness of the U.S. second-strike capability or its continued power to perform its primary function of deterring the Soviet Union from using its nuclear forces against us. None of the evidence on the Soviet buildup points beyond an effort to move close to a crude equality with us in numbers of offensive missiles, nor is there evidence of a widespread program of ABM deployment or of a Soviet MIRV program.

The rapidity of the recent buildup in Soviet forces tempts some to project that buildup into the future and to see it as a try for "strategic superiority." The absence of official announcements of force goals by the Soviet Union—such as the U.S. Secretary of Defense makes in his annual budget presentations—reinforces the temptation; and the demonstration of the illusory nature of such a goal seems an insufficient response. Yet our past experience with the projected "defense gap" of the early fifties and the "missile gap" of 1959–61 shows the dangers of such an interpretation. In both these cases we clearly overreacted. In the first, the result was our concentration on a large, expensive, and not very effective defense system against Soviet bombers that was soon to be obsolete since the Soviet

Union was moving on to missiles. In the second, the scale of our reaction may have had the direct result of stimulating the current Soviet buildup. If our aim remains that of maintaining deterrence, we can clearly afford to wait for the event rather than begin now to respond to our projections of the future.

However, technical developments point to the coming of a time when mutual deterrence can no longer rest reliably on mutual watchfulness and forbearance without explicit arms-control agreements over the deployment of strategic forces. The decision (July 1968) of our own and the Soviet governments to initiate talks on a leveling-off in the deployment of strategic weapons indicates an acceptance of something like the line of argument given above by both governments. Yet it is clear that a freeze would present a host of difficult political and technical problems. First is the question of how much reliance we would be willing to place on unilateral—that is, intelligence—verification of Soviet deployments rather than inspection procedures established by agreement. Second, equally important and even more difficult to resolve, is the question of whether and to what extent we should seek control over technical improvements in existing warheads and vehicles and the research and development efforts leading thereto. No risk-free answer to these questions is likely to be found even in conceptual terms, much less in terms of negotiable arrangements between the two countries. Third, and probably most important and most difficult, is the political problem of gaining acceptance for a Soviet claim to some kind of "equality" in strategic forces, however defined. There is among us a widely shared popular feeling that our wealth, our power, and our virtue entitle us to be first and that any claim to equality by the morally and economically inferior Soviet Union is presumptuous if not dangerous. The new administration must conquer this sentiment, since it should be clear that we cannot expect to persuade the Soviet Union to accept a freeze under which its position is defined as "inferior." This counsel is easier to give than to execute; but peace and security are widely and deeply desired, and strong presidential leadership can mobilize these desires in support of a relationship of "safe equality" by explaining that in matters of strategic systems we cannot be usefully and effectively "first."

Difficult as these problems are, the alternative prospects arising from the uncontrolled forward thrust of technical change in weaponry that we have sketched above are much grimmer. The atmosphere of mutual distrust and fear produced by increased uncertainty will hardly promote the success of what will at best always be difficult negotiations for arms control, and the balance resulting from any particular agreement will be much more difficult to calculate.

The present and near future offer a peculiarly favorable period for such a discussion. A freeze at something like next year's numbers of offensive missiles and an agreement on modest ABM deployments on each side, combined with a ban on new systems (specifically, MIRVs and new launching platforms or vehicles), would allow each side fixed, hardened land-based and mobile sea-based offensive systems and some sharply limited defensive deployments; yet it would prevent the introduction of MIRVs, the widespread deployment of new land- and sea-based systems that would be undertaken as a natural counter to MIRV, and the move to "thick" ABM systems of very high cost. The prevention of greatly increased deployments of mobile missiles is important because of the problems they would create for unilateral surveillance, or even for effective mutual inspection, and the consequent further destabilization of the strategic competition.

Another argument for pressing negotiations with the Soviet Union on the deployment of strategic weapons is the need to contain the further spread of nuclear weapons. Even the initiation of such negotiations would give an important stimulus to the completion of the nonproliferation treaty; success would make much more likely wide adherence to the treaty, especially by those nations which are capable of making nuclear weapons and which have criticized the one-sided character of the treaty's restraints. Failure to initiate discussions—especially if coincident with a visible acceleration of Soviet-American competition—would probably not only kill the treaty but stimulate more nations to "go nuclear," as they lost hope of great-power restraint. This, of course, would add a further destabilizer to the international scene.

Because of the technical complexities of the subject and its political sensitivity in the Congress, the military services, and large segments of the public, the new President and his Secretaries of State and Defense must place a very high priority on the task and give it a significant and continuing share of their personal attention if there is to be any prospect of a useful negotiation. It should be made the major arms-control effort and one of the major foreign policy initiatives of a new administration.

Negotiations are likely to prove long and difficult, even if they get underway immediately. There may be some virtue during their course—especially if they are not progressing—in exploring the possibilities of simpler measures of arms control, which could contribute to the domestic and international sense of forward motion in this area, as well as have some significance in themselves. Especially worth considering are a cutoff in the production of fissionable material, a complete test-ban treaty, a ban on placing nuclear weapons in the seabed, and a declaration against the first use of nuclear weapons, either in unconditional form or limited to use against nonnuclear powers. Each has its dilemma. For the first two, it is the difficulties of negotiating meaningful inspection versus the magnitude of risks entailed in reliance on unilateral verification. For the second two, it is the limitation on deployment versus the possible weakening of deterrence against conventional attacks in force and the consequent decline in our allies' confidence in our security guarantees, especially that of West Germany and South Korea. A thorough discussion of these problems would go beyond the purpose of this paper. It is sufficient to say that the values that may be gained by arms control are increasing and of enough importance to justify a reexamination of the balance of advantages and risks in each case.

NATO Forces

Next to our strategic forces, our commitment to NATO is our most important military commitment. It, too, has been affected by a changing political context and, though to a much less important extent, by changes in military technology.

Currently, NATO forces on the central front are roughly in balance with the opposing Warsaw Pact forces west of the Soviet frontier, measured in terms of capacity to fight a conventional ground war; indeed, the NATO forces immediately available probably have some qualitative superiority on the central front, especially in terms of aircraft. This has now been the case for several years. Further, the total forces and total military budgets of the NATO powers (excluding U.S. forces in Vietnam and the expenditures in support of them) are greater than those of the Warsaw Pact nations. Table 1 gives a selection of the relevant statistics.

In the critical central region, the German component of NATO's ground forces is the largest, followed by that of the United States. In tactical airpower, the United States has the largest force, with Italy and Germany next. In addition, of course, the U.S. forces in NATO are equipped with a vast array of tactical nuclear weapons, currently some 7,000 in num-

TABLE 1. *NATO and Warsaw Pact Defense Budgets and Military Strengths in 1968*

Item	NATO[a]	Warsaw Pact[b]
I. Armed forces manpower		
Total men under arms	6,300,000	About 4,300,000
Total army personnel	3,600,000	About 2,900,000
Troops in combat-available divisions		
a. In the central region on M-day	680,000	About 620,000
b. In all European regions on M-day	900,000	About 960,000
II. Aircraft		
Inventory value of tactical combat aircraft at nominal cost	$27,000,000,000	About $16,000,000,000
Tactical aircraft inventory	11,000	9,000
III. Total defense budget	$75,000,000,000	About $50,000,000,000

Source: Department of Defense, Office of Assistant Secretary for Systems Analysis. Data are given in round numbers and U.S. dollars.
M-day. Mobilization day.
a. Does not include U.S. forces and costs in Vietnam.
b. For this purpose the pact comprises USSR, Bulgaria, Czechoslovakia, East Germany, Hungary, Poland, and Rumania.

ber. The Soviet forces also have a sizable nuclear component at the tactical level, but its precise magnitude is not known. Together, there are clearly enough nuclear explosives deployed in tactical formations to destroy most of Europe, without the assistance of strategic forces on either side.

The balance represented by the figures in Table 1 has not been significantly changed by the Soviet invasion of Czechoslovakia. On the one hand, the Soviet Union called up some reserves and moved troops from western Russia into Czechoslovakia. On the other, the Czech forces can hardly be counted among the combat-available, and indeed, if an allowance is made for the minimum Soviet force required for occupation duties inside Czechoslovakia, the net change is probably negative. Further, the movement represented no particular surprise in military terms. Some two or three months was available for preparation, and NATO was well aware of Soviet moves during the period. Only the immediate political decision was a surprise.

If we consider not only the statistics of military deployment but also the less easily measurable but more important factors of political will, the advantages on the side of NATO in terms of its defensive purpose are even stronger. For all their disagreements and divisions, there is a clear will to self-defense among European members of NATO. By contrast it is difficult to conceive of enthusiastic Czech, Hungarian, and Polish participation in offensive operations directed westward across the frontiers of the Federal Republic of Germany. Of course, the same could be said of a corresponding move by the West; but it is the essence of a wise NATO policy to emphasize the treaty's defensive purpose and to present the Soviet Union with the alternatives of peace or the offensive.

The large NATO deployments reflect two different sets of politicomilitary concerns: the desire of the Germans for a "forward strategy," so that any attack will be met and, if possible, repulsed at the borders of the Federal Republic before the attackers can occupy any substantial part of its territory, and the anxieties of U.S. and British defense planners—especially the political chiefs of defense departments—about the consequences of the use of tactical nuclear weapons in Europe.

The first of these has been more or less constant since the Germans found their political voice in the alliance. The second, however, represents a more recent development and a turn away from a previous policy of relying on the heavy use of tactical nuclear weapons in Europe, which was initiated in the mid-fifties and, at the time, only grudgingly accepted by our allies. As we came to recognize that the game of tactical nuclear weapons was a two-sided one—and to calculate the consequences of their bilateral use and to contemplate the difficulties of drawing a line between their use in Europe and general strategic warfare—we tried, beginning in the sixties, to deemphasize nuclear weapons. We set an example for the alliance by building up conventional strength and urged the other members, especially the Germans, to follow it.

Over the same period, however, and indeed, beginning rather earlier, the politicians and people of Western Europe became less and less convinced of the likelihood of a massive Soviet attack. Parliaments became increasingly unwilling to vote increases in military budgets or to extend periods of military service. We have argued above that this perception of Soviet intent is correct and, accordingly, that current strategy must be evaluated in the light of it. To be sure, the need for deterrence remains; but the means will have to be changed. Three requirements must still be met: first, the American commitment embodied in the treaty; second, enough involvement of American troops on the central front to make it clear to the Soviet Union that the commitment will be honored and that no military action on any significant scale in Europe is possible without engaging the United States in war; third, a U.S. strategic striking force of a size and capacity that will continue to rule out the rational choice of a major war by the Soviet Union.

In addition to helping deter a massive Soviet attack, no matter how unlikely, the U.S. troops in Germany have at least three other important functions. First is that of assisting in maintaining ground access to West Berlin and Western rule in West Berlin. The presence of properly deployed American forces in enough strength so that "incidents" on the Autobahn or at the Berlin boundaries can be met with a proportionate, but not an undue, response that is clearly American, provides a constant reminder to the Soviet Union of the dangers of attempting to change the situation of West Berlin by force. The Americans in West Berlin serve a corresponding function with respect to possible incursions by East German police or troops, the use of Soviet forces for political intimidation, and the like. These functions will remain vital until the political arrangements governing the relations of West Berlin, the Federal Republic, and the German Democratic Republic are clearly accepted by all of the parties. The second function of U.S. troops is that of maintaining a presence and a forward deployment sufficient to reassure the Germans in particular and Western Europe in general of our continued commitment to their defense. While this deployment is inseparably connected with the prime task of displaying our intentions to the Soviet Union, it, so to speak, plays to a different audience. Finally, U.S. troops in Germany assure other members of NATO that immediate management of the alliance's confrontation with the Soviet Union is not solely in the hands of the West Germans, and they provide the means of integrating German forces into the NATO command system. This is an important element in alliance solidarity, whose value even the German government accepts.

While all these functions are separable for analytical purposes, the demands they make for U.S. forces are by no means additive. The tasks of garrisoning West Berlin and providing a large enough mobile force to make clear that access to the city cannot be closed off without a major military confrontation require about two and one-half U.S. divisions: one-half in Berlin, one for deployment at the Autobahn approaches, and one as a general reserve. One more division would make possible enough forward deployment of U.S. troops in southern Germany to provide assurance to the Germans and the other NATO members of the seriousness of our commitment. We now have almost twice as large a ground combat force in Germany as this. General supporting forces and air forces are probably not so much larger than necessary, but units now manning a large variety of tactical nuclear weapons could usefully be viewed as even more redundant than the ground combat forces. Altogether, at a crude estimate, present U.S. forces in Europe may be on the order of 30 to 40 percent larger than would strictly be needed to meet the current strategic requirements of the alliance, if these requirements were defined in politically realistic terms.

If any sizable reduction were to be made in U.S. forces, it would almost certainly be paralleled by some reduction—though not necessarily a proportionate one—in force levels and budgets of the European members of NATO; the United States would no longer be able to exert its customary pressure in NATO for large budgets and stronger forces. Thus, any changes that a new administration may make must be considered in terms of their total effects on NATO's deployments.

Three kinds of arguments can be made for sizable reductions in U.S. forces in Europe. The first, and probably most persuasive, is a budgetary one. At present levels of defense and total federal expenditures, any deployment that is not strictly necessary is a luxury. In particular, our paying for extra insurance that the Europeans do not themselves believe necessary, as shown by their own expenditures, is most inappropriate. To realize significant budgetary savings, we must not only withdraw forces from Europe to the United States; they must also be scaled down in total numbers. The second argument stresses the desirability of shifting more responsibility to the now prosperous Europeans for their own defense; but this cannot be accomplished by exhortation, as we have discovered over some years. It can only be done by facing them with the facts of our decisions. The third argument concerns the significant possibilities for arms-control arrangements affecting Europe that force reductions might open up.

These arrangements are of two kinds. First is the parallel reduction of forces on the central front, matching U.S. troop reductions with withdrawal of Soviet forces stationed west of the Soviet borders, and reductions by other NATO members with those of the Eastern European countries. Second is the creation of a substantial denuclearized zone on both sides of the dividing line in Germany. Both of these are items which, in one shape or another, have long figured in Soviet arms-control proposals and propaganda and which we have steadfastly rejected. Our past attitude rested on both military and political grounds. Militarily, these changes appeared to undermine our forward strategy by removing from the central front both the troops and weapons on which it was based. Further, our removal of troops across the Atlantic could not be compared with a Soviet removal to just behind its own western borders, some 700 miles from the German dividing line. Politically, they were viewed as threatening the unity of the NATO alliance at two levels. Until fairly recently, discussing them would have appeared to be a sharp reversal of U.S. strategic doctrines; in a dangerous situation, such a reversal would have been alarming, especially to the Germans. On an ideological level, the negotiations required for such arrangements would have appeared to "equate" NATO and the Warsaw Pact or would have involved the recognition of East Germany.

Today the military grounds are no longer relevant to our current strategic concepts and the appraisal of the military balance which they embody. While the particular political objectives raised in the past are not now apposite, there are significant political problems that would be raised by the discussion of such proposals. They turn essentially on the role of the Federal Republic. It has always been difficult for Germans to accept their exclusion from Soviet-American discussions on matters that concern them so intimately. On the other hand, it would be difficult for them to negotiate in a forum which included the GDR as a legitimate party; indeed, it is difficult to see how negotiations of the requisite sort could be carried on if all the alliance members on both sides participated. This is not to say that a process of negotiation cannot be found but to emphasize the important role of the relations between the Federal Republic and the United States and the views of the Germans in any such process.

Further, there is the difficult problem of whether it is wise for the United States and NATO to move unilaterally on force reductions and redeployments of tactical nuclear weapons or whether changes should be restricted to those on which there are reciprocal undertakings by the Warsaw Pact nations. A case for some unilateral action exists: such action may provide an important or even a necessary initial impetus to the negotiating process, both for the Soviet Union and for the Europeans, who may then have a clearer idea of how much defense they need and want to pay for. Yet, if there are to be negotiations, we cannot simply give away our bargaining position, and too much unilateral change can make negotiation appear unnecessary to the Russians.

In the area of strategic nuclear forces, bilateral Soviet-American discussions are clearly appropriate, and the arms-control issues themselves are central to the discussions. In the area of European military deployments, arms-control problems are inevitably closely linked to the larger political issues of the German settlement; and the character and pace of the discussions depend heavily on views in the Federal Republic about how to regulate its relations with the GDR in particular and the Communist governments of Eastern Europe in general. Therefore, negotiations on the arms-control issues cannot be separated from broader political negotiations on Germany and a European settlement. These, in turn, will bear heavily on the political relations of the Federal Republic, the United States, and the other members of NATO.

Further, the interests of the other side in such arms-control negotiations are not clear. The westward deployment of Soviet troops has always been at least as much for their value as a political instrument in dealing with the bloc countries as for their role in confronting the forces of NATO. The invasion of Czechoslovakia underlines this point; and it is doubtful that the Soviet Union would want to discuss troop withdrawals or reductions now. Neither would the Western Europeans. Thus, unlike negotiations on the deployment of strategic weapons, arms-control discussions are probably an item for the future; nonetheless, they should not be dropped out of sight.

Other General Purpose Forces

The foregoing discussions of the strategic military balance and the needs of NATO dealt with situations in which the basic military and political considerations governing the possible use of force can be translated into the kind of quantitative terms necessary for decisions on force levels and budgets; in Europe there is a reasonably coherent and explicit rationale for policy, dominated neither by arbitrary political assumptions nor by forecasts of complex chains of future contingencies, though, to be sure, both elements cannot be entirely dispensed with. When we consider the military forces required for other purposes, however—namely, the general purpose forces for world-wide use, the strategic reserves, and the supporting forces for air-lift, sea-lift, general overhead, training, and reserve strength—we move into an area much more difficult to deal with in quantitative terms. However, we can make some progress by dividing the problem in two and considering, first, forces in East and South Asia and, second, U.S. strategic reserves and other supporting forces.

At the present, of course, our deployments in Asia are dominated by the war in Vietnam. We have some 550 thousand military personnel in South Vietnam, nearly 100 thousand more in Thailand, in Strategic Air Command (SAC) units engaged in bombing Vietnam, and naval personnel in Southeast Asian waters. This total is a little short of 20 percent of our total armed forces; it is also only a little short of the whole increase in forces—700 thousand men—added since the levels planned for 1964, the last year before we began the sharp increase in our military commitments in Vietnam.

In addition, we still maintain two army divisions in South Korea, somewhat less than one division elsewhere in the Pacific, some air force units in Japan, Okinawa, and the Philippines, and Seventh Fleet forces over the whole of the western Pacific.

On the assumption that the Vietnam war will be settled in a way that involves the total withdrawal of all American forces from the country—at some near future, but unspecified, time—what do the political prospects outlined above demand in the way of military commitments? One division in South Korea will certainly suffice for deterrence purposes; it may not even be necessary, since South Korean forces are adequate for defense against the possibility of another invasion. A second division, which we have considered withdrawing for some time, now functions essentially as a trade for South Korean troops in Vietnam. Considerable naval and air deployments will still be needed in the western Pacific to perform the general function of deterrence and low-key political support of neutral and allied countries against communist threats to use force and the particular function of protecting the independence of Taiwan. These functions, of course, involve not only the direct presence of the Seventh Fleet but also the less visible total power of the United States. Deterrence on this basis can be expected with high confidence to continue to be effective in protecting Japan, Taiwan, the Philippines, Australia, New Zealand, and Indonesia in view of the low capability of the military forces of the Asian communist nations for overseas or long-distance operations and their overall strategic weakness.

Given a fair degree of internal unity and economic growth, the same can be said about India. Its own military capabilities for defending its border with China are not negligible, and the logistical problems for the Chinese of mounting an invasion of India that reaches at all deeply into the plains beyond the Himalayan foothills are formidable. With sufficient political will, India can make a repetition of the frontier attack of October 1962 unattractive to China as long as American, and perhaps even Soviet, assistance seems to be in the offing. Without a stable political underpinning, of course, even a large U.S. force would be of little help. There is a case for extending the patrol range of some Seventh Fleet forces westward into the Indian Ocean—and even into the Bay of Bengal—simply to make the American military presence more visible. The basing problems this would present must be faced; and if the fleet's range cannot be extended without any forward land bases, or with bases involving no political problems, such as Australia, it is doubtful whether the gains would compensate for the problems created by the bases.

The value of peripheral deterrent forces for Thailand, Burma, Malaysia, and Singapore, however, is less certain and depends very much on the course of internal political developments in those countries, as well as in China and North Vietnam. We have learned from Vietnam that even a very large and more immediately present force may be incapable of restoring a political balance once it has tipped far enough in favor of insurgent forces of the left, especially when they can draw on outside encouragement and support. A further lesson from Vietnam is that the American people do not believe we have a vital interest in trying to redress such a balance, regardless of the means. To say this is not at all to condemn the countries of the Southeast Asian peninsula to Chinese or North Vietnamese domination or even to communist governments. It is merely to recognize the limitations on the instruments available to the United States to affect political events in one way or another and, above all, the weakness of military force for this purpose.

The only area outside of Asia in which we have recognized a more than marginal possibility of U.S. military action on short notice is the Middle East. A renewal of the Arab-Israeli conflict might conceivably occur in circumstances that would generate a strong demand for U.S. military action to save Israel. But such action, to be effective, must be as much symbolic as forceful: it must warn the Arab states and their Soviet supporters to stop their military action immediately and return the conflict to the political and diplomatic level. As long as we maintain sizable naval forces in the Mediterranean, we will have that capability; it seems most unlikely that it will be necessary in advance to deploy forces to do more. Further, the likelihood of renewed major conflict in the Middle East appears to depend to a great extent on the general state of relations between the Soviet Union and the United States; if the whole perspective of this paper is correct, that likelihood will be diminishing rather than increasing.

Prior to the large troop commitments to Vietnam, the United States maintained about ten active divisions in the continental United States in addition to forces occupied in logistic, training, and administrative functions. Four-plus of these were specifically earmarked as NATO reinforcements; the rest formed a general strategic reserve. Within this general reserve force, of course, were tactical air and naval units. The size of this force was rationalized in terms of the need to meet, on short notice, the contingency of three military involvements at once: one in Europe, one in South or East Asia, both on a substantial scale, and a small third one elsewhere in the world.

The foregoing discussion suggests that we should determine our force needs on the basis of more modest plans. These plans would include the capability of meeting simultaneously on short notice a large troop requirement in Europe and a small one elsewhere in the world. On top of the reductions of overseas commitments suggested above, amounting to between three and four divisions, these more modest contingency requirements might permit a total reduction of between five and six divisions in our active organized ground combat forces. To allow for a somewhat increased capability of reinforcing Europe, however, in view of the proposed reduction in forces deployed there, we should probably cut this figure for the total reduction to between four and five divisions, with corresponding, or perhaps proportionately somewhat smaller, internal reductions in naval and tactical air forces. This would leave a reserve in the United States of more than five divisions to back up NATO plus nearly four divisions for other simultaneous contingencies. In addition, of course, there would remain a mobilization base of ready reserve units, which at present stands at eight divisions, with between one and two months required to bring them to active status.

This level of forces would be more than adequate for whatever non-European contingencies might demand a show of force. But it would rule out emergency interventions in substantial force on short notice on a world-wide basis and, more particularly, in the two areas far from the deployments we have considered: sub-Saharan Africa and Latin America. For both these areas, arguments against intervention exactly parallel those made above with regard to Asia and are even more strongly applicable, since neither area is near a large or communist power. The reduction in our forces that has been suggested would in no way prevent us from making some contributions under the United Nations or other international organization to peacekeeping forces, should these be authorized.

Another element in our overseas deployment of forces that could usefully be greatly reduced is our world-wide structure of military bases. Many of these were originally sought from foreign governments to accommodate the relatively short-range B-47 bombers when these formed the major part of our strategic striking force. As the bombers grew obsolete, new functions were found for the bases: air transport, communications and intelligence installations, association with training missions. Changing technologies in communication and related fields and the increasing political costs associated with bases in countries outside Europe argue for a stringent reevaluation of their continuing utility.

Other Means of Keeping the Peace

If the United States were to reassess the balance of costs and advantages of military action outside Europe and to change deployments accordingly as sketched above, the potential for American involvement in violent conflicts would be automatically reduced. However, with some few exceptions, these changes would not work toward reducing the likelihood and level of violence along with the prospects of our own participation in it. The possibility that violent conflict will erupt in many places throughout the world is sufficiently high that means must be devised to reduce and control it. The control of violence is important only in part because of the risk that conflict may spread and may ultimately involve the superpowers as partisans of one side or another. Beyond that, international order and peace are important ends in themselves—though not always all-important ones—and the United States has some responsibility for attempting to shape its policies to serve these ends.

Unfortunately, useful specific prescriptions in this area are few indeed; but there are two possibilities worth mentioning. One is control of the international traffic in arms, especially the larger conventional weapons such as tanks, heavy artillery, combat aircraft, and combat ships. Only the United States, the Soviet Union, and a few of their allies, especially the United Kingdom, France, and Czechoslovakia, have so far had major roles as suppliers in this trade; the Chinese have played only a small part. Much of the supply, especially that provided by the United States and the Soviet Union, has been a by-product of military assistance agreements, alliances, and the like; little is sold in ordinary commercial transactions. The most promising way to control arms in most of the world outside the major alliances would be to regulate and limit this trade. At the outset two steps commend themselves: UN registration of transactions in specific categories of arms; and a large reduction on our own part of credit sales, military assistance programs, and the like. On balance and with some exceptions—in particular, NATO—the latter step would simply be in our own interest, irrespective of wider agreements. The record of return on similar investments by the Soviet Union is equally or more dismal; whether they have learned the lesson remains to be seen. The competitive element on both sides has been sufficiently strong to justify some hope that an initiative by the United States might have wider effects.

The other measure, or rather set of measures, to control arms is the strengthening of the peacekeeping capacities of the United Nations. A variety of ways of doing this has been discussed at great length. All depend on the political agreement of the great powers; so far this has been lacking. But clearly, an important use of détente would be to renew these efforts, perhaps with a greater realization on both sides of their potential significance. On the assumption that such an agreement will eventually be reached, a particularly promising path to explore would be the earmarking by a large number of member nations of troops for UN duties and their training to this end. The Canadians and Scandinavians have pioneered along these lines, and they can offer much useful experience. Joint training exercises of such contingents from several nations could be a valuable step in the process of moving toward a usable international peacekeeping force.

A Summary of Force Sizes and Budgets

In summary, the proposals that have been sketched here in varying degrees of detail look to a substantial reduction in the role of military force in our foreign policy and consequent and corresponding reductions in the scale of our military establishment. In part, they are offered to encourage recognition (that will be mirrored in our force structure) of what have already become the facts of international politics. In part, particularly with respect to the control of strategic weapons and the deployments of both nuclear weapons and conventional forces in NATO, they are offered as possibilities for important U.S. initiatives in foreign policy, on the grounds that our policies should determine our weapons, and not vice versa.

Ideally, it would be desirable to measure our proposals in terms of their effects on future force structures and military budgets. It is extremely difficult to do this with any pretense to accuracy with publicly available figures, since they do not, as a matter of principle, show either the details of deployments, in terms of men and weapons, or the costs associated with particular elements and deployments of forces. Nonetheless, the figures presented in the unclassified part of the annual military posture statements made each year since 1961 by the Secretary of Defense to the relevant committees of the Congress provide a basis for some crude estimates.

First, the scattered estimates of changes for particular areas have been translated into an integrated figure for the total number of men in the armed forces. The starting point was the planned size of the force for fiscal year 1964 (before the dispatch of U.S. combat troops to South

Vietnam), some 2.7 million men, which was used as a standard. That figure represented active organized combat forces of nineteen-plus divisions. The proposals in this paper have suggested reducing combat forces by between four and five divisions, or about 21 percent. If the whole force were reduced in this proportion, the resulting total would be 2.1 million men, or 1.4 million less than the previous level. However, it has also been suggested that other forces than combat troops should probably be reduced by a smaller proportion; the goal to be sought then becomes a total force level of some 2.2 to 2.4 million men.

For a corresponding estimate of the budget, two sets of figures have been used as bench marks: the proposed budget for fiscal year 1969, and the actual budget (in terms of total obligational authority) for fiscal year 1964, with costs classified by military programs. (Fiscal year 1964 was the last year before the budget began to reflect heavy commitments in Southeast Asia.) These and other data from the 1969 budget document are given in Table 2. It offers two alternate bases for estimating future outlays. The total of column 3, 1964 expenditures in 1969 prices, is $62 billion; this could serve as a crude estimate of the post-Vietnam level of expenditures. The plausibility of this figure is reinforced by the major increases between 1964 and 1969 in those accounts strongly associated with the war in Southeast Asia. A somewhat more refined and much more speculative set of figures is set down in column 6, to show the result for some future year of putting the reductions and redeployments suggested above into effect. Four items show substantial reductions as compared with 1964: strategic forces, general purpose forces, supply and maintenance, and military assistance. The 40 percent reduction in the costs of strategic forces reflects the institution of a freeze and the beginning of force reductions via the phasing out of obsolete weapons. The costs of general purpose forces, and of supply and maintenance going chiefly to them, are reduced 20 percent, roughly in proportion to the reduction in total force levels suggested above. The military assistance program is reduced to a nominal level. The program for intelligence and communications reflects the assumption that smaller and less widely deployed forces will be needed; that in research and development, the sharp slow-down of efforts to create new strategic weapons systems. With a smaller active force, National Guard expenditures are left at 1969 levels to allow for higher levels of readiness and manpower. Finally, air/sea-lift is left unchanged, as mobility relative to smaller forces assumes more importance. The total is more than $12 billion (in 1969 prices) less than the 1964 figure, a very considerable saving and the smallest defense budget in more than a decade.

TABLE 2. Recent and Proposed Military Budgets
In billions of dollars

Military program	TOA for fiscal year 1964	TOA for fiscal year 1964[a] (1969 prices)	TOA for fiscal year 1969	Increase of 1969 over 1964 (1969 prices)	Synthetic budget for fiscal year 197x (1969 prices)
(1)	(2)	(3)	(4)	(5)	(6)
Strategic forces	9.3	11.1	9.6	−1.5	6.5[b c]
General purpose forces	17.9	21.7	35.2	+13.5[d]	17.4[b]
Intelligence and communications	4.3	5.0	6.3	+1.3[d]	4.5[e]
Air/sea-lift	1.1	1.3	1.8	+0.5	1.3
National Guard, Reserves	1.9	2.5	3.0	+0.5[d]	3.0
Research and development	5.0	6.2	5.1	−1.1	5.6[e]
Supply and maintenance	4.1	4.9	7.3	+2.4[d]	3.9[b]
Training	5.5	6.8	9.8	+3.0[d]	6.1[e]
Administration	1.2	1.3	1.7	+0.4[d]	1.2[e]
Military assistance	1.3	1.3	2.7	+1.4[d]	0.5[b]
Total	51.6	62.1	82.5	+20.4	50.0

TOA. Total obligational authority.
a. Derived from column 2 by assuming each account experienced the same degree of price increase. Total taken from the "Statement of Secretary of Defense Robert S. McNamara before the Senate Armed Forces Committee on the Fiscal Year 1969–73 Defense Program and 1969 Budget," Table 1 ("Financial Summary"), p. 214.
b. Large reduction from 1964 level (in 1969 prices).
c. Especially large reduction to take account of fact that fiscal year 1964 was a year of very rapid procurement of missiles. Reduced amount would still allow for some procurement.
d. Increase of 1969 over 1964 in 1969 prices heavily influenced by activity in Vietnam.
e. Small reduction from 1964 level (in 1969 prices).

The total figure for 197x presented in Table 2 is obviously a crude one. It reflects no examination of the detailed composition of each of the individual accounts which make it up nor the inevitable changes in that composition from the base year of fiscal year 1964. Thus, for example, it does not take into account the fact that new weapons tend to be both more complicated and more expensive than those they replace and also more effective in performance. In some cases, as a consequence, smaller numbers of weapons and smaller numbers of men to operate them are required as one generation of weapons replaces another. The relations between numbers of men, dollars, and military units (battalions, squadrons, and so on) therefore change, with the result that simple projections of past figures or the use of overall price indices may be misleading. Further, from one year to the next, the figures in each particular program account may involve different mixtures of expenditures for procurement of new weapons and for operation of existing ones. A more precise estimate would require detailed consideration of just what new procurement programs are under way or planned in each functional category. Nonetheless, despite their crudity, and their lack of realism in any detailed sense, these figures are still useful as indicating plausible and achievable orders of magnitude.

Ideally, the table should have several more columns, each showing a different synthetic budget for the same future year, 197x, calculated on alternate assumptions about military policy. In particular, the budgetary consequences of maintaining or even increasing our overseas deployments (for example, in South Asia) and of embarking on the next round of development and procurement in strategic weapons, both offensive and defensive, should be examined. Even without detailed computations, it is clear that presently authorized programs for procuring new strategic offensive and defensive weapons, including Minuteman III, Poseidon, and Sentinel, could add in the neighborhood of $5 billion per year to the budget levels shown for 197x. Beyond that, new weapons which have been seriously proposed by the services, including a new strategic bomber, a new land-based missile, a sea-based ABM, a new undersea long-range missile, and a new surface-ship-based long-range missile system, could add, first, several billions per year to the research and development budget and, later, $5 billion or more per year for procurement. An expansion of the ABM system to provide a "thick" defense could move its annual procurement cost from between $1 billion and $2 billion to as much as four times that amount. It is unlikely that *all* these things will be done, or all done at once, but it is not at all unlikely that if we decide to maintain "strategic superiority" in the coming years $7 billion or $8 billion per year will have to be added to the totals for research and development and strategic weapons shown in column 6. The large difference between columns 3 and 4 for general purpose forces gives some idea of what maintaining large overseas deployments and force sizes might mean.

If the estimates in Table 2 are taken as having some validity, then the question naturally arises, How soon might we be able to reach 197x and what do we have to do to get there? In part, of course, it depends on what happens in Vietnam, the kind of settlement that is achieved and how soon. Decisions on redeployments in the Pacific cannot readily be made until the shape of settlement begins to emerge; reductions in the total size of the general purpose forces probably also must wait. In part these reductions may depend on the progress of arms-control negotiations, though these may prove to be more useful in keeping future budgets at low levels than in moving sharply in the direction of lower budgets now. The initial steps to hold down expenditures on strategic weapons can be taken immediately, since they depend solely on our acceptance of the proposition that there is no urgency in beginning either deployment or procurement of new systems of offensive and defensive weapons. However, we probably cannot maintain this position for more than a few years in the face of continued failure to make progress in negotiations with the Soviet Union on mutual limitation of strategic weapons. With respect to force redeployments in Europe, timing depends primarily on the pace of diplomatic tactics in dealing with our NATO allies, especially the Germans, but, as suggested above, some prior initiative on our part may be indispensable to begin the process. All in all, the budget set down is not an unreasonable target for the new administration to aim for by the end of its first term.

But if it is to do so, the "how" becomes all important. Radical change in our military policy will cut across all kinds of vested interests, emotional, bureaucratic, political, and economic. Only determined and persistent efforts by the political leadership of the administration can bring about such changes. The President, the Secretary of Defense, and the Secretary of State must make this goal a major concern in all their actions, and direct their efforts equally at creating public understanding of their course of action, persuading Congress of its wisdom, and guiding the civil and military bureaucracies of the national security establishment along this path.

Finally, the question arises, Does not the whole structure of argument that has been erected in these pages really depend on a fundamental assumption of Soviet benevolence and good faith that does not correspond to the facts? The answer to this is that reliance on neither benevolence nor good faith—in the sense of sheer moral obligation—is involved. Rather, it is expected that *both* the Soviet Union and the United States are capable of recognizing a mutual interest in an increase in international stability, a decrease in the prospect of the use of force, especially when either of them is involved, and a relief from the economic burdens of rising military budgets. Both sides have already begun to make this recognition and to guide their policy by it. What is urged here is that—realizing the great importance of this course and the grim consequences of seeking military "superiority" and relying on the use of force as the chief instrument of our foreign policy—we put the direct pursuit of these interests at the center of our security policy for the period ahead.

HENRY A. KISSINGER

CENTRAL ISSUES OF
AMERICAN FOREIGN POLICY

The twentieth century has known little repose. Since the turn of the century, international crises have been increasing in both frequency and severity. The contemporary unrest, although less apocalyptic than the two world wars which spawned it, is even more profoundly revolutionary in nature.

The essence of a revolution is that it appears to contemporaries as a series of more or less unrelated upheavals. The temptation is great to treat each issue as an immediate and isolated problem which once surmounted will permit the fundamental stability of the international order to reassert itself. But the crises which form the headlines of the day are symptoms of deep-seated structural problems. The international system which produced stability for a century collapsed under the impact of two world wars. The age of the superpowers, which temporarily replaced it, is nearing its end. The current international environment is in turmoil because its essential elements are all in flux simultaneously. This paper will concentrate on structural and conceptual problems; earlier papers in this volume have dealt with specific policy issues.

The Structural Problem

For the first time, foreign policy has become global. In the past, the various continents conducted their foreign policy essentially in isolation. Throughout much of history, the foreign policy of Europe was scarcely affected by events in Asia. When, in the late eighteenth and nineteenth centuries, the European powers were extending their influence throughout the world, the effective decisions continued to be made in only a few great European capitals. Today, statesmen face the unprecedented problem of formulating policy for well over a hundred countries. Every nation, no matter how insignificant, participates in international affairs. Ideas are transmitted almost instantaneously. What used to be considered domestic events can now have world-wide consequences.

The revolutionary character of our age can be summed up in three general statements: (a) the number of participants in the international order has increased and their nature has altered; (b) their technical ability to affect each other has vastly grown; (c) the scope of their purposes has expanded.

Whenever the participants of the international system change, a period of profound dislocation is inevitable. They can change because new states enter the political system, or because there is a change in values as to what constitutes legitimate rule, or finally, because of the reduction in influence of some traditional units. In our period, all of these factors have combined. Since the end of the Second World War, several score of new states have come into being. In the nineteenth century the emergence of even a few new nations produced decades of adjustment, and after the First World War, the successor states of the Austro-Hungarian Empire were never assimilated. Our age has yet to find a structure which matches the responsibilities of the new nations to their aspirations.

As the number of participants has increased, technology has multiplied the resources available for the conduct of foreign policy. A scientific revolution has, for all practical purposes, removed technical limits from the exercise of power in foreign policy. It has magnified insecurities because it has made survival seem to depend on the accidents of a technological breakthrough.

This trend has been compounded by the nature of contemporary domestic structures. As long as the states' ability to mobilize resources was limited, the severity of their conflicts had definite bounds. In the eighteenth century, custom restricted the demands rulers by "divine right" could make upon their subjects; a philosophy of minimum government performed the same role through much of the nineteenth century. Our period has seen the culmination of a process started by the French Revolution: the basing of governmental legitimacy on popular support. Even totalitarian regimes are aberrations of a democratic legitimacy; they depend on popular consensus even when they manufacture it through propaganda and pressure. In such a situation, the consensus is decisive; limitations of tradition are essentially irrelevant. It is an ironic result of the democratization of politics that it has enabled states to marshal ever more resources for their competition.

Ideological conflict compounds these instabilities. In the great periods of cabinet diplomacy, diplomats spoke the same language, not only in the sense that French was the lingua franca, but more importantly because they tended to understand intangibles in the same manner. A similar outlook about aims and methods eases the tasks of diplomacy—it may even be a precondition for it. In the absence of such a consensus, diplomats can still meet, but they lose the ability to persuade. More time is spent on defining contending positions than in resolving them. What seems most reasonable to one side will appear most problematical to the other.

When there is ideological conflict, political loyalties no longer coincide with political boundaries. Conflicts among states merge with divisions within nations; the dividing line between domestic and foreign policy begins to disappear. At least some states feel threatened not only by the foreign policy of other countries but also, and perhaps especially, by domestic transformations. A liberalized communist regime in Prague—which had in no way challenged Soviet preeminence in foreign policy—caused the Kremlin to believe that its vital interests were threatened and to respond by occupying the country without even the pretext of legality.

The tensions produced by ideological conflict are exacerbated by the reduction in influence of the states that were considered great powers before the First World War. The world has become militarily bipolar. Only two powers—the United States and the Union of Soviet Socialist Republics—possess the full panoply of military might. Over the next decade, no other country or group of countries will be capable of challenging their physical preeminence. Indeed, the gap in military strength between the two giant nuclear countries and the rest of the world is likely to increase rather than diminish over that period.

Military bipolarity is a source of rigidity in foreign policy. The guardians of the equilibrium of the nineteenth century were prepared to respond to change with counteradjustment; the policy makers of the superpowers in the second half of the twentieth century have much less confidence in the ability of the equilibrium to right itself after disturbance. Whatever "balance" there is between the superpowers is regarded as both precarious and inflexible. A bipolar world loses the perspective for nuance; a gain for one side appears as an absolute loss for the other. Every issue seems to involve a question of survival. The smaller countries are torn between a desire for protection and a wish to escape big power dominance. Each of the superpowers is beset by the desire to maintain its preeminence among its allies, to increase its influence among the uncommitted, and to enhance its security vis-à-vis its opponent. The fact that some of these objectives may well prove incompatible adds to the strain on the international system.

But the age of the superpowers is now drawing to an end. Military bipolarity has not only failed to prevent, it has actually encouraged, political multipolarity. Weaker allies have good reason to believe that their defense is in the overwhelming interest of their senior partner. Hence, they see no need to purchase its support by acquiescence in its policies. The new nations feel protected by the rivalry of the superpowers, and their nationalism leads to ever bolder assertions of self-will. Traditional uses of power have become less feasible, and new forms of pressure have emerged as a result of transnational loyalties and weak domestic structures.

This political multipolarity does not necessarily guarantee stability. Rigidity is diminished, but so is manageability. Nationalism may succeed in curbing the preeminence of the superpowers; it remains to be seen whether it can supply an integrating concept more successfully in this century than in the last. Few countries have the interest and only the superpowers have the resources to become informed about global issues. As a result, diplomacy is often geared to domestic politics and more concerned with striking a pose than contributing to international order. Equilibrium is difficult to achieve among states widely divergent in values, goals, expectations, and previous experience.

The greatest need of the contemporary international system is an agreed concept of order. In its absence, the awesome available power is unrestrained by any consensus as to legitimacy; ideology and nationalism, in their different ways, deepen international schisms. Many of the elements of stability which characterized the international system in the nineteenth century cannot be re-created in the modern age. The stable technology, the multiplicity of major powers, the limited domestic claims, and the frontiers which permitted adjustments are gone forever. A new concept of international order is essential; without it stability will prove elusive.

This problem is particularly serious for the United States. Whatever our intentions or policies, the fact that the United States disposes of the greatest single aggregate of material power in the world is inescapable. A new international order is inconceivable without a significant American contribution. But the nature of this contribution has altered. For the two decades after 1945, our international activities were based on the assumption that technology plus managerial skills gave us the ability to reshape the international system and to bring about domestic transformations in "emerging countries." This direct "operational" concept of international order has proved too simple. Political multipolarity makes it impossible to impose an American design. Our deepest challenge will be to evoke the creativity of a pluralistic world, to base order on political multipolarity even though overwhelming military strength will remain with the two superpowers.

The Limits of Bipolarity: The Nature of Power in the Modern Period

Throughout history, military power was considered the final recourse. Statesmen treated the acquisition of additional power as an obvious and paramount objective. As recently as twenty-five years ago, it would have been inconceivable that a country could possess *too much* strength for effective political use; every increment of power was—at least theoretically—politically effective. The minimum aim was to assure the impermeability of the territory. Until the Second World War, a state's strength could be measured by its ability to protect its population from attack.

The nuclear age has destroyed this traditional measure. Increasing strength no longer necessarily confers the ability to protect the population. No foreseeable force level—not even full-scale ballistic missile defenses—can prevent levels of damage eclipsing those of the two world wars. In these conditions, the major problem is to discipline power so that it bears a rational relationship to the objectives likely to be in dispute. The paradox of contemporary military strength is that a gargantuan increase in power has eroded its relationship to policy. The major nuclear powers are capable of devastating each other. But they have great difficulty translating this capability into policy except to prevent direct challenges to their own survival—and this condition is interpreted with increasing strictness. The capacity to destroy is difficult to translate into a plausible threat even against countries with no capacity for retaliation. The margin of superiority of the superpowers over the other states is widening; yet other nations have an unprecedented scope for autonomous action. In relations with many domestically weak countries, a radio transmitter can be a more effective form of pressure than a squadron of B-52s. In other words, power no longer translates automatically into influence. This does not mean that impotence increases influence, only that power does not automatically confer it.

This state of affairs has profound consequences for traditional notions of balance of power. In the past, stability has always presupposed the existence of an equilibrium of power which prevented one state from imposing its will on the others.

The traditional criteria for the balance of power were territorial. A state could gain overwhelming superiority only by conquest; hence, as long as territorial expansion was foreclosed, or severely limited, the equilibrium was likely to be preserved. In the contemporary period, this is no longer true. Some conquests add little to effective military strength; major increases in power are possible entirely through developments within the territory of a sovereign state. China gained more in real military power through the acquisition of nuclear weapons than if it had conquered all of Southeast Asia. If the Soviet Union had occupied Western Europe but had remained without nuclear weapons, it would be less powerful than it is now with its existing nuclear arsenal within its present borders. In other words, the really fundamental changes in the balance of power have all occurred *within* the territorial limits of sovereign states. Clearly, there is an urgent need to analyze just what is understood by power—as well as by balance of power—in the nuclear age.

This would be difficult enough were technology stable. It becomes enormously complicated when a scientific revolution produces an upheaval in weapons technology at five-year intervals. Slogans like "superiority," "parity," "assured destruction," compete unencumbered by clear definitions of their operational military significance, much less a consensus on their political implications. The gap between experts and decision makers is widening. The decision maker rarely has as many hours to study a problem as the expert has years. The result is that the decision maker runs the risk of unprecedented dependence on his technical staff. He is informed by "briefings," a procedure which stresses theatrical qualities and leaves its target with the uneasy feeling that he has been "taken," even—or perhaps especially—when he does not know exactly how. Decisions may reflect an attempt to ward off conflicting pressures rather than a clear conception of long-range purposes.

In short, as power has grown more awesome, it has also turned abstract, intangible, elusive. Deterrence has become the dominant military policy. But deterrence depends above all on psychological criteria. It seeks to keep an opponent from a given course by posing unacceptable risks. For purposes of deterrence, the opponent's calculations are decisive. A bluff taken seriously is more useful than a serious threat interpreted as a bluff. For political purposes, the meaningful measurement of military strength is the assessment of it by the other side. Psychological criteria vie in importance with strategic doctrine.

The abstract nature of modern power affects domestic disputes profoundly. Deterrence is tested negatively by things which do *not* happen. But it is never possible to demonstrate *why* something has not occurred. Is it because we are pursuing the best possible policy or only a marginally effective one? Bitter debate even among those who believe in the necessity of defense policy is inevitable and bound to be inconclusive. Moreover, the longer peace is maintained—or the more successful deterrence is—the more it furnishes arguments for those who are opposed to the very premises of defense policy. Perhaps there was no need for preparedness in the first place because the opponent never meant to attack. In the modern state, national security is likely to be a highly divisive domestic issue.

The enormity of modern power has destroyed its cumulative impact to a considerable extent. Throughout history the use of force set a precedent; it demonstrated a capacity to use power for national ends. In the twentieth century any use of force sets up inhibitions against resorting to it again. Whatever the outcome of the war in Vietnam, it is clear that it has greatly diminished American willingness to become involved in this form of warfare elsewhere. Its utility as a precedent has therefore been importantly undermined.

The difficulty of forming a conception of power is paralleled by the problem of how to use it diplomatically. In the past, measures to increase readiness signaled the mounting seriousness with which an issue was viewed.[1] But such measures have become less obvious and more dangerous when weapons are always at a high state of readiness—solid-fuel missiles require less than ten minutes to be fired—and are hidden either under the ground or under the oceans. With respect to nuclear weapons, signaling increased readiness has to take place in a narrow range between the danger of failure and the risk of a preemptive strike.

Even when only conventional weapons are involved, the question of what constitutes a politically meaningful threat is increasingly com-

---

1. Sometimes these measures got out of control; the mobilization schedules were one of the principal reasons for the outbreak of the First World War.

plicated. After the capture of the *Pueblo*, the United States called up thirteen thousand reservists and moved an aircraft carrier into the waters off the shores of Korea. Did the fact that we had to call up reserves when challenged by a fifth-rate military power convey that we meant to act or that we were overextended? Did the move of the aircraft carrier indicate a decision to retaliate or was it intended primarily to strike a pose?

The problem is illustrated dramatically by the war in Vietnam. A massive breakdown of communication occurred not only within the policy-making machinery in the United States but also between the United States and Hanoi. Over the past five years, the U.S. government has found it difficult, if not impossible, to define what it understood by victory. President Johnson extended an open-ended offer for unconditional negotiations. Yet our troops were deployed as if this offer had not been made. The deployment was based on purely military considerations; it did not take into account the possibility that our troops might have to support a negotiation—the timing of which we had, in effect, left to the opponent. Strategy divorced from foreign policy proved sterile.

These perplexities have spurred new interest in arms-control negotiations, especially those dealing with strategic missiles. These negotiations can be important for the peace and security of the world. But to be effective, they require an intellectual resolution of the issues which have bedeviled the formulation of military policy. Unless we are able to give an operational meaning to terms such as "superiority" or "stability," negotiations will lack criteria by which to judge progress.

Thus, whatever the course—a continuation of the arms race or arms control—a new look at American national security policy is essential. Over ten years have passed since the last comprehensive, bipartisan, high-level reevaluation of all aspects of national security: the Gaither Committee. A new administration should move quickly to bring about such a review. It should deal with some of the following problems: (a) a definition of the national interest and national security over the next decade; (b) the nature of military power in that period; (c) the relationship of military power to political influence; (d) implications and feasibility (both military and political) of various postures—superiority, parity, and so on; (e) the implications (both political and military) of new developments such as MIRV (multiple individually targeted reentry vehicles) and ballistic missile defenses; (f) the prospects for arms control including specific measures to moderate the arms race.

Political Multipolarity: The Changed Nature of Alliances

No area of policy illustrates more dramatically the tensions between political multipolarity and military bipolarity than the field of alliance policy. For a decade and a half after the Second World War, the United States identified security with alliances. A global network of relationships grew up based on the proposition that deterrence of aggression required the largest possible grouping of powers.

This system of alliances was always in difficulty outside the Atlantic area because it tried to apply principles drawn from the multipolar world of the eighteenth and nineteenth centuries when several major powers of roughly equal strength existed. Then, indeed, it was impossible for one country to achieve dominance if several others combined to prevent it. But this was not the case in the era of the superpowers of the forties and fifties. Outside Europe, our allies added to our strength only marginally; they were in no position to reinforce each other's capabilities.

Alliances, to be effective, must meet four conditions: (1) a common objective—usually defense against a common danger; (2) a degree of joint policy at least sufficient to define the *casus belli*; (3) some technical means of cooperation in case common action is decided upon; (4) a penalty for noncooperation—that is, the possibility of being refused assistance must exist—otherwise protection will be taken for granted and the mutuality of obligation will break down.

In the system of alliances developed by the United States after the Second World War, these conditions have never been met outside the North Atlantic Treaty Organization (NATO). In the Southeast Asia Treaty Organization (SEATO) and the Central Treaty Organization (CENTO), to which we belong in all but name, there has been no consensus as to the danger. Pakistan's motive for obtaining U.S. arms was not security against a communist attack but protection against India. Iran, as a member of CENTO, armed not against the USSR but against the UAR. Lacking a conception of common interests, the members of these alliances have never been able to develop common policies with respect to issues of war and peace. Had they been able to do so, such policies might well have been stillborn anyway, because the technical means of cooperation have been lacking. Most allies have neither the resources nor the will to render mutual support. A state which finds it difficult to maintain order or coherence of policy at home does not increase its strength by combining with states suffering similar disabilities.

In these circumstances, SEATO and CENTO have grown moribund as instruments of collective action. Because the United States has often seemed more eager to engage in the defense of its SEATO and CENTO allies than they themselves, they have become convinced that noncooperation will have no cost. In fact, they have been able to give the impression that it would be worse for us than for them if they fell to communism. SEATO and CENTO have become, in effect, unilateral American guarantees. At best, they provide a legal basis for bilateral U.S. aid.

The case is different with NATO. Here we are united with countries of similar traditions and domestic structures. At the start, there was a common conception of the threat. The technical means for cooperation existed. Mechanisms for developing common policies came into being—especially in the military field. Thus in its first decade and a half, NATO was a dynamic and creative institution.

Today, however, NATO is in disarray as well. Actions by the United States—above all, frequent unilateral changes of policy—are partially responsible. But the most important cause is the transformation of the international environment, specifically the decline in the preeminence of the superpowers and the emergence of political multipolarity. Where the alliances outside of Europe have never been vital because they failed to take into account the military bipolarity of the fifties, NATO is in difficulties because it has yet to adjust to the political multipolarity of the late sixties.

When NATO was founded in 1949, Europeans had a dual fear: the danger of an imminent Soviet attack and the prospect of eventual U.S. withdrawal. In the late 1960s, however, the fear of Soviet invasion has declined. Even the attack on Czechoslovakia is likely to restore anxiety about Soviet military aggression only temporarily. At the same time, two decades of American military presence in Europe coupled with American predominance in NATO planning have sharply reduced the fear that America might wash its hands of European concerns.

When NATO was formed, moreover, the principal threat to world peace seemed to lie in a Soviet attack on Europe. In recent years, the view has grown that equally grave risks are likely to arise in trouble spots outside Europe. To most Europeans, these do not appear as immediate threats to their independence or security. The irony here is striking. In the fifties, Europeans were asking for American assistance in Asia and the Middle

East with the argument that they were defending the greater interests of freedom. The United States replied that these very interests required American aloofness. Today, the roles are precisely reversed. It is Europe that evades our entreaties to play a global role; that is to say, Europeans do not consider their interests at stake in America's extra-European involvement.

These are symptoms of deeper, structural problems, however. One problem, paradoxically, is the growth of European economic strength and political self-confidence. At the end of the Second World War, Europe was dependent on the United States for economic assistance, political stability, and military protection. As long as Europe needed the shelter of a superpower, American predominance was inevitable. In relations with the United States, European statesmen acted as lobbyists rather than as diplomats. Their influence depended less on the weight of their countries than on the impact of their personalities. A form of consultation evolved whereby Europeans sought to influence American actions by giving us a reputation to uphold or—to put it more crudely—by oscillating between flattery and almost plaintive appeals for reassurance. The United States, secure in its predominance, in turn concentrated on soothing occasional European outbreaks of insecurity rather than on analyzing their causes.

Tutelage is a comfortable relationship for the senior partner, but it is demoralizing in the long run. It breeds illusions of omniscience on one side and attitudes of impotent irresponsibility on the other. In any event, the United States could not expect to perpetuate the accident of Europe's postwar exhaustion into a permanent pattern of international relations. Europe's economic recovery inevitably led to a return to more traditional political pressures.

These changes in Europe were bound to lead to a difficult transitional period. They could have resulted in a new partnership between the United States and an economically resurgent and politically united Europe, as had been envisaged by many of the early advocates of Atlantic unity. However, the European situation has not resolved itself in that way. Thoughtful Europeans know that Europe must unite in some form if it is to play a major role in the long run. They are aware, too, that Europe does not make even approximately the defense effort of which it is capable. But European unity is stymied, and domestic politics has almost everywhere dominated security policy. The result is a massive frustration which expresses itself in special testiness toward the United States.

These strains have been complicated by the growth of Soviet nuclear power. The changed nature of power in the modern period has affected NATO profoundly. As the risks of nuclear war have become enormous, the credibility of traditional pledges of support has inevitably been reduced. In the past, a country would carry out a commitment because, it could plausibly be argued, the consequences of not doing so were worse than those of coming to the ally's assistance. This is no longer self-evident. In each of the last three annual statements by the Secretary of Defense on the U.S. defense posture, the estimate of *dead* in a general nuclear war ranged from 40 to 120 million. This figure will, if anything, increase. It will become more and more difficult to demonstrate that *anything* is worse than the elimination of over half of a society in a matter of days. The more NATO relies on strategic nuclear war as a counter to all forms of attack, the less credible its pledges will be.

The consciousness of nuclear threat by the two superpowers has undermined allied relationships in yet another way. For understandable reasons, the superpowers have sought to make the nuclear environment more predictable, witness the nuclear test ban treaty and the nonproliferation treaty. But the blind spot in our policy has been the failure to understand that, in the absence of full consultation, our allies see in these talks the possible forerunner of a more comprehensive arrangement affecting their vital interests negotiated without them. Strategic arms talks thus emphasize the need of political understanding in acute form. The pattern of negotiating an agreement first and then giving our allies an opportunity— even a full one—to comment is intolerable in the long run. It puts the onus of failure on them, and it prevents them from doing more than quibble about a framework with which they may disagree. Strains have been reinforced by the uncertain American response to the Soviet invasion of Czechoslovakia—especially the reluctance to give up the prospect of a summit meeting. Atlantic relations, for all their seeming normalcy, thus face a profound crisis.

This state of affairs has been especially difficult for those Americans who deserve most credit for forging existing Atlantic relations. Two decades of hegemony have produced the illusion that present Atlantic arrangements are "natural," that wise policy consists of making the existing framework more tolerable. "Leadership" and "partnership" are invoked, but the content given to these words is usually that which will support the existing pattern. European unity is advocated to enable Europeans to share burdens on a world-wide scale.

Such a view fails to take into account the realities of political multipolarity. The aim of returning to the "great days of the Marshall Plan" is impossible. Nothing would sunder Atlantic relationships so surely as the attempt to reassert the notions of leadership appropriate to the early days of NATO. In the bipolar world of the forties and fifties, order could be equated with military security; integrated command arrangements sufficed as the principal bond of unity. In the sixties, security, while still important, has not been enough. Every crisis from Berlin to Czechoslovakia has seen the call for "strengthening NATO" confined to military dispositions. Within months a malaise has become obvious again because the overriding need for a common political conception has not been recognized. The challenge of the seventies will be to forge unity with political measures.

It is not "natural" that the major decisions about the defense of an area so potentially powerful as Western Europe should be made three thousand miles away. It is not "normal" that Atlantic policies should be geared to American conceptions. In the forties and fifties, practicing unity—through formal resolutions and periodic reassurances—was profoundly important as a symbol of the end of our isolationism. In the decade ahead, we cannot aim at unity as an end in itself; it must emerge from common conceptions and new structures.

"Burden-sharing" will not supply that impetus. Countries do not assume burdens because it is fair, only because it is necessary. While there are strong arguments for Atlantic partnership and European unity, enabling Europe to play a global role is not one of them. A nation assumes responsibilities not only because it has resources but because it has a certain view of its own destiny. Through the greater part of its history—until the Second World War—the United States possessed the resources but not the philosophy for a global role. Today, the poorest Western European country—Portugal—has the widest commitments outside Europe because its historic image of itself has become bound up with its overseas possessions. This condition is unlikely to be met by any other European country—with the possible exception of Great Britain—no matter what its increase in power. Partially as the result of decolonization, Europeans are unlikely to conduct a significant global policy whatever their resources or their degree of unity. Cooperation between the United States and Europe must concentrate on issues within the Atlantic area rather than global partnership.

Even within the Atlantic area, a more equitable distribution of responsibilities has two prerequisites: there must be some consensus in the analysis of the international situation, at least as it affects Europe; there must be a conviction that the United States cannot or will not carry all the burdens alone. Neither condition is met today. The traditional notion of American leadership tends to stifle European incentives for autonomy. Improved consultation—the remedy usually proposed—can only alleviate, not remove, the difficulty.

The problem of consultation is complex, of course. No doubt unilateral American action has compounded the uneasiness produced by American predominance and European weakness. The shift in emphasis of American policy, from the NATO multilateral force to the nonproliferation treaty, the frequent unilateral changes in strategic doctrine, have all tended to produce disquiet and to undermine the domestic position of ministers who had staked their futures on supporting the American viewpoint.

It is far from self-evident, however, that more extensive consultation within the existing framework can be more than a palliative. One problem concerns technical competence. In any large bureaucracy—and an international consultative process has many similarities to domestic administrative procedures—the weight given to advice bears some relation to the competence it reflects. If one partner possesses all the technical competence, the process of consultation is likely to remain barren. The minimum requirement for effective consultation is that each ally have enough knowledge to give meaningful advice.

But there are even more important limits to the process of consultation. The losing party in a domestic dispute has three choices: (a) it can accept the setback with the expectation of winning another battle later on—this is the usual bureaucratic attitude and it is based on the assurance of another hearing; (b) if advice is consistently ignored, it can resign and go into opposition; (c) as the opposition party, it can have the purpose either of inducing the existing government to change its course or of replacing it. If all these avenues are closed, violence or mounting frustration are the consequences.

Only the first option is open to sovereign states bound together by an alliance, since they obviously cannot resign or go into opposition without wrecking the alliance. They cannot affect the process by which their partners' decision makers are chosen despite the fact that this may be crucial for their fate. Indeed, as long as the need to maintain the alliance overrides all other concerns, disagreement is likely to be stifled. Advice without responsibility and disagreement without an outlet can turn consultation into a frustrating exercise which compounds rather than alleviates discord.

Consultation is especially difficult when it lacks an integrating overall framework. The consultation about the nonproliferation treaty concerned specific provisions but not the underlying general philosophy which was of the deepest concern to many of our allies, especially the Federal Republic of Germany and Italy. During periods of détente, each ally makes its own approach to Eastern Europe or the USSR without attempting to further a coherent Western enterprise. During periods of crisis, there is pressure for American reassurance but not for a clearly defined common philosophy. In these circumstances, consultation runs the risk of being irrelevant. The issues it "solves" are peripheral; the central issues are inadequately articulated. It deals haphazardly in answers to undefined questions.

Such a relationship is not healthy in the long run. Even with the best will, the present structure encourages American unilateralism and European irresponsibility. This is a serious problem for the United States. If the United States remains the trustee of every noncommunist area, it will exhaust its psychological resources. No country can act wisely simultaneously in every part of the globe at every moment of time. A more pluralistic world—especially in relationships with friends—is profoundly in our long-term interest. Political multipolarity, while difficult to get used to, is the precondition for a new period of creativity. Painful as it may be to admit, we could benefit from a counterweight that would discipline our occasional impetuosity and, by supplying historical perspective, modify our penchant for abstract and "final" solutions.

All of this suggests that there is no alternative to European unity either for the United States or for Europe. In its absence, the malaise can only be alleviated, not ended. Ultimately, this is a problem primarily for the Europeans. In the recent past, the United States has often defeated its purposes by committing itself to one particular form of European unity— that of federalism. It has also complicated British membership in the Common Market by making it a direct objective of American policy.

In the next decade the architectonic approach to Atlantic policy will no longer be possible. The American contribution must be more philosophical; it will have to consist more of understanding and quiet, behind-the-scenes encouragement than of the propagation of formal institutional structures. Involved here is the American conception of how nations cooperate. A tradition of legalism and habits of predominance have produced a tendency to multiply formal arrangements.

But growing European autonomy forces us to learn that nations cooperate less because they have a legal obligation to do so than because they have common purposes. Command arrangements cannot substitute for common interests. Coordinated strategy will be empty unless it reflects shared political concepts. The chance of disagreements on peripheral issues may be the price for unity on issues that really matter. The memory of European impotence and American tutelage should not delude us into believing that we understand Europe's problems better than it does itself. Third force dangers are not avoided by legal formulas, and more important, they have been overdrawn. It is hard to visualize a "deal" between the Soviet Union and Europe which would jeopardize our interests without jeopardizing European interests first. In any event, a sense of responsibility in Europe will be a much better counter to Soviet efforts to undermine unity than American tutelage.

In short, our relations with Europeans are better founded on developing a community of interests than on the elaboration of formal legal obligations. No precise blueprint for such an arrangement is possible because different fields of activity have different needs. In the military sphere, for example, modern technology will impose a greater degree of integration than is necessary in other areas. Whatever their formal autonomy, it is almost inconceivable that our allies would prefer to go to war *without* the support of the United States, given the relatively small nuclear forces in prospect for them. Close coordination between Europe and the United States in the military sphere is dictated by self-interest, and Europe has more to gain from it than the United States.

For this very reason, it is in our interest that Europeans should assume much greater responsibility for developing doctrine and force levels in NATO, perhaps by vitalizing such institutions as the West European Union (WEU), perhaps by alternative arrangements. The Supreme Allied Commander should in time be a European.

Military arrangements are not enough, however. Under current conditions, no statesman will risk a cataclysm simply to fulfill a legal obligation. He will do so only if a degree of *political* cooperation has been established which links the fate of each partner with the survival of all the others. This requires an entirely new order of political creativity.

Coordination is especially necessary in East-West relations. The conventional view is that NATO can be as useful an instrument for détente as for defense. This is doubtful—at least in NATO's present form. A military alliance, one of the chief cohesive links of which is its integrated command arrangement, is not the best instrument for flexible diplomacy. Turning NATO into an instrument of détente might reduce its security contribution without achieving a relaxation of tensions. A diplomatic confrontation of NATO and the Warsaw Pact would have all the rigidities of the bipolar military world. It would raise fears in Western Europe of an American-Soviet condominium, and it would tend to legitimize the Soviet hegemonical position in Eastern Europe. Above all, it would fail to take advantage of the flexibility afforded by greater Western European unity and autonomy. As Europe gains structure, its attraction for Eastern Europe is bound to increase. The major initiatives to improve relations between Western and Eastern Europe should originate in Europe with the United States in a reserve position.

Such an approach can work only if there is a real consensus as to objectives. Philosophical agreement can make possible flexibility of method. This will require a form of consultation much more substantial than that which now exists and a far more effective and coherent European contribution.

To be sure, events in Czechoslovakia demonstrate the limits of Eastern European autonomy that the Soviet Union is now prepared to tolerate. But the Soviet Union may not be willing indefinitely to use the Red Army primarily against allies as it has done three times in a decade and a half. In any event, no Western policy can guarantee a more favorable evolution in Central Europe; all it can do is to take advantage of an opportunity if it arises.

Policy outside Europe is likely to be divergent. Given the changed European perspective, an effort to bring about global burden-sharing might only produce stagnation. The allies would be able to agree primarily on doing nothing. Any crisis occurring anywhere would turn automatically and organically world-wide. American acceptance of European autonomy implies also European acceptance of a degree of American autonomy with respect to areas in which, for understandable reasons, European concern has lessened.

There may be opportunities for cooperation in hitherto purely national efforts, for example, our space program. European participation in it could help to remedy, the "technological gap."

Finally, under present circumstances, an especially meaningful community of interests can be developed in the social sphere. All modern states face problems of bureaucratization, pollution, environmental control, urban growth. These problems know no national considerations. If the nations of the Atlantic work together on these issues—either through private or governmental channels or both—a new generation habituated to cooperative efforts could develop similar to that spawned in different circumstances by the Marshall Plan.

It is high time that the nations bordering the Atlantic deal—formally, systematically, and at the highest level—with questions such as these: (a) What are the relative roles of Europe and the United States in East-West contacts? (b) Is a division of functions conceivable in which Western Europe plays the principal role in relation to Eastern Europe while the United States concentrates on relationships with the USSR? (c) What forms of political consultation does this require? (d) In what areas of the world is common action possible? Where are divergent courses indicated? How are differences to be handled?

Thus, we face the root questions of a multipolar world. How much unity should we want? How much diversity can we stand? These questions never have a final answer within a pluralistic society. Adjusting the balance between integration and autonomy will be the key challenge of emerging Atlantic relations.

Bipolarity and Multipolarity: The Conceptual Problem

In the years ahead, the most profound challenge to American policy will be philosophical: to develop some concept of order in a world which is bipolar militarily but multipolar politically. But a philosophical deepening will not come easily to those brought up in the American tradition of foreign policy.

Our political society was one of the few which was *consciously created* at a point in time. At least until the emergence of the race problem, we were blessed by the absence of conflicts between classes and over ultimate ends. These factors produced the characteristic aspects of American foreign policy: a certain manipulativeness and pragmatism, a conviction that the normal pattern of international relations was harmonious, a reluctance to think in structural terms, a belief in final answers—all qualities which reflect a sense of self-sufficiency not far removed from a sense of omnipotence. Yet the contemporary dilemma is that there are no total solutions; we live in a world gripped by revolutions in technology, values, and institutions. We are immersed in an unending process, not in a quest for a final destination. The deepest problems of equilibrium are not physical but psychological or moral. The shape of the future will depend ultimately on convictions which far transcend the physical balance of power.

THE NEW NATIONS AND POLITICAL LEGITIMACY

This challenge is especially crucial with respect to the new nations. Future historians are likely to class the confusion and torment in the emerging countries with the great movements of religious awakening. Continents which had been dormant for centuries suddenly develop political consciousness. Regions which for scores of years had considered foreign rule as natural struggle for independence. Yet it is a curious nationalism which defines itself not as in Europe by common language or culture but often primarily by the common experience of foreign rule. Boundaries—especially in Africa—have tended to follow the administrative convenience of the colonial powers rather than linguistic or tribal lines. The new nations have faced problems both of identity and of political authority. They often lack social cohesiveness entirely, or they are split into competing groups each with a highly developed sense of identity.

It is no accident that between the Berlin crisis and the invasion of Czechoslovakia, the principal threats to peace came from the emerging areas. Domestic weakness encourages foreign intervention. The temptation to deflect domestic dissatisfactions into foreign adventures is ever present. Leaders feel little sense of responsibility to an overall international equilibrium; they are much more conscious of their local grievances. The rivalry of the superpowers offers many opportunities for blackmail.

Yet their relations with other countries are not the most significant aspect of the turmoil of the new countries. It is in the new countries that questions of the purpose of political life and the meaning of political legitimacy—key issues also in the modern state—pose themselves in their most acute form. The new nations weigh little in the physical balance of power. But the forces unleashed in the emergence of so many new states may well affect the moral balance of the world—the convictions which form the structure for the world of tomorrow. This adds a new dimension to the problem of multipolarity.

Almost all of the new countries suffer from a revolutionary malaise: revolutions succeed through the coming together of all resentments. But the elimination of existing structures compounds the difficulty of establishing political consensus. A successful revolution leaves as its legacy a profound dislocation. In the new countries, contrary to all revolutionary expectations, the task of construction emerges as less glamorous and more complex than the struggle for freedom; the exaltation of the quest for independence cannot be perpetuated. Sooner or later, positive goals must replace resentment of the former colonial power as a motive force. In the absence of autonomous social forces, this unifying role tends to be performed by the state.

But the assumption of this role by the state does not produce stability. When social cohesiveness is slight, the struggle for control of authority is correspondingly more bitter. When government is the principal, sometimes the sole, expression of national identity, opposition comes to be considered treason. The profound social or religious schisms of many of the new nations turn the control of political authority quite literally into a matter of life and death. Where political obligation follows racial, religious, or tribal lines, self-restraint breaks down. Domestic conflicts assume the character of civil war. Such traditional authority as exists is personal or feudal. The problem is to make it "legitimate"—to develop a notion of political obligation which depends on legal norms rather than on coercive power or personal loyalty.

This process took centuries in Europe. It must be accomplished in decades in the new nations, where preconditions of success are less favorable than at comparable periods in Europe. The new countries are subject to outside pressures; there is a premium on foreign adventures to bring about domestic cohesiveness. Their lack of domestic structure compounds the already great international instabilities.

The American role in the new nations' efforts to build legitimate authority is in need of serious reexamination. The dominant American view about political structure has been that it will follow more or less automatically upon economic progress and that it will take the form of constitutional democracy.

Both assumptions are subject to serious questions. In every advanced country, political stability preceded rather than emerged from the process of industrialization. Where the rudiments of popular institutions did not exist at the beginning of the Industrial Revolution, they did not receive their impetus from it. To be sure, representative institutions were broadened and elaborated as the countries prospered, but their significant features antedated economic development and are not attributable to it. In fact, the system of government which brought about industrialization—whether popular or authoritarian—has tended to be confirmed rather than radically changed by this achievement.

Nor is democracy a natural evolution of nationalism. In the last century, democracy was accepted by a ruling class whose estimate of itself was founded outside the political process. It was buttressed by a middle class, holding a political philosophy in which the state was considered to be a referee of the ultimately important social forces rather than the principal focus of national consciousness. Professional revolutionaries were rarely involved; their bias is seldom democratic.

The pluralism of the West had many causes which cannot be duplicated elsewhere. These included a church organization outside the control of the state and therefore symbolizing the limitation of government power; the Greco-Roman philosophical tradition of justice based on human dignity, reinforced later by the Christian ethic; an emerging bourgeoisie; a stalemate in religious wars imposing tolerance as a practical necessity and a multiplicity of states. Industrialization was by no means the most significant of these factors. Had any of the others been missing, the Western political evolution could have been quite different.

This is why communism has never succeeded in the industrialized Western countries for which its theory was devised; its greatest successes have been in developing societies. This is no accident. Industrialization—in its early phases—multiplies dislocations. It smashes the traditional framework. It requires a system of values which makes the sacrifices involved in capital formation tolerable and which furnishes some integrating principles to contain psychological frustrations.

Communism is able to supply legitimacy for the sacrifices inseparably connected with capital formation in an age when the maxims of laissez faire are no longer acceptable. And Leninism has the attraction of providing a rationale for holding on to power. Many of the leaders of the new countries are revolutionaries who sustained themselves through the struggle for independence by visions of the transformations to be brought about after victory. They are not predisposed even to admit the possibility of giving up power in their hour of triumph. Since they usually began their struggle for independence while in a small minority and sustained it against heavy odds, they are not likely to be repelled by the notion that it is possible to "force men to be free."

The ironic feature of the current situation is that Marxism, professing a materialistic philosophy, is accepted only where it does not exist: in some new countries and among protest movements of the advanced democratic countries. Its appeal is its idealistic component and not its economic theory. It offers a doctrine of substantive change and an explanation of final purposes. Its philosophy has totally failed to inspire the younger generation in communist countries where its bureaucratic reality is obvious.

On the other hand, the United States, professing an idealistic philosophy, often fails to gain acceptance for democratic values because of its heavy reliance on economic factors. It has answers to technical dislocations but has not been able to contribute much to building a political and moral consensus. It offers a procedure for change but little content for it.

The problem of political legitimacy is the key to political stability in regions containing two-thirds of the world's population. A stable domestic system in the new countries will not automatically produce international order, but international order is impossible without it. An American agenda must include some conception of what we understand by political legitimacy. In an age of instantaneous communication, we cannot pretend that what happens to over two-thirds of humanity is of no concern or interest to the United States. This does not mean that our goal should be to transfer American institutions to the new nations—even less that we should impose them. Nor should we define the problem as how to prevent the spread of communism. Our goal should be to build a moral consensus which can make a pluralistic world creative rather than destructive.

Irrelevance to one of the great revolutions of our time will mean that we will ultimately be engulfed by it—if not physically, then psychologically. Already some of the protest movements have made heroes of leaders in repressive new countries. The absurdity of founding a claim for freedom on protagonists of the totalitarian state—such as Guevara or Ho or Mao—underlines the impact of the travail of the new countries on older societies which share none of their technical but some of their spiritual problems, especially the problem of the nature of authority in the modern world. To a young generation in rebellion against bureaucracy and bored with material comfort, these societies offer at least the challenge of unlimited opportunity (and occasionally unlimited manipulativeness) in the quest for justice.

A world which is bipolar militarily and multipolar politically thus confronts an additional problem. Side by side with the physical balance of power, there exists a psychological balance based on intangibles of value and belief. The presuppositions of the physical equilibrium have changed drastically; those of the psychological balance remain to be discovered.

THE PROBLEM OF SOVIET INTENTIONS

Nothing has been more difficult for Americans to assimilate in the nuclear age than the fact that even enmity is complex. In the Soviet Union, we confront an opponent whose public pronouncements are insistently hostile. Yet the nuclear age imposes a degree of cooperation and an absolute limit to conflicts.

The military relationship with the Soviet Union is difficult enough; the political one confronts us with a profound conceptual problem. A society which regards peace as the normal condition tends to ascribe tension not to structural causes but to wicked or shortsighted individuals. Peace is thought to result either from the automatic operation of economic forces or from the emergence of a more benign leadership abroad.

The debate about Soviet trends between "hard-liners" and "soft-liners" illustrates this problem. Both sides tend to agree that the purpose of American policy is to encourage a more benign evolution of Soviet society—the original purpose of containment was, after all, to bring about the *domestic* transformation of the USSR. They are at one that a settlement presupposes a change in the Soviet system. Both groups imply that the nature of a possible settlement is perfectly obvious. But the apostles of containment have never specified the American negotiating program to be undertaken from the position of strength their policy was designed to achieve. The advocates of relaxation of tensions have been no more precise; they have been more concerned with atmosphere than with the substance of talks.

In fact, the difference between the "hawks" and "doves" has usually concerned timing: the hawks have maintained that a Soviet change of heart, while inevitable, was still in the future, whereas the doves have argued that it has already taken place. Many of the hawks tend to consider all negotiations as fruitless. Many of the doves argue—or did before Czechoslovakia—that the biggest step toward peace has already been accomplished by a Soviet change of heart about the cold war; negotiations need only remove some essentially technical obstacles.

This difference affects—and sometimes poisons—the entire American debate about foreign policy. Left-wing critics of American foreign policy seem incapable of attacking U.S. actions without elevating our opponent (whether it happens to be Mao or Castro or Ho) to a pedestal. If they discern some stupidity or self-interest on our side, they assume that the other side must be virtuous. They then criticize the United States for opposing the other side. The right follows the same logic in reverse: they presuppose our good intentions and conclude that the other side must be perverse in opposing us. Both the left and the right judge largely in terms of intentions. In the process, whatever the issue—whether Berlin or Vietnam—more attention is paid to whether to get to the conference room than what to do once we arrive there. The dispute over communist intentions has diverted attention from elaborating our own purposes. In some quarters, the test of dedication to peace has been whether one interprets Soviet intentions in the most favorable manner.

It should be obvious, however, that the Soviet domestic situation is complex and its relationship to foreign policy far from obvious. It is true that the risks of general nuclear war should be as unacceptable to Moscow as to Washington; but this truism does not automatically produce détente. It also seems to lessen the risks involved in local intervention. No doubt the current generation of communist leaders lacks the ideological dynamism of their predecessors who made the revolution; at the same time, they have at their disposal a military machine of unprecedented strength, and they must deal with a bureaucracy of formidable vested interests. Unquestionably, Soviet consumers press their leaders to satisfy their demands; but it is equally true that an expanding modern economy is able to supply *both* guns and butter. Some Soviet leaders may have become more pragmatic; but in an elaborated communist state, the results of pragmatism are complex. Once power is seized and industrialization is largely accomplished, the Communist party faces a difficult situation. It is not needed to conduct the government, and it has no real function in running the economy (though it tries to do both). In order to justify its continued existence and command, it may develop a vested interest in vigilance against outside danger and thus in perpetuating a fairly high level of tension.

It is beyond the scope of this essay to go into detail on the issue of internal communist evolution. But it may be appropriate to inquire why, in the past, every period of détente has proved stillborn. There have been at least five periods of peaceful coexistence since the Bolshevik seizure of power, one in each decade of the Soviet state. Each was hailed in the West as ushering in a new era of reconciliation and as signifying the long-awaited final change in Soviet purposes. Each ended abruptly with a new period of intransigence, which was generally ascribed to a victory of Soviet hardliners rather than to the dynamics of the system. There were undoubtedly many reasons for this. But the tendency of many in the West to be content with changes of Soviet tone and to confuse atmosphere with substance surely did not help matters. It has enabled the Communist leaders to postpone the choice which they must make sooner or later: Whether to use détente as a device to lull the West or whether to move toward a resolution of the outstanding differences. As long as this choice is postponed, the possibility exists that latent crises may run away with the principal protagonists as happened in the Middle East and perhaps even in Czechoslovakia.

The eagerness of many in the West to emphasize the liberalizing implications of Soviet economic trends and to make favorable interpretation of Soviet intentions a test of good faith may have the paradoxical consequence of strengthening the Soviet hard-liners. Soviet troops had hardly arrived in Prague when some Western leaders began to insist that the invasion would not affect the quest for détente while others continued to indicate a nostalgia for high-level meetings. Such an attitude hardly serves the cause of peace. The risk is great that if there is no penalty for intransigence there is no incentive for conciliation. The Kremlin may use negotiations—including arms control—as a safety valve to dissipate Western suspicions rather than as a serious endeavor to resolve concrete disputes or to remove the scourge of nuclear war.

If we focus our policy discussions on Soviet purposes, we confuse the debate in two ways: Soviet trends are too ambiguous to offer a reliable guide—it is possible that not even Soviet leaders fully understand the dynamics of their system; it deflects us from articulating the purposes we should pursue, whatever Soviet intentions. Peace will not, in any event, result from one grand settlement but from a long diplomatic process, and this process requires some clarity as to our destination. Confusing foreign policy with psychotherapy deprives us of criteria by which to judge the political foundations of international order.

The obsession with Soviet intentions causes the West to be smug during periods of détente and panicky during crises. A benign Soviet tone is equated with the achievement of peace; Soviet hostility is considered to be the signal for a new period of tension and usually evokes purely military countermeasures. The West is thus never ready for a Soviet change of course; it has been equally unprepared for détente and intransigence.

These lines are being written while outrage at the Soviet invasion of Czechoslovakia is still strong. There is a tendency to focus on military implications or to speak of strengthening unity in the abstract. But if history is a guide, there will be a new Soviet peace offensive sooner or later. Thus, reflecting about the nature of détente seems most important while its achievement appears most problematical. If we are not to be doomed to repeat the past, it may be well to learn some of its lessons: We should not again confuse a change of tone with a change of heart. We should not pose false inconsistencies between allied unity and détente; indeed, a true relaxation of tensions presupposes Western unity. We should concentrate negotiations on the concrete issues that threaten peace such as intervention in the third world. Moderating the arms race must also be high on the agenda. None of this is possible without a concrete idea of what we understand by peace and a creative world order.

An Inquiry into the American National Interest

Wherever we turn, then, the central task of American foreign policy is to analyze anew the current international environment and to develop some concepts which will enable us to contribute to the emergence of a stable order.

First, we must recognize the existence of profound structural problems that are to a considerable extent independent of the intentions of the principal protagonists and that cannot be solved merely by good will. The vacuum in Central Europe and the decline of the Western European countries would have disturbed the world equilibrium regardless of the domestic structure of the Soviet Union. A strong China has historically tended to establish suzerainty over its neighbors; in fact, one special problem of dealing with China—communism apart—is that it has had no experience in conducting foreign policy with equals. China has been either dominant or subjected.

To understand the structural issue, it is necessary to undertake an inquiry, from which we have historically shied away, into the essence of our national interest and into the premises of our foreign policy. It is part of American folklore that, while other nations have interests, we have responsibilites; while other nations are concerned with equilibrium, we are concerned with the legal requirements of peace. We have a tendency to offer our altruism as a guarantee of our reliability: "We have no quarrel with the Communists," Secretary of State Rusk said on one occasion, "all of our quarrels are on behalf of other people."

Such an attitude makes it difficult to develop a conception of our role in the world. It inhibits other nations from gearing their policy to ours in a confident way—a "disinterested" policy is likely to be considered "unreliable." A mature conception of our interest in the world would obviously have to take into account the widespread interest in stability and peaceful change. It would deal with two fundamental questions: What is it in our interest to prevent? What should we seek to accomplish?

The answer to the first question is complicated by an often repeated proposition that we must resist aggression anywhere it occurs since peace is indivisible. A corollary is the argument that we do not oppose the fact of particular changes but the method by which they are brought about. We find it hard to articulate a truly vital interest which we would defend however "legal" the challenge. This leads to an undifferentiated globalism and confusion about our purposes. The abstract concept of aggression causes us to multiply our commitments. But the denial that our interests are involved diminishes our staying power when we try to carry out these commitments.

Part of the reason for our difficulties is our reluctance to think in terms of power and equilibrium. In 1949, for example, a State Department memorandum justified NATO as follows: "[The treaty] obligates the parties to defend the purposes and principles of the United Nations, the freedom, common heritage and civilization of the parties and their free institutions based upon the principles of democracy, individual liberty and the role of law. It obligates them to act in defense of peace and security. It is directed against no one; it is directed solely against aggression. It seeks not to influence any shifting balance of power but to strengthen a balance of principle."

But principle, however lofty, must at some point be related to practice; historically, stability has always coincided with an equilibrium that made physical domination difficult. Interest is not necessarily amoral; moral consequences can spring from interested acts. Britain did not contribute any the less to international order for having a clear-cut concept of its interest which required it to prevent the domination of the Continent by a single power (no matter in what way it was threatened) and the control of the seas by anybody (even if the immediate intentions were not hostile). A new American administration confronts the challenge of relating our commitments to our interests and our obligations to our purposes.

The task of defining positive goals is more difficult but even more important. The first two decades after the end of the Second World War posed problems well suited to the American approach to international relations. Wherever we turned, massive dislocations required attention. Our pragmatic, ad hoc tendency was an advantage in a world clamoring for technical remedies. Our legal bent contributed to the development of many instruments of stability.

In the late sixties, the situation is more complex. The United States is no longer in a position to operate programs globally; it has to encourage them. It can no longer impose its preferred solution; it must seek to evoke it. In the forties and fifties, we offered remedies; in the late sixties and in the seventies our role will have to be to contribute to a structure that will foster the initiative of others. We are a superpower physically, but our designs can be meaningful only if they generate willing cooperation. We can continue to contribute to defense and positive programs, but we must seek to encourage and not stifle a sense of local responsibility. Our contribution should not be the sole or principal effort, but it should make the difference between success and failure.

This task requires a different kind of creativity and another form of patience than we have displayed in the past. Enthusiasm, belief in progress, and the invincible conviction that American remedies can work everywhere must give way to an understanding of historical trends, an ordering of our preferences, and above all an understanding of the difference our preferences can in fact make.

The dilemma is that there can be no stability without equilibrium, but equally, equilibrium is not a purpose with which we can respond to the travail of our world. A sense of mission is clearly a legacy of American history; to most Americans, America has always stood for something other than its own grandeur. But a clearer understanding of America's interests and of the requirements of equilibrium can give perspective to our idealism and lead to humane and moderate objectives, especially in relation to political and social change. Thus our conception of world order must have deeper purposes than stability but greater restraints on our behavior than would result if it were approached only in a fit of enthusiasm.

Whether such a leap of the imagination is possible in the modern bureaucratic state remains to be seen. New administrations come to power convinced of the need for goals and for comprehensive concepts. Sooner, rather than later, they find themselves subjected to the pressures of the immediate and the particular. Part of the reason is the pragmatic, issue-oriented bias of our decision makers. But the fundamental reason may be the pervasiveness of modern bureaucracy. What started out as an aid to decision making has developed a momentum of its own. Increasingly, the policy maker is more conscious of the pressures and the morale of his staff than of the purpose this staff is supposed to serve. The policy maker becomes a referee among quasi-autonomous bureaucratic bodies. Success consists of moving the administrative machinery to the point of decision, leaving relatively little energy for analyzing the decision's merit. The modern bureaucratic state widens the range of technical choices while limiting the capacity to make them.

An even more serious problem is posed by the change of ethic of precisely the most idealistic element of American youth. The idealism of the fifties during the Kennedy era expressed itself in self-confident, often zealous institution building. Today, however, many in the younger generation consider the management of power irrelevant, perhaps even immoral. While the idea of service retains a potent influence, it does so largely with respect to problems which are clearly *not* connected with the strategic aspects of American foreign policy; the Peace Corps is a good example. The new ethic of freedom is not "civic"; it is indifferent or even hostile to systems and notions of order. Management is equated with manipulation. Structural designs are perceived as systems of "domination" —not of order. The generation which has come of age after the fifties has had Vietnam as its introduction to world politics. It has no memory of occasions when American-supported structural innovations were successful or of the motivations which prompted these enterprises.

Partly as a result of the generation gap, the American mood oscillates dangerously between being ashamed of power and expecting too much of it. The former attitude deprecates the use or possession of force; the latter is overly receptive to the possibilities of absolute action and overly indifferent to the likely consequences. The danger of a rejection of power is that it may result in a nihilistic perfectionism which disdains the gradual and seeks to destroy what does not conform to its notion of utopia. The danger of an overconcern with force is that policy makers may respond to clamor by a series of spasmodic gestures and stylistic maneuvers and then recoil before their implications.

These essentially psychological problems cannot be overemphasized. It is the essence of a satisfied, advanced society that it puts a premium on operating within familiar procedures and concepts. It draws its motivation from the present, and it defines excellence by the ability to manipulate an established framework. But for the major part of humanity, the present becomes endurable only through a vision of the future. To most Americans—including most American leaders—the significant reality is what they see around them. But for most of the world—including many of the leaders of the new nations—the significant reality is what they wish to bring about. If we remain nothing but the managers of our physical patrimony, we will grow increasingly irrelevant. And since there can be no stability without us, the prospects of world order will decline.

We require a new burst of creativity, however, not so much for the sake of other countries as for our own people, especially the youth. The contemporary unrest is no doubt exploited by some whose purposes are all too clear. But that it is there to exploit is proof of a profound dissatisfaction with the merely managerial and consumer-oriented qualities of the modern state and with a world which seems to generate crises by inertia. The modern bureaucratic state, for all its panoply of strength, often finds itself shaken to its foundations by seemingly trivial causes. Its brittleness and the world-wide revolution of youth—especially in advanced countries and among the relatively affluent—suggest a spiritual void, an almost metaphysical boredom with a political environment that increasingly emphasizes bureaucratic challenges and is dedicated to no deeper purpose than material comfort.

Our unrest has no easy remedy. Nor is the solution to be found primarily in the realm of foreign policy. Yet a deeper nontechnical challenge would surely help us regain a sense of direction. The best and most prideful expressions of American purposes in the world have been those in which we acted in concert with others. Our influence in these situations has depended on achieving a reputation as a member of such a concert. To act consistently abroad we must be able to generate coalitions of shared purposes. Regional groupings supported by the United States will have to take over major responsibility for their immediate areas, with the United States being concerned more with the overall framework of order than with the management of every regional enterprise.

In the best of circumstances, the next administration will be beset by crises. In almost every area of the world, we have been living off capital—warding off the immediate, rarely dealing with underlying problems. These difficulties are likely to multiply when it becomes apparent that one of the legacies of the war in Vietnam will be a strong American reluctance to risk overseas involvements.

A new administration has the right to ask for compassion and understanding from the American people. But it must found its claim not on pat technical answers to difficult issues; it must above all ask the right questions. It must recognize that, in the field of foreign policy, we will never be able to contribute to building a stable and creative world order unless we first form some conception of it.

BIOGRAPHICAL NOTES

Introduction

KERMIT GORDON is president of the Brookings Institution. He was a member of the Council of Economic Advisers under President Kennedy and U.S. Budget Director under Presidents Kennedy and Johnson. Mr. Gordon taught at Williams College, where he was David E. Wells professor of political economy. A graduate of Swarthmore, he studied at University College, Oxford, as a Rhodes Scholar.

Budget Alternatives after Vietnam

CHARLES L. SCHULTZE is a senior fellow at the Brookings Institution and professor of economics at the University of Maryland. He was U.S. Budget Director under President Johnson and served on the staff of the Council of Economic Advisers. Mr. Schultze is a graduate of Georgetown University and received the Ph.D. from the University of Maryland.

CRITICS: Wilfred Lewis, Jr., senior fellow, Brookings Institution; Murray L. Weidenbaum, chairman, Department of Economics, Washington University.

Jobs, Training, and Welfare for the Underclass

JAMES L. SUNDQUIST is a senior fellow at the Brookings Institution. He was a Deputy Under Secretary of Agriculture under Presidents Kennedy and Johnson and a Senate legislative aide. He participated in the preparation of the Appalachian regional development plan, the war on poverty, the Manpower Development and Training Act, and other employment legislation. He is the author of *Politics and Policy: The Eisenhower, Kennedy, and Johnson Years*.

CRITICS: Eli Ginzberg, professor of economics, Graduate School of Business, and director, Conservation of Human Resources Project, Columbia University; George P. Schultz, dean, Graduate School of Business, University of Chicago.

Raising the Incomes of the Poor

JAMES TOBIN is Sterling professor of economics at Yale University. He was a member of the Council of Economic Advisers under President Kennedy and director of the Cowles Foundation for Research in Economics at Yale University. He received the Ph.D. from Harvard University. Mr. Tobin is the author of *National Economic Policy* and a coauthor of *The American Business Creed*.

CRITICS: Victor R. Fuchs, vice president for research, National Bureau of Economic Research, Inc.; Robert Lampman, Institute for Research on Poverty, University of Wisconsin.

The Negro and the Urban Crisis

KENNETH B. CLARK is president of the Metropolitan Applied Research Center, Inc., and professor of psychology at the City College of the City University of New York. He is a graduate of Howard University and received the Ph.D. from Columbia University. Mr. Clark is the author of *Prejudice and Your Child* and *Dark Ghetto*.

CRITICS: Charles V. Hamilton, professor of political science and director of the Graduate Program in Urban Studies, Roosevelt University; Thomas F. Pettigrew, professor of social psychology, Harvard University.

Moving toward Realistic Housing Goals

ANTHONY DOWNS is senior vice president of the Real Estate Research Corporation and its affiliate, SYSTEMETRICS, and a member of the National Commission on Urban Problems. He was on the faculty of the University of Chicago and has served as a consultant to the RAND Corporation, the National Advisory Commission on Civil Disorders, the Department of Housing and Urban Development, and the U.S. Civil Rights Commission. Mr. Downs is the author of *An Economic Theory of Democracy* and *Inside Bureaucracy*.

CRITICS: Victor H. Palmieri, consultant, University of California at Los Angeles, and former deputy executive director of the National Advisory Commission on Civil Disorders; Nathaniel H. Rogg, executive vice president, National Association of Home Builders.

Crime and Law Enforcement

JAMES Q. WILSON is professor of government at Harvard University. He was director of the Joint Center for Urban Studies of the Massachusetts Institute of Technology and Harvard University. He served on the Science Advisory Committee of the President's Commission on Law Enforcement and Administration of Justice and has worked with a number of government agencies on problems of crime and police work. He received the Ph.D. from the University of Chicago. He is the author of *Varieties of Police Behavior* and a coauthor of *City Politics*.

CRITICS: Alfred Blumstein, Institute for Defense Analyses; James Vorenberg, professor of law, Harvard Law School.

Investing in Better Schools

RALPH W. TYLER is president of the National Academy of Education and emeritus director of the Center for Advanced Study in the Behavioral Sciences, Stanford, California. He was dean of the Division of the Social Sciences at the University of Chicago and has served on the faculties of the University of Nebraska, the University of North Carolina, and Ohio State University.

CRITICS: H. Thomas James, dean, School of Education, Stanford University; S. P. Marland, Jr., former superintendent, Pittsburgh public schools.

New Challenges to the College and University

CLARK KERR is chairman of the Carnegie Commission on the Future of Higher Education and professor of economics at the University of California at Berkeley. He was president of the University of California and chancellor of the University of California at Berkeley. He is the author of *The Uses of the University* and *Labor and Management in Industrial Society* and a coauthor of *Industrialism and Industrial Man*.

CRITICS: Harold Howe II, U.S. Commissioner of Education; David Riesman, Center for Advanced Study in the Behavioral Sciences, Stanford, California (on leave from Harvard University).

Unemployment, Inflation, and Economic Stability

HERBERT STEIN is a senior fellow at the Brookings Institution and chief economic consultant of the Committee for Economic Development. He was research director and vice president of the Committee for Economic Development. He received the Ph.D. from the University of Chicago. He is a coauthor of "High Employment and Growth in the American Economy," in *Goals for Americans*.

618 Agenda for the Nation

CRITICS: Arthur F. Burns, chairman, National Bureau of Economic Research, Inc.; Robert M. Solow, professor of economics, Massachusetts Institute of Technology.

Managing the Federal Government

STEPHEN K. BAILEY is dean of the Maxwell Graduate School of Citizenship and Public Affairs, Syracuse University, and a regent of the State of New York. He is a past president of the American Society for Public Administration and a former mayor of Middletown, Connecticut. Mr. Bailey's most recent book (with Edith Mosher) is *ESEA: The Office of Education Administers a Law*.

CRITICS: Rufus E. Miles, Jr., director, Mid-Career Program, Woodrow Wilson School of Public and International Affairs, Princeton University; Wallace S. Sayre, chairman, Department of Public Law and Government, Columbia University.

The Politics of Alliance: The United States and Western Europe

FRANCIS M. BATOR is professor of political economy and director of studies in the Institute of Politics, John F. Kennedy School of Government, Harvard University; special consultant to the Secretary of the Treasury; and a member of the Advisory Committee on International Monetary Arrangements. He was Deputy Special Assistant to the President for National Security Affairs and a member of the senior staff of the National Security Council under President Johnson. He received the Ph.D. from the Massachusetts Institute of Technology. He is the author of *The Question of Government Spending*.

CRITICS: Robert R. Bowie, director, Center for International Affairs, Harvard University; Joseph Kraft, syndicated newspaper columnist.

Relations with the Soviet Union

MARSHALL D. SHULMAN is professor of government and director of the Russian Institute at Columbia University. He was professor of international politics at the Fletcher School of Law and Diplomacy, Tufts University; associate director of the Russian Research Center at Harvard University; and Special Assistant to the Secretary of State. Mr. Shulman is the author of *Stalin's Foreign Policy Reappraised* and *Beyond the Cold War*.

CRITICS: Cyril E. Black, director of international studies, Princeton University; Henry L. Roberts, professor of history, Dartmouth College.

Transpacific Relations

EDWIN O. REISCHAUER is University Professor at Harvard University. He was Ambassador to Japan under Presidents Kennedy and Johnson, director of the Harvard-Yenching Institute, and professor of far eastern languages at Harvard University. He received the Ph.D. from Harvard University and studied in France, Japan, and China. He is the author of *Wanted: An Asian Policy* and *Beyond Vietnam: The United States and Asia*.

CRITICS: Lucian W. Pye, Center for International Studies, Massachusetts Institute of Technology; James C. Thomson, Jr., Institute of Politics, John F. Kennedy School of Government, Harvard University.

The Middle East

JOHN C. CAMPBELL is senior research fellow at the Council on Foreign Relations and vice president of the Middle East Institute. He was on the staff of the Department of State, most recently as a member of the Policy Planning Council. He received the Ph.D. from Harvard University. Mr. Campbell is the author of *The United States in World Affairs* and *Defense of the Middle East*.

CRITICS: Richard H. Nolte, executive director, Institute of Current World Affairs; Nadav Safran, Center for Advanced Study in the Behavioral Sciences, Stanford, California (on leave from Harvard University).

The Dollar and the World Economy

RICHARD N. COOPER is professor of economics at Yale University. He was Deputy Assistant Secretary of State for International Monetary Affairs and served on the staff of the Council of Economic Advisers. He was educated at Oberlin College, the London School of Economics, and Harvard University. He is the author of *The Economics of Interdependence: Economic Policy in the Atlantic Community* and an associate author of *Britain's Economic Prospects*.

CRITICS: Charles P. Kindleberger, professor of economics, Massachusetts Institute of Technology; Robert Solomon, director, Division of International Finance, Board of Governors of the Federal Reserve System.

The United States and Low-Income Countries

MAX F. MILLIKAN is professor of economics and director of the Center for International Studies at the Massachusetts Institute of Technology. He is a member of the Advisory Committee on Economic Development of the Agency for International Development and of the United Nations Committee on Development Planning. Mr. Millikan is a coauthor of *No Easy Harvest: The Dilemma of Agriculture in Underdeveloped Countries* and a coeditor of *The Global Partnership*.

CRITICS: Robert E. Asher, acting director, Foreign Policy Studies Program, Brookings Institution; David E. Bell, vice president, Ford Foundation.

Military Strategy, Military Forces, and Arms Control

CARL KAYSEN is director of the Institute for Advanced Study, Princeton, New Jersey, and a consultant to the RAND Corporation. He was professor of economics and political economy and associate dean of the Graduate School of Public Administration at Harvard University. He served as Deputy Special Assistant to the President for National Security Affairs under President Kennedy. He received the Ph.D. from Harvard University.

CRITICS: Roswell L. Gilpatric, partner, Cravath, Swaine & Moore, New York; Albert J. Wohlstetter, University professor of political science, University of Chicago.

Central Issues of American Foreign Policy

HENRY A. KISSINGER is a member of the faculty of the Center for International Affairs, professor of government, and director of the Defense Studies Program at Harvard University; and a consultant to the Department of State and the RAND Corporation. He is the author of *The Troubled Partnership: A Reappraisal of the Atlantic Alliance*, *The Necessity for Choice: Prospects of American Foreign Policy*, and *Nuclear Weapons and Foreign Policy*.

CRITICS: Caryl P. Haskins, president, Carnegie Institution of Washington; Paul Seabury, professor of political science, University of California at Berkeley.